CALIFORNIA REAL ESTATE

ESCROW

DR. DONNA L. GROGAN

Dearborn™
Real Estate Education

This publication is designed to provide accurate and authoritative information in regard to the subject matter covered. It is sold with the understanding that the publisher is not engaged in rendering legal, accounting, or other professional service. If legal advice or other expert assistance is required, the services of a competent professional person should be sought.

President: Roy Lipner
Vice-President of Product Development and Publishing: Evan Butterfield
Associate Publisher: Louise Benzer
Managing Editor, Production: Daniel Frey
Quality Assurance Editor: David Shaw
Typesetter: Todd Bowman
Creative Director: Lucy Jenkins

Published by Dearborn™ Real Estate Education,
a division of Dearborn Financial Publishing, Inc.®
30 South Wacker Drive, Suite 2500
Chicago, IL 60606-7481
(312) 836-4400
http://www.dearbornRE.com

Printed in the United States of America.

06 07 10 9 8 7 6 5 4 3

Library of Congress Cataloging—in—Publication Data

Grogan, D. L. (Donna L.)
  California real estate escrow / Donna Grogan.
    p. cm.
    Includes bibliographical references and index.
  ISBN 0-7931-8574-2
    1. Escrows—California. 2. Real estate business—Law and legislation—California.
I. Title.
KFC256.E8G76   2004
  346.79404'373—dc22   2004005142

CONTENTS

ABOUT THE AUTHOR

Donna Grogan, MBA, PhD, GRI, CRS, CPM

Professor Donna Grogan began her real estate career in 1974 as a sales associate before buying two Century 21 residential offices. She earned her GRI designation in 1977 and Certified Residential Specialist (CRS) in 1979 after closing 100 escrows. Grogan completed two bachelor degrees, one in Business Management (1980) and one in Finance/Real Estate (1982). Her master's thesis, *Property Management Training and Education,* was completed in 1985. Her associate's degree coursework was at Cerritos College and Los Angeles Trade Tech College with completion and degree from Los Angeles City College. Her bachelor and master's degrees were received from California Polytechnic University, Pomona, California. She was awarded her Certified Property Manager (CPM) designation in 1985 and then wrote *California Property Management* in 1987. Grogan has written and edited numerous DRE-approved continuing education courses and edited college-level real estate textbooks for many publishers. In 1989 she coauthored *California Loan Brokerage and Lending,* and in 2002 she wrote the study guide on the same subject for the Real Estate Education Center (REEC). Pepperdine University conferred the doctorate degree on Grogan in 2000 with her dissertation *A Needs Assessment for the Skills for the Real Estate Assistant.* In 2003 on sabbatical she completed the *Computer Applications in Real Estate* textbook and *California Real Estate Escrow.*

Grogan has taught real estate courses since 1980 at five community colleges: Cerritos, El Camino, Glendale, Mount San Antonio, and Rio Hondo, and at three universities: Woodbury, California State Los Angeles, and California Polytechnic Pomona. She has taught distance education real estate computer courses and initiated curriculum for computer courses to accompany real estate lecture courses to increase computer literacy among agents, such as finance/loan brokering, practice, appraisal, and property management.

Grogan has served on several California community colleges REEC committees for curriculum, conference planning, state study guide review and edit, in addition to committees at her current full time position at El Camino College in Torrance, California, such as academic Senate Vice President and Business Division Curriculum Representative. In 1998 her peers selected her as the recipient for the Norm Woest Award as the "Most Outstanding California Instructor of the Year."

She served as the 1999 president for the California Real Estate Educator's Association (CREEA) and presented her dissertation work at the Real Estate Educators Association (REEA) Conference to national peers in 2000. Since 2001 she has served on the California Department of Real Estate (DRE) education advisory committee that reviewed, edited, and rewrote many questions for the state text bank for exam questions. She served the real estate commissioner as part of the committee that added the criteria that new licensees must complete Real Estate Practice within 18 months of licensing, in addition to the existing requirement for completion of Real Estate Principles, to meet the commissioner's desire to raise the standards for educational requirements. The belief is that increased education will decrease litigation and infractions by licensees. You may contact Dr. Donna Grogan by e-mail at *real_estate@earthlink.net*.

ACKNOWLEDGMENTS

This book is dedicated to three persons who have greatly influenced the correctness of information in real estate transactions: (1) Pat Grogan, spouse and broker, who has given support and materials used in Southern California escrows and transactions; (2) Pat Grogan's granddaughter, Becky Ripp, with Fidelity Title in Chico, California, for her contribution of Northern California escrow instructions information; and (3) Richard Grogan, Architect, of San Diego and Orange Counties, California, for contributing construction technical information and material on closing an escrow with his dad. Each of these is an invaluable person to the author on both a personal and professional level.

The author would like to offer a special thanks to the following reviewers whose expertise has been invaluable: Thurza B. Andrew, Butte Community College and Chico Valley Mortgage; Leonel "Leo" Bello, City College of San Francisco; Sandy Gadow, *escrowhelp.com* and *allaboutescrow.com*; and Ignacio Gonzalez, Mendocino Community College.

The author would also like to acknowledge the publisher's team of editors and production professionals for their manuscript assistance, including graphics and artwork. Students from El Camino College, Cerritos College, Rio Hondo College, Mount San Antonio College, and Glendale Community College are gratefully thanked for the contributions of their real estate projects to the knowledge of the author in the real estate matters. Special thanks goes to the guest speakers who took their time and shared specific subject expertise on the various escrow topics that students brought to the classroom.

SCOPE OF THE ESCROW BUSINESS

CHAPTER ONE

1

BACKGROUND

■ KEY TERMS

abstract attorney	electronic recordation	land grants
barristers	electronic signatures	neutral
Board of Land	engineers	perfect escrow
Commissioners	escroue	stakeholders
chain of title	escrow	surveyor
complete escrow	grant	title ownership
electronic funds	grantor	Treaty of Guadalupe
transfer	instruments	Hidalgo

■ CHAPTER OVERVIEW

The role of **escrow** in a real estate transaction is critical. Escrow acts as the clearinghouse for documents and the exchange of funds. Escrow provides the detailed, itemized costs for each party to the transaction. Therefore, a clear understanding of the escrow process is vital to anyone involved in a real estate transaction. This includes the lender, the seller (and his or her agent), the borrower, the buyer (and his or her agent), the company that issues the title insurance policy, the termite company, the hazard insurance carrier, the tax assessor, and many others.

The background of events surrounding the transfer of title between individuals has led to the current actions for the escrow industry. As with most other industries today, many changes will occur in how escrow will be handled in the future. This is partly due to the emergence of new technology and new efficiencies as companies align and merge with real estate related entities.

This book is designed to meet the needs of several real estate groups. Consumers will gain knowledge on the various aspects of escrow used for a particular type of transaction. Real estate agents will learn how the escrow process works for their transactions. The professionals working in the escrow field will enhance their understanding of the business today so they can better prepare for future business success. A career in escrow can be rewarding for those who seek to help others through an often emotionally charged real estate transaction.

■ LEARNING OBJECTIVES

At the conclusion of Chapter 1, you will be able to

- understand the structure of this book;
- give a definition of escrow;
- outline the history of the real estate escrow business;
- differentiate between residential and nonresidential types of escrows;
- describe professional escrow trade associations; and
- explain the escrow process.

■ OVERVIEW OF THE BOOK

This book is divided into three sections: (1) scope of the escrow business, (2) processing the escrow, and (3) escrow specialization. Figure 1.1 gives a graphic overview of the book. Figure 1.2 shows where specific types of escrow transactions are discussed in the book. Words shown in bold in the text indicate that they are defined in the Glossary.

Chapter 1 gives an overview of the escrow process. This chapter also includes information about the background of the industry and professional organizations.

Chapter 2 presents the types of entities that perform escrows, followed by an explanation of the legal requirements for an escrow provider. The emphasis is on describing career opportunities for people in the escrow business. Thus, the two chapters in Section 1 form an introduction to the escrow profession.

FIGURE 1.1

Overview of the Book

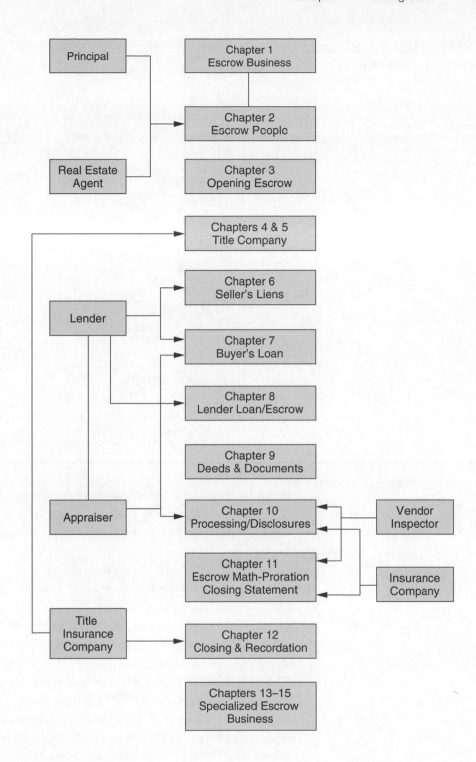

Section 2 of this book covers the step-by-step process for handling and processing an escrow. The ten chapters in Section 2 are directed at the most common escrow transaction, a residential sale. In Chapters 3 through 12, the reader will follow a typical escrow from its opening to the close of escrow. While the emphasis is on the part played by the licensed real estate agent, the chapters present sufficient

FIGURE 1.2

Types of Escrows

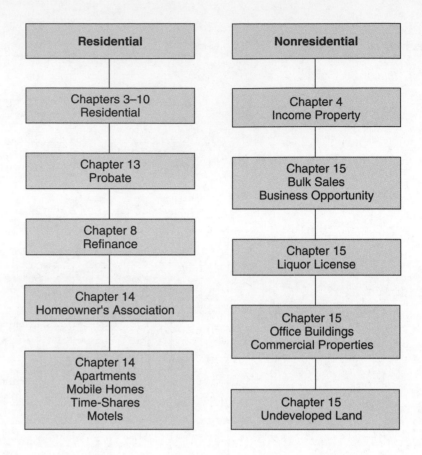

detail to prepare the reader for entry-level employment in the escrow field. Also, the intent is to familiarize non-real estate individuals, the public, with the process involved in either the purchase or sale of a home.

Chapter 3 begins with the relationship that the buyer, seller, and licensed real estate agent have with the opening of escrow. This chapter introduces the reader to the initial escrow instructions and the subsequent memorandums and amendments. It also discusses the differences in escrow practices for out-of-state, Northern California, and Southern California.

Chapters 4 and 5 discuss the title insurance company aspects. A key element for the consumer is the method in which the entity holds title, which is briefly described in Chapter 4. In addition, Chapter 4 describes the preliminary title report. The types of title insurance policies for various properties, typical endorsements, and the policy exclusions are discussed in Chapter 5.

Chapters 6, 7, and 8 explain the role that lenders play in an escrow transaction and deal with the buyer, seller, and loan escrows. Chapter 6 explains how the seller's liens are paid off and the interaction of the seller's existing payoffs with escrow, including the beneficiary demand statement. Chapter 7 outlines the interaction between escrow and the buyer when the buyer is obtaining a new loan. Other types of loans, such as assumption of the seller's existing loan, are discussed in a later chapter. Chapter 8 is about the loan escrow, foreclosure, and creative financing escrow.

Chapter 9 discusses the documents that escrow or others must prepare in the transaction, such as the deed. Required legal disclosures are a big part of any California real estate transaction, and Chapter 10 describes many items handled during processing, such as the termite clearance report.

Chapter 11 reviews the mathematics involved in an escrow, including impounds, prorations, and closing costs. Chapter 12 covers disbursements and the relationship between escrow officers, title company, and the County Recorders' Offices. Escrow handles many documents after the close of escrow.

Section 3 of this book covers various specialized escrow fields, such as probate, refinances, mobile homes, income-producing property, business properties, and nonresidential properties.

Chapter 13 covers the role of escrow in common occurrences such as probate. Chapter 14 explains the additional paperwork involved in an escrow handling income-producing property and exchanges, time-shares, construction, and homeowners' associations. Also, it discusses the role of the accommodator in the escrow.

Nonresidential transactions are covered in Chapter 15, detailing the additional items associated with bulk sales transactions, business opportunities, and the transfer of a liquor license through an escrow upon the sale of a business. Chapter 15 also covers real estate specialties, such as office buildings, commercial properties, and undeveloped land.

Each chapter begins with an overview and learning objectives. Each chapter concludes with a summary and a chapter quiz. Some words are shown in bold print the first time the word appears in the chapter. This indicates that the full definition may be found in the glossary at the back of the book. See page 451 for information on accessing common escrow forms.

■ PROPERTY TRANSFER: PAST, PRESENT, AND FUTURE

Escrow Definition   The average consumer usually cannot provide a clear definition of what escrow is or does. Even some real estate agents are not able to explain what is meant by escrow in concise words to their clients. Thus, a dictionary definition is a great place to begin, which most clearly corresponds to the California Department of Real Estate (DRE) test.

Webster's New World College Dictionary of the American Language defines escrow as

> a written agreement, as a bond or deed, put in the care of a third party and not delivered or put in effect until certain conditions are fulfilled.

According to *Black's Law Dictionary*, escrow is

> a legal document or property delivered by a promisor to a third party to be held by the third party for a given amount of time or until the occurrence of a condition, at which time the third party is to hand over the document or property to the promisee.

Perhaps the following online definition of escrow is easier to understand:

> It's simply an arrangement where a third party—such as a title insurance company or a lawyer—holds money or documents and distributes them according to instructions from both parties.

> In a commercial real estate transaction, for example, the escrow agent may obtain funds and documents from the buyer, the seller, and the commercial lender. When everything is ready, the escrow agents make sure the money and papers wind up in the right hands. Escrow agents make transactions flow smoothly and reliably.

WEB LINK

> *http://real-estate-law.freeadvice.com/commercial_real_estate/escrow.htm*

Escrow Past

The word "escrow" can be traced back to the French word **escroue.** The French referred to a scroll or a roll of writing as *escroue*. In America, *escrow* is the writing of the agreements made between the parties involved in a real property transaction. Real estate law and judicial law have different codes and sections regarding escrow, as seen in the box that follows.

> The California Civil Code Section 1057 states the following:
>
> A **grant** may be deposited by the **grantor** with a third person, to be delivered on performance of a condition, and, on delivery by the depository, it will take effect. While in the possession of the third party, and subject to condition, it is called an escrow.

A basic real estate principles book often describes escrow as the deposit of **instruments** and funds to a third **neutral** party with instructions to carry out the provisions of an agreement or contract. When everything is deposited into escrow to enable carrying out the instructions, it is referred to as a **complete escrow** or **perfect escrow.**

A real estate law textbook often explains the limits of what an escrow agent can do. The escrow agent is not an arbitrator or a mediator of disputes. The role of the escrow agent is to follow instructions. Because an escrow is an agency, the escrow agent does not hold any discretionary powers. An escrow never acquires title either because it is always an agency. An essential element of an escrow is the irrevocability of the deposit of both the deed and the purchase money.

Escrow History

Most present-day U.S. real estate business practices have their origins in Europe. The early settlers brought the customs of their homeland. In Europe, most of the people who handled real property transactions came from engineering or **surveyor** backgrounds, such as the first U.S. President, George Washington. These **engineers** acted as conveyancers for handling the transfer of title for real property. The engineers conducted title searches to determine the rights to ownership. The surveyors conducted searches to establish property lines. The conveyancers signed abstracts describing the respective titles. The engineers oversaw the surveyors who established property line boundaries and parcel measurements.

Barristers, the early European lawyers, handled the legal issues of real property transfer during that era. A barrister who specialized in real property transactions was often referred to as an **abstract attorney.** In many eastern U.S. states, the abstract attorney still handles the escrow and title functions in the transfer of real property because there is no escrow officer involved in a transaction. Early eastern U.S. colonials handled real estate transfers by following English, French, and Dutch European practices. In the East, King Charles of England owned the land and delegated to Lord Fairfax the authority to divide up that land into large **land grants.** The East Coast record system uses many metes (measurements) and bounds (boundaries) land descriptions for early title information. As properties were later subdivided, the lot, block, and tract system was also used. The South-western states, including California, also use both the metes-and-bounds and the tract-land systems. But California is different from the East in that many land descriptions came from the Spanish, not the French and Dutch land grant system. When East Coast properties are transferred from a seller to a buyer with a warranty deed, the seller warrants that he or she has ownership and the ability to transfer title ownership. It is similar to a personal guarantee.

California consists of 58 counties. Each area has a different past and operates in a different manner today. Some counties are still primarily undeveloped or pre-dominantly government controlled while other counties are mainly agriculturally developed or are residential/commercial urban centers. Northern California developed from Russian fur-trapper settlements and from mining towns. The custom prior to statehood often included merely settling on the land and using the resources available, with no escrow or ownership.

Southern California has a different history. In 1542, Juan Rodriguez Cabrillo arrived at San Diego Bay and proclaimed that the title ownership to all the land was to be held in the name of King Ferdinand of Spain. The King funded the California mission system while retaining ultimate ownership of the land. The mission leaders served as the property managers, overseeing the property assets and sent "rent/profit" on ships back to Spain. The locals could not own property unless the King gave them the right through a Spanish land grant. By establishing missions, the Spanish spread the concept of permanent land ownership in California rather than the nomadic concept of migrating with the animals and seasons. Spanish influence continued even after California was no longer a part of Spain.

In 1822, Spain left North America when Mexico claimed its independence. From 1822 to 1846, sizable rancho grants were conferred upon Mexican citizens and foreigners who adopted Mexican citizenship. Over 500 such grants were granted by 1846. Immigrants from the U.S. East Coast were not allowed to own property in the Mexican territory of California.

Property in most states is transferred by a warranty deed, which conveys fee **title ownership** to real property. This document gives warranties by the grantor to the grantee for recovery for defective title. But under the land grant system from Spain, then Mexico, California uses the grant deed to transfer title ownership to real property.

At the end of the Mexican-American War (1846–1848), the **Treaty of Guadalupe Hidalgo** in February 1848 addressed ownership under Mexican land grant customs. Each rancho owner had to reregister his or her land ownership to affiliate with the new U.S. government through the Land Commissioner. The California territory became one of the six states associated with Mexican rules, customs, and practices, including retaining the Mexican concept for community property.

After gold was discovered near Sutter's Fort in 1848, Washington, D.C., politicians decided that the California territory would make a valuable addition to the U.S. government to help fund East Coast interests. On September 9, 1850, California became a state of the United States, based on English common law as the basis for regulations.

In 1851 the U.S. Congress appointed a **Board of Land Commissioners** to settle California land disputes. The board held the power to rule upon and make settlements for all claims to private land ownership in California.

It was common for a buyer and seller to meet at a barrister's office to transfer ownership title. A seller signed over the item of value, such as real property, to a buyer, in the presence of a witness, such as the attorney and his secretary or law clerk. A common problem arose when the two parties were not available at the same time at the same place. Even though people in the past might have entrusted a friend, relative, or community leader to hold ownership papers until the other party delivered the item of value, it is said that the foundation for modern escrow practices is based on actions taken in San Diego, California, in 1895. The February 1959 issue of *The Stakeholder* quoted L. J. Beynon's account in April 1928 describing the event:

> One day in 1895, a man was obligated to leave town immediately but needed to leave documents, to be held in trust for another party. He asked the clerk at a depository business if he would, as a matter of convenience, take his executed deed, deliver it to the buyer together with a Certificate of Title, and collect from the buyer and send him the sum of $1,000. Thus, the man left an order to exchange documents for funds, and this became the first independent escrow in San Diego, California.

> From time to time, other people requested the same service. Not only people who lived out of town, but those who were going away on a trip.

As more and more people needed to find a neutral third person to hold documents or cash pending the final settlement of instructions by the parties and as more demand for such services grew, the neutral depository, such as a bank or insurance company, could not handle this business incidental to the main function of the company.

Title Insurance and Trust Company in San Diego appointed Elijah Unger and L. J. Beynon as the first two escrow clerks in the United States to act as the neutral **stakeholders** for real property transactions. While parties may still have met to handle the transfer paperwork among themselves, the escrow business kept growing because of the differences in dealing with the Mexican land grants, the Land Commissioner's Office, and technicalities in clearing ownership interests in California. The title insurance company, not a barrister, as the escrow holder handled the transfer of real property.

Present Property Transfer

Gradually, other title insurance companies were formed. The title insurance companies collected document copies of each successive land transfer ownership in California. These companies evolved into the modern title companies of today. Their primary purpose is to have a continuous record of the succession of land ownership, like connected links in a chain. Each link represents each owner. This is referred to as the **chain of title.** The title insurance company today collects an insurance premium to ensure that one party (typically the seller) is conveying clear title to the buyer, for transfer ownership purposes. Also, a one-time premium is charged to a borrower when obtaining a loan (new loan with purchase or refinance). This title policy is taken to assure the lender that no prior liens exist ahead of the new loan, except what the lender agrees to have as a priority ahead of them, such as property taxes. This is referred to as the "exceptions," as found in the title policy. Title insurance is explained in more detail in Chapter 4.

Thus, the escrow system as we know it today has grown into a highly developed operation. Escrow today involves so many more technical elements than the definition would have involved from its origins over 100 years ago. Escrow is no longer just a place to leave documents or money to hold for an absentee person. In the past, it was easy for one person to just hand the money to the other person and get a signed deed. While the basic stakeholder element is still present today from its roots, the escrow holder of today has evolved into a person who has many other responsibilities, duties, and liabilities to many other parties besides the buyer and seller. For example, the escrow holder must now comply with and report to the Internal Revenue Service. Escrow has to follow specific instructions from the lender placing the new loan even if the parties did not request the item. More is involved with disclosure requirements today. A person who had worked in the escrow business 50 years ago would most likely not recognize the escrow business practices used today.

Escrow Future

The real estate industry is rapidly changing to meet technology-driven demands. New trends in the escrow field continue to reshape the business.

First, the escrow clients are more educated in real estate transactions. Existing homeowners have more information and experience. Most property owners have owned several properties in their life and have therefore experienced several escrows. These experienced persons are knowledgeable and expect an escrow agent to know and handle things professionally. Sellers demand more, especially in the area of service.

The people who work in real estate have found that buyers have a greater need for service. Because some buyers are mentored by relatives who may assist in part of the purchase, the buyers gain knowledge from previous real estate transactions. Other buyers are required to complete a formal class on budgeting, finance, and the real estate transaction as specified by certain loan types. This is especially true for some first-time homebuyer or government-subsidized loan programs. Many other buyers cannot buy until they sell their present property. These move-up buyers use the information gained from when they bought the property in the past and the information on the process for the current buyer of their home. Some of the public is apt to complete a general real estate principles course to gain the body of knowledge necessary to protect themselves in a real estate transaction. Many licensees acquired their licenses for the primary purpose of selling homes to use the commissions as the down payment to purchase homes. Increased education about real estate means increased demands on escrow performance.

The demographics show that over 1 percent of the population in California is licensed to sell real estate. Large influxes in population are expected over the next few decades. In 2000 California was home to over 30 million people; in 2040 over 60 million will live here. An escrow agent can expect many first-time homebuyers to be unaccustomed to California escrow procedures, especially if they have closed escrow in another state where they expect to meet with an attorney to handle the escrow duties. Even within California, Northern and Southern California handle escrow in different ways. Therefore, a buyer from a different region of California may expect escrow to be handled in another manner than the common custom in the local area. The future shows a trend toward drastic changes in this area as electronic escrow, online escrow, and escrow software change the shape of old business practices.

Some buyers are not familiar with escrow practices because they come from countries where individuals are not allowed to own property. Also, a large number of first-time homebuyers are not native English speakers. The escrow officer can expect more demand for multilingual communications and requests for explanations and forms printed in languages other than English.

The real estate business is undergoing major changes. Smaller real estate sales firms are forming alliances with a network of service providers for their real estate transactions. The brokerage firm may have a working relationship with an online lender, a particular title provider, and others. Most escrow instructions will be electronically delivered to the parties where they can print and sign documents at the consumer's home or office. A real estate agent will have a password to access Internet escrow signatures, **electronic signatures.** The escrow practices of yesterday have been greatly altered. Buyers, however, still may bring in large sums of cash, or obtain a bank draft or cashier's check. The seller frequently instructs escrow to electronically transfer his or her net proceeds to another escrow or directly to his or her bank account. **Electronic funds transfer,** due to safety, surety, and convenience, is replacing manual delivery of funds. This is especially true for electronic transfer of mortgage and lender funds for title company reconveyance, loan payoff, and new loan funding.

The real estate sales agents have combined transaction forms and thereby have changed the industry. In the past, the real estate licensee wrote up the sales contract. After all parties signed and agreed to the terms and conditions, the agent telephoned the escrow holder and dictated escrow instructions. The escrow holder had the title company or messenger deliver typewritten escrow instructions to be signed by the various parties and then delivered back to escrow. This process could take one to two weeks to complete.

The California Association of REALTORS® has recently created the purchase contract and joint escrow instructions. The escrow officer does not need to rewrite what had already been signed and agreed to by the parties to the transaction. Computer keyboarded instructions are still used to alter, amend, clarify, or change the original contract/escrow instructions while the transaction proceeds to closure.

With the new method, the agents go to a Web site, enter a password, enter the data one time, which will then automatically be entered onto multiple forms, press "print" for the client, and send this information to the person processing the escrow to its closing. At each step, from the beginning of the contract process, through the various changes as the transaction proceeds, to the electronic transfer of the buyer's funds, **electronic recordation** of the deed, and electronic transfer of the seller's closing funds, escrow is ever changing. The future will require more knowledge of the escrow officer as the sellers demand better service, buyers demand better communications, and the industry demands better technological skills.

■ BASIC INDUSTRY INFORMATION

Demand for a third-party escrow entity arose from local practices by individuals who sought to transfer ownership of real property. An industry grew to meet consumer needs with a variety of specializations.

In the early days of California's development, the population consisted of smaller communities where almost everyone knew their neighbors. Usually a buyer could feel confident that the seller actually owned the property. A local attorney or bank official could easily prepare the documents needed to transfer ownership.

The usual practice was for buyers, sellers, real estate agents, and their respective attorneys to collectively negotiate the agreement. This process was often a noisy and an expensive arrangement. As the railroads brought in a multitude of newcomers, the need for more consistent and dependable procedures became apparent. Population increased as people moved from the Midwest to California during the Great Depression and the Dust Bowl. Figure 1.3 shows the population growth from 1900 to 2000. Great demand put pressure on multiple-family construction and on the escrow business. Builders met this demand by creating more housing units.

After World War II, many soldiers were discharged at one of the numerous California military bases. This created a higher demand for escrow entities that specialized in processing the paperwork for government loans. The end of World War II saw a gigantic leap in California's population. Individuals who had never seen California prior to the war were discharged in the "golden" state, married, then started their new families in California. Between 1945 and 1960 new tract

FIGURE 1.3

**Population Growth
1900 to 2000**

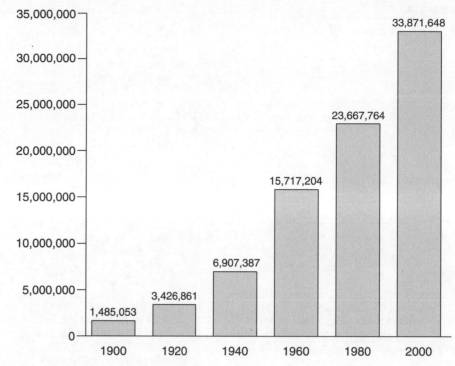

Source: Negative Population Growth, Inc. (*www.npg.org*).

homes sprang up overnight to form many new communities financed through government loan programs.

As the baby boomers acquired greater wealth from the 1970s through the early 2000s, escrow operations have continued to have high demand. The escrow holder needs to be able to handle short sales, foreclosures, exchanges, various financing arrangements, and other types of transactions. The basic elements of a real property transaction do not change; the end result remains the transfer of title ownership.

Different escrow holders handle a typical escrow in California with vast differences in operations. Some differences arise from the regulatory agency governing the escrow entity. Other differences are due to affiliation or ownership by or with a parent company that is often involved in some other phase of the transaction, such as the sales, loan, or title company. Specific types of escrow are handled according to government regulations, such as bulk sale and transfer of a liquor license.

It is projected that the demand to handle large bulk transfer of wealth among generations will increase. Special knowledge of probate transactions and transfer of title ownership within a trust will be a large part of future escrow business. Figure 1.4 is a diagram of the life of an escrow.

Life of an Escrow

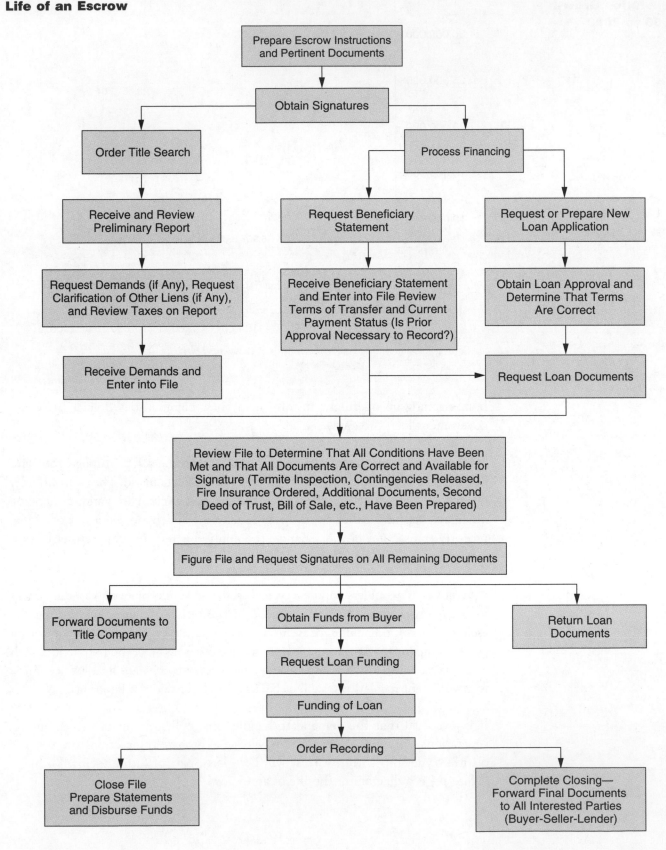

THINK ABOUT IT   Must every escrow do ALL the steps listed in Figure 1.4?

What are the advantages for the buyer and seller to use an escrow holder?

What are the advantages for the seller to have an escrow?

What are the advantages for the real estate agent?

What are the advantages for the lender?

■ CHAPTER SUMMARY

Escrow officers act as neutral parties. They hold the deposited funds and required documents until all conditions have been met. This is why the term "stakeholder" is an appropriate description of an escrow officer's role.

When communities were smaller and everyone seemed to know and trust their neighbors, buyers could rely upon the seller's ownership and right to sell. But as California's population increased, the need for an independent, reliable, inexpensive process to transfer property ownership became obvious. Gradually the escrow industry evolved.

From the opening to the closing, the escrow process normally follows several steps. These steps are practiced in the same general way throughout the state. However, the specific timing of these steps is different in Northern and Southern California. These steps will be described in greater detail throughout the book.

■ CHAPTER 1 QUIZ

1. The term that best describes the escrow holder is
   a. stakeholder.
   b. holder in due course.
   c. engineer's survey.
   d. abstractor.

2. The need for escrow was developed because
   a. the increased population needed a speedy and efficient way to transfer ownership of real property.
   b. buyers and sellers needed a dependable neutral party to prepare documents.
   c. lenders needed a bridge to communicate with buyers.
   d. of all of the above.

3. The term *escrow* originated from the
   a. Latin word used by barristers.
   b. financial term of bankers.
   c. French word for scroll.
   d. Spanish phrase in the Treaty of Guadalupe Hidalgo.

4. Escrow is a
   a. person.
   b. process.
   c. company.
   d. law.

5. The principal purpose for an escrow is to hold documents until the
   a. buyer brings in all the deposit funds required.
   b. seller gets release of liability from his or her lienholder(s).
   c. seller approves the buyer's loan request.
   d. buyer signs the transfer documents.

6. The Board of Land Commissioners was formed by
   a. the Mexican government.
   b. a California licensing agency.
   c. the Spanish government.
   d. the U.S. Congress.

7. Escrow acts as a(n)
   a. trustee.
   b. valuator.
   c. clearinghouse.
   d. abstractor.

8. The primary reason for escrow processes changing so fast is due to
   a. laws and regulations.
   b. electronic technology.
   c. buyer demands.
   d. seller demands.

9. Which of the following is NOT part of the escrow process?
   a. A third party
   b. A licensee meeting the occurrence of a French bond
   c. Where a grantor deposits a grant with conditions
   d. Delivery by the depository makes the grant take effect

10. The increase in demand for escrow is a result of
    a. population growth.
    b. increased competition.
    c. legislative action.
    d. regulation codes.

CHAPTER TWO

ESCROW:
THE PROFESSION
AND THE PEOPLE

■ KEY TERMS

American Escrow
  Association (AEA)
California Escrow
  Association (CEA)
closer

Department of
  Corporations
escrow agent
escrow law
escrow officer
fiduciary

independent escrow
licensee
person
title
thrift institution

■ CHAPTER OVERVIEW

Licensing may or may not be required of an escrow officer, depending upon the company structure. Chapter 2 reviews the legal aspects of escrow and discusses the differences in the legal organization of various escrow companies. The **independent escrow** firms are formed as corporations. Other escrow operations are operated as a department of a bank or thrift institution. Lawyers or real estate brokers may handle the escrow in a real estate transaction if it is in the normal course of their business of handling the balance of the transfer of real property ownership.

Professional organizations offer escrow designations, representing various levels of education, experience, and skill obtained by an individual officer. Success and job opportunities for employment in the field of escrow are closely connected with professional designations that are granted by the industry escrow trade associations. Some states refer to the person who performs the close of escrow as the settlement agent, because that business entity handles the settlement costs and the closing document, often referred to as the settlement statement. Other states call the individual the **closer.** In California the term for the person who handles the escrow is the **escrow officer.**

■ LEARNING OBJECTIVES

At the conclusion of Chapter 2, you will be able to

- explain licensing requirements for positions in escrow;
- differentiate the six classifications of escrow holders;
- distinguish among the various state commissioner regulations and requirements;
- explain the different employment positions in the escrow industry; and
- describe various careers in escrow.

■ LICENSING

The definition of escrow does not include the word fiduciary. A **fiduciary** is a person held in a position of trust and confidence. If the parties to a transaction expect the escrow company to maintain trust and confidence, then why is fiduciary responsibility not a part of the definition of escrow? The answer lies in the difference between the role of an escrow officer and the role of a real estate licensed agent. The relationship of the real estate agent to the principal is one where the broker is acting as a fiduciary for the principal and owes certain loyalty that cannot be breached under the rules of agency. The escrow officer is under no agency laws and is primarily a neutral intermediary who only acts based upon the written instructions signed by the principals. The escrow officer is not licensed by the government agency to act for the buyer or for the seller or for real estate agents. An escrow agent must remain neutral.

A real estate agent must obtain a state license from the California Department of Real Estate in order to handle real estate sales activities. An appraiser must obtain a state license from the Office of Real Estate Appraisal to give an opinion of value. State or federal bodies oversee financial institutions, such as banks and thrift institutions. An attorney works under the state bar association rules.

FIGURE 2.1

How Do I Start an Escrow Company in California?

Any person who desires to engage in business as an escrow agent in California must be a corporation organized for that purpose. In addition, there are several criteria which must be met:

a. you must have a $50,000 tangible net worth and $25,000 in liquid assets,

b. you must obtain a surety bond of at least $25,000,

c. the manager of the company must have at least 5 years experience of responsible escrow experience,

d. you must be a member of Escrow Agents Fidelity corporation and pay them an initial membership fee of $3,000,

e. all officers, directors, stockholders, managers, and employees will be required to file fingerprints with the initial application, and

f. you must pay a filing fee of $625 and an investigation fee of $100.

Persons licensed by the Department of Corporations as an escrow agent are subject to the provisions of the Escrow Law (Division 6 of the California Financial Code [FC]) and the Escrow Regulations (Title 10, Chapter 3, Subchapter 9 of the California Code of Regulations [CCR]). Copies of the California Financial Code may be purchased from Barclays Law Publishers, 400 Oyster Point Blvd., South San Francisco, CA 94080.

Source: Excerpt from *www.escrowhelp.com.* Reprinted with permission from Sandy Gadow, author, *The Complete Guide to Your Real Estate Closing.*

The procedures used for closing an escrow are not controlled by law. State law regulates licensed real estate agents and licensed escrow corporations. County laws dictate the recordation requirements for documents. Federal law regulates when certain disclosures are required, such as the Real Estate Settlement Procedures Act (RESPA) and the Foreign Investment in Real Property Tax Act (FIRPTA). But local custom dictates practices for commonly used escrow procedures. Thus, some laws do regulate certain procedures required for closing the escrow. It is legal for a buyer and seller to handle all the details of a transaction with no real estate **licensee** and no third-party escrow settlement agent with some type of property. Most transactions and transfers of real property, however, do utilize the services of an **escrow agent.** See Figure 2.1 on how to start an escrow company in California.

The escrow person who is employed to handle an escrow is not required to have any state or federal license to practice business activities, unless the firm is under the California **Department of Corporations.** If the escrow is broker-owned, the broker must have a California Department of Real Estate license, but the escrow officer does not need any license. The escrow entity, however, is not bound to require escrow officers to hold any form of governmental background check or minimum level of education or hours of supervised experience. Instead, the industry monitors its own activities. In addition, the industry has created professional designations to take the place of licensing individuals. See page 451 for information on accessing many of the rules and regulations from the various government agencies that should be thoroughly reviewed for more specific details as to the rules and regulations set forth by the commissioners and legislation.

■ ESCROW HOLDERS

The word "stakeholder" is sometimes used to designate the escrow holder. A stakeholder is considered as the agent of the respective parties until such time as the escrow is closed. After the escrow has closed, then the escrow holder becomes a trustee for the money and the documents until the escrow holder distributes and disperses the instruments and funds in accordance with the escrow instructions.

People who work with different escrow officers and handle dissimilar real property transactions, such as probate or foreclosures, are often confused about how differently the whole process is executed. One escrow person handles a transaction one way, while another does things entirely differently. Many new real estate salesperson licensees do not understand why there are so many variances. The public, who has infrequent purchases and sales, is usually even more confused.

To discuss why escrow personnel handle things so differently, one must discuss the escrow company first, not the person working at the escrow company. Each type of escrow entity may be under a different government entity, thus having different regulations to observe. An escrow holder may be a corporation, a division of a bank or savings association, an attorney, a department of a title insurance company, or a real estate broker licensed by the California Department of Real Estate (DRE). Figure 2.2 shows the different entities that may act as an escrow holder. Each of the six different entities falls under five different government agencies, and one is directly under the bar association jurisdiction.

Each commissioner is a political appointee made by the state governor. Thus, the term of each commissioner is generally the same length as the term of the governor. In California, the governor is elected for four years, thus each commissioner serves for four years. Each commissioner brings to the position his or her own particular experiences, background, and areas of expertise. Some commissioners are extremely knowledgeable in the field of real property matters while other commissioners are more knowledgeable in non-real estate matters. It would be rare to find a commissioner with a long-term relationship knowledgeable on current escrow operations and practices.

FIGURE 2.2

Escrow Entities: Who May Act

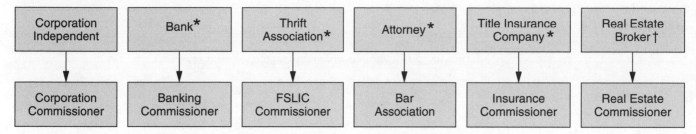

* Exempt from escrow license law.   † Only if the broker is an agent in the transaction.

Corporation Commissioner

A license to act as an escrow holder can be held only by a corporation in the state of California, according to Section 17200 of the California Finance Code. This section states that it shall be unlawful for any person to engage in business as an escrow agent within this state except by means of a corporation duly organized for that purpose and licensed by the Commissioner of Corporations as an escrow agent.

Section 17004 of the Finance Code states that an *escrow agent* means any person engaged in the business of receiving escrows for deposit or delivery. No individual person or unincorporated entity may act as the escrow agent unless its business acts fall under the categories that are exempt. An independent escrow corporation must be licensed by the California Department of Corporations in order to handle an escrow in California. Section 17005 of the Finance Code states that a *licensee* means any person holding a valid unrevoked license as an escrow agent. The code further states that a **person** means, in addition to the singular, persons, groups of persons, cooperatives, associations, company, firm, partnership, corporation, or other legal entity.

The California Financial Code (see Figure 2.3) contains the **escrow law** for those who are required to hold a license. This law describes the legal requirements for those who act as an escrow agent.

Among other requirements, under the Corporation Commissioner, the corporation must be solvent and furnish a surety bond. The corporation must have a minimum level of liquidity, and there are tangible net worth minimum requirements. The codes for escrow law that are found in the Finance Code, Division 6, under the California Department of Corporations, specifically describe the what, who, where, when, and how of being an escrow agent. These regulations identify those activities that are considered escrow functions and those excluded from following these rules.

FIGURE 2.3

**Independent Escrow
Company—Department
of Corporations**

Finance Code, Division 6, Sections		17000–17702
Chapter 1.	Application of this Division	17000–17010
Chapter 2.	License and Bond	17200–17215
Chapter 2.5	Escrow Agents' Fidelity Corporation	
	Article 1. Definitions	17300–17305
	Article 2. Purpose: Scope of Guarantee	17310–17315
	Article 3. Membership Fees & Assessments	17320–17324
	Article 4. General Provisions	17330–17350
Chapter 3.	Escrow Regulations	17400–17423.1
Chapter 4.	Revocation of License	17600–17609.2
Chapter 5.	Hearings	17610–17614
Chapter 6.	Liquidation and Conservatorship	
	Article 1. Possession by Commissioner	17621–17629
	Article 2. Conservatorship	17630–17634
	Article 3. Liquidation by the Commissioner	17635–17654
Chapter 7.	Crimes and Civil Penalties	17700–17702

The escrow that uses this form of business status is the independent escrow corporation, most frequently used in Southern California. Figure 2.4 shows a list of some requirements for escrow companies performing acts under the corporation commissioner rules and regulations. Many safeguards are required to serve as protection for the consumer for independent escrow corporations that are not subject to the same specifications, such as the escrow department handling by the title insurance business and operations.

There are two primary differences between the corporation escrow entity and all other types of escrow operations. The first is that only the independent escrow corporation must have an escrow license in order to conduct escrow business. The second is the requirement for an annual state audit. The California Department of Corporations bills each escrow corporation for a specific fee that pays the typical rate for checking the company for the accuracy of the records and account of client funds. Each fiscal year the corporation escrow firm must submit to the California Corporation Commissioner's office an independent audit prepared by a public accounting firm or a certified public accountant (CPA). The purpose for the audit is to ensure that no funds are carried over until the next year that should have been collected from the parties to the transaction or that should have been disbursed to any entity, including appraisers, financial lending

FIGURE 2.4

Corporation Escrow Requirements

- Obtain license from California Department of Corporations
- Provide surety bond and solvent, tangible, liquid net worth information
- Furnish annual CPA audit for fiscal year to Corporation Commissioner
- Conduct primary business as escrow and not substantially related to real estate sales
- Maintain client funds in demand deposit financial institution trust account

institutions, or the principals. This ensures current year fiscal responsibility for all funds handled by the escrow company. No other escrow holder has these stringent requirements. The additional cost for the audit does, however, increase the cost of doing business for the independent escrow corporation.

Escrow agents must be licensed by the California Commissioner of Corporations, unless they fall under the list of those that are exempt from licensing. In 1972 a legal action was filed by the Escrow Institute of California against the Commissioner of Corporations. The court judgment, subsequently upheld on appeal, affirmed that "individuals and entities designated as exempt from the provisions of escrow law were subject to stringent statutes and regulations provisions governing conduct of their business or profession; and, it was not unreasonable for the legislature to exempt them from the escrow law; and, the exemption did not give rise to an unconstitutional classification or impose discriminatory burden on independent escrow agents." Exemptions from escrow licensing law requirements include

- banks,

- thrift institutions,

- attorneys,

- title insurance companies, and

- real estate brokers.

Section 17005.5 of the Finance Code states that unless specifically exempted, as in Section 17006, the definition of escrow shall not be used to exclude anyone. Section 17006 states that this Finance Code Division 6 does *not* apply to: "(1) Any person doing business under any law of this state or the United States relating to banks, trust companies, building and loan or savings and loan associations or insurance companies; (2) Any person licensed to practice law in California who is not actively engaged in conducting an escrow agency; (3) Any person whose principal business is that of preparing abstracts or making searches of title that are used as the basis for the issuance of a policy of title insurance by a company doing business under any law of the state relating to insurance companies; and, (4) Any broker licensed by the Real Estate commissioner while performing acts in the course of or incidental to a real estate transaction to which the broker is an agent or a party to the transaction and in which the broker is performing an act for which a real estate license is required."

Banking Commissioner

Under the Banking Commissioner, banks are regulated by the State Banking Law and work closely with interstate commerce, which is monitored by the Federal Reserve System. During the normal course of handling banking transactions, all phases of operations are subject to audit for the handling of all bank funds. The California Finance Code, Division 1, Banks, Section 99, is also known as the State Banking Law. The codes refer to escrow activity of performing escrow work for clients. The codes indicate that while authorized to act as escrow holders for all transactions requiring escrow, banks act most commonly as depositories for escrow trust fund accounts for their business customers.

Other codes, such as a DRE regulation for a broker trust account, require the establishment of escrow accounts to be placed in state chartered banks. In fact, oversight of the organization and operations of the bank, including the escrow department and its activities, is provided by the State Superintendent of Banks. This superintendent is the chief officer of the State Banking Department, under authority established by the State Bank Act of 1909, which also authorized commercial bank institutions and savings and trust institutions. The escrow department is usually a small part of the banks' business operations. During the normal course of a bank audit, the bank's escrow department funds and procedures would also be subject to audit.

The Federal Deposit Insurance Corporation (FDIC) regulations apply to escrow company operations in several places. Code Section 3500 is about escrow accounts in regard to real estate loans, while codes 4187 through 6994 concern escrow operations, and code sections in the 7000s are concerned with the Real Estate Settlement Procedures Act (RESPA) escrow information. Use the FDIC outline in Figure 2.5 for easy reference. For more detailed information go to the following Web site: *http://www.fdic.gov/regulations/laws/rules/*.

WEB LINK

@

Both banks and thrift institutions commonly handle escrow accounts in conjunction with real estate loans. See Figure 2.6 for other FDIC law regarding RESPA and Figure 2.7 for selected individual definitions that are cited in this government regulation for escrow accounts. These codes pertain to escrow accounts held by a lender, when the bank is the lender, in the handling of the escrow impound account for collection, handling, and disbursement of client escrow funds. These regulations are designed to assist in protection of the consumer's funds when the handling of the payments on behalf of the client is outside the client's control. When borrowers are prohibited from paying their taxes and insurance outside of the bank loan payment on their own behalf, and when the lender makes these payments directly to the tax or insurance source, the lender/bank has certain obligations to comply with in order to ensure that the client funds are handled and maintained according to strict guidelines to protect the consumer.

Several publications by Housing and Urban Development (HUD), called "Public Guidance Documents" give specific information regarding escrow account information, including those escrow accounts established in connection with any federally related mortgage loan. HUD sets limits for escrow accounts using calculations based on monthly payments and disbursements.

FIGURE 2.6

**FDIC Law:
Section 3500—RESPA**

Section 3500—REAL ESTATE SETTLEMENT PROCEDURES ACT (RESPA)

3500.17—Escrow Accounts

  (a) General

  (b) Definitions

  (c) Limits on payments to escrow accounts; acceptable accounting methods

  (d) Methods of escrow account analysis

  (e) Transfer of servicing

  (f) Shortages, surpluses, and deficiencies requirements

  (g) Initial escrow account statement

  (h) Format for initial account statement

  (i) Annual escrow account statement

  (j) Formats for annual escrow account statement

  (k) Timely payments

  (l) System of record keeping

  (m) Penalties

  (n) Civil penalties procedures

Source: *http://www.fdic.gov/regulations/laws/rules/6500-2520.html#7008.*

No license is required to be a bank employee who works exclusively on handling bank escrow transactions. The bank normally handles only escrows for its own customer transactions, for example, when a family sets up a trust or estate that has real estate holdings, such as for a minor child. The bank escrow department might handle the transfer of property on behalf of the minor between holders within the trust, or the transfer upon death to another person upon the death of the trustees. An attorney, however, most often handles these kinds of transactions.

Thrift Institution Commissioner

The **thrift institutions,** formerly the savings and loan associations in California, are usually either state or federally chartered. The state thrift institution Commissioner oversees the entire operations of the thrift business, under the Finance Code, Division 2, Savings and Loan, Section 5000. The State Bank Act of 1909 authorized savings and trust institutions. See Figure 2.6 for FDIC law, regulations, and related acts.

Savings and thrift institutions can and do offer escrow services but usually only to their own depositors. Thrift operations are governed under the provisions of the Office of Thrift Supervision (OST), which is responsible for the oversight of the savings and thrift institution activities.

FIGURE 2.7

Definitions of Escrow Account Terms

REAL ESTATE SETTLEMENT PROCEDURES ACT (RESPA) Section 3500.17

Annual Escrow Account Statement. As noted in 3500.17(i) a servicer shall submit an annual escrow account statement to the borrower within 30 calendar days of the end of the escrow account computation year, after conducting an escrow account analysis.

Disbursement date means the date on which the servicer actually pays an escrow item from the escrow account.

Escrow account means any account that a servicer establishes or controls on behalf of a borrower to pay taxes, insurance premiums or other charges with respect to a federally related mortgage loan, including charges that the borrower and servicer have voluntarily agreed that the servicer should collect and pay. The definition includes trust account, reserve account and impound account.

Escrow account computation year is a 12-month period established for the escrow account beginning with the borrower's initial payment date.

Single-item analysis means an accounting method used by computing the sufficiency of escrow account funds by considering each escrow item separately.

Source: *http://www.fdic.gov/regulations/laws/rules/6500-2520.html#7008.*

The guidelines for their escrow operations are strictly limited in scope to those transactions under the direct control of the thrift institution, such as transfer on a foreclosed property back to the thrift institution and then subsequently transferred to another person upon sale at a public auction. The escrow can be handled by the escrow department of the thrift institution for certain limited types of transactions.

Bar Association

Attorneys are required to take a college course on real property specifically as part of the law school curriculum. In most other states, except California and a few adjoining states, an attorney acts as the settlement agent and handles what is known as the escrow process, overseeing title search and settlement. The real estate licensee shows the property, gets the purchase contract signed and agreed upon by both parties, then makes the appointment for the buyer and the seller to meet at the law office. The attorney has both parties sit down at a law office table and asks standard questions about the understanding and agreement between the parties, such as the address, spelling of names, price, terms, conditions, restrictions, etc. The attorney draws up a legally binding contract. Once the contract is executed, few amendments occur later. All principals know that an attorney is representing the transaction. The attorney can give legal advice on the consequences of actions.

In many Midwest states, transactions are often handled by an abstract attorney. The abstract attorney summarizes the content(s) of the material or records involving the property. These specialized attorneys actually abstract the title of record on the real property, in the same manner as a title insurance company would perform a title search of records against the property and the people, as is done in California. On the East Coast this individual is referred to as a title insurance attorney.

A person who has passed the state bar exam is required to be a real estate agent if he or she performs acts that require a license for a fee. If an attorney handles an escrow, the attorney is required to have a corporation escrow license, unless the act is within the normal scope of his or her business, such as a transfer between spouses in a divorce settlement or for heirs upon the settling of an estate.

In California, the Business and Professions Code, Division 3, Chapter 4 is commonly referred to as the State Bar Act. The State Bar Act is a public corporation organized under the Corporations Code. All persons permitted and licensed to practice law in the state may become members of the State Bar. The Board of Governors of the State Bar provides oversight of all the professional activities of their members, and there is no Law Commissioner.

Under the State Bar Act, an attorney can act as an escrow for all transactions for which an escrow agent is desired or required so long as the attorney is "not actively engaged in conducting an escrow agency," according to Finance Code, Section 17006(b).

The State Bar of California Rule 3-110 concerns *Failing to Act Competently* and requires bar members to have sufficient learning and skill when the legal service is undertaken. The skill must be acquired prior to performance of the act. Thus when dealing with any attorney on the handling of any escrow, it is prudent to ask about his or her experience in escrow, title, and transfer of real property. For example, when an attorney transfers property from the individuals to title held in an inter vivos trust, a living trust, or similar trust, some attorneys use a quitclaim deed. This type of deed may not guarantee that the parties have any current interest in the property. If one of the parties signed a grant deed, transferring the property to another, an hour before signing the quitclaim deed, a cloud would exist on the title to the property. A quitclaim transfers "all that I have," and the individual may have 100 percent or 0 percent interest in the property at the time of signing. A grant deed transfers "all that I have, and I have some," indicating that the transferee will receive all the interest that the transferrer has, and it also indicates that the transferrer actually does have some interest in the property at the time of signing.

Also, if any additional title is acquired afterward, the grant deed would include this additional after-acquired title, but a quitclaim deed would not. For example, three siblings inherit property from their parents and place the property into a newly formed trust. The trust states that if any one of them dies with no heirs, their interest is transferred to the remaining siblings. Thereafter, one sibling dies with no heirs. With a quitclaim, A, B, and C held title of ⅓ each. After the death of C, it was intended that A and B end up with ½ each. Thus A increased from ⅓ up to ½ interest in the property, as did B. The additional after-acquired title would not be covered with the quitclaim deed.

Rule 4-100 of the State Bar of California concerns *Preserving Identity of Funds and Property of a Client*. This rule states that all funds received or held for the benefit of clients by a member of the bar or law firm must be deposited into an identifiable bank account labeled "Trust Account" or "Client's Fund Account" or similar words. The account must be maintained in the State of California unless written instruction from the client indicates otherwise. No funds of the client may be commingled except (1) funds reasonably sufficient to pay bank charges, and (2) when funds belong part to the client and in part to the member or law firm (such as receipt of a settlement awarded), the funds belonging to the member or firm must be withdrawn at the earliest reasonable time after the member's interest in that portion becomes fixed.

The member must (1) promptly notify a client of receipt of client funds; (2) identify and label client funds and place them in safekeeping as soon as practicable; (3) maintain complete records of all funds of the client coming into possession of the member or law firm; (4) preserve all records of client funds for a period not less than five years after final appropriate distribution of such funds; (5) comply with any audit of such records; and (6) promptly pay or deliver to the client any funds requested by the client that client is entitled to receive.

The Standard under Rules of Professional Conduct Rule 4-100(C) states the following about maintenance of records: "(1) a member shall, from the date of receipt of client funds through the period of five years from the date of appropriate disbursement of such funds, maintain: (a) a written ledger for EACH client with client name; the date, amount and source of funds; the date, amount paid, and purpose of each disbursement; and, current balance for each client; (2) a written journal for each bank account that sets forth the name of the account; the date, amount, and client affected by each debit and credit; and, the current balance in the account; and, (3) the member shall maintain a written journal that specifies each item held, the person on whose behalf it is held, the date of receipt, the date of distribution, to whom distributed." These rules can be found on the State Bar of California Web site at *http://www.calbar.ca.gov/state/calbar/calbar_home.jsp*. Do a search for "professional conduct" to locate the rules.

WEB LINK

@

Insurance Commissioner

When average persons think of insurance, they typically think of auto or life insurance. They rarely think of insurance for real property. But, in California, the insurance commissioner is very much involved in regulating operations for homeowner insurance and **title** insurance company escrow operations. Although only a department of the title insurance business entity, the title company escrow department in Northern California handles the bulk of escrows. As the single largest handler of the transfer of real property in that part of the state, the insurance commissioner is responsible for overseeing the insurance industry escrow operations as part of the commissioner's required insurance operations.

When a title insurance company both handles the escrow settlement and issues the title insurance policy, each with separate fees for both the buyer and the seller, the cost per person may be less than charged by other escrow providers. The combined operation is more cost efficient and is safer for the title insurance company that insures the title. The less the risk the lower the charge. When the title company knows that its own escrow department employee handled the loan payoff (reconvened) for the prior recorded liens and resolved mechanic's lien threats (such as an unpaid termite report for corrective work performed) during escrow, the title insurance company may perceive less of a threat of potential loss.

Escrow service divisions of insurance companies, specifically title insurance companies, are classified as controlled escrow companies. They can provide the same type of services as the independent escrow company. Their activities are normally limited to those transactions that complement the primary title insurance business. This is similar to the rules under the real estate commissioner for DRE licensees. The conveniences of collection that title insurance company escrows offer facilitate the escrow process. The advantage of the convenience is somewhat offset by the limited flexibility of the fee structure when compared to independent escrow firms.

The state Insurance Commissioner oversees title insurance companies, which are governed by the California Insurance Code. The Insurance Code, Division 2, Part 6, Chapter 1 contains Section 12340.3c. This section states that among the activities conducted by the business of insurance is "the performance by a title insurer, and underwritten title company or a controlled escrow company of any service in conjunction with the issuance or contemplated issuance of a title policy including, but not limited to, the handling of any escrow, settlement, or closing in connection therewith; or the doing of or proposing to do any business which is in substance the equivalent of any of the above." Further, Section 12340.6 defines *controlled escrow company* to mean

- any person, natural or artificial, other than a title insurer or underwritten title company,

- whose principal business is the handling of escrow of real property transactions in connection with which title policies are issued,

- is controlled by or controls, or is under common control with a title insurer,

- or controls or is controlled by, or is under common control with an underwritten title company,

- or if a natural person is employed by or controlled by a title insurer or by an underwritten title company.

Real Estate Commissioner

The California licensed real estate broker is not required to be licensed as a licensed escrow agent to perform the duties of an escrow holder because the escrow company would have to follow the rules and regulations of two different state commissioners. However, the California Department of Corporations does, through its Real Estate Commissioner, administer strict requirements for the conditions under which licensed real estate brokers can conduct their business in order to comply with the exemption from the escrow license law.

A real estate salesperson cannot act as an escrow agent because all acts of the salesperson must be conducted under a state licensed broker. The salesperson may, however, be employed as an escrow officer employed by a real estate broker to conduct escrow business on behalf of that employing broker. Because of the employing broker requirement, the salesperson escrow officer cannot handle any escrow in which the employing broker is not acting as a licensed real estate broker in the handling of the transfer of the property. The employing broker must be conducting business to act as a licensed real estate broker in the transaction.

The licensed real estate broker may handle the escrow for a fee only if that broker is acting as a licensed real estate broker in that particular transaction. It is typical in Southern California for the larger real estate brokerage corporate offices to have a broker-owned escrow company that conducts escrows for the transactions handled by the agents licensed under that employing brokerage firm and under the designated broker who is liable for the activities of that firm. The real estate broker is given a personal right to act as the escrow agent under the normal real estate license awarded by the California real estate law, supervised under the California Real Estate Commissioner. Under California real estate practices rules and regulations, the broker may delegate the duties performed for the escrow portion of the transaction. Brokers may not delegate the personal right given to them to anyone else, including no sales associate, salesperson, or associate broker employed by the firm. The broker may employ a person to perform clerical type secretarial work under that broker to assist with the escrow paperwork. Figure 2.8 shows the California Department of Corporations acts governing real estate brokers.

When a California licensed real estate broker is performing the duties and acting as the escrow agent, special disclosures are required. Among other things, the broker must give a written statement in not less than 10-point type that the broker is a California Department of Real Estate licensed broker. Because real

FIGURE 2.8

Broker-Owned Escrow

- License law applies only to the California licensed real estate broker.

- The escrow broker must represent the buyer or the seller in the transaction, or the broker may act on his or her own behalf as a party to the transaction and conduct the escrow operations.

- Escrow may not be the primary business of the broker, but it is only incidental to the transaction.

- No group broker association escrow can be conducted under the real estate broker license.

- The broker cannot advertise using the word *escrow* to lead the public to believe escrow is the business of the broker.

- All escrow funds must be kept in a trust fund that both the California Department of Real Estate and the California Department of Corporations may inspect.

estate contracts must be in writing, according to the Statute of Frauds, a disclosure statement must be part of the written escrow instructions that are executed by the buyer and the seller.

The California Business and Profession's (B&P) Code Division 4, Sections 10000 through 11020 are the consolidated and revised laws that are supervised, administered, and enforced by the California Department of Real Estate. These codes regulate transactions affecting interests in real property by licensed brokers and salespersons with respect to dealings in real property. The codes carry disciplinary and criminal penalties for violations for these real estate activities in California. Section 10141.5 states that within *one month* after the closing of a transaction in which title to real property, or in the sale of a business when real property, is conveyed from a seller to a purchaser, through a licensed real estate broker, that broker must inform, or cause the information to be given to, the seller and purchaser in writing of the selling price. In the event of an exchange of real property or a business opportunity, the information must include a description of the property and the amount of money paid as consideration. This same code section states that within *one week* after the closing of a transaction negotiated by a real estate broker where title passes and a deed of trust secured by the real property is executed, the broker must cause the deed to be recorded with the county recorder of the county where the property is located. Or the broker may cause the deed to be delivered to the beneficiary as a written recommendation that the deed be recorded forthwith, unless written instructions not to record are received from the beneficiary.

Section 10145(a) of the B&P indicates that the client funds must be deposited immediately into a neutral escrow depository, or into the hands of the broker's principal, or placed into a bank trust account maintained by the broker. All funds deposited by the broker into a broker trust account must be maintained there until disbursed by the broker according to the person entitled to the funds.

The regulations of the Real Estate Commissioner are found in Chapter 6. Article 19 pertains to Escrows and Article 15 covers Trust Fund Accounts. See Figure 2.9 for a list of regulations. These Articles contain various sections that elaborate on the handling of escrow and client trust funds by the California Department of Real Estate licensed broker. When handling client funds, "the broker must maintain a written columnar record in chronological sequence showing the following: (a) date funds received, (b) from whom, (c) amount received, (d) date deposited into bank, (e) date of disbursement, (f) check number, (g) to whom disbursement made, (h) amount disbursed, (i) amount of interest earned, if any, and (j) daily bank balance of the escrow/trust bank account."

In the past, it was not economical to establish an escrow department of a real estate broker's office activities because of the amount of work required and the added liability exposure for the work incurred. However, as real estate firms become larger with several hundreds of agents working under one broker, the volume of escrow activity carried on by these agents employed under that one broker for that one firm becomes far more economically reasonable. And, as the broker's errors and omissions insurance coverage is better written to protect against potential liabilities in conjunction with the handling of an escrow, the escrow procedures seem more economically reasonable. But the primary reason for broker-owned escrow company expansion of business is due to electronic escrows. With "e-escrow" now available at a reasonable cost to the consumer and providing added income for the broker, it is likely that this area of the escrow business should continue to grow.

Many differences exist between the various types of escrow entities. Each escrow service provider must meet the written legal requirements issued by the governing state commissioner. Each state commissioner follows the rules and regulations of his or her respective state department regulations. In practice, many operations seem the same or similar. The escrow entity is trying to get from the opening of escrow, say Point A, to the close of the escrow and transfer of title, Point B. How each travels during the interim is drastically different. Table 2.1 shows some of the differences.

In addition to the various types of different escrow company operations—because of their respective regulators—other escrow entities not discussed in further detail also exist. While state chartered banks are under the control of the State Banking Commissioner, national banks are under the Comptroller of the Currency. If a state chartered bank is a member of the Federal Reserve, then the Federal Reserve Board oversees that escrow department's operations under that bank's rules and regulations of operation. Both state and national banks are under the Federal

Article 19 Escrows

Section 2950: When Broker Handles Escrow

When the broker handles an escrow the broker is prohibited from the following:

(a) Accepting forms containing any blank to be filled in after signing or initialing escrow instructions

(b) Permitting any person to make addition, deletion, or alteration unless signed by all persons who initiated the escrow instructions

(c) Failing to deliver at the time of execution a copy of escrow instructions or any form any person signed

(d) Failing to maintain books, records, and accounts according to accepted principles of accounting and good business practices

(e) Failing to maintain the office, place of books, records, accounts, safes, files, and papers relating to such escrows freely accessible and available for audit, inspection and examination by the commissioner

(f) Failing to deposit all money received in a bank trust/escrow account before the close of the next full working day after receipt

(g) Withdrawing or paying out any money deposited in such trust account without the written instruction of the parties

(h) Failing to advise all parties in writing that any licensee in the transaction has any interest in the escrow company

(i) Failing upon close of escrow to render each principal a written statement of all receipts and disbursements and payable to whom

(j) Delivering or recording any instrument which purportedly transfers a party's title or interest in real property without obtaining the written consent of that party

Section 2951: Record Keeping and Funds Handling

Article 15 Trust Fund Accounts

28230.1 Interest-Bearing Trust Account

2831 Trust Fund Records to Be Maintained

2831.1 Separate Record for Each Beneficiary or Transaction

2831.2 Trust Account Reconciliation

2832 Trust Fund Handling

2832.1 Trust Fund Handling for Multiple Beneficiaries

2834 Trust Account Withdrawals

TABLE 2.1

Escrow Entity Differences

Escrow Type	Independent	Broker-Owned	Title Insurance Company	Attorney	Bank	Savings Association
Regulator	California Department of Corporations	California Department of Real Estate (DRE)	California Department of Insurance	California Bar Association	Federal Reserve	Federal Office of Thrift Supervision (OTS)
Boss	Corporation Commissioner	Real Estate Commissioner	Insurance Commissioner	Bar Association	Banking Commissioner	Savings-Thrift Commissioner
Protection	$4M Fidelity Bond (minimum) and $2,500 Surety Bond	DRE Recovery Fund: Maximum $20,000 per person			FDIC Insurance Up to Maximum per Signatory	
License Requirement	Escrow License	DRE Broker License	None	None	None	None
Experience of Escrow Officer	Yes (5 year minimum)	None	None			
Net Worth Requirement	Yes	None		None	None	None
Liquidity Requirement	Yes	No		None	None	None
Background investigation	Yes	Yes (FBI Search)			*	*
Fingerprints	Yes (and Photo)	Yes (Live Scan)				

* Employer investigation possible for employment.

Deposit Insurance Corporation regulatory body also. State chartered savings associations are now referred to as "thrift institutions." Federally chartered savings and thrift institutions are under the Office of Thrift Supervision (OTS). The escrow operations for a builder would fall under the corporation commissioner, as would the escrow department of a mortgage loan banker. Likewise, a credit union escrow department would fall under the corporation commissioner.

■ PROFESSIONAL ESCROW ORGANIZATIONS AND DESIGNATIONS

Six escrow officers and supervisors met in 1924 to discuss mutual problems, which eventually led to the formation of the Los Angeles Escrow Association (LAEA). Many lawyers became concerned that these escrow holders were perhaps trying to practice law. In 1936, the California Bar Association, representing attorneys, entered into an agreement with the newly formed California Land Title Association. The formal agreement outlined the activities allowed to be performed by the title companies and those duties to be reserved for an attorney only, to perform as the practice of law.

A similar agreement was prepared between the State Bar and the California Bankers Association, which stated: "Where a bank is employed to act as an escrow agent, it is entitled to prepare, or cause to be prepared, the escrow instructions defining its rights, duties, and liabilities as an escrow agent." These agreements formed the foundation for the current practice of using escrow holders as the primary vehicle for the transfer of title between parties.

In 1966, an agreement between the State Bar of California and Escrow Institute of California was signed establishing the guidelines for the future professional functions of each organization. This agreement allowed escrow holders to perform certain specified duties without violating the prohibition of practicing law without meeting the requirements of a lawyer. The State Bar of California had to terminate all the earlier agreements in 1979 because the mutual agreement was considered similar to price fixing. The Sherman Antitrust Act (1890) prohibits competing businesses within the same industry from conspiring together to set uniform practices. The earlier agreements were used as the foundation for the current duties and functions for escrow holders.

Much has changed since the 1930s in the law profession, real estate practices, and escrow procedures. Many of the items commonly handled today did not exist over three quarters of a century ago. The handling of probate, holding title as joint tenant with the right of survivorship or in a living trust, and title insurance to guarantee lenders' protection did not exist. The majority of the changes that have led to common practices today have come about due to escrow associations. An *association* is a group of people who join together with a common purpose, usually to promote the business, protect its members, and direct legislative guidelines for legal practices within the profession. The various different escrow personnel has led to the current laws and operations within the escrow business today in California. Because practices in escrow vary between different states, the national organization, discussed on page 39, holds conferences and meetings that discuss local practices to aid in setting national standards of practices for intrastate title firms, while exchanging differing mandated regulations for specific states.

California Escrow Association

In the mid-1950s, the Los Angeles Escrow Association helped initiate the formation of other escrow groups. One group, the Escrow Institute, consisted of several local escrow associations from the San Gabriel Valley, Long Beach, Riverside, San Bernardino, and Santa Barbara areas. These groups joined together to form the statewide **California Escrow Association (CEA).** The first President of the California Escrow Association was Fred Tichenor of California Bank.

Education was emphasized by CEA from its inception. In the early 1960s the CEA members served as advisers when community college real estate escrow educators began a program to award a certificate for escrow separate from the real estate certificate. The separation between the certificates led additional, non-real estate licensees to the classroom to further their knowledge and understanding of the transfer of property. People who worked in the title insurance industry, tax office employees, bank trust employees, and refinance loan processors were attracted to the specialized education, as well as various escrow personnel. Since the late 1960s, CEA members continue to present educational seminars at many colleges and universities statewide.

In 1969, CEA inaugurated a program for Professional Designations. Still in effect today, escrow officers proudly display their plaques, which proclaim that they have obtained the coveted Certified Escrow Officer (CEO) designation or Certified Senior Escrow Officer (CSEO) designation. CEA also has examinations for Certified Escrow Instructor (CEI), Bulk Sale Specialist (BSS), and Mobile Home Specialist (MHS). Each year, escrow professionals throughout the state and experts in selected areas participate in CEA's Education Conference where well-known speakers discuss specialized topics of current importance. The organization's primary goals are focused on education and legislation for the escrow business.

The mission statement for the California Escrow Association is as follows:

> To both lead and support the escrow closing, real estate and financial communities through our commitment to the professional and personal growth of the escrow practitioner; to do this by sharing knowledge and experience and by granting recognition within our profession.

In addition, the California Escrow Association created an online publication, the *Reality Statement*. The purpose of the documents published there is to encourage members of CEA to deliver and receive information through modern technology. CEA members are encouraged to continue to be effective, educated, professional, and involved. The organization set up a legislative hotline, utilized modern training methods, and provided membership information. CEA continues to identify and address the changing needs of the escrow professional and to provide an aggressive forum for addressing the issues of its diverse membership. For more information, this professional organization may be reached by telephone at (916) 325-0600; by fax at (916) 325-9990; by writing its offices at California Escrow Association, 530 Bercut Drive, Suite G, Sacramento, CA 95814; or by going to its Web site: *www.ceaescrow.org*.

WEB LINK

American Escrow Association (AEA)

In 1980 the California Escrow Association worked together with similar state groups in Oregon, Washington, Arizona, and Nevada to form the **American Escrow Association (AEA).** The first president was Earl Barrett, a Californian. The individuals who belong to this organization work for a title company, escrow company,

FIGURE 2.10

AEA Web Site Sample

~ <u>Consumers Info</u> ~ <u>News Flashes!</u> ~ <u>President's Message</u> ~ <u>Board of Directors</u> ~ <u>National Standards</u> ~
<u>Annual Conference</u> ~ ~<u>Membership</u> ~ <u>Creating Alliances</u> ~

Mission Statement:

- Enhance the education of the escrow/settlement professional.
- Improve escrow and closing services.
- Disseminate information as to the difference in such services between states.
- Promote more uniformity in such services.
- Increase the public knowledge and understanding of such services.
- Coordinate legislative efforts throughout the United States, the District of Colombia, its possessions and territories.

The American Escrow Association prides itself on being the **representative of** its member states and individual members in **the escrow and settlement industry.**

Our Goals

The goals of the Association are to **further the education and professionalism of the escrow industry** as a whole. These goals are the backbone of the Association and remain today as guidelines for our continued growth.

Source: *http://www.a-e-a.org.* Reproduced with the permission of the American Escrow Association.

or loan broker. Today less than half of the states have escrow associations because the majority of the escrow work in most states is performed by an attorney.

AEA activities and membership are growing for a number of reasons. One advantage for having an independent escrow rather than an attorney do the basic escrow mechanics of a transaction is often the more moderate price. Another benefit is the consistency of the procedure and reliability for doing only one job that is used in the transfer of property by the escrow company.

On a national level, the AEA assists members in networking various individual state interests into a national coalition. The AEA is helping to establish closing practices for real estate transactions worldwide. Many areas of the world are changing from government ownership of property to private land ownership. This increases the demand for escrow practices and procedures on a global basis. You may contact the AEA by telephone at (800) 877-7414; by writing it at American Escrow Association, c/o Grant Enterprises, 4623 SW Alaska Street, Seattle, WA 98116; or by visiting its Web site (see Figure 2.10): *www.a-e-a.org.*

WEB LINK

■ CAREERS IN ESCROW

Escrow is a neutral depository that conducts business for the principals. The employees of the escrow company may not be licensed to act as escrow agents. The employing body may or may not be licensed, depending upon the structure of the firm. Some individuals may be licensed in another capacity, such as the licensed salesperson acting under the licensed broker and employed to act as the escrow officer. However, most persons who work in escrow positions are not licensed. Many opportunities for employment are available for a career in escrow. It is important to know the various positions in the field and the duties and responsibilities expected for each.

Escrow Agent or Escrow Holder

This business entity (individual or company) is responsible and liable for the escrow transaction; this is the employing firm. The business may be conducted as an independent escrow corporation, as a department of a title insurance company or a bank, or as part of an attorney's or a real estate broker's practice.

Escrow Officer

The **escrow officer** is trained to have the full skills and competencies necessary to complete a variety of types of escrows. This person must know how to prepare documents, check details on loans and title reports, work with various vendors who do work on the property during escrow, and interpret data and instructions. In addition, the escrow officer should possess skills in handling difficult people and stressful situations. The ability to resolve problems and offer a variety of possible solutions is a great help to the other parties involved, such as agents, lenders, or contractors. The escrow officer will work with the many real estate agents, pest controllers, loan brokers, etc., in addition to the principals to the transaction, the buyer and the seller.

Complex transactions are often the easiest because the principals and agents are often more knowledgeable. Conversely, the simplest transfer of a low-priced condominium may be the hardest transaction if the parties are not knowledgeable about escrow procedures, real estate transactions, homeowner associations, or the transfer of real property. The escrow officer must be efficient and be able to generate a profit for the firm; should have an analytical mind to assimilate, coordinate, organize, and resolve problems; and should have the type of formal training and knowledge that is similar to that of a paralegal or real estate assistant. Good skills in accounting, computer escrow programs, communications, and time management are a must for a position as an escrow officer.

The escrow holder acts as the agent of each principal. A limited agency relationship exists between the escrow officer and the principals. When the escrow is first opened, the escrow officer is the agent of both parties. Written instructions determine the duties of the agent.

International Escrow Agent

With the enormous growth in global real estate transactions, the demand for a global escrow provider has dramatically increased. Customers and suppliers need a global provider who can service both of their respective needs, regardless of the physical, geographic location of the parties. The international escrow agent must be able to meet the specific legal requirements for the global principals and their agents. The online documents must be secure, the international funds transfer must be readily available, and the transaction must be available in multiple languages. The international escrow agent must understand the idiosyncrasies of various cultures and the business practices that go with European, Asian, American, and other countries' real property transactions. The escrow software of today often translates the escrow documents into whatever language is desired, but an individual with multiple languages and a background based upon living and working in the business and real property environment in another culture is especially helpful for a position as an international escrow officer.

Escrow Receptionist

The individual who begins working in the escrow business in this position becomes familiar with the demands of the rest of the entire office operation. The key to this position is the ability to be friendly but firm in handling incoming callers who insist on reaching other escrow office personnel who may not be immediately available to handle the call. Confidentiality is a key concern. When a caller demands to talk about the Jones file on Elm Street, the escrow receptionist may not even acknowledge that the office has such a file until and unless the caller is identified as a principal to the transaction. A loose tongue can end up with extraneous liens being placed into the escrow, which might hold up the close of escrow until disposition of the alleged encumbrance on the transaction. Learning the vocabulary of the business is an important first step in obtaining a job as an escrow receptionist.

Escrow Assistant

This is an entry-level position where individuals can learn the escrow business. The key to advancement is to learn the progression of steps from opening an escrow to disbursements after the close of escrow and transfer of title. The more experience one obtains in the various, detailed progression of the escrow stages, the more opportunities will be available. The escrow officer under whom the assistant is trained will also greatly influence the body of knowledge obtained in this position. If the assistant works under an escrow officer who only handles refinance loans in a position at a loan brokerage office, the assistant will have limited escrow knowledge. The same is true if the assistant's work experience has previously been only at a bank trust department. It would be wise to look into the escrow associations' job availability notices to see which positions would best broaden the assistant's variety of experience for different types of escrows, such as bulk sales, new tract sales, exchanges, income or commercial property sales, and others.

Escrow Office Manager

This person is in charge of an escrow department. The escrow office manager is responsible for the office operations and reporting these to the company owners. Because the office must run at a profit, the bottom line is important. This person needs a background in financial management, personnel, marketing, communications, and education; that is, the ability to teach others. Coordination of the escrow files of an entire office and all the escrow officers working for the firm is a career that calls for a background in escrow knowledge in order to have the technical and people skills to monitor, evaluate, and supervise all the other office personnel.

Escrow Administrator

The escrow administrator has all the responsibilities and duties of the escrow office manager, except instead of overseeing a single office operation, the manager may oversee several escrow branches, such as at a bank chain. Strong managerial skills are required for success in this career, as well as personnel skills.

THINK ABOUT IT

Interview and observe an individual in the escrow profession and complete the chart below. In the first column, list the skill. In the second column, place a mark if the skill is primarily mathematical. Mark the third column if the skill is predominantly a written job skill. Mark the fourth column if the skill is primarily a verbal communications skill.

Skill	Math	Written	Verbal
1.			
2.			
3.			
4.			
5.			
6.			
7.			
8.			
9.			
10.			

■ CHAPTER SUMMARY

Where escrow is practiced, the participants are called settlement agents, closers, or, as in California, escrow officer. Some escrows handle the transfer of title to real property through the escrow department at a bank or a savings association. In many Midwestern states escrow is handled by an abstract attorney. On the East Coast, escrow is often handled by a title insurance attorney. In Northern California escrow is predominantly handled by a department of the title insurance company that insures the title in the transaction. In Southern California independent escrow companies handle the escrow process, and they are licensed to do escrow from the California Department of Corporations. Independent escrow companies are not otherwise affiliated with any part of the transaction.

Several escrow associations united to form the California Escrow Association in the 1950s. Then in 1980, organizations from five states created the national American Escrow Association. These two professional organizations are recognized as educational and employment networks. Each organization aids members in maintaining professional standards and in uniting to gain political support for the industry.

■ CHAPTER 2 QUIZ

1. Which of the following is *NOT* true?
   a. CEA awards specialized professional designations to qualified individuals.
   b. An escrow holder is legally the same as an attorney.
   c. The term escrow is actually from the French word *escroue*.
   d. The California Escrow Association helped form the American Escrow Association.

2. The California Escrow Association
   a. helped create the American Escrow Association.
   b. began as federal legislation.
   c. is a subsidiary of the California Bar Association.
   d. was created by the California Land Title Association.

3. Escrow is expected to do all *EXCEPT* which of the following?
   a. Gather documents
   b. Determine prorations
   c. Insure the title and record the deed
   d. Disburse proceeds and papers after the close of escrow

4. The escrow process is handled by the
   a. title officer.
   b. real estate salesperson.
   c. loan officer.
   d. escrow agent.

5. The California Bar and Department of Real Estate
   a. prohibit members/licensees from handling any part of the escrow process.
   b. issue a special escrow license for members/salesperson licensees performing escrow operations.
   c. allow members/brokers to handle escrow if it is in the normal scope of their business in which they are handling the transfer of title as part of their other business.
   d. developed the foundation for the two organized escrow associations and instituted federal legislation to monitor and support escrow licensing operations.

6. Bank and savings thrift institution escrow departments
   a. must obtain an escrow license to perform services when handling escrow in conjunction with trust or probate clients.
   b. handle escrows in conjunction with the normal course of their other banking business operations.
   c. are governed under the California Insurance Commissioner.
   d. are prohibited from handling any and all escrow operations.

7. Who may handle an escrow in California?
   a. Title attorney, abstract attorney, or California attorney
   b. California Department of Real Estate broker
   c. Title insurance company employee in its escrow department
   d. All of the above

8. The individual escrow company operation that requires a minimum of five years of escrow officer experience is licensed under which California Commissioner?
   a. Corporation
   c. Insurance
   b. Real Estate
   d. Banking

9. The regulator who oversees the escrow department of a title company is the
   a. Department of Corporations.
   b. Department of Real Estate.
   c. Department of Insurance.
   d. Department of Banking.

10. Who requires a background investigation and fingerprints?
    a. Insurance Commissioner and Real Estate Commissioner
    b. Corporation Commissioner and Insurance Commissioner
    c. Corporation Commissioner and Real Estate Commissioner
    d. None of the above

SECTION TWO

PROCESSING THE ESCROW

CHAPTER THREE

OPENING THE ESCROW

■ KEY TERMS

agent	escrow	principal
AIN	escrow holder	promise for a promise
APN	estate	property
capacity	fees	real property
certified escrow	FSBO	take sheet
instructions	liquor license	TIN
CLAP FACTS	mutual agreement	vesting
consideration	ownership	Zone Disclosure
contract	personal property	Statement fee
earnest money		

■ CHAPTER OVERVIEW

The requirements for a legal contract are much the same as the requirements for a valid escrow. The escrow practices differ in other states and between Northern and Southern California. An experienced escrow officer will ask for all items required to have a valid escrow and will know the practices for real estate escrow in the local area. The escrow holder knows what he or she needs in order to have a valid escrow.

The real estate agent and principal need to know what information the escrow officer will request to open escrow. Some required items usually include the purchase contract, vesting, real property description, **personal property,** commission, financing terms, and possession details.

■ LEARNING OBJECTIVES

At the conclusion of Chapter 3, you will be able to

- understand the elements required for a valid escrow;
- give a definition of opening an escrow;
- outline the areas contained in escrow instructions;
- differentiate between various state and regional escrow practices;
- explain the necessity for escrow instructions; and
- describe requirements for a valid escrow.

■ REQUIREMENTS FOR A VALID ESCROW

Any discussion of the requirements for a valid escrow must include the agreement, the parties, the instructions, and contract law.

Agreement

An *agreement* is a binding **contract** between parties in a real property transaction. It is a mutual promise for a promise. The first misunderstanding in an escrow is determining who the parties are. Most people assume the escrow instructions are a binding contract between a buyer and a seller in a sales transaction. This is not the case.

The buyer and the seller should already have a mutually agreed upon binding sales contract prior to obtaining escrow instructions. The binding contract between the buyer and the seller may be a purchase agreement, an exchange agreement, a rent with option to purchase, a land contract, wraparound agreement, some agreement of sale, or any other legally binding agreement.

In the case of a For Sale By Owner, **FSBO** (pronounced FISBO), the principals often believe that the original oral agreement is all that is needed. The parties might agree on the date escrow is to close, the buyer agrees to obtain a loan, and the seller agrees to sell at a specific price. The critical elements are often not discussed. Closing costs are negotiable by the parties in most all transactions, yet they are often not discussed between the buyer and FSBO seller. Some common items not fully agreed upon by the parties may include

- an appraisal;

- termite preventive work; and

- termite report with corrective work.

When no licensee is involved, the principals may not understand that in a court of law in California, a **real property** transaction must be in writing to be enforceable, according to the Statutes of Frauds. Because the escrow instructions are not a contract between the buyer and seller, no contract exists.

When a licensed real estate agent is involved, a written binding contract is already in place and executed by the parties. The most commonly used contract is the California Association of REALTORS® (CAR) purchase agreement form, although other forms are also used. The CAR details most of the major items needed to close the escrow. The contract contains the price and the date escrow is to close. The CAR contract also has how many days each party has to review and/or disapprove items such as an inspection, disclosure, personal property, and who is responsible for the payment of closing costs and fees.

Parties

If escrow instructions are not between the buyer and the seller, then who are the parties to the escrow instructions? Escrow instructions are between the escrow company and each individual entity to the transactions. When escrow instructions are created, one set of instructions is between the buyer and the escrow company, another set of instructions is between the seller and the escrow holder, and yet another set is between the borrower and the lender.

Instructions

The set of escrow instructions for the buyer indicates many items that are only for the buyer, such as instructions to escrow stating that the buyer wants a copy of the "Certified Escrow Instructions" delivered to the buyer's prospective lender or loan agent. The seller's escrow instructions indicate that the escrow holder is to pay off the seller's existing loan. These instructions are specific to the individual party and not applicable to the other principal.

In addition, the escrow instructions indicate specific items that must be complied with when working with a lender, even though the lender does not sign any set of escrow instructions agreeing to any of the terms that the buyer and the seller agreed to. Herein lies the first area of conflict. If escrow instructions state that the interest rate is not to exceed a specific rate, this does not mean that the principal will actually get that rate. If the property owner is refinancing, or if the buyer is obtaining a new loan during the course of the escrow, the interest rates are subject to market conditions and might increase. The shorter the time between escrow opening and the close of escrow, the less likely interest rate changes will occur. The longer the escrow period, the more likely the rate will change. If the rate and terms at the *end* of escrow are above the amounts specified in the escrow instructions, the escrow company cannot close escrow without the signed, written permission of the principal. The **principal** may not agree to the change in terms and instead may prefer to cancel escrow rather than agree to go ahead with an unfavorable loan. However, this has consequences for the seller, who does not care if the buyer pays all cash for the property or finances part of the purchase price. If the real estate contract does not state differently, and if the escrow instructions do not state otherwise, the buyer may be held to breach of contract with the seller for nonperformance of closing of the escrow. Therefore, the buyer must specify that if the lender changes the terms, the consequences for the seller are finding another purchaser.

The buyer signs a set of escrow instructions that are binding between the buyer and the escrow holder. The seller signs a set of escrow instructions that are binding between the seller and the escrow holder. Often the same items are placed in one writing, on one set of escrow instructions for such items as the price, property address, **vesting,** escrow period, and personal property. However, each principal often has separate pages that only one side is a party to. For example, only the seller would have a deed to sign to transfer title to the buyer. Likewise, only the buyer would receive a page instructing the escrow holder regarding the new property insurance policy.

When separate escrow instructions are prepared, the buyer and the seller do not sign the same set of instructions. On the purchase agreement contract, both principals sign on the "original" of the same document. The buyers sign a set of instructions to the escrow holder authorizing escrow to do specific items on their behalf. The same is true of the seller. When both sets of the signed documents are returned to the escrow holder, then the escrow is open.

Sometimes the real estate agents and principals do not know about the need to follow up. If one side signs and returns the escrow instructions, but the other side does not, the escrow is not open. It is therefore very important that when one side returns their documents that they check with the escrow holder to confirm if the other side has returned signed documents. Again, if they have, then the escrow is open. But if the other side has not yet returned the documents signed by all the required parties, then it is time for the agent or principal to contact the other side to determine when this will be completed. Check each day until this has been completed.

Contract Law

The principals need to have executed a binding agreement.

Legal contract.   To have a valid escrow, it is required to have a valid contract. As was stated above, all the elements necessary for contract law apply, which are discussed below.

Capacity.   **Capacity** means that it is necessary for all parties to the escrow to be legally competent. If an individual is signing for himself or herself, escrow need go no further. But often one person is acting for another person or entity. Escrow must have documents that confirm the ability for one to sign for another. For example, if the party to the escrow is a corporation, the secretary of the corporation, not the president, is usually the signatory. A corporate resolution or the articles of incorporation is the document that usually states who may sign for the corporation. Likewise, many people hold title in a trust. The parties to the escrow may or may not be the signatories for the trust. The trust document authorizes the individuals who may sign on behalf of the trust.

Consideration.   The term **consideration** means something of value, usually the cash down payment. Contract law says there must be adequate consideration to bind the contract. The consideration may be equity, as in an exchange. Normally when the buyer's down payment is placed into escrow, the escrow instructions between the buyer and escrow holder would comply with contract law because consideration was given in good faith with instructions on what to do with these funds. It is not unusual for the buyer's broker to have the down payment in the broker trust account. In this case, the escrow instructions may state the location of the consideration is in the broker's trust account or in a bank CD account. The escrow instructions should indicate when and how the funds get from the broker trust account to the escrow holder.

Lawful object.   The legal system will not enforce an illegal contract. If a contract violates a law, it may be held to not have lawful object and, therefore, be illegal and unenforceable in a court of law. In a real **estate** transaction, this could be a note drawn up for a loan that violates the usury law regarding interest rates. Not having lawful object includes when a party waives a right the law does not allow them to waive, such as a written statement waiving a mandated disclosure. Contract law requires an understanding of lawful object but prohibits the practice of law by the escrow officer. In California, the escrow association entered into a series of treaties with the state bar association for the practice of real estate transfer of property **ownership** using an escrow entity.

Mutual agreement.   For a contract to be binding, all the parties to the contract must agree to the terms and conditions of the contract. The meeting of the minds when signatures from all parties are executed is referred to as **mutual agreement.**

Promise for a promise.   In the purchase agreement, the **promise for a promise** is the offer and acceptance between the principals. The buyer promised to perform by delivering all the money necessary to close escrow, including the closing costs. The seller promised to deliver clear title to the buyer. In escrow instructions, the principals promise to deliver the items called for in the escrow instructions. The buyer principal promises to deliver the funds to escrow prior to the close of escrow. The seller principal promises to execute a notarized deed to escrow. The escrow officer promises to perform many duties, such as to give a certified copy of escrow instructions to the buyer's lender and to keep the information obtained in the escrow confidential.

■ SELECTION OF THE ESCROW HOLDER

Selection of the **escrow holder** involves California law, local custom, and the qualifications of the escrow holder, all discussed below.

Law

California law does not state that an escrow is required for the majority of real estate transactions, except in the transfer of specific types of transactions as discussed above. The acronym LIPS is often used to remember the four types of transactions that require an escrow, as shown in Figure 3.1. It is possible for the seller to sign a deed to a buyer and for the buyer to give the seller all the cash necessary for the consideration to be met, and then the deed to be recorded at the county recorder's office to transfer title between the parties. However, if a new loan is to be obtained, the lender will require certified escrow instruction and title insurance for the lender.

Practices

When an escrow will be used, as is typically the case, local custom and real estate practices dictate how the escrow holder is selected. This varies throughout California and is negotiable between the parties. Typically the party who pays for the item, such as loan fees, termite treatment, or title insurance, makes the selection of the company performing that service. However, this is not the case with selection of the escrow holder.

Often the purchase agreement contract between the buyer and the seller does not state the actual name of the escrow company. The specific name of the escrow company should have been indicated so as not to have an ambiguous contract. Most contracts leave the name blank or indicate "to be decided," and each agent often wants a different company.

The party who selected the escrow holder may not be the party to pay for the services. The selection of the service provider is negotiated in the contract between the principles. In Southern California the seller usually selects the services and the buyer normally agrees. In Northern California it is typical for the buyer to select services and the seller usually agrees. Generally, because neither the buyer nor the seller knows any particular service provider, the real estate licensees often make the selection. In the Bay area and often in the central coastal areas surrounding San Francisco, typically the buyer pays the escrow fee. In some parts of the state the escrow fee is split between the buyer and the seller, as is

FIGURE 3.1

Transactions Requiring an Escrow

Liquor
Impounds
Probate
Securities

common in Southern California. For a refinance, the borrower usually pays the entire escrow fee. Again, local custom varies.

Qualified Escrow Holder

Not all escrow holders handle all types of escrows. Most escrow officers are qualified to perform services for transactions, such as the following:

- Sale of real property between a seller and a buyer, with licensed DRE agents

- Sale of real property between a seller and a buyer, with no sales agents

- Refinance for an existing property owner, with no sales agent

- Land sale contract, all-inclusive trust deed, or wraparound mortgage between a buyer and seller, with or without sales agents

- Sale of a trust deed to an investor

A broker-owned escrow company also is unqualified to accept performing the duties of the escrow when only outside agents are involved or when no agent is involved. If the broker is not the agent handling the sale transaction, the escrow officer employed to work under that broker cannot handle the escrow. The transaction must involve the employing broker.

Many escrow officers are not trained to handle specialized escrows and would usually refer the parties to an escrow agent who is capable of performing the transaction. Some escrow companies specialize in the following types of transactions:

- Mobile home unit transfer of ownership or financing of the module

- Mobile home park with pads or time-share ownership

- Leasehold interests of tenants

- Exchange of real property, with or without use of an accommodator

- Business property transfer of ownership or financing of commercial or industrial property that may or may not include personal property and fixtures

- **Liquor license** transfer of ownership
- Bulk sales with a liquor license
- Combinations of any of the above

■ DIFFERENCES IN ESCROW PRACTICES

Prior to opening escrow, two questions should be answered by each principal:

1. Are you currently under contract with any licensed agent?

   The answer to this question reveals issues involving agency disclosure, buyer-broker or listing contracts, and lender commitment requirements.

2. Have you ever been involved in any escrow anywhere?

   The answer will reveal if the principal has experience with escrow procedures in other countries, states, or regions of California.

When a principal has closed more transactions than their current real estate salesperson, all of which are out-of-state, problems in procedures often arise. When escrow presents the principal with different documents than have been previously experienced on other transactions, a lot more explanation will be required. Due to the higher prices, purchasers often have acquired the funds needed to close escrow in California from the proceeds of the sale of some other property, often from an out-of-state transaction. Some differences are discussed below.

Other Countries

The real estate practices in other countries vary considerably. Formerly, because many countries would not allow private ownership of property, there was no need for escrow. The government owned all the land and basically rented it to the citizens of that country. In countries where the citizens allow private ownership of real property, the transfer ownership is handled in many different ways. In most of Europe the current practices follow the past feudal system, where the king owned all the land. The common practice is for the use of a barrister, or attorney, to handle a real property transaction. The appraisers usually come from a background of engineering and are called evaluators, rather than appraisers. Evaluators in much of Europe are more interested in the cost approach to value, rather than the comparable market analysis approach to value used by U.S. real estate practitioners.

Other States

In most of the New England states, an independent escrow company does not handle the escrow. Typically, the real estate **agent** shows the **property** to the buyer and writes an offer to purchase, as is done in a California transaction. This is where the similarity stops. After the seller accepts the offer to purchase and a mutually agreed-upon contract agreement is established, an appointment is set with an attorney. The lawyer has the buyer and the seller meet at the law office, and the attorney draws up a binding contract between the parties. Then the attorney either searches the title or hires another attorney to search title, often referred to as an abstract attorney, because they abstract the title.

A list of specific state information can be found using the online resources in the Appendix. The information shows items such as whether a mortgage or deed of trust (trust deed) is used, transfer tax, who usually pays the title insurance, recording fee, closing costs, and required disclosures. The Appendix also shows state agency contact information.

California

In California, attorneys are rarely involved in escrow instructions except when the real estate transaction is part of the normal course of their other business, such as handling a probate estate or in the case of transferring ownership under a divorce decree. A thorough explanation of the state differences should be disclosed at the beginning of every transaction.

Northern California and Southern California operate in many similar ways for a real estate escrow. However, some differences do apply. See page 451 for information on accessing a set of sample Southern California escrow instructions and Northern California escrow instructions. When reading and comparing the two sets, the differences seem subtle yet several things are handled differently.

The areas where the procedures are most different are timing and contract law.

Timing.   The most notable difference is usually the timing of when something is performed. In most Southern regions, escrow is opened immediately after the purchase contract is executed. In the Northern areas, the escrow is opened just before the close of the escrow. The types of documents and basic set of instructions between the principals and the escrow holder would remain the same.

The Southern areas therefore have a greater need for the use of an escrow amendment because of changes that occur during the normal course of a transaction. The Northern area would have less or no amendments because all the items would already have been resolved before the end of the transaction, and prior to escrow instruction being typed.

Items that typically might have to be amended in an escrow include price, loan amount, loan interest rate, and cash. For example, the buyer and the seller agree upon the price, but often the value that the appraiser provides for the property could change the closing price. When the appraised evaluation differs from the sales price, the lender may become involved because the loan criteria are based on a percentage of the appraised value, not a percent of the sales price. When an appraisal is less than the sales price, the buyer may place additional cash down payment or the seller may carry back a second trust deed for the difference if mutually agreed.

Contract law. Typically in Northern California, the general practice is that the documents between the escrow holder and the principals are unilateral escrow instructions. Because the escrow instructions are at the end of the transaction, just prior to closing, and everything is virtually already finished, the escrow instructions created at the end of the process contain all the items already agreed to and already performed. The two principles are jointly agreeing on one set of instructions that directs the escrow holder to perform his or her duties. The terms are usually set in the final stages at this point, and all parties are in full agreement with no changes made prior to the close of escrow. Both principals are acting as one person, and the unilateral escrow instructions state what has already been agreed upon by all parties, including the lender. The principals then ratify the escrow instructions. Because the parties ratify the writing after most of the work is completed, the summary box showing the cash and loans is not normally completed at the beginning of the escrow instructions. The escrow instructions merely state the cash down payment and the amount of the loan(s) with the final terms and conditions for the loan.

In Southern California, bilateral escrow instructions are the most commonly used in practice. In this case the two parties are both instructing the escrow holder to perform certain authorized items on their behalf. However, as the transaction goes on, many items are subject to change. The buyer and seller can change vesting, the buyer's loan terms and conditions are subject to change, the appraised price may change the contract sales price, the date of possession may change, and a lump sum credit to the buyer from the seller for repairs found during the disclosure process may be requested. The escrow instructions will contain a summary box of total consideration at the beginning of the document to indicate the cash and loans that make up the total price. The principals, lender, and agents can quickly and easily see the breakdown of the transaction funds in the summary.

Performance. In Southern California, once escrow is opened, the escrow officer handles virtually all of the communications with the new lender, the seller's existing lender to obtain beneficiary demand statement, and the title insurance company. In Northern California, the broker performs more duties because the escrow is not officially open. The broker stays in contact with the buyer's lender and requests a preliminary title report. The broker may place the buyer's deposit with an escrow company.

Joint escrow instructions. An increasingly popular practice in California is for the real estate agents in the transaction to use the Residential Purchase Agreement and Joint Escrow Instructions document released by the California Association of REALTORS®. This document contains all the items of agreement between the buyer and seller, or the purchase information, in addition to the instructions for escrow. See Figure 3.2 for an example of the joint escrow instructions form.

FIGURE 3.2

Joint Escrow Instructions Form

CALIFORNIA ASSOCIATION OF REALTORS®

**CALIFORNIA
RESIDENTIAL PURCHASE AGREEMENT
AND JOINT ESCROW INSTRUCTIONS**
For Use With Single Family Residential Property — Attached or Detached
(C.A.R. Form RPA-CA, Revised 10/02)

Date _____, at _____, California.
1. **OFFER:**
    A. **THIS IS AN OFFER FROM** _____ ("Buyer").
    B. **THE REAL PROPERTY TO BE ACQUIRED** is described as _____
        _____, Assessor's Parcel No. _____, situated in
        _____, County of _____, California, ("Property").
    C. **THE PURCHASE PRICE** offered is _____
        _____ Dollars $ _____
    D. **CLOSE OF ESCROW** shall occur on _____ (date)(or ☐ _____ **Days** After Acceptance).
2. **FINANCE TERMS:** Obtaining the loans below **is a contingency** of this Agreement unless: **(i)** either 2K or 2L is checked below; or

REAL ESTATE BROKERS:
A. **Real Estate Brokers are not parties to the Agreement between Buyer and Seller.**
B. **Agency relationships are confirmed as stated in paragraph 27.**
C. If specified in paragraph 2A, Agent who submitted the offer for Buyer acknowledges receipt of deposit.
D. **COOPERATING BROKER COMPENSATION:** Listing Broker agrees to pay Cooperating Broker (**Selling Firm**) and Cooperating Broker agrees to accept, out of Listing Broker's proceeds in escrow: **(i)** the amount specified in the MLS, provided Cooperating Broker is a Participant of the MLS in which the Property is offered for sale or a reciprocal MLS; or **(ii)** ☐ (if checked) the amount specified in a separate written agreement (C.A.R. Form CBC) between Listing Broker and Cooperating Broker.
Real Estate Broker (Selling Firm) _____
By _____ Date _____
Address _____ City _____ State _____ Zip _____
Telephone _____ Fax _____ E-mail _____

Real Estate Broker (Listing Firm) _____
By _____ Date _____
Address _____ City _____ State _____ Zip _____
Telephone _____ Fax _____ E-mail _____

ESCROW HOLDER ACKNOWLEDGMENT:
Escrow Holder acknowledges receipt of a Copy of this Agreement, (if checked, ☐ a deposit in the amount of $ _____),
counter offer numbers _____ and _____
_____, and agrees to act as Escrow Holder subject to paragraph 28 of this Agreement, any
supplemental escrow instructions and the terms of Escrow Holder's general provisions.

Escrow Holder is advised that the date of Confirmation of Acceptance of the Agreement as between Buyer and Seller is _____

Escrow Holder _____ Escrow # _____
By _____ Date _____
Address _____
Phone/Fax/E-mail_____
Escrow Holder is licensed by the California Department of ☐ Corporations, ☐ Insurance, ☐ Real Estate. License # _____

(____/____)   **REJECTION OF OFFER:** No counter offer is being made. This offer was reviewed and rejected by Seller on _____
(Seller's Initials) _____ (Date)

Source: Reprinted with permission, CALIFORNIA ASSOCIATION OF REALTORS®. Endorsement not implied.

When the joint escrow instructions form is used, it is common for additional documents to be added to the preprinted escrow instructions at a later date. It is typical for the escrow company to issue a separate set of supplementary pages of boiler-plate clauses. These clauses most often contain language that releases the escrow holder from liability or limits escrow involvement in specific items, such as the handling of personal property between the parties. Another example of an additional necessary document to the joint instructions would be the execution of the deed that transfers ownership that would be handled at a later date. The signed note and trust deed executed by the buyer are also executed as an additional document at a later date. However, the basic elements for a valid escrow are contained within the combined document.

Be aware, however, that some areas use a purchase agreement that does not contain joint escrow instructions. In some areas of practice within California it is typical for the original deposit receipt and purchase agreement to be faxed over to the escrow holder so that the escrow holder may read and ascertain the clauses and agreements where the parties have reached mutual agreement. This procedure would be very similar to that of the joint instructions. However, in other parts of the state, the escrow holder does not want a copy of the purchase agreement, because there may a conflict between the purchase agreement contract between the principals and the escrow instructions typed up by the escrow holder. In these areas the agents typically telephone the escrow officer. The escrow officer takes charge by asking the questions he or she wishes to have answered in order to prepare the escrow instructions.

■ INFORMATION NEEDED TO OPEN THE ESCROW

The responsibility for the successful opening of escrow rests on the agent, the principals, and the escrow holder.

Agent Responsibility

In every case the principals and agents need to know what the escrow holder will need to have to create a full set of valid escrow instructions. Each party should have a thorough overview of the escrow process before opening the escrow. A diagram of the escrow process is shown in Figure 3.3.

A checklist is a good way for these individuals to make sure they have all the necessary information to give to the escrow holder. If the escrow holder has a copy of the purchase agreement, additional information not contained on that contract is still needed, such as the name of the loan agent or the actual lender. A list is shown below to assist the agent or principals in having the necessary information before opening escrow.

- *Names:* Full legal name and marital status of each principal is basic.

- *Consideration:* Cash down payment and who holds the deposit during escrow and the balance of all cash needed to close escrow including the balance of the down payment plus the amount needed for closing costs must be provided.

FIGURE 3.3

The Escrow Process

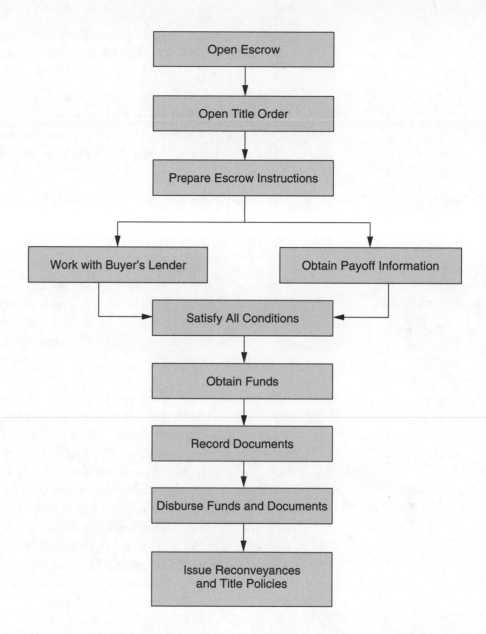

- *Financing:* Loan broker, lender, type of loan terms, and conditions of the loan must be determined. Is the obtaining of financing a contingency of the transaction? If so, what are the consequences if the borrower does not obtain a loan in terms of costs incurred and the buyer's deposit?

- *Encumbrances:* Homeowner association documents, title insurance, easements and the rights of tenants must be made specific. For an escrow involving income property, the buyer often assumes the seller's obligations and agreements, such as tenant security deposits and laundry machine contracts.

- *Inspections and Disclosures:* Both compliance that the event has occurred and determination of who will pay for such services are part of the escrow process.

- *Services:* The names of all services should be provided to the escrow holder for any bill that will be authorized for payment by escrow, such as the broker name for the real estate commission, the company name for the title insurance, and the termite company for the termite clearance report.

Principal Responsibility

Each side of the transaction must be informed of what they are to do to help close the escrow. Although most all items are negotiable, each principal must perform specific items as shown in Figure 3.4.

Escrow Responsibility

The escrow holder knows what items are needed to close a typical escrow. Problems often arise from not being able to obtain the pertinent information about the transaction from the parties to the transaction, such as vesting for the buyer or the legal description of the named property when an exchange is part of the seller's transaction.

The escrow holder must ask permission to proceed with the escrow on those agreed-upon escrow items pending the outcome by the parties of any disputed item. For example, the escrow officer would ask both parties if the escrow holder should proceed in obtaining the seller's loan payoff beneficiary demand information, and should proceed with working with the lender on obtaining loan approval and loan documents, at the time when the appraisal valuation does not match the sales price. With permission to proceed on the other matters, such as working with the loan and title officers, the escrow can proceed forward while the parties decide, outside of escrow, on the manner in which they will mutually agree to handle the disputed situation. The real estate agents or principals may ask the escrow holder what the options are, because the escrow officer may have seen other closed transactions with similar problems in the past. The mere providing of information on options that the escrow holder has experienced in the past, when asked for the information, is not a recommendation by the escrow agent. Escrow officers must never give legal, tax, or real estate advice, unless they actually hold a license to practice law, prepare taxes, or hold a Department of Real Estate (DRE) license.

Today it is common for the escrow to receive a faxed copy of the purchase agreement, which is kept in the escrow file. The escrow holder will often transfer the information contained on the purchase agreement onto a **take sheet** as is shown in Figure 3.5. The purpose of the take sheet is to assist the escrow holder with the information needed to prepare the escrow instructions by outlining the data required in an orderly fashion. The take sheet is not meant to dictate any of the terms or conditions of the transaction. The take sheet is a pre-escrow

FIGURE 3.4

Duties Each Principal Must Perform

The following are items for which the seller is responsible:

- Sign and return the escrow instructions
- Provide copies of lien information, such as existing loans, judgments, or other liens
- Execute a deed notarized by the buyer
- Comply with existing lien holder demands and beneficiary statement requirements, including tax liens and impound account shortages
- Complete the statement of information for title insurance purposes
- Provide tenant information (names, contracts, deposits, etc.)
- Provide all required disclosure information and comply with lender requirements for repairs or work requirements, such as pest control clearance
- Provide insurance information
- Pay all seller agreed-upon fees and costs, such as commission
- The buyer responsible for various items in the escrow as provided in the following list:
    - Sign and return the escrow instructions
    - Designate the method for holding title ownership to the property
    - Provide information for liens, such as judgments and tax liens
    - Execute notarized trust deed(s) and sign the note for indebtedness for the loan(s)

The following list includes items for which the buyer is typically responsible:

- Comply with new lender loan requirements including credit report information
- Complete the statement of information for title insurance purposes
- Review and approve the preliminary title report, disclosure statements, and inspection reports provided
- Execute all information needed by the title company, lender, and homeowner association
- Provide insurance information
- Pay all fees and costs, including the buyer-broker agreement instructions

instruction worksheet. The process of gathering the data that will eventually go on the escrow instructions familiarizes the escrow holder with the information that will be used in the file.

It is common for the items gathered for the take sheet to be keyed into the same escrow software program that will also be used to generate the escrow instructions. The original escrow instructions are then either printed by the escrow holder and

FIGURE 3.5

Escrow Take Sheet

ESCROW TAKE SHEET

FILE NUMBER:		CONSIDERATION	
Office Name:		Buyer Will Deposit:	$
Officer Code:		Deposited by Buyer:	$
Date of Opening:		Deposited by Broker:	$
Estimated Close Date:		Cash to Come:	$
Type of Transaction:		Paid Outside Escrow:	$
Estimated Fee:		Equity Exchanged:	$
Exchange Party:		Credit for Note:	$
Concurrent Escrow Number:		Trust Deed:	$
PROPERTY ADDRESS		Trust Deed:	$
County:		Trust Deed:	$
City:		Trust Deed:	$
Zip Code:		Trust Deed:	$
Unincorporated Area:			
Unit Number:	Lot:		
Block:	Tract Number:	Total Consideration:	$

LEGAL DESCRIPTION:

SELLER

Name:

Marital Status:	Vesting:
Mailing Address:	Phone:

Forwarding Address:

Name:

Marital Status:	Vesting:
Mailing Address:	Phone:

Forwarding Address:

BUYER

Name:

Marital Status:	Vesting:
Mailing Address:	Phone:

Forwarding Address:

Name:

Marital Status:	Vesting:
Mailing Address:	Phone:

Forwarding Address:

FIGURE 3.5

Escrow Take Sheet (Continued)

NEW LOAN

Loan Amount: $	Type of Loan: Priority	
In Favor of:		
Address:		
Phone:	Fax:	E-mail:
Attention:		Loan Number:
Interest Rate: %	Per Diem: $	Maximum Points:
Interest From: / /		Monthly Payment $
Term of Loan:		
Alienation Clause ❑ Yes ❑ No	Prepayment ❑ Yes ❑ No $	
Late Fee Amount: $	Days for Late Fee:	Balloon Payment ❑ Yes ❑ No

PRORATION INFORMATION FOR ESCROW INSTRUCTIONS

Tax Year:		Taxes Subject To:
Prorate ❑ Yes ❑ No	Adjust ❑ Yes ❑ No	Impound Account ❑ Yes ❑ No
Impound Balance: $		Held by:
Documentary Transfer Tax: $		Paid by:
County Transfer Tax: $		Paid by:
City Transfer Tax: $		Paid by:

TITLE COMPANY

Address:	
Phone: Fax:	E-mail:
Title Officer:	Order Number:
Prelim Number:	Policy Number:
Endorsement Codes:	Exclusions:

EXISTING LOAN(S)

Loan Number:	Interest Rate: %	Per Diem ❑ Yes ❑ No
Appx Unpaid Loan Balance: $		Original Loan Amount: $
Monthly Payment: $		Original Recording Date:
Type of Loan:	In Favor of:	
Address:		
Phone:	Fax:	E-mail:
Attention:		Priority
Book Number:	Page Number:	Date recorded:

Loan Number:	Interest Rate: %	Per Diem ❑ Yes ❑ No
Appx Unpaid Loan Balance: $		Original Loan Amount: $
Monthly Payment: $		Original Recording Date:
Type of Loan:	In Favor of:	
Address:		

FIGURE 3.5

Escrow Take Sheet (Continued)

Phone:	Fax:	E-mail:
Attention:		Priority
Book Number:	Page Number:	Date recorded:

BROKERAGE FEES/COMMISSION		Total Commission:	%
Commission to Listing Office:	%	Commission to Selling Office:	%
Amount $		Amount: $	
Name of Agent:		Name of Agent:	
Phone:	Fax:	Phone:	Fax:
Name of Broker/Company:		Name of Broker/Company:	
Address:		Address:	
City, State, Zip:		City, State, Zip:	
Phone:	Fax:	Phone:	Fax:

ADDITIONAL CHARGES			
Association Name:		Amount of Dues: $	
Address:		Phone:	Fax:
Management Company Name:		Manager:	
Address:		Phone:	Fax:
Pest Control Company Name:			Paid by:
Buyer Protection Policy Company Name:			Paid by:
Buyer Hazard Insurance Company Name:			Paid by:
Buyer Flood Insurance Company Name:			Paid by:
Buyer Earthquake Insurance Company Name:			Paid by:

the hard copy sent to the parties or they are transmitted electronically to the agent for the buyer and the agent for the seller. The escrow holder can electronically send **certified escrow instructions** to the buyer's lender and send the data to the title insurance company for preparation of the preliminary title report.

■ SAMPLE ESCROW INSTRUMENTS

Once the take sheet, or escrow memo form, has been completed, the escrow officer has sufficient information to prepare the escrow instructions. The pertinent information had to be obtained from the parties first. The escrow officer then confirms or clarifies some of the information received by speaking to the agents or principals on the phone. The verbal information solicited from the parties is obtained to clarify or add additional information not contained in the purchase agreement. See page 451 for information on accessing a sample of Southern California escrow instructions and a sample of Northern California escrow instructions.

At this point of the escrow processing, information may not yet be available. The escrow holder would make a notation on the file to request the information at a later date, such as vesting or final loan terms or certain disclosures. When all information is received by escrow, the escrow can close. In Northern California almost all of the information is available when escrow instructions are prepared at the end of the transaction. Loans, however, are always subject to change until actually funded and closed. The lender, appraiser, title officer, and escrow officer are part of a group of real estate related entities referred to as third party interests.

After receiving the data and requesting additional information, the escrow officer will organize the data and sort through the list of items that will need to be decided upon, such as what exactly will happen and the order in which each item will be placed. The events must be timed in a sequential order that will aid in the closing of the escrow. No two escrows are alike, but this book will attempt to describe the order of events in one logical method of operation. The type of escrow for the type of property and the type of clients will often determine the actual chain of events. Different principals and agents dictate that instructions must be written in a specific manner; and the escrow officer must be flexible in handling clients if future business is to be expected. Uncooperative escrow personnel will result in future business with another escrow company.

The following section involves a brief explanation of the common areas of standard escrow instructions. Specialized escrow transactions are covered in the areas found in Section 3 of this book. All escrow instructions, no matter the type of property or location of the property in California, have some common basic data that usually include the following:

- *Names:* The full, legal name of each seller and of each buyer or legal entity is essential. Initials and nicknames are not usually used for legal title to real property.

- *Property:* The full, legal description is obtained for the title search and to be placed on the deed used to transfer title. The street address may be included as a memorandum item, usually indicated after the legal description as "aka," meaning "also known as."

- *Tax identification:* Most county recording offices insist on the tax assessor's parcel number (**APN**) or assessor's identification number (**AIN**), or tax identification number (**TIN**) to be placed on the documents to be recorded.

FIGURE 3.6

Contract Requirements and Transaction Costs

Cash to be paid through escrow by each party (down payment)

Loan information (existing, new 1st, new 2nd)

Agreements (inspections, appraisal, disclosures)

Possession (close of escrow, seller rent back, buyer rent)

Fees paid by whom

Agents (salesperson, brokers, loan representative, lender, and insurance agent)

Consideration (deposit, increase deposit, price)

Title (name of the parties, subject property data)

Services performed by whom (escrow, title company, termite company)

- *Time:* Maximum time to perform the conditions and terms of the contract. Escrow has no control over third party performance, such as the date the appraisal is ordered and received, or the date the lender has the loan documents ready for signatures. The parties specify a required date, such as "on or before" a date; or a set date, such as "not before January 1, 2XXX" or "must record prior to December 31, 2XXX." In the first case, any time the escrow conditions have been met, the escrow holder is authorized to close the transaction. In the second case, the escrow officer is prohibited from allowing recordation prior to a specific date. In the third case, the escrow officer must see that everything is ready to close before the date, otherwise the transaction "falls out of escrow" and cannot close escrow because the escrow cannot meet the agreed-upon terms and conditions.

Escrow Instrument Basic Requirements

A basic real estate principles course teaches that the purchase contract and subsequent escrow instructions must contain specific items, as shown in Figure 3.6. The acronym of CLAP FACTS is often referred to as a memory aid for items needed by the escrow officer. **CLAP** stands for the following: **C**ash, **L**oans, **A**greements, and **P**ossession. **FACTS** means the **F**ees, **A**gents, **C**onsideration, **T**itle, and **S**ervices.

C

Cash. The cash includes the initial deposit, **earnest money,** accepted by the broker at the time of creating the initial offer-to-purchase contract, and prior to the seller's acceptance. If the seller insisted on the deposit amount being increased and if the buyer agreed to increase the deposit, then the additional deposit funds are also part of the cash. These funds may be left in the broker trust account, or more commonly, are transferred to the escrow holder during the escrow period.

Additional cash funds are needed to close the escrow for both the balance of the total down payment and for the closing costs.

Noncash.   The second type of consideration is anything of value used in lieu of cash as all or part of the consideration. The noncash item is noted in the escrow instructions as equivalent to cash, and escrow is not concerned with the actual appraised value of this type of consideration that is often transferred between the parties outside of escrow. If a boat or motor home is given to the seller instead of cash as the down payment, **escrow** would not be a party of transaction unless the transfer of title and bill of sale were handled through the escrow. More commonly given for noncash consideration, instead of personal property, is equity in another property, such as when owners exchange property. When the owner carries back a trust deed in lieu of receiving cash at the close of escrow, the amount of the note would be considered a noncash part of the total consideration.

L   **Loans.**   The terms and conditions of the loan are specified in the escrow instructions. Time limits are usually part of loan criteria, such as expiration of the interest rate or loan documents. The time in which work is to be performed is limited, such as receiving the appraisal report. The escrow has no control over these, and the work is often performed outside of escrow.

A   **Agreements.**   The following is a discussion of the various types of agreements commonly used in an escrow, which are contained in various escrow clauses as part of the escrow instructions. Additional clauses may be used in a geographic area of California, for a particular type of property, or as agreed upon by the parties. The agreements between the parties include the various disclosures required, including any type of homeowner association.

Disclosures.   Almost all disclosures are handled by the agents and principals outside of escrow. The escrow holder is not concerned with disclosures, and they are often not contained in any writing of the escrow instructions. All disclosure items that have been furnished and agreed upon between the parties may be listed as part of the escrow instructions as a memorandum item. The only disclosure that escrow is usually involved with is the Zone Disclosure Statement, usually ordered by escrow with an independent firm. The **Zone Disclosure Statement fee** is billed to and paid through escrow. A third party firm searches the government maps of California on behalf of the seller. Any areas affecting the subject property are disclosed to the buyer. The buyer's lender obtains the same information and often requires the buyer to obtain flood insurance if the property is located on a known flood plain. However, if the report discloses that the property is located near an earthquake fault line, the lender does not require earthquake insurance. Therefore, the Zone Disclosure Statement gives the buyers information so they can make the decision about adding quake coverage.

Associations. The covenants, conditions, and restrictions (CC&Rs) of any association contain agreements and legal restrictions on property use by which the property owner must abide. The lender will require a copy for its file. Many California communities are subject to association or Architectural Committee review for proposed construction or remodeling. These single-family homes or attached condominium units have express easements, right-of-ways, restrictions, and provisions in recorded documents affecting ownership use and rights.

P

Possession. Three options are available for possession. The buyer may rent the property prior to the close of escrow and have possession of the premises in advance of ownership. This is typical when the buyer is an existing tenant or may occur when the property is vacant when placed for sale. Also, a lease with option to purchase transaction would involve advance possession. Another option is when the seller rents back the property after the close of escrow. In this case the seller may be required to pay the buyer's loan payment during the possession period. Here the seller does not give up possession at the close of escrow. The seller obtains all of his or her funds at close of escrow, except some amount held back for rent, usually payable in advance, for the agreed-upon period. This is typically used in areas where the purchaser is a contractor and is obtaining the necessary architectural, engineering, and city plans, permits, and approvals prior to tearing down the existing property to build a new structure. The most common practice, however, is the option where the buyer obtains possession at or just after the close of escrow. It is common for the agreement of possession to include that the seller has up to three days after the close of escrow to vacate the premises.

F

Fees and costs. Each item is usually specified in the escrow instructions. Unless prohibited by law, all costs and **fees** are freely negotiable between the parties, and either principal may pay for the item. Chapter 9 has detailed information about prorations and the calculation of closing costs. FHA and VA loans and first-time homebuyer programs may prohibit the buyer from paying certain fees.

Prorations. The escrow instructions contain language where the principals have directed, in writing, how the escrow officer is to handle the division of certain expenses. This involves expenses already paid by the seller that need to be reimbursed to the seller by the buyer, such as prepaid property taxes. It also involves items collected by the seller that need to be transferred to the buyer, such as the security deposit held by the property owner on behalf of the tenant and not yet earned by the landlord.

Taxes.   Real property taxes are usually prorated between the parties. Escrow will indicate the transfer between the parties on a specific form. A county Documentary Transfer Tax is a one-time tax imposed on all California transfers of ownership payable at the time of recordation. Many cities in California have added a City Transfer Tax, as well as a one-time charge that may be paid by either party. During escrow, a form is faxed to the IRS to determine if any unpaid income taxes are a lien against any of the parties. All state and federal income taxes must be cleared before escrow may close because prior tax liens would be a priority above any new loan placed on the property. Escrow is also involved in both the FIRPTA and the Cal-FIRPTA, where the seller is obtaining the sale proceeds at the close of escrow on which income taxes may be due.

A

Agent.   Typical agents involved in a real estate transaction include the DRE-licensed real estate agents, including the sales and loan agents, in addition to the insurance agents.

Sales agents.   The DRE-licensed agents normally handle the required agency disclosure outside of escrow. Escrow is most involved with each real estate salesperson. Most transactions have one salesperson agent for the seller and one salesperson agent for the buyer. Each licensed salesperson works for a DRE-licensed broker. The employing broker may be an individual or a corporation. Escrow will require the employer to sign for the commission agreement, including any referral fee paid to another broker.

Loan agents.   Loan representatives and their employing brokers are usually DRE-licensed agents who handle the financing outside of escrow, such as loan qualification, type of loan, loan terms, approved appraisal, and credit rating of the purchaser. The financing of real property uses recorded trust deeds in California. The order of recordation determines the priority in case of default. The escrow instructions specify the priority order for all the loans. The loan amount, interest rate, length of the loan, and other terms and conditions are shown on the escrow instructions. The costs and charges associated with obtaining a new loan are part of the escrow instructions, including the points, appraisal, origination fee, and document preparation fee. The contract often specifies the timeline for the loan application.

Insurance agents.   The principals may make agreements regarding the title, life, flood, earthquake, mortgage, and hazard insurance policies required by either principal, the lender, or the government. The ALTA and CLTA title insurance policy endorsements, exclusions, and premium payments are specified in the contract. Some government loans, such as a Cal-Vet loan, require a borrower to have a life insurance policy. Lenders require flood insurance for properties within identified areas according to government survey maps. The buyer receives a disclosure so he or she may determine if earthquake insurance is desired. Loans with a smaller down payment and some government program loans require mortgage insurance. All lenders require a hazard insurance policy to cover fire damage. Optional insurance policies include contents coverage or renter's insurance.

C

Consideration.   A summary box is normally provided on the first page of the escrow instructions, that includes the cash, the loans, and the total price, or total consideration. The summary helps all parties see the transaction details. Additional information is contained in the body of the escrow instructions, especially loan terms and conditions. Two types of consideration are used in a real estate transaction, the cash and the loan information. The cash, loan, and down payment constitute the total consideration, or price.

T

Title.   Escrow prepares the transfer document, the deed. The name of the seller and the name of the buyer are placed on the deed. The manner that the buyer will hold title to the property is indicated on the deed. The method of holding title has legal and tax consequences that may affect not only the buyer but also future generations. The ways to hold title are discussed in Chapter 4.

S

Services.   Many third party companies are involved in a real estate transaction. Many are not named in the binding, legal contract that is executed between the principals. Most are determined after escrow is opened. The escrow sometimes does not see the report performed by the third party but only receives the bill to pay through escrow for the services performed, such as the termite, home warranty, and any physical inspection. Escrow does receive, review, and pay for the title report. Even the services of the escrow company for the escrow instructions may or may not be agreed upon when the principals have executed the purchase agreement.

Termite clearance.   It has become standard practice for the purchase agreement to spell out two areas for the pest control report. One area is corrective, to rectify existing damage to the premises. Almost all lenders insist that termite damage be corrected as a condition prior to funding the loan. The other area is the preventive work that is recommended to the buyer for future problems. The buyer usually pays for this part of the work because the items benefit the buyer after the seller no longer owns the property. Escrow is normally not concerned with the contents of the termite inspection, but it is usually presented with the bill to pay for the clearance report through escrow.

Home warranty.   A third party company provides the buyer with coverage for a limited time. Typically the period of time is for one year from the date of issuance. If the seller elects to obtain a home warranty at the time the listing begins and prior to the close of escrow, the seller benefits from coverage during both the listing period and the escrow period, which can be up to six months. If the hot water tank went out during this time, the coverage would replace the old one with a new one for a standard deductible. Either party may pay for the policy.

Physical inspection.   A third party performs a diligent physical inspection and furnishes the report to the principals, usually through the agents. The report is often handled outside of escrow, but the bill for the inspection may be paid through escrow by one of the parties. Escrow is not concerned with the contents of the report.

THINK ABOUT IT   What personal experience do you have with escrow?

How would you explain to a principal the differences in the escrow process between Northern California and Southern California?

■ CHAPTER SUMMARY

A valid escrow must meet the legal requirements of a valid contract, including capacity of the parties, lawful object, adequate consideration, and mutual promises. Each party involved in the escrow has responsibilities and obligations to assist in closing of the escrow. The practices in other countries and other states differ on how escrow is handled. Northern California and Southern California escrow practices differ also. While the end result in all cases is still the transfer of ownership, the procedural steps vary.

In most transactions the escrow holder receives information to open escrow, which the escrow officer places on a take sheet. Then a copy of the purchase agreement is often delivered to the escrow officer for preparation of the escrow instructions. Escrow is not open until the escrow holder receives signed copies of the escrow instructions. The instructions state the consideration, loans, agreements, and possession information.

■ CHAPTER 3 QUIZ

1. In Southern California escrow instructions are prepared
   a. in bilateral form.
   b. in unilateral form.
   c. sequentially.
   d. under duress.

2. In Northern California escrow instructions are prepared
   a. in bilateral form.
   b. in unilateral form.
   c. sequentially.
   d. under duress.

3. Real estate brokers are more active in the escrow process in
   a. Northern California.
   b. Southern California.
   c. other states.
   d. none of the above.

4. Compared to the standard California deposit receipt and purchase agreement, the vesting (method of holding) title shown on the title report
   a. always agrees.   c. has no relation.
   b. must agree.   d. must be stated.

5. An encumbrance
   a. refers to liens only.
   b. includes any burden on title.
   c. is a title exemption.
   d. covers the principals' transfer obligation.

6. The take sheet is used by the escrow holder
   a. to organize information for the escrow instructions.
   b. so that all disbursement checks are cleared properly.
   c. but has been replaced with automated computer processing.
   d. but seldom involves escrow information and primarily is used by the title company.

7. The take sheet
   a. is used to obtain details on the new loan requested by the purchaser.
   b. assists the escrow officer in preparing the escrow instructions.
   c. obtains data that will be needed by the title company for the preliminary title report.
   d. is all of the above.

8. The escrow officer may never give
   a. legal advice.
   b. tax advice.
   c. real estate advice.
   d. any of the advice listed above.

9. The most common way that the escrow officer receives the information to prepare the escrow instructions is by
   a. face-to-face interview with the principals.
   b. fax of deposit receipt to the principals.
   c. telephone call by the real estate agents, with fax of purchase agreement.
   d. lender fax to the title company just prior to the close of escrow.

10. The escrow instructions
    a. act as the final binding contract for the loan terms and conditions agreed to by the purchaser.
    b. always supersede any prior written agreements.
    c. are the instructions to the escrow holder.
    d. are the only binding contract that is needed by the principals.

CHAPTER FOUR

TITLE INSURANCE: CONSUMERS AND REAL ESTATE PROFESSIONALS

■ KEY TERMS

abstract of title
chain of title
deed
encumbrances
exclusion
liens
patent

policy of title
   insurance
preliminary title
   report
statement of
   information (SI)
title

title defect
title insurance
   company
title officer
title plant
title search

■ CHAPTER OVERVIEW

The single most important third party firm that the escrow company will work
with during a transaction is usually the **title insurance company.** While the buyer
is working with the lender, and the seller is dealing with the appraiser, escrow
will be working closely with the title insurance company. Each title company will
use the records found in the title plant to trace title ownership back to the 1850
statehood. Earlier title record searches are used when the land grant records are

traceable for previously deeded ownership. The title company will have all parties to the transaction complete a **statement of information (SI)** form that will be included with escrow instructions and will be given to the title officer to open the title order.

The title company will use the information on the SI to search records about the people to determine if there are any outstanding liens against any of these principals for unpaid judgment, unpaid taxes, or other liens. The title company will also search public records to determine if any encumbrances are recorded against the real property involved in the transaction. The title company will establish the **chain of title** showing ownership and title vesting. As a result of the initial searches, the title company will produce a preliminary title report that indicates what was initially found. This is the basis for the title company's initial offer to issue a **policy of title insurance.** Not all property is insurable, and a title policy will have **exclusions** that are not covered by the new title insurance policy.

Many things can occur from the time the preliminary title report is issued until the close of escrow. In most cases, the buyers indicate how they will hold title; the new lender will indicate the minimum title insurance coverage as a contingency for the new loan; and the seller will explain in the escrow instructions which liens have to be paid at close of escrow (COE).

■ LEARNING OBJECTIVES

At the conclusion of Chapter 4, you will be able to

- explain why principals should make informed decisions in the selection of the title insurance company;

- give a definition of title insurance;

- differentiate between a preliminary title report and a policy of title insurance;

- outline the steps used to obtain a preliminary title report;

- understand how a title search is performed; and

- distinguish between property and people title issues.

■ SELECTION OF THE TITLE INSURANCE COMPANY

The principal parties negotiate the selection of services used in the real estate transaction. No law requires any particular party to the transaction to select the escrow or title insurance company. Local practices usually dictate normal procedures. When no agents are involved, and with the principals infrequently involved in a real estate transaction, then local practices would be unknown to the principals. If the transaction falls within the Real Estate Settlement Procedures Act (RESPA), the buyer has the right to select the title and escrow company.

Some types of financing do not allow the borrower to pay certain fees and/or may limit the amount the borrower may pay for items, such as the escrow fee or loan fees. This prohibition is typical for low-income borrowers, government insured or guaranteed loans, and special city or area programs for first-time home borrowers. In these cases the seller generally selects the transaction services, including the escrow and title insurance provider, because the buyer has no prior real estate transaction experience and does not know which firm to use.

There are several logical reasons for the seller to select the service provider. As indicated above, the seller may be required to pay for the service. In most instances, the party who pays for the service has the right to select the service provider.

The current seller probably purchased the property from another seller, which involved the current seller going through the process of qualifying and obtaining a new loan, and at the close of that escrow, receiving a policy of title insurance. In addition, many owners have gone through the process of refinancing property they own, and that involves escrow and title. All of these activities involve the current seller and may mean that he is or she is more experienced and understands the escrow and title process better than the buyer. The buyer may never have owned real property prior to this transaction and may have little understanding of or experience in the process involved. For first-time buyers, the selection of the service is not based upon their prior business expertise, but it is rather negotiated by the parties or handled according to local practices.

The title insurance company searches the records to establish the chain of property ownership for prior ownership interest and current lien records. The insurance company would prefer to have to search back to only the last policy of title insurance that was issued on the property. For example, if a title insurance company placed a policy on the property ten years ago when the current seller bought the property with Title Company X, and if a title insurance company placed a policy on the property when the current seller refinanced the property five years ago with Title Company Y, the new Title Company Z will look back to both X and Y policy file reports. It makes no sense to go back over the information that has already been obtained. In the old days, physical folders were kept with the paper documents obtained for each policy, such as copies of deeds and public record liens. Each title insurance company would establish its own file folder with all the documents obtained.

Today, with the capability of scanning documents and electronic transmission of data, the computer records for the last **title search** can be e-mailed to another title company searcher. In fact, many of the former title companies have merged or been acquired by another title insurance company. The current search may include a report from a former title company that the current title company now owns.

No matter how the title company acquired the prior information, the current title insurance company **title officer** will still do an independent validation of the documents and records found. Even if a prior title policy was issued from the current title company, and thus is using the file records already acquired and owned by the current title company, the current title officer will still verify the information. In fact, some of the past data that have already been approved after review in the past may be questioned on the current transaction due to current knowledge on past events that might affect the title to the property.

A discount for the current policy may be available, if the title insurance company hired for the current transaction is the same company that recently performed a thorough title search. The seller may have knowledge of the most recent title insurance policy, and the buyer would most likely not have any prior contact with any title company. The selection for the buyer would not improve the transaction, but the selection by the seller of the former title insurance company may save time, effort, and money.

■ WHAT THE TITLE INSURANCE COMPANY INSURES

Like any insurance vendor, a title insurance company insures against loss. Unlike many insurance company policies, a title policy is not a recurring expense. Once the premium is paid and a policy is issued, the coverage is valid for as long as the same named insured owns the property. The one-time premium is paid through escrow in advance of property ownership, at the escrow, and the policy covers all future title ownership for the life of the property ownership.

The title insurance coverage covers past events that would affect ownership rights to the property, including items shown in Figure 4.1. All previous financial **liens,** such as bank loans, tax liens, special assessments, and mechanic's liens, would be included. All previous financial liens against the seller would be cleared so that after the close of escrow no tax or court liens against the previous owners would remain against the property. Likewise, any financial liens against the buyer must be paid off and cleared before the buyer may take title to the property. The title company uses a set of records referred to as the **title plant.** More than one title company often uses the set of recorded documents held by a title insurance company on real property. All past encumbrances on

FIGURE 4.1

Title Report Condition

> **Events Affecting Title Condition**
> - The estate or interest in property
> - The recorded owner of the estate or interest
> - The legal description of the parcel of land involved
> - Taxes (city and county)
> - Bonds and special assessments, such as street lighting, sewers, sidewalk, and repairs
> - Easements, such as public utility purposes, alleys, sewers, light and air, and driveways
> - CC&Rs (Covenants, Conditions, and Restrictions) that affect their use of the land such as types of buildings, setbacks, and fences
> - Existing deeds of trust
>
> **Condition of Title**
> - Judgment liens recorded against persons (sellers) affecting the ownership, such as federal income tax liens, money judgments, etc.
> - Recorded leases, including building, ground, and mineral
> - Recorded declaration of homestead
> - List of printed exceptions and exclusions

the property or the individual people must be taken care of to clear title at the time of close of escrow.

When after the transfer of ownership and the issuance of the new policy of title insurance anyone claims to have any interest against the property, the property owner would go to the title policy and demand that the title insurance company take care of the matter. For example, if the termite inspection made prior to the close of escrow indicated that fascia boards had to be replaced prior to issuance of a clear termite certificate report, the buyer would assume that the termite company did the work. The seller, however, got a lower bid for the cost of the repairs. After the work was completed, the termite company reinspected, approved the work, and issued a final certificate report. However, the repair worker, who was never paid, filed a mechanic's lien against the property. After the close of escrow, the worker contacts the buyers to demand payment. The worker states that the buyers must pay for the services because they are now the property owners and they benefit from the completion of the work performed on the premises. In this case the new property owners, the buyers, would contact the title insurance company. The title insurance company would handle the problem.

■ HOW THE TITLE SEARCH IS PERFORMED

When a property sells, it is standard procedure for an escrow to be opened with an escrow company. After the escrow company gathers the initial information for the transfer of ownership or financing of the property, it almost immediately contacts the title company to open a title search. (Note that the escrow company may be a department of a title insurance company or may be a separate business entity.)

The title search is performed by reviewing paper documents, by computer searches, and by going to the courthouse, county recorder, Internal Revenue Service, and tax assessor office. From these sources the title company obtains information about the property and the principals involved in the transaction. The information may be acquired manually, as hard copy data, or it may be retrieved by automated computer systems.

The initial search is referred to as an **abstract of title.** In some cases, an attorney will offer an opinion or certificate of title, such as in out-of-state transactions. If the principal accepts only the abstract of title, preliminary title report, or attorney opinion or certificate, without obtaining an actual policy of title insurance, the individual is assuming great risk if a future claim is made against the property. An abstract is a condensed version of the recorded documents affecting title to the property. A preliminary title report is an offering by a title insurance company of the items it preliminarily found that would affect the property, but it is not the firm's offer that insurance coverage is available for the property. The firm will approve the actual policy only after a more thorough and detailed investigation is conducted of the records.

Any gap in the chain of title results in a cloud on the title and would usually result in a court action to establish ownership. Any break in the property's chain of title means that the current owner does not have valid title to the property and therefore cannot convey title to a subsequent purchaser and cannot obtain a policy of title insurance. The abstractor must validate any gap in the title. A gap usually occurs when the name of a person who obtained title to the property is not the same name conveying the title to the subsequent titleholder, as is the case when a foreclosure or a sale by an executor/administrator occurs.

In other states, a buyer is often given a warranty deed, rather than the grant deed used in California. With a warranty deed the seller warrants that the grantor can pass **title** to the grantee in good condition. The grantor is giving all the title he or she has to the property, which may be 100 percent of the ownership or it may be nothing. If an attack against the title fails and the property owner suffers a financial loss, the property owner would go back to the grantor from whom title to the property was received. One problem with this method is that locating the grantor after the close of escrow may be impossible. The second problem is that if the grantor can be found, the chance of recovery is dependent upon the financial ability of the grantor to pay the claim made on the judgment. Another problem is the time and expense to bring an action against the grantor, in hopes of gaining recovery from loss. The warranty deed is not used in California.

In California, title insurance companies are corporations whose assets are reviewed by the governmental agency under which they are licensed to do business, as shown in Table 2.1 on page 37. For example, the insurance commissioner reviews the financial stability of a company to see that the firm is acting in good faith for consumer protection. The rules and regulations for operating in California include insurance commissioner review of the company's past performance, current claims, and projected resources. Because the title insurance companies are private business entities that are in business to make a profit, it must always be remembered that the security of the title is afforded by the insurance policy coverage and exclusions that are controlled by the integrity and financial structure of the company that issues the policy. In addition, some of the other states also have title insurance company coverage available, while others don't.

The next phase performed in the title search is that someone must review the data after all information of record is obtained. The process involves someone trained to make a decision. Several individuals may participate in the decision. The purpose of the review is to determine if the data can be eliminated because they do *not* involve any of the parties to the transaction and do *not* involve any property liens, encumbrances, or other ownership rights or interests. If the data cannot be eliminated, then they remain as part of the file that must be kept and processed by a decision maker.

The documents are compiled in order, usually by date of recordation, to establish the past chain of events. The process of conducting the title search is called "running the chain of title." In this way, a prior loan that was later paid off would show both the original loan and the document showing that the loan had been paid in full—or reconveyed. The chain of events occurring from one event to the next is called the *chain of title* in the real estate business and refers to the history of interest in the property.

Just as each link in a chain connects to the next to form a complete chain, so too each event connects the links from one owner to another, whether by land **patent,** land grant, or from previous other sources, including foreign countries and federal government transfers of land ownership. Each one event links from the prior event. When any period of time or event has a missing link, the chain of title has a missing event. The title insurance company cannot insure the title when an event is missing. For example, a loan made 100 years ago may be found on a property, but the subsequent loan payoff cannot be found. The title insurance company will first attempt to obtain the original documents and the proper parties to complete the reconveyance document. Failing to locate the necessary paper-work, the title insurance company will then usually insist that a bond be purchased to cover 2½ times the original amount of the loan. It wants not only the original principal amount covered but also an amount that would cover any unpaid interest should the note surface and the holder of the note demand the full amount of the loan and all accrued interest. Because the original note is not available to determine the interest rate, the nominal rate in normal use at the date the original note would have begun is usually used to calculate the approximate amount of interest that would have accrued.

■ WHAT TASKS ARE PERFORMED BY A TITLE INSURANCE COMPANY?

A title company performs a thorough and diligent search of the title records and public documents. Title experts who are proficient in the field perform a thorough search of the title. The title is the foundation on which property ownership is based. The title company insures a principal against hazards inherent to real property ownership interests. The title company insures the legal right for an individual entity to possess and use the property within the restrictions found on the property. The restrictions are provided to the principal prior to obtaining an ownership interest. This disclosure is made preliminarily and before the principal acquires title, usually in the preliminary title report.

Some individuals believe that the recordation of a **deed** proves that they own the property and they need no further protection. In truth, however, the deed only delivers all the rights that the grantor had in the property. If, for any reason, at some future date a claim is found to the title to the property by an heir of the party who transferred title to the current seller, then the buyer might not have received any interest in the property when it is found that the seller did not have title to the property. With title insurance two protections are offered. First, the title insurance company ensures that the best possible legal defense will be provided if the title to the property is under attack. Second, the title insurance policy is insurance up to the face amount of the policy should a legal action be awarded against the insured title or ownership interest in the real property.

The title company recites the current conditions of the title, according to the investigation made by the title experts. The company will recite the conditions under which coverage will be offered, if not rejected and denied because of risk of loss because title to the property is found to be uninsurable. The title policy defines the coverage afforded, lists any exceptions made, then guarantees that the title company will defend against any proposed claim of a right to title or interest in the property. Any actual loss usually takes years to settle after a claim is made against the title. The courts establish the settlement based upon the title dispute and the rights of the parties.

No further premium is due. The firm then is representing that it will defend against any attack on the title to the property insured at no additional expense to the property owner. The insured is protected against financial losses caused by any found title defects, no matter how long after the date the policy is issued. What the company does is safeguard against financial loss due to an issue of title. The policy is effective as long as the insureds or their heirs have an interest in the property.

■ PAYMENT FOR THE TITLE INSURANCE POLICY AND TITLE SEARCH

The party requesting the service is normally the one responsible for the expense. The cost of title insurance is handled differently, however, depending on local practices. In some states, title insurance is handled by a government agency as part of the recordation fees and processing. However, in California the insurance commissioner regulates the insurance industry, including title insurance, but does not set the premium rates. Due to free market competition, local conditions for premium rates are in the same general range. The significant difference between title insurance companies in California is not the difference in premium rates so much as the difference in services.

The basic owner's title insurance policy premium rate usually varies within a narrow range. For the most part, the cost of a basic premium will range from $3.50 to $5.50 per $1,000 of coverage. The basic owner's policy rate is referred to as the base rate, or the standard rate for both CLTA and ALTA policies, as shown in columns 2, 3, and 6 in Figure 4.2. Note that the fourth column is also referred to as the concurrent rate, meaning the policy must include both the CLTA *and* ALTA coverage endorsement.

When a refinance loan occurs there is no seller to pay the CLTA rate. The owner-borrower on a refinance pays the ALTA refinance rate as shown in column three of Figure 4.2. The owner may wish to also purchase the CLTA refinance policy as shown in the fourth column as the CLTA lenders refinance rate.

Other types of policies or additional endorsements are available at specific rates quoted by the title insurance company, too numerous for details contained in this book. The short rate, however, is the most common special type of title insurance coverage. As the name implies, the coverage is intended to be for only a short period of time, with a subsequent policy to be issued at the end of the period. The short rate period varies among insurance providers and can be 12 or 24 months. The original premium rate is usually 10 percent to 20 percent higher with the subsequent policy rate 20 percent to 30 percent lower.

A single, nonrecurring premium is paid only once to purchase the title insurance policy.

The cost for a title search is not the same as the cost for the title insurance premium. In most areas, the rate quoted is a combined charge for both the title

FIGURE 4.2

Title Company Rate Chart

Amount of Insurance	ALTA Basic Rate	ALTA 5 yr. Short	Concurrent ALTA Rate	Refinance Rate	CLTA Lenders Basic Loan Rate
$50,000	$400.00	$395.00	$220.00	$395.00	$395.00
100,000	620.00	496.00	286.00	434.00	496.00
150,000	760.00	608.00	328.00	532.00	608.00
200,000	900.00	720.00	370.00	630.00	720.00
250,000	1,025.00	820.00	407.50	717.50	820.00
300,000	1,150.00	920.00	445.00	805.00	920.00
350,000	1,262.50	1,010.00	478.75	883.75	1,010.00
400,000	1,375.00	1,100.00	512.50	962.50	1,100.00
450,000	1,475.00	1,180.00	542.50	1,032.50	1,180.00
500,000	1,575.00	1,260.00	572.50	1,102.50	1,260.00
550,000	1,675.00	1,340.00	602.50	1,172.50	1,340.00
600,000	1,775.00	1,420.00	632.50	1,242.50	1,420.00
650,000	1,875.00	1,500.00	662.50	1,312.50	1,500.00
700,000	1,975.00	1,580.00	692.50	1,382.50	1,580.00
750,000	2,075.00	1,660.00	722.50	1,452.50	1,660.00
800,000	2,175.00	1,740.00	752.50	1,522.50	1,740.00
850,000	2,275.00	1,820.00	782.50	1,592.50	1,820.00
900,000	2,375.00	1,900.00	812.50	1,662.50	1,900.00
950,000	2,475.00	1,980.00	842.50	1,732.50	1,980.00
1,000,000	2,575.00	2,060.00	872.50	1,802.50	2,060.00

search and the title insurance. A separate fee may be charged for services individually. Most title companies quote the package rate that would include the cost for the title officer, the researcher, the attorney, and the abstracter search fees, if any of these are used. In California, the combined package rate is usually referred to simply as the title insurance premium rate.

■ OPENING THE TITLE ORDER

The real estate agent could contact the title insurance company to open a title order, but that is not common practice. In Northern California, the agent opens the escrow with the title company escrow division that opens the title order. Normally, the real estate professional obtains an online or faxed property profile from the title company to determine initial information, such as the name of the seller, the legal description, and tax identification number (APN, AIN, or TIN).

It is common for the independent escrow officer or title company escrow officer to open the title order. This can be performed online, or by fax or telephone, but practice today is usually a telephone call to the title insurance company by the escrow officer. If a title company is handling the escrow, the escrow officer could type the report via the company computer that would link the escrow instructions to ordering the preliminary title report.

Once the escrow officer has contacted the title receptionist or order entry clerk, the basic file information is transmitted to the title insurance company employee for the property data, seller information, and the name of the buyer and vesting, along with any existing known liens and the type of financing the buyer will be obtaining. The statement of information will be forwarded to the title company so the title technician can gather data on the people.

■ ANALYZING THE STATEMENT OF INFORMATION

The statement of information (SI) is completed by each principal in the transaction on a form such as the one shown in Figure 4.3. If a married couple is selling the property and two individuals are purchasing the property, then four SIs would be used. Each principal gives personal information on employment, residences, Social Security number, and former marriages. The title insurance company uses this information to search both state and Internal Revenue Service (IRS) records to obtain an income tax search. The court index records are also used to seek out tax lien records and any judgments or suits against any of the principals.

The majority of the information obtained is used to eliminate debts against other individuals who are not the person involved in the transaction but who have the same name as the principal. When a title company searches the general index (GI) with the name of the person, it is not unusual that a common surname, such as Brown, Chen, Lee, Fernandez, Garcia, Hernandez, Smith, or Johnson would have page-after-page of data showing records against someone with that name. The title examiner uses the place of residence and employment to establish the likelihood of the record not matching the proposed insured. All clouds would have to be cleared off before the insurance policy will be written by the title insurance company. Once all the items indicated on the report are eliminated that do not pertain to the individual involved, then the items that are remaining are attributable to the principal. The results of the information found by the title technician and the title division will determine if the title officer will allow the title insurance company to place the insurance policy on the transaction. Not all property is insurable. Some easements or liens may not be able to be resolved.

FIGURE 4.3

Statement of Information

> *Proper completion of this form will help protect you by enabling the title company to eliminate title problems that might arise through similarity of your name with the name of another person against whom there may be judgments, tax liens, or other matters affecting property ownership.*
>
> Escrow Number _____   Title Order Number _____

First	Middle	Last		First	Middle	Last

Birthplace _____ Year of Birth   Birthplace _____ Year of Birth
Social Security No. _____   Social Security No. _____

I have lived in California since_____   I have lived in California since_____

We were married on_____at_____   Wife's maiden Name_____

* * RESIDENCE(S) FOR LAST 10 YEARS * * *

NUMBER AND STREET	CITY	FROM (DATE) TO (DATE)
NUMBER AND STREET	CITY	FROM (DATE) TO (DATE)
NUMBER AND STREET	CITY	FROM (DATE) TO (DATE)

* * OCCUPATION(S) FOR LAST 10 YEARS * * *

Husband's

Present Occupation	Firm Name	Address	No. Years
Prior Occupation	Firm Name	Address	No. Years

Wife's

Present Occupation	Firm Name	Address	No. Years
Prior Occupation	Firm Name	Address	No. Years

* * FORMER MARRIAGE(S) * * *

If no former marriages write "None"_____

Name of former wife _____

Deceased _____Divorced_____When_____Where_____

Name of former husband_____

Deceased _____Divorced_____When_____Where_____

The Street Address of the property in this transaction is _____
Improvements: _____ Single residence _____ Multiple residence _____Commerical
Occupied by: ____Owner _____Leasee ____Tenants Any portion of new loan funds to be used for construction: ___ Yes ___No
Date:_____   Home phone:_____   Business phones:_____

Signature: _____

Signature: _____

FIGURE 4.4

Sample Face Page of a Preliminary Title Report

Pacific Ocean Title Insurance Company   4412 Pacific Coast Highway #17
                                               Torrance, CA 90604
                                               (800) 555-2222

(1) Pacific Ocean Escrow
      22234 Western Avenue
      Torrance, CA 90604

Attn: Donna Grogan, Escrow Officer   (2) Your No. 1111-DG
                                         (3) Our No. 1212212-45PS

(4) Dated as of _____ April 1, 20XX _____ at 7:30 A.M.

In response to the above referenced application for a policy of title insurance,

PACIFIC OCEAN TITLE INSURANCE COMPANY

hereby reports that it is prepared to issue, as of the date hereof, a California Land Title
Association Standard Coverage Form Policy of Title Insurance describing the land and the
estate of interest therein hereinafter set forth in Schedule A, insuring against loss which may
(5) be sustained by reason of any defect, lien or encumbrance not shown or referred to as an
Exception in Schedule B or not excluded from coverage pursuant to the printed Schedules,
Conditions and Stipulations of said policy form.

Please read carefully the exceptions shown or referred to below and the exceptions
and exclusions set forth in Exhibit A attached to this report. The exceptions and exclusions
are meant to provide you with notice of matters which are not covered under the terms of the
title insurance policy and should be carefully considered. It is important to note that this
preliminary report is not a written representation as to the condition of title and may not list
all liens, defects, and encumbrances affecting title to the land.

This report (and any supplements or amendments thereto) is issued solely for the purpose of
(6) facilitating the issuance of a policy of title insurance and no liability is assumed hereby. If it
is desired that liability be assumed prior to the issuance of a policy of title insurance, a Binder
or Commitment should be requested

Pacific Ocean Title Insurance Company

(7) By:_____ **Fred Dyer** _____
          Fred Dyer, Title Officer

Order No. 1212212-45PS

FIGURE 4.4

Sample Face Page of a Preliminary Title Report (Continued)

Explanation of the Face Page of a Preliminary Title Report

1. The firm's name, address, and name of the individual who placed the order for the preliminary report. It is also used for mailing purposes.

2. This number identifies the customer's escrow file for the property and includes the escrow officer's initials for easy identification.

3. This number identifies the title company's title order for the property and includes the title officer's number and initials for easy identification.

4. This date represents the date and time, up to which matters affecting the title to the real property therein described have been examined and reported. This normally is the same as the "plant date," i.e., the date to which the plant or "lot books" and the General Index (GI) have been posted.

5. This paragraph specifies the type of coverage form on the policy of title insurance that will be prepared by the title insurance company to issue and the general scope of the insurance.

6. This paragraph specifies that no liability is ever intended under a preliminary report; it further indicates what should be requested if the customer desires assumption of liability prior to policy issuance.

7. Signature of title officer indicates that he or she has reviewed and approved the preliminary report for issuance.

■ THE PRELIMINARY TITLE REPORT

The **preliminary title report,** or prelim, is a signed and dated report used to facilitate the issuance of a policy of title insurance. The prelim is a report of the conditions found on the property upon which the title insurance company is willing to issue a policy of title insurance. The prelim is issued before, or preliminary to, the issuance of a title insurance policy.

The prelim is sent to escrow for distribution to appropriate parties to the transaction—the principals and the lender. These parties review the preliminary title report to determine the conditions on which the eventual insurance policy will be issued. The prelim shows existing items that are currently recorded or are of record against the property. Any item found on the title in the prelim will have to be cleared off the record or approved to remain on title before the insurance policy is issued.

A sample preliminary title report, including Schedule A and Schedule B portions, is shown in Figures 4.4, 4.5, and 4.6.

FIGURE 4.5

Sample Schedule A of Preliminary Title Report

SCHEDULE A

The estate or interest in the land described or referred to in this schedule covered by this report is:

(1) A fee

Title to said estate or interest at the date hereof is vested in:

(2) SAM SELLER AND MARY SELLER,
Husband and wife, as joint tenants

The land referred to in this report is situated in the State of California, County of Los Angeles and is described as follows:

(3) Lots 10 & 11 of Tract 16969, as shown on a map thereof recorded in Book 284, Pages 1 to 3 inclusive, of Maps, records of said Los Angeles County.

(4) EXCEPTING therefrom the Northeasterly 11 feet of said Lot 10.

Order No. 1212212-45PS

Explanation of Schedule A of Preliminary Title Report

1. A fee estate (the word "estate" is used to express the degree, quantity, nature, duration, or extent of an interest in land). A "fee" is the highest type of estate or interest an owner can have in land—freely transferable and inheritable, and whose owner is entitled to possession. (There are a number of other estates or interests in land that the title company could insure.)

2. This shows who the owner of record is and how they hold title to the property (vesting).

3. The legal description of the land covered by the preliminary title report.

   NOTE: Many times, minerals, e.g., oil and gas, etc., have been reserved or accepted in previous conveyances. In these instances, an "exception" to the legal description would be added, such as:

4. "EXCEPTING THEREFROM all oil, gas, and other hydrocarbon substances in and under or that may be produced from a depth of 500 feet below the surface of said land, but without the right of surface entry, as reserved in deed recorded . . . "

FIGURE 4.6

Sample Schedule B of Preliminary Title Report

SCHEDULE B

At the date hereof, exceptions to coverage in addition to the printed exceptions and exclusions in said policy form would be as follows:

EXCEPTIONS:

① 1. Property taxes, including any assessments collected with taxes, for the fiscal year 2003–2004, are as follows:

Assessor's Parcel No:	111-2222-333
Code Area:	03-111
Bill No.:	04000000
Land:	$ 50,000.00
Improvements:	$200,000.00
Exemptions:	$ 7,000.00
1st Installment:	$ 1,253.97
2nd Installment:	$ 1,253.96

② 2. A sale to the state of California for delinquent taxes for the fiscal year 2000–2001, and subsequent delinquencies. Amount to redeem prior to July 31, 2003, $2,859.42.

③ 3. Bond No. 123, Series No. 5, County Improvement No. (none shown) Assessment District No. 116A, issued June 10, 2000, for lights, in the original amount of $595.30. Principal payable annually beginning April 15, 2001, interest payable semiannually.

④ 4. An easement for ingress and egress and incidental purposes as provided in the deed recorded August 23, 1950, as Instrument No. 1277.

Affects: Easterly 20 feet of said property

⑤ 5. Covenants, conditions, and restrictions (deleting therefrom any restrictions based on race, color, or creed), as provided in deed recorded in Book 8530, Page 350, Official Records.

Said Covenants, conditions, and restrictions provide that a violation thereof shall not defeat nor render invalid the lien of any mortgage or deed of trust made in good faith and for value.

⑥ 6. An easement for electrical lines and incidental purposes as provided in the Deed recorded March 6, 2000, in Book 6789, Page 123, Official Records.

FIGURE 4.6

Sample Schedule B of Preliminary Title Report (Continued)

(7) 7. A deed of trust to secure an indebtedness of $500,000.00, and any other amounts as therein provided, recorded October 20, 1972, as Instrument No. 12333, in Book 7936, Page 43, Official Records.
Dated: October 10, 1972
Trustor: Robert M. Sellerman and Mary Sellerman, husband and wife
Trustee: First City Title Company
Beneficiary: California Sunshine Savings & Loan Association

(8) The beneficial interest under said deed of trust was assigned of record to Anthony Christensen and Terri Christensen, husband and wife, by assignment Recorded April 12, 1973, in Book 8001, Page 220, Official Records.

(9) Newport Beach Trustees, Incorporated was substituted as trustee in said deed of trust, by an instrument recorded May 6, 1973, in Book 8003, Page 7, Official Records.

(10) Notice of Default under the terms of the above deed of trust by California Sunshine Savings & Loan Association as the alleged owner and/or holder of the note secured thereby, was recorded May 8, 1974, in Book 8106, Page 410, Official Records.

8. A deed of trust to secure an indebtedness of $20,000.00, and any other amounts as therein provided, recorded October 20, 1972, as Instrument No. 63976, in Book 7936, Page 45, Official Records.
(11) Dated: October 12, 1972
Trustor: Vaughn Myers and Judith Myers, husband and wife
Trustee: Pacific Ocean Title Company
Beneficiary: William A. Brown and Mary C. Brown, husband and wife, as joint tenants

(12) The lien or charge of said deed of trust was subordinated to the lien or charge of the deed of trust referred to in Item 7, by an agreement dated October 20, 1972, recorded October 20, 1972, in Book 7936, Page 47, Official Records.

(13) An instrument dated December 12, 1973 executed by Vaughn Myers and Judith Myers and William A. Brown and Mary C. Brown, which modifies the Terms of said deed of trust as therein provided, recorded January 13, 1974, in Book 8088, page 330, Official Records.

(14) The beneficial interest under said deed of trust was assigned of record to R. F. Jones Realty, by assignment recorded January 20, 1974 and by other Assignments of record.

FIGURE 4.6

Sample Schedule B of Preliminary Title Report (Continued)

(15) Said deed of trust also secures an additional advance in the amount of $5,000.00, as evidenced by an Instrument recorded August 9, 1974, in Book 8109, Page 614, Official Records.

(16) 9. A judgment for $2,365.10 against Vaughn Myers and Judith Myers, in favor of Cool Pool, Incorporated, a California Corporation, entered June 2, 1978, in (none shown) Court, North County Judicial District, Case No. 743611, an abstract of which judgment was recorded June 17, 1978, as Instrument No. 78-687755, Official Records.

(17) 10. A lien for $936.50 due the United States of America from Vaughn Myers and Judith Myers, as evidenced by a Certificate No. 93641, recorded September 20, 1979, as Instrument No. 79-912234, Official Records.

(18) 11. A lien for $320.50 due the State of California from Vaughn Myers and Judith Myers, as evidenced by Certificate No. 73492, recorded October 12, 1980, as Instrument No. 80-1199891, Official Records.

12. A lien for $193.60 DUE TO THE County of Oakdale from Vaughn Myers and Judith Myers, as evidenced by a Certificate No. HO-3941, recorded November 5, 1980, as Instrument No. 80-1199891, Official Records.

(19) NOTE NO. 1:   This report is incomplete as to matters which may affect the title to or impose liens or encumbrances on, said land, unless eliminated by statements(s) of identity from all parties.

Your order can be expedited by furnishing such statement(s) of identity as soon as possible so that the records can be examined further and your escrow closing will not be delayed.

NOTE NO. 2:   The premium for a policy of title insurance, if issued, will be based on the short-term rate.

Explanation of Schedule B of Preliminary Title Report

1. *Taxes.* The first item (encumbrance) shown in "Schedule B" is a statement regarding the amount and status of the current year's taxes, e.g., taxes now a lien, now due, or respective installments paid or unpaid.

2. *Tax Sale.* If there are tax delinquencies for a prior year or years, the amount including penalty and interest to redeem prior to a certain future date is shown here.

3. *Bond.* Bonds or assessments (if any) levied at the inception of construction of improvements, e.g., streets, gutters, sidewalks, sewers, etc., under an approved district are shown here, on a parity with taxes.

FIGURE 4.6

Sample Schedule B of Preliminary Title Report (Continued)

From this point on, the remaining items shown in the preliminary report will be shown in order of their respective priority (usually, but not always, based on recording dates), the oldest first, and so on.

4. *An Easement.* This is a right or interest in the land of another which entitles the holder thereof to some use or benefit, e.g., to install poles and wires, pipelines, roadways, etc., "dedicated" on the tract map (subdivision), which affects the herein described property.

5. *Protective Restrictions.* Many times these are imposed by owners to help regulate setbacks, side yards, architectural matters, and such other items of common interest to those living within the development. These restrictions are usually placed of record at the inception of the development.

   Most protective restrictions will state, as these do, that a violation of the terms will not disturb the trust deed of the property ("good faith provision").

6. A further easement was granted for electrical purposes.

7. *Deed of Trust.* A (recorded) deed of trust conveys title to particular land to a neutral third party (trustee) with limited powers (such as powers of sale) for the purpose of securing a loan (debt). It is similar to a mortgage.

8. *Assignment.* An assignment of the beneficial (lender's interest under the deed of trust from the original beneficiary to another).

9. *Substitution of Trustee.* Here a new trustee is substituted for the original trustee.

10. *Notice of Default.* The terms of the trust deed were violated, e.g., failure to pay monthly installments, and therefore, a notice of said default was recorded. (Notice here the chronology of the items affecting the first deed of trust.)

11. *Deed of trust.* Another deed of trust was recorded on the same day as the previous deed of trust shown as described above.

12. *Subordination Agreement.* The parties have agreed that this last deed of trust is to be a "second" trust deed or a junior lien to the trust deed shown previously above. The recorded subordination agreement states this fact. The agreement may be a separate instrument or it may be incorporated within the deed of trust which is to become subordinate.

13. *Modification Agreement.* The terms of a trust deed may be modified in a number of ways, e.g., provisions for additional advances, extension of maturity dates, etc., by agreement executed by the trustor and beneficiary, or their successors.

14. *Assignments.* Except that there were several assignments. (Note also the chronology of the items affecting the second deed of trust.)

15. *Additional Advance.* Recording of a notice of additional advance is not required by law. However, most lenders will require the recording of a notice.

16. *An Abstract of Judgment.* Imposes a lien on this and most other real property now owned or hereafter acquired by the debtor until satisfaction or expiration thereof.

FIGURE 4.6

Sample Schedule B of Preliminary Title Report (Continued)

17. *Federal Tax Liens.* Under federal law, any revenue tax, unpaid after demand, becomes a lien on all property and rights to property of the person liable thereof, from the time the assessment is made, valid, however, against any purchaser, holder of a security interest, mechanic's lien, and judgment lien creditor only when notice thereof is previously filed in the county recorder's office.

18. *State and County Liens.* Most have the force, effect, and priority of judgments. An increasing number of legislative enactments imposing a wide variety of taxes, assessments, and charges provide that the same shall generally have the force, effect, and priority of a judgment against the party responsible for payment. These liens are evidenced by a recording in the form of a certificate and abstract or a notice of lien; but regardless of the form, they are generally treated for title insurance purposes similar to judgment liens. *However,* the specific statutes should be referred to before relying upon a release, expiration, or subordination.

19. *Statement of Information (Identity).* This confidential information statement is used to enable the title officer to eliminate the title problems which may arise through similarity of the name of seller and/or buyer with the name of another person against whom there may be judgments, tax liens, or other matters affecting property ownership.

Explanation of a Preliminary Report

A preliminary report is a signed and dated formal report, which sets out in detail the condition of title to a particular parcel of land.

Within a short time after a title order has been opened, all of the existing matters of record relative to the title on the subject property are assembled in a title search package and examined by skilled technicians. This is the time when the preliminary report is prepared and sent to the customer. The report reflects the existing conditions of title so that parties to the transaction will become aware of all matters of record that affect the title. This report is issued before the title policy—hence the name preliminary report.

The four matters shown in the report are the estate or interest covered; the record owner of the estate or interest; the parcel of land involved; and the exceptions, liens, and encumbrances that affect the land at the date and time of the report.

The Lender's Supplemental Report

The lender's supplemental report (shown in Figure 4.7) includes all preliminary title report information contained and explained above. This page indicates three additional items. The first is the stipulation by the lender that the ALTA and CLTA standard coverage will be included. The second is that the ALTA lender physical inspection is to be included to verify the single-family residence, which is the collateral for the lender's loan and required for mortgage insurance coverage. The third, and last, item required is that there be no encumbrances in the chain of title.

FIGURE 4.7

Sample of Lender's Supplemental Preliminary Title Report

Pacific Ocean Title
Insurance Company
Office: Torrance

South Bay Mortgage Company
8765 Long Beach Boulevard
Long Beach, CA 90804

Attn: Charles Crown

Your No. 1111-MJ
Our No. 1212212-45PS

Gentlemen,

The above numbered report (including any supplements or amendments thereto) is hereby modified and/or supplemented in order to reflect the following additional items relating to the issuance of an American Land Title Association Loan Form Policy of Title Insurance.

Dated as of:_____May 17, 20XX_____at 7:30 A.M. By: *Fred Dyer*_____
Fred Dyer, Title Officer

NOTE 1: Our American Land Title Association (ALTA) Policy when issued, will contain standard No. 100 California Land Title Association (CLTA)

NOTE 2: An inspection of said land discloses improvements thereon designated as a single family residence, known as: 123 Elm Street, Coastal Inlet, CA 99999

NOTE 3:   CHAIN OF TITLE REPORT

The following is furnished for information only:

The only fee conveyance affecting said land recorded within six (6) months of the date of this report are as follows:

NONE

* * * * * * * *

FIGURE 4.8

Sample Plat Map for Preliminary Title Report

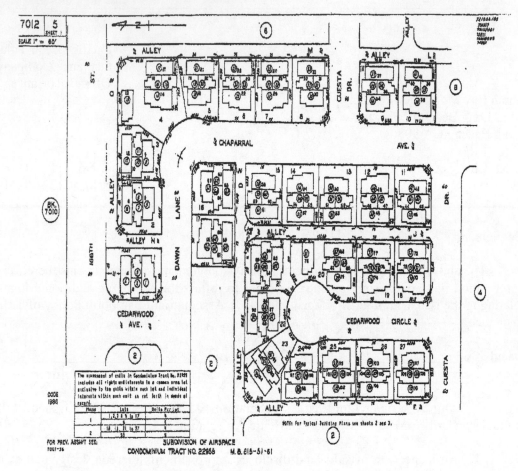

Plat Map for Preliminary Title Report

The plat (shown in Figure 4.8) normally is a reduced size copy of the recorded subdivision map or the pertinent county assessor's map, included for information purposes only. The escrow officer and searcher and/or title officer should check for errors, e.g., proper dimensions or distances shown; any excepted property excluded; any reference to acreage deleted if map shows same, etc.

■ WHAT THE TITLE SEARCH REVEALS

When a title searcher obtains the data about the property or the people involved in the transaction on the real property that the title insurance company has been asked to insure, many items are revealed. The voluntary and involuntary liens and **encumbrances** of record are disclosed to the parties, usually in the preliminary title report.

Some properties cannot obtain title insurance. When a title defect is found on a property, the title insurance company may not be able to clear the problem and therefore will not issue insurance coverage. A **title defect** is anything in the entire history of the real property ownership that may encumber all or any part of the property owner's right to quiet enjoyment of the property. The defect may cause the owner to lose some portion of the property. Title companies do turn down some applications if the company determines that the title cannot be cleared. The title company will not provide insurance when the title is found to be uninsurable. This makes it important that the contract between the parties and the escrow instructions state that the transfer of ownership and closing of escrow are contingent upon good title being passed to the purchaser. The documents should state that the buyer is under no obligation to purchase property with an uninsurable title.

The transfer of property ownership may still occur between the parties involved, but the principals become self-insured in case a future claim is made. In this case the financial position invested in the property by the principal is the assumed risk inherent in property ownership. Because a lender usually will not loan funds on a property that cannot be insured by a title company with a policy of title insurance, the transaction would probably need to be an all-cash transaction directly between the principals.

Figure 4.9 shows the path taken from the preliminary title report to the actual policy of title insurance. A review of this overview explains the steps and procedures taken by the title company personnel to ensure that the insurance policy covers all the basic information needed to assure the lender and purchaser that no liens and encumbrances of the seller, such as the seller's loan, remain on the property after the transfer of title to the buyer except for those items the buyer agrees to prior to the transfer, such as property taxes and a new loan. The personnel mentioned in Figure 4.9 are discussed in Chapter 5.

■ HOW TITLE IS HELD

Vesting may be translated as holding title. To *vest* title to property means to secure a person's authority or right to title ownership of property. A person or entity has many methods available to hold title to real property. The legal and tax consequences of vesting are discussed in the next section. The common methods of holding title when only one legal entity takes title to real property are shown in Figure 4.10 and detailed in Table 4.1. The common methods of holding title where more than one individual entity takes title to property, commonly referred to as multiple, or concurrent, ownership of real property, are seen in Figure 4.11 and detailed in Table 4.2.

FIGURE 4.9

Path of a Preliminary Report to a Title Policy

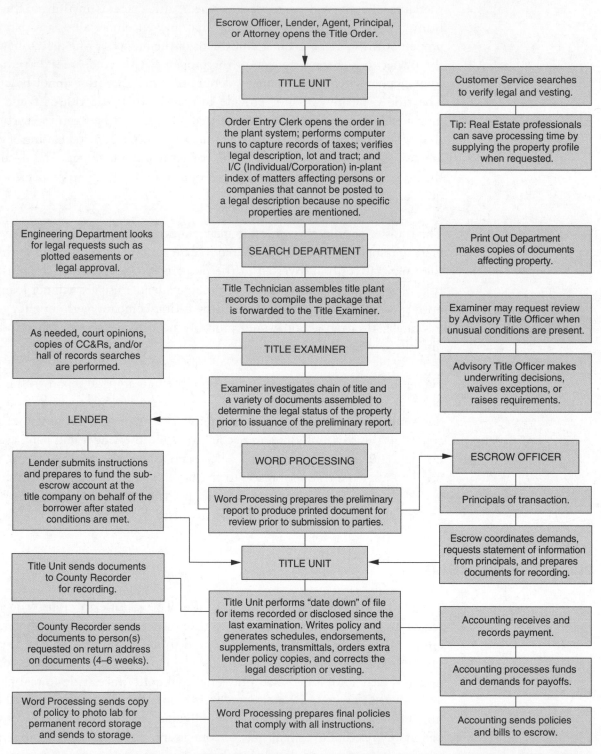

Escrow Officer, Lender, Agent, Principal, or Attorney opens the Title Order.

TITLE UNIT

Customer Service searches to verify legal and vesting.

Order Entry Clerk opens the order in the plant system; performs computer runs to capture records of taxes; verifies legal description, lot and tract; and I/C (Individual/Corporation) in-plant index of matters affecting persons or companies that cannot be posted to a legal description because no specific properties are mentioned.

Tip: Real Estate professionals can save processing time by supplying the property profile when requested.

Engineering Department looks for legal requests such as plotted easements or legal approval.

SEARCH DEPARTMENT

Print Out Department makes copies of documents affecting property.

Title Technician assembles title plant records to compile the package that is forwarded to the Title Examiner.

Examiner may request review by Advisory Title Officer when unusual conditions are present.

As needed, court opinions, copies of CC&Rs, and/or hall of records searches are performed.

TITLE EXAMINER

Advisory Title Officer makes underwriting decisions, waives exceptions, or raises requirements.

Examiner investigates chain of title and a variety of documents assembled to determine the legal status of the property prior to issuance of the preliminary report.

LENDER

WORD PROCESSING

ESCROW OFFICER

Lender submits instructions and prepares to fund the sub-escrow account at the title company on behalf of the borrower after stated conditions are met.

Word Processing prepares the preliminary report to produce printed document for review prior to submission to parties.

Principals of transaction.

Escrow coordinates demands, requests statement of information from principals, and prepares documents for recording.

Title Unit sends documents to County Recorder for recording.

TITLE UNIT

County Recorder sends documents to person(s) requested on return address on documents (4–6 weeks).

Title Unit performs "date down" of file for items recorded or disclosed since the last examination. Writes policy and generates schedules, endorsements, supplements, transmittals, orders extra lender policy copies, and corrects the legal description or vesting.

Accounting receives and records payment.

Accounting processes funds and demands for payoffs.

Word Processing sends copy of policy to photo lab for permanent record storage and sends to storage.

Word Processing prepares final policies that comply with all instructions.

Accounting sends policies and bills to escrow.

Note: This is an example of a simple title order, identifying the most basic elements in a title search. More complex situations can and do occur routinely. Your title representatives will be happy to assist you in understanding more difficult transactions.

FIGURE 4.10

Ownership by One Entity

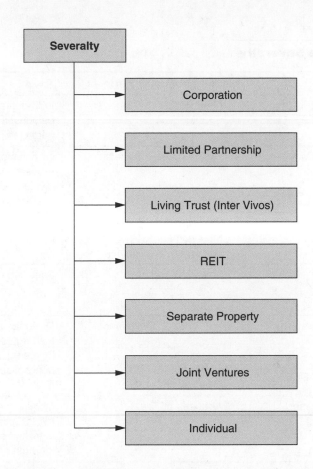

■ TITLE PARTICIPATION AT CLOSE OF ESCROW AND BEYOND

Several events can happen after the close of escrow (COE) that keeps the title insurance company involved. One of the negative activities is when someone makes a challenge to the ownership of the property, often years after the transfer of title took place. In this case the insured would simply notify the title insurance company. In accordance with the terms of the policy, the title insurance company undertakes to defend the title at the expense of the title company. The title company investigates the claim using its in-house researchers and often a staff attorney. If the claim reaches the courts, the title company retains the legal team necessary to defend the title. Again, the title company bears the expense of the court suit.

Even though the title insurance policy provides coverage only from the time of issuance of the policy back to the origin of the title in the United States, future claims against the title can come from many directions. The title insurance company would defend the title for the heirs and devisees against an attack as if the original insured were still alive. This can be important in claims resulting in prior claims made under a subordination clause for new construction and for

TABLE 4.1

Ownership in Severalty

	Sole Proprietorship	Trust	Tenancy in Partnership
Who takes title.	One person.	Individuals, groups of persons, a living trust partnership, corporations.	Only partners.
Ownership is divided.	One undivided ownership.	Ownership is a personal property interest and can be divided into any number of interests.	Ownership interest is in relation to interest in partnership.
Title is held.	One title: As a single man/woman; as an unmarried man/woman.	Legal and equitable title is held by the trustee.	Title is in the partnership.
Possession.	Sole possession.	Specified in trust provisions.	Equal right of possession; only for partnership purposes.
Interest conveyed.	Part of total conveyance.	Designated parties in the trust agreement authorized by the trustees to convey; a beneficiary's interest in the trust may be transferred.	No partner can sell interest in the partnership without consent of the other partners. Convey whole partnership.
Status of purchaser.	Acquires all title.	Obtains beneficial interest by assignment; or obtains legal and equitable title from the trust.	Acquires all title.
Upon death.	Passes to heirs.	Successor beneficiaries named in the trust agreement; no probate.	Partnership interests pass to surviving partner, pending liquidation of partnership. The share of deceased partner goes to that partner's estate.
Successor status.	One undivided interest.	Defined by trust agreement; successor becomes the beneficiary and the trust continues.	Heirs of devisees have rights in partnership interest, but not in specific property.
Creditor's interest.	Whole property can be sold to satisfy creditors.	Creditor may seek an order of execution sale of beneficial interest or seek order that the trust be liquidated and proceeds distributed.	Partner's interest cannot be seized or sold separately by personal creditor. Partner's shares may be obtained by a personal creditor.
Presumption of law.	None.	Trust is expressly created by an executed trust agreement.	Arises only by virtue of partnership status in property placed in partnership.
Federal estate tax.	Full estate is taxed.	None.	Each partner is taxed separately.

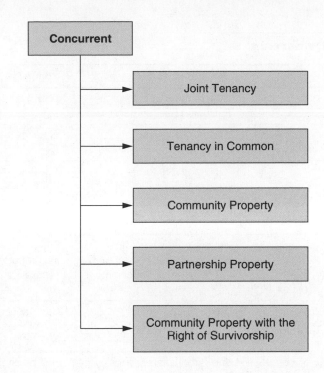

homeowner association rights to title. The improvements that are owned by a seller may be built upon leasehold lands. The government, Native Americans, and religious organizations own large parcels of land in California, especially in the mountain and desert areas. When an individual buys the improvements from the seller the buyer obtains only the interest that the seller had. The seller may have a 99-year lease that has already had 80 years used, with only 19 years remaining. In this case, when a buyer asks a bank to place a 30-year loan on the property, the lender will refuse. The lender would seek title insurance for the full period that the loan is placed on the property. In this case the buyer would have only 18 remaining years on the lease with a 30-year loan that would run for 12 years after the buyer no longer owned the property.

THINK ABOUT IT

Two real estate students, A and B, decide to buy an investment property duplex together. A has more funds available than B and puts up ⅔ of the cash needed to close escrow and B pays ⅓. The grant deed states only their names with no other mention about vesting. A and B live in one side of the three-bedroom duplex, and they rent out the other side of the duplex for the rental income.

After a while they begin to disagree on everything. A asserts the greater ownership interest and orders B to use only one bedroom because A will be using the other two bedrooms.

How is the title to the property held? What are the rights of A and B?

TABLE 4.2

Concurrent Ownership

	Joint Tenancy	Community Property	Tenancy-in-Common
Who takes title.	Any number of people, including husband and wife.	Only husband and wife.	Any number of persons, including husband and wife.
Ownership is divided.	Cannot be divided.	Equal ownership.	Can be divided into any number.
Title is held.	Only one title to the whole property.	Title held in the "community."	Each co-owner has a separate legal title to his/her own undivided interest.
Possession.	Equal right of possession.	Equal right of possession.	Equal right of possession.
Interest conveyed.	All are co-owners; if one breaks his/her interest, new owner is tenant-in-common.	Both owners must convey the property; cannot convey separate interest upon death.	Each co-owner may convey separately.
Status of purchaser.	Becomes a tenant-in-common with other co-owners.	Can acquire only the whole title of the community; cannot acquire a part of it.	Becomes a tenant-in-common with other co-owners.
Upon death.	Individual interest ends; cannot will; survivors own equally.	Half belongs to survivor, in severalty. Half goes by will to descendant's devisee or by succession to survivor.	No right of survivorship; interest passes by will to devisee or heirs.
Successor status.	Last survivor owns all the property in severalty.	Tenancy in common between devisee and survivor.	Devisees or heirs become tenants in common.
Creditor's interest.	Co-owner interest may be sold on execution sale to satisfy creditor who becomes tenant in common.	Co-owner interest cannot be seized and sold separately; whole property may be sold to satisfy debts of co-owner.	Co-owner interest may be sold on execution sale to satisfy creditor who becomes tenant in common.
Presumption of law.	Must be expressly stated on document.	Presumed all property acquired is community.	Favored in most cases, except spouses.
Federal estate tax.	Full estate tax; spouse can claim marital deduction.	Half of estate taxed; spouse can claim marital deduction.	Estate tax according to property split; spouse can claim marital deduction.

Answer: The interests are not equal, and because no vesting was stated at the time they acquired the property, each holds title as a tenant-in-common (TIC).

Each has a right to possession to the entire property with no limit on specific portions of the property. B could sue A to regain possession.

B could also sue for partition. The judge would most likely have one buy out the other or order the property sold and the proceeds split with A getting ⅔ of the net proceeds and B getting ⅓.

Escrow would need the signature of both A and B to transfer ownership to a third party in the event of a sale. Escrow would need the signature of B to grant all interest to A if A and B agreed that A could refinance the property and pay B his or her ⅓ net proceeds.

■ CHAPTER SUMMARY

Consumers and professionals alike, including investors and agents, often debate and have counteroffers over the selection of the real estate services, including selection of the escrow company and the title insurance company (which may be the same firm). No law in California dictates the selection, which is freely negotiable between the parties. However, Fannie Mae does state that the seller cannot make his or her choice of title insurance a condition of sale. The federal RESPA law indicates that the buyer has the choice of title insurance company.

The title company performs a search of the title records to obtain the chain of title. This chain links every owner, one-at-a-time, back to the original source of ownership of the real property. Many steps are taken in the process to ascertain that each owner has a direct link to the past owner.

Once the title order has been opened with the title company, the statement of information (SI) is obtained from each principal. The title company uses the SI plus public and court records to furnish the preliminary title report, prior to issuing the actual title insurance policy. The principals must instruct escrow on the method in which they are planning to take title to the property in order for the documents to be prepared for signatures and approvals by the parties to the transaction as well as approval by any lender involved and approval by the title insurer.

■ CHAPTER 4 QUIZ

1. A statement of information is
   a. an invasion of the principal's privacy.
   b. used to prosecute principals.
   c. used by the title insurer to properly identify principals.
   d. an intrusive document required by the credit reporting agency.

2. A title search includes all *EXCEPT*
   a. checking records.
   b. filing documents at the County Recorder's office.
   c. reviewing public records.
   d. assembling documents and facts affecting real property.

3. A preliminary title report
   a. is a title company's formal report as of a particular date.
   b. insures the loan in case of foreclosure.
   c. insures ownership of a particular property, with exceptions.
   d. is a contract to indemnify.

4. An abstract is
   a. data compiled after the preliminary title report.
   b. data compiled after the policy of title insurance.
   c. made for the purpose of title examination.
   d. a land registration system showing ownership.

5. The chronological list of documents showing the recorded history of a property is called a(n)
   a. official record.
   b. date down.
   c. title insurance policy.
   d. chain of title.

6. The evidence of a person's right or interest in real property is referred to as
   a. vesting.   c. estate.
   b. title.   d. instrument.

7. When a financial obligation is shown against a property, the term used is
   a. conveyance.   c. patent.
   b. easement.   d. lien.

8. The document that is used by the title company to enable the elimination of problems caused from the names of the individuals is called
   a. patent
   b. title plant
   c. chain of title
   d. statement of information

9. Which is *NOT* part of the escrow?
   a. Determine the vesting, encumbrances, and liens
   b. Hold deposited money as a third party
   c. Perform certain conditions as instructed
   d. Handle instruments given to a third party

10. Another word used for instrument is
    a. document.   c. plant.
    b. patent.   d. Torrens.

CHAPTER FIVE

TITLE INSURANCE:
TECHNICAL DOCUMENTS

■ KEY TERMS

access	exceptions	order entry clerk
advisory title officer	exclusions	public street access
ALTA	grantor-grantee index	short-term rate
assignment	homeowner policy	survey plat map
CLTA	interim binder	title representative
condo ALTA	lis pendens	title searcher
contiguous land	mechanic's lien	title technician
easement	mineral extraction	title unit
endorsement	off-record	tract index

■ CHAPTER OVERVIEW

An insurance policy is designed to safeguard the insured against loss. Title insurance is designed to safeguard the property owner or lender against an attack on title to the property. Several types of standard policies are available, including ALTA, CLTA, homeowner, and binder. The standard policy often includes many types of endorsements. Not all matters are insured, and many of the exclusions are written to specifically exempt many kinds of issues pertaining to the property.

The chain of title uses the grantor-grantee index (GI) found at the county recorder's office in addition to other types of public records. The links between past owners must be sufficient to establish a clear ownership by the party transferring some right to real property. The right may be ownership from a seller to a buyer or a lienholder for financing property. Each party to the transaction is checked for the various maiden, married, divorced, or any other name used by the principals.

Various title company personnel handle the technical documents at the title insurance company. Brief descriptions of some of the jobs associated with employees in the title insurance industry are described.

■ LEARNING OBJECTIVES

At the conclusion of Chapter 5, you will be able to

- outline endorsements contained in a title insurance policy;
- understand the coverage of a title insurance policy;
- explain the types of title insurance policies;
- give definitions for CLTA and ALTA title insurance; and
- differentiate between the various kinds of title policy exceptions and exclusions.

■ TYPES OF TITLE INSURANCE POLICIES

The U.S. system of laws recognizes more rights and interests in real property than in personal property. Some of these rights include life estates, future interests, subsurface and air rights, right-of-ways and easements, and liens. Because the purchase of real property is usually the most expensive and long-term financial commitment most people make in a lifetime, the protection of the owner of real property is a major concern in any real estate transaction. The protection expected covers construction, transfer between buyer and seller, financing, and leasehold interests.

In California almost every real estate transaction is closed with the issuance of a policy of title insurance in favor of the property owner or the lender, or both. The insurance company indemnifies against loss up to the face amount of the policy. Because the primary purpose of title insurance is to eliminate risks and prevent loss caused by defects that might arise out of past events, the title insurer takes affirmative steps to minimize its risk so it won't have to pay a claim to a policyholder. If title companies do their job correctly, the policyholder will never suffer any loss and will never have to be subject to any adverse claim.

Most title insurance companies offer insurance policies for real property that contain specific endorsements to the insurance contract that alter the scope and application of the coverage. The most common types of title insurance coverage are the American Land Title Association (ALTA), California Land Title Association (CLTA), joint policy, homeowner policy, and interim binder policy.

Policies for owners are also issued covering various estates other than fee title, such as for leaseholds. Variations occur in the clauses of the title policy and in the pricing for the different types of coverage. These special policies would include transactions involving churches and charitable institutions. Insurance covering the new owner following a foreclosure is a special type of policy. Whenever a holder of minerals interests or noncontiguous parcels is involved, variance coverage is established.

American Land Title Association

Of the different types of title insurance policies available, the most common kind is the American Land Title Association or **ALTA** lender's policy that protects only the lender and is used for a purchase and on a refinance. The typical types of coverage found for a one-unit to four-unit residential property in an ALTA policy are shown in Figure 5.1. The ALTA policy is acquired when a property changes ownership because few buyers can pay all cash for a property. Any financing, whether it be with a new purchase or when obtained for a refinance of an existing loan, will usually require a policy of title insurance to protect the lender's interests.

FIGURE 5.1

ALTA Policy Coverage

- Mechanic's lien protection
- Unrecorded lien by the homeowners' association
- Unrecorded easements
- Rights arising out of leases, contracts, or options
- Pay rent for substitute land or facilities
- Inflation protection
- The legal right of access to the property
- Forced removal of a structure because it
  - extends onto the land owned by another;
  - extends onto an easement;
  - violates a restriction; or
  - violates an existing zoning law

The ALTA policy is designed to meet the needs of institutional lenders. These lenders act as financial intermediaries for the depositors, investors, and employees whose funds the institution holds in trust and care to be invested in real estate matters. The lending institution seeks relative security for these investments. The security that lenders seek is that the loan they place on real property be a valid first trust deed lien. This means that the lenders want their loan to take priority over any other claim or interest in and to the real property, except items disclosed to and approved by the lender. The kinds of liens allowed by the first trust deed holder are property taxes and assessments. The lenders want assurance that the party to whom the loan was funded is the party who actually holds title ownership to the property.

The lender is concerned about anything that would affect the loan security. The lender is worried about **off-record** matters that might have a priority ahead of the lender's interest. Another concern is assuring that the property has **access** to a public street. A lender is always concerned that a mechanic's lien might have a priority over the trust deed.

Lenders (extended coverage, ALTA). The lenders' ALTA extended coverage is normally issued to institutional lenders, with coverage extended to include such off-record matters as lack of access, marketability, encroachments, and possible statutory liens for labor or materials arising out of work on the improvement or the land. If this title insurance policy is issued in conjunction with a sale policy, a concurrent rate is applicable as discussed on page 83. If a refinance (with no sale) is to be issued, the basic schedule rate is usually charged, with a **short-term rate** applicable.

Lender policy (extended coverage, ALTA). The ALTA lender policy for a construction loan policy is used when insuring deeds of trust on improved land, with work of improvement being additional to existing improvements. The initial policy is an extended coverage ALTA policy without some of the endorsements. The lender of first priority is included within the ALTA insurance coverage. This policy is also rewritten at the completion period of the construction as another ALTA policy with specific affixed endorsements. The liability coverage is for the loan amount and not the appraised value, the sales price, or the construction costs. The short-term rate is applied to the loan policy portion only. The pricing totals 130 percent of the basic rate: 100 percent for the extended coverage loan policy plus 30 percent for the ALTA rewrite.

California Land Title Association

The second most common title insurance policy is the California Land Title Association or **CLTA** owner's policy that is usually purchased at the time of transfer of title. The typical coverage found in a CLTA policy is shown in Figure 5.2. In Southern California common practice is for the seller to pay for this policy, and in Northern California it is more common that the buyer pay for the CLTA

FIGURE 5.2

CLTA Policy Coverage

- Ownership interest in title to the property by someone else
- A document not properly signed
- Forgery
- Fraud
- Duress
- Defective recording of any document
- Restrictive covenants
- Unmarketable title
- Lack of right of access to and from the land (ingress and egress)
- A lien on the title for a deed of trust
- A judgment against the property
- A charge by a homeowners' association
- Any tax or special assessment against the property

title insurance policy. Naturally, all costs are negotiable, except on certain FHA, VA, and Cal-Vet loans according to federal RESPA guidelines.

Owners (standard coverage, CLTA). This policy insures the buyer(s) in a sale transaction, with a liability equivalent to the total sales price. This policy may be issued for a loan assumption or for sales involving a new institutional loan or when the transaction does not require "secondary" financing. The pricing is from the basic schedule of rates, with the short-term rate used. This policy includes homeowner's endorsements and inflationary endorsements when applicable at no additional charge.

Owners (extended coverage, CLTA or ALTA). The insured includes the property owner, with coverage extended to also include the institutional lender, including marketability of the property. This additional coverage requires that a survey be submitted prior to escrow closing. The pricing is 200 percent of the basic schedule rate, with a liability equal to the total sales price.

Joint protection (standard coverage, CLTA). This policy coverage is identical to the standard owner's policy described above, with the insurance extended to "jointly" insure the lender. In most cases, this policy is used to issue coverage to the "secondary" lender, or the primary lender. Extended coverage is not required. The pricing is also the basic schedule rate, with a liability equal to the total sales price—and not less than the total of all deeds of trust. Homeowner's and inflationary endorsements are affixed when applicable.

Lenders (standard coverage, CLTA). This policy insures any lender who does not require the above described extended coverage policy. The coverage is commonly issued to individual beneficiaries, makers of "hard money" second trust deeds, and credit unions. This policy is not necessary in a sales transaction, inasmuch as equivalent coverage is afforded to a lender under the joint protection policy. The exception to this rule would occur if a binder were issued to the buyer. The premium is 80 percent of the basic schedule rate, or usually a small flat fee, if issued concurrent with the binder. The short-term rate is applicable, with a liability equal to the amount of the loan.

Lender policy–mechanic's lien (standard coverage, CLTA). This policy is the standard loan policy with endorsement affixed to include priority insurance covering mechanic's liens. This policy is issued when loan funds are to be used for construction purposes. The liability is the loan amount with a premium of 90 percent the basic rate: 80 percent for the standard loan coverage; 10 percent for the special construction endorsement. The short-term rate is applicable to the policy portion.

Lender policy–construction (standard coverage, CLTA). This policy is also a standard loan policy for construction loans secured by a deed of trust on vacant land, with a specific endorsement for priority coverage. This policy is rewritten at the completion of the construction project as an extended coverage ALTA policy. The liability is the loan amount, with the short-term rate being applicable to the loan policy portion only. The pricing totals 125 percent of the basic rate: 80 percent for the standard loan; 10 percent for the priority endorsement; with 35 percent for the ALTA rewrite.

Vendee (standard coverage, CLTA). This policy insures a buyer under a sales contract, with no initial conveyance, where the transfer of ownership title to the buyer is at a future date. Pricing is the basic schedule rate, with the short-term rate applicable. A standard owner's policy can be issued at the time the vendee acquires fee title with only a 25 percent premium charge. The liability is equal to the sales price.

The exception is where the transaction is with the California Department of Veterans Affairs, or Cal-Vet. A Cal-Vet transaction requires a joint protection policy because the vested owner is, in fact, the lender and this requires a lender's policy of title insurance. The buyer, or vendee, holds the equitable title in a Cal-Vet loan transaction.

Homeowner Policy Coverage

The coverage for a **homeowner policy** includes the coverage in the CLTA and the ALTA, plus the additional items shown in Figure 5.3. In fact, it is almost impossible to obtain financing on any real property in California without obtaining the required policy of title insurance. A less common policy is known as a leasehold policy that

FIGURE 5.3

Homeowner Policy Coverage—CLTA and ALTA

- Restrictive covenant violations
- Enhanced access—vehicular and pedestrian
- Damage to structure from use of an easement
- Street address is correct
- Map not consistent with legal description
- Coverage for spouse acquiring through divorce
- Violations of building setbacks
- Discriminatory covenants
- Insurance coverage forever
- Post policy
  - Defect in title
  - Contract or lease rights
  - Forgery
  - Easement
  - Limitation on use of the land
  - Damage from minerals or water extraction
  - Living trust coverage
  - Encroachment by a neighbor, other than for a wall or fence
  - Automatic increase in value up to 150 percent
  - Correction of existing violation of covenant
  - Limitation of use
  - Prescriptive easement

is used primarily by commercial and industrial organizations that rent property on long-term leases. The interim binder has become more popular as more investors are flipping property with a relatively short-term ownership period.

The Interim Binder

As more and more people buy property for investment and speculation, the **interim binder** policy becomes a more important tool for the real estate broker. By utilizing the interim binder, principals to a transaction can realize a substantial savings in the cost of title insurance. Insurance in excess of the original binder amount is priced on an increased liability basis. A sample ALTA interim binder is shown in Figure 5.4. This binder is a single page written by the title insurance company to add to the owner's policy that is written at the same time. This type of policy automatically expires 45 days after one year from the date of issuance. This allows for the one year of coverage plus a normal escrow period of additional time. After the 410 days, an additional fee would have to be paid for coverage of additional time.

FIGURE 5.4

Sample Interim Binder

FEE $XXX.xx

Pacific Ocean Title Insurance Company
a corporation,

HEREBY AGREES WITH THE VESTEE NAMED HEREIN THAT IT WILL ISSUE, FROM AND AFTER THE DATE SHOWN BELOW, ITS **AMERICAN LAND TITLE ASSOCIATION (ALTA) PLAIN LANGUAGE POLICY** OF TITLE INSURANCE WITH A LIABILITY NOT EXCEEDING **$XXX,XXX.xx,** SHOWING TITLE TO THE ESTATE OR INTEREST DESCRIBED AND TO BE VESTED IN THE VESTEE NAMED HEREIN, SUBJECT ONLY TO THE EXCEPTIONS SHOWN HEREIN, AND TO ALL OF THE PROVISIONS OF THE POLICY; OR, IF A VALID AND SUFFICIENT INSTRUMENT CREATING AN INSURABLE ESTATE OR INTEREST IN FAVOR OF THE NOMINEE OF THE VESTEE NAMED HEREIN IS EXECUTED, DELIVERED AND RECORDED WITHIN TWO YEARS FROM THE DATE STATED BELOW, THE POLICY WILL BE ISSUED AS OF THE DATE OF RECORDING THE INSTRUMENT, INSURING THE ESTATE OR INTEREST SUBJECT ONLY TO THE AFORESAID EXCEPTIONS AND PROVISIONS OF THE POLICY AND TO LIENS, ENCUMBRANCES, AND ANY OTHER MATTERS WHICH SHALL HAVE INTERVENED, OCCURRED OR ATTACHED, OR BECOME FOR THE FIRST TIME DISCLOSED BETWEEN THE DATE STATED BELOW AND THE DATE OF RECORDING THE INSTRUMENT, INCLUDING THOSE MATTERS WHICH MAY ATTACH AS A RESULT OF THE RECORDING.

THE BINDER IS PRELIMINARY TO THE ISSUANCE OF THE POLICY OF TITLE INSURANCE AND SHALL BECOME NULL AND VOID 410 DAYS FROM THE DATE SHOWN BELOW OR WHEN THE POLICY IS ISSUED, WHICHEVER SHALL FIRST OCCUR.

DATED: JULY 2, 20XX AT 8:00 A.M.

In lieu of an owner's policy, a binder to insure a resale within 24 months of the date of closing may be issued for a fee of 10 percent of the base rate depending upon the liability amount. This fee is in addition to the applicable fee for an owner's policy. Prior to its expiration, a binder may be extended for an additional 12 months for an additional fee of 10 percent of the base rate based upon the liability amount.

Provided that an owner's policy is issued prior to the expiration of a binder insuring the nominee of the vestee named as the insured, there shall be no additional charge for the liability amounts up to the amount stated in the interim binder for the same form of coverage. When a binder is issued for a standard coverage policy, but the new policy is extended coverage, an additional 25 percent is added to the base rate, based upon the policy liability amount. A binder may be reissued to reflect an interim transfer of title prior to the ultimate resale purchaser for an additional charge of 25 percent of the base rate, based upon the binder amount.

Commitment to insure (interim binder). The format of the "temporary" binder assures an equity purchaser of obtaining title insurance for the individual investor, contractor, or homebuyer who intends to resell within a 24-month period. This reduces the ultimate insurance cost. The pricing is usually 110 percent of the basic schedule rate, which includes the standard owner's policy for the ultimate buyer(s) for only a small additional liability charge. This binder is extended to the buyers only and cannot be extended to cover lenders.

■ TITLE EXCEPTIONS

By design, after the title insurance policy is written and the escrow closes, the title ownership is not free and clear of all liens and encumbrances. Some items remain on the property after the transfer of ownership. Lien items may be voluntary or involuntary.

The title insurance company writes the policy with standard **exceptions** to the endorsements or **exclusions** to limit risk. The exclusions are spelled out in the policy, but few people take the time to read and understand what is *not* covered by the title insurance policy. Figure 5.5 lists the ALTA residential exclusions, and explanations of some of these exceptions to the policy are discussed. The main items not included in policy coverage are government and mining rights, items that occur after the policy date, anything not of public record, and anything known to any party and not disclosed.

The title insurance company cannot insure property free of property taxes, thus no title policy could contain a title exception for taxes. The most common involuntary lien against a property is the government's right to tax real property and to levy special assessments. The title company indicates that the principal will receive title to the property subject to the property tax lien, which remains as a recurring expense.

Another area of governmental rights that is excluded in the title insurance policy is political governmental items that are subject to change at the whim of a local constituency. These meetings include groups who influence building codes, zoning, and condemnation. A local government can easily hold public hearings to change the use of parcels of land, sections of a city, or areas of a municipality. The title insurance company could not insure for such items that are so subject to change by the local political climate. Even when an area is studied for redevelopment, and then approved for a change, it takes time to actually finish a condemnation project when many properties are involved in a large block of land amassed together. In the end, without actually receiving the funding for the project, often dependent upon matching federal funds or the selling of municipal

FIGURE 5.5

ALTA Residential Title Insurance Policy Exclusions

> ## AMERICAN LAND TITLE ASSOCIATION (ALTA) RESIDENTIAL TITLE INSURANCE POLICY EXCLUSIONS
>
> *This policy does not insure against loss or damage (and the company will not pay costs, attorneys' fees, or expenses) that arise by reason of or resulting from the following:*

1. Governmental policy power, and the existence or violation of any law or governmental regulation. This includes building and zoning ordinances and also laws and regulations concerning the following:
   * land use
   * improvements on the land
   * land division
   * environmental protection

   This exclusion does not apply to violations or the enforcement of these matters that appear in the public records at policy date.

   This exclusion does not limit the zoning coverage described in the covered title risks.

2. The right to take the land by condemning it, unless
   * a notice of exercising the right appears in the public records on the policy date; and
   * the taking happened prior to the policy date and is binding on you if you bought the land without knowing of the taking.

3. Title Risks
   * that are created, allowed, or agreed to by you;
   * that are known to you, but not to us, on the policy date—unless they appeared in the public records;
   * that result in no loss to you; and
   * that first affect your title after the policy date—this does not limit the labor or material lien coverage in covered title risks.

4. Failure to pay value for your title.

5. Lack of a right
   * to any land outside the area specifically described and referred to in Schedule A; or
   * in streets, alleys, or waterways that touch your land.

6. Taxes or assessments, which are not shown as existing liens by the records of any taxing authority that levies taxes or assessments on real property or by the public records. Proceedings by a public agency, which may result in taxes or assessments, or notices of such proceedings, whether or not shown by the records of such agency or by the public records.

7. Any facts, rights, interests, or claims which are not shown by the public records but which could be ascertained by an inspection of the land or by making inquiry of persons in possession thereof.

8. Easements, liens, or encumbrances or claims thereof, which are not shown by the public records.

9. Discrepancies, conflicts in boundary lines, shortage in area, encroachments, or any other facts which a correct survey would disclose, and which are not shown by the public records.

10. (a) Unpatented mining claims; (b) reservations or exceptions in patents or in Acts authorizing the issuance thereof; (c) water rights, claims, or title to water, whether or not the matters excepted under (a), (b), or (c) are shown by the public records.

    This exclusion does not limit the access coverage in covered title risks.

bonds, the project will not come to fruition. The title company could not bear the loss for individuals claiming a loss due to political actions.

The most common involuntary encumbrance is the right granted to utility companies for property access, including underground or overhead electric lines, telephone lines, gas lines, sewer lines, and cable lines. The right of the utility company includes the right to read the meter and bill for services. The right to discontinue services for nonpayment is normally a part of the utility company powers. A principal cannot sever the rights of a utility company after the title insurance policy is issued and make a claim against the title company. Disclosure of a utility company easement is made prior to transfer of ownership, usually in the preliminary title report.

Another common exclusion by the title policy is the item that arises after the title insurance policy is written. Because the policy is written to cover the time from origination of title records up to the date the policy is issued, it does not cover subsequent changes. Any future coverage for title after a policy is written would require a new policy. This is why it is common for a person to resist paying another premium when refinancing. If the person purchased the home and obtained both a CLTA and an ALTA policy at the close of escrow, then the individual refinances the property six months later, the lender for the new loan would require a new ALTA policy. This is where knowledge of coverage by the real estate professional can help decrease costs for the principal. At the time of the purchase, a short-term special rate could be arranged if it is known ahead of time that another loan will be financed on the property in a relatively short period of time. When a buyer indicates refinancing relatively soon to do a remodel or add a large capital improvement such as a pool, then the buyer should have the opportunity to save money at the later refinance by having an explanation of policy options that meet his or her needs. This requires depth of knowledge by the individual handling the original transaction.

In addition, the title insurance company requires that the policyholder pay value for the title because a legal requirement of any contract is that consideration be made by the party. At the same time, any information that any party knew about but did not disclose is not included in policy coverage. For example, the seller received a notice from the city that curbs, gutters, and sidewalks were going to be installed along the front of the property. Each property owner would be charged a per linear foot amount for the improvement. Letters are sent to all the property owners on the street who are affected by the proposed improvements. Yet, no lien is yet placed on the property because public hearings are required and the city is putting together a proposed financing package for the project. The seller receives a letter that the city will allow the property owner to pay $3,000 in one lump sum for the proposed improvements that will be a lien on the property three months after completion of the work. Or the city indicates that the property owner may finance the improvements by paying only $100 a year, collectible as part of the property tax bill. At the time of the transfer of ownership to the property, because no lien is yet placed on the property, there is no lump sum bill that could be paid in escrow to eliminate the future lien. Because it could be proven that the property owner along with all the neighbors would have knowledge of the upcoming lien, yet the seller did not disclose the lien to anyone in the transaction, the title insurance company would not cover the event. The buyers could try to sue the seller for nondisclosure of a material fact, but the buyers would be ultimately stuck paying the bill because they are the ones who received the benefit. The courts usually require the individual who receives the benefit from the item to pay the bill for that item. The last area commonly excluded from policy coverage is about the dirt itself. In California, the policy covers all items about the parcel of land with the exception of most mineral rights. This is not true in other states where ownership of the surface includes ownership of the subsurface substances. Most all below-surface substances are owned by a different entity and not included in policy coverage.

Also, property lines are often a problem. It is advisable to require a **survey plat map,** if any boundary area seems to be questionable. When a property is located on a street where vacant lots are common, or where new construction is still being performed immediately around the property, or when custom homes are involved, a physical survey and title coverage of property lines is highly recommended.

For example, it was found that as an avenue developed off the main street, each structure was developed by separate individuals. No tract map was filed showing the development of the entire street by one builder, with easements, right-of-ways, alleys, and accesses approved and insured at the time of original construction. The property was developed when the owner of a large chunk of land sold off individual lots privately. Each person who bought each lot built a separate type of home by placing the home in the middle of the lot. The street held 15 lots on each side of the street, with a cul-de-sac at the end. A problem arose when the last lot at the end of the street was developed.

The first property was developed 20 years ago with a house and a garage. The block wall fence placed around the corner lot was ten feet over onto the adjoining property. All subsequent property owners built 10 feet over and ran their fence from the first error. An encroachment of 10 feet onto each neighbor's property continued as each new house was built. None of the property owners obtained a survey of the land. The last person to develop the last house on the last vacant lot did get a survey. As a result, the last house ended up being placed with the required 5-foot side lot setback, which happened to be only 10 feet from the neighbor's front door. Instead of each house being on a large lot that had 20 to 25 feet between each house, the existing home and the newly constructed house ended up only 10 feet apart. This created a large loss in value for the existing adjoining property owner who purchased the property when the adjoining lot was vacant. The title insurance policy did not cover this claim because the original policy did not include extended coverage, a survey, or further search for adequate property line definitions that was available for the buyers to request at the time they purchased a neighboring lot.

A potential error such as this is another reason why a real estate professional would seek knowledge of types of policies, coverage, exceptions, and pricing. For only a few hundred dollars at the time of purchase, the buyer of the adjoining property could have received disclosure of this item prior to taking ownership of the property. Because of the disclosure during the survey and title search, the individual might never have taken title to the property. The adjoining property owner would not have suffered a loss in value due to the proximity to the new home. Or, with the disclosure, the price would have been negotiated to reflect the reduced value of the much smaller lot. The lot was thought to have been $75' \times 150'$ and turned out to be $65' \times 150'$, which reduced the lot by 1,500 square feet. Many homes are about 1,500 square feet in total area. This represents a large difference in value. If land in that area sold for $100 a square foot, this loss in value is $150,000, a substantial and significant amount. Policy coverage would have been about $350.

The regular ALTA policy shown in Figure 5.5 is often an add-on policy when a CLTA title insurance policy is purchased in a buyer-seller sale transaction. However, many real estate transactions occur daily where there is no seller, such as the numerous refinance escrow transactions. The lender will require an ALTA policy before the loan may fund. All of the items discussed above regarding the ALTA coverage in Figure 5.5 are part of this policy, in addition to more clauses that restrict or exclude coverage by the title insurance company. Figure 5.6 indicates the typical lender ALTA policy with its exclusion clauses covering government rights after the policy date, payment of value for title, items not of public record, a property survey, and mineral rights. Additional items for the ALTA lender policy include environmental issues, change in lot dimensions, eminent domain, results that end with no loss, and liens where no value is paid or that are unenforceable.

Plottage is when a group of smaller properties are combined to create a single, larger parcel. A result is that the new property is a change in the lot dimensions. The title insurance company insured the old, smaller lots with a title insurance policy. If the owner of the smaller property acquired and joined together the neighboring properties for a large development, the old title insurance policy would not cover the new larger parcel. A new policy would have to be obtained. This new policy would search the history for each one of the smaller parcels to determine if any adverse liens or encumbrances existed on any one of the smaller parcels.

FIGURE 5.6

ALTA Loan Title Insurance Policy Exclusions

AMERICAN LAND TITLE ASSOCIATION LOAN POLICY (ALTA)
WITH ALTA ENDORSEMENT—COVERAGE
and
AMERICAN LAND TITLE ASSOCIATION LEASEHOLD LOAN POLICY
WITH ALTA ENDORSEMENT COVERAGE
AND EXCLUSIONS FROM COVERAGE

The following matters are expressly excluded from the coverage of this policy, and the company will not pay loss or damage, costs, attorneys' fees, or expenses that arise by reason of the following:

1. Any law, ordinance, or governmental regulation (including but not limited to building and zoning laws, ordinances, or regulations) restricting, regulating, prohibiting, or relating to
   (i) the occupancy, use, or enjoyment of the land;
   (ii) the character, dimensions, or location of any improvement now or hereafter erected on the land;
   (iii) a separation in ownership or a change in the dimensions or area of the land or any parcel of which the land is or was a part; or
   (iv) environmental protection, or the effect of any violation of these laws, ordinances, or governmental regulations, except to the extent that a notice of the enforcement thereof or a notice of a defect, lien, or encumbrance resulting from a violation or alleged violation affecting the land has been recorded in the public records at date of policy.

2. Rights of eminent domain unless notice of the exercise thereof has been recorded in the public records at date of policy, but not excluding from coverage any taking which has occurred prior to date of policy which would be binding on the rights of a purchaser for value without knowledge.

3. Defects, liens, encumbrances, adverse claims, or other matters, including those
   (a) created, suffered, assumed or agreed to by the insured claimant;
   (b) not known to the company, not recorded in the public records at date of policy, but known to the insured claimant and not disclosed in writing to the company by the insured claimant prior to the date the insured claimant became an insured under this policy;
   (c) resulting in no loss or damage to the insured claimant;
   (d) attaching or created subsequent to date of policy (except to the extent that this policy insures the priority of the lien of the insured mortgage over any statutory lien for services, labor, or material or to the extent insurance is afforded herein as to assessments for street improvements under construction or completed at date of policy); or
   (e) resulting in loss or damage that would not have been sustained if the insured claimant had paid value for the insured mortgage.

4. Unenforceability of the lien of the insured mortgage because of the inability or failure of the insured at date of policy, or the inability or failure of any subsequent owner of the indebtedness, to comply with applicable doing business laws of the state in which the land is situated.

5. Invalidity or unenforceability of the lien of the insured mortgage, or claim thereof, which arises out of the transaction evidenced by the insured mortgage and is based upon usury or any consumer credit protection or truth in lending law.

6. Any statutory lien for services, labor, or materials (or the claim of priority of any statutory lien for services, labor, or materials over the lien of the insured mortgage) arising from an improvement or work related to the land which is contracted for and commenced subsequent to date of policy and is not financed in whole or in part by proceeds of the indebtedness secured by the insured mortgage, which at dates of policy the insured, has advanced or is obligated to advance.

FIGURE 5.6

ALTA Loan Title Insurance Policy Exclusions (Continued)

7. Any claim, which arises out of the transaction creating the interest of the mortgagee insured by this policy, by reason of the operation of federal bankruptcy, state insolvency, or similar creditors' rights laws, that is based on

    (a) the transaction creating the interest of the insured mortgagee being deemed a fraudulent conveyance or fraudulent transfer; or

    (b) the subordination of the interest of the insured mortgagee as a result of the application of the doctrine of equitable subordination; or

    (c) the transaction creating the interest of the insured mortgagee being deemed a preferential transfer except where the preferential transfer results from the failure

    (i) to timely record the instrument of transfer; or

    (ii) of such recordation to impart notice to a purchaser for value or a judgment or lien creditor.

The above policy forms may be issued to afford either standard coverage or extended coverage. In addition to the above exclusions from coverage, the exceptions from coverage in a standard coverage policy will also include the general exceptions as found in the joint CLTA coverage.

The title insurance policy states that environmental coverage is excluded, unless already known and cited before the policy issue date. If income property has written citations for mold or lead-based paint prior to the policy date, this fact would need to be disclosed prior to the transfer of title and could not be excluded from the policy coverage date.

The policy excludes any eminent domain action unless disclosed to all parties prior to change of ownership and policy issue date. Some purchasers buy property for redevelopment under governmental redevelopment action through condemnation and eminent domain action. The purchaser and policyholder want the old property improvements allowed to be removed and the new zoning, new use, and new building to be allowed. However, the title insurance company must be made aware of such action prior to coverage so that the correct policy may be issued that would cover the new property owner and the lender who is financing the new project. The insurance company cannot insure what it does not know about and that may or may not actually happen at some future date. Just because plans to make changes are approved, this does not mean that actual funding and completion of a new project is always carried out.

Another exclusion is that the insured suffered no loss. The burden of proof is on the insured to show that he or she did suffer a loss. In the examples already given in this chapter, the person did not know about the tax lien for the new curbs, gutters, and sidewalk prior to the policy issue date, but the insurance company can get an appraisal after the work is completed to show the actual increase in value to the property because of the undisclosed lien. Any change in zoning that increased the property value or a change in lot dimensions that improved the value of the property would not be an insurance claim. An insurance claim is to reimburse an insured for some loss.

Another area of title insurance policy coverage relates to liens. Under the rules of the "holder in due course," it must be proven that the person holding the note at the time of default paid consideration for the note and is subsequently suffering a loss by the nonpayment on the note. If a note is received by someone who paid no consideration for the lien, then this also violates the policy. If no value was paid, then the insurance company will not pay because no one has suffered any loss.

The lien clause exclusion provides that the insurance company will not cover any note that is unenforceable. For example, a note that is found to violate the usury laws because of high interest rates, high fees, and a short term would not be able to be a claim paid by the insurance company. Because the terms of the rate are illegal or unenforceable, there is no contract.

The CLTA policy is issued at the close of escrow by the title insurance company to the buyer. The typical clauses contained in a CLTA title insurance policy are similar to the description of the clauses contained in an ALTA policy coverage. Normally items such as governmental building, zoning, condemnation, eminent domain, mineral rights, and similar items are exceptions to the CLTA title policy. (See Figure 5.7.) Coverage is not for after the policy date and excludes payment by the insurance company if there is no resulting loss or no value paid or if the documents are unenforceable. Items that the parties knew but did not disclose are also excluded. All real estate professionals should read all insurance clauses thoroughly at least once to gain the knowledge of coverages and exclusions and ask the **title representative** to explain clauses they do not understand.

The most common voluntary lien is the new loan that the principal will obtain in order to be able to complete purchase. Because most buyers cannot pay all cash for real property, they ask a lender to loan the balance of the purchase price above the buyers' down payment. New loan funds are delivered to the escrow company as a credit for the buyers, and treated in the same manner as if the loan funds were cash on debit/credit side of the closing statement. When escrow obtains the funds from the buyers' lender, the amount is applied toward the entire purchase price and given to the seller, less the seller's closing costs.

The most common private voluntary encumbrance is homeowner association covenants, conditions, and restrictions (CC&Rs) with the association rules and regulations. The most common public voluntary encumbrance is the construction and building ordinances with setbacks and zoning restrictions. The right to *ingress and egress* for street access to real property is a common public encumbrance that allows the principal to drive on the street and park at the curb, but it is only a temporary use. Homeowners cannot park their motor homes or boats at the curb

FIGURE 5.7

CLTA Title Insurance Exclusions

CLTA PRELIMINARY REPORT FORM
LIST OF PRINTED EXCEPTIONS AND EXCLUSIONS

SCHEDULE B

CALIFORNIA LAND TITLE ASSOCIATION (CLTA)
STANDARD COVERAGE POLICY
EXCLUSIONS FROM COVERAGE

The following matters are expressly excluded from the coverage of this policy and the company will not pay loss or damage, costs, attorneys' fees, or expenses which arise by reason of the following:

1. (a) Any law, ordinance, or governmental regulation (including but not limited to building or zoning laws, ordinances, or regulations) restricting, regulating, prohibiting, or relating to
    (i)   the occupancy, use, or enjoyment of the land;
    (ii) the character, dimensions, or location of any improvement now or hereafter erected on the land;
    (iii) a separation in ownership or a change in the dimensions or area of the land or any parcel of which the land is or was a part; or
    (iv) environmental protection, or the effect of any violation of laws or ordinances or governmental regulations, except to the extent that a notice of the enforcement thereof or a notice of a defect, lien, or encumbrance resulting from a violation or alleged violation affecting the land has been recorded in the public records at Date of Policy.
    (b) Any governmental police power not excluded by (a) above, except to the extent that a notice of the exercise thereof or a notice of defect, lien, or encumbrance resulting from a violation affecting the land has been recorded in the public records at Date of Policy.

2. Rights of eminent domain unless notice of the exercise thereof has been recorded in the public records at Date of Policy, but not excluding from coverage any taking which has occurred prior to Date of Policy which would be binding on the rights of a purchaser for value without knowledge.

3. Defects, liens, encumbrances, adverse claims, or other matters:
    (a) whether or not recorded in the public records at Date of Policy, but created, suffered, assumed, or agreed to by the insured claimant;
    (b) not known to the Company, not recorded in the public records at Date of Policy, but known to the insured claimant and not disclosed in writing to the Company by the insured claimant prior to the date the insured claimant became an insured under this policy;
    (c) resulting in no loss or damage to the insured claimant;
    (d) attaching or created subsequent to Date of Policy; or
    (e) resulting in loss or damage which would not have been sustained if the insured claimant had paid value for the insured mortgage or for the estate or interest insured by this policy.

4. Unenforceability of the lien of the insured mortgage because of the inability or failure of the insured at Date of Policy, or the inability or failure of any subsequent owner of the indebtedness, to comply with the applicable doing business laws, or the state in which the land is situated.

5. Invalidity or unenforceability of the lien of the insured mortgage, or claim thereof, which arises out of the transaction evidenced by the insured mortgage and is based upon usury or any consumer credit protection or truth in lending law.

6. Any claim, which arises out of the transaction vesting in the insured the estate or interest of the insured lender, by reason of the operation of federal bankruptcy, state insolvency, or similar creditors' rights laws.

for an extended period of time in most communities because of the legal ordinance by a city or municipality enforcing that right as an easement. An **easement** is the *temporary* right to use real property.

A common private restriction in many California deeds is for the exclusion of subsurface mineral rights. The surface right to build a home and use the top portion of the land is common, but the portion of earth below a specific depth is owned by another entity. Other than the surface primary owner, the other entity may use this ownership for the extraction of minerals, including slant-drilling rights.

■ TITLE INSURANCE COMPANY ENDORSEMENTS

A standard title insurance company policy includes many commonly used endorsements. **Endorsements** are additions that can expand coverage of the title insurance policy, thus fulfilling specific requirements for the insured. Also, there is no use to spend extra funds to obtain additional endorsements unless the coverage is necessary or recommended. Often, too, because endorsements that may be available in one state may not be available in another state or area, the differences should be determined by checking with the title insurance officer to determine whether an endorsement is available, at what additional cost, and what the coverage includes. A summary list of some of the kinds of additional endorsements available is given in Figure 5.8.

The outline of listed endorsements in Figure 5.8 demonstrates the detail of what is available for those who seek additional endorsement coverage. However, a further explanation is needed for those who studied detailed insurance policy endorsements. The endorsements listed below are an explanation for general information on the topic and meant only as an introduction. Actual title insurance company endorsements and exclusions change over time to represent current practices. Although the exact wording and actual form may vary between states and among title insurance companies in differing areas of California, the basic explanation should give the real estate professional a better understanding of title insurance policy endorsements.

ALTA Endorsements

Assessments—ALTA. This endorsement is designed for use with the ALTA loan policy to provide the insured lender with protection against loss sustained by reason of any assessments for street improvements under construction or completed as of the date of the endorsement having priority over the lien of the insured mortgage. California and several other states included this endorsement as part of the ALTA loan policy as insuring a property, thus avoiding the necessity of adding the endorsement to the policy.

FIGURE 5.8

Samples of Commonly Requested Endorsements

ACCESS
Insured easement provides access to public street (owner or lender).

ADDITIONAL ADVANCE (Optional)
Additional advance under deed of trust (standard coverage lender).
Additional advance under deed of trust (ALTA lender).

ADDITIONAL ADVANCE (Obligatory)
Advance under deed of trust—broad coverage—liability limited to amount of policy (ALTA lender).
Advance under deed of trust—broad coverage—liability increased by amount of advance (ALTA lender).

ASSIGNMENTS
Assignment of lessor's interest in lease (ALTA lender).
Assignment of rents contained in mortgage or deed of trust (standard or ALTA lender).

COVENANTS, CONDITIONS, AND RESTRICTIONS
CC&Rs do not impair lien of deed of trust (ALTA lender).
CC&Rs do not impair lien of deed of trust (standard coverage lender).
No present enforceable violation (ALTA lender).
No present enforceable violations (standard coverage lender).
Future violations (ALTA lender).
Future violations (standard coverage lender).
Unmarketability of title—violations (ALTA lender).
Unmarketability of title—violations (standard coverage lender).
Present violation of particular CC&R (ALTA or standard coverage lender).
Enforceability of reverter provision (owner or ALTA lender).
Enforceability of reverter provision—unmarketability of title (ALTA lender).
Location of foundation does not violate CC&R (standard or ALTA lender).

DESCRIPTION
Policy description—later subdivision (owner or lender).

EASEMENTS
Foundation does not encroach onto easement (standard or ALTA lender).
Improvements do not encroach onto easement (ALTA lender).
Improvements do not encroach onto easement (standard coverage lender).
Forced removal of encroaching improvements (standard or ALTA lender).
Exercise of right of use or maintenance of easement (owner, standard, or ALTA lender).
Insured easement affords ingress and egress to street (owner or lender).
Foundation does not encroach (standard or ALTA lender).
No existing encroachments (ALTA lender).
No existing encroachments (standard coverage lender).
Forced removal of encroaching improvements (ALTA lender).
Forced removal of improvements encroaching onto easement (standard or ALTA lender).

FOUNDATION
Does not violate CC&R nor encroach (ALTA or standard coverage lender).

FIGURE 5.8

Samples of Commonly Requested Endorsements (Continued)

IMPROVEMENTS

No existing encroachments (ALTA lender).

No existing encroachments (standard coverage lender).

No damage by reason of encroachment onto easement (ALTA lender).

No damage by reason of encroachment onto easement (standard coverage lender).

No damage by reason of surface mineral development (owner or ALTA lender).

No damage by reason of surface mineral development (standard coverage lender).

Forced removal of encroaching improvements (ALTA lender).

Forced removal of encroaching improvements (standard coverage lender).

Forced removal of improvements encroaching onto easement (standard or ALTA lender).

Designation of improvements, street address (ALTA lender).

Designation of improvements and street address—condominium (owner or lender).

LEASES

Assignment of lessor's interest in lease (ALTA lender).

Assignment of rents in mortgage or deed of trust (standard or ALTA lender).

MARKETABILITY

Unmarketability of title—CC&R violations (ALTA lender).

Unmarketability of title—CC&R violations (standard coverage lender).

Unmarketability due to reverter provision in CC&R (ALTA lender).

MECHANICS' LIENS

Priority of trust deed—commencement of work (standard coverage lender).

Work of improvement disclosed by notice of completion (owner).

Priority of trust deed—work of improvement disclosed by notice of completion (standard or ALTA lender).

Priority of trust deed—work of improvement disclosed by notice of completion on portion of land (standard or ALTA lender).

Priority of trust deed—work of improvement on portion of land—no notice of completion (standard or ALTA lender).

Work of improvement disclosed by notice of completion (standard or ALTA lender).

Priority of additional advance (standard or ALTA lender).

Priority of obligatory advance (ALTA lender).

MINERALS

Surface entry damage (owner or ALTA lender).

Surface entry damage (standard coverage).

MODIFICATION

Modification of trust deed to provide for advances (standard coverage lender).

Modification of trust deed to provide for advances (ALTA lender).

OIL

Surface entry damage (owner or ALTA lender).

Surface entry damage (standard coverage lender).

RENTS

Assignment of lessor's interest in lease (ALTA lender).

Assignment of rents contained in mortgage or deed of trust (standard or ALTA lender).

FIGURE 5.8

Samples of Commonly Requested Endorsements (Continued)

STREETS
Insured easement provides access to street (owner or lender).

SURFACE ENTRY
By owner of minerals (owner or ALTA lender).
By owner of minerals (standard coverage lender).

SURVEY-MAP-PLAT (ALTA lender)
Policy plat shows correct location and dimensions of land.
Condominium project correctly shown on recorded map (owner or lender).
Land described in policy may be described by reference to later subdivision map (owner or lender).

TAXES
Estate or interest is a condominium and entitled to be assessed and taxed as a separate parcel (lender).

TRUST DEEDS
Assignment of lessor's interest in lease (ALTA lender)
Assignment of rents contained in mortgage or deed of trust (standard or ALTA lender).
Optional advance under trust deed (lender).
Obligatory advance under trust deed (ALTA lender).

Federal Truth in Lending—ALTA.   This ALTA endorsement covers a lender for a loss arising from a judicial determination terminating the lien of an insured mortgage due to the exercise of a right of rescission granted by the federal Truth in Lending Act or Consumer Credit Protection Act. The above acts provide for certain exemptions. If the insured loan involves an exempt transaction, for example the borrower is not a natural person but a corporation, partnership, or other organization, the endorsement may be issued.

Zoning—ALTA.   This endorsement insures certain zoning matters as they pertain to *unimproved* property or where the insured is not interested in full building code insurance. The endorsement specifies the zoning classification and the use or uses of what is permitted. Issuance of this coverage requires an examination of the applicable zoning ordinances and amendments to determine the particular zone and permitted uses of the insured loan.

Condominium—ALTA.   The **condo ALTA** endorsement provides insurance that the condominium estate is created in accordance with local laws. In addition, it covers violations of covenants, conditions, and restrictions, as well as certain encroachment matters. This endorsement may be issued after a review of the association bylaws, the condominiums declarations map, and related documents.

Planned unit development—ALTA. This endorsement provides coverage for planned unit developments that is similar to the condominium coverage for an ALTA policy. The ALTA endorsement insures against loss or damage due to violations of restrictive covenants, forfeiture, or reversion provisions of restrictive covenants, assessments gaining priority over an insured mortgage, compelled removal of improvements due to encroachment, and failure of title by reason of a right of first refusal.

In order to consider issuance of this ALTA endorsement, the covenants must be reviewed for violations, forfeiture and reversions provisions, creation of assessments and any provisions subordinating them to mortgages, and any right of first refusal provisions. Known encroachment of the improvements must also be provided.

Modification of deed of trust. This endorsement is designed for use with ALTA lenders' policies for the purpose of giving assurance to the lender that the insured mortgage or the obligation secured thereby has been modified and as modified retains its priority. The endorsement may be issued once it is determined that the holder of the note is a party to the modification agreement and the modification agreement is recorded.

Variable rate mortgage—ALTA. This endorsement protects insured lenders against loss by reason of the invalidity, loss of priority, or unenforceability of the lien of the insured mortgage resulting from the provisions that provide for changes in the rate of interest (variable rate, convertible, renegotiable rate, adjustable rate, or shared appreciation mortgages).

Another ALTA endorsement provides similar coverage for those jurisdictions where a lender must rely on a specific state act or federal preemption to override local state law in making the variable interest rate loan. Issuance of these variable rate endorsements depends on the disclosure of the variable provisions, as in issuance of other ALTA endorsements, and information establishing the right to a federal preemption or state statute. Disclosure of variable interest and negative amortization provisions in the recorded instrument is necessary to consider issuance of the ALTA policy. Requests to issue this endorsement will usually be accompanied with a request to issue the policy with a liability for 110 percent to 125 percent of the loan amount.

Manufactured housing—ALTA. In order to remove any doubts as to whether or not a manufactured housing unit or mobile home on the subject property is included within the policy coverage, this ALTA endorsement is available. It expands the definition of "land" as used in the policy to include the manufactured housing unit as real property. Issuance of this endorsement relies on provisions in state laws allowing the manufactured housing unit to be converted into real property. If the conversion has been proper and if such unit is now being taxed as a real property improvement, the endorsement may be issued.

Environmental protection/residential.   This endorsement is designed for use with any ALTA loan policy when the loan is secured by a deed of trust or mortgage on property used primarily for residential purposes to provide the insured lender with certain protection against loss or damage sustained by reason of loss of priority of the lien of the insured mortgage over any environmental protection liens recorded in the public records or created pursuant to certain state statutes. This coverage is not available for owner's policies.

CLTA and ALTA Endorsements

"Off-record"—CLTA.   This endorsement is designed as an explicit extension of coverage otherwise provided to insure lenders under an ALTA loan policy. CLTA standard coverage was developed from the lender's need for assurance against loss from certain "off-record" occurrences. The endorsement contains clauses that extend the lender's coverage in three general areas: (1) covenants, conditions, and restrictions; (2) encroachments; and (3) rights of others to use the surface of the land for mineral development.

The title company may attach the CLTA endorsement to ALTA loan policy, provided

1. the insured loan *does not* cover raw land;

2. the loan is *not* for construction purposes (including remodeling); or

3. upon inspection there are *no* title reasons why the coverage cannot be given.

It is the practice of most title companies to issue the endorsement *only at the time of recording* the insured deed of trust. *It is not* to be issued at a later date, except with a new or reissue policy, as in the case of a construction loan package.

Reverter—CLTA.   This endorsement is designed for use with the CLTA and ALTA lenders' or owners' policies to assure a lender that existing covenants, conditions, and restrictions do not contain any enforceable reverter, right of reentry, or right or power of termination. To a large extent, the same coverage is provided by the standard CLTA endorsement that insures against loss occasioned by present and future violations of covenants, conditions, and restrictions. Certain lenders are not satisfied with insurance against loss caused by reversion, but require specific assurance that, in fact, there can be no reversion of title. This endorsement may be given with the approval of local managements in the following five circumstances:

1. The restrictions have been imposed in a deed or declarations of restrictions in the form of covenants only without express provisions for reversion and without the use of the word "condition" or "conditions" in relation to the imposition.

2. When the holder of the reversion has expressly waived his power of termination.

3. When the holder of the reversion has by implication waived his power of reversion by permitting uniform violations through the neighborhood.

4. Where the only effective conditions relate to liquor and it appears that the property in question is in a residential neighborhood and will be used for residential purposes throughout the life of the loan.

5. Where the restrictions contain no express provisions for enforcing a reversion but there is language to "conditions" or "reversions"—provided that a specific method of enforcement by injunction or abatement is affordable to other owners in the tract.

This endorsement may also provide the insured ALTA lender or owner with coverage against loss by reason of the exercise of or attempt to exercise reverter rights in CC&Rs. An endorsement may be obtained that provides an insured ALTA lender with coverage against loss by reason of the exercise of surface rights for the extraction or development of minerals leased under an oil and gas lease.

Mechanics' liens—CLTA. This endorsement is used with CLTA loan policies insuring construction loans in instances where lenders seek protection against loss if mechanics' liens gain priority over the insured deed of trust, where such priority is based on the claim that construction began prior to the recording of the insured loan. This endorsement is not designed for use with ALTA policies.

This endorsement may be issued, provided

- an inspection discloses that at the time of recording no work has commenced and no materials were delivered, or

- there is a sufficient and approved indemnity if there has been commencement.

A **mechanic's lien** endorsement is designed for use with ALTA or CLTA loan policies after a valid notice of completion describing all land in the policy has been recorded. Lenders often request an endorsement in connection with construction loans when they are planning either to make a "take-out" (permanent) loan to the borrower or to sell the construction loan to another lender who will make the permanent loan.

Foundations—CLTA. This endorsement is used with ALTA or CLTA loan policies where a construction loan previously has been insured and the lender requires assurance that the foundations do not encroach upon adjoining lands or violate existing covenants, conditions, and restrictions. A variation of this endorsement assures the lender that the foundations do not, at the date of the endorsement, encroach onto any easements referred to in the policy.

Usually following a physical inspection of the property in question, the endorsement may be issued assuring the insured lender that

- the foundations of the structure under construction on the subject land are within the boundary lines of said land, and

- the locations of the foundations do not violate the covenants, conditions, and restrictions referred to in other endorsements of a policy of title insurance.

Easement—CLTA. This endorsement is designed for use with ALTA or CLTA lenders' policies. The coverage is broader than that afforded by the standard CLTA form endorsement. Loss is limited to a claim resulting from damage to existing improvements located or encroaching upon the easement. It is usually requested by lenders when an item or items appearing in the preliminary title report are unlocatable "blanket" easements. A modified endorsement is also available. The lender is insured against loss that might occur should the owner of the easement, for purposes specified in the endorsement, compel removal of encroaching improvements.

Before issuing an easement endorsement, the title company must conduct considerable research, possibly inspect the land, and carefully make an analysis of the following six areas:

1. Is the easement fixed, or is it unlocated?

2. What is the purpose of the easement (e.g., pole lines, storm drains, etc.)?

3. What are the possibilities that the easement will be exercised?

4. To what extent will the improvements be damaged if the easement privileges are exercised? The extent of the investigation or inspections necessary to reach a conclusion.

5. Will damage occur from maintenance of the easement (e.g., storm drains)?

6. Will the use or maintenance of the easement necessitate the removal of any encroaching improvements?

Assignment—CLTA. The **assignment** endorsement is used with ALTA or CLTA loan policies when the beneficial interest in the insured deed of trust has been assigned and the assignee requests the limited assurance that the public records disclose no reconveyance, modification, or subordination of the issued deed of trust.

The title company may issue the endorsement after reviewing the following four searches:

1. The note secured by the deed of trust must be examined to determine that the chain of endorsements from the original payee to the insured is unbroken. *Exception:* If the assignment is handled by a reputable escrow firm, the note need not be examined. The escrow officer would state, by letter, that the note is endorsed as required, and the deed of trust has been delivered to the assignee through escrow.

2. A lot book search must be made to disclose inconsistent assignments, reconveyances, either full or partial, modifications, or any other matters that could affect the deed of trust under the coverage.

3. A general index (GI) search must be run on the assignor and all uninsured intervening assignors for any matters that would affect the competency of the assignor or the validity of the assignment (e.g., federal tax liens).

4. A search is made to ensure that all assignments of beneficial interest are recorded.

Note: If the assignment is a collateral assignment, this endorsement may not be used. The CLTA endorsement is designed for use with collateral assignments or insurance that may be afforded by issuing a new title policy.

CLTA Endorsements

Optional advances—CLTA. Frequently, deed of trust forms are drawn to provide security not only for specified, current obligations but also to secure future advances (i.e., the form contains an "open-end provision"). In general, the priority of an advance, so secured, against liens and interest arising between the date of trust deed record and the date the advance is made depends on whether or not the advance is obligatory or optional by the lender. When the advances are optional, priority is contingent upon the lender's knowledge of intervening rights at the date the advance is made.

The endorsement may be issued, provided

■ a review is made of the note to determine that an additional advance has been made to a named person, the insured, in a certain sum, evidenced by the promissory note for that amount and secured by a deed of trust, with property information identifying it.

- the deed of trust provides for an advance to the insured ("open-end provision").

- a lot book search and general index run must be made to determine
  - that the maker of the note is the present record owner of the encumbered land;
  - that there are no defects in, or liens or encumbrances prior to such advances;
  - that there have been no reconveyances, full or partial, or any modification or subordination of the deed of trust; and
  - matters relating to the status and capacity of the maker of the note.

- a new tax and lien report must be obtained and tax or assessments liens arising after the date of the policy must be shown.

Violation of CC&RS—CLTA. This endorsement provides coverage to an owner against judicial enforcement of covenants, conditions, and restrictions. The coverage extends to present or future violations. The endorsement is typically predicated on either a uniform noncompliance with the covenants, conditions, and restrictions indicating that a court would be reluctant to enforce them or previous litigation setting a precedent for nonenforcement.

Surface rights for mineral extraction—CLTA. Protection against damage to existing improvements resulting from exercise or use of a surface right for **mineral extraction** or development of reserved mineral rights is available. If the surface rights were either expressly waived at the time the minerals were reserved or subsequently released, the endorsement may be issued. If rights of surface entry have not been waived, issuance of the endorsement may be considered depending on the particular case with specific facts, including the nature and value of the mineral interest, local geology, local zoning restrictions of mining activity, and existing improvements on the property.

Public street access—CLTA. The **public street access** endorsement provides affirmative assurances that the named street is in fact a physically open public street, that the land in question abuts the street, and that there is nothing to prohibit access from the land to the street. Before issuing this endorsement, the title company will conduct research and inspect the land.

A complete title search and tax and lien search must be made to determine the following four items:

1. That the parties to the modification agreement appear of record as the owners of the land and of the beneficial interest.

2. Matters relating to the status and capacity of the parties to the modification agreement.

3. That there has been no full or partial reconveyance of the deed of trust. If a partial reconveyance has been issued, coverage under this endorsement must be limited to lands presently encumbered by the deed of trust.

4. That there are no liens or encumbrances subsequent to the subject deed of trust. If any matters are found, they must be set forth as exceptions in the endorsement unless the parties holding liens or encumbrances subject their interest to the deed of trust as modified by appropriate recorded subordination agreements.

Additional CLTA endorsement. This endorsement provides the following four assurances.

1. Provides insured ALTA residential lender with coverage against loss by reason of lack of priority over (a) any federal or state environmental protection lien which is recorded in the public records except as disclosed in writing in the title policy, and (b) any state environmental protection lien provided for by any state statute in effect at date of policy, except as provided for by state statutes specified in the endorsement.

2. Provides assurance to the lender that future advances made under a "revolving line of credit" will have the same priority as advances made as of the date of the policy.

3. Provides insured ALTA variable rate mortgage lender with coverage against loss by reason of (a) invalidity or unenforceability of the insured mortgage resulting from terms therein providing for changes in the rate of interest, or (b) loss of priority of the insured mortgage lien caused by the changes in the rate of interest, unpaid interest added to principal, and/or interest on interest.

4. Provides insured lender with assurance that the estate or interest covered by the policy is a condominium in fee, and as such is entitled to be assessed and taxed as a separate parcel.

Address—CLTA. This endorsement is used with ALTA loan policies when a lender is requiring specific coverage determining the address of the insured land and the type of improvement located therein. It also assures the lender that the map attached to the policy shows the current location and dimension of the parcel as disclosed by records imparting constructive notice.

Survey—CLTA. This endorsement is designed for use with CLTA and ALTA owners' policies and affords assurance that the land described in the policy is the same as that delineated on the plat of survey attached to, and made a part of, the policy. The endorsement may be issued, provided a title officer or the engineering department for the company has examined the survey plat and determined that the area delineated thereon corresponds exactly with land described or to be described in the policy.

Contiguous land—CLTA.   A **contiguous land** endorsement may be used with CLTA or ALTA owners' or lenders' policies for contiguous land concern. The need for this endorsement arises under differing circumstances. An example is when a purchaser acquired land adjacent to land already owned by the purchaser, and it is intended that the two parcels shall be used together. In this situation, ownership of a strip between the two parcels, by a stranger, would frustrate the proposed usage. It always requires a title search of all parcels in question.

Mandatory advance—CLTA.   This endorsement is designed for use with ALTA lenders' policies when several advances, all secured by the same insured mortgage, are contemplated and a separate endorsement is to be issued as each advance is made.

The title company may issue the endorsement, provided

- the lender has furnished a written statement that an advance in a specified sum has been made to a named person; that the advance is evidenced by a promissory note that recites that it is secured by the insured deed of trust (identifying it by recording reference or otherwise) or in lieu of such statement, the note evidencing the advances, or a copy delivered to the title office for examination; and

- a complete search from the date of the base policy of the date of the most recently issued endorsement must in every case be made and the matters disclosed thereby must be treated in relation to each paragraph of the endorsement after being reported to and approved by the lender.

Revolving line of credit.   The revolving line of credit loan allows the borrower to obtain any amount up to an established credit limit, pay down the outstanding balance, and reborrow up to the credit limit.

The endorsement for this type of loan is designed to provide coverage to the insured lender against loss sustained by reason of a loss of priority as to future advances (with certain exceptions) made pursuant to a note or revolving credit loan agreement, secured by the insured mortgage. Additionally, the FA-21 provides coverage against loss caused by invalidity, unenforceability, or loss of priority due to provision in the loan providing for variable interest rates.

Typically, these revolving credit endorsements may be issued if the loan agreement clearly creates a revolving line of credit that is disclosed in and secured by the record mortgage and further creates an obligation on the lender to honor requests for advance so long as the borrower is not in default. Additionally, issuance of this endorsement necessitates disclosure of the variable interest rate provisions contained in the note.

■ DATE DOWN THE FILE

Before the title insurance policy is written and before the close of escrow and transfer of ownership and prior to funding of the loan, a thorough title examination is performed by title insurance personnel having special training and expertise. The title insurance company checks the county recorder's office for deeds and documents recorded against the property. The county tax collector's office must be searched to obtain records that ensure that all real property taxes and special assessments will be paid current at the time of recordation. The court records must be checked to obtain data on any title transfer, trust deeds and loans, judgments, liens, probate action, quiet title action or any other **lis pendens,** suit, or judicial decision.

To *date down the file* is to list in sequential order the items the escrow company needs from the title insurance company. Many items that the title insurance company needs are furnished by the escrow company, such as the statement of information (SI). Other items are available inside the title company records and the technical documents used only by title company personnel. The title company file contains a date down sheet, or similar control sheet, that gives sequential order to documents for ease in following the chain of title.

The chain of title must be consecutive, showing the transfer of all interest in the property by all subsequent individuals. The search of the chain of title often leads to issues such as a change in the manner in which title is held and changes in names of the principals. It is not uncommon for the principals to have originally acquired title as "Mary Smith and Bob Jones, as joint tenants" and a later change to "Mary Smith Jones and Robert Jones, husband and wife, as community property (with the right of survivorship)" and to later have changed title to "The Jones Family Trust dated June 1, 20XX" with Mary Jones, Co-Trustee and Robert Jones, Co-Trustee.

In this case Mary Smith changed her name on title to the property three times. First she took title in her unmarried name of Mary Smith. Later, after she married Robert/Bob Jones, she took title as his wife as Mary Smith Jones. When the property was placed into their trust, she became Mary Jones, Co-Trustee of The Jones Family Trust dated June 1, 20XX. Also, he changed his name three times. He originally took title as Bob Jones, who is not married to Mary Smith. Then he changed his ownership title to Robert Jones after he married Mary Smith Jones. When the two formed their trust, he then took title as Robert Jones, Co-

Trustee of The Jones Family Trust dated June 1, 20XX. Each of these transfers should have shown a conveyance that said "Mary Jones, who acquired title as Mary Smith" or "Robert Jones, who acquired title as Bob Jones" to help clarify the apparent gaps in the chain of title.

It is common for a father and son to have the same first and last name. It is common for a girl and her aunt to have the same name. Therefore, each transfer should clearly denote the "transfer from" and the "transfer to" so that no gap in the chain of title and no further explanation or examination is necessary. The title searcher must show each item that will have to be resolved prior to transfer of property ownership. The abstractor would have to check public records for civil court actions, foreclosures, probate court, personal income tax records, judgments, liens, and any judicial decision for all of the following names: Mary Smith, Mary Jones, Bob Jones, Robert Jones, and The Jones Family Trust dated June 1, 20XX.

■ INDEX SYSTEM

As discussed in Chapter 4, the chain of title goes back to the oldest history of ownership for the property. Some states became part of the United States from the Louisiana Purchase. In many cases, such as with the Oklahoma Land Rush, ownership was obtained from a U.S. government patent issued by the U.S. government showing an individual's ownership of the land. After the Revolutionary War, the new country had no treasury with which to pay soldiers for their service. Instead of a paycheck, some individuals received a land patent. Some states originated from the original 13 colonies that originated under the rule of England. In those areas where the chain of title to property is known from before the U.S. federal government owned or governed any lands, ownership to real property already existed. In California this is also the case from the previous Mexican rule that followed the former Spanish rule. If a break is found in a chain of title dating way back to some previous claim, the matter is usually settled with a court action to establish the rights of the claimant, if any.

FIGURE 5.9

Grantor Index—Cleyburne, Arkansas

Grantor	Grantee	Instrument	Date Filed	Book	Page
John Chandler	Jm. F. Hazlewood	QC	2/12/1872	1	394
James M. Smith	W. C. Hazlewood	Will	5/20/1872	1	448
W. F. Ramsey	W. H. Saudberry	Mtg	3/23/1878	2	221
Joseph McHoffey	B. V. Cummings	Will	6/20/1888	7	672
Will Johnson	W. F. Ramsey	Deed	4/2/1891	9	518
State of Arkansas	A. J. Cummings	Patent	9/25/1900	14	67

FIGURE 5.10

Grantee Index

Grantor	Grantee	Instrument	Date Filed	Book	Page
E. P. Hazlewood	Elizabeth Norrad	Deed	11/17/1886	B	74
J. Mitchell	W. C. & Emma Ramsey	M	1/19/1895	1	170
John T. & Jane Hazlewood	Jno. D. Smith	Deed	11/18/1896	1	573
E. C. Ramsey	W. F. Ramsey	QC	10/28/1899	10	242
J. T. Hazlewood & wife Jane	G. W. Hazlewood	QC	5/29/1900	13	54
Jesse Hazlewood	Tom Hazlewood & wife Ida	QC	2/4/1901	14	162

Two types of index systems are used predominantly in the United States. The least used system is called the **tract index.** This system is used in the northern areas of the United States, much of which was part of the Louisiana Purchase, such as from Oklahoma to North Dakota and from Wisconsin to Utah and Wyoming. This system is not used in California.

In California the most common index is the **grantor-grantee index.** Figure 5.9 shows an example of a grantor index and Figure 5.10 shows the grantee index. These are two separate indexes, one for the transferor and one for the transferee. Each index is kept in alphabetic order for each calendar year. Each index shows the names of the two parties, the date the document was filed with the recorder's office, and the reference. The reference number is usually shown by stating the number of the book in which the transfer information is found, and the page number where the transfer is actually written. In very old records the signatures of the parties and the signature of the clerk as witness are shown on the page. A brief legal description is usually shown in the index book for reference, with the full legal description shown on the actual document, such as a deed.

■ TITLE COMPANY PERSONNEL

Each title insurance company operates in its own manner, but similarities have evolved over the years for the various personnel positions there. The title company may have an active escrow division that has a separate set of personnel who perform duties similar to any other escrow entity operation. The title portion, excluding the escrow operation, has specific operational procedures to perform title tasks. An organizational chart is shown in Figure 4.9 on page 98. Some of the job descriptions for these positions are discussed below.

In obtaining a title insurance policy, the process begins with the opening of escrow, followed by the escrow officer opening the title order with the title unit. The title unit may consist of only two people, the title officer and an assistant, or it may be an entire department. After the title order has been opened, customer service verifies the legal and vesting; that is, customer service determines the legal owners and the manner in which title is currently held.

The title order then goes to the search department. The search department verifies liens, easements, encumbrances, covenants, conditions, and restrictions. It prepares a computerized property chain of title and a general index for each principal. Then a thorough examination is made by the searcher who looks to see if any break in the chain or any apparent discrepancy occurs. The searcher looks at the hall of records for unrecorded and unforeseen easements, liens, and more. Tax and bonds are prepared by municipal lien services to search for property tax liens, judgment liens, mechanics' liens, and federal or state liens. The engineering department prepares the plat map for the property in the transaction.

The examination with combined information results in the preliminary title report. The title officer examines the search package and writes the preliminary title report. Then an investigation is made to verify the legal vesting, encumbrances, liens, CC&Rs, the removal of some items shown, the conditions under which a policy may be issued, and any objections from the buyer made prior to close of escrow or issuance of a policy.

After completion of performance of any defects to the title, the word processing department types the preliminary title report and enters the information into the computer retrieval software system of the title insurance company.

A messenger service or an electronic delivery is made to the escrow and lender. Any new documents, demands, and the statement of information are submitted to the title unit.

When escrow has everything in order, escrow will then instruct the title insurance company to record the documents. The title insurance company records by messenger or electronically at the county recorder's office; the deeds show a recordation time of 8:00 A.M. the following morning. This would include the grant deed transferring title between principals. This also includes any new trust deed and the deed of reconveyance to pay off the seller's encumbrance from the escrow proceeds.

The title officer then writes the policy of title insurance for CLTA, ALTA, or other authorized coverage and endorsements. The word processing operator retrieves the computer information and prepares the final title insurance policy that will be released to the principals and lenders.

All these title insurance company employees have job descriptions and have differing rates and methods of payment. It is not uncommon for persons in the escrow field to work their way up the ladder from an original position at an escrow company or with a beginning at a title insurance company. Some of the positions are presented below.

The *receptionist* is the individual responsible for answering the telephone to direct information to the personnel who work for the title company. Handling messenger pick up and delivery and mail delivery are often part of the duties of this job.

The *title rep*, or representative, is responsible for generating new business. These salespeople call on individual real estate and/or escrow companies. The position once included picking up escrow instructions from the escrow company and delivering them to the real estate sales agent. After the agent had the principals sign the documents, the title rep would pick up the signed papers and deliver them back to escrow. With electronic transfer of funds, this is less common. Software programs that aid in real estate production are now common title rep aids in sales offices. Also, continuing education credit seminars and training classes are often given to the sales agent by the title rep to assist real estate sales agents or escrow personnel. Many laws and court cases have disallowed insurance companies from giving sales agents gifts, now termed illegal kickbacks. This is because the court has determined that these items increase the cost to the consumer of doing business in a real estate transaction, which violates RESPA law. To decrease consumer costs, all such gifts have been outlawed.

The *abstractor*, or **title searcher,** is the individual who gathers the documents and information and places them into the file. Past files on the parties or property previously handled by the title company might be retrieved. The searcher looks up public records to compile the data. This individual conducts the task of title examination.

The *title officer* is the one who is senior in charge of the file. This person reviews all the data to determine if the information is complete and if the chain of title is insurable. In other words, this individual is responsible for ensuring that there is no risk to the insurance company that a future claim will be made against the insurance policy for clear title.

The **order entry clerk** opens the title order in the title plant system, performs computer runs to capture records, verifies the legal description, and searches individual and corporate general indexes (GI).

The **title technician** assembles the title plant records, compiles file data in a specific order, and forwards the file to the title examiner.

The *title examiner* investigates the chain of title and documents and determines the legal status of the property.

The *word processor* prepares the preliminary title report, prints documents, reviews information, prepares the final policy of title insurance that complies with instructions, and copies the policy for permanent record storage.

The *title unit* date-downs the file to indicate items recorded or disclosed since the last title examination; writes the policy of title insurance; generates schedules, endorsements, supplements, and transmittals; and makes corrections on the legal description or vesting.

The *advisory title officer* reviews unusual conditions; makes underwriting decisions and conditions; and sets, approves, and waives exceptions.

THINK ABOUT IT

Does the title company have to defend against a claim?

A buyer bought land with a title-company-issued policy. The title company search discovered a recorded deed granting an easement to a third party, which was not disclosed in the preliminary title report to the buyer.

After the close of escrow a third party notified the buyer of the easement. The buyer contacted the title company, which refused to take action.

The buyer cleared the title himself, proving the conveyance of the easement was void, then sued the title company for breach of contract for not defending the title against the third party.

The court found that the title company acted in bad faith and awarded the buyer several hundred thousand dollars.

[*Jarchow v. Transamerica Title Ins. Co.*, 122 Cal. Rptr. 470 (975)]

■ CHAPTER SUMMARY

The technical documents used by title insurance company personnel will vary little between various title insurance companies. Each title insurance firm offers many types of insurance policies, endorsements, and exclusions. The statement of information (SI) and public recorded documents found in the grantor-grantee indexes (GI) are used to determine insurability of the property. This chapter discussed title company personnel and positions, including job titles and duties.

■ CHAPTER 5 QUIZ

1. Among the choices given, the most common title insurance policy would be the
   a. binder.
   b. short term.
   c. ALTA.
   d. foundation endorsement.

2. What is the name of the index most commonly used in California?
   a. General
   b. Grantor-grantee
   c. Grantee
   d. Tract

3. The schedule of prices for a policy of title insurance is referred to as
   a. schedule rate.
   b. quote rate.
   c. estimate price.
   d. quote price.

4. The point from where the last title policy was issued to where the current title order is to begin is termed
   a. subdivision.
   b. recording.
   c. title.
   d. starter.

5. The term used when a portion of property is taken from a larger parcel on an arb map is
   a. constructive notice.
   b. cut out.
   d. easement.
   d. encroachment.

6. The date down that covers the time from the original title examination to present is a(n)
   a. claim of title.
   b. estate.
   c. reexamination.
   d. escrow.

7. The area of a title company that generates schedules and endorsements is called the
   a. title technician.
   b. title representative.
   c. title officer.
   d. None of the above are correct.

8. The title examiner
   a. writes the policy of title insurance.
   b. performs the computer run of records.
   c. makes underwriting decisions.
   d. investigates the chain of title.

9. The person who would compile data in a specific order in a title file would most likely be the
   a. order entry clerk.
   b. title technician.
   c. title examiner.
   d. title officer.

10. The advisory title officer does NOT
    a. review unusual conditions.
    b. prepare the preliminary title report.
    c. make underwriting decisions.
    d. approve and waive exceptions.

CHAPTER SIX

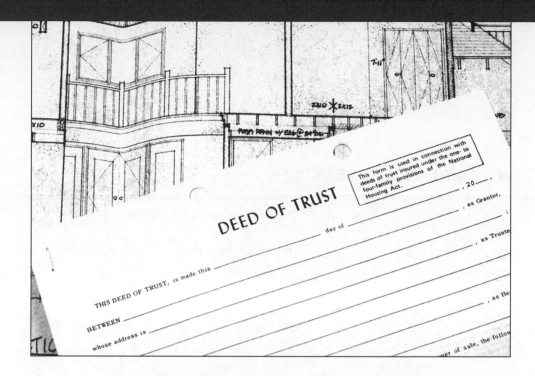

SELLER'S ESCROW AND LIENS

■ KEY TERMS

beneficiary	lien information sheet	seller affidavit
beneficiary demand	mechanic's lien	tax liens
beneficiary statement	mortgagee	transferor
demand for payoff	mortgagor	trustee
due-on-sale clause	reconveyance deed	trustor
judgment lien	satisfaction of	trust deed
Lane Guide	judgment	

■ CHAPTER OVERVIEW

The preliminary title report shows various items of record against the property for which the seller is responsible, either liens (monetary items) or encumbrances (nonmonetary items). For the liens that will be paid off, the escrow officer will obtain information from the seller so that the escrow officer can contact the various lien holders for payoff or loan status information. The escrow officer provides this information to the title company. The title company will make the wire transfer to pay off the loan at the direction of the escrow officer according to the lien holder instructions. The title company records the document showing that the lien has been paid off.

■ LEARNING OBJECTIVES

At the conclusion of Chapter 6, you will be able to

- understand the relationship between escrow and a lien holder versus the principals;

- give a definition for reconveyance;

- outline the steps for escrow to take to pay off a seller's lien;

- differentiate between a demand and beneficiary statement; and

- explain the Lane Guide and how it is used.

■ OBTAINING THE PAYOFF INFORMATION

As part of the escrow instructions, the escrow officer includes a form, referred to as the **lien information sheet,** for the seller to complete. The form is usually returned to escrow along with the signed documents or may be returned separately. On the form, the seller indicates the name of each of his or her lenders, the loan number, mailing address, approximate unpaid balance, and other information as shown in Figure 6.1.

For loan information, the escrow officer will write to each lien holder to request and obtain the data. The escrow officer cannot rely on the information obtained directly from the seller. Most principals do not remember all the terms of the loan(s). The escrow officer knows that the information obtained from the seller is not the conclusive information to rely on when recording documents.

Escrow officers know that they must make direct contact with each lien holder to obtain the detailed data required by the escrow instructions. The escrow holder might not be able to proceed with escrow until the seller's lien holder agrees to the terms of the escrow agreement created by the principals. The lender is not bound by agreements made by the principals.

■ PARTIES TO A DEED OF TRUST

The parties to a deed of trust, unlike a mortgage used in many other states, consist of three parties, rather than two. Mortgages are not commonly used in California. Under the mortgage system, the entity that loans the funds is called the **mortgagee**

FIGURE 6.1

Lien Information Sheet

Escrow Number _____   Property Address: _____

City:_____ CA Zip Code _____

1st Trust Deed:

    Name of Lender: _____

    Mailing Address: _____

    City: _____ State_____ Zip Code:_____

    Loan Number: _____   Phone (_____)_____

    Appx. Unpaid Loan Balance: _____ Interest Rate: _____%

2nd Trust Deed:

    Name of Lender: _____

    Mailing Address: _____

    City: _____ State_____ Zip Code:_____

    Loan Number: _____   Phone (_____)_____

    Appx. Unpaid Loan Balance: _____ Interest Rate: _____%

3rd Trust Deed:

    Name of Lender: _____

    Mailing Address: _____

    City: _____ State_____ Zip Code:_____

    Loan Number: _____   Phone (_____)_____

    Appx. Unpaid Loan Balance: _____ Interest Rate: _____%

_____ Date: _____
    Seller

_____ Date: _____
    Seller

and the borrower is called the **mortgagor.** In California, the trust deed system calls the entity that loans the funds the **beneficiary** (bank) and the borrower is called the **trustor** (debtor). The third party is called the **trustee** who holds bare legal title to the property for only loan default or loan payoff. When a loan is in default, the beneficiary notifies the trustee to begin foreclosure procedures under the power of sale clause contained in the deed of trust. The trustee handles notifying the trustor of the default, advertises the auction, and conveys title to the subsequent purchaser for a foreclosure, as will be discussed in Chapter 8. Also, when a loan has been paid off and the beneficiary receives all funds due or agreed upon, the beneficiary instructs the trustee to record the deed of reconveyance to convey the ownership interest back to the trustor.

The escrow officer has a set of signed escrow instructions from the seller that contain written instructions to the escrow officer to comply with certain lender requirements. Although the seller's existing lien holder is not a direct party to the escrow, such as the principals who are, the escrow officer may not deceive the lender as to the facts of the transaction. This is even more important for the buyer's lender, which is discussed in Chapter 7.

Normal escrow instruction clauses include the following or a similar statement:

> You are instructed to provide title to the subject real property in the condition identified in the escrow instructions by the parties. You are not responsible for the contents or accuracy of any beneficiary demands and/or beneficiary statements delivered to you by the existing lien holders. You are not required to submit any such beneficiary statements and/or demand to the parties for approval before the close of escrow unless expressly instructed to do so in writing. Should the parties desire to preapprove any such beneficiary statement and/or demand, the parties requesting the same shall deliver separate and specific written escrow instructions to you.

This statement means that whether or not the amount stated on the beneficiary demand (also called the bene) is correct or not, the escrow officer is instructed to pay the amount without any approval of the seller. If a real estate professional wants to protect the seller, a separate written instruction must be given to the escrow officer for the seller to approve.

■ BENEFICIARY DEMAND VERSUS BENEFICIARY STATEMENT

The first step in ordering a demand statement is to obtain the lien information sheet for all liens of record known by the property owner. The escrow officer will then obtain information from the preliminary title report showing liens on record

FIGURE 6.2

Request for Payoff Demand—Beneficiary Demand

Date:

Lender of Record
PO Box XXXX
Anytown, CA 90000

ATTN: Loan Pay-off Department

RE: Loan #: XX-00000-XX

Property address: 123 Elm Street, Somecity, CA 91234

Title Vested as: Mr. and Mrs. IMA borrower

Legal description: Lot 12 in Tract 24 in pages 12 to 14 of book 32 in the office
of the county recorder in a California County.

Mary Belle Smith, Escrow Officer   John James, Title Officer
Escrow No. MBS-112   Title Order No. 7-765432
A California Escrow Company   A California Title Company
789 Maple Avenue
Somecity, CA 91234

---

that may or may not have been provided by the seller. Once the escrow officer obtains the lien holder information, the process begins.

For each loan, the escrow officer must obtain a written statement. If the loan is to be paid in full through escrow the escrow officer will order from the beneficiary a **demand for payoff,** or **beneficiary demand,** as is shown in Figure 6.2.

Thus, even though the seller may be the trustor who is trying to obtain information to pay off the existing loan, the escrow officer is required to process the information received directly from the beneficiary regarding the amount due at the close of escrow to the lender. The escrow officer should always communicate the beneficiary information to the principal, whether directly with the seller or through the seller's real estate agent. If the beneficiary information closely matches the information obtained on the lien information sheet, the escrow officer should feel fairly comfortable in closing escrow with the payoff figure furnished by the trustee. If the unpaid loan balance is not close to the amount shown on the lien information sheet, the escrow officer should notify the seller. An acknowledgment of the contents of the beneficiary statement allows the seller to challenge, correct, or resolve disputed issues directly with the beneficiary.

It is common for the beneficiary demand to be faxed directly to the lender. Some lenders require the original signature(s) of the trustor(s). If the title insurance company demands an original signature of the trustee, along with the original note, then the escrow can still use the faxed bene for file reference in calculating the seller proceeds. The escrow could not close without obtaining the required original documents.

If the beneficiary demand is not returned in a reasonable turnaround time, it will be necessary for the escrow officer to have the telephone number in order to follow up to see if the escrow demand request was received. It is not uncommon that closing is held up because the loan servicing company has actually received the request and forwarded the request to the investor who actually owns the loan note and that investor does not follow up with a quick turnaround time in returning the information.

If the buyer will take over an existing loan of record, then the escrow officer will order a **beneficiary statement** stating the current status of the loan, as is shown in Figure 6.3. The principal may take over the existing loan of record by assumption or subject to the existing loan. With the beneficiary statement, the escrow officer needs more than just the current unpaid balance. The loan status is also required: the currency of the loan payments, amount in or shortage of the impound account, amount of the monthly payment, amount of late fee, due date of the next payment, and due date of a late assessment. Many lenders have a provision that allows another principal to take over the existing loan after providing a loan assumption fee, such as 1 percent of the then current unpaid loan balance. A credit report or other information may also be required. An FHA loan, for example, is assumable under specific terms and conditions, whereas a Cal-Vet loan is never assumable.

The escrow holder should know the type of loan being paid off, whether government or conventional, to check the beneficiary demand statement received to determine if possible errors have occurred. For example, DVA and FHA loans have no prepayment penalty, whereas Cal-Vet loans and some conventional loans do.

■ OUT-OF-STATE BENEFICIARIES

The escrow officer begins writing to lien holders by using the information contained in the **Lane Guide.** The Lane Guide contains detailed information that shows proper mailing address for a specific lender, and it includes the fax number and telephone contact. The guide also shows information for acquiring loan payoff and loan status information. The address shown in this booklet is not usually the local branch office, but it is the address where the loan servicing is handled. Most lenders have one address for the monthly payment, another for insurance, another for foreclosure, and yet another for the beneficiary statement request. Many lenders have mailing addresses outside California.

FIGURE 6.3

Beneficiary Statement

Date:

Lender of Record
PO Box XXXX
Anytown, CA 90000

      ATTN: Loan Status Department   RE: Loan #: XX-00000-XX

Property address: 123 Elm Street, Somecity, CA 91234

Title Vested as: Mr. and Mrs. IMA Borrower

Legal description: Lot 12 in Tract 24 in pages 12 to 14 of book 32 in the office
                of the county recorder in a California County.

Current unpaid balance: $_____   Interest rate on the loan _____ %

The monthly payment is $_____   Due on the _____ day of each month.

The next date a payment is due is _____   The amount of the late fee is $_____

The late fee is assessed and due on what day of each month _____

The impound account status is:
        There is no impound connected with this loan _____
        There is an impound shortage of $_____
        The impound account contains $_____

The loan terms for assumption are: _____

_____

The loan terms for taking title subject to the existing title are: _____

_____

Mary Belle Smith, Escrow Officer   John James, Title Officer
Escrow No. MBS-112_____   Title Order No. 7-765432
A California Escrow Company   A California Title Company
789 Maple Avenue
Somecity, CA 91234

The Lane Guide is a helpful source of information that the processor will frequently use as a reference. Most lenders usually keep the loan information database records in a centralized location. The Lane Guide gives the complete street address and zip code of the verified address, fax numbers, 800 numbers, special departments for collections, wholesale lending, REO, assumptions, and administrative offices. It also provides the service center information to obtain account ratings or verifications of deposit, complete information for obtaining payoff quotes, loan verifications, ratings, and schedule of fees, as well as providing detailed information on rating policies, hours, and locations of installment loan accounts.

When a borrower is trying to obtain a loan, the contact is usually a local loan representative who obtains the actual loan funds from a financial backer. The backer may be a lender who is active in the state in which the loan is originated, but more often than not the backer gets the funds from out-of-state sources. After the close of escrow, most loans are sold in the secondary money market to investors from all over the world. The borrower, however, may not see any change when the loan is sold from the originator to the investor. This is because a different branch of the same firm that originated the loan often handles the loan servicing, which is the ongoing collection of the payment obligation.

Many loans contain clauses, such as prepayment penalties, that would increase the amount of the unpaid balance to pay the loan off entirely. In the case of negative amortization, the final payoff may be more than the original loan amount. Past due late fees or impound shortages also increase the amount that escrow needs for loan payoff.

For example, the seller has a current loan with XYZ Finance Corporation on a property located in Visalia, California, where a mortgage loan broker in Visalia originated that loan several years ago. Subsequently, the loan was sold in the secondary market and is currently with a loan servicing firm located in Oklahoma. What mailing address would be used for ordering the beneficiary demand? By using the Lane Guide, the processor would be able to ascertain that the mailing address for the loan servicing agent is 17671 Vine Blvd. #104, Yourtown, OK 55555-3164. Without the Lane Guide, the processor may have sent the beneficiary demand to the Visalia office where the loan originated, and this would cause a delay in the processing time. For information, call 1-800-LANE GUIDE; write to National Subscription Center, P.O. Box 70610, Reno, NV 89570-0610; FAX (800) 526-3650; or visit the Web site: *www.laneguide.com.*

WEB LINK

@

The contents of the Lane Guide include the contact information for various lenders all over the state and the country, ranging from the head offices of large financial corporations to individual branches and even private party investors. The most common way to order the bene is to send a fax to the lender, and, by using the Lane Guide the escrow officer can obtain the lender fax number.

■ DUE-ON-SALE CLAUSE

When the demand statement indicates a **due-on-sale clause,** the buyer is prohibited by the lender from taking over the seller's existing unpaid loan balance under the terms and conditions given to the seller. The terms and conditions that the original borrower agreed to included that only that individual is approved for liability on the loan. This is based upon the credit worthiness of the borrower. A different borrower would have different credit, different income, and different past experiences with real estate. These differences mean that the beneficiary wants to know who is responsible for repayment of the debt.

During times of rising interest rates, the buyers want to take over the seller's existing, lower interest rate loan rather than see a new, higher rate loan. In addition, it is more expensive to obtain a new loan with the associated costs. Points, prepaid interest, ALTA title insurance, loan origination fee, and a new appraisal are costs that may be reduced or waived when a loan is taken over by a borrower.

When interest rates are relatively stable or decreasing, fewer principals seek to take over the seller's loan, unless loan costs, such as points, are high, or when a principal could not qualify for a new loan. In these cases, the buyer would merely obtain his or her own new loan.

A due-on-sale clause in a note says basically that "I will loan *you* the money, but not a stranger." This makes the due-on-sale clause common when private parties make loans to one another. In the case where the seller carries back a loan on the property, the seller would not want that buyer to subsequently sell the property to another individual who started making payments on the loan.

When the escrow officer takes the initial escrow instructions, a checklist of questions should be established for various types of escrows. In the case of an owner carryback loan that will be in secondary position of priority, the escrow officer should ask if any type of acceleration clause will be placed in the note. The escrow officer is usually the party that draws up both the note and the **trust deed** in the case of seller secondary financing.

■ FHA LOAN BENEFICIARIES

In addition to determining the terms and conditions of taking over an existing loan, other terms of the existing note affect the escrow. For example, in the case of an FHA loan, subsequent borrowers may assume the existing loan, provided that they furnish credit and employment information to the lender. FHA requires payment of a loan assumption fee to assume an FHA loan, and the escrow officer would be responsible for ascertaining that the FHA lender has approved the buyer.

The escrow officer also must be cognizant of the special FHA note requirements on notification for loan payoff. Most textbooks and FHA seminars indicate that there is no prepayment penalty on an FHA loan. This is not true if escrow fails to adequately notify the lender within the required time lines. The standard FHA clause states the beneficiary is entitled to collect 30 additional full days of interest for loan payoff. Thus, if the escrow is supposed to be from June 1 to July 30, approximately 60 days, the escrow officer would have to make the beneficiary demand no later than June 25 to ensure that the FHA lender received the demand request by July 1. If escrow is waiting for approval of the appraisal or any other contingency that would delay making the demand request until later in the escrow, then the seller would be penalized by the delay. Thus, if the demand was not faxed over to the beneficiary until July 15 and the escrow was to close July 30, the seller would be charged 30 full days' interest rather than the 14 days' interest that would have been due. Because many people do not know of this rule, the real estate professional needs to make sure the escrow officer has sent the beneficiary demand within the correct time frame to avoid any extra expense to the seller. Professionals try to close near the end of the month when an existing FHA loan is to be paid off.

■ MAINTAINING THE FILE CALENDAR

The file calendar is very important for an escrow officer. The usual turnaround time for many items, such as the beneficiary demand statements, will range anywhere from two working days to a month or more. For example, a demand request faxed to a lender may be back to escrow within 24 hours. Or the appraisal may take up to six weeks to obtain.

The escrow file calendar would note the date that each item was originally sent out to another individual or entity. The date that such items as the preliminary title report request and beneficiary demand request and other items were ordered would be noted in the file. The calendar would be marked with the follow-up date for a second request or a phone-call follow-up.

Each item received would be marked in the file so that no further follow-up would be needed. When all items are received, the escrow officer notifies all parties that they are in a position to close. Even if everything is in place, the escrow officer may not order that the escrow close on his or her own initiative. It is not uncommon that a particular party does not want the escrow to close due to taxes or because of another escrow that is tied to this escrow. If all parties agrees to close the escrow early, then the escrow officer would do so; otherwise, the closing would have to wait for approval.

■ REQUIRING STATEMENT FEE IN ADVANCE

Some beneficiaries will not release any information on the status of the existing loan until a payment is made for the information. The lender may charge a fee for furnishing the payoff information, or beneficiary statement. When an FHA-insured or a DVA-guaranteed loan is being paid off, the lender is not allowed to charge this fee.

If the information is released with a billing statement indicating that the fee charged by the trustee is paid through the costs and expenses at the close of escrow, then if the escrow does not close, the trustee costs would not be paid. Therefore, some lenders request that a fee be paid in advance. In addition, some lenders in a real estate market where interest rates are rising fear releasing the information because the escrow may not close with a loan assumption. Rather the parties may have agreed to an all-inclusive trust deed (AITD) or a transaction involving a contract of sale or wraparound financing. In these cases, the fee may never be paid. Any credit line loan and most stand-alone second trust deed lenders usually want an up-front, beneficiary demand fee for the current loan status. This is especially true when the second is staying in second position. When an advance fee is required for the trustee's statement of the loan status, the escrow officer must request the funds from the seller. The seller has no funds placed into the escrow and the seller expects all costs to be paid from the proceeds at the close of escrow. Only the buyer's initial deposit funds may be on deposit in the escrow account. The buyer has not given the escrow written instructions allowing the spending of his or her funds to pay off the seller's trustee costs.

■ UNDERSTANDING THE DEMAND WHEN IT ARRIVES

Once the beneficiary statement or demand has been received, the escrow officer should immediately send a copy to the principal for approval by faxing a copy to the real estate agents or sending a copy directly to the principal. The principal is sent a copy for approval so he or she can make sure the charges and fees being assessed are correct before escrow closes.

Confusion often arises about making the last payment before the close of escrow. If the escrow officer cannot prove that a payment has been made and if the lender does not acknowledge that the payment has been credited to the account, then the seller/trustor often makes two final loan payments. As an example, assume that the monthly loan payment is due on the first day of the month. Assume that the seller made the payment and the lender has credited the trustor with this payment for the month of July. The escrow is supposed to close on July 30 so that the seller would not make the August 1 payment. Delay happens and the escrow does not close on July 30.

Does the seller send the August 1 payment to the lender? The answer is no. If the seller mails in the monthly payment between August 1 and August 10, before the date a late fee is assessed on this loan, the payment would not have cleared the bank and the beneficiary statement would not reflect the reduced principal payment. So, if the seller sent the payment to the lender, escrow would also have to take from the seller's closing proceeds the per diem amount that the beneficiary demand indicated. This means that the seller would have made the payment twice. In this case, after the close of escrow, the lender would eventually credit all sums due and process a refund check back to the trustor.

The trustor fears that as August 10 arrives and the escrow was supposed to have closed that if the payment is not made to the lender, a late fee will be assessed. All payments made during an open escrow fall under the same rules as any regular payment. If not paid by the 15th of the month, a late fee is assessed by the lender, which would negatively affect the credit of the seller who most often is in escrow to purchase another property. A late fee can lower the FICO credit rating score for any borrower and could cause less favorable loan terms.

The solution for this potential problem is to use the already open escrow. The seller should make the payment to the lender, with the loan number and full amount due, attach the loan payment coupon, and deliver the monthly payment to escrow. The escrow company will work with the title company to ensure that the payment is received and credited by the lender of record and will adjust the escrow closing statement accordingly.

A sample beneficiary payoff demand statement is shown in Figure 6.4. The information contained in the document is the loan payoff amount and current status of the payment. The amount of interest to charge on a per day basis is also shown. In the early days of escrow, the escrow officer would take the unpaid loan balance and multiply by the interest rate to determine the annual interest. Then that amount would be divided by the number of days in a year to calculate the daily or per diem rate of interest in dollars. This amount would be multiplied by the number of days of the month from close of escrow back to the last loan payment.

Today the escrow officer rarely calculates the daily interest. The beneficiary demand statement usually indicates the per diem rate of interest in dollars that escrow will use. The statement also shows the date through which the loan is paid. Thus, if the beneficiary demand shows that the loan is paid through the last day of previous month, then the escrow officer would use the per diem rate times the days from the first of the month to and including the date of close of escrow. Other items found on the statement constitute the status of the impound account.

FIGURE 6.4

Beneficiary Payoff Demand Statement

Country Loans for Homes, Inc.
Payoff Department
1000 Country Avenue
Kansas City, MO XXXXX
1-800-123-4567
Fax: 1-702-222-1212

Amended
PAYOFF DEMAND STATEMENT
Statement Void After: December 31, 20XX
Statement Date: December 1, 20XX
This loan is in Foreclosure.

Mailed to: Property Address:
City Escrow Company, Inc.   Neil S. Howell
Escrow Officer: Donna Grogan   Frances J. Howell
22254 Vermont Avenue   7932 Lomita Blvd #17
Anytown, CA 91224   Somecity, CA 94321
Escrow # 32235DG   Account No. 766201-D
                                                Case # 23766 CA

Principal Balance as of 06/01/20XX	$ 276,728.01
Interest from 06/01/20XX to 12/31/20XX	$ 10,754.99
County Recording Fee	$ 12.00
Fees Due	$ 825.00
Additional Fees and Costs	$ 336.82

Total Due on Account No. 766201-D	**$291,653.82**

- Your loan is currently in default and has been accelerated. If you cure the default before you payoff your loan, your loan will be reinstated and deemed current. If you payoff your loan after your default is cured, you may be liable for the payment of a prepayment penalty. The amount of any prepayment penalty would be in addition to the payoff amount shown on this statement.

Daily Interest*	From	To	Interest Rate
$55.5813	06/01/20XX	12/31/20XX	6.55%

*Daily Interest = Principal Balance x Interest Rate ÷ 365.
AMENDED DEMAND STATEMENTS ARE SENT AUTOMATICALLY IF THE TOTAL AMOUNT DUE INCREASES ON OR BEFORE DECEMBER 31, 20XX.
Payoff funds must be made payable to Country Loans for Homes, Inc. Pay offs will be accepted by WIRE or CERTIFIED FUNDS ONLY. Funds MUST reference Country Loans for Homes, with Loan # Account No. 766201-D, Property Address: 7932 Lomita Blvd #17 Somecity, CA 90712 for Borrower: Neil S. Howell and Frances J. Howell or they will be RETURNED. Funds received after 3:00 Central Time may be posted the following business day:

WIRE funds to: **MAIL funds to:**
BANK OF THE MIDWEST   COUNTRY LOANS FOR HOMES, INC.
  ABA Routing #1110000111   Attention: Payoff Department, Foreclosure V-04
  MRC Account # 12345-12345   1000 Country Avenue, Kansas City, MO XXXXX

Please reference the Loan Number on the face of the check and DO NOT STAPLE the contents.
Payoff amount is subject to change for various reasons, including but not limited to the following:
- A recent mailed payment not shown on this statement-(DO NOT place a stop payment on any check.)
- Payments returned to us by the finanacial institution for any reason.
- Scheduled payment(s) from the escrow account (for taxes, insurance premiums or other escrow items)
- Potential collection charges (if the account is past due)
- Late charges for delinquent payments received subsequent to Dec 31, 20XX

This communication is from a debt collector.

■ PRIVATE PARTY LIENS

When one of the beneficiary entities cannot be located to obtain the loan payoff information, escrow will notify the principal and title company. For example, 30 years ago a seller sells a home to a young couple. Because the seller owns the property free and clear of any real property loan, the seller carries the loan as the first trust deed holder.

After the close of escrow, the monthly payments are made from the buyer to the bank that the seller has designated as a collection and loan service. The funds accumulate over time in the commercial bank trust department managed account. The bank acts as a trustee for collection of funds on behalf of the beneficiary.

Eventually the trustor pays all the loan payments, the loan is paid off, and a reconveyance deed is requested of the trustee. The trustor is notified by the trustee that the reconveyance deed instructions can only be directed by the beneficiary. In addition, the letter from the bank indicates that the beneficiary cannot be located. Therefore, no reconveyance deed can be made even though the bank has all the payments.

This matter would be referred to the title insurance company. The trustor, three decades later, wants to refinance the property and finds he or she is unable to obtain a new loan unless the public record shows that the old loan is paid off. In this case the title insurance company would require a bond to be paid by the trustor to the title company to cover an amount equal to two and one half times the original principal loan amount. The bond covers the principal and all accrued interest on that note should an heir find the original note years later and claim she was never paid.

Private party liens have these types of problems in cases where an original signature from the beneficiary on a reconveyance deed cannot be obtained. In the case above the private party beneficiary and trustee died shortly after creating the loan and before the loan was reconveyed with no known heirs. The trustee cannot just release the trustor. A cloud on the title has been created. The property owner cannot obtain a new loan or sell the property until the reconveyance matter is handled.

Once the beneficiary demands are received, forwarded to the parties, and approved, the information is then entered into the file. The amount for each lien is entered on the estimated closing statement so that the seller's net proceeds may be calculated. It is very important to see that this first step is completed as far in advance as possible of the actual closing of the escrow, especially if the seller is purchasing another property with the proceeds from this escrow. This allows for the parties to double-check figures ahead of time to ensure that adequate

FIGURE 6.5

Instruction to Pay Tax Liens and Assessments

The foregoing terms, provisions, conditions, and instructions are hereby approved and accepted in their entirety and concurred with by me. I will hand you necessary documents called for on my part to cause title to be shown as set out herein, which you are authorized to deliver when you hold or have caused to be applied to funds set forth herein within the time as herein provided. You are authorized to pay, on my behalf, any recording fees, charges for evidence of title as called for, whether or not this escrow is consummated, except those the buyer agreed to pay. You are hereby authorized to pay bonds, assessments, taxes, and any liens of record, including prepayment penalties, if any, to show title as called for within these instructions.

funds are available for the closing of the other property. This is a time when keeping the principals informed about the progress of the escrow helps to maintain good client-agent communications and trust.

■ TAX LIENS

The escrow instructions pertaining to the seller usually contain standard clauses that instruct the escrow officer to pay any **tax liens** of record. The wording shown in Figure 6.5—or similar type phrases or sentences—is usually contained in preprinted escrow instructions. This boiler-plate wording specifically instructs that no further notice is needed from the seller to the escrow officer.

Real property taxes are governed by California state law, including Proposition 13, Proposition 60, Proposition 90, and the many other legislative and initiative acts that affect real property taxes. Property taxes are collected by the county in which the property is located. The County Assessor first assesses the value of the property to determine the amount of property tax due. Generally, the assessed value is the cash or market value at the time of the purchase. This value increases not more than 2 percent per year until the property is sold or new construction is completed. The Auditor-Controller applies the appropriate tax rate for the general tax levy. Locally voted special assessment taxes for city or district areas are added as a direct property tax to the parcels affected.

The Tax Collector prepares the property tax bill and distributes the real property tax bills each year. The property owner receives a copy of the annual property tax bill that allows for the payment to be made in two installments. The first installment covers the property taxes from July 1 to December 31 for the current year in which the property tax bill is sent to the property owner of record. This tax bill for one half the annual amount is due on November 1. Most people do not pay the tax at that time. The date that the taxes are more often paid is just

TABLE 6.1

Seller Tax Lien Debit or Credit Chart

Month	+ Credit +	– Debit –
January		X
February 1–9		X
February 11–28/29		X
March		X
April 1–9		X
April 11–30	X	
May	X	
June	X	
July		X
August		X
September		X
October		X
November		X
December 1–9		X
December 11–31	X	

before the date that a late fee assessment would be incurred. The first installment is paid by December 10, the delinquent date. Most lenders pay the taxes just prior to the delinquency date and not on the due date.

The property taxes are based upon the government's fiscal tax year beginning July 1 of the current year and ending June 30 of the following year. The second installment covers the property taxes from January 1 to June 30 of the subsequent tax year. This second installment is due on February 1 but not delinquent until April 10.

The escrow officer will take the amount shown on the annual property tax information for each installment and prorate using that amount, as shown on the preliminary title report. The escrow officer handles the seller's property tax information on whether the seller gets back a credit for taxes that have been paid in advance or debits the seller to charge the seller for unpaid property taxes that the seller owes and have not yet been paid.

Because the payment made on December 10 only pays through December 31, the seller always owes taxes during most of the first installment period. The only time a credit balance is reflected is after the payment is made by December 10 for a credit for the balance of only that month before the January 1 date when the second half of taxes would become a charge to the seller. The payment made on April 10 would have paid the past month's taxes from January 1 to April 10, and would pay in advance up to June 30. Table 6.1 shows a chart for the seller under normal circumstances where the tax payments are not delinquent and not past due.

■ OTHER SELLER LIENS AND SELLER EXPENSES

Common liens for which the sellers will be charged through escrow are for mechanics' liens, judgment liens, and income tax liens. The priority of liens is that federal government liens, such as federal income tax, are senior to state or local government liens, such as property taxes. All government liens take priority over private party liens, such as loans. The time and date of recordation sets the lien priority for nongovernment liens, including mechanics' liens and judgments.

Mechanic's Lien

A **mechanic's lien** is an encumbrance against real property for unpaid work performed or materials delivered for the property. Because the worker, or materialman, was unpaid, a lien was filed against the real property. The worker must file a court action within 90 days to settle the matter once the mechanic's lien is filed. Should the worker file a notice on a homeowner, but not follow up with an actual court date, then the item would appear to the title company as a cloud on the title. During the 90-day period, the matter would have to be resolved. However, if the worker and owner never had a court date, or if they did have a court date but the worker did not win the court lawsuit, then the title company would simply remove the cloud and clear the title. If the worker and owner did go to court and if the worker won the suit, then an actual lien would be recorded against the property. In this case, the amount of the debt would have to be paid prior to having clear title to the property. A sample form is shown in Figure 6.6 for a mechanic's lien that would be recorded to show an outstanding lien on a property.

Judgment Lien

A **judgment lien** is an award given by a court against a person who is a party to a lawsuit. The person who wins the case is awarded an amount of money to collect against the other party. The amount of money becomes a judgment award and may be recorded against the real and personal property owned by the party whom the judgment is against. Providing there is adequate equity in the real property, the judgment creditor could force the real property to be sold to satisfy the judgment. This will be discussed in Chapter 10. A federal bankruptcy is also a court action, and the escrow and title company handles it as it does any other judgment lien against the escrow funds that would be due to the seller. In most cases, however, the individual who has to pay the judgment will simply sell the property voluntarily to satisfy the debt and receive a release, called the **satisfaction of judgment.**

Closely related to the judgment lien is a lis pendens, which means a pending action. This is filed against the real property of persons who are being sued so that they cannot sell the property before the final disposition of the court action. If the property is sold, there could be nothing that the creditor may collect against after the award is given by the judge or jury. Thus the property is tied up and

FIGURE 6.6

Mechanic's Lien

RECORDING REQUESTED BY
First City Title Company

**AND WHEN RECORDED MAIL
THIS DEED AND
UNLESS OTHERWISE SHOWN BELOW
MAIL TAX STATEMENTS TO**

Name
Address
City & State
Zip

Book
Page
File No.

Recorded on
_____at_____
Official Records
County of Los Angeles, California
C. B. McCormack
Registrar-Recorder/County Clerk

Fees:
$ _____
B.

SPACE ABOVE THIS LINE FOR RECORDER'S USE

MECHANIC'S LIEN

NOTICE IS HEREBY GIVEN that, Pursuant to the provisions of the California Civil Code
_____
hereafter referred to as "Claimant" (whether singular or plural), claims a lien upon the real property and buildings, improvements, or structures thereon, described in Paragraph Five (5) below, and states the following:

(1) That demand of Claimant after deducting all just credits and offsets is _____ together with interest thereon at the rate of ____% per annum from _____, 20____.

(2) That the name of the owner(s) or reputed owner(s) of said property, is (are)
_____
(name, or state "unknown')

(3) That Claimant did from _____, until _____ perform labor and/or supply materials as follow:
(general statement of a kind of work done or materials furnished, or both)
_____
_____
_____

for the construction, alteration, or repair of said buildings, improvements, or structures, which labor, or materials, or both of them, were in fact used in the construction, alteration, or repair of said buildings, improvements or structures, the location of which is set forth in Paragraph Five (5) below.

(4) Claimant furnished work and materials under contract with or at the request of:
_____
_____

(5) That the property upon which said lien is sought to be charged is situated in the City of _____, County of _____, State of California, commonly known as _____and more particularly described as:
(Street address): _____
DATED: This _____ day of _____, 20____ Firm Name: _____

(Verification for Individual Claim)   (Verification for other than Individual Claim)

STATE OF CALIFORNIA
COUNTY OF_____

_____ begin first duly sworn, deposes and says: That _____be is the _____Claimant named in the foregoing claim of lien, that_____ has read the same and knows the contents thereof, and that the statements therein contain are true and that it contains, among other things, a correct statement of _____ demand, after credits and offsets.

Dated: this ____day of _____,20___at_____
(City& State)
_____
(Signature of Affiant)

Subscribed and sworn to before me
_____
_____

Notary Public in and for said State

STATE OF CALIFORNIA
COUNTY OF _____

_____
being first duly sworn, deposes and says That ____
_____the Claimant herein, is a _____that affiant is _____ and for that reason ____makes his affidavit on behalf of said _____that he was read the same & knows the contents thereof, and that the statements therein contained are true and that it contains among other things, a correct statement of the demand of Claimant, after deducting all just credits and offsets.

Dated: this ____day of _____,20___at_____
_____(City& State)
_____
(Signature of Affiant)

Subscribed and sworn to before me
_____
_____

Notary Public in and for said State

cannot be sold until after the action is finalized. The Notice of Action is filed in conjunction with the lis pendens.

Income Taxes

Income taxes are an encumbrance against an individual person. Each individual seller could have a separate state or separate federal income tax lien for unpaid personal income taxes or for business income taxes. The government could force the sale of the property, but it is more common for the property owner to sell the property voluntarily and pay the debt.

The loan officer who initiates a new loan will be required to obtain an IRS Form 4506 for the loan file before loan approval is given by the loan committee in order to meet investor criteria. The form is the Request for Copy of Transcript of Tax Form as is shown in Figure 6.7. Similarly, the title officer must obtain a release from IRS for both the buyer and the seller. Each principal must have a separate release from state and federal tax liens.

For the seller, unpaid income taxes mean less proceeds at the close of escrow. For the buyer, unpaid income taxes would be a lien that would have priority over all other liens and therefore be before the first trust deed loan. The title company handles the payoff of any income tax lien against the party. But often the escrow agent is the party responsible for obtaining the demand from IRS. When the form is sent to IRS, the return fax answer may indicate that no income tax is due or outstanding against that particular Social Security Number (SSN) or tax identification number (TIN). In this case, no taxes would be paid from escrow. In most escrows, because none of the principals has any tax lien from either federal or state agencies, the item is cleared.

The escrow officer must comply with legislation in both California and the United States regarding the personal income of the principals. The information contained in Figure 6.8 shows typical escrow wording that might be included in escrow instructions.

Other Expenses

The seller agrees to pay specific charges in escrow. As part of the signed escrow instructions the following are typical phrases that would be included where the seller is instructing the escrow officer to pay certain items on the seller's behalf. The wording for these items is shown in Figure 6.9.

■ THE RECONVEYANCE

The seller wants to make sure he or she is no longer liable for any debt or liens after escrow closes. No debts or liens are to remain against the seller after the close of escrow in conjunction with the subject property. Likewise, the buyer

FIGURE 6.7

Request for Copy of Transcript of Tax Form

Form **4506**
(Rev. January 2004)

Department of the Treasury
Internal Revenue Service

Request for Copy of Tax Return

► Do not sign this form unless all applicable parts have been completed.
Read the instructions on page 2.
► Request may be rejected if the form is incomplete, illegible, or any required
part was blank at the time of signature.

OMB No. 1545-0429

TIP: You may be able to get your tax return or return information from other sources. If you had your tax return completed by a paid preparer, they should be able to provide you a copy of the return. The IRS can provide a **Tax Return Transcript** for many returns free of charge. The transcript provides most of the line entries from the tax return and usually contains the information that a third party (such as a mortgage company) requires. See new **Form 4506-T,** Request for Transcript of Tax Return, to order a transcript or you can call 1-800-829-1040 to order a transcript.

1a	Name shown on tax return. If a joint return, enter the name shown first.	1b	First social security number on tax return or employer identification number (see instructions)
2a	If a joint return, enter spouse's name shown on tax return	2b	Second social security number if joint tax return

3 Current name, address (including apt., room, or suite no.), city, state, and ZIP code

4 Address, (including apt., room, or suite no.), city, state, and ZIP code shown on the last return filed if different from line 3

5 If the tax return is to be mailed to a third party (such as a mortgage company), enter the third party's name, address, and telephone number. The IRS has no control over what the third party does with the tax return.

CAUTION: *Lines 6 and 7 must be completed if the third party requires you to complete Form 4506.* **Do not** *sign Form 4506 if the third party requests that you sign Form 4506 and lines 6 and 7 are blank.*

6 **Tax return requested** (Form 1040, 1120, 941, etc.) and all attachments as originally submitted to the IRS, including Form(s) W-2, schedules, or amended returns. Copies of Forms 1040, 1040A, and 1040EZ are generally available for 7 years from filing before they are destroyed by law. Other returns may be available for a longer period of time. Enter only one return number. If you need more than one type of return, you must complete another Form 4506. ► _____

 Note: *If the copies must be certified for court or administrative proceedings, check here.* . . . . ☐

7 **Year or period requested.** Enter the ending date of the year or period, using the mm/dd/yyyy format. If you are requesting more than four years or periods, you must attach another Form 4506.

___ / ___ / ___   ___ / ___ / ___   ___ / ___ / ___   ___ / ___ / ___

8 **Fee.** There is a $39 fee for each return requested. **Full payment must be included with your request or it will be rejected. Make your check or money order payable to "United States Treasury."** Enter your SSN or EIN and "Form 4506 request" on your check or money order.

a	Cost for each return	$	39.00
b	Number of returns requested on line 7		
c	Total cost. Multiply line 8a by line 8b	$	

9 If we cannot find the tax return, we will refund the fee. If the refund should go to the third party listed on line 5, check here . . ☐

Signature of taxpayer(s). I declare that I am either the taxpayer whose name is shown on line 1a or 2a, or a person authorized to obtain the tax return requested. If the request applies to a joint return, **either** husband or wife must sign. If signed by a corporate officer, partner, guardian, tax matters partner, executor, receiver, administrator, trustee, or party other than the taxpayer, I certify that I have the authority to execute Form 4506 on behalf of the taxpayer.

Telephone number of taxpayer on line 1a or 2a
(   )

Sign Here

► Signature (see instructions)   Date

► Title (If line 1a above is a corporation, partnership, estate, or trust)

► Spouse's signature   Date

For Privacy Act and Paperwork Reduction Act Notice, see page 2.   Cat. No. 41721E   Form **4506** (Rev. 1-2004)

FIGURE 6.7

Request for Copy of Transcript of Tax Form (Continued)

Form 4506 (Rev. 1-2004)   Page **2**

Changes To Note

Section references are to the Internal Revenue Code.

• **Form 4506,** Request for Copy of Tax Return, is now used to request copies of tax returns. Use **new Form 4506-T**, Request for Transcript of Tax Return, to request tax return transcripts, tax account information, W-2 information, 1099 information, verification of non-filing, and record of account.

• The fee for a photocopy of a tax return has increased to $39.

Instructions

Purpose of form. Use Form 4506 to request a copy of your tax return. You can also designate a third party to receive the tax return. See line 5.

How long will it take? It may take up to 60 calendar days for us to process your request.

Where to file. Attach payment and mail Form 4506 to the address below for the state you lived in when that return was filed. There are two address charts: one for individual returns (Form 1040 series) and one for all other returns.

Note: *If you are requesting more than one return and the chart below shows two different service centers, mail your request to the service center based on the address of your most recent return.*

Chart for individual returns (Form 1040 series)

If you lived in and filed an individual return:	Mail to the Internal Revenue Service at:
Maine, Massachusetts, New Hampshire, New York, Vermont	RAIVS Team 310 Lowell St. Stop 679 Andover, MA 01810
Alabama, Florida, Georgia, Mississippi, North Carolina, South Carolina, West Virginia, Rhode Island	RAIVS Team 4800 Buford Hwy. Stop 91 Chamblee, GA 30341
Arkansas, Colorado, Kentucky, Louisiana, New Mexico, Oklahoma, Tennessee, Texas	RAIVS Team 3651 South Interregional Hwy. Stop 6716 Austin, TX 78741
Alaska, Arizona, California, Hawaii, Idaho, Montana, Nevada, Oregon, Utah, Washington, Wyoming	RAIVS Team Stop 38101 Fresno, CA 93888
Delaware, Illinois, Indiana, Iowa, Kansas, Michigan, Minnesota, Missouri, Nebraska, North Dakota, South Dakota, Wisconsin	RAIVS Team Stop B41-6700 Kansas City, MO 64999
Ohio, Virginia	RAIVS Team 5333 Getwell Rd. Stop 2826 Memphis, TN 38118

Connecticut, District of Columbia, Maryland, New Jersey, Pennsylvania, a foreign country, or A.P.O. or F.P.O. address	RAIVS Team DP SE 135 Philadelphia, PA 19255-0695

Chart for all other returns

If you lived in:	Mail to the Internal Revenue Service at:
Alabama, Alaska, Arizona, Arkansas, California, Colorado, Florida, Georgia, Hawaii, Idaho, Iowa, Kansas, Louisiana, Minnesota, Mississippi, Missouri, Montana, Nebraska, Nevada, New Mexico, North Dakota, Oklahoma, Oregon, South Dakota, Tennessee, Texas, Utah, Washington, Wyoming	RAIVS Team Mail Stop 6734 Ogden, UT 84201
Connecticut, Delaware, District of Columbia, Illinois, Indiana, Kentucky, Maine, Maryland, Massachusetts, Michigan, New Hampshire, New Jersey, New York, North Carolina, Ohio, Pennsylvania, Rhode Island, South Carolina, Vermont, Virginia, West Virginia, Wisconsin	RAIVS Team P.O. Box 145500 Stop 2800F Cincinnati, OH 45250

Line 1b. Enter your employer identification number if you are requesting a copy of a business return. Otherwise, enter the first social security number (SSN) shown on the return. For example, if you are requesting Form 1040 that includes Schedule C (Form 1040), enter your SSN.

Signature and date. Form 4506 must be signed and dated by the taxpayer listed on line 1a or 2a. If you completed line 5 requesting the return be sent to a third party, the IRS must receive Form 4506 within 60 days of the date signed by the taxpayer or it will be rejected.

Individuals. Copies of jointly filed tax returns may be furnished to either spouse. Only one signature is required. Sign Form 4506 exactly as your name appeared on the original return. If you changed your name, also sign your current name.

Corporations. Generally, Form 4506 can be signed by: (1) an officer having legal authority to bind the corporation, (2) any person designated by the board of directors or other governing body, or (3) any officer or employee on written request by any principal officer and attested to by the secretary or other officer.

Partnerships. Generally, Form 4506 can be signed by any person who was a member of the partnership during any part of the tax period requested on line 7.

All others. See section 6103(e) if the taxpayer has died, is insolvent, is a dissolved corporation, or if a trustee, guardian, executor, receiver, or administrator is acting for the taxpayer.

Documentation. For entities other than individuals, you must attach the authorization document. For example, this could be the letter from the principal officer authorizing an employee of the corporation or the Letters Testamentary authorizing an individual to act for an estate.

Signature by a representative. A representative can sign Form 4506 for a taxpayer only if this authority has been specifically delegated to the representative on Form 2848, line 5. Form 2848 showing the delegation must be attached to Form 4506.

Privacy Act and Paperwork Reduction Act Notice. We ask for the information on this form to establish your right to gain access to the requested return(s) under the Internal Revenue Code. We need this information to properly identify the return(s) and respond to your request. Sections 6103 and 6109 require you to provide this information, including your SSN or EIN, to process your request. If you do not provide this information, we may not be able to process your request. Providing false or fraudulent information may subject you to penalties.

Routine uses of this information include giving it to the Department of Justice for civil and criminal litigation, and cities, states, and the District of Columbia for use in administering their tax laws. We may also disclose this information to Federal and state agencies to enforce Federal nontax criminal laws and to combat terrorism.

You are not required to provide the information requested on a form that is subject to the Paperwork Reduction Act unless the form displays a valid OMB control number. Books or records relating to a form or its instructions must be retained as long as their contents may become material in the administration of any Internal Revenue law. Generally, tax returns and return information are confidential, as required by section 6103.

The time needed to complete and file Form 4506 will vary depending on individual circumstances. The estimated average time is: **Learning about the law or the form,** 10 min.; **Preparing the form,** 16 min.; and **Copying, assembling, and sending the form to the IRS,** 20 min.

If you have comments concerning the accuracy of these time estimates or suggestions for making Form 4506 simpler, we would be happy to hear from you. You can write to the Tax Products Coordinating Committee, Western Area Distribution Center, Rancho Cordova, CA 95743-0001. **Do not** send the form to this address. Instead, see **Where to file** on this page.

FIGURE 6.8

Seller Instruction to Pay Income Taxes

IRS 1099 REPORTING DISCLOSURE: Parties are made aware that we are required by law to report the total "gross" proceeds (total consideration/sales price) on all real estate sales to the IRS at closing. In addition, parties are further made aware that the escrow holder will also be required by H.R. 639 "Home Sale Tax Fairness Act of 1992" to report to the IRS the amount of real estate property taxes apportioned between the parties at close of escrow. Seller is to complete, sign, and return the amount of real estate property taxes apportioned between the parties at close of escrow. Seller is to complete, sign, and return the attached certification form to escrow holder (all sellers must sign), and this escrow may not close if this form is not received prior to closing. This is an IRS requirement, and any questions should be directed to the Treasury Department and not to the escrow holder.

NOTE: Corporations are automatically exempt from IRS 1099 reporting.

FTRA: The Federal Tax Reform Act of 1986, as amended, and the U.S. Revenue and Taxation Code, require certain transactions to be reported to the Internal Revenue Service and the State Franchise Tax Board. In those transactions seller will furnish a correct tax identification number to you so you can report this transaction as required by law. Seller understands that seller may be subject to civil or criminal penalties for failure to do so.

FIGURE 6.9

Seller Instructions to Pay Expenses

You are further instructed to pay documentary transfer tax on deed as required.

You are further authorized and instructed to pay commission as set forth on separate instructions made a part hereof.

wants only his or her own debts and liens showing against the property after the transfer of ownership that the buyer signed and agreed to. To accomplish this, the title insurance company has the responsibility of recording the executed document to comply with both the buyer's and the seller's desires to terminate certain liens.

Once a deed is recorded it cannot be unrecorded. To show that a debt has been paid in full, a **reconveyance deed** is recorded. A *partial reconveyance*, although less frequently used, shows that a part of a loan has been paid to satisfy part of a debt. One example of a partial reconveyance is when a developer has a blanket loan encumbrance on a parcel of land. The parcel is being subdivided and sold off as several smaller individual lots. As each smaller lot is sold, the lender can release that individual lot by using a partial reconveyance that would be issued for the one lot sold. A reconveyance deed is shown in Figure 6.10.

FIGURE 6.10

Reconveyance Deed

RECORDING REQUESTED BY

First City Title Company

AND WHEN RECORDED MAIL
THIS DEED AND UNLESS OTHERWISE
SHOWN BELOW MAIL TAX
STATEMENTS TO
Name
Address
City & State
Zip
Title Order No.   Escrow No.

Book
Page
File No.

Recorded on
_____at_____
Official Records
County of Anywhere, California
Conny B. McCormack
Registrar-Recorder/County Clerk

Fees:
$ _____
B.

SPACE ABOVE THIS LINE FOR RECORDER'S USE

FULL RECONVEYANCE

Any **Title Insurance Company,** a corporation,

Trustee under deed of trust executed by_____,
Trustor, dated _____ and recorded as Instrument No. _____, on _____, 20XX,
in Book _____, Page _____ of Official Records, in the office of the County Recorder of _____
_____ County, California having been requested in writing, by the holder
of the obligation secured by said deed of trust , to reconvey the estate granted to trustee under said deed of trust,
DOES HEREBY RECONVEY to the person or persons legally entitled thereto, without warranty, all the estate,
title, and interest acquired by trustee under said deed of trust:

(legal description here)

APN or AIN: xxx-xxx-xx
AKA: _____

Any Title Insurance Company

Dated:_____   By:_____
                                              Title

STATE OF CALIFORNIA
COUNTY OF_____
On this the _____day of _____ , 20XX
The undersigned, a Notary Public in and for said
County and State, personally appeared _____
_____, known to me
to be an Assistant Secretary of ___Any__Title
Company, the corporation that executed said instrument
on behalf of the corporation therein named, and
Acknowledged to me that such corporation executed
the same, and acknowledged to me that such corporation
executed the within instrument pursuant to its by laws
or a resolution of its board of directors

FOR NOTARY SEAL OR
STAMP

_____
       Signature of Notary
_____
    Name (Typed or Printed) of Notary

The beneficiary notifies the trustee that the debt has been cleared by giving the trustee a document called a request for reconveyance. The trustee cannot act without written instructions from the beneficiary. The reconveyance deed is executed by the trustee. This means that the beneficiary is authorizing the trustee to return title to the property back to the trustor because the debt is paid off.

■ SELLER AFFIDAVIT

In the standard California Association of REALTORS® (CAR) Residential Listing Agreement (LA) the seller makes the following representations not only to the buyer but also to the escrow company and title company representing liens:

> SELLER REPRESENTATIONS: Seller represents that, unless otherwise specified in writing, Seller is unaware of: (i) any Notice of Default recorded against the Property; (ii) any delinquent amounts due under any loan secured by, or other obligation affecting the Property; (iii) any bankruptcy, insolvency, or similar proceeding affecting the Property; (iv) any litigation, arbitration, administrative action, government investigation, or other pending or threatened action that affects or may affect the Property or Seller's ability to transfer it; and, (v) any current, pending, or proposed special assessments affecting the Property. Seller shall promptly notify Broker in writing if Seller becomes aware of any of these items during the Listing Period or any extension thereof.

The CAR Seller's Affidavit of Nonforeign Status and/or California Withholding exemption (SA) contains the topic paragraphs shown in the list below. The clauses comply with the federal Internal Revenue Service Code and the state California Revenue and Taxation Code sections. The **seller affidavit** form advises the parties to seek an appropriate tax professional for tax advice. The form indicates that the sales price of the property is subject to withholding tax unless the transaction complies with some exemptions.

- Property address.
  - Address of subject property being transferred.
- Transferor's information.
  - Name of the transferor.
  - Telephone of the transferor.
  - Tax identification number of the transferor (Social Security or corporation).
- Authority to sign.
  - States that the signer has the authority to sign for the transferor.
- Federal law exemptions from withholding tax.

- States that individual transferor is not a nonresident alien for tax purposes.

- States that the transferor is not a foreign corporation/partnership, LLC, or trust.

■ California law exemptions from withholding tax.

- If the total sales price is $100,000 or less, the transaction is exempt from the tax.

- Individuals or those with a revocable trust.

- The principal residence is being transferred as per IRC Section 121.

- The property is being exchanged as per IRC Section 1031 (voluntary).

- The property is being exchanged as per IRC Section 1033 (involuntary).

- The transfer will result in a tax loss.

■ Corporation transferors.

- The transferor has a permanent California place of business.

- The LLC or partnership will file a California tax return on the sale.

- The irrevocable trust transferor has at least one trustee in California who will file a California tax return on the sale.

- The **transferor** is exempt under state or federal law.

■ CONTINGENCIES

In virtually all transactions the sellers have many contingencies in the transaction to protect their position. One of the main concerns is that when a buyer takes the seller's property off the market from all other prospective purchasers while the buyer is yet obtaining items necessary to close escrow, the seller desires to minimize the risk. Therefore, the most common contingency imposed by the seller in a real property transaction is the time lines within which the buyer must approve or disapprove specific items that may not have been revealed in advance of opening escrow.

The area of contingencies is one of the larger areas of differences between a real property transaction in Northern California and in Southern California. In the south, the property is taken off the market, then the buyer obtains the buyer's loan approval, property appraisal, and the disclosures after the escrow is opened. In the northern part of the state, the buyer must have already satisfied himself or herself prior to the seller accepting the purchaser's offer. In either case, the seller desires to limit the amount of time that the property is off the market if the buyer fails to perform. Below is a list of common seller contingencies that are to be removed within a specified number of days:

- Increase of buyer's deposit

- Remove loan contingency

- Approve completed inspection reports

- Approve completed disclosure reports

- Sale of the buyer's current residence

■ SELLER-CAUSED ESCROW FALL OUT

There are a variety of reasons why an escrow does not close. Because escrow is a means for enabling ownership transfer to occur fairly with the required document, escrow involves many areas where the seller can hinder the close of escrow. The following is a list of typical reasons where the seller was the major cause for the transaction falling out of escrow:

- Seller's sentimental reasons about the property

- Seller's proposed purchase fell out of escrow

- Property defect, such as faulty plumbing or a leaky roof

- Failure to disclose, such as a change in school district

- Seller dissatisfaction, such as lack of due diligence by the other parties

- Failure of the parties to agree on certain terms, such as payment of points

THINK ABOUT IT

The preliminary title report shows a judgment lien against Thurston Miller on the escrow for Thurston and Evelyn Miller. The escrow officer contacts the title officer to determine additional information about the lien. The title officer indicates that the lien appears to be nonpayment of child support with a lien date of September 20, 1985. Escrow recalculated the file and indicated that with the amount of the lien showing on the judgment plus estimated interest and additional court costs to obtain a release of judgment lien should the amount be paid, that the seller would net nothing. In fact, escrow indicates that the seller would have to bring in $5,000 to close the escrow. What steps should be taken?

1. Pull the copy of the statement of information (SI) to determine if Mr. Miller lists any previous marriage.

2. Finding no previous marriage indicated on the SI, look at the other information contained on that document. Upon looking at the balance of the information, the SI shows his date of birth as January 25, 1980.

3. Notify the title officer about the facts found so the officer can determine that the lien might be seller's father and is most likely not part of this escrow because this person in escrow would only have been five years old at the time of the lien.

4. Due to the confidentiality and the Right to Privacy Act, do *not* notify any principal of any lien that is not for that individual. The son may not know about the judgment lien, and you could be liable for the disclosure.

■ CHAPTER SUMMARY

The escrow officer provides the seller with the lien information sheet where the seller states the name and loan number for each lien holder. The escrow officer uses this information and the information found on the preliminary title report obtained from public records to obtain payoff information for liens of record and for encumbrances to be paid through escrow. Some ongoing items such as property taxes are to be paid current to the close of escrow or prorated between the parties.

For liens to be paid off in escrow, the escrow holder contacts each lien holder to obtain the status of the loan and the amount to pay at the close of escrow. The statement is referred to as a bene, which is trade jargon used to describe the beneficiary. If the loan is to be paid off in full, it is referred to as the beneficiary demand, or the demand for payoff amount. If the buyer is to assume the existing lien of record, the beneficiary statement is used to state the current status of the loan.

At the close of escrow, the escrow officer directs the title company to pay the amounts found on the beneficiary demand statement, including any payoff of any income tax lien, unpaid property taxes, judgment liens, mechanics' liens, or other amounts due from the seller's proceeds or due from the buyer. After the payoff, a reconveyance deed is recorded at the county recorder's office to indicate that the lien has been paid in full. A satisfaction of judgment is recorded to show that a court suit lien has been satisfied.

■ CHAPTER 6 QUIZ

1. A demand is a
   a. written statement indicating the conditions under which an existing loan can be paid in full.
   b. statement to escrow that prevents its closing.
   c. threat to the escrow officer.
   d. statement of loan condition from an existing lender, when a loan is being assumed.

2. A beneficiary statement is a
   a. written statement indicating the conditions under which an existing loan can be paid in full.
   b. statement to escrow that prevents its closing.
   c. threat to the escrow officer.
   d. statement of loan condition from an existing lender, when a loan is being assumed.

3. The lien information sheet is
   a. completed by a buyer so title insurer can look for outstanding liens.
   b. completed by the seller so escrow can write for loan status and payoff information.
   c. required by the lender before the new buyer may be funded.
   d. all of the above.

4. The reconveyance is used to show
   a. the amount of income taxes due from the seller.
   b. the amount of income taxes due from the buyer.
   c. that the lien has been satisfied and paid off.
   d. that the loan has been taken over by a subsequent purchaser.

5. The party responsible for making a wire transfer of the funds to the existing lien holder after the close of escrow and recordation of the deed transferring ownership title to the property would be the
   a. buyer.
   b. seller.
   c. escrow company.
   d. title insurance company.

6. The party who furnishes the information on the lien information sheet is the
   a. seller.
   b. buyer.
   c. escrow officer.
   d. title insurance company.

7. The two sources for finding lien holders are the
   a. beneficiary demand and lien information sheet.
   b. lien information sheet and preliminary title report.
   c. preliminary title report and policy of title insurance.
   d. policy of title insurance and beneficiary statement.

8. Which statement is correct about an assumed FHA loan?
   a. The lender may receive a prepayment penalty of six months' interest on the unpaid loan balance after first deducting 20 percent of the principal.
   b. The lender may charge a fee of 1 percent of the original loan balance for a new principal.
   c. The lender may receive 30 days' interest on the unpaid loan balance at payoff.
   d. All the above are correct.

9. Private party lien holders and institutional lenders
   a. are under the same rules and regulations and must offer the same services.
   b. are so different that escrow cannot close if both are involved in the same transaction.
   c. coordinate with escrow and title to assist in reducing closing costs.
   d. have different rules and regulations regarding seller lien payoffs.

10. The parties to a trust deed consist of
    a. trustor, beneficiary, and trustee.
    b. mortgagor and mortgagee.
    c. trustor and mortgagor.
    d. beneficiary and mortgagee.

CHAPTER SEVEN

LOAN ESCROW AND BUYER ESCROW

■ KEY TERMS

buyer affidavit
California Department
  of Veterans Affairs
  (Cal-Vet)
contingency
conventional loan
Department of Veterans
  Affairs (DVA)

Federal Housing
  Administration
  (FHA)
loan approval
loan docs
loan officer
loan originator
loan processor

locked
mortgage insurance
  premium (MIP)
prequalified
private mortgage
  insurance (PMI)
trust deed
vesting

■ CHAPTER OVERVIEW

The escrow officer will often handle a transaction where no buyer and seller are involved, such as in a refinance. Whether a new loan is obtained with a purchase or as a refinance, the escrow officer is involved directly with the lender, due to the clauses contained in the escrow instructions that specifically instruct the escrow officer to work with the lender. The documents that the borrower signs instruct the escrow officer to provide certified escrow instructions to the lender. The escrow officer often meets with the borrower to have the loan documents

171

signed and notarized at the escrow company. The escrow officer instructs the title department to record the trust deed that is evidence for the debt.

In order for an escrow officer to be effective in handling a loan escrow, he or she must know the different types of lenders and different types of loan programs. Each loan program has different criteria, and the escrow officer will meet all in his or her normal work. A thorough understanding of the loan process, without being an expert on the specific loan details, is an important part of the escrow job. Most real estate contract agreements are contingent upon the borrower obtaining a loan. Thus, if the borrower does not obtain the loan, the escrow most likely will not close. Part of the loan approval process is the federal legislature requiring a good-faith estimate showing the annual percentage rate (APR) and estimated closing costs. Many lender disclosures are required.

■ LEARNING OBJECTIVES

At the conclusion of Chapter 7, you will be able to

- understand the relationship between escrow and the buyer's new lender;
- list the components of a trust deed;
- outline the steps for escrow to take to meet the requirements of the buyer's new loan;
- differentiate between various types of buyer loans for the requirements for escrow; and
- explain the loan process from buyer prequalification to funding and recordation of the documents evidencing the new loan on the property.

■ TYPES OF LENDERS

Although there are others who handle some real estate loans, four types of lenders dominate the real estate loan market: institutional lenders, loan brokers, loan bankers, and private lenders. The escrow officer should distinguish between the different types of lenders to better understand how the transaction is processed. Each type of lender has its own guidelines and requirements from escrow to allow the loan to be funded, recorded, and closed. Without understanding the differences, the escrow officer cannot anticipate problems and resolve lender issues.

Institutional Lenders   These lenders are the larger firms with known names, such as Bank of America, Wells Fargo, Countrywide, and Chase. They may make loans directly to the public, and these lenders have a tendency to advertise directly to consumers to market loans. The source of their funds to make loans to consumers comes from their own clients, through savings accounts and investors, or from investments. As investors in real estate and other markets, these institutions buy and sell blocks of real estate loans in the secondary money market to generate cash for new loans secured by real property. They also place real estate loans through loan brokers rather than rely only on the employees of the institutions processing all of their business.

Institutional lenders tend to prefer conforming loans that are freely tradable on the secondary money market where real estate loans are bought and sold. These loans adhere to FNMA, Freddie Mac, GNMA, FHA, DVA, or similar loan criteria. The borrower must have a minimum FICO credit score, and the property must meet appraisal standards in relation to the loan-to-value ratio, or LTV. Once the escrow officer has closed several of these types of transactions, he or she will realize the procedure to follow with regards to the lender is somewhat standard in processing and closing. The escrow officer knows what to expect and would then be in a position to meet the needs of the lender to make the transaction run smoothly and efficiently.

Loan Brokers

Loan brokers work just like any other real estate broker—on a fee basis based on the service they provide. They commit institutional lender or private lender funds on real estate loans and receive a commission. The loan funds come from another source and are not the broker's own money.

The loan broker must meet the criteria of the actual source of the funds being placed for the loan. The loan broker has no voice in the loan criteria. Therefore, these loans may have a problem during the escrow period when rates are rapidly changing. The loan may begin at one rate that was quoted to the loan broker by the lender, which was in turn quoted to the consumer. Near the close of escrow, however, the lender may state that the rate or points will be higher or may add less favorable terms as criteria for obtaining the loan. The loan broker has no control over the funds unless the loan was **locked** prior to drawing the loan documents (docs). Loans are typically locked from 45 to 120 days. One advantage of using a loan broker is that they may shop many different institutional lending sources to obtain the best loan available. A disadvantage is that if market conditions change before the close of escrow, and in markets where the broker cannot or did not guarantee to lock the ultimate loan offered to the consumer, little can be done. When interest rates are falling or relatively stable, the lender will allow a rate to be locked, and brokers obtain the locked rate for the client. In markets where interest rates are rapidly rising, lenders will not offer or allow locks, or may charge a fee to lock a loan rate.

Loan Bankers

The loan banker is a bank. Loan bankers may use their own funds to place real estate loans directly to clients or may use the services of a loan broker. They set their own rules of acceptability of the loan to meet their own criteria. So long as their lending practices are not discriminatory, they are allowed great latitude and fill a wide gap in the lending community to fit loans needed for nonconforming property or for borrowers with lower than average FICO credit scores. With experience, it is fairly easy for the escrow officer to understand the procedures for a loan bank. This allows the escrow officer to plan ahead for what will be needed by the lender to consummate the loan. A loan banker, like the loan broker, may also use funds that are not its own.

Private Lenders

A credit union is a group of savers with pooled funds to make loans to their own group. An individual investor is a private lender. Private lenders often specialize in a particular type of property or a particular type of loan. For example, specific investors make loans only for miniwarehouse storage facilities or for gas stations or for retail mall construction. When an owner carries back part of his or her equity in the form of a second trust deed as an extension of credit from the seller to the buyer, that seller is a private lender. Because private lenders set their own terms and conditions, the escrow officer cannot usually prepare in advance for the type of loan conditions that may be asked of the escrow. The escrow officer must wait until actually receiving the documents in order to determine what must next be done to comply with the loan requirements. Each individual investor has instructions that may be different and unique to the type of loan funded.

■ TYPES OF LOANS

In addition to understanding the types of lenders, as noted above, each lender has preferences on the types of loans it can fund. Some lenders can make all types of loans, but the majority of lenders specialize in just a very limited few types. The major types of loan programs are summarized in Figure 7.1.

Government Loans

The criteria for a government-backed loan require the escrow officer to execute different types of documents for the various loans. Government loans are FHA, DVA, or Cal-Vet. Each loan type has criteria and loan procedures that the escrow holder should know.

The **Federal Housing Administration (FHA)** loans are handled through a loan broker, just as the same loan broker can handle a conventional loan. The FHA is administered under the Housing and Urban Development loan; FHA insures the loan in case of default. Escrow handles FHA loans with the following characteristics:

FIGURE 7.1

Loan Program Types

	FHA	DVA	Cal-Vet	FNMA/FNLMC
What	1–4 units	1–4 units	1–4 units	1–4 units
Who	Anyone	Any veteran	Any veteran	Anyone
Maximum price	NONE	NONE	NONE	NONE
Interest rate	Set by lender/market	Set by lender/market	Set by State of California	Set by lender/market
Type of Interest	Fixed or variable	Fixed or GPM	Variable interest rate	Fixed or Variable
Prepayment Penalty	None	None	2% of loan for 1st 5 years	Negotiable
Title Held By	Borrower	Borrower	State of California	Borrower
Program Name	Federal Housing Administration	Department of Veterans Affairs	California Department of Veterans Affairs	Conforming Conventional
Max Loan	as of 10-1-02	as of 9-25-02	as of 8-1-02	as of 1-1-03
Units: 1 2 3 4	$253,650.00 $285,650.00 $347,100.00 $400,500.00	$322,700.00	Cal-Vet/VA $240,000.00 Cal-Vet 2000/97 $250,000.00 Cal-Vet 80/20 $250,000.00	$322,700.00 $413,100.00 $499,300.00 $620,500.00
Down Payment	3%	0%	VA/2% 97/3% 20%	Negotiable
Costs	1% Loan Origination Fee	1% Loan Origination Fee	1% Loan Origination Fee	Negotiable

- No secondary financing is allowed at the time of the original first trust deed loan.

- Buyers must contribute a minimum of 3 percent of their own funds to close the escrow.

- Mortgage insurance premium (MIP) is always required, requiring an MIP disclosure.

- Seller may pay anything above the 3 percent required of the total funds from the buyer.

- The FHA loan amount may not exceed the FHA appraisal.

- The FHA 203(b) and (i) are the most common FHA loan programs.

- FHA recurring closing costs include property taxes, fire insurance, and mortgage insurance.

- FHA nonrecurring closing costs are title insurance, appraisal, and escrow fees.

- Closing costs may be financed and added to loan amount, so long as the maximum loan amount is not exceeded and the buyer placed 3 percent of the sales price into escrow.

- FHA loans charge the buyer a one-time up-front premium (UFMIP).

- FHA loans charge the buyer an annual renewal premium, payable monthly.

- Lender requires certified escrow instructions from escrow.

- FHA loans require an impound account for taxes, hazard, and mortgage insurance.

WEB LINK

- The maximum loan amount varies in each county in California, and current information may be found at the following Web address: *https://entp.hud.gov/idapp/html/hicost1.cfm*.

The **Department of Veterans Affairs (DVA)** loan is handled through a loan broker, just as is the FHA loan. The Department of Veterans Affairs, once called the Veterans Administration (VA), does not take government funds and make real estate loans. The lender makes the loan, and the DVA becomes involved only in case of default. When a borrower defaults on a DVA loan, the lender applies to the DVA to be reimbursed for any loss. Escrow handles the loan similarly to any other loan, with the following specific exceptions:

- DVA allows 100 percent financing with zero cash down payment.

- The veteran is required to occupy the premises.

- The loan may have a fixed or variable interest rate.

- DVA loans have a funding fee that is determined by the type of loan and down payment.

- The buyer or the seller may pay the funding fee, or it may be added to the loan amount, provided the maximum loan amount is not exceeded.

- DVA allows a second trust deed with a DVA loan, so long as the total of all loans does not exceed the CRV and the interest rate on the second does not exceed the interest rate on the first trust deed.

- The seller may pay all of the veteran's normal closing costs.

- The veteran cannot be charged an escrow fee.

- Requires impound account for taxes and hazard insurance.

- Closing costs are regulated for what a veteran may pay for the following:
  - Appraisal report (certificate of reasonable value, or CRV);
  - Credit report;

– Funding fee;

– Loan origination fee;

– Recording fees; and

– Survey, inspection, or similar reports.

The **California Department of Veterans Affairs (Cal-Vet)** program may be handled by a loan broker as well as directly by the Cal-Vet offices. Cal-Vet escrows are not handled by independent escrow companies or by title insurance companies. The Cal-Vet escrow is handled by the Cal-Vet offices. When a non-Cal-Vet escrow officer is working with a **loan officer** who is handling a Cal-Vet loan, the following differences from other loans should be noted:

■ Cal-Vet loans typically have short escrows of under 35 days.

■ The veteran must occupy the property.

■ Secondary financing is allowed if approved by Cal-Vet.

■ Only 5 percent down payment is required, with as low as 2 percent down payment for those veterans who qualify.

■ Loan origination cost is minimal, approximately $50.

■ Each California county has a maximum loan amount, by area, based on the average county sales price.

■ Cal-Vet loans have a low, variable interest rate with no cap.

WEB LINK

■ Cal-Vet loans require an impound account for taxes, hazard, and life insurance.

■ For additional information visit: *http://www.cdva.ca.gov*.

Conventional Loans

The most common type of new loan obtained on real property is a conventional loan. The **conventional loan** market has the most flexible options available if the borrower has sufficient down payment to qualify for the loan. Some loans are unique to California for a particular area or to specific buyer qualifying criteria, such as California Housing Finance Agency (CHFA), Southern California Home Financing Authority (SCHFA), and Public Employees Retirement System (PERS) buyers. The escrow officer should be aware of the basics concerning most every new conventional loan, such as the following:

■ Conventional loans can be used for different types of property: residential, commercial, industrial, etc.

■ Conventionals have no maximum sales price, with limits usually set by a particular loan program.

- Large loan amounts outside of FNMA conforming limits are referred to as *jumbo loans*.

- Nonconforming loans are sometimes offered at higher rates and less favorable terms.

- LTVs can be up to 95 percent of appraised value with only 5 percent down payment.

- An impound account for taxes and insurance is required only if loan is greater than 80 percent LTV.

- Interest rates may be fixed, variable, biweekly, or tied to an independent index.

- Private mortgage insurance (PMI) is required for loans greater than 80 percent LTV.

- PMI has a single-premium payment at the beginning of the loan as a lump sum, and then ongoing monthly premiums are paid to the lender and prorated through escrow.

- Closing costs are negotiable by the parties to the escrow and a loan requirement.

The fixed-rate loan allows the escrow officer to precalculate the anticipated proration of interest so that the escrow officer can let the principal know the amount of the balance of cash that will be needed to close the loan. In the case of loans that are not fixed rate, the escrow officer often does not know until the last minute, when the loan documents arrive, the amount to charge on a per-day basis for the proration for the new loan. A few of the most common loan terms are discussed below so the escrow officer can be familiar with the most common ones that will be typically used in a normal escrow.

Jumbo.   The *jumbo loan* is one where the loan amount, not the sales price, exceeds the conforming FNMA or similar maximum loan amount. The maximum loan amount has continued to increase over time. At any particular time, a specific maximum dollar amount is considered a conforming loan. The escrow officer would need to be familiar with the jumbo loan terms. California's inland valleys have loans that are not high-cost loans, while the coastal, mountain, or desert resort regions are usually considered jumbo loan areas.

Fixed.   The *fixed-rate loan* is a loan that has the same consistent rate of interest from the beginning to the end of the loan term. The amount of interest per day is easy to calculate. Some fixed-rate loans may be converted to a variable-rate loan, just as many adjustable-rate loans may be converted to a fixed-rate loan at a later date.

Variable. The *variable-rate loan,* or *variable-rate mortgage* (VRM) or *variable interest rate* (VIR) loan, has an interest rate that goes up or down depending upon some extraneous event. The loan is usually tied to one of many types of an index. The fluctuations in the index would change the rate of the real estate loan interest rate. The escrow officer would need to have the actual loan documents in hand to calculate the closing cost information from the lender for a variable-rate loan.

Adjustable. The *adjustable-rate loan* is different from the variable-rate loan in that this type of loan usually remains at one rate for a fixed period of time, say one year, then adjusts at a particular date, such as on the annual anniversary date of the loan. The adjustment periods are spelled out in the loan in advance and usually have limits. These loans usually have what is referred to as a "cap." The maximum, or *cap,* that the interest rate and the payment may be increased over the life of the loan is set in the loan documents.

The escrow officer is frequently asked by the prospective borrower to explain what the terms mean in the loan documents that are being signed at escrow. The escrow officer should know how to explain normal clauses, how to contact the agent or loan officer if a more detailed explanation is required, and how to obtain the information from the loan documents to calculate the closing.

The escrow officer usually is required to provide information only about the closing costs and the various disclosures.

See page 451 for information on accessing common escrow forms.

■ LENDER PERSONNEL AND THE LOAN PROCESS

The escrow officer works closely with the buyer's lender to close escrow. It is important for the escrow officer to know the differences between various types of lenders and the personnel who work for lenders that the escrow officer would interact with in a normal real estate transaction. The **loan originator** may be either a mortgage loan broker, a mortgage loan banker, a commercial bank, or a savings or thrift institution. A private party or a credit union could originate a loan, but these are only a small part of the marketplace. The borrower works with the loan originator. Escrow has little contact with the loan originator.

After the loan is originated, the loan package is sent to the **loan processor,** who orders the credit report, the appraisal, and asks for a copy of the certified escrow instructions. The escrow officer works mostly with the loan processor.

In order to close the escrow, the loan is sent to the loan underwriter to approve or deny the loan based on the qualifications of both the property and the borrower.

Terms of Transaction

1. Buyer has deposited to escrow by Personal Check the sum of $4,000
2. Buyer will deposit, prior to close of escrow, the sum of $36,000
3. Buyer to obtain a New 1st Trust Deed loan in the amount of $360,000
4. To Complete the Total Consideration of $400,000

Furthermore, I will execute and deliver any instruments and/or funds which this escrow requires to show title as called for, all of which you are instructed to use on or before **March 17, 2XXX,** provided you hold a Policy of Title insurance with the usual title company's exceptions, with a liability of not less than **$400,000.00,** covering property in the City of Anytown, County of Anywhere, State of the USA, described as follows:

SUBJECT TO:
(1) General and special County and City (if any) Taxes for the current fiscal year, not due or delinquent, including any special levies, payments for which are included therein and collected therewith.

(2) Lien of Supplemental Taxes, if any, assessed pursuant to the provisions of Chapter 3.5 (commencing with Section 75) of the Revenue and Taxation Code of the USA.

(3) Covenants, Conditions and Restrictions, reservations easements for public utilities, districts, water companies, alleys and streets, rights and rights of way of record, if any; also exceptions of oil, has minerals and hydrocarbons, and/or lease, if any, without the right of surface entry.

(4) A New Conventional First Trust Deed to record, executed by Vestee herein, securing a Note for $360,000.00 in favor of National Mutual Savings, or order, bearing interest at a rate determined by the Lender, payable as required by the Lender. Buyers' execution of the loan documents shall be deemed approval of all terms and conditions contained therein. Escrow Holder is instructed to comply with all of the lender's requirements in connection with said new loan.

BUYER & PROPERTY TO QUALIFY FOR NEW LOAN: Buyer and property to qualify for and obtain the new loan(s) as set out above, and the depositing herein of the Lender's loan documents shall constitute satisfaction of this condition. The Buyer's signatures on the Lender's loan documents shall constitute their acceptance and approval of the terms and conditions contained therein.

You are not to be responsible in any way whatsoever nor to be concerned with the terms of any new loan or the content of any loan documents obtained

(Continued on next page)

by any party in connection with this escrow except to order such loan documents into the escrow file, transmit the loan documents to Buyer for execution and transmit the executed loan documents to lender. The parties understand and agree that you are not involved nor concerned with the approval and/or processing of any loan or the contents and effect of loan documents prepared by a lender.

The parties expressly indemnify and hold you harmless against third-party claims for any fees, costs or expenses where you have acted in good faith, with reasonable care and prudence and/or in compliance with these escrow instructions. You are not required to submit any such beneficiary statement and/or beneficiary demand to the parties for approval before the close of escrow unless expressly instructed to do so in writing. Should the party(ies) desire to preapprove any such beneficiary statement and/or beneficiary demand, the party(ies) requesting the same shall deliver separate and specific written escrow instructions to you.

When the underwriter approves the loan package, the file is sent to the loan committee for final approval. If approved, the loan is then sent to funding just prior to recordation. The recordation includes the grant deed, the reconveyance deed, and the trust deed.

After the loan has closed escrow, the escrow officer sends the loan documents to loan servicing, called "shipping the loan." The *servicing* is the process whereby an entity will collect the monthly payment according to the terms of the trust note.

■ LOAN PREQUALIFICATION

The loan process began before escrow was opened. At some point the borrower is **prequalified** by one or more prospective lenders or a loan broker/banker. The lender will determine the type of loan for which this particular borrower is qualified. The experienced lender knows the amount of reserves and cash the borrower will need.

The escrow officer could ask the real estate agent and the lender the following types of questions during the course of the escrow to be alert to transaction phases:

■ Is the transaction contingent upon the appraisal? If so, is the appraisal in?

■ Was the buyer prequalified for this particular loan? If so, is another loan available as a backup should the lender change the loan at the terms stated?

- Does the buyer have adequate reserves for additional closing costs if required? Or for additional down payment should the original loan desired not be approved?

- Does the buyer in this transaction have another property that must close escrow prior to the close of this transaction?

- Are tax exchange benefits important to any party to the transaction?

■ SENDING PRELIMINARY TITLE REPORT AND CERTIFIED ESCROW INSTRUCTIONS

The escrow officer composed the original set of escrow instructions, most likely using an escrow software program. The escrow officer would make the following copies of the original instructions: (1) copy for buyer to sign and return to escrow with an original signature; (2) copy for the buyer to retain as a copy for his or her records; (3) copy for the seller to sign and return to escrow with an original signature; (4) copy for the seller to retain as a copy for his or her records; (5) copy for the real estate brokerage office that handles the buyer; (6) copy for the real estate brokerage office that handles the seller.

The escrow officer will receive a copy of one set of original escrow instructions with signatures from the buyer and one set with original signatures from the seller. A copy of the commission authorization signed by the principals will also come back from each broker to the escrow holder. The seller will also return a signed, notarized grant deed prior to close of escrow.

Once the escrow holder receives the fully executed set of documents, escrow is open. When the escrow is officially opened, after having received all the original signatures, then the escrow holder can give the lender the certified copy of escrow instructions. The buyer and the seller do not sign the same set of escrow instructions. The escrow officer certifies that they have a copy of original signatures in their files. The lender must have certified escrow instructions and a copy of the sales contract purchase agreement. The lender's underwriter will look at both of these documents prior to loan approval to see that both contain information that matches on the loan requirements. For example, if the loan is an owner-occupied type of loan or a DVA loan that requires the veteran to occupy the property, the escrow instructions should not show that security deposits for a tenant in possession are being transferred from the seller to the buyer. The tenant occupying the property should have all interests terminated if the buyer is planning to occupy the premises.

After the escrow instructions have been prepared and sent out to the parties for signature, the escrow officer will be working with the title insurance company.

It is common that at this point the preliminary title report will be received from the title company. The escrow instructions normally call out that the buyer has a certain number of days from receipt of the preliminary title report for approval or disapproval. The escrow officer forwards the preliminary title report to the buyer and would note the number of days from delivery in order to comply with the written instructions. The number of days may vary, but in California the amount of time is typically printed on the purchase agreement. See the following textbox for the wording contained in the escrow instructions for Southern California (see page 451 for information on accessing sample instructions) that address the handling of the preliminary title.

> **PRELIMINARY TITLE REPORT:** Escrow Holder is instructed to order a copy of the Preliminary Title Report and, if any, covenants, conditions, and restrictions. Upon receipt, forward same to Buyer who will then have 14 days from receipt of same in which to approve or disapprove in writing. Absence of written notification by Buyer(s) of disapproval within specified time shall be deemed Buyer's approval of all documents and deposit of final closing funds by Buyer shall satisfy this condition in full.

The escrow officer will review the preliminary title report and compare the information with that found in the escrow instructions. See page 451 for information on accessing a sample preliminary title report. Note the following breakdown in the categories shown on the sample preliminary title report:

- General policy provisions
  - Offer to insure
  - Exceptions
  - Exclusions
- Schedule A
  - Existing title: Fee
  - Seller's name(s)
  - Legal description of the real property
  - Exceptions to ownership, usually mineral rights are excluded
- Schedule A-1
  - Note 1: Escrow funds and wire transfer information
  - Note 2: Beneficiary must sign off for loan payoff
  - Note 3: Statement of Information (SI) required from all parties
  - Note 4: Existing real property taxes; prorations

- Note 5: No conveyance within past six months
- Note 6: Nothing in this report would cause a decline in title insurance coverage
- Note 7: Situs. The physical property address and type of property: single family
- Note 8: The title insurance rate that is offered

■ Schedule B
- A: Property tax
- B: Supplementary property tax
- 1: Easement: Utility: Pipe
- 2: Easement: Utility: Electric
- 3: Easement: Utility: Phone
- 4: CC&Rs
- 5: Seller's existing first trust deed at time of loan origination
- 6: Seller's existing second trust deed at time of loan origination
- 7: Judgment against the seller
- 8: IRS lien against the seller
- 9: California Board of Equalization tax lien
- 10: Unsecured property tax lien
- 11: Child support lien

It is unlikely that the seller would have disclosed each of the above liens that may appear on the preliminary title report. Even if the liens had been disclosed by the seller, only the beneficiary can provide the actual current unpaid balance on each lien. Therefore, this would alert the escrow officer to recalculate the file to determine if there are enough proceeds to pay off all these liens to determine the net proceeds. It is not uncommon for sellers to realize that they are behind on a payment on their loan, but they are also unaware and unable to calculate the trustee's fees, accrued interest, late fees, and other penalties that may be assessed by the beneficiary. The title insurance company requires the original signature of the trustee on the reconveyance deed to perform a full loan payoff.

■ KEEP IN TOUCH: USING THE CONVERSATION LOG

To close escrow from the standpoint of the licensed agent, the key is follow-up and following the paper trail. There is always some type of problem to be resolved with all escrows. The key is good communications skills with everyone involved. Both agents need to stay in touch with their principals, and each needs to make sure to follow up on all contingencies. Expect no one else to follow up on the required details. The agents need to keep in contact with everyone who can cause any delay in the closing.

To close escrow from the title company standpoint means following the closing instructions. Upon receipt of the statement of information (SI), the title personnel must conduct the general index search. The reported information needs to be analyzed to see if it pertains to this particular escrow. Title personnel are responsible for property searches, people's names, liens, judgments, recording of documents, issuance of title insurance, paying off liens, and getting the balance of funds to escrow to be distributed to the seller and others. The key for title personnel is to clear all items as soon as possible. Complicated matters of public record can be cleared given adequate time and not rushed at the last minute. Timing is everything.

The escrow officer can close the escrow almost every time when all the parties follow the instructions in a timely manner. The escrow officer needs many items executed, such as the written escrow instructions, notarized deeds, signed IRS and other tax release forms, local and city property reports, disclosure forms, SI, insurance policies, and third party reports such as the termite clearance report.

■ LOAN FEES

Escrow instructions may indicate that a consumer is paying any loan fees through escrow, or the loan fee may be added into the unpaid loan balance. For example, refinance loan borrowers who want to obtain $100,000 net proceeds will sign loan documents indicating that they owe $105,000. The $5,000 in costs and fees may be added to the unpaid loan balance.

When the loan fees are paid through the escrow, several calculations must be made. Typically, one point equals 1 percent of the loan amount, not 1 percent of the sales price. The lender does not charge the borrower fees on the cash down payment placed into the escrow that is not being financed as part of the loan. Therefore, on a loan of $100,000, each point would be determined by multiplying the $100,000 times 1 percent. Points are commonly used to buy down an interest rate on a loan. This is used when a buyer has more cash than the minimum needed to close this transaction but wants a lower interest rate. In many cases the lower interest rate allows borrowers to qualify for a loan that they might otherwise not be able to obtain.

■ PRIVATE MORTGAGE INSURANCE

When a borrower applies for a loan where the LTV is greater than 80 percent of the appraised value, the lender will require mortgage insurance for most residential home loans. For property that is a second home or for rental-income property, mortgage insurance is required if the equity position of the borrower is less than 25 percent or 30 percent. Many buyers do not have 20 percent to 30 percent cash down payment. The mortgage insurance is a premium that is paid by the borrower on a loan and covers loss to the lender in case of default by the borrower. If the insurance policy is activated, the mortgage insurance company reimburses the lender or its assignee for losses that may be incurred if the loan is in default. Mortgage insurance allows lenders to offer a loan program with a lower down payment requirement to borrowers. The escrow officer must be aware of the up-front cost for the premium, if any, to calculate the amount of cash a borrower needs to close escrow. The escrow officer must calculate the final closing statement with any up-front mortgage insurance premium (UFMIP) premium and disclose these costs to the borrower.

The insurance premium is payable monthly together with the loan payment. Most policies require an initial premium amount to be paid at the close of escrow for one year in advance as part of the closing costs. This insurance premium payment is generally not tax deductible. The usual fee for the monthly premium payment is ½ of 1 percent, or 0.50 percent of the unpaid loan balance or original loan amount, whereas the one time fee is usually a flat fee. Calculations are shown in Chapter 11. One name for this insurance policy is mutual mortgage insurance (MMI).

An FHA loan requires the borrower to pay a **mortgage insurance premium (MIP).** The up-front mortgage insurance premium (UFMIP) is 1.5 percent of the loan amount. The escrow officer should note that if the transaction is for a condominium and the borrower is obtaining a new FHA loan, there is no UFMIP, only the monthly premium of ½ of 1 percent of the loan amount, divided by 12. If the borrower pays a UFMIP premium, the mortgage insurance is calculated at 2.25 percent of the loan amount. The FHA MIP may be financed. A veterans loan, a DVA Cal-Vet loan, does not have any mortgage insurance premium.

For a conventional loan, with nongovernment financing, the insurance is termed **private mortgage insurance (PMI).** The escrow officer is usually given a bill for the amount of the mortgage insurance premium. The entire loan is not insured, only the top percentage of the loan. Although rates are always subject to change in the financial community, the typical conforming loan insures the lender's risk by using the following coverage:

80.01 to 85 percent   Insurance covers the top 12 percent

85.01 to 90 percent   Insurance covers the top 25 percent

90.01 to 95 percent   Insurance covers the top 30 percent

■ LOAN CONDITIONS PRIOR TO LOAN DOCS

The loan usually is approved by the loan broker or lender with the following wording: "subject to condition." The reason the loan is not just approved or denied is because some pending information may not yet be available or completed. Some of the most common items that may not yet be received by the escrow company or the lender would include the following:

- Termite clearance final report
- Title insurance policy
- Flood insurance endorsement
- Mortgage insurance policy
- Reinspection by appraiser or lender that work requirements have been met
- Hazard insurance endorsement

The standard clause in the escrow instructions for Southern California (see page 451 for information on accessing sample instructions) states the following:

> **FIRE INSURANCE:** Buyer herein agrees to furnish new fire insurance prior to the close of escrow with sufficient coverage on the dwelling for replacement of subject property. Buyer to deposit sufficient funds as called for by Escrow Holder to pay first year premium at close of escrow. Lender's release of loan funds shall be deemed its approval of said insurance coverage.

The underwriter has approved the loan pending the obtaining of missing items. The missing item may be some additional credit verification on the borrower, or some work requirement on the property. Either way, the actual completion of the item may be handled outside of escrow, or it may be something that is handled by escrow. The escrow officer should determine which items are contained in the conditions.

A common item required prior to final loan approval is homeowner association information. If the association indicates a pending legal action and lawsuit in place, or work being performed currently on the property, then the lender would be concerned about the lien priority. The title insurance company and the lender want to make sure that the first trust deed is in first position. If a worker files a mechanic's lien for something performed on the property, the commencement date of that work is highly likely to be prior to the lender's original date of interest in the property. Likewise, a judgment from a lawsuit would also become an issue for the lender. The ALTA title insurance policy ensures that the first trust deed is in first position and that the second trust deed is in second position, if there is a second. No other liens are to interfere with the order of priority designated in the escrow instruction.

■ LOAN APPROVAL

The actual **loan approval** is handled by the lender's loan committee. Depending upon the size of the loan and the size of the firm, the loan committee may consist of only one person or be only the one underwriter. For very large loans, and nonconforming property, the loan committee may consist of many qualified experts who actually discuss the merits or risks of the particular loan. This portion of the transaction is handled outside of escrow and is of no concern to the escrow officer.

Notification to escrow of loan approval usually consists of a telephone call to inform the parties that it is okay to proceed with the loan and a faxed approval, allowing escrow to close. At this point in the transaction, the lender may call the escrow holder to verify specific information, such as the amount of cash down payment actually received by the escrow holder and placed into the escrow trust fund. In cases where the broker is acting as the loan agent and the transaction is handled by a broker-owned escrow, the escrow officer would be more closely aware of both the loan approval process and the drawing of the loan documents.

■ PREPARING LOAN DOCS

Once the conditions have been met to the satisfaction of the underwriter, the loan is forwarded to the document department where the actual loan documents are prepared on a computer. Industry software, such as DOC MGIC or MORT PRO, is used to generate the loan documents. These loan software programs are not linked to, nor are they part of, the escrow software programs currently on the market. The escrow software program, however, is often the same as that used by the title insurance company. This is especially true where the title company handles the escrow, such as in Northern California. The loan documents include the trust note that contains the terms and conditions of the loan.

When the loan documents are printed and ready for the buyer/borrower to sign, the lender may have the **loan docs** handled in one of the following ways:

- Retain loan docs; trustor will come to the lender to sign docs.
- Loan docs go to the mortgage loan broker for signature(s).

- Title company picks up loan docs; trustor signs loan docs at the title company.

- Title company picks up loan docs; trustor signs loan docs at the title company escrow company.

- Loan docs go to the escrow company for signature(s).

- Loan docs go to the real estate broker/escrow for signature(s).

- Traveling notary delivers loan docs to the trustor for signature(s).

■ GOOD-FAITH ESTIMATE AND REGULATIONS X AND Z

Federal law requires the lender to provide the borrower with a written estimate of proposed closing costs within three days of loan application, and another copy prior to closing. The law was designed to prevent the charging of illegal fees, such as kickbacks. One result of this law is that the borrower is provided with an idea of the costs and fees so that the borrower will have sufficient cash needed to close the escrow. The prescribed form also allows the borrower to compare one loan against another by comparing the annual percentage rate (APR) for the loan.

Regulation X requires the lender to provide the following specific disclosures:

- A good-faith estimate of closing costs on a prescribed settlement statement form

- Servicing disclosure statement indicating if the lender plans to collect the ongoing loan payments after the close of escrow or if someone else will likely perform this job

- Related business between the lender and affiliated business partners (escrow, title, real estate sales office, builder/developer, insurance, etc.)

- HUD-1(A) Final settlement cost statement (Regulation Z [Reg Z])

- Impound account statement showing the first year projected income and expenses

Regulation Z is a federal law that requires the settlement agent, the escrow officer, to itemize all charges imposed on the principals. The two-page form falls under the Real Estate Settlement Procedures Act (RESPA). All fees, commissions, costs, and expenses affiliated with the escrow must be placed on the form. The first page of the form contains the following:

- Summary of totals for the borrower's side of the transaction

- Summary of totals for the seller's side of the transaction

- Total gross amount of funds that are due from the borrower to close the escrow

- Total funds paid by or for the borrower

- Total gross amount of funds due to the seller at the close of escrow

- Total expenses paid by or for the seller that reduce the amount due to the seller

The first page of the form splits each side of the document. One side is for the buyer and one side is for the seller. The second page does not distinguish separate sides, but lists one column for the costs of the buyer and one column for the costs of the seller. Either party may pay a particular fee in a specific transaction, and when a cost is split between the principals, the fee is shown in both columns. All costs are listed. A HUD-1 form is shown in Chapter 11 with details on how escrow calculates each item.

■ FUNDING

After the signed loan docs are returned to the lender, a reviewer performs a final check to see that everything in the file is in order. The common questions to be asked include the following:

- Is every signature signed exactly as it is typed?

- Have all the places indicated been initialed by the trustor?

- Has a date been placed on all documents?

- Will all liens be cleared for taxes, judgments, and other unpaid items as shown on the prelim?

- Has the borrower instructed escrow on vesting?

- Are all required places properly notarized with a notary seal that is current?

- Has the source of funds been verified and delivered to escrow?

- Are all required inspections, maintenance, and repairs completed?

- Is the final credit check report in the file and checked against the original credit report?

- Is the desk/review appraisal information in the file?

Some lenders will then have the file sent to the audit department if discrepancies are found for another review. However, most files just move forward to be funded, where the money is transferred from the lender to the title insurance company.

The title insurance company pays off the existing lender of record. The title company deducts its own fees. The balance of the funds is transferred to the escrow account. The escrow officer writes checks to make the account end up with a zero balance after all disbursements. For the seller, the escrow officer writes the commission check, the termite company check, and a check to the seller for the balance of the proceeds. For the buyer, the escrow officer writes a check for any extra funds that were not spent on the escrow from the funds that were received. Some escrows close with funds held back with written instructions for future disbursement.

The loan documents are a very large package of documents that have many places that must be signed. The loan docs consist of agreements and disclosures. A brief list of loan docs consists of the following:

- Escrow instructions and title insurance company copy

- Insurance requirements

- Title wire instruction

- HUD-1 Settlement Statement and Truth-in-Lending (TIL), Regulation Z

- Interest rate disclosure (ARM, fixed rate, balloon, etc.)

- Riders: second home, condominium, 1–4 family, planned unit development (PUD)

- Occupancy affidavit

- Borrower's certification

- Notice: fair housing, flood

- Tax forms: W-9, IRS Forms 4506, 1099

- Loan service disclosure, impound account, assignment of deed of trust

- Deed of trust and trust note

It is extremely important that the escrow officer understand that most all loan docs are good only for the calendar month in which they are written. The docs automatically expire at the end of the current month. If the loan docs are drawn for the current month, but for some reason the signed documents were not returned to the lender in time to fund the loan in the same month, then new loan docs for the subsequent month would have to be redrawn. The reason for this involves the proration of the interest on the loan that the lender charges. Part of the loan documents consist of a page of instructions to the escrow officer and a page of instructions to the title insurance company. Sometimes lender instructions are good only for the day of closing. Part of the instructions is that the documents are only good for the current month. The title insurance company is instructed *not* to record the trust deed unless it is still the same calendar month.

Most lenders require from 48 hours' to 72 hours' advance notice from the escrow officer or title company that the loan will be closing. This is the time period where the actual money is wire transferred from the lender to the title insurance company.

Should the loan docs expire, a new complete set of loan docs would have to be prepared by the lender. This means extra costs to the borrower. In some cases, the actual loan commitment may also expire so that the terms and conditions of the loan are no longer available. If new loan terms come into play, the buyer may no longer qualify for the loan if the rate has been increased. This is where the "time is of the essence" clause in the real estate agreements is critical.

■ TRUST DEED

The first **trust deed** for a new conventional loan with an institutional lender is shown in Figure 7.2. The document is divided into several areas, as discussed in detail in the following list:

- Recordation information. The upper left corner contains the name of the title or escrow company, and the name of the beneficiary or trustor to whom the document will be mailed after recordation.

- County *recorder* information. The upper right corner contains the revenue tax stamps, and recordation information with date and time of recordation for the county in which the real property is located.

- Document title. The document is named with deed of trust or the deed of trust and assignment of rents. In case of default by the trustor, this later document gives the beneficiary the right to collect the rents, if any, and use these funds to offset the costs of the default. A review of a deed is given in Chapter 9, detailing the various areas of a grant deed, which is similar to a trust deed. A grant deed and a trust deed do, however, have differences. The items specific to the trust deed and not contained in the grant deed are described below. Some highlights of the body of the document include the following:

  - *Name of the trustor(s) and trustor vesting.* Names of trustor individuals or entity/entities who are conveying the title to the trustee, along with the manner in which the trustor holds title. **Vesting** is the manner in which an individual holds title to real property that may limit an owner's ability to possess or dispose of real property and may affect the party's income taxes.

FIGURE 7.2

Trust Deed

RECORDING REQUESTED BY
First City Title Company
**AND WHEN RECORDED MAIL THIS
DEED AND UNLESS OTHER WISE
SHOWN BELOW MAIL TAX
STATEMENTS TO**
Name
Address
City & State
Zip
Title Order No.   Escrow No.

Book _____

Page _____

File No. _____
_____ Recorded On _____
_____ at _____ A.M.
Official Records
Any County, CA
Anthony Bryce
County Recorder

Fees:
$ _____
B.

SPACE ABOVE THIS LINE FOR RECORDER'S USE

DEED OF TRUST AND ASSIGNMENT OF RENTS

The center section of many trust deeds contain an area with wording such as: On May 17, 1973 identical fictitious deeds of trust were recorded in the offices of the County Recorders at the Counties of the State of California, the first page thereof appearing in the book and at the page of the records of the respective County Recorder as follows:

COUNTY	Book	Page	COUNTY	Book	Page	COUNTY	Book	Page
Alameda	3540	89	Marin	2736	463	Santa Barbara	2486	1244
Alpine	19	753	Mariposa	143	717	Santa Clara	0623	713
Amador	250	243	Mendocino	942	242	Santa Cruz	2358	744
Butte	1870	678	Merced	1980	381	Shasta	1195	293
Calaveras	368	92	Modoc	225	689	Sierra	59	439
Colusa	409	347	Mono	160	215	Siskiyou	687	407
Contra Costa	7077	178	Monterey	877	243	Solano	1860	581
Del Norte	174	526	Napa	922	96	Sonoma	2610	975
El Dorado	1229	594	Nevada	663	303	Stanislaus	2587	332
Fresno	6227	411	Orange	10961	398	Sutter	817	182
Glenn	563	290	Placer	1528	440	Tehama	630	522
Humboldt	1213	31	Plumas	227	443	Trinity	161	393
Imperial	1355	801	Riverside	1973	139405	Tulare	3137	567
Inyo	205	660	Sacramento	731025	59	Tuolumne	396	509
Kern	4809	2351	San Benito	386	94	Ventura	4182	662
Kings	1018	394	San Bernardino	8294	877	Yolo	1081	335
Lake	743	552	San Francisco	8820	587	Yuba	564	153
Lassen	271	367	San Joaquin	2813	6		File No.	
Los Angeles	T8512	751	San Luis Obispo	1750	491	San Diego	73-299568	
Madera	1176	234	San Mateo	6491	600	Oakdale	565	290

The provisions contained in Section A, including paragraphs 1 through 5, and the provisions contained in Section B, including paragraphs 1 through 9 of said fictitious Deeds of Trust are incorporated herein as fully as though set forth at length and full herein. The undersigned, Trustor, requests that a copy of any notice of default and any notice of sale herein shall be served at the address hereinabove set forth, being the address designated for the purpose of receiving such notice or documents.

Signature of Trustor

STATE OF CALIFORNIA
COUNTY OF LOS ANGELES
On November 15, 20XX, the undersigned, a Notary Public in and for said County and State, personally appeared _____

known to me to be the person(s) whose name(s) (is)(are) subscribed to the within instrument and acknowledged that they executed the same.

Signature of Trustor

For Notary Seal or Stamp

- *Name of the trustee.* The name of the individual or entity (usually a company with perpetual life) that receives the bare title to the property.

- *Name of the beneficiary.* The individual or entity that the borrower is obligated to repay the debt to; the lender.

- *Operative words of conveyance.* The specific phrase that indicates the intent to convey or transfer title to the trustee that confers the power to "grant, transfer, and assign to trustee, in trust, with power of sale."

- *Assignment of rents.* The trustor assigns all rents, issues, and profits to the beneficiary. In a default, the beneficiary instructs the trustee to hire property management expertise to collect the rents. Default on rents from mismanagement is often the reason for the default on the loan.

- *Obligation.* The debt obligation stating the original loan amount is shown; the trustor agrees to pay this amount to the beneficiary as defined in the trust note and as described on the trust deed secured by the real property.

- *Trustor signature.* Each trustor must sign to acknowledge liability for the debt.

- *Notary.* A public notary acknowledges the signature of the trustor.

Figure 7.2 is a device that saves a great deal of recording fees, which reduces expenses to the principals. The beneficiary has the reverse side of the document recorded once in each county. The information contained on this side of the page is the preprinted fine print contained on the reverse side of the trust deed with standard clauses. No information that would be for any individual particular escrow, loan, or transfer would be contained on this side of the document. By recording each page once in each county, the 60 pages would cost a total of $600 if the average recording fee were $10 per county. Each county sets its own fees, and they vary over time. If this blanket recordation process were not used, then the title company would have to pay each time the page was recorded again.

For example, if a title company recorded 1,000 trust deed transactions in one year at $10 each, the lender would be charging buyers $10,000 for the front side of each document, which contains the transaction-specific information (name of the party, address, loan amount, etc.) as is shown in Figure 7.3, plus another $10,000 to record the back side of the page with the fine print clauses. This is a total of $20,000. If the title company recorded only the front page of 1,000 loans that gave reference to the recorded second page, the total expense would be only $10,000. This is a real cost savings when the borrower is the one who usually is responsible for the cost of the recording fees at the county recorder's office.

FIGURE 7.3

Deed of Trust

76 306693

Order No.   **CC 55555**

Escrow No.   **55555**

RECORDING REQUESTED BY:

GOLDEN FEDERAL SAVINGS & LOAN

When Recorded Mail to:

P.O. BOX 1677

GLENDALE, CA. 91206

FEE $5   R

4

LOAN No. 781290

SPACE ABOVE THIS LINE FOR RECORDER'S USE

DEED OF TRUST

THIS DEED OF TRUST is made this   12th   day of   NOVEMBER   19 76   amoung the Trustor,

_____ , HUSBAND AND WIFE   (herein "Borrower")

GOLDEN FEDERAL SAVINGS AND LOAN ASSOCIATION OF CALIFORNIA, a corporation   (herein "Trustee")

and the beneficiary, GOLDEN FEDERAL SAVINGS AND LOAN ASSOCIATION OF CALIFORNIA, a corporation organized and existing under the laws of THE UNITED STATES OF AMERICA, whose address is_____ San Francisco, California (herein "Lender")

Borrower, in consideration of the indebtedness herein recited and the trust herein created, irrevocably grants and conveys to Trustee, in trust, with power of sale, the following described property located in the County of
LOS ANGELES _____ State of California:

PARCEL 1:   THE NORTHERLY 150 FEET OF THE SOUTHERLY 480 FEET OF THE WEST HALF OF THE NORTHWEST QUARTER OF THE SOUTHWEST QUARTER OF THE NORTHEAST QUARTER OF SECTION 29, TOWNSHIP 4 SOUTH, RANGE 13 WEST, SAN BERNARDINO MERIDIAN ACCORDING TO THE OFFICIAL PLAT OF SAID LAND FILED IN THE DISTRICT LAND OFFICE OCTOBER 30, 1884, EXCEPT THEREFROM THE WESTERLY 179 FEET THEREOF.

PARCEL 2:   THE EASTERLY 12 FEET OF THE WEST HALF OF THE NORTHWEST QUARTER OF THE SOUTHWEST QUARTER OF THE NORTHEAST QUARTER OF SECTION 29, TOWNSHIP 4 SOUTH, RANGE 13 WEST, SAN BERNARDINO MERIDIAN, ACCORDING TO THE OFFICIAL PLAT OF SAID LAND FILED IN THE DISTRICT LAND OFFICE OCTOBER 30, 1884

EXCEPT THEREFROM THE NORTHERLY 20 FEET THEREOF, INCLUDED WITHIN THE LINES OF THE ELM VISTA DRIVE.

ALSO EXCEPT THEREFROM THE SOUTHERLY 480 FEET THEREOF.

which has the address of _____ Lomita
                                    (Street)   (City)

California 90717   (Herein "Property Address") ; (If Unknown, So State)
(State and Zipcode)

Together with all the improvements now or hereafter erected on the property, and all easements, rights appurtenances, rents (subject however to the rights and authorities given herein to Lender to collect and apply such rents) royalties, mineral, oil and gas rights and profits, water, water rights, and water stock, and all fixtures now or hereafter attached to the property, all of which, including replacements and additions thereto, shall be deemed to be and remain a part of the property covered by this Deed of Trust: and all of the foregoing, together with said property (or the leasehold estate if this Deed of Trust is on a leasehold): are herein referred in as the "Property":

To Secure to Lender (s) the repayment of the indebtedness evidenced by Borrower's note dated:
        NOVEMBER 12, 1976   (herein "Note"), in the principal sum of
SIXTY THOUSAND AND NO/100   Dollars,
with interest thereon, providing for monthly installments of principal and interest, with the balance of the indebtedness, if not sooner paid, due and payable on   NOVEMBER 15, 2006   : the payment of all other sums, with interest thereon advanced in accordance herewith to protect the security of this Deed of Trust: and the performance of the covenants and agreements of Borrower herein contained; and (b) the repayment of any future advances, with interest thereon, made to Borrower by Lender pursuant to paragraph 21 hereof (herein "Future Advances").
Borrower covenants that Borrower is lawfully seised of the estate hereby conveyed and has the right to grant and convey the Property, that the Property is unencumbered, and that Borrower will warrant and defend generally the title to the Property against all claims and demands, subject to any declarations, easements or restrictions listed in a schedule of exceptions to coverage in any title insurance ploicy insuring Lender's interest in the Property.

California 1 to 4 Family

■ BUYER AFFIDAVIT

Whereas the seller's affidavit is a statement signed by the seller to authorize escrow to pay any possible income taxes generated from the sale of the property, the buyer's affidavit is drastically different. In the first place, the seller could be receiving a large amount of cash at the close of escrow and could try to take those funds and place them where the seller would pay no income taxes on the gain realized from the sale of the property. However, the buyer is not receiving cash at the close of escrow under normal circumstances. Therefore, the buyer affidavit has far different rules.

The buyer affidavit is used only for properties with a sales price of under $300,000. The **buyer affidavit** is also called the Foreign Investment in Real Property Tax Act (FIRPTA). The purpose is to avoid paying 10 percent of the sales price to the Internal Revenue Service under IRC §1445. For a transaction where the price is greater than $300,000, the party should be advised to obtain information from a professional tax adviser. A sample of the standard California Association of REALTORS® (CAR) Buyer's Affidavit is shown in Figure 7.4.

■ CONTINGENCIES

The escrow officer must constantly watch the contingencies in the escrow that have not yet been met, meaning that escrow cannot yet close. The buyer usually has several contingencies that must be met. The most likely **contingency** found in virtually all escrow instructions is that the entire transaction is contingent upon the buyer obtaining the loan. The escrow officer would follow up on the status of the new loan to ensure the closing, especially if no agents are involved. However, other common contingencies also arise that keep the escrow from closing, such as the following:

- Loan commitment from the lender
- Increase in the amount of the initial deposit and placing the additional funds into the escrow by a specific date
- Approval of the termite report, inspections, roof certification, etc.
- Obtaining of a city permit, occupancy permit, or construction plans
- Delivery of the insurance policies (hazard, earthquake, flood, mortgage) endorsements
- Closing statement on the property the buyer is selling to have the funds to close this escrow
- Lease agreements on rental properties and security deposit information

FIGURE 7.4

Buyer's Affidavit

CALIFORNIA
ASSOCIATION
OF REALTORS®

BUYER'S AFFIDAVIT
That Buyer is acquiring property for use as a residence
and that sales price does not exceed $300,000.
(FOREIGN INVESTMENT IN REAL PROPERTY TAX ACT)

1. I am the transferee (buyer) of real property located at _____
_____.

2. The sales price (total of all consideration in the sale) does not exceed $300,000.

3. I am acquiring the real property for use as a residence. I have definite plans that I or a member of my family will reside in it for at least 50 percent of the number of days it will be in use during each of the first two 12 month periods following the transfer of the property to me. I understand that the members of my family that are included in the last sentence are my brothers, sisters, ancestors, descendents, or spouse.

4. I am making this affidavit in order to establish an exemption from withholding a portion of the sales price of the property under Internal Revenue Code §1445.

5. I understand that if the information in this affidavit is not correct, I may be liable to the Internal Revenue Service for up to 10 percent of the sales price of the property, plus interest and penalties.

   Under penalties of perjury, I declare that the statements above are true, correct and complete.

Date _____   Signature _____

                               Typed or Printed Name _____

Date _____   Signature _____

                               Typed or Printed Name _____

IMPORTANT NOTICE: An affidavit should be signed by each individual transferee to whom it applies. Before you sign, any questions relating to the legal sufficiency of this form, or to whether it applies to a particular transaction, or to the definition of any of the terms used, should be referred to an attorney, certified public accountant, other professional tax advisor, or the Internal Revenue Service.

Published and Distributed by:
REAL ESTATE BUSINESS SERVICES, INC.
a subsidiary of the CALIFORNIA ASSOCIATION OF REALTORS®
525 South Virgil Avenue, Los Angeles, California 90020

PRINT DATE

OFFICE USE ONLY
Reviewed by Broker
or Designee _____
Date _____

EQUAL HOUSING
OPPORTUNITY

FORM AB-11 REVISED 2/91

Source: Reprinted with permission, CALIFORNIA ASSOCIATION OF REALTORS®. Endorsement not implied.

■ BUYER-CAUSED ESCROW FALL OUT

Escrow is the neutral third party with legal obligations and responsibilities to safeguard the interest of everyone involved in the outcome of a real property transaction. The escrow officer is to see that the principals conduct business with minimum risk. The principals place the responsibility for handling the funds and documents in the hands and under the control of someone who is not the least bit affected by the outcome of the transaction. Even with all the safeguards taken by the impartial escrow party in the transaction, there are times when the buyer causes the transaction to fall out of escrow. A list of some typical items where the buyer was the major cause for the transaction falling out of escrow is as following:

- The buyer backs out because of lack of funds.

- A defect in the property is disclosed to the buyer after escrow opens.

- Buyer fails to disclose hidden costs.

- Buyer is dissatisfied because of poor treatment by the agent, lender, or others.

- Parties fail to agree on certain terms, such as points and closing costs.

- The lender fails to approve the property.

- The lender fails to approve the borrower(s).

- Buyer is frustrated by the purchase process and by lack of understanding of the normal events in closing an escrow.

THINK ABOUT IT

A buyer purchased a new home directly from a builder, which closed escrow on January 2, 2004. The contract required the buyer to pay all closing costs. To reduce costs, the buyer did not purchase title insurance.

On September 15, 2004, a mechanic's lien was filed in connection with work on the property in conjunction with the construction. The buyer tried to contact the builder who could not be located. Upon checking the records, the buyer found that the July 1 to June 30, 2003, property taxes had not been paid. What does the buyer owe?

Answer: The buyer bought the property subject to *all* existing liens, whether aware of any specific lien or not, and whether or not disclosed to the buyer. The buyer has primary responsibility for paying the lien holders for both the mechanic's lien and the property taxes.

By September, however, all of the mechanics' liens for the construction period would have expired. Over nine months later, the buyer is notified of the mechanic's lien. The unpaid worker would have had a maximum of 90 days after construction was completed to file on the property and notify the owner, which would have been no later than April 30, 2004. This assumes that the builder did not file a Notice of Completion. By September the legal period had expired and the buyer owes nothing.

The buyer does owe the property taxes, but not the mechanic's lien because the house was purchased subject to all existing liens, and real property taxes never go away until they are paid in full, including the late fee penalty.

■ CHAPTER SUMMARY

The escrow officer should become familiar with the types of lenders and the types of loans offered in the marketplace. An understanding of the loan criteria is important to closing the escrow. To accommodate an understanding of the loan process, this chapter reviewed many items regarding the obtaining of a new loan from various types of lenders for various types of loans. The federal government imposes several regulations that may be handled by the lender and by the escrow officer. The RESPA, Regulation X, and Regulation Z must be complied with. The lender must give the buyer a good-faith estimate of the cash needed to close the escrow and the annual percentage rate (APR) within three days of loan application. The HUD-1 closing cost statement must be given at the close of escrow on required qualifying properties and is often prepared by the escrow officer. The chapter ends with a discussion on problems with buyers causing the escrow to not close.

■ CHAPTER 7 QUIZ

1. The buyer affidavit is used for
   a. disclosing closing costs.
   b. tax purposes.
   c. prequalification.
   d. annual percentage rate (APR).

2. Which is a type of lender?
   a. Mutual mortgage insurance
   b. Private mortgage insurance
   c. Private party
   d. Mortgage loan broker

3. A type of government loan would include
   a. conventional.
   b. private party.
   c. Federal Housing Administration (FHA).
   d. Federal Deposit Insurance Corporation (FDIC).

4. A fictitious deed is
   a. where the same identical document is recorded in different counties on the same date.
   b. a phony document where forgery and fraud were most likely used.
   c. a deed used to record ownership to property for famous people who use an alias.
   d. where the title insurance company handles the funds rather than the escrow company.

5. When the escrow officer receives the preliminary title report, the document
   a. is forwarded to the buyer to review and approve or disapprove.
   b. is reviewed by the escrow officer to check details, such as the legal description.
   c. allows a specific number of days for the buyer to disapprove or it is approved.
   d. allows all of the above.

6. Mortgage insurance is usually always required on which type of loan?
   a. 80 percent conventional
   b. Cal-Vet
   c. Veteran's loan
   d. FHA

7. The escrow officer should know that the loan process would follow in which order?
   a. Conditions, approval, docs, funding
   b. Regulation X, recording trust deed, conditions
   c. Funding, approval, docs, recording trust
   d. Regulation Z, conditions, funding, approval

8. Which document requires a public notary stamp/seal prior to recordation?
   a. Preliminary title
   b. Trust deed
   c. Trust note
   d. Title insurance policy

9. Which is *NOT* a federal regulation regarding a real estate transaction?
   a. RESSTA   c. REG Z
   b. RESPA   d. HUD-1

10. Loan documents would most likely consist of
    a. preliminary title report, insurance requirements, and occupancy affidavit.
    b. loan application, FICO credit rating score, fair housing notice.
    c. title wire instruction, tax forms, review appraisal, underwriter take sheet.
    d. trust deed and note, HUD-1 settlement statement, impound account disclosure.

CHAPTER EIGHT

LOAN ESCROWS

■ KEY TERMS

all-inclusive trust
   deed (AITD)

annual percentage
   rate (APR)

assumption

foreclosure

loan documents

loan servicing
   disclosure

notice of sale

private party loan

publishing period

real estate owned
   (REO)

refinance (refi)

Regulation B

Regulation X

Regulation Z

reinstatement period

repossession

request for notice
   of default

RESPA

short sale

subject to

three-day right of
   rescission

Truth-in-Lending
   (TIL)

wraparound

■ CHAPTER OVERVIEW

Chapter 6 dealt with the seller's existing loan on the property, and Chapter 7 concerned the buyer's obtaining of a new loan with the purchase of the property. Chapter 8 deals with the refinance of the property by the existing property owner and the areas of real estate finance termed "creative financing."

Some buyers seek to purchase a property where the lender has taken back the property under a default or foreclosure under some term of the loan. When the finance company or bank owns the property after the original trustor has lost the property through a foreclosure action, it is termed real estate owned (REO).

Chapter 8 also discusses the documents used and the tasks performed by the escrow officer when a private party carries back a second trust deed for some part of the purchase price. The all-inclusive trust deed (AITD), assumption, taking title subject to an existing loan, and wraparound loan are described and discussed. The chapter ends with information about the buyer's acceptance of the loan offered by the lender.

■ LEARNING OBJECTIVES

At the conclusion of Chapter 8, you will be able to

- understand why the escrow officer must comply with lender requirements;
- give a definition for each request used for a private party loan;
- list and explain the common forms used in a refinance loan escrow;
- differentiate between loan assumption or subject to existing loan escrows; and
- explain the procedures for an escrow involving a foreclosure.

■ THE LOAN ESCROW (REFINANCE—REFI)

One of the most common types of escrows handled by an escrow officer during times of relatively low interest rates is the refinance escrow. The existing property owner probably has an existing loan on the property. The existing loan may be at a higher interest rate, and the **refinance (refi)** may lower the rate on the loan that would lower the owner's monthly payments. Or, because the property may have appreciated in value, the owner may wish to pull equity out of the property, referred to as a "cash out loan." The escrow officer should be familiar with the various forms and procedures needed to close the escrow. The escrow instructions would include something similar to the following wording:

> Escrow is instructed to obtain a Deed of Trust, securing One Note, payable as per its terms, with an approximate unpaid balance of $_____, in favor of _____ payable in _____ installments of $_____, including interest at the rate of _____ % per annum. Borrower's execution of the **loan documents** constitutes their full approval of all terms and conditions contained therein.

Prior to the escrow instructions being ordered, the borrower has probably already contacted a lender. In most cases the Good Faith Estimate has already been sent to the borrower that shows the projected closing costs. At this point, the lender may call to open the loan escrow. See page 451 for information on accessing a sample loan escrow for the transaction. Many documents and forms will be used as part of a refinance transaction, a list of which is provided below, along with discussion of each item:

- Loan escrow instructions. These pages spell out the terms and conditions that the escrow must abide by.

- Federal **Regulation Z,** or **Truth-in-Lending (TIL),** Disclosure. The lender must disclose to the applicant, prior to being committed to the loan, the **annual percentage rate (APR)** according to federal law. The form shows the finance charge, the amount financed if all payments were made over the life of the loan, and the amount of total payments that would be made to the lender. The form also indicates if the loan is a variable-rate loan, the insurance requirements, the security for the loan, late fee charge, prepayment penalty, assumption information, and life/disability insurance information. In the case of a refinance, and not on a new loan made with the purchase of a home, the borrower has a **three-day right of rescission.** The creditor must notify the borrower in writing that he or she has a three-day right of rescission to cancel the loan by giving the lender written notice.

- Federal **Regulation X,** or Real Estate Settlement Act, Estimate. The HUD good-faith estimate of closing costs is a federal law that requires the lender to disclose the estimated amount of fees, commission, costs, and expenses that the borrower will have to pay. It also gives the estimated monthly payment, including impounds. The HUD-1 form gives the final figures of closing costs.

- Federal **Regulation B,** or Disclosure Regarding Settlement Service Provider. A federal law that requires the lender to tell the borrower if it will or will not service the loan after the close of escrow.

- **RESPA** Servicing Disclosure Statement. Disclosure to the borrower that the loan originator plans to keep the loan or plans to assign/transfer the loan after the close of escrow to another entity. The loan servicer collects the ongoing monthly payments and maintains the impound account and monitors the ongoing hazard insurance policy on the property to protect the lender.

- California Insurance Notice. Indicates that the lender cannot require its own insurance affiliated firm as a condition of the loan and that the borrower may seek his or her own insurance.

■ Notice of Right to Copy of Appraisal Report. Indicates that the borrower is entitled to receive a copy of the written appraisal report for the property securing the loan.

■ Quitclaim Deed. The lender will require the borrowers to transfer the property out of their trust and back into their individual names of the trustees. The borrowers need to remember to transfer the property back into their trust after the close of escrow. Escrow usually will not prepare the deed to transfer from the individuals back into the trust agreement as an accommodation to that party.

■ Preliminary Change of Ownership Report. This form must be completed *prior* to the transfer of the subject property and is discussed in Chapter 9 and seen in Figure 9.10.

■ Hardship. When the first monthly payment is less than 30 full days after the close of escrow, the borrower signs a statement indicating that making the payment is not a hardship on the borrower. If a loan closes on the second day of this month, and the first payment is made on the first day of next month, a hardship letter would be required.

■ **Loan Servicing Disclosure** Statement. This statement gives the percentage of loans transferred for the past several years and indicates that the originating lender either (1) intends to keep the loan and handle the loan servicing; or (2) does not intend to keep the loan and will not handle the servicing of the loan after the close of escrow.

■ Important Notice Regarding California Property Taxes—Supplemental Tax Bill. This form advises the borrower that the tax assessor may revalue the real property and charge an additional, supplemental tax bill payable to the tax collector. The supplemental tax bill covers the remaining portion of the current fiscal tax year until the next, full-year assessment.

■ Request for Copy or Transcript of Tax Form—IRC Form 4506. This form allows the lender to contact IRS directly to obtain a transcript of or verification within 7 to 10 working days. The form must be received within 60 days from date of signature. The figures given on the loan application and the copies of tax returns provided to the lender must match the records that IRS indicates for the borrower.

■ Privacy Notice. The lender indicates that it will not give private, personal information about the borrower to nonaffiliated third parties.

■ Hazard Insurance Disclosure. A disclosure stating that the lender cannot require hazard insurance for any amount greater than the amount of coverage to replace the improvements. Land is not insured, only improvements.

- California Consumer Credit Score Disclosure (Civil Code 1785.20.2). Indicates the credit agency and the credit score given by each agency.

- Address Certification. A form that indicates where the payment books and future correspondence are to be mailed.

- Borrower's Certification. The borrower guarantees that all the facts represented are true.

- Flood Zone Notification. This form tells the borrower if the property on which the loan is secured is or is not located in a specified flood hazard zone area and whether or not the lender will require flood insurance to be paid by the borrower if it is. The area is identified by the Federal Emergency Management Agency (FEMA) and may or may not have the National Flood Insurance Program (NFIP) available.

- Notice to Borrower—Impound/Escrow Account. The borrower is given three options: (1) a voluntary impound account on a loan where such is not required by the lender but the borrower prefers to have the taxes and insurance collected as part of the normal loan payment; or (2) the borrower does not want to have an impound account, and the borrower will pay his or her own property taxes and insurance separate from the lender; or (3) the lender requires that an impound account be established as part of the loan approval process. An escrow where the loan amount does not exceed 80 percent of the LTV does not usually require an impound account.

- Fair Lending Notice. Under the Housing Financial Discrimination Act of 1977, a lender may not discriminate against making a loan due to neighborhood or geographic area or based on race, color, religion, sex, marital status, national origin, or ancestry. An alleged violation would be filed with the California Department of Real Estate for "redlining."

- W-9, Request for Taxpayer Identification Number and Certification. The purpose of this form is to report income paid to the borrower and interest paid on the loan for income taxes.

- Specific Closing Instructions. This form specifies which documents are part of the loan documents required prior to funding. The payoff requirements and loan terms are included on the form. Title insurance requirements and secondary financing disclosure are stated.

The escrow procedures for a refinance escrow would include the following 13 procedures:

1. Print the escrow computer generated instructions; make two additional copies of the escrow instructions, and one copy of everything else to be mailed out.

2. Upon receipt of the beneficiary demands, as shown in Figure 6.2, fax a copy of the demand to the seller/broker to enable him or her to review the figures, along with a place for the trustor to sign, and return to acknowledge receipt of the dollar amounts.

3. Upon receipt of the borrower's signed instructions, keep the original in the office file, make a copy of the statement of information (SI), as shown in Figure 4.3, and fax to the title officer with the title order number on the document for reference.

4. Key the terms of the approved loan into the computer along with any special closing requests for amendments and deeds, as shown in Figures 6.10, 7.2, 7.3, and 9.3.

5. Fax the order for loan documents to the lender with instructions on where the prepared loan documents are to be sent, e.g., escrow, title company, broker, lender.

6. Fax a request to receive the lender's closing instructions to enable escrow to create an estimated closing statement, or ask the lender to fax escrow the estimated closing statement that the lender prepared for the borrower.

7. Deliver the estimated closing statement, amendments, and any deeds requiring signatures.

8. Fax the order for the insurance request with directions on where the policy or endorsement is to be delivered, e.g., escrow, title company, lender, etc. Instruct the insurance company to fax the evidence of insurance for approval to escrow before the original policy is sent to the lender.

9. Have the borrower(s) sign the loan documents.

10. Return the signed loan documents to the lender.

11. Send the original documents that are being recorded, along with attachments and the original preliminary change of ownership report (PCOR), as shown in Figure 9.10, to the title officer and instruct the officer to set up for recording.

12. Instruct the title company to forward the final funding figures to escrow after the loan has funded. (The lender should receive instructions that the lender is not allowed to fund the loan until *all* conditions of the escrow have been met, such as all demands have been received, the escrow has received clear funds from the borrower, and all parties have signed all documents.)

13. Create the final closing statement, HUD-1 form, as shown in Figure 12.5, and checks to be disbursed to the principals.

■ FORECLOSURES

A **foreclosure** occurs when a borrower defaults on a loan. Law prescribes the foreclosure procedure, and a judge or the trustee determines how the assets of the borrower will be allocated and applied toward debts. In California, any person having an interest in the real property—on which the debt property was attached as security for the loan debt—has the right to redeem the property at any time after the obligation is in default, but only up to five days prior to the date of the foreclosure sale. Then the redemption period ends. During the last five days prior to the sale, the debtor must deliver all funds due: unpaid loan balance, late fees, trustee fees, etc. Under the trust deed system, all sales are final and no one has the right to any subsequent interest after a final foreclosure sale and transfer of property ownership to a subsequent purchaser of a foreclosure.

California uses the nonjudicial trust deed foreclosure procedure because the original trust deed and note contained a clause or "working" indicating power of sale language. The proceedings most often take place without a court date, saving time and money. Eliminating the need for a court action speeds up the recovery time for the lender.

The escrow officer may be alerted that the existing loan is in default by the agents who open the escrow on the beneficiary demand statement or by the principal. Under foreclosure proceedings, the escrow officer needs to be especially cognizant of the time periods. The borrower may be refinancing an existing loan to pay for the defaulted loan or may be selling the property to try to beat the date of the foreclosure proceedings. Virtually all lenders will try to work with the escrow officer if a buyer is already in escrow to purchase the property so that the lender does not actually have to hold a foreclosure auction to regain funds for the property under a default on the loan.

The escrow officer should be aware that when a lender actually takes a property back and the banking system audits that lender, the assets of the bank may be tied up or the bank rating of the bank might be reduced. This has a negative effect on the financial institution. The bank would prefer to have the escrow close with a disassociated purchaser of the property who pays off the loan in full, along with the foreclosure costs. However, the escrow officer should also be aware that the bank must proceed with the foreclosure action during the time period that the current escrow is also being processed. It is often a neck-and-neck race, sometimes appearing to be a tie, over which will close first, the escrow or the foreclosure. The bank has an agreement with all the investors who placed funds with the bank to continue to proceed with the foreclosure action. The escrow officer must remember that acceleration of the loan in order to exercise the due-on-sale clause in the event of default on the loan is at the option of the lender.

In the case where a junior lien is also on the property, that investor has the legal right to make up all the payments, penalties, and costs accrued for the default on the senior lien(s), and add those sums to the junior lien, then start a foreclosure action on the junior lien. More discussion in this area is given below in the private party loans section on page 220. In the case of junior liens in default, the holder of the note may wish to obtain rights to ownership of the property rather than just recovery of the money. When the junior lien holder exercises the right to foreclose, even though an escrow is already open with a buyer who would pay off all debts on the property, the escrow may not close fast enough to stop the foreclosure action by that junior loan. When the escrow officer sends out the beneficiary demand statement, careful attention should be paid to determine whether or not the junior lien holder is returning the document. If the escrow holder has obtained the beneficiary demand and is in a position to close fast enough, the junior lien holder has no recourse except to accept the funds and be paid off in full with no further interest in the property. If the junior lien holder is holding up the close of escrow by not returning the documents needed so escrow can proceed with action to transfer ownership to the property, the escrow officer should notify the parties as to the lack of receipt of the demand.

The beneficiary demand shown in Chapter 6, Figure 6.4, is for a senior loan that is in default. The document shows that the loan is in foreclosure and gives a specific date that must be met to avoid the foreclosure sale date. In most cases, there is adequate time to close the escrow without undue concern about the trustee's foreclosure date.

Repossession

When a borrower defaults on a loan, the lender has the legal right to take possession of the item on which the loan was based, termed **repossession.** Two sets of loans are common. An unsecured loan is one made on the good-faith promise to repay the loan. A collateralized loan is based on the value of the asset pledged, called a "secured loan." Real estate loans use the appraisal to determine the value of the property at the time the loan is placed, and the real property is the ultimate security for the loan in case of default.

If property sells for a higher amount than the existing loan amount in the foreclosure transaction, then the value of the appraisal is irrelevant because the sale generated enough funds to retire the debt. However, when a loan is not paid off and the borrower is not making the monthly payment obligation, the lender must take action to acquire the property on which the security of the loan was based.

Once the lender has acquired the legal rights to the premises, then the lender may sell the property to recover the funds necessary to retire the debt. The foreclosure auction is where the lender sells the property at a public auction to recover the unpaid balance on the original loan. But, before the auction can take

FIGURE 8.1

**Trust Deed Foreclosure
Procedures**

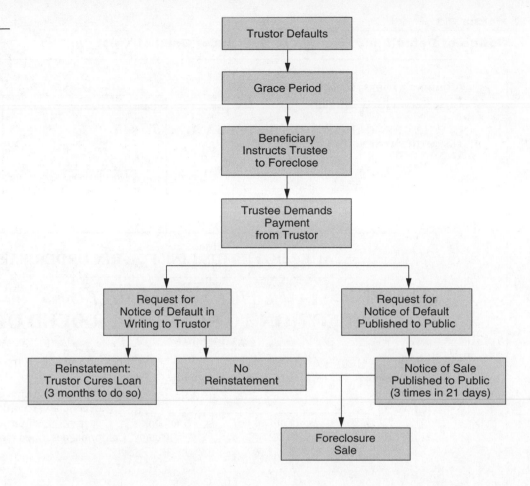

place, the lender must take the proper legal steps. Figure 8.1 shows the trust deed foreclosure steps in flowchart format. A default action includes the following:

■ Written notice in the trust note for what constitutes default.

■ Written notice for the number of days that constitute a grace period or remedy to default.

■ Written notice to trustor making a "demand" for the payment that is past due.

■ Beneficiary notifies the trustee of trustor's default and instruction default action.

■ Trustee gives written notice by recording a **request for notice of default** (see Figure 8.2).

■ Trustor has three-month **reinstatement period** on the loan in which to pay all past due payments, late fees, plus trustee costs, fees, and charges (runs until five days before the sale date).

FIGURE 8.2

Notice of Default and Election to Sell Under Deed of Trust

RECORDING REQUESTED BY

First City Title Company

AND WHEN RECORDED MAIL THIS DEED AND
UNLESS OTHER WISE SHOWN BELOW MAIL TAX
STATEMENTS TO

Name
Address
City & State
Zip
Title Order No.   APN:

Book
Page
File No.
          Recorded on

_____at_____
Official Records of the
County of Western, California
C. B. McCormack
Registrar-Recorder/County Clerk

Fees:
$ _____
B.

SPACE ABOVE THIS LINE FOR RECORDER'S USE

NOTICE OF DEFAULT
AND ELECTION TO SELL UNDER DEED OF TRUST

NOTICE IS HEREBY GIVEN: That _____ TITLE INSURANCE COMPANY, a
Corporation, is Trustee under a deed of trust dated _____, 20____
executed by_____ Trustor, to secure obligations
in favor of _____ Beneficiary, recorded _____
_____, 20____ as document no. _____, in book _____, page _____ of Official Records
in the office of the Recorder of _____ County, California, described land therein as:

(legal description)

said obligations including _____ note for the sum of $ _____.

That the beneficial interest under such deed and the obligations secured thereby are owned
By the undersigned;

That a breach of, and default in, the obligations for which such deed is security has
occurred in that payment has not been made of:

*** sample *** *The February 1, 2005, and all subsequent installments are now in
default with interest paid to January 1, 2005.*

That by reason thereof, the undersigned, present beneficiary under such deed, has executed
and delivered to said Trustee a written Declaration of Default and Demand for Sale, and has
deposited with said Trustee such deed and all documents evidencing obligations secured thereby,
and has declared and does hereby declare all sums secured thereby immediately due and payable,
and has elected and does hereby elect to cause the trust property to be sold to satisfy the obligations
secured thereby.

Dated:_____   _____

_____*Real Estate Owned*

- Trustee has 21 days to place three ads for the **publishing period** to place a foreclosure notice in a public paper of local circulation where the property is physically located (situs), not where the defaulting trustor lives, for the **notice of sale.**

- Foreclosure sale takes place at the date, time, and location published to the public with all sales final and no period of redemption or further action available to the defaulting trustor.

Real Estate Owned (REO)

A property that has been foreclosed upon by a lender where the lender now owns the property is referred to as **real estate owned (REO).** Once a lender on a defaulting trustor has foreclosed a property, the property may not be immediately available for sale to the public. Sometimes the lender cannot get clear title to the problem because of a cloud on the title, such as a mechanic's lien interest or the rights of other entities.

A borrower and lender may agree not to hold a foreclosure sale, but may instead use a deed in lieu of foreclosure. In this case the trustor voluntarily surrenders ownership interest to the property by signing over a deed of ownership to the lender. This saves the lender a great deal of legal expenses and may lessen the damage to the trustor's credit.

The Short Sale

A **short sale** occurs when the lender has to sell the property for less than the amount that would retire the debt. A deficiency judgment in California where a trust deed is used is almost unheard of because the lender will often accept a short sale.

The total amount of proceeds received from the forced sale would be applied toward all the expenses, which include other items in addition to the unpaid loan. In the event of an actual foreclosure auction as shown in Figure 8.3, the escrow officer should understand the lien priority order. The following is the order in which proceeds are distributed:

- Trustee's costs to sell. They include notifying junior lien holders of default and intent to sell, publishing the auction, holding the auction, and distributing the funds.

- Federal income tax lien. Often a trustor in default on the loan payment is also behind on the payment of income or property taxes. The escrow officer should expect tax liens as part of a short sale or foreclosure escrow. The federal tax lien has priority over the state income tax as state income tax has priority over local property tax liens.

- State taxes. Personal income taxes, business income taxes, business sales tax, and payroll taxes for a defaulting trustor who owns a business as a sole proprietor are common. Because the business is held as an individual, the taxes may also be a lien against the individual who is in default on the home loan that may have been used to finance the business.

- Property taxes. When a trustor does not make the house payment, the taxes, insurance, and homeowner association fees are expected to be in default. Only the local property taxes take priority over all other items except trustees' costs and income taxes.

- Homeowner association (HOA) dues and assessment(s). The unpaid house payment usually always means that the association fees are also in default. Because the HOA was recorded prior to the current property owner taking title to the property, the HOA is normally in a priority position.

- Trust deed (TD) lien(s). The lender of record for the property is usually next in position. The first TD usually has the first position. Junior liens may or may not come next. The priority order would depend upon the time and date of recordation of the subsequent holder of trust deeds.

- Mechanic's lien(s). If the work began prior to the first TD, then the mechanic's lien would have priority above the first TD. If the worker began work for the benefit of the property (architect, lumber yard materials, contractor, etc.) after the first TD was recorded, but before the second TD was recorded, then the order of payoff would be the first TD, then the mechanic's lien, then the second TD. The date and time of recordation would not prevail as the commencement of the work sets the mechanic's lien priority.

- Homestead. If the owner has filed a homestead, the amount due on the homestead would come after all of the above list of priority items.

- Judgment creditor. Any unsecured lien, such as a credit card debt or an auto loan in default would fall into the next category. The default on the unsecured loan, meaning not secured by the real property but may be secured by the car, may include a personal injury award or lawsuit award. The judgment creditor may be the party seeking to sell the property and may not realize that the lien priority list above will be paid prior to the court judgment payment.

- Homeowner/trustor. Should any funds remain after all creditors have been paid, the amount, if any, would then be paid to the defaulting trustor, as determined by law.

The escrow instructions will indicate that all items requested by the lender must be fully complied with as per the written beneficiary demand. In addition, the lender will stipulate that the terms of the short pay are only as of a specific date. In the foreclosure sale, the lender either gets the property back (to sell at a future date) or gets *all* of the money due on the defaulting loan. In the case of the short pay, the lender is agreeing to accept less than the full amount that is due. The lender will also demand a copy of all documents of the escrow and additional documents on the part of the defaulting trustor to make sure that the trustor is not making money off the transaction while the lender is taking less than the full amount due. The lender will demand a form showing all the assets of the defaulting trustor to see if there is any other source of funds the trustor could use to make up the difference in the loss.

For the buyer, the transaction is simply a regular purchase, usually with a short escrow. The buyer obtains an appraisal with the new lender and signs loan documents for a new loan to close the escrow. If the escrow is not in a position to close until one day too late, the buyer will lose the purchase, and the trustee may transfer title to another entity at the foreclosure sale.

The escrow officer has to be aware of last-minute liens placed on the property that the title insurance company picks up late because the lien was not placed until the last minute. For example, a buyer is purchasing a property that is in foreclosure and just prior to close of escrow the title company runs an update title search and discovers a previous undisclosed lien. The defaulting trustor has failed to pay the local water bill for the past six months, and the agent tells escrow that the full-sized back-yard swimming pool was empty a few weeks ago but is now full, heated, and being used by the trustor and all the neighbors for a going-away party by the defaulting trustor. Some surprise, last-minute utility bills show up as liens totaling a very large amount. This situation is not all that uncommon.

The lender will accept less than the full amount because of the mortgage insurance. When the lender takes 97 percent of the amount that is due, the lender must show all the documentation under the terms of the mortgage insurance policy and then, after the close of escrow on the short sale, must file a claim with the insurance company to recover the 3 percent that was not realized at the time of the close of escrow. In other words, the lender actually receives no loss. The lender first goes after the defaulting trustor, then goes to recover any loss from the insurance.

HUD/VA REO

When a conventional lender has property held by the REO department, a quick sale is utilized to turn around the lender's portfolio to remove the negative collection from the lender's record. When government-guaranteed or government-insured loans are involved, the process is slower and requires more paperwork from all parties.

Should the escrow officer become involved in a Department of Veterans Affairs (DVA) REO, then the VA Form 26-6705c, as shown in Figure 8.3, is used for the purchase offer to DVA. The form would show the property address, the amount of net cash offered to DVA after adjusting the price and costs of the

FIGURE 8.3

DVA Offer to Purchase Foreclosure Property

OMB Approved No. 2900-0029
Respondent Burden: 5 Mins.

Department of Veterans Affairs

ADDENDUM TO OFFER TO PURCHASE AND CONTRACT OF SALE

PRIVACY ACT STATEMENT: The information collected on this form will serve as an offer to purchase a VA-acquired property. The acquisition and sale of such property is authorized by law (38 U.S.C. 3720(a)(5j). You are not required to furnish the information but are urged to do so since it is vital to proper action by VA in processing your offer to purchase the subject property. Responses may be disclosed outside the VA only if the disclosure is authorized under the Privacy Act, including the routine uses identified in VA system of records, 55VA26, Loan Guaranty Home, Condominium and Manufactured Home Loan Applicant Records, Specially Adapted Housing Applicant Records; and Vendee Loan Applicant Records - VA, published in the **Federal Register.**

RESPONDENT BURDEN: Public reporting burden for this collection of information is estimated to average 5 minutes per response, including the time for reviewing instructions, searching existing data sources, gathering and maintaining the data needed, and completing and reviewing the collection of information. Send comments regarding this burden estimate or any other aspect of this collection of information, including suggestions for reducing this burden, to VA Clearance Officer (723), 810 Vermont Ave NW Washington, DC 20420; and to the Office of Management and Budget, Paperwork Reduction Project (2900-0029), Washington, DC 20503

ADDENDUM TO PURCHASE OFFER DATED	PM NO.

1. PROPERTY ADDRESS *(Include No., Street or Rural Route, City or P.O., State and ZIP Code)*

NOTICE: On cash sales with outside financing, the amount of any discount points, loan origination fees and closing costs which the buyer expects VA to pay, must be itemized below. VA reserves the right not to pay costs which in VA's judgment are unreasonable or not customary, and the purchaser will be liable for any additional monies required to close. The amount of the sales commission and for sales bonus to be paid (up to the maximum authorized by VA) must also be itemized below. <u>All spaces must either contain an amount or the word "none".</u> If an amount is not entered, it will not be paid by VA.

2. CASH OFFER ☐			3. TERM OFFER ☐		
A. OFFERED PRICE			A. OFFERED PRICE	$	
DEDUCTIONS:			LESS (-) DOWNPAYMENT	$	
B. DISCOUNT POINTS	$		C- AMOUNT OF VENDEE LOAN REQUESTED *(Item A - Item B)*		$
C. LOAN ORIGINATION FEE	$		D. TIMES W CASH EQUIVALENT FACTOR		%
D. CLOSING COSTS	$		E. CASH EQUIVALENT VALUE (CEV) OF LOAN AMOUNT		$
E. SALES COMMISSION	$		F. PLUS (+) FUNDING FEE (% of Item C)		
F. SALES BONUS	$		G. PLUS (+) DOWNPAYMENT *(Item B)*	$	
G. TOTAL DEDUCTIONS		$	H. ADDITIONS TO CEV OF LOAN AMOUNT *(Item F + Item G)*		$
H. NET TO VA		$	I- CASH EQUIVALENT VALUE OF TOTAL OFFER *(Item E + Item H)*		$
			J. LESS (-) SALES COMMISSION	$	
			K. LESS H SALES BONUS	$	
			L. TOTAL DEDUCTIONS *(Item J + Item K)*		$
			M. NET TO VA *(Item I - Item L)*		$

<u>VA WILL ACCEPT THE OFFER WHICH PROVIDES THE HIGHEST NET RETURN TO VA, BASED ON CORRECT CALCULATIONS. ERRORS IN THE COMPUTATION OF THE NET TO VA MAY RESULT IN THE OFFER BEING REJECTED AND ANOTHER OFFER ACCEPTED.</u>

4A. PURCHASER	4B. CO-PURCHASER
5. AGENT	6. BROKER

7. BROKER'S TAX ID NO/SOCIAL SECURITY NO.

VA FORM *SEP 1992* **26-6705C**	PURCHASE OFFER NO.	* U.S. G.P.O. 1993 343-134174109

subject offer, and the terms of the offer. The DVA accepts the offer that nets the DVA the highest net amount after all income and all expenses. Because the DVA guarantees the lender against any loss, the lender must document any actual loss. Once all the required documentation is approved, the lender submits the loss for the difference between the funds realized from the sale and the funds expended to obtain the guaranteed amount up to the maximum.

The Housing and Urban Development (HUD) agency oversees the Federal Housing Administration (FHA) homes. In order to make a bid on a HUD-owned repossessed REO home, the brokers and buyers must go through the HUD approved real estate office that has exclusive rights to the list of properties available. To find information on California properties, access the HUD Web site and click on the Northern or Southern California link (see Figure 8.4). This will direct you to the appropriate broker Web site, which lists various information, some of which is the following:

- E-bids
- Results of bids
- Broker registration
- Broker information
- Law enforcement officer program
- Teacher certification program
- Forms

WEB LINK

The Web site address is as follows: *http://www.hud.gov/homes/index.cfm.*

The HUD-9548 form is shown in Figure 8.5 as the sales contract to be prepared by a HUD-approved broker and electronically transmitted with the following information for the property disposition program:

- Purchaser's names and complete property address
- Manner in which the buyer will take title to the property
- Bid amount and initial deposit
- Occupancy information

In addition to completion of the form, the buyer must also submit the following forms:

- Disclosure and release regarding mold

FIGURE 8.4

HUD Web Site

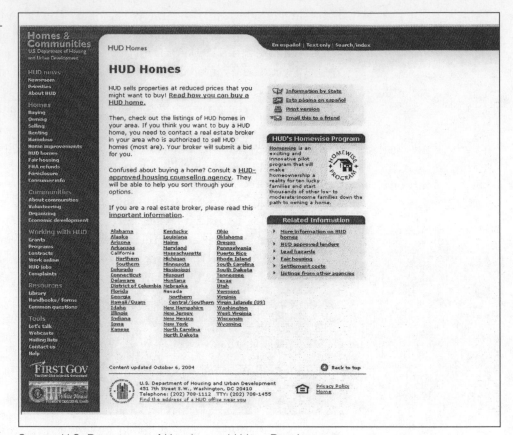

Source: U.S. Department of Housing and Urban Development

■ Letter of commitment on lender's letterhead

■ Photocopy of earnest money deposit—cashier's check payable to HUD or the buyer's name

■ HUD Addendum A—forfeiture and extension policy, covering:
  – Allowable closing costs paid by buyer, including the following:

Appraisal fee

Credit report

Flood certification

Home inspection

Homeowner's warranty

Loan discount points

Loan origination fee

Prepaid and escrow items for owner-occupied purchases

Recording fees and transfer tax

FIGURE 8.5

HUD Foreclosure Bid Form for Electronic Submission

Sales Contract

Property Disposition Program

U.S. Department of Housing and Urban Development
Office of Housing
Federal Housing Commissioner

HUD Case No.

1. I (We), _____
   (Purchaser(s)) agree to purchase on the terms set forth herein, the following property, as more particularly described in the deed conveying the property to the Secretary of Housing and Urban Development:

   _____ .
   (street number, street name, unit number, if applicable, city, county, State)

2. The Secretary of Housing and Urban Development (Seller) agrees to sell the property at the price and terms set forth herein, and to prepare a deed containing a covenant which warrants against the acts of the Seller and all claiming by, through or under him. Title will be taken in the following name(s) and style: _____ .

3. The agreed purchase price of the property is .... ➤ 3. $_____

   Purchaser has paid $_____ as earnest money to be applied on the purchase price, and agrees to pay the balance of the purchase price, plus or minus prorations, at the time of closing, in cash to Seller.   The earnest money deposit shall be held by _____ .

4. ☐ Purchaser is applying for FHA insured financing [☐ 203(b), ☐ 203(b) repair escrow, ☐ 203(k)] with a cash

   down payment of $_____ due at closing and the balance secured by a mortgage in the amount of

   $_____ for_____ months (does not include FHA Mortgage Insurance Premium,
   prepaid expenses or closing costs Seller has agreed to fund into mortgage.).

   ☐ Said mortgage involves a repair escrow amounting to $_____
   ☐ Purchaser is paying cash or applying for conventional or other financing not involving FHA.

5. Seller will pay reasonable and customary costs, but not more than actual costs, nor more than paid by a typical Seller in the area, of obtaining financing and/or closing (excluding broker's commission) in an amount not to exceed .... ➤ 5. $_____

6a. Upon sales closing, Seller agrees to pay to the broker identified below a commission (including
    selling bonus, if offered by seller) of .... ➤ 6a. $_____

6b. If broker identified below is not the broad listing broker, broad listing broker will receive a commission of: .... ➤ 6b. $_____

7. The net amount due Seller is (Purchase price [Item 3] less Items 5 and 6) .... ➤ **7. $**_____

8. Purchaser is: ☐ owner-occupant (will occupy this property as primary residence) ☐ investor
   ☐ nonprofit organization ☐ public housing agency ☐ other government agency.   Discount at closing: _____ %
   Discount will reduced by amounts, if any, listed on Line Items 5 and 6.

9. Time is of the essence as to closing. The sale shall close not later than _____ days from Seller's acceptance of contract. Closing shall be held at the office of Seller's designated closing agent or _____ .

10. If Seller does not accept this offer, Seller ☐ may ☐ may not hold such offer as a back-up to accepted offer.

11. Lead based paint addendum ☐ is ☐ is not attached; Other addendum ☐ is ☐ is not attached hereto and made part of this contract.

12. **Should Purchaser refuse or otherwise fail to perform in accordance with this contract, including the time limitation, Seller may, at Seller's sole option, retain all or a portion of the deposit as liquidated damages. The Seller reserves the right to apply the earnest money, or any portion thereof, to any sums which may be owed by the Purchaser to the Seller for rent.** Purchaser(s) Initials:_____   Seller's Initials:_____

13. This contract is subject to the Conditions of Sale on the reverse hereof, which are incorporated herein and made part of this contract.
    Certification of Purchaser: The undersigned certifies that in affixing his/her/its signature to this contract he/she/it understands: (1) all the contents thereof (including the Conditions of Sale) and is in agreement therewith without protest; (2) he/she/it is responsible for satisfying itself as to the full condition of the property; and (3) that Seller will not perform repairs after acceptance of this contract.
    Purchaser(s): (type or print names & sign)   Purchaser(s) Address:

Purchaser(s) Social Security Number (SSN) or Employer Identification Number (EIN) (include hyphens) Phone No:	Date Purchaser(s)Signed Contract:
Seller: Secretary of Housing and Urban Development By: (type name & title, & sign) X	Date Contract Accepted by HUD:

Certification of Broker: The undersigned certifies that: (1) neither he/she nor anyone authorized to act for him/her has declined to sell the property described herein to or to make it available for inspection or consideration by a prospective purchaser because of his/her race, color, religion, sex, familial status, national origin, or disability; (2) he/she has both provided and explained to the purchaser the notice regarding use of Seller's closing agent; (3) he/she has explained fully to the purchaser the entire terms of the contract, including Condition B on the reverse hereof; and (4) he/she is in compliance with Seller's earnest money policy as set forth on HUD forms SAMS-1111, Payee Name and Address, and SAMS-1111-A, Selling Broker Certification, which he/she has executed and filed with Seller.

Broker's Business Name & Address: (for IRS reporting) (include Zip Code)	Broker's EIN or SSN: (include hyphens)	SAMS NAID:
	Signature of Broker: X	Broker's Phone No:
Type or print the name and phone number of sales person:		

This section for HUD use only. Broker notified of:	Authorizing Signature & Date:
☐ Acceptance ☐ Back-Up No. _____	X
☐ Rejection ☐ Return Earnest Money Deposit	

Previous editions are obsolete   ref. Handbook 4310.5   form HUD-9548 (1/99)

FIGURE 8.5

HUD Foreclosure Bid Form for Electronic Submission (Continued)

Conditions of Sale

A. All assessments, including improvement assessments which are available for payment without interest or penalty for advance payment, taxes, rent, and ground rent, if any, shall be prorated as of the closing date.

B. **Seller makes no representations or warranties concerning the condition of the property, including but not limited to mechanical systems, dry basement, foundation, structural, or compliance with code, zoning or building requirements and will make no repairs to the property after execution of this contract. Purchaser understands that regardless of whether the property is being financed with an FHA-insured mortgage, Seller does not guarantee or warrant that the property is free of visible or hidden structural defects, termite damage, lead-based paint, or any other condition that may render the property uninhabitable or otherwise unusable. Purchaser acknowledges responsibility for taking such action as it believes necessary to satisfy itself that the property is in a condition acceptable to it, of laws, regulations and ordinances affecting the property, and agrees to accept the property in the condition existing on the date of this contract. It is important for Purchaser to have a home inspection performed on the property in order to identify any possible defects. If FHA insured financing is used, up to $200 of the cost to perform the inspection may be financed into the mortgage. Names of home inspection companies can be found in the yellow pages of your telephone directory under the heading "Home Inspection Services.**

C. If financing is involved in this transaction (Item 4), Purchaser agrees that should he/she/it fail to provide documentation indicating that proper loan application was made in good faith within 10 calendar days of the date this contract was accepted by Seller, and/or thereafter otherwise to put forth good faith efforts to obtain necessary financing, Seller shall have the option of rescinding this contract and retaining all or a portion of Purchaser's earnest money deposit.

D. Seller may rescind this contract and return all or a portion of Purchaser's earnest money deposit under the following conditions:
1. Seller has not acquired the property.
2. Seller is unable or unwilling to remove valid objections to the title prior to closing.
3. Seller determines that purchaser is not an acceptable borrower.

Tender of the deposit shall release the Seller from any and all claims arising from this transaction.

E. Purchaser may not perform repairs nor take possession of the property until sale is closed. Risk of loss or damage is assumed by Seller until sale is closed, unless Purchaser takes possession of the property prior thereto, in which case State law shall apply. (1) If sale involves FHA insured financing and after damage the property no longer meets the intent of Minimum Property Standards (MPS), Seller may, at its option, perform repairs or cancel the contract and return Purchaser's full earnest money deposit. If, after damage, the property still meets the intent of MPS, Purchaser has the option of accepting the property as-is, with a purchase price adjustment at Seller's sole discretion, or cancelling the contract and receiving refund of full earnest money deposit. (2) If sale does not involve FHA insured financing, Seller will not repair damage but may, at Seller's sole discretion, reduce the sale price. Purchaser has option to cancel the contract and receive refund of full earnest money deposit. Tender of the earnest money shall release Seller from any claims arising from this transaction.

F. If this property is being offered with FHA insured mortgage financing available, Seller's acceptance of this contract constitutes a commitment to insure, conditioned upon Purchaser being determined by Seller or Direct Endorsement Underwriter to be an acceptable borrower and further conditioned upon Seller's authority to insure the mortgage at the time the sale is closed.

G. **Purchaser understands that Seller's listing price is Seller's estimate of current fair market value.**

H. No member of or Delegate to Congress or Resident Commissioner shall be admitted to any share or part of this contract or to any benefit that may arise therefrom, but this provision shall not be construed to extend to this contract if made with a corporation for its general benefit.

I. Purchaser and Seller agree that this contract shall be binding upon their respective heirs, executors, administrators, successors or assigns but is assignable only by written consent of the Seller.

J. If this property was constructed prior to 1978, Seller has inspected for defective paint surfaces (defined as cracking, scaling, chipping, peeling or loose paint on all interior and exterior surfaces). Seller's inspection found no defective paint surfaces, or if defective paint surfaces were found, Seller has treated or will treat such defective surfaces in a manner prescribed by Seller prior to closing. **Purchaser understands and agrees that the Seller's inspection and/or treatment is not intended to, nor does it guarantee or warrant that all lead-based paint and all potential lead-based paint hazards have been eliminated from this property.** Purchaser acknowledges that he/she/it has received a copy of a pamphlet which discusses lead-based paint hazards and has signed, on or before the date of this contract, the Lead-Based Paint Addendum to Sales Contact - Property Built Before 1978. Purchaser understands that the Lead-Based Paint Addendum must be signed by all Purchasers and forwarded to Seller **with** this contract. Contracts which are not in conformance with these requirements will not be accepted by Seller.

K. The effective date of this contract is the date it is accepted (signed) by the Seller.

L. If the amount stated in Item 5 exceeds actual and typical financing and/or closing costs, such excess shall not be paid by Seller and may not be used by Purchaser to reduce amount(s) due Seller.

M. Seller's policies and requirements with regard to earnest money (including forfeiture thereof), extensions of time in which to close the sale, back-up offers, and allowable financing and/or closing costs are detailed in instructions issued to selling brokers.

N. Seller makes no representations or guarantees that the property will, in the future, be eligible for FHA insured mortgage financing, regardless of its condition or the repairs which may be made.

O. **Warning: Falsifying information on this or any other form of the Department of Housing and Urban Development is felony. It is punishable by a fine not to exceed $250,000 and/or a prison sentence of not more than two years. (18 U.S.C. 1010, 3559; 3571)**

P. This contract contains the final and entire agreement between Purchaser and Seller and they shall not be bound by any terms, conditions, statements, or representations, oral or written, not contained in this contract.

Previous editions are obsolete   ref. Handbook 4310.5   form **HUD-9548** (1/99)

Survey

Title insurance

– Allowable closing costs paid by HUD/seller, including the following:

Brokerage commission

Proration of property taxes, special assessments, HOA fees, utility bills

Escrow fee

Recording fees

HOA transfer fee

HOA documents cost

– Seller disclosure

– Walkthrough inspection

– Buyer certification

– Lead-based paint addendum—property built before 1978

WEB LINK

@

When a successful bidder is awarded a HUD home, the HUD-approved escrow will handle the transaction. The current escrow firm that answered a request for proposal (RFP) to bid on handling HUD escrow business in California and other states is Escrow Max. Escrow Max's Web site address is as follows: *escrowmax.com*.

Because no other escrow firm may be used, any real estate professional working in the business would need to know the forms and procedures required for this type of escrow where items are not negotiable but are set by the seller, HUD. Some of the cost requirements are listed above, and other items are available from the escrow company.

All HUD-REO escrows are handled by the government-agency-approved firm that varies by area. All approved forms and procedures must be followed, even though the existing loan is being paid off and the buyer is obtaining a new loan.

The purpose of the property disposition is to have FHA property that has been foreclosed on put back into the general public circulation so that the subsequent purchaser, after the defaulted trustor no longer has any ownership interest in the property, can improve the property and start paying the new lender and paying the property taxes. These properties are usually sold on an "as is" basis with specific warranties from the seller excluded in writing with no recourse available to the buyer should the buyer find problems after change in ownership.

■ PRIVATE PARTY LOANS

Sellers may not need all of the cash equity they could receive at the close of escrow upon the sale of their property. When the buyer gets a new 80 percent conventional loan through a new lender, the sellers will often have adequate funds to pay any debts they may have and be able to purchase a new property with the remaining cash, even after paying the costs to sell.

In this case the seller may bank or invest the balance of the extra funds and live off the interest received from that principal amount. However, the interest rate that banks pay is relatively low. The amount received in invested funds may be at higher risk of loss of the principal than the seller is willing to accept. Therefore, using the funds to assist the buyer to obtain the property is often in the seller's best interest. If the banks are paying 2 percent to 5 percent interest on savings, an owner carryback second trust deed secured against the property they are selling is often a better investment, where the seller may get 8 percent to 10 percent. If the seller receives interest-only payments, this lowers the monthly payment for the borrower and makes it easier for the buyer to qualify. The terms of **private party loans** such as these are usually more favorable. The escrow officer will normally include some phrase in the escrow instructions regarding the usury law for the interest rate, such as the following:

> You shall not be responsible in any way whatsoever nor are you to be concerned with any question of usury in any loan or encumbrance, whether new or of record, which may arise during the processing of this escrow.

The buyer benefits due to lower closing costs because the seller does not usually charge points on the loan, and the buyer does not pay a loan origination fee or other lender fees.

One reason for a small second trust deed is the benefit on cost reduction for the buyer. If a buyer has 15 percent cash down payment but not the balance of the 5 percent cash to put as a down payment, the buyer cannot obtain an 80 percent LTV. Any loan amount above the 80 percent requires mortgage insurance, in addition to any other extra expenses that may be incurred.

For example, as is shown in Table 8.1, for an 80 percent loan based upon a $400,000 sales price, the cash down payment required would be $80,000, but the buyer only has $60,000 in cash. The loan payment on the 80 percent loan of $320,000 at 7 percent interest would be $2,129 per month. The buyer cannot get this loan with only 15 percent down. If the seller carried back a 5 percent second of $20,000 at 7 percent with interest-only payments, the interest payment would be $116.67. The buyer's payment would be the $2,129 + $116.67 for a total monthly payment of $2,245.67. Each year the benefit of home ownership should

TABLE 8.1

80–15–5 Versus 85–15 Loan Comparison

	80–15–5	85–15
Price	$400,000.00	$400,000.00
Down	− $60,000.00	− $60,000.00
New 1st Mortgage	$320,000.00	$340,000.00
2nd Mortgage	$20,000.00	$0.00
Monthly Payment on 1st; Years 1–5	$2,129.00	$2,262.06
Monthly Payment on 2nd; Years 1–5	$116.67	$0.00
Mortgage Insurance	+ $0.00	+ $141.67
	$2,245.67	$2,403.73
Monthly Payment on 1st; Years 6–30	$2,129.00	$2,262.06
Tax Return Paid on 2nd	$4,000/year	$0.00
Up-front mortgage insurance	$0.00	$5,590.00

allow the buyer to receive at least $2,000 in an income tax refund due to income tax laws. If the buyer sends the seller $2,000 each year for only 5 years, the second would be paid off in half the time, thus reducing the total monthly payment to only $2,129 per month.

However, if the buyer placed the 15 percent cash down payment and obtained an 85 percent loan, the lender would require mortgage insurance. The 85 percent loan at 7 percent for 30 years on the $400,000 purchase price would mean a loan amount of $340,000 with a monthly payment of $2,262.06 plus the mortgage insurance. The mortgage insurance has two components, the one-time up-front fee paid as part of the closing costs, plus the ongoing monthly insurance premium. The up-front fee varies, depending upon the type of loan. For a first-time home-buyer where the rate is 1.75 percent of the $340,000 loan amount, the additional cash needed to close the escrow would increase $5,590. Because the buyer did not have $20,000, an extra $6,000 at closing is to be paid. In addition, the monthly fee is 0.5 percent of the $340,000 divided by 12 months for an additional $141.67 per month on the $340,000 loan amount. The total monthly payment would be the $2,262.06 plus the $141.67, for a total of $2,403.73.

By having the seller carry back a 5 percent second, the buyer's monthly payment is reduced by $200 per month. The $200 per month could also be applied toward reducing the unpaid principal on the loan, if desired. Therefore, the escrow officer can see why principals would request that the escrow draw up the necessary documents to effect a second trust deed.

The escrow officer is the entity that draws up the trust deed and fills in the promissory trust note. The seller is accepting a note in lieu of cash at the close of escrow. The escrow officer fills in the beginning date of the trust note as the date of the close of escrow. The escrow officer would need to obtain from the seller the terms for the following:

- Interest rate

- Monthly payment

- Due date for monthly payment

- Late fee and date when due

- Ending date on the term of the loan

- Notice requirements in case of default

Several clauses are included in the documents that the escrow officer would complete. In order for the escrow officer to have the authority to insert the clauses, written instruction to that end would be required in the escrow instructions themselves. These same instructions should be in the purchase contract between the principals. One common clause is the alienation clause that does not allow another person to take over the existing loan. Should the trustor put another name, an individual that is currently alien, or foreign, to the existing title, then the alienation clause would be triggered by the beneficiary lender. The following phrases commonly convey the words:

Alienation clause. If the trustor or his or her successors in interest shall sell, convey, or alienate the property described herein, or any part thereof, or any interest herein, in any manner or way, whether voluntary or involuntary, any indebtedness or obligation secured hereby, at the option of the holder hereof, and without demand or notice, shall immediately become due and payable.

Late charge. The trust note would typically contain a clause regarding the late fee made for any late payment. The escrow officer would insert the following words:

In the event any payment is not paid within 10 15 [circle one] days of the due date, the trustor shall pay to the beneficiary a late charge of $_____ or _____ percent of the then unpaid balance, in addition to each payment due and unpaid.

Seller financing disclosure. A second trust deed would be prepared by the escrow officer. California Civil Code 2956-2967 gives information on the regulation covering seller-financing disclosures. The parties specify the terms and conditions that the trust note or financing security instrument, such as an all-inclusive trust deed, or AITD, will contain. The escrow officer is responsible for completion of the form and ensuring that the document is recorded. The escrow instructions would normally include the following type of wording in connection with the trust deed and trust note information:

> You shall not be responsible in any way whatsoever nor are you to be concerned with any question of usury in any loan or encumbrance, whether new or of record, which may arise during the processing of this escrow.

Even though the seller agreed to help finance part of the purchase price to assist the buyer, the benefit may be a higher sales price or a more secure and higher interest rate than the seller could obtain from other investment opportunities. The seller's largest concern is not the security of the property, which has a recorded second trust deed placed upon the title records to the property, but is default. The seller is always concerned about what happens if the buyer continues to make the small monthly payment on the second but does not have the funds to make the payment on the new first trust deed. To protect the seller, the escrow officer is instructed to prepare another document to be recorded with the trust deed, termed the Request for Notice of Default.

The Request for Notice of Default instructs the beneficiary of the first trust deed to notify the beneficiary of the junior lien holder(s) that the payment on the first has not been made. In this event the holder of the second can make up the payment on the first, add that amount to the unpaid balance of the second, and start foreclosure on the second.

The escrow officer prepares the Request for Notice of Default with the information on the first trust-deed holder. The form instructs the trustee of the first trust deed to notify the holder of the second trust deed when a default has caused the beneficiary of the first trust deed to begin foreclosure procedures. The trustee notifies the holder of the second trust deed within ten days after the notice of default is recorded. The form that the escrow officer would complete is shown in Figure 8.6.

■ THE LOAN ASSUMPTION OR SUBJECT TO ESCROW

When a written assumption agreement is executed between the lender and a prospective purchaser of real property, then the loan is assumed. An **assumption** always requires that the existing lender be notified about the transfer of ownership to the property. The escrow officer would include in the escrow instructions written direction to write the beneficiary for a demand, or beneficiary statement, often called a "statement of condition." Most beneficiaries charge a fee for providing the demand information.

FIGURE 8.6

Request for Notice

RECORDING REQUESTED BY
First City Title Company

AND WHEN RECORDED MAIL
THIS DEED AND
UNLESS OTHER WISE SHOWN BELOW MAIL TAX
STATEMENTS TO

Name
Address
City & State
Zip
Title Order No.   Escrow No.

Book
Page
File No.

Recorded on
_____at_____
Official Records
County of Los Angeles, California
Conny B. McCormack
Registrar-Recorder/County Clerk

Fees:
$ _____
B.

SPACE ABOVE THIS LINE FOR RECORDER'S USE

REQUEST FOR NOTICE

In accordance with Section 2921b, Civil Code, request is hereby made that a copy of any notice of

Default and a copy of any notice of sale under of deed of trust recorded _____, 20___

In Book _____ Page _____ of official records of _____County, (or filed for record

with recorder's serial No._____, County) California, executed by_____

as trustor in which _____

is named as beneficiary and _____

as trustee be mailed to _____ where the address is:

_____

Signature_____

APN or AIN: xxx-xxx-xx

Dated:_____   _____

                                                            _____

STATE OF CALIFORNIA   _____
COUNTY OF_____
On this the _____day of _____ , 20___   _____
The undersigned, a Notary Public in and for said
County and State, personally appeared _____
_____, known to me
to be the person ___whose name ____subscribed
to the within instrument and acknowledged that   **FOR NOTARY SEAL OR**
_____executed the same.   **STAMP**

_____
          Signature of Notary
_____
         Name (Typed or Printed)

Some lenders insist that a buyer formally assume the loan, except in the case of an FHA or DVA loan. Conventional loans are usually only assumable if they are adjustable-rate loans, and then only for one time. Fixed-rate conventional loans are usually not assumable. The primary liability for repayment of the debt shifts from the original trustor to the subsequent, or new, trustor. In the case where a due-on-sale provision is contained within the terms of the trust note, the escrow officer would notify the lender of the proposed transfer of ownership and obtain the terms and conditions under which the lender would allow the assumption. The escrow officer would record a Substitution of Liability form at the county recorder's office as part of the formal loan assumption. The escrow instructions would typically contain the following wording for a loan assumption:

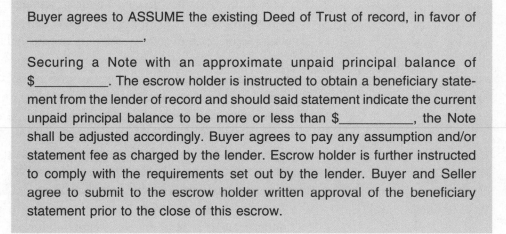

Buyer agrees to ASSUME the existing Deed of Trust of record, in favor of

_____,

Securing a Note with an approximate unpaid principal balance of $_____. The escrow holder is instructed to obtain a beneficiary statement from the lender of record and should said statement indicate the current unpaid principal balance to be more or less than $_____, the Note shall be adjusted accordingly. Buyer agrees to pay any assumption and/or statement fee as charged by the lender. Escrow holder is further instructed to comply with the requirements set out by the lender. Buyer and Seller agree to submit to the escrow holder written approval of the beneficiary statement prior to the close of this escrow.

Most lenders have standard forms, fees, and procedures when using an assumption agreement. If no due-on-sale clause is contained in the trust note, the lender cannot change the terms of the loan by raising the interest rate on the loan or making any other demands of the borrower that are not in the original note. Thus, if a note contains an assumption clause, it is normal that the terms of assumption also be contained. The escrow officer should expect to see instruction from the existing lender to pay 1 percent of the current unpaid balance as a one point assumption fee. Some government loans contain a clause that indicate that the lender must approve the subsequent borrower's credit report and pay a flat fee of $100 to change the beneficiary records to mail the subsequent payments to the new borrower.

Where no due-on-sale clause exists in the trust note, the lender cannot require the purchaser to sign an assumption agreement, so that the borrower could take title **subject to** the existing loan, rather than execute an assumption agreement with the existing lender. In markets where interest rates are rising or a prepayment penalty is contained in the note, the subject to clause becomes very popular. The borrower would rather have the lower interest rate and lower payment on the existing loan than pay the cost for a new loan. Typical escrow instruction wording is:

> Buyer agrees to take title "SUBJECT TO" the existing Deed of Trust of record, in favor of _____, securing a Note with an approximate unpaid principal loan balance of $_____, bearing interest at the rate of _____ % per annum, payable in _____ installments of approximately $_____ each.

If the buyer will take title subject to an existing loan of record then the escrow officer will order a beneficiary statement stating the current status of the loan, as is shown in Figure 6.3. In the case of the beneficiary statement, the information needed is more than just the current unpaid balance, but also must state if the payments are current, the amount in or shortage of the impound account, the amount of the monthly payment, the amount of late fee, the due date of the next payment, and when a late assessment would be due. The terms and conditions of a different entity taking over the loan would be required. Many lenders have a provision that allows another to take over the existing loan after providing a loan assumption fee, such as 1 percent of the then current unpaid loan balance, along with a credit report or other information. An FHA loan, for example, is assumable under specific terms and conditions, whereas a Cal-Vet loan is never assumable. VA and Cal-Vet loans may be taken over by only another veteran who meets the same criteria as if he or she were applying for a new government loan.

In the case of taking title subject to the existing loan of record, the primary liability rests with the original trustor who borrowed the funds from the lender of record. In case of default by the subsequent purchaser, the lender would go back on the original trustor's credit and funds to cure the default in the loan. The lender had a written contractual obligation only with the original trustor. Because all real estate transactions in California for real property must be in writing according to the Statute of Frauds and because the subsequent property owner had no written agreement with the lender, the lender will ignore the subsequent purchaser's interest in the property. The lender will treat the purchaser's interest similar to a tenant in possession's rights of possession and hold the party's interest in possession as a cloud on the title, not as the lender's obligation to work with a subsequent purchaser.

■ WRAPAROUND

A **wraparound** may be used when no acceleration clause and alienation clause is contained in the trust note. The escrow instruction phrase would be worded as one of the following: regular **all-inclusive trust deed (AITD),** AITD interest included, or AITD interest extra, as seen in the text box below.

AITD—All-Inclusive Trust Deed.
The escrow holder is directed to create an All-Inclusive Trust Deed, securing One Note, payable as per its terms with an approximate unpaid balance of $_____, in favor of _____, payable in _____ installments of approximately $_____, including interest at the rate of _____ % per annum.

AITD—Installment Note—Interest Included.
The buyer and the seller will execute an All-Inclusive Deed of Trust and Note, on a form handed to you, in the amount of $_____, in favor of _____, dated during escrow, with interest at _____ % per annum, accruing from the date of funding, payable at the place where holder designates; principal and interest is payable in _____ installments of $_____, or more, beginning 30 days from the close of escrow and continuing until _____ from the close of escrow, at which time the then unpaid principal balance, plus accrued interest thereon, shall become due and payable. The escrow holder is hereby authorized and instructed to complete and/or endorse said note, at the close of escrow, to comply herein.

AITD—Installment Note—Interest Extra.
The buyer and seller will execute an All-Inclusive Deed of Trust and Note, on a form handed to you, in the amount of $_____, in favor of _____ _____, dated during escrow, with interest on the unpaid principal balance at the rate of _____ % per annum, from the date of funding; principal payable in _____ installments of $_____, or more, beginning 30 days from close of escrow and continuing until _____ from the date of close of escrow, at which time the unpaid principal balance and accrued interest thereon shall become due and payable. The escrow holder is hereby authorized and instructed to complete and/or endorse said Note, at the close of escrow, to comply herewith.

When the transaction is completed, the loan wraps around the existing loan adding additional debt on the property, and the borrower makes only one payment. For example, an existing first trust deed is at 6 percent with a current unpaid loan balance of $250,000 with existing monthly payments of $1,498.90.

The buyer purchases the property for $400,000 and places $50,000 cash as a down payment. The buyer does not have the additional $100,000 needed to close escrow. If the buyer went to a finance company or institutional lender for a loan, the interest rate on the $100,000 might be 9 percent to 12 percent. If the buyer tried to borrow the $100,000 on a credit card, the interest rate would be even higher, if the borrower would qualify for that much credit card debt.

One alternative is for the seller to carry back a junior, second trust deed. Because there is higher risk, the interest rate is also higher. The seller might agree to carry the $100,000 second trust deed at 8 percent amortized over 30 years, but due and payable in 10 years. The payment would be $733.82. This would mean that the borrower is making a payment of both a first and a second loan, which buyers often do not want to do. The total of the two payments would be the $1,498.90 on the $250,000 first plus the $733.82 on the $100,000 second, for a total monthly payment of $2,232.72.

The alternative to having two separate payments is for the seller to include the remaining balance of the existing first trust deed unpaid loan balance, plus the additional amount carried by the seller. In other words, the buyers would have one loan, under one recorded document showing their interest in the property. The purchaser could obtain title insurance as a secured all-inclusive trust deed, or AITD. The buyers would have one loan for $350,000 after they placed their $50,000 cash down payment. If the current interest rate for a new loan is at 7 percent, the $350,000 AITD could set the terms as amortized over 30 years but due in 10 years at 7 percent interest payable monthly. The buyer would have only one monthly payment of $2,328.59.

The wraparound loan includes both the remaining balance on the existing loan plus some additional amount carried back by the seller for part of his or her equity. The AITD is different from the land contract or contract of sale because title to the property is actually transferred. The seller may desire to use the AITD in a market where interest rates are rapidly rising and fewer buyers would qualify at the higher rate. If the appraisal is lower than the sales price, the AITD benefits the seller. If the seller has a large prepayment penalty if his or her loan is paid off, the AITD would greatly reduce the costs that the seller would pay. Benefits to the buyer include one single payment that is normally about the same as the two combined, lower down payment accepted than a conventional lender might require, and lower closing costs at a shorter time because only the seller has to approve the buyer and the escrow draws up the transfer documents.

Should the principals elect to utilize the AITD, the escrow officer draws the transfer documents instead of the lender. The grant deed, for change of ownership, and the trust deed, for security of the debt, recorded against the property is not used. The AITD combines both in the one recorded deed. The first step in executing an AITD is the examination of the underlying, existing trust note by the real estate licensees and the principals to determine if an acceleration clause exists that would prohibit this type of transfer.

Often, the terms of the AITD are drawn up in a written contract by an attorney, and the terms and conditions of the transaction are dictated and presented to the escrow officer, who sees that all necessary documents are recorded. The escrow officer would need a copy of the original trust deed and trust note to draw up the new AITD. The escrow officer would fill in the AITD with the monthly payment, the interest rate, any balloon payment information, and due date for each payment as well as the late date and the late fee information. The trust note usually includes property tax, insurance, and impound account information. The AITD payment is often due 10 days to 15 days prior to the seller's underlying payment due date to allow time for processing and for the buyer's check to clear before the seller has to make the payment on the underlying loan.

The escrow officer fills in the total value of the AITD, which is the total price minus the down payment made. The remaining amount would be the original loan amount of the AITD. The principals must give instruction to escrow for the monthly payment made by the buyer and for the monthly payment on the underlying loan. The seller may be the responsible party. Servicing may be an institution, such as a bank trust department, a property management firm, or a collection agency.

If the owner carryback trust deed was a straight or term note the escrow instructions would contain a clause that states the following:

> The escrow holder is instructed to execute a Deed of Trust to record as part of the total consideration, on our normal form, or on a form handed to you, executed by the Vestee(s) herein, to secure one Note for $_____ in favor of _____, dated during escrow, with interest at _____ % per annum, accruing from the date of funding; the principal and interest is all due and payable _____ from the close of escrow. The escrow holder is hereby authorized and instructed to complete and/or endorse said Note, at the close of escrow, to comply herewith.

The parties also must instruct the escrow officer who will pay for the cost of the loan servicing—the collections and disbursements, including impounds, and the preparation and distribution of who will obtain the income tax benefits for preparation, distribution, and payment of IRS Form 1099 information on the loan interest portion of the payment. All funds should be clearly delineated in the written contract prior to execution of the documents.

The law is clear about the exact procedures to be followed in case of default on the loan, but the parties to the transaction may have little knowledge as to the legal requirements. The exact circumstances constituting a default should be made very clear in the contract. In addition to any default on the payment of the loan and default on the payment of taxes or insurance, a default can be brought about for the condition of the property that is the security for the loan.

All parties should seek legal council when entering into an AITD agreement to assure that no misunderstandings occur. The AITD is the same in that if the borrower does not make the payment, the lender will foreclose, whether a conventional lender or a private party. If the buyer makes the payments, the seller/lender has no legal recourse to the property.

One important issue that the seller should have in writing and that the buyer should agree to is a clause in the escrow instructions and the note stating that the seller must be named on all insurance policies as a comortgagee. A standard clause in the escrow instructions is typically as follows:

Where the assignment of any insurance policy from Seller to Buyer is concerned, Seller guarantees to you any insurance policy handed you in this escrow is policy in force, the policy has not been hypothecated and that all necessary premiums have been paid. You are authorized to execute on behalf of the parties assignments of interest in any insurance policy (other than title insurance policies) called for in this escrow, you are authorized to transmit for assignment any insurance policy to the insurance agent requesting that the insurer consent to such assignment, to request that a loss payee clause or such other endorsements as may be required be issued and to forward such policy to the lenders and entitled parties. You shall not be responsible for verifying the acceptance of the request for assignment and policy of insurance by the insurance company. The parties mutually agree that you will make no attempt to verify the receipt of the request for assignments by the issuing insurance company. All parties are placed on notice that if the insurance company should fail to receive the assignment, the issuing company may deny coverage for any loss suffered by Buyer. IT IS THE OBLIGATION OF THE INSURED OR THE INSURED'S REPRESENTATIVE TO VERIFY THE ISSUING COMPANY'S ACCEPTANCE OF THE ASSIGNMENT OF THE POLICY.

■ BUYER'S ACCEPTANCE OF LOAN

The escrow instructions usually refer to how the buyer indicates acceptance of the loan. When an escrow is opened, the amount of the loan was negotiated between the buyer and the seller. However, after the lender obtains the written appraisal report, the price may be later changed. The purchase agreement should also have an executed addendum to the original purchase agreement if the price is changed.

The purchase agreement may have stated a specific loan amount with the interest rate not to exceed a certain amount, such as not to exceed 7 percent. However, the buyer may not qualify for a 7 percent loan. Interest rates may rise during the escrow period. The buyer should approve any change in the loan program, loan terms and conditions, or loan rate. Typically the language used is similar to the following: "Buyer's signature on loan documents constitutes full approval of all loan terms and conditions."

Most all lenders require the following items to be executed by the buyer, in addition to other specific items required by a specific lender for a specific loan:

- Loan documents executed by the buyer, notarized where required, and delivered back to the lender to review and approve prior to funding of the loan.

- Title insurance (ALTA) in an amount equal to the loan amount to insure the interest of the lender.

- Each exception on the title insurance policy must have the prior approval of the lender.

- Policy of hazard insurance endorsement for the loan amount or replacement cost, naming the lender as loss payee.

THINK ABOUT IT

A home is sold on a land contract with the buyer to pay $3,500 a month for 15 years. After the 60th payment, the buyer stops making payments. What are the remedies available for the seller?

Answer: The seller could rescind the contract by returning all the payments made of $3,500 a month, minus the fair rental value of $2,500 a month for the 60 months if the buyer agrees to relinquish the property.

The seller could sue for monetary damages to get a judgment ordering the buyer to pay the seller what is owed under the contract and the buyer would keep the house.

The buyer would sell the house, and the seller would collect from the sale proceeds.

The land contract terms might declare a forfeiture if the buyer defaults. In this case the buyer could lose all payments and the right to possession.

The escrow officer must establish that the parties have sought legal counsel covering the principals' rights under a land contract.

■ CHAPTER SUMMARY

Creative financing real estate transactions require expertise from the escrow officer. This chapter listed and described the common loan refinance transaction documents that are found using the Appendix resources on page 451. When some buyers purchase a foreclosure or repossessed property, the escrow officer is then under pressure during the escrow to try to beat the foreclosure date to close the transaction for the buyer where the lender is the seller.

Many documents are prepared by the escrow officer, such as the private party trust deeds for an owner carryback loan. A buyer can take title subject to the existing loan, or with acceptance of the lender the buyer may assume the loan and have primary liability. The all-inclusive trust deed (AITD) is popular when interest rates are rising. The escrow officer is asked to prepare the documents necessary for recordation, frequently dictated by an attorney who prepares the purchase contract.

No matter what kind of transaction or creative financing transaction, the escrow officer must obtain the buyer's acceptance of the loan terms and conditions being offered or arranged or before the transaction can close.

■ CHAPTER 8 QUIZ

1. Loan processing involves
   a. arranging assumption or payoff.
   b. requesting beneficiary statements.
   c. qualifying the borrower.
   d. all of the above.

2. The escrow officer must comply with the written instructions of the
   a. buyer.
   b. seller.
   c. lender.
   d. the entities above.

3. The Request for Notice of Default form is used
   a. by the lender to ascertain if the buyers are making the current payments on their existing loan.
   b. to determine the rate and terms under which a borrower qualifies for a new loan.
   c. to notify the junior lien holder when the senior lien is in default.
   d. by the seller who carries back a loan to obtain the borrower's credit rating.

4. Which is correct?
   a. A wraparound loan usually costs the buyer a little extra in closing cost fees.
   b. The seller encourages the buyer to obtain a loan at or above the maximum usury law limit.
   c. The borrower has a three-day right of rescission in a refinance loan from the date of delivery of the Truth-in-Lending disclosure.
   d. An AITD is the same as a refinance or a land sales contract.

5. The hardship letter, privacy notice, and California credit disclosure would be part of
   a. escrow instructions.
   b. loan documents.
   c. policy of title insurance.
   d. preliminary title report.

6. The difference between a short pay and a foreclosure is that in a
   a. short pay, the escrow cannot close without full reimbursement of the lender's unpaid principal, plus accrued interest, plus foreclosure and the trustee's cost of sale.
   b. short pay, the lender takes less total funds than are required for full payoff.
   c. foreclosure, the lender always takes a loss due to the extra costs.
   d. foreclosure, the escrow can close with less than the funds that are needed.

7. When a borrower takes title subject to the existing loan of record the
   a. existing loan cannot contain an acceleration clause in the trust note.
   b. lender is notified and the borrower signs full liability papers with the lender.
   c. new lender allows the existing lender to retain an interest in the property.
   d. seller is relieved of all liability relating to the loan.

8. When the escrow instructions state that the buyers' signatures on the documents constitute their full approval of the terms and conditions contained in the document, this is referred to as
   a. buyer's approval of the loan.
   b. seller's affidavit.
   c. buyer's affidavit.
   d. lender's instruction to charge maximum fees allowable by law.

9. A Request for Notice of Default is used to
   a. transfer title from an individual into a trust to obtain a loan.
   b. allow a borrower to take over an existing loan.
   c. initiate a seller carryback loan.
   d. instruct a trustee to notify a junior lien holder of loan default.

10. To have primary liability for an existing loan, a borrower could
    a. assume the existing loan by executing an assumption agreement.
    b. qualify and obtain a new loan with a lender.
    c. do neither of the above.
    d. do both a and b.

CHAPTER NINE

PREPARING DOCUMENTS

■ KEY TERMS

acknowledged
attorney-in-fact
corporation grant deed
documentary transfer
  tax
grant deed
grantee

grantor
interspousal grant deed
notary public
power of attorney
Preliminary Change
  of Ownership
  Report (PCOR)

quitclaim deed
recital clause
request for notice
reservation
substitution of trustee
trust deed
trust note

■ CHAPTER OVERVIEW

The escrow officer works with many documents and must be familiar with the forms commonly used in an escrow. The escrow officer is often the person who completes preprinted forms, such as the various deeds, the preliminary change in ownership form for tax purposes, and the forms relating to real estate loans. Chapter 9 reviews many of the documents, explains them in detail, and provides sample forms.

■ LEARNING OBJECTIVES

At the conclusion of Chapter 9, you will be able to

- understand how to complete the preliminary change of ownership report;
- give a definition for a deed;
- outline the steps required to transfer ownership of a trust deed;
- differentiate between a grant deed and a quitclaim deed; and
- explain the various transfer taxes.

■ TRANSFER OF OWNERSHIP AND DEEDS

The content of a deed does not require prescribed wording or format. In early U.S. history, deeds were predominantly handwritten by the individual transferring the property from themselves to another party. The deed shown in Figure 9.1 is a valid deed executed during a period in early California history, and Figure 9.3 is a more recently used deed that meets the legal requirements as upheld by the court system for the transfer of ownership to property in the format commonly used today.

A deed that conveys title to real property must have been properly prepared, delivered, and accepted. According to the Statute of Frauds, a deed must meet the following criteria to be valid:

- Must be in writing to be enforceable in court
- Must name the grantee who is to receive the property
- Must have some form of consideration
  - Price paid
  - For love and affection
- Must contain words that clearly convey the intent to transfer
  - Interest in the property
  - Giving and receiving of the interest
- Must name the grantor
- Must contain the signature of the grantor on the document
- Must have a public notary seal if it is to be recorded
- Must be delivered by the grantor to the grantee
- Must be accepted by the grantee

FIGURE 9.1

Early California Deed

I, Virgil W. Earp of the city of Colton, County of San Bernardino and State of California, for and in <u>consideration</u> of the love and affection which I bear towards my wife and as an expression of my heartfelt gratitude to her for her constant, patient and heroic attendance of my bedside while I lay dangerously wounded at Tombstone Arizona, **do grant** unto my wife, Mrs. Olivia Earp **as her separate estate,** all that **real property** situated in the City of Colton, County of San Bernardino, State of California, Described as follows, To wit: Lots 5 and 6 in Block 113 in and of said City of Colton; being the same lots <u>conveyed</u> to me by J.F. Walin by **deed** bearing date April 30th, 1888; now of record at page 172 in Vol. 74 of deeds, records of said San Bernardino County.

A full, true and correct copy of original, recorded at request of V.W. Earp. July 9, 1888, at 10:35 A.M. Lugona Allen, County Recorder.

A person may owe someone money without the evidence for the debt recorded against the real property owned by the debtor. Private parties may borrow money from another individual without recording a trust deed, as was described in Chapter 7. Likewise, a person can own property without evidence of a recorded grant deed. In the case of title acquired through adverse possession, title did not pass by grant deed. When title is acquired through the life estate, a deed may not have been used to evidence the ownership. Instead of using a grant deed, warranty deed, quitclaim deed, or corporate deed, a last will and testament may also serve to convey title to real property.

Successor trustees may transfer property under a trust. A surviving joint tenant may acquire additional title to property. An owner may have received title through a will without receiving a grant deed. The voluntary transfer of ownership to real property can be evidenced in many ways. Some of the types of deeds commonly used to transfer ownership are discussed in this chapter.

The escrow officer is often the party responsible for preparing these documents. Other entities may prepare documents such as the trust deed. The escrow officer often notarizes documents. The escrow officer sees that the document is delivered to the title company for recordation at the close of escrow. The deed has several purposes, which include the following:

- Conveys or transfers title
- Serves as evidence of ownership

■ USING PREPARED FORMS

The real estate industry has devised preprinted blank forms for most real estate transactions. These documents require only the pertinent data to be filled in correctly. However, once a deed has been recorded, it cannot be "unrecorded." The subsequent change from one form of ownership to another could carry substantial tax consequences or the exclusion of intended heirs or the inclusion of unintended heirs.

The tax consequences of how title is held and how a transfer is structured should involve both an experienced real estate licensee and a tax preparer who can analyze the consequences and look at the future implications. In the case of estate planning and the rights of the heirs, an experienced real estate licensee and an attorney who specializes in real estate and estate law should be consulted.

Prepared forms are often obtained from software programs or from a local stationery store. Always check the bottom left corner of any prepared form for the date, usually shown in a form such as "Rev 6/95," meaning that June of 1995 was the revision date. Older forms should probably not be used.

Another source of prepared forms for real estate is the title insurance company. The title insurance company often prints forms, especially deeds, at its expense and furnishes the forms to the real estate agents, attorneys, and escrow companies. The name of the trustee included on the form is often preprinted and may be a wholly owned subsidiary or an affiliated company of the title insurance company. Trustee fees more than offset the cost of printing and distributing the forms.

The escrow officer usually uses escrow-specific software that prints the current forms. The prepared forms from the escrow computer software have usually been reviewed by the bar association, the California Association of REALTORS® (CAR), the escrow association, the ALTA and CLTA title associations and other interested parties. Figure 9.2 has a list of some of the typical forms the escrow officer might prepare during the normal course of an escrow.

■ SUBSTITUTION OF TRUSTEE

Many deeds prepared for recordation contain the name of the trustee preprinted on the form. When a loan is to be paid off, the beneficiary instructs the trustee to prepare a reconveyance deed. The trustee charges a fee for preparing the reconveyance deed, for the recordation costs, and for handling the matter with the beneficiary and the trustor. A typical transaction where the first trust deed is with a financial institution is handled in this manner. However, in private

FIGURE 9.2

Sample Documents

Title of Document	
Abandonment of Homestead	Notice of Additional Advance
Abstract of Judgment	Notice of Completion
Affidavit—Death of Joint Tenant	Notice of Default
All-Inclusive Deed of Trust	Notice of Nonresponsibility
Assignment of Deed of Trust	Notice of Rescission
Contract of Sale	Notice of Trustee's Sale
Declaration of Homestead	Power of Attorney
Declaration of Restrictions	Reconveyance, Full
Decree of Distribution	Reconveyance, Partial
Deed, Easement	Release of Mechanic's Lien
Deed, Grant	Request for Notice
Deed, Tax	Revocation of Power of Attorney
Deed, Trustee's	Satisfaction of Judgment
Deed, Quitclaim	Satisfaction of Mortgage
Deed of Trust (All-Inclusive)	Subordination Agreement
Deed of Trust (Trust Deed)	Substitution of Trustee
Lis Pendens	Trust Deed (All-Inclusive)
Mechanic's Lien	Trust Deed (Deed of Trust)
Notice of Action (Lis Pendens)	

transactions a **substitution of trustee** is often used. When the property is sold, the seller carries back a junior and becomes a beneficiary. The buyer of the property is the trustor. The parties may use a Substitution of Trustee form to record the change from a corporation to an individual to perform the trustee duties. Figure 9.3 shows a Substitution of Trustee prepared form, ready for recordation.

When a larger institutional lender acts as the beneficiary, it is common for the trustee to be a title company or bank affiliate. An individual person may also act as the trustee. The trustee needs to live long enough to perform the duties required for future reconveyance. This is why a corporation, that does not die but has perpetual life, is usually named as the trustee in most documents.

FIGURE 9.3

Substitution of Trustee

RECORDING REQUESTED BY
Pacific Ocean Title Company
AND WHEN RECORDED MAIL
THIS DEED AND
UNLESS OTHER WISE SHOWN BELOW MAIL TAX
STATEMENTS TO
Name
Address
City & State
Zip

Book
Page
File No.

Recorded on
_____ at _____
Official Records
County of Los Angeles, California
Conny B. McCormack
Registrar-Recorder/County Clerk

Fees:
$ _____
B.

SPACE ABOVE THIS LINE FOR RECORDER'S USE

SUBSTITUTION OF TRUSTEE

NOTICE IS HEREBY GIVEN that, Pursuant to the provisions of the California Civil Code

_____

hereafter referred to as "Claimant" (whether singular or plural), claims a lien upon the real property
and buildings, improvements, or structures thereon, described in Paragraph Five (5) below, and states
the following:

(1) That demand of Claimant after deducting all just credits and offsets is _____
together with interest thereon at the rate of ____% per annum from _____, 20____.

(2) That the name of the owner(s) or reputed owner(s) of said property, is (are)

_____
(name, or state "unknown")

(3) That Claimant did from _____, until _____
perform labor and/or supply materials as follows: _____
(general statement of a kind of work done or materials furnished, or both)
_____

for the construction, alteration, or repair of said buildings, improvements, or structures, which labor, or
materials, or both of them, were in fact used in the construction, alteration, or repair of said buildings,
improvements, or structures, the location of which is set forth in Paragraph Five (5) below.

(4) Claimant furnished work and materials under contract with or at the request of:

_____
_____

(5)   That the property upon which said lien is sought to be charged is situated in the City of
_____, County of _____, State of California, commonly known as
_____and more particularly described as:
(Street address)
_____
_____

DATED: This _____ day of _____, 20____   Firm Name: _____

_____   _____
(Verification for Individual Claim)   (Verification for other than Individual Claim)

■ GRANT DEED

A **grant deed** may convey all of the ownership of the property or only a portion. In the case of a life estate, the deed may contain wording that indicates that the grantee is receiving all of the title to the property after the death of a particular person, which may or may not be the grantor. Or the grant deed may contain a clause that gives all the real property to the grantee with the exclusion of specific portions of the land, such as a driveway right-of-way easement. This is known as a **reservation.** A grant deed may also contain a deed restriction that does not allow for certain acts to be performed on the premises. It is typical that when certain religious organizations sell property, they include a clause stating that the subsequent owners may not produce, manufacture, or sell alcoholic beverages on the premises or else the property ownership reverts back to the religious organization. This is known as "reversion."

In the case of a grant deed, the party who is transferring the property out of his or her name is called the **grantor.** The party receiving title to the property is called the **grantee.** The grantor may sell the property or give it away. The grantee may purchase the property or may have been given ownership of the property. The grantee may not receive all of the property. A typical trust deed in California will give the full legal description to the real property and usually contains language for an exception, usually the exclusion of the mineral rights. Figure 9.4 shows a typical grant deed. A step-by-step explanation of the grant deed is shown after the deed in Figure 9.5, and because this explanation is detailed enough, it will not be repeated for the following various other types of deeds that are very similar in format.

Consideration

California does not require that the amount of consideration (price paid) be shown on the deed. Most grant deeds in California begin with the phrase "for valuable consideration" to meet the contract law that requires consideration. A will would show the consideration to be "for love and affection" rather than monetary value.

Name of the Grantors and Grantor Vesting

Grantors are individuals or entities conveying the title to the grantee, along with the manner in which the grantor holds title; that is, the names of the parties giving up ownership to the property. The grantor must be competent, meaning of legal age and of sound mind who is not being forced to execute the document. While each grantor may execute a separate deed, it is most common for all parties to be named on the same document.

FIGURE 9.4

Grant Deed

RECORDING REQUESTED BY (4)
First City Title Company

AND WHEN RECORDED MAIL (5)
THIS DEED AND
UNLESS OTHER WISE SHOWN BELOW MAIL TAX
STATEMENTS TO
Name
Address (6)
City & State
Zip
Title Order No. (17)   Escrow No.

Book
Page (1)
File No.

Recorded on
_____at_____
Official Records
County of _____, California
Conny B. McCormack
Registrar/Recorder/County Clerk

Fees: (2)
$ ____
B.

SPACE ABOVE THIS LINE FOR RECORDER'S USE

GRANT DEED

(3)

The undersigned declares that the documentary transfer tax is $_____and is
____ computed on the full value of the interest or property conveyed, or is
____ computed on the full value less the value of liens or encumbrances remaining thereon at the time of sale.
The land, tenements or realty is located in
____ unincorporated area   ____ city of _____

(7) FOR A VALUABLE CONSIDERATION, receipt of which is hereby acknowledged,
* (8)

(9) hereby GRANT(S) to
* (10)

the following described real property in the City of_____, County of _____
state of California:

(11) (legal description here)

(18) APN or AIN: xxx-xxx-xx
AKA:
Dated:_____ (12)   _____ (13)

_____

STATE OF CALIFORNIA (15)
COUNTY OF_____
On this the _____ day of _____ , 20___
(14) The undersigned, a Notary Public in and for said
County and State, personally appeared _____
_____, known to me
to be the person ___whose name ____subscribed
to the within instrument and acknowledged that
_____executed the same.

_____
Signature of Notary

_____
Name (Typed or Printed) of Notary

**FOR NOTARY SEAL OR
STAMP**

(16)

Mail Tax Statements to Party shown on following line: If no Party so shown, mail as directed above.

_____
Name   Street Address   City & State

FIGURE 9.5

Commentary for Grant Deed

A deed is a written instrument by which title to or an interest in real property is transferred from one person or legal entity (the grantor) to another (the grantee). Two kinds of deeds are most commonly used in California—the grant deed, as discussed here, and the quitclaim deed. The basic difference between the grant deed and the quitclaim deed lies in the operative words of conveyance. A grant deed is a grant deed because it uses the unqualified wording "grant(s)" (see item 9 below) to convey the transfer of title ownership.

1. *Recording Information.* The book and page numbers of the official records where the document is entered, the file number (sometimes called the document or instrument number) assigned by the county recorder and the date and time of recordation are noted on the document, constituting the recording reference.

2. *County Recorder's Stamps.* The large stamp reflects the recording reference of the document and makes reference to the name of the county and the county recorder. The smaller stamp indicates the recording fees. These stamps are placed on the document by the clerk in the county recorder's office.

3. *Documentary Transfer Tax.* This is a tax levied on the sale of the property by the county (and sometimes the city) where the property is located.

4. *Recording Requested By.* This identifies the party requesting that the document be recorded. It appears above the name of the title company when groups of documents are submitted to the county for recording.

5. *And When Recorded Mail To.* After recording, the document will be mailed by the county to the addressee shown in this section.

6. *Tax Statement Address.* This is the party (and address) to whom a statement regarding real property taxes will be mailed by the county tax office. It is usually the same party in the "And When Recorded Mail To" section (item 5). If so, there is no need to complete this section. If the tax statement is to be mailed elsewhere, then the appropriate information must be inserted.

7. *For a Valuable Consideration.* This is a statement that reflects that money or some legal consideration is being given in exchange for the property. (This is a holdover from earlier times and is no longer necessary in a voluntary conveyance.)

8. *Grantor.* This identifies the party selling or transferring the property, called the grantor.

9. *Operative Words of Conveyance.* Wording in this section indicates a present intent to transfer the title to the real property. It is an essential part of any deed. In the grant deed, the wording "hereby grant(s)" is used.

10. *Grantee.* This identifies the party receiving title ownership to the property, called the grantee. The status, e.g., husband and wife, and method of acquiring title, e.g., as joint tenants, should also be set out. The status and method of acquiring title is referred to as "the vesting."

11. *Legal Description.* This legally describes the real property. This is usually accomplished by a lot/block tract lot, metes-and-bounds, or U.S. government survey type of legal description. A lengthy description may include a separate street, referred to on the documents as an addendum or attachment.

FIGURE 9.5

Commentary for Grant Deed (Continued)

12. *Date of Execution.* This is often the date on which the document is executed (signed), but generally it is also the date on which it is prepared (drawn).

13. *Signature of the Grantor(s).* The signature of the grantor (seller) will appear on the line in this section and his/her name should be printed or typed beneath the signature.

14. *Acknowledgment.* An acknowledgment is a formal declaration made before an authorized official (usually a notary public) by the person who has executed (signed) a document that such execution is his/her own act and deed. This declaration is then reduced to writing and attested to by said authorized official. In most instances, a document must be **acknowledged** ("notarized") before it can be accepted for recording.

15. *Venue.* This identifies the state and county where the acknowledgment is taken.

16. *Notary Seal or Stamp.* In this section the official seal of the notary public or other authorized official must be affixed or stamped.

17. *Title Order No. and Escrow No.* On this line the title company's order number will appear, along with the customer's escrow number, if the document was recorded as part of a title order which culminated in the closing of an escrow. These numbers are assigned by the title/escrow companies as a control number for "in-house" use.

18. *Assessor's Parcel Number (APN) or also known as Assessor's Identification Number (AIN).* In many counties, as a prerequisite to recording, many types of documents must contain the Tax Assessor's Parcel Number, AKA Assessor's Identification Number for the real property.

Name of the Grantees and Grantee Vesting

The grantee must be named on the document. A deed may transfer title to a fictitious name, such as an assumed name. A valid transfer of a deed may also be made to an incompetent person or to a minor grantee with a guardian. The grantee, however, must exist, and title cannot be transferred to a deceased grantee.

Legal Description

The full legal description to the real property. If it is long, such as in lengthy metes-and-bounds descriptions, with homeowner association ownership and with exceptions, this area may state "See attached Exhibit A" so a separate page can list more information. The bottom of this area often states "AKA 123 Elm Street." Deeds show both the technical legal description and the common street mailing address as assigned by the U.S. Postal Service for that particular property. In the chain of title, the current legal description is derived from previous legal descriptions. The same legal description previously used should be used whenever possible with the exact same order of the words. If property has been subdivided or otherwise altered, this may not be possible. In very old deeds, a **recital clause** was used to show from whom the property was received and how the current grantor acquired title, such as the following:

Middlebury, Connecticut August 23, 1843

To Whom It May Concern: Know ye that the subscriber having heretofore settled upon Harvey F. Johnson by this Deed may real estate accumulated by the same considerations which induced me to do that I would by this Instrument make known that *I give* and settle all my personal Estate of every name and description on the said H. F. Johnson as my adopted son and heir, to be his, with the following provision and understanding: He the said H. F. Johnson is to provide for and support me during my natural life, to pay all reasonable debts and funeral charges which may be due for me at my decease, also that he the said Johnson within three months after my decease pay to Benjamin F. Clark, son of Elon Clark of Waterbury as a balance of what I designed to give him twenty eight dollars and to Charles son of said Elon one hundred dollars.

■ QUITCLAIM DEED AND INTERSPOUSAL GRANT DEED

A **quitclaim deed** is a written document that operates as a release. The deed describes the parties and the property. The quitclaim deed is intended to pass any title, interest, or claim that the grantor may have in the real property, but it does not contain any warranty or covenant of any valid or implied interest or title ownership. The transferor may have no interest in the property at the time the transfer is made, and thus may be giving 100 percent of zero. The grantee receives 100 percent of all that the transferor gives and thus may have acquired nothing. The word *quitclaim* literally means to quit all claims against the property; it means to renounce all possession, right, or interest in the property forever. The form is most often used by a family law attorney when transferring real property between spouses obtaining a divorce. In every single case that the quitclaim deed could be used, a grant deed could also have been used to affect the actual transfer of all ownership interest held in the property and representing that some interest is held in the property.

A quitclaim deed is usually used instead of the lengthy court action referred to as a "quiet title action" to clear a cloud on the title. A cloud on the title is some claim, right, condition, or encumbrance that impairs clear title to real property. See Figure 9.6 for an example of a quitclaim deed. The words that are critical to a valid quitclaim deed include language similar to a statement such as: "Transferor does hereby remise, release, and quitclaim forever all rights, interest, and ownership to the real property."

The grant deed is the most commonly used deed to transfer real property ownership in California, followed by the quitclaim deed. However, the **interspousal grant deed** is a document used when the transfer is between individuals in a

FIGURE 9.6

Quitclaim Deed

RECORDING REQUESTED BY
First City Title Company

AND WHEN RECORDED MAIL THIS DEED AND

UNLESS OTHER WISE SHOWN BELOW MAIL TAX STATEMENTS TO
Name
Address
City & State
Zip

Title Order No. _____ Escrow No. _____

Book
Page
File No.

Recorded on
_____at_____
Official Records
County of _____, California
Conny B. McCormack
Registrar-Recorder/County Clerk

Fees:
$ _____
R

SPACE ABOVE THIS LINE FOR RECORDER'S USE

QUITCLAIM DEED

The undersigned declares that the documentary transfer tax is $_____and is

____ computed on the full value of the interest or property conveyed, or is

____ computed on the full value less the value of liens or encumbrances remaining thereon at the time of sale.

The land, tenements or realty is located in

____ unincorporated area   ____ city of _____

FOR A VALUABLE CONSIDERATION, receipt of which is hereby acknowledged,*

do (es), hereby remise, release and forever quitclaims to*

the following described real property in the City of_____, County of _____ state of California:

(legal description here)

APN or AIN: xxx-xxx-xx
AKA:
This deed is given to carry out the mutual desire and agreement of the parties hereto, that said property become vested in the grantee herein as her separate property.

Dated:_____   _____

_____

STATE OF CALIFORNIA   _____
COUNTY OF_____
On this the _____day of _____ , 20___   _____
The undersigned, a Notary Public in and for said
County and State, personally appeared _____
_____, known to me
to be the person ___whose name ____subscribed
to the within instrument and acknowledged that
_____executed the same.

FOR NOTARY SEAL OR STAMP

_____
        Signature of Notary

_____
    Name (Typed or Printed) of Notary

Mail Tax Statements to Party shown on following line: If no Party so shown, mail as directed above.

Name   Street Address   City & State

marriage; see Figure 9.7. The document would be used when one spouse deeds all interest in real property to the other spouse. This document gives greater strength than a quitclaim deed. Another use for the document is when the married individuals are not divorcing or separating, but wish to transfer ownership interest to real property out of one of the spouses' names. This deed may be used when one party inherits a property, which is the sole and separate property of that individual. Because of the possibility of commingling of funds during the marriage to pay the loan, insurance, or taxes, the quitclaim deed may be used to distinguish and exclude a spouse from property ownership.

■ ACKNOWLEDGMENT AND JURAT'S NOTARY

The California state real estate exam likes to ask the question: "Who acknowledges the deed?" with answer choices typically: (a) buyer, (b) seller, or (c) notary. Clearly, the seller must acknowledge the contents of the document to be true and correct.

The **notary public** acknowledges the authenticity of signatures of the person signing the document. Notaries sign either one of two things. One is that they are stating that the individual is "personally known to me to be" because they actually know the person is who they represent to be. Or else, the notaries sign that they have verified proper identification that the signers are the persons they say that they are, usually using a picture identification, such as a driver's license, and an ink thumb print in the notary book along with the party's signature in the notary book. The party seeking the notary seal on the document signs twice, once in the notary book and also on the document itself, in the presence of the notary.

When a document does not have enough room for all the required wording and the seal, a jurat is used. Or when a document is signed separately from the notary stamp being affixed, a separate notary form is attached to the document, called a "jurat's notary." Most deeds have the notary affixed to the face of the document. But as some documents have become larger with more phrases contained on the printed form, especially in the case of a trust deed, the notary space may not be available on the face of the document and a separate part is attached. This happens because the county recorder in many California counties is restricting the size of the face of each recorded document. If the document is outside the prescribed borders the document is sent back, without being recorded, with instructions as to the size limitation for each page. If the information runs into another page, each separate page must be within the measurements and recorded separately. Hence, many documents have the notary as a separate page with an additional recording fee for the page containing the notary seal or jurat's notary.

FIGURE 9.7

Interspousal Grant Deed

Loan No. 694-33280
Escrow No. JR 4961-505

87 336693

When Recorded Mail to:
Mary Anne Davis
7421 Elm Vista Drive
Anytown, CA 94321
MAIL STATEMENTS TO:

Mary Anne Davis
7421 Elm Vista Drive
Anytown, CA 94321

RECORDED IN OFFICIAL RECORDS
OF _____ COUNTY, CA
May 6, 1999 at 8:00 A.M.
Recorder's Office

FEE $5   R
        4

DOCUMENTARY TRANSFER TAX
$xx a conveyance from any transfer of the
Documentary Transfer Tax per the
Revenue and Taxation Code #119
as complimentary value at no
consideration between the parties
Larry H. Davis
Signature of delivery to grantee by grantor

Interspousal Transfer Grant Deed
(a recordation transfer document under California Constitution Article 13 A & 1 et seq)

This is an interspousal Transfer Grant Deed and a change of grantor under #119 of the Revenue and Taxation Code as the instrument for the transfer agreement
[ ] A transfer to a trustee for the transfer of real property for the purposes of deceased or legally incompetent estate trust of the grantor.
[X] A transfer to a spouse or grantor spouse as conveyance with a property settlement agreement as estrangement or separation of an estate of the grantor.
[ ] The separate transfer of equity as connected with a property settlement agreement.
FOR A VALUABLE CONSIDERATION, receipt of which is hereby acknowledged
                    Larry H. Davis
hereby GRANT(S) to
                    Mary Anne Davis, an unmarried woman, as her sole and separate property
the real property in the City of Anytown County of _____
State of California, described as:
PARCEL 1: The northerly 150 feet of the southerly 480 feet of the west half of the northwest quarter of
            the southwest quarter of the northeast quarter of section 29, township 4 south, range 13 west,
            San Bernardino Meridian according to the official plat of said land filed in the district land
            office October 30, 1884.
EXCEPT there from the westerly 179 feet thereof.
PARCEL 2: The easterly 12 feet of the west half of the northwest quarter of the southwest quarter of the
            northeast quarter of Section 29, township 4 south, range 13 west, San Bernardino Meridian,
            according to the official plat of said land filed in the district land office October 30, 1884.
EXCEPT there from the northerly 20 feet thereof, including the lines of the Elm Vista Drive.

ALSO EXCEPT there from the southerly 480 feet thereof.
Dated: 11-10-98

Larry H. Davis
Larry H. Davis

STATE OF CALIFORNIA
COUNTY OF _____ __}SS
On November 10, 1998 before
me, the undersigned, a Notary Public in and for said State
            Larry H. Davis
Personally known to me or proved to me on the basis of satis-
Factory evidence to be the person whose name
Subscribed to the within instrument and acknowledged
That he executed the same.
WITNESS My hand and official seal.
Signature Jeremy Cox

OFFICIAL SEAL
JEREMY COX
Notary Public, California
_____County
Commission Expires June 15, 2000

FIGURE 9.8

**Instructions for Use
of a Notary with the
Document**

> Please sign and acknowledge this instrument before a notary public. Be sure the notary seal is legible; sign your name exactly as it is printed on this document.

When escrow sends escrow instructions, amendments, or other documents to the parties to be signed, the wording shown in Figure 9.8 is often attached to each document requiring the use of a notary. Another item to always check is the expiration date of the notary seal. It is not uncommon for a document to be returned from the lender or title company or county recorder's office with the document not recorded, along with a statement indicating that the public notary's seal has expired.

This delays the escrow and can have serious financial consequences for the parties involved. The delay in time changes the prorations and the amount of funds needed by the buyer and the amount of funds the seller will receive. It may mean that the loan documents, which are also time sensitive, also expire. If the lender has to draw new loan documents additional charges will be assessed.

■ DOCUMENTARY TRANSFER TAX

The county charges a tax for the transfer of property from one owner to another. In many areas the city also charges a transfer tax that must also be paid at the close of escrow. A chart showing the normal **documentary transfer tax** is shown in Chapter 11 on page 322. The wording used in the escrow instructions allowing the collection and payment of this tax is usually as follows:

> You are further instructed to pay documentary transfer tax on deed as required.

When a document is recorded and no stamps are shown and no fee is charged, it is as an accommodation recordation made by the title insurance company. The lack of the amount of documentary transfer tax does not mean that a transfer did not take place. When a transfer is made where the consideration is love and affection, as in the transfer of real property from a parent to his or her child, no consideration is paid by cash and thus no document transfer tax is paid. Many categories are exempt from the payment of the documentary transfer tax as is discussed in the next section on the preliminary change of ownership report. A chart with the fee for the documentary transfer tax is shown in Figure 9.9 based upon the $0.55 per $500 of value of the property.

FIGURE 9.9

Documentary Transfer Tax Stamp Chart

Consideration	Tax	Consideration	Tax	Consideration	Tax
00001-500	00.55	33501-34000	37.40	67001-67500	74.25
00501-1000	01.10	34001-34500	27.95	67501-68000	74.80
01001-1500	01.65	34501-35000	38.50	68001-68500	75.35
01501-2000	02.20	35001-35500	39.05	68501-69000	75.90
02001-2500	02.75	35501-36000	39.60	69001-69500	76.45
02501-3000	03.30	36001-36500	40.15	69501-70000	77.00
03001-3500	03.85	36501-37000	40.70	70001-70500	77.55
03501-4000	04.40	37001-37500	41.25	70501-71000	78.10
04001-4500	04.95	37501-38000	41.80	71001-71500	78.65
04501-5000	05.50	38001-38500	42.35	71501-72000	79.20
05001-5500	06.05	38501-39000	42.90	72001-72500	79.75
05501-6000	06.60	39001-39500	43.45	72501-73000	80.30
06001-6500	07.15	39501-40000	44.00	73001-73500	80.85
06501-7000	07.70	40001-40500	44.55	73501-74000	81.40
07001-7500	08.25	40501-41000	45.10	74001-74500	81.95
07501-8000	08.80	41001-41500	45.65	74501-75000	82.50
08001-8500	09.35	41501-42000	46.20	75001-75500	83.05
08501-9000	09.90	42501-42500	46.75	75001-76000	83.60
09001-9500	10.45	42501-43000	47.30	76001-76500	84.15
09501-10000	11.00	43001-43500	47.85	76501-77000	84.70
10001-10500	11.55	43501-44000	48.40	77001-77500	85.25
10501-11000	12.10	44001-44500	48.95	77501-78000	85.80
11001-11500	12.65	44501-45000	49.50	78001-78500	86.35
11501-12000	13.20	45001-45500	50.05	78501-79000	86.90
12001-12500	13.75	45501-46000	50.60	79001-79500	87.45
12501-13000	14.30	46001-46500	51.15	79501-80000	88.00
13001-13500	14.85	46501-47000	51.70	80001-80500	88.55
13501-14000	15.40	47001-47500	52.25	80501-81000	89.10
14001-14500	15.95	47501-48000	52.80	81001-81500	89.65
14501-15000	16.50	48001-48500	53.35	80501-82000	90.20
15001-15500	17.05	48501-49000	53.90	82001-82500	90.75
15501-16000	17.60	49001-49500	54.45	82501-83000	91.30
16001-16500	18.15	49501-50000	55.00	83001-83500	91.85
16501-17000	18.70	50001-50500	55.55	83501-84000	92.40
17001-17500	19.25	50501-51000	56.10	84001-84500	92.95
17501-18000	19.80	51001-51500	56.65	84501-85000	93.50
18001-18500	20.35	51501-52000	57.20	85001-85500	94.05
18501-19000	20.90	52001-52500	57.75	85001-86000	94.60
19001-19500	21.45	52501-53000	58.30	86001-86500	95.15
19501-20000	22.00	53001-53500	58.85	86501-87000	95.70
20001-20500	22.55	53501-54000	59.40	87001-87500	96.25
20501-21000	23.10	54001-54500	59.95	87501-88000	96.80

FIGURE 9.9

Documentary Transfer Tax Stamp Chart (Continued)

Consideration	Tax	Consideration	Tax	Consideration	Tax
21001-21500	23.65	54501-55000	60.50	88001-88500	97.35
21501-22000	24.20	55001-55500	61.05	88501-89000	97.90
22001-22500	24.75	55501-56000	61.60	89001-89500	98.45
22501-23000	25.30	56001-56500	62.15	89501-90000	99.00
23001-23500	25.85	56501-57000	62.70	90001-90500	99.55
23501-24000	26.40	57001-57500	63.25	90501-91000	100.10
24001-24500	26.95	57501-58000	63.80	91001-91500	100.65
24501-25000	27.50	58001-58500	64.35	91501-92000	101.20
25001-25500	28.05	58501-59000	64.90	92001-92500	101.75
25501-26000	28.60	59001-59500	65.45	92500-93000	102.30
26001-26500	29.15	59501-60000	65.00	93001-93500	102.85
26501-27000	29.70	60001-60500	66.55	92501-94000	103.40
27001-27500	30.25	60501-61000	67.10	94001-94500	103.95
27501-28000	30.80	61001-61500	67.65	94501-95000	104.50
28001-28500	31.35	61501-62000	68.20	95001-95500	105.05
28501-29000	31.90	62001-62500	68.75	95001-96000	105.60
29001-29500	32.45	62501-63000	69.30	96001-96500	106.15
29501-30000	33.00	63001-63500	69.85	96501-97000	106.70
30001-30500	33.55	63501-64000	70.40	97001-97500	107.25
30501-31000	34.10	64001-64500	70.95	97501-98000	107.80
31001-31500	34.65	64501-65000	71.50	98001-98500	108.35
31501-32000	35.20	65001-65500	72.05	98501-99000	108.90
32001-32500	35.75	65501-66000	72.60	99001-99500	109.45
32501-33000	36.30	66001-66500	73.15	99501-100000	110.00
33001-33500	36.85	66501-67000	73.70		

■ PRELIMINARY CHANGE OF OWNERSHIP REPORT

The wording used in the escrow instructions to direct the escrow officer to comply with the law requiring the reporting of the details of a transfer of ownership to the tax entity for the purpose of generating tax revenue to the government is shown in the text box below. The words are intended to relieve the escrow holder from any liability or responsibility in connection with completion of the form should the parties to the transaction elect not to comply with the tax laws.

The penalty and amount the escrow officer must pay to the tax entity is spelled out so that a clear understanding by the principals is indicated in writing for all parties to have for disclosure purposes. The real estate agents may explain the effects as may the lender or the tax or legal consultant of the principal. The wording also states where the buyer may obtain additional information on completing the form or questions about the form. The buyer is the party responsible for the form. The common words used in the escrow instructions are the same or similar to the following:

PRELIMINARY CHANGE OF OWNERSHIP REPORT Prior to the close of escrow, Grantee shall cause to be handed to Escrow Holder a fully completed and executed "Preliminary Change of Ownership Report" pursuant to the requirements and in accordance with Section 480.3 of the USA Revenue and Taxation Code. If Grantee so chooses, Grantee may elect not to complete and execute said form prior to the close of escrow. Buyer is aware that if Buyer does not complete the form in full, sign and return it to you before closing, a penalty will be assessed by the county recorder. Escrow Holder's sole duty shall be the delivery of said form to the County Recorder at the time of recordation of transfer documents.

Buyer acknowledges that if the Change of Ownership form is not filed after the close of escrow within the time limits set forth by the county recorder, severe additional penalties will be assessed against the Buyer.

The **Preliminary Change of Ownership Report (PCOR)** is shown in Figure 9.10. This form must be completed *prior* to the transfer of the subject property (California Revenue and Taxation Code 480.3). The form has four parts. Part one is where the borrower indicates if the transaction is for a transfer of the property to a trust or to return the property to the original transferor. Part 2 gives other information. Part 3 is where the price and terms of a sale are given. Part 4 gives information about the property. The document is presented to the county recorder at the time of recordation of transfer ownership documents.

■ TRUST CERTIFICATION AND CORPORATION OWNERSHIP

Trust

Many property owners hold title to property in some form of a trust. In the event the escrow officer notes that the title report indicates that a trust is involved, the escrow officer must then make sure that the documents are signed by the correct parties. For the sample trust shown in Figure 9.11, the parties cannot sign as Sandra Anna Gonzales and Juan Ivan Gonzales. Instead, she must sign as "Sandra Anna Gonzales, Trustee for The Gonzales Family Trust dated June 1, 1988," and he must sign as "Juan Ivan Gonzales, Trustee for The Gonzales Family Trust dated June 1, 1988."

FIGURE 9.10

Preliminary Change of Ownership Report (PCOR)

To be completed by transferee (buyer) prior to transfer of subject property in accordance with Section 480.3 of the Revenue & Taxation Code. A preliminary Change of Ownership Report must be filed with each conveyance in the County Recorder's office for the county where the property is located. This particular form may be used in all 58 counties of California.

THIS REPORT IS NOT A PUBLIC DOCUMENT

	FOR ASSESSOR'S USE ONLY

SELLER/TRANSFEROR:_____
BUYER/TRANSFEREE:_____
ASSESSOR'S PARCEL NUMBER:_____
LEGAL DESCRIPTION:_____
ADDRESS/LOCATION OF PROPERTY:_____
MAIL TAX INFORMATION TO: Name_____
Address_____

APN_____
RA _____ YES ____ NO _____
GRID _____ MULT _____
RECORD DATE _____
PP _____
NV _____

NOTICE: A lien of property taxes applies to your property on March 1 of each year for the taxes owing in the following fiscal year. July 1 through June 30. One-half of these is due November 1, and one-half is due February 1. The first installment becomes delinquent on December 10, and the second installment becomes delinquent on April 10. One tax bill is mailed before November 1 to the owner of record. IF THIS TRANSFER OCCURS AFTER MARCH 1 AND ON OR BEFORE DECEMBER 31, YOU MAY BE RESPONSIBLE FOR THE SECOND INSTALLMENT OF TAXES DUE FEBRUARY 1.

The property which you acquired may be subject to a supplemental assessment in an amount to be determined by your County Assessor. For further information on your supplemental roll obligation, please call your County Assessor.

PART 1: TRANSFER INFORMATION
Please answer all questions.

YES   NO

____ ____ A, Is this transfer solely between husband and wife (addition of a spouse, death of a spouse, divorce settlement, etc.)?

____ ____ B. Is this transaction only a correction of the name(s) of the person(s) holding title to the property (for example, a name change upon marriage)?

____ ____ C. Is this document recorded to create, terminate, or reconvey a lender's interest in the property?

____ ____ D. Is this transaction recorded only to create, terminate, or reconvey a security interest (e.g., cosigner)?

____ ____ E. Is this document recorded to substitute a trustee under a deed of trust, mortgage, or other similar document?

____ ____ F. Did this transfer result in the creation of a joint tenancy in which the seller (transferor) remains as one of the joint tenants?

____ ____ G. Does this transfer return property to the person who created the joint tenancy (original transferor)?

____ ____ H. Is this transfer of property:

____ ____   1. to a trust for the benefit of the grantor, or grantor's spouse?

____ ____   2. to a trust revocable by the transferor?

____ ____   3. to a trust from which the property reverts to the grantor within 12 years?

____ ____ I. If this property is subject to a lease, is the remaining lease term 35 years or more including written options?

____ ____ J. Is this an transfer from parent to children or from children to parents?

____ ____ K. Is this transaction to replace a principal residence by a person 55 years of age or older?

____ ____ L. Is this transaction to replace a principal residence by a person severely disabled as defined by Revenue and Taxation Code Section 69.5?

If you checked **yes** to J, K, or L, an applicable claim form must be filed with the County Assessor.

Please provide any other information that would help the Assessor to understand the nature of the transfer.

_____

FIGURE 9.10

Preliminary Change of Ownership Report (PCOR) (Continued)

IF YOU HAVE ANSWERED YES TO ANY OF THE ABOVE QUESTIONS, EXCEPT J, K OR L, PLEASE
SIGN AND DATE: _____ DATE _____

OTHERWISE, COMPLETE BALANCE OF THE FORM

PART II: OTHER TRANSFER INFORMTION

A.   Date of transfer if other than recording date_____

B.   Type of transfer. Please check appropriate line.

    ____Purchase   ____Foreclosure   ____Gift   ____Trade or Exchange

    ____Merger, Stock, or Partnership Acquisition

    ____Contract of Sale ----Date of Contract_____

    ____Inheritance ---- Date of Death_____

    ____Other: Please explain:_____

    ____Creation of a Lease   ____Assignment of a Lease

    ____Termination of a Lease   Date lease began_____

    Original term in years (including written options)_____

    Remaining term in years (including written options)_____

C.   Was only a partial interest in the property transferred?   ____Yes   ____No

    If yes, indicate the percentage transferred_____%

PART III: TRANSFER INFORMATION

A.   CASH DOWN PAYMENT OR Value of Trade or Exchange (excluding cost)   Amount $_____

B.   FIRST DEED OF TRUST @_____% interest for _____ years.

        Payments./Mo.(Prin.& Int. only) = $_____   Loan Amt. $_____

    ____FHA   ____Fixed Rate   ____New Loan

    ____Conventional   ____Variable Rate   ____Assumed Existing Loan Balance

    ____VA   ____All Inclusive D.T. ($_____Wrapped)

    ____Bank or Savings & Loan   ____Finance Company

    ____Cal-Vet   ____Loan Carried by Seller

    ____Balloon Payment   ____Yes   ____No   Due Date_____   Amount $_____

C.   SECOND DEED OF TRUST @_____% interest for _____years.

        Paymts./Mo.(Prin. & Int. only) = $_____   Loan Amt. $_____

        Due Date_____   Amount $_____

    ____Bank or Savings & Loan   ____Fixed Rate   ____New Loan

    ____Loan Carried by Seller   ____Variable Rate   ____Assumed Existing Loan Balance

    Balloon Payment   ____Yes   ____No

D.   OTHER FINANCING: Is other financing involved not covered in (b) or (c) above?   ____Yes   ____No

    Type_____ @_____% interest for _____ years.

        Paymts./Mo.(Prin. & Int. only) = $_____   Loan Amt. $_____

    ____Bank or Savings & Loan   ____Fixed Rate   ____New Loan

    ____Loan Carried by Seller   ____Variable Rate   ____Assumed Existing Loan Balance

    ____Balloon Payment   ____Yes   ____No   Due Date_____   Amount $_____

E.   IMPROVEMENT BOND   ____Yes   ____No   Outstanding Balance: Amount $_____

F.   TOTAL PURCHASE PRICE (or acquisition price, if traded or exchanged,

    incl. Real estate commission if pd.)   Total Items A through E | $ |

G.   PROPERTY PURCHASED: ____through a broker;   ____direct from seller;   ____Other

    (explain)_____

    If purchased through a broker, provide broker's name and phone number : _____

    Please explain any special terms or financing and any other information that would help the Assessor

    understand the Purchase price and terms of the sale:_____

FIGURE 9.10

Preliminary Change of Ownership Report (PCOR) (Continued)

PART IV: PROPERTY INFORMATION

A. IS PERSONAL PROPERTY INCLUDED IN THE PURCHASE PRICE?
(other than a mobilehome subject to local property tax?)   ____Yes ____No
If yes, enter the value of the personal property included in the purchase price &   _____
(Attach itemized list of personal property)

B. IS THE PROPERTY INTENDED AS YOUR PRINCIPAL RESIDENCE?   ____Yes ____No
If yes, enter the date of occupancy _____/ _____, 20_____ or intended occupancy _____/ _____, 20_____
                            Month   Day   Month   Day

C. TYPE OF PROPERTY TRANSFERRED:
____ Single-family residence   ____ Agricultural   ____ Time-share
____Multiple-family residence (no. of units:____) ____ Co-op/Own-your-own   ____ Mobile Home
____Commercial/Industrial   ____ Condominium   ____ Unimproved lot
____Other (Description: _____)

D. DOES THE PROPERTY PRODUCE INCOME?   ____Yes ____No

E. IF THE ANSWER TO QUESTION D IS YES, IS THE INCOME FROM:
____Lease/Rent   ____Contract   ____Mineral Rights____Other----explain:_____

F. WHAT WAS THE CONDITION OF THE PROPERTY AT THE TIME OF SALE?
____ Good   ____ Average   ____Fair   ____Poor
Enter here, or on an attached sheet, any other information that would assist the Assessor in determining value
of the property, such as the physical condition of the property, restrictions, etc.
_____
_____

I certify that the foregoing is true, correct and complete to the best of my knowledge and belief

Signed_____ Date: _____
           (New Owner/Corporate Officer)

Please Print Name of New Owner/Corporate Officer _____
Phone No. where you are available from 8:00 a.m. — 5:00 p.m. (   )_____

(NOTE: The Assessor may contact you for further information.)

If a document evidencing a change of ownership is presented to the recorder for recordation without the
concurrent filing of a preliminary change of ownership report, the recorder may charge an additional
recording fee of twenty dollars ($20).

The information contained within the trust agreement will indicate the powers of the individuals. If the trust does not specify the act in the trust agreement in writing, then the escrow officer and lender will assume that the individual does not have the power to do the thing or to perform the act. Where ownership is in a trust, in order for the transfer of title from the trust-seller to the buyer, then the above information is correct. However, in the case of a refinance, or if the buyer wants to hold title in the trust, many lenders will require a change in the vesting. The individual trustees may have to deed the property out of the trust and back into their individual names with a recorded grant deed, then execute the loan documents and complete the recordation for the trust deed in the name of the

FIGURE 9.11

Certificate of Revocable Trust

The undersigned, creators and trustees of the below described trust, hereby certify the following facts with respect thereto:

1. Name of Trust: The Gonzales Family Trust
2. Date of Trust: May 17, 1999
3. Name of Creators: Sandra Anna Gonzales and Juan Ivan Gonzales
4. Name of Trustees: Sandra Anna Gonzales and Juan Ivan Gonzales, or the survivor of them.
5. Successor Trustees: Alex Paul Gonzales, succeeded by Andrew Fernando Gonzales.
6. Beneficiaries: The creators of this trust, while they are both living, shall hold all beneficial interest in the assets placed in this trust.
7. Revocability: The creators of this trust may revoke this trust in part or in whole while they are both living, by an instrument in writing signed by the creators and delivered to the trustee.
8. Powers of Trustee: In order to carry out the provisions of the trust, the trustee shall have these powers and discretions to:
   a. Sell Assets: Sell, convey, exchange, convert, improve, repair, partition, divide, allot, subdivide, create restrictions, easements, or other servitudes thereon, and otherwise operate and control;
   b. Lease Assets: Lease for terms within or beyond the term of any trust provided for in this Declaration and for any purpose, including exploration for the removal of gas, oil, and other minerals; and enter into any covenants and agreements relating to the property so leased or any improvements which may then or thereafter be erected on such property;
   c. Encumber Assets: Encumber or hypothecate for any trust purpose by mortgage, deed of trust, pledge, or otherwise;
   d. Administer Insurance: Carry insurance of such kinds and in such amounts as the Trustee may deem advisable at the expense of the Trust provided for in this Declaration; Alex Paul Gonzales shall act as Special Trustee over any insurance policies owned by the Trust, and shall make all decisions with respect thereto; while either Creator shall act as Trustee under this instrument, he or she shall execute any documents necessary or appropriate to implement the actions taken by the Special Trustee on the request of any insurance company.
   e. Litigate: Commence or defend at the expense of the trust provided for in this Declaration as such litigation with respect to any such trust or any property of the Trust Estate as Trustee may deem advisable and employ, for reasonable compensation payable by any such trust, such counsel as the Trustee deems advisable for that purpose;
   f. Invest: Invest and reinvest the Trust funds in such property as the Trustee, exercising reasonable business judgment, may deem advisable, whether or not such property is of the character specifically permitted by law for the investment of Trust funds; provided, however, that the Trustee is not authorized to invest or reinvest the Trust funds in property which is nonproductive of income; provided, further, that in the event that any income producing property of the Trust

FIGURE 9.11

Certificate of Revocable Trust (Continued)

subsequently becomes nonproductive of income, the Trustee is directed at such time to convert such nonproductive property to property productive of income;

g. Vote: Vote, by proxy or otherwise, in such manner as Trustee may determine to be the best interest of the Trust provided for in this Declaration any securities having voting right held by the Trustee pursuant to this Declaration;

h. Pay bills: Pay any assessments or other charges levied on any stock or other security held by Trustee in trust pursuant to this Declaration;

i. Foreclose: Participate in any plans or proceedings for the foreclosure, reorganization, consolidation, merger or liquidation of any corporation or organization that has issued securities held by the Trustee or will issue securities to be held by Trustee in trust pursuant to the terms of this Declaration, to deposit securities with the transfer title or securities on such terms as Trustee may deem in the best interest of the trusts to any protective or other committee established to further or defeat any such plan or proceeding;

j. Compromise claims: Compromise, submit to arbitration, release with or without consideration and otherwise adjust any claims in favor of or against any trust provided for in this Declaration;

k. Borrow: The Trustee shall have the power to borrow money for any trust purpose (including from the probate estate for the purpose of paying taxes) on such terms and conditions as the Trustee may deem proper from any person, firm or corporation; this includes the power to borrow money on behalf of one trust from any other trust provided for in this Declaration, and to obligate the trusts, or any of them provided for in this Declaration to repay such borrowed money;

l. Manner of Holding Title: The Trustees may hold securities or other property held by Trustee in the trust pursuant to this Declaration in Trustee's name as Trustee under this Declaration, or the Trustee may hold securities unregistered in such condition that ownership will pass by delivery.

m. Signature Powers:

   i. During the joint lives of the Creators, only ONE signature of either Creator as Trustee shall be required to transact any transfer of Trust assets held by banks, savings and loans, credit unions, stock companies, or brokers or similar entities holding cash, stocks, bonds, or similar assets which belong to the trust.

   ii. It is the Creators' intent that the Trustee shall have no more extensive power over any Community Property transferred to the Trust Estate than either of them would have had under California Civil Code Section 5125 had this Declaration of Trust not been created. This instrument shall be interpreted to achieve this intention. This limitation shall terminate on the death of either Creator.

EXECUTED ON THIS 17TH DAY OF MAY 1999 AT ___Any City___, California.

BY: _Sandra Anna Gonzales_____, CREATOR

BY: _Sandra Anna Gonzales_____, TRUSTEE

BY: _Juan Ivan Gonzales_____, CREATOR

BY: _Juan Ivan Gonzales_____, TRUSTEE

individuals. The individuals are the ones who hold a job and earn income that is used to qualify for the loan. Therefore, some lenders will insist that the individuals sign for the funds. After the close of escrow, the individuals would need to then create a new grant deed to place the title back into the trust, if the trustees want the trust to hold title to the real property asset.

Corporation

Another form of ownership involving more than one person is when a group of stockholders owns real property in the name of the corporation. This is common when the builder/developer of the property builds new homes, then gives a corporation deed to each individual purchaser. Also, when a property has been foreclosed, the trustee who passes title to the successful bidder gives a corporation deed to transfer ownership to the new buyer.

The escrow officer must make sure to have the correct signer for the escrow documents and for the **corporation grant deed** or the corporation quitclaim deed as is shown in Figure 9.12. The president of the corporation is rarely the person having the authority to sign the assets for the corporation. Most likely the secretary is the party who signs for the corporation. And the secretary of the corporation needs to obtain a corporate resolution authorizing the sale of the assets of the corporation. If only the president signs the grant deed to transfer ownership to a buyer for the property, the title company may reject approval of recordation of the document without having evidence of the authority for the person doing the signing. The escrow officer may request a corporate resolution and minutes of a corporate meeting given the written authority for the signer of all documents as related to the escrow.

The title company will perform a search on the corporation, just as it would on an individual who obtains a policy of title insurance. People with a common name will have a much longer list of assets, as is shown in Figure 9.13 showing the results of a sample search for a Corporation.

■ NOTES AND TRUST DEEDS

A **trust note** contains the terms and conditions for a loan secured by real property in California. The holder of the first trust deed usually prepares the trust note when an institutional lender is used in the transaction. However, junior lien holders and private parties, such as when the seller carries the loan, do not usually furnish the trust note. This note is often prepared by the escrow officer. The terms of the note may have been contained in the written purchase agreement, or they may be a dictated amendment to the original escrow instructions. The common reasons that the seller carries back a loan usually fall into the following categories:

FIGURE 9.12

Ownership by a Corporation

RECORDING REQUESTED BY
First City Title Company

**AND WHEN RECORDED MAIL
THIS DEED AND**
UNLESS OTHER WISE SHOWN BELOW MAIL TAX
STATEMENTS TO
Name
Address
City & State
Zip
Title Order No.   Escrow No.

Book
Page
File No.

Recorded on
_____at_____
Official Records
County of_____, California
Conny B. McCormack
Registrar-Recorder/County Clerk

Fees:
$ _____
R

SPACE ABOVE THIS LINE FOR RECORDER'S USE

CORPORATION QUITCLAIM DEED

The undersigned declares that the documentary transfer tax is $_____and is
____ computed on the full value of the interest or property conveyed, or is
____ computed on the full value less the value of liens or encumbrances remaining thereon at the time of sale. The land,
tenements or realty is located in
____ unincorporated area   ____ city of _____

FOR A VALUABLE CONSIDERATION, receipt of which is hereby acknowledged,
a corporation organized under the laws of the State of
do (es), hereby remise, release and forever quitclaims to

the following described real property in the City of_____, County of _____
state of California:

  (legal description here)

Dated:_____   _____

                                                 _____

STATE OF CALIFORNIA   _____
COUNTY OF_____
On this the _____day of _____ , 20___   _____
The undersigned, a Notary Public in and for said
County and State, personally appeared _____
_____, known to me
to be the _____President, and_____
_____known to me to be Secretary of the
corporation that executed the within Instrument,
known to me to be the persons who executed the
within Instrument on behalf of the corporation
therein named, and acknowledged to me that
such corporation executed the within instrument
pursuant to its by-laws or resolution of its board
of directors.

**FOR NOTARY SEAL OR
STAMP**

_____
          Signature of Notary

_____
     Name (Typed or Printed) of Notary

Mail Tax Statements to Party shown on following line: If no Party so shown, mail as directed above.

Name   Street Address   City & State

FIGURE 9.13

Individual Corporation Name Run (General Search Sample)

Type		Date Filed	Doc #	% Trans	Name
LN	04400238	12 FEB 90	01B7-44538 03	75% INDIV	GONZAL 1:S,1157, ABC Lane
DV	42700302	26 FEB 90	01C7-52811 00	100% MALE	GONZALEZ J: DISSOL
DC	42700304	26 FEB 90	01C7-96212 00	80% FEMALE	GONZALEZ J: CT ORDER 24700
BY	011C9005	02 MAR 90		75% INDIV	GONZALES J: CA, 123 Street
JG	87300402	13 MAR 90	01C7-4744600	100% MALE	GONZALEZ J: MC 001078 4045
LN	34300575	26 MAR 90	01D7-5442001	100% INDIV	GONZALES J: O,156, CBA Lane
LN	35400575	26 MAR 90	01D7-5552001	100% MALE	GONZALEZ J: O,123, 321 Street
DC	25700596	28 MAR 90	01D7-2582602	100% MALE	GONZALEZ J: CT ORDER SC 035
LN	69600617	30 MAR 90	01D7-8973401	75% INDIV	GONZAL J: S,622, XYZ Lane
LN	27900629	02 APR 90	01D7-2803801	99% INDIV	GONZALEZ: S, 109, BCA Avenue
BY	49509008	09 APR 90		100% MALE	GONZALEZ J: RR ILK Boulevard
DC	54700725	18 APR 90	01E7-34822012	75% MALE	GONZALEZ, J: CT ORDER SC
JG	80400813	03 MAY 90	01F7-2050401	100% MALE	GONZALEZ J: MC 00613
LN	53500838	07 MAY 90	01F7-9361201	100% MALE	GONZALEZ J: S,4350, 010 Lane
LN	99600885	15 MAY 90	01F7-7972802	88% MALE	GONSALEZ J: S,125, HLI Street
LN	36300934	23 MAY 90	01F7-96446017	100% MALE	GONZALES J: S, 213, 123 Lane
JG	03801135	26 JUN 90	01H7-309110	100% MALE	GONZALEZ J: MC 00549
LN	18801153	28 JUN 90	01H7-1891802	99% INDIV	GONZALES J: S,941, 001 Avenue
BY	35209021	27 AUG 90		100% MALE	GONZALES J: JD, 111 Street
DC	12201520	04 SEP 90	01J7-5234500	100% MALE	GONZALEZ J CT ORDER SC 257
DC	12201520	04 SEP 90	01J7-5234500	80% FEMALE	GONZALEZ J: CT ORDER SC 25
JG	46201580	13 SEP 90	01K7-4631402	75% MALE	GONZALES J MC00897 21
JG	46201580	13 SEP 90	01K7-4631402	75% MALE	GONZALES J: MC008 22
BY	27909023	17 SEP 90		100% MALE	GONZALEZ J; KL ZEE Street
LN	98401647	26 SEP 90	01K7-3853800	99% INDIV	GONZALEZ J: S.S. EXTE
LN	49101707	05 OCT 90	01L7-3851000	100% MALE	GONZALEZ J: S 458, 004 Boulevard
BY	53309026	18 OCT 90		88% FEMALE	GONZALEZ J: KM SRQ Road
BY	05809027	24 OCT 90		100% MALE	GONZALEZ J: BR HIJ Lane
DC	24801825	29 OCT 90	01L7-24903	100% MALE	GONZALES J: CT ORDER SC 005
BY	93309028	13 NOV 90		100% MALE	GONZALES J: KL, MN Avenue
LN	37301935	19 NOV 90	01A8-7743800	100% MALE	GONZALEZ J: S 31, 654 Street
LN	47901991	30 NOV 90	01B8-4800999	100% MALE	GONZALES J: S 34, QPO Road
LN	28201989	30 NOV 90	01B8-6830800	80% INDIV	GONZALEZ J: S 13, 765 Lane
LN	49602014	05 DEC 90	01B8-2971603	100% MALE	GONZALEZ J: S 13, 987 Street
JG	45102107	21 DEC 90	01B8-0525000	100% MALE	GONZALEZ J: MC 00, 111 Lane
LN	68900004	02 JAN 91	01B8-6901601	100% MALE	GONZALEZ J: S 64, UVW Boulevard
JG	76500023	07 JAN 91	01C8-7662103	100% MALE	GONZALEZ J: MC 0058, 888 Road
JG	97900051	11 JAN 91	01C8-380 3000	75% FEMALE	GONZALEZ J: MC 0027, WVU Avenue
DC	18200137	30 JAN 91	01D8-7830101	100% MALE	GONZALES J: MADER CT ORD
BY	99209162	30 JAN 91		100% MALE	GONZALEZ J: 543 Street
BY	95109166	05 MAR 91		100% MALE	GONZALEZ J: WL 862 Road
BY	59609169	27 MAR 91		100% MALE	GONZALEZ J: GM 268 Lane
DC	77908464	02 APR 91	01F8-2802003	80% FEMALE	GONZALEZ J: CT ORD, ZZ Street

KEY TO TERMS

BY = BANKRUPTCY	LN = LIEN	JG = JUDGMENT	DC = DOCUMENT OF THE COURT

- The appraisal is lower than the agreed loan amount with purchaser not having adequate cash to cover the difference.

- Sellers can earn a higher interest rate on the note than if they placed the cash in a financial institution.

- Seller does not need the cash and would place the extra funds on this or another property if the seller received cash on this transaction.

- Seller hopes the buyer defaults in the future so seller can reobtain ownership to the property under foreclosure laws, allowing the holder of a junior lien to take over the senior lien without qualifying for the senior loan.

- Seller wants to postpone collection of taxable principal to spread the balance of the cash to be received from the sale until a different tax year where a lower tax rate is expected, usually under an installment sale agreement.

- Because buyer cannot qualify in the current market with conventional lenders, the transfer is made until the property has more equity and the buyer has established a payment record.

- Seller avoids a prepayment penalty that deeply cuts into the seller's profit proceeds.

A deed of trust, also called a **trust deed,** is the most commonly used document evidencing debt on real property in California. The trust deed is used by a borrower (trustor) to convey bare, equitable title to real property that is owned by the trustor. The trustor transfers this title to a neutral third party, the trustee, in order to secure the obligation. The obligation is usually the repayment of a debt under the terms of a promissory note, called the trust note. The debt is payable to a lender, the beneficiary.

The trustee is usually a corporation. The trustee holds the title until the beneficiary gives instructions to either begin foreclosure or to show the debt has been repaid in full. The trustee is given the power of sale to perform a nonjudicial foreclosure. The proceeds received from the trustee's sale where the successful bidder received a trust deed are used to apply toward the payment on the defaulted obligation. The trustee also issues the deed of reconveyance, commonly referred to as the "reconveyance deed," that is recorded at the county recorder's office to act as evidence that the obligation has been paid in full.

■ POWER OF ATTORNEY

A **power of attorney** is when one individual gives another person the power to act on his or her behalf, such as to negotiate a real estate transaction. Persons given a power of attorney sign as if they were the actual property owner or the buyer. The individual who is acting on behalf of the actual owner, buyer, landlord, or tenant is called the **attorney-in-fact.**

In California, a valid power of attorney must have been recorded at the county recorder's office where the property is physically located for the attorney-in-fact to carry out the powers delegated. This means that the document must be in writing. An unrecorded power of attorney is useful to the escrow officer to see that the other parties intend to convey powers for the attorney-in-fact to carry out the real estate transaction matters on their behalf; however, only an acknowledged and recorded document is valid to actually convey title to land.

Two types are commonly used. The *general power of attorney* grants the right to sign all documents, no matter what kind, during a person's absence. This is typically used between spouses. The other, the *specific power of attorney*, stipulates exactly what may be signed, such as granting the real estate broker the right to reject any offers below a specific price when the broker has a valid listing agreement contract. In Northern California, most escrows require using a specific power of attorney.

A power of attorney is often used in a transaction where one of the parties is out of state, such as when one spouse leaves to begin a new job while the other spouse remains behind until the house is sold and in escrow. Therefore, it is important to let the escrow officer know as soon as applicable when a power of attorney will be used. This allows time for the escrow officer to draw up the document; deliver the document to the appropriate party; have the document signed, notarized, and returned to escrow; then get the document to the title company for recording.

Both parties must remain legally competent and both must remain alive to the termination of the transaction. The power of attorney may be terminated by filing a Notice of Revocation. A Power of Attorney form is shown in Figure 9.14.

THINK ABOUT IT

Grant Deed or Quitclaim Deed?

An unmarried brother and sister co-own property with a grant deed. The sister executes a grant deed to a third party for payment of her debt. The brother is very upset. He jumps in his car to drive over to fight over the matter, but he gets into a car crash and dies. The brother had willed all his property to his sister. Who has title to the property?

Answer: The grant deed transferred only the sister's interest to the third party. The brother did not sign a deed to transfer his interest to the third party. However,

FIGURE 9.14

Power of Attorney Form

RECORDING REQUESTED BY

WHEN RECORDED MAIL TO

NAME

ADDRESS

CITY

STATE&ZIP

Title Order No.   Escrow No.

SPACE **ABOVE** THIS LINE FOR RECORDER'S USE

POWER OF ATTORNEY—GENERAL

KNOW ALL MEN BY THESE PRESENTS

that _____ _____ have   made,
constituted and appointed, and by these presents do hereby make, constitute and appoint _____
_____ true and lawful Attorney for _____ and in _____ name , place and
stead to ask, demand, sue for, recover, collect and receive all such sums of money, debts, dues, accounts, legacies, bequests,
interests, dividends, annuities, and demands whatsoever as are now or shall hereafter become due, owing, payable, or belonging to the
under-signed; and have, use, and take all lawful ways and means in the name of the undersigned, or otherwise, for the recovery
thereof, by legal process, and to compromise and agree for the same, and grant acquittances or other sufficient discharges for the
same, for the undersigned, and in the name of the undersigned to make, seal, and deliver the same; to compromise any and all debts
owing by the undersigned, and to convey, transfer, and/or assign any property of any kind or character belonging to the undersigned in
satisfaction of any debt owing by us or either of us; to bargain, contract. agree for, purchase, receive, and take lands, tenements,
hereditaments, and accept the seizen and possession of all lands, and all deeds, and other assurances in the law therefor; and to
lease, let, demise, bargain, sell, remise, release, convey, mortgage, convey in trust, and hypothecate lands, tenements, and
hereditaments, upon such terms and conditions, and under such covenants as said attorney shall think fit; to exchange real or personal
property for other real or personal property, and to execute and deliver the necessary instruments of transfer or conveyance to
consummate such exchange and deliver subordination agreements subordinating any lien, encumbrance or other right in real or
personal property to any other lien, encumbrance, or other right therein; also to bargain and agree for, buy, sell, mortgage, hypothecate,
convey in trust or otherwise, and in any and every way and manner deal in and with goods, wares and merchandise, chooses in action,
and other property in possession or in action, including authority to utilize my eligibility for VA Guaranty; also to transfer, assign, and
deliver stock and the certificate or certificates evidencing the ownership of the same; and to make, do, and transact all and every kind of
business of what nature and kind soever; and, also for the undersigned and in the name _____
and as the act and deed of the undersigned, to sign, seal, execute, deliver, and acknowledge such deeds, covenants, leases,
indentures, agreements, mortgages, deeds of trust, hypothecations, assignments, bottomries, charter parties,bills of lading, bills,
bounds, notes, receipts, evidences of debts, releases, and satisfactions of mortgage, judgment and other debts, and such other
instruments in writing, of whatever kind of nature, as may be reasonable, advisable, necessary, or proper in the premises.

Giving and granting unto said Attorney _____ full power and authority to do and perform
all and every act and thing whatsoever requisite and necessary to be done in and about the premises, as fully to all intents and purposes
as the undersigned might or could do if personally present, the undersigned herebyexpressly ratifying and confirming all that said
Attorney shall lawfully do or cause to be done by virtue of these presents.

Dated _____

STATE OF CALIFORNIA
COUNTY OF _____   } SS

On _____ before me, _____
personally appeared _____   _____
_____
personally known to me or proved to me on the basis of satisfactory
evidence to be the person(s) whose name(s) is/are subscribed to the
within instrument and acknowledged to me that he/she/they executed
the same in his/her/their authorized capacity(ies), and that by
his/her/their signature(s) on the instrument the person(s), or the entity
upon behalf of which the person(s) acted, executed the instrument.

WITNESS my hand and official seal.

Signature _____   (Notary Seal)

when the sister acquired the brother's interest from the will, all the brother's interest was automatically transferred to the sister and a grant deed conveys both the current title ownership interest plus any after-acquired title.

If the sister had used a quitclaim deed, the third party would own half and the sister would own half of the property.

■ CHAPTER SUMMARY

The escrow officer is often required to prepare various documents in conjunction with the normal escrow transaction. These may include the deed that transfers ownership to the real property, as well as the trust deed and trust note that may secure a loan on the property. The use of prepared, preprinted legal forms is common, especially using the escrow software programs of today's escrow practices. This chapter discussed the sections found on common deeds.

Other documents commonly used in a real estate transaction include the preliminary change of ownership report and calculation of the documentary transfer tax. The escrow officer makes sure the public notary seal is properly affixed to any document that must be recorded to give notice to the world of the contents of the document, including the change of ownership from a trust to an individual, a power of attorney so someone may act for another, and the substitute of trustee form. This chapter helped explain many of the documents in detail for escrow personnel.

■ CHAPTER 9 QUIZ

1. The most common method to transfer owner-ship to real property is by
   a. grant deed.
   b. trust deed.
   c. trust certification.
   d. power of attorney.

2. In the preparation of documents used in an escrow transaction, the escrow officer
   a. must create each paper with original word-ing each time so as to not violate current federal copyright laws.
   b. uses preprinted or computer prepared forms.
   c. has the seller direct the trustee in writing to prepare all forms.
   d. works with the buyer to obtain the forms from the stationery store or similar places.

3. The substitute of trustee is used when
   a. one of the sellers will be out of area at the time of closing so the other seller needs a form to legally allow him or her to sign for the absentee party.
   b. a lender sells a loan to another lender and assigns its interest in the property.
   c. the property owner wants to reduce the fees to refinance by having the trustee changed from a title insurance company or lender affiliated company to a private individual who will handle signing the reconveyance deed.
   d. a loan is in default and the lender assigns its interest to a collection agency.

4. The grant deed is used
   a. to show a debt lien on the property.
   b. to transfer off ownership by one spouse to another.
   c. for tax purposes to calculate the trust cer-tification revenue.
   d. for conveying real property ownership from one party to another.

5. The trust deed indicates
   a. a change in ownership of the property from one trustor to the trustee.
   b. a change in ownership of the property from the trustee to the beneficiary.
   c. a loan recorded against the property.
   d. that the revenue tax code has proper filing and payment of required fees.

6. The purpose of a power of attorney when used in conjunction with an escrow is to
   a. qualify for the financing of the loan.
   b. allow one party to sign documents for a principal to the escrow.
   c. authorize the appraisal report.
   d. order the credit report and have authoriza-tion to provide the information to the lender.

7. A trust certification is used to
   a. allow the loan to be recorded on the real property.
   b. verify that the appraiser was independent of the transaction.
   c. indicate the authorized trustee who may act on behalf of the trust.
   d. finalize the divorce agreement for the sale of the community property asset.

8. The documentary transfer tax
   a. may be in addition to any local city transfer tax.
   b. is at the rate of $0.55 per $500, or $1.10 per thousand of valuations.
   c. is neither a nor b.
   d. is both a and b.

9. A public notary acknowledges the
   a. signature of the lender.
   b. authenticity of the appraisal report.
   c. signature of the signer.
   d. content of the document.

10. The preliminary change of ownership report is used to
    a. create a security interest in personal property.
    b. determine the total sales price used for the supplementary property tax bill.
    c. allow one party to sign for another in an escrow situation.
    d. discourage disputes between the buyer and seller when reconveying a partial interest in property.

PROCESSING AND DISCLOSURES

■ KEY TERMS

amendment	insurance policy	termite clearance
bill of sale	irrevocable demand	termite report
disclosures	order	transfer disclosure
electronic signature	personal property	statement (TDS)
good funds law	possession agreement	walk-through
home warranty	real property	wire transfer
inspection	special recording	

■ CHAPTER OVERVIEW

Chapter 10 discusses the various disclosures that are a natural part of a real estate transaction. The written purchase agreement contract between the buyer and the seller contains many clauses pertaining to the topic of disclosure. In addition, the appraiser is involved in making disclosures directly to the lender that are normally outside of escrow, unless a payment for services is made through escrow to correct a default. In fact, when a loan is involved, the lender insists on many disclosures, such as a structure pest control clearance report. The real estate sales agents and the loan broker are usually licensed by the California Department of Real Estate, which requires every transaction to have a transfer disclosure statement (TDS). The TDS is handled between the parties and outside of escrow, in which the escrow officer is not involved, unless specified in the transaction.

Escrow is involved in many documents, such as insurance coverage, the possession agreement, and anything that involves the closing, such as a wire transfer or irrevocable demand order from another escrow. The title company is very involved with the funds at the close of escrow to pay off the existing liens and to ensure recordation of the new funds placed into the escrow. All funds transfers include written instructions on the handling of money and disclosures of the restrictions on when funds are available to the various parties, including the principals, agents, and vendors.

■ LEARNING OBJECTIVES

At the conclusion of Chapter 10, you will be able to

- understand the various types of disclosures required for a typical escrow;
- give a definition for the good funds law;
- outline the wire transfer and electronic signature elements of an escrow;
- differentiate between escrow disclosures and sales disclosures; and
- explain inspections and disclosures.

■ INSPECTIONS AND DISCLOSURES

An **inspection** is a visual investigation of a physical component of real property. The inspection may be performed by a variety of individuals or companies. When the property is listed for sale, the California Department of Real Estate (DRE) licensee is required to make a diligent visual inspection of the premises. This would require the agent to have access to the premises to investigate the condition there. No additional expertise is needed above that required to obtain the level of license that the individual holds. The real estate sales agent does not need to have the level of knowledge that a contractor or appraiser might have, unless they also hold that license.

Prior to a licensed agent showing the property, the buyer's agent is responsible for asking the listing agent if there are any special disclosures that should be made to the buyer based on the listing agent's physical inspection. The buyer's agent, referred to as the selling agent, must also perform a diligent physical inspection.

The standard purchase agreement between the buyer and the seller includes the requirement that a transfer disclosure statement (TDS) be given from the seller to the buyer. If no licensed real estate agent is involved, as in the case of the for sale by owner (FSBO) transaction, the seller is still obligated to furnish the TDS, according to California State Law Civil Code 1105. The seller must give the legally prescribed wording to the buyer that describes physical defects, landfill, homeowner association, and other disclosures.

All of the TDS information is handled outside of escrow, with which the escrow officer is not concerned. If the TDS disclosure is not given, the buyer can cancel the transaction. The wording found in the following text box is commonly agreed to between the parties to the real estate transaction.

> **PHYSICAL INSPECTION:** Within __ calendar days after Seller's acceptance, Buyer shall have the right, at Buyer's expense, to select a licensed contractor or other qualified professional(s), to inspect and investigate the subject property, including, but not limited to, structural, plumbing, sewer/septic systems, well, heating, electrical, built-in appliances, roof, soils, foundation, mechanical systems, pool, pool heater, pool filter, air conditioner, if any, possible environmental hazards such as asbestos, formaldehyde, radon gas, and other substances/products. Buyer shall keep the subject property free and clear of any liens, indemnify and hold Seller harmless from all liability, claims, demands, damages or costs, and repair all damages to the property arising from the inspections. All claimed defects concerning the condition of the property that adversely affect the continued use of the property for the purposes for which it is presently being used shall be in writing, supported by written reports, if any, and delivered to the Seller within __ calendar days after Seller acceptance. Buyer shall furnish Seller copies, at no cost, of all reports concerning the property obtained by the Buyer. When such reports disclose conditions or information unsatisfactory to the Buyer, which the Seller is unwilling or unable to correct, Buyer may cancel this agreement. Seller shall make the premises available for all inspections. BUYER'S FAILURE TO NOTIFY SELLER IN WRITING SHALL CONCLUSIVELY BE CONSIDERED APPROVAL.

Closely related to the physical inspection and TDS are the issues relating to retrofit. These items are also handled outside of escrow, with which escrow is not concerned. However, the payment for compliance with the retrofit and governmental requirements for a property are a great concern of the escrow holder. The escrow agent must obtain the signature of the seller who is paying for the retrofit compliance. In addition, the escrow holder must make sure that full disclosure is made to both the new lender and the buyer. Often, a condition prior to funding will be that the retrofit work has been complied with. It is common for the retrofit work to be paid for after the close of escrow from the seller's proceeds, similar to the payment for the termite clearance report. The wording for the preprinted purchase contract is shown in the following text box, and if this wording does not reflect the intent of the parties, then a document or phrase would need to be drawn in writing to show the special arrangements being made that are different from the standard wording.

> **RETROFIT:** Compliance with any minimum mandatory government retrofit standards, including proof of compliance, shall be paid for by Seller.
>
> **ENERGY CONSERVATION RETROFIT:** If local ordinance requires that the property be brought in compliance with minimum energy Conservation Standards as a condition of transfer, Buyer shall comply with and pay for these requirements.

The portions of the agreement that would be unique to a specific transaction are shown as underlined material in the example in the text box below. The escrow officer would include those items with the same or similar words that would apply to the individual transaction. A **bill of sale** is issued for the individual items of personal property transferred to the buyer. In some transactions, this is an important part of the consideration. For apartment and rental income property, the depreciation for the structure may be about 30 years, whereas the depreciation for personal property items, such as stoves and refrigerators, can be as few as five years. This can represent a large financial difference to a buyer. In the case of the sale of a business, the trade fixtures are usually transferred with a bill of sale, and the seller is often required to pay sales tax on the items. The escrow holder then would become involved with obtaining a release from the state sales tax collection agency. Business personal property fixtures often include the tables, chairs, desks, counter, cash register, office equipment, restaurant equipment, or similar items.

> **PERSONAL PROPERTY:** The following items of **personal property,** free of liens and without warranty of condition are included in the purchase price and shall convey to Buyer at closing: <u>**family room surround sound wiring and speakers (but not the equipment), courtyard fountain and pump, and large wind chime.**</u> Parties acknowledge that no monetary value is given to said items in regard to the purchase price. All parties acknowledge that all personal property items are handled outside of escrow, between the parties, for which escrow is not responsible. No bill of sale is provided by escrow.
>
> *(Continued on next page)*

FIXTURES: All existing fixtures and fittings that are attached to the property or for which special openings have been made are included in the purchase price (unless excluded elsewhere in these instructions) and are transferred free of liens, including, but not limited to, electrical, light, plumbing, and heating fixtures, solar systems, fireplace inserts, built-in appliances, screens, awnings, shutters, window coverings, attached floor coverings, TV antennas/satellite dishes, and related equipment (if owned by Seller), private integrated telephone systems, air cooler or conditioner, pool and spa equipment, water softeners (if owned by Seller), security systems and/or alarms (if owned by Seller), garage door openers/remote controls, attached fireplace equipment, mailbox, all in-ground landscaping including trees and shrubs.

The phrase that the escrow holder usually includes in the escrow instructions when personal property is being transferred between the parties is shown in the text box below. It should be remembered that the lender and the escrow holder are the two parties working on the transaction who never see the premises. The lender gets a copy of the appraisal, with photographs of the property and area. But the escrow holder does not get a copy of the appraisal and never sees the property. This means that escrow cannot be held accountable for any of the items that would be obvious on a visual inspection of the premises. Escrow must relieve itself of a liability in connection with the physical parts of the transaction, which is the collateral for the entire event. Remember that escrow is only concerned with being the neutral third party that holds the funds and documents in safe keeping until transfer of ownership.

The paragraph in the following text box is typically found in standard residential escrow instructions regarding the personal property and the fixtures involved in the transaction. According to the basic principles of real estate, the transfer of ownership to real property is by deed and to personal property by a bill of sale. **Real property** is thought to be immovable, whereas **personal property** is the portable personal belongings of an individual. However, real property can become personal property and personal property can become real property. Therefore, it is always wise to spell out in the escrow the specific agreements between the parties to the transaction.

You shall make no physical inspection of the real property or personal property described in any instruments deposited in, or which is the subject of this escrow. You have made no representations or warranties concerning any such real property or personal property and are not to be concerned with nor liable for the condition of real property.

The escrow entity, who has never seen the premises, is not to be liable for any matters where special expertise is required, such as chemical pest or termite control and in any of the areas regarding hazardous substances. The paragraph in the next text box represents typical wording found in the escrow instructions.

> The parties agree to release you from any and all liability of any kind or nature and to indemnify you from any loss, damages, claims, judgments or costs of any kind or nature resulting from or related to the release or discharge of hazardous or toxic wastes on the subject property whether it occurred in the past or present or may occur in the future which release or discharge is in violation of law, in excess of any state and federal standards, permit requirements and/or disclosure requirements existing at this time or which may exist at a future time. The parties represent that they made their own assessment of the condition of the subject property and have not relied on any of your representations in making the assessment. The parties are advised to seek independent legal and technical environmental expert advice in assessing the risks associated with potential hazardous or toxic wastes.

The **transfer disclosure statement (TDS)** became effective on January 1, 1987, and requires the seller and the seller's licensed agent, if any, and the buyer's licensed agent, if any, to provide specific disclosure information to a prospective purchaser. The buyer has three days in which to rescind the purchase from the date of delivery of the TDS form. Civil Code Section 1102.3 is a California law that has three major areas of **disclosures.** The first area is where a check-box list of features for the property is listed. The second area specifically asks if any significant defects or malfunctions are known for selected items listed, such as roof, plumbing, or electrical circuits. The third area asks the seller if he or she is aware of a list of specific items, such as landfill, lead-based paint, common walls with adjoining landowners, structural additions or modifications with or without permits, flooding, homeowner association issues, and similar areas. Because the escrow holder never sees the property, the disclosures are usually a memorandum in the escrow instructions that state that the TDS types of disclosures, including the home inspection report, are of no concern to escrow and with which escrow is not to be concerned. The parties will sign that they have complied with a law or been given a report, with the escrow holder noting only that the parties have agreed that the items have met with their approval outside of escrow. This often includes the walk-through conducted just prior to the close of escrow and may even include the written appraisal report. Typically, the escrow holder will have some kind of checklist to ensure that the items called out in the purchase contract and escrow instructions have been completed so that the escrow is in a position to close. An example of one such checklist is shown in Figure 10.1.

FIGURE 10.1

Checklist Required to Close Escrow

THE FOLLOWING IS A CHECKLIST REQUIRED TO COMPLETE YOUR FINAL CLOSING STATEMENT PRIOR TO CLOSING TO AVOID MISSING ANY ITEMS AT CLOSING:

_____Home Protection Policy

_____Property Disclosure

_____Termite Report

_____Home Inspection Report

_____Notary

_____Messenger/Overnight Mail

_____Demand—1st T.D.

_____Demand—2nd T.D.

_____Misc. _____

PLEASE FAX ACTUAL BILL WITH AUTHORIZATION IN WRITING FOR THE BILL TO BE PAID BY ESCROW

The escrow officer would have some kind of checklist to notify the other parties in the transaction of items that are needed in order to close. The initial list that the escrow officer might use for the internal escrow file might be similar to the example shown in Figure 10.2.

A year after the TDS became required, in January 1, 1988, the disclosure regarding real estate agency relationships became effective. The provisions of the law are found in Article 2.5, Section 2373 of Chapter 2 of Title 9 of Part 4 of Division 3 of the Civil Code in California for real estate licensees. If the escrow holder is not licensed by the DRE, then the escrow officer would not need to comply with making any disclosure. By definition, escrow is to remain a neutral third party to the transaction. However, if the escrow is being handled by a DRE broker-owned licensee, the DRE-licensed individual would need to comply with the agency disclosure. Again, in normal escrow instructions, the agency disclosure is handled outside of escrow with which the escrow officer is not concerned because it is not between the principals.

California Assembly Bill AB 6 (Civil Code §1102) requires a disclosure report to be given to a buyer regarding the property address of the transaction based upon a review of maps and data cited from public information. Site-specific information is required by a registered geologist or licensed professional engineer to conduct a site investigation. Geotechnical and other reports are available with a city, county, state, or federal agency or office and may be required. The following

FIGURE 10.2

Internal Escrow Checklist

	Need	Requested	Received	Remarks
Instructions:				
Seller			X	No forwarding address
Buyer		X		
Borrower				
S I				
Seller			X	Sent to escrow
Buyer/Borrower		X		
Lender Info Sheet	X			
Property Info Sheet		X		
Bene Demand	X			
1st T.D.		X		
2nd T.D.		X		
3rd T.D.				
New Lender				
Cert. Esc. Inst.				Copy to escrow
Prelim. Title		X		
Approval		X		Notified escrow
Docs Ordered	X			
Docs Signed	X			
Docs to Lender	X			
Funding	X			
Amendments				
Seller Signed		X		
Buyer Signed		X		
Copy to Lender	X			
Vesting				
Trust Certificate		X		
Deed			X	Sent to Title Co.
Estimated Stmt.		X		
Recording	X			
HUD-1 to Borrower	X			
HUD-1 to Lender	X			
Misc. Docs				
Grant Deed		X		Original @ escrow
Homestead Release	X			
Other				

are the typical categories reported for a typical residential disclosure report, for which the report will indicate either "not situated" or "situated" in a:

- Special Flood Hazard Area (Zone A or Zone V) designated by the Federal Emergency Management Agency (FEMA);

- Dam or Reservoir Inundation Area mapped by the State Department of Water Resources;

- State of California Very High Fire Hazard Severity Zone;

- State of California Fire Responsibility Area for which the owner of the property is subject to the maintenance requirements of Section 4291 of the Public Resources Code;

- State of California Alquist-Priolo Earthquake Fault Zone;

- Program run by the State of California Division of Mines and Geology Seismic Hazard Mapping Act;

- Earthquake-induced Landslide Hazard Zone on official maps of the Seismic Hazard Mapping Act;

- Liquefaction Hazard Zone on official maps of the Seismic Hazard Mapping Act;

- Tsunami Inundation Area mapped in the County General Plan Safety Element;

- County where sites on slopes or in hillside areas may be subject to Slope Instability; and

- Mello-Roos Community Facilities District that is currently being assessed, as reported by available records from the county auditor-controller, as of the date of this report. Seller of property in Mello-Roos Districts must provide a Notice of Special Tax and Notice of Special Assessment to the buyer disclosing a summary and details for all 1915 Bond Act & Mello-Roos Assessment districts levying taxes against real property. (Mello-Roos is explained in detail in Chapter 11 on page 321.)

■ HOME WARRANTY

The word warranty has different meanings in a real estate transaction depending upon the state and the area of the country. In eastern states the transfer of ownership between the seller and the buyer is *not* with a grant deed, but is with a warranty deed. In this case, the seller warrants to the buyer that the seller actually owns the property and is giving the buyer all ownership title to full ownership of the property. In California, a warranty has different meaning. It refers to the warranty as a guarantee as to the physical premises, also called a **home warranty.** The seller, however, does give certain warranties to the buyer, namely as to the legal use of the premises approved by government permits for alterations, and so forth, as is seen in the text box below.

SELLER REPRESENTATION: Seller warrants that Seller has no knowledge of any notice of violations of City, County, State, Federal, Building, Zoning, Fire, Health Codes or ordinances, or other governmental regulation filed or issued against the property. This warranty shall be effective until date of close of escrow.

STRUCTURAL MODIFICATIONS: Within _____ calendar days after Seller's acceptance, Seller shall disclose to Buyer, in writing, any known structural additions or alterations, or the installation, alteration, repair or replacement of significant components of the structure upon the property made with or without necessary permit(s). Buyer is allowed _____ calendar days after receipt of such disclosure to notify Seller, in writing, of disapproval. When the disclosed conditions or information are unsatisfactory to buyer, which Seller is unwilling or unable to correct, buyer may cancel this agreement.

The seller and buyer make warranties to each other and make representations to other parties involved in the transaction, such as the lender. The two standard clauses below are between the two parties with which the escrow holder is not normally concerned. However, in the case of liquidated damages, a clear misunderstanding often occurs. When an escrow does not go as anticipated and does not close after the buyer's deposit has been placed into escrow, the seller believes that the purchase contract says that the seller automatically gets 3 percent of the sales price because of the buyer's default on closing of the escrow. This is *not* the case. The escrow officer must have mutual instructions that are signed and agreed upon by all parties. If this is not possible, the escrow holder follows the preprinted portion of the original escrow instructions that indicate the escrow holder must stop and do nothing until mutual agreement is reached. If mutual agreement is never obtained, then the escrow holder may exercise other remedies, such as going to court in an interpleader action to have a judge determine the outcome of the deposit (see the text box below).

LIQUIDATED DAMAGES CLAUSE: Buyer and Seller have initialed the "Liquidated Damages" clause contained in the Real Estate Purchase Contract for the subject property.

ARBITRATION CLAUSE: Buyer and Seller have initialed the "Arbitration" clause contained in the Real Estate Purchase Contract for the subject property.

Because the TDS allows the buyer to cancel the transaction three days after receipt of the form, the escrow officer should ascertain if the agents have already given the buyer the required form. The information contained on the form is of no concern to the escrow holder, unless it holds up the close of the escrow, such as appraisal noted work requirements. A home warranty policy is handled similar to the TDS.

■ LIENS, JUDGMENTS, AND CHILD SUPPORT DISCLOSURE

A title search would reveal any outstanding liens against any of the parties to the real estate transaction. The title company could not issue clear title until any items found as a lien are first cleared. In order to clear a lien a release form must be obtained from the court to show that the creditor no longer has a claim. Escrow cannot accept a statement from the principal or a letter from the creditor. Once a legal court action has been filed, the court must give the release to clear the record.

If a lien is paid from the escrow proceeds, the escrow officer would make the disbursement. A lien release form would be completed and given to the title company for recordation. Chapter 12 shows several of the types of documents that would be recorded at the close of escrow, such as the Satisfaction of Judgment form and the Release of Mechanic's Lien forms.

■ AMENDMENTS

Amendments are not common in Northern California transactions because the escrow instructions are not drawn up until toward the end of the transaction when most items have already been settled. A last-minute change could occur and an amendment could be used.

In Southern California amendments are common occurrences due to the numerous changes that are normal from the beginning to the end of the escrow process. The vesting of the parties may change; the loan amount often differs from the original contract sales information; and corrections such as the legal description are often made with an escrow amendment.

The escrow officer would use some form of checklist system to determine if all items are in writing that are required and that all documents are as represented. If not, the escrow officer would draw up an amendment for signatures. The escrow **amendment** usually states that all other terms and conditions remain the same except only the specific item being changed in the amendment. A copy of all amendments would also be required to be forwarded to the buyer's lender as part of the original instructions for delivery of certified escrow instructions to the lender.

■ BUYER'S WALK-THROUGH

The **walk-through** was originally designed to let the seller show the buyer unique nuances about the property. The seller would show the buyer how to operate such items as the sprinklers and time box, automatic garage door openers, and any permanent built-in safe. It is the final inspection for the buyer prior to ownership of the property. The typical wordings in the escrow instructions are seen in the next text box:

> **CONDITION OF PROPERTY:** Seller warrants that on the date possession is made available to Buyer: The built-in appliances and plumbing, heating/air conditioning, electrical, water, sewer/septic, and pool/spa systems, if any, shall be operative. The roof shall be free of known leaks. All broken or cracked glass shall have been replaced. All other items, including landscaping, grounds, and pool/spa, if any, shall be maintained in the same condition as on the date of acceptance of the offer.

In some cases, the buyer may never have seen the inside of the structure, such as with uncooperative tenants in possession at the time the offer was accepted. In most cases, the buyer has not been inside the structure since prior to acceptance of the original offer to purchase. It has probably been weeks or several months since the buyer saw the property, if at all. This is the chance for the buyer to review the property in more detail, such as obtaining window measurements, measuring door widths for larger furniture, or more careful inspection of appliances that are part of the purchase price.

It is most helpful if the escrow instructions include a clause indicating that the buyer has a walk-through prior to close of escrow, that the escrow officer obtain a sign-off release when the inspection has been completed. See the next text box for possible typical wording for this part of the transaction.

> **WALK-THROUGH INSPECTIONS:** Buyer to have a walk-through inspection five days prior to close of escrow.

Reminding the seller's agent that this is required, as a part of the written instruction, if that is the case, may be helpful. It is advisable to reinforce that the utilities should remain on until after the walk-through has been performed so that the buyer may check all the necessary items with light from electricity, heating, plumbing, etc. If the escrow instructions indicate that all mechanical systems are to be in working order at the close of escrow, the buyer should flush the toilets, test the garbage disposal and dishwasher, activate the furnace thermostat, use the hot water from the hot water tank, turn on the shower and tub, stove, air conditioner, and pool equipment, if applicable. Check to see that sinks drain. Verify that the landscaping is still in place, as are the floor and window coverings.

The escrow is not concerned with the results of the walk-through, but only that this item is signed off and agreed to by the principals. The walk-through does not represent a "work order" form where the buyer requests anything to be done to the premises. It is, in fact, too late for work on the premises or it would hold up the close of escrow. All the work requests needed to have been part of the original offer to purchase, or handled over a month prior to when the home inspection should have been conducted by a home inspector, a warranty professional, a licensed appraiser, or some similar person.

The purpose of the final walk-through is to assure the buyers that they are getting what they bargained for. It is to ensure that the seller is giving to the buyer what was agreed to by the parties. And should items be discovered that are faulty, several methods of correction are available, as follows:

- Cancel the escrow and incur the costs of cancellation. This would be used when the premises are substantially different than represented and have major faults. In this case the buyer may incur costs for the credit report, appraisal, and escrow cancellation fee.

- Notify the lender/appraiser of substantially different premises components and determine if the lender will make the loan with the differences. If the lender will not make the loan with the problem, and the escrow instructions are contingent upon the buyer obtaining the loan, then this places the problem for the seller to rectify.

- Obtain one or more estimates for the corrections, submit them to the seller to select and approve, and transfer the cash at the close of escrow from the seller to the buyer to rectify the defaults and correct the problems.

- Proceed to close the escrow with the faults and take no action. This is especially good in a market where prices are rapidly rising and the seller may already have another offer at a higher price than the current transaction. This is also used where the buyer is planning major remodeling to the premises and would have removed the items in question anyway. The problem items should be noted on the walk-through in any event.

■ SMOKE DETECTORS AND ENVIRONMENTAL, GEOLOGIC/SEISMIC, AND FLOOD DISCLOSURES

Many items are not part of the escrow, and the escrow officer assumes no responsibility or liability for those items. However, if the contract between the buyer and seller requires delivery of a document or requires a report or a clearance for an item, then escrow would be involved because the escrow could not close until compliance is made. Some other items are required by the buyer's lender and are not items that the buyer or the seller would pay extra to obtain. Yet other items are required by law and not required by the principals or the lender. The clauses in the next text box usually appear in the sales contract and become part of the requirements that must be met before escrow can close.

SMOKE DETECTOR(S): State Law requires that residences be equipped with operable smoke detector(s). Local ordinances may have additional requirements. Unless exempt, Seller shall deliver to Buyer a written statement of compliance in accordance with applicable state and local law prior to close of escrow.

ENVIRONMENTAL DISCLOSURE: The parties agree to release you from any and all liability of any kind or nature and to indemnify you from any loss, damages, claims, judgments, or costs of any kind or nature resulting from or related to the release or discharge of hazardous or toxic wastes on the subject property whether it occurred in the past or present or may occur in the future which release or discharge is in violation of law, in excess of any state and federal standards, permit requirements, and/or disclosure requirements existing at this time or which may exist at a future time. The parties represent that they made their own assessment of the condition of the subject property and have not relied on any of your representations in making the assessment. The parties are advised to seek independent legal and technical environmental expert advice in assessing the risks associated with potential hazardous or toxic wastes.

GEOLOGIC/SEISMIC HAZARD DISCLOSURE: If the Property is situated in a Special Studies Zone (SSZ) or Seismic Hazard Zone (SHZ) designated under Public Resources Code 262102625 or 2690-2699.6, or in a locally designated geologic hazard zone(s) or area(s) where disclosure is required by local ordinance, Seller shall, within ____ calendar days after acceptance of the offer, disclose in writing to Buyer this fact(s) and any other information required by law. Construction or development of any structure may be restricted. Disclosure of SSZs and SHZs is required only where the maps, or information contained in the maps, are "reasonably available." Buyer is

(Continued on next page)

allowed ____ calendar days after receipt of the disclosure(s) to make further inquiries at appropriate government agencies, lenders, insurance agents, or other appropriate entities concerning use of the Property under local building, zoning, fire, health, and safety codes as may be applicable under the Special Studies Zone Act, Seismic Hazards Mapping Act, and local geologic ordinance(s). Buyer shall provide written notice to Seller of any items disapproved within this latter time period.

FLOOD HAZARD DISCLOSURE: If the Property is situated in a Special Flood Hazard Area designated by the Federal Emergency Management Agency, Seller shall, within ____ calendar days after acceptance of the offer, disclose this fact in writing to Buyer. Flood insurance may be required by lender. Buyer is allowed ____ calendar days from receipt of the disclosure to make further inquiries at appropriate governmental agencies, lenders, insurance agents, or other appropriate entities. Buyer shall provide written notice to Seller of any items disapproved within this latter time period.

■ PEST CONTROL INSPECTION AND TERMITE REPORT CLEARANCE

Many people associated with real estate matters do not know that the state licenses persons and firms who are allowed to use the dangerous chemicals necessary to eradicate specific types of pests. A pest control company is authorized to spray for, or otherwise treat, such pests as fleas, ants, and roaches. The chemicals used for these types of pests are not the same as the allowable treatment or chemicals used for termites. Some termites are present in most of the ground in California and are referred to in a termite report as subterranean termites. Some termites, like other flying insects, swarm and move from one property to another. A more thorough explanation can be found with the Structural Pest Control Board, see Figure 10.3. The Board's Web address is *http://www.pestboard.ca.gov/forms.htm.*

WEB LINK

Some buyers request a pest control inspection report for residential income property. The buyer wants to make sure the property is free of ants, roaches, spiders, and other pests that annoy occupants or cause the premises to be uninhabitable under landlord-tenant laws. The state license for use of the chemicals to perform this type of service is different from the chemicals used and the state license obtained for termite eradication.

The **termite report** is a statement of the condition found on the improvements on the property as of the date of the inspection by a licensed and qualified termite company. The escrow officer receives a copy of all authorized termite report inspections made by a termite firm.

FIGURE 10.3

Structural Pest Control Board Web Site

Source: Structural Pest Control Board (*www.pestboard.ca.gov/forms.htm*).

Should more than one inspection be issued, the escrow holder would include all such reports in the file that would be disclosed to the buyer and the buyer's lender. Normally loan requirements state that a termite clearance is required. A typical termite report might reflect that some boards must be replaced because of the findings of infestation by wood destroying insects. In this case, the termite company may replace the boards or it may work with a subcontractor who would replace the damaged boards. It is not uncommon for the property owner to have the boards replaced at a lower cost by another, independent worker. Or the independent worker may include other work for the same price that the termite company estimated to make the repair. Typically, the termite company will remove the existing, infested board, and will replace it with new wood. However, the termite company will not paint the board so that if nothing else is done until close of escrow the buyer receives the property with new, raw wood. This is where the seller will hire an outside person at the same price, but that price must include one coat of primer to seal the new wood, then another coat of exterior trim paint to match the existing wood on the property.

One concern is the bill for each termite inspection and for the worker who performed any work on the premises prior to the close of escrow. Should the worker not be paid through the escrow or by the property owner, the worker could file a mechanic's lien. If such a lien were found valid, the lien would have priority over the new first trust deed holder and a claim would be made against the ALTA title insurance policy.

The escrow officer must answer several questions, such as the following:

- Are there multiple reports?

- Was corrective work required?

- Was corrective work performed and completed?

- Was preventive work recommended?

- Was preventive work performed and completed?

- Has the termite report been disclosed to the buyer and buyer's lender?

- Has escrow received written authorization to pay for the termite clearance?

The escrow officer is instructed in the original escrow instructions whether or not the principals required a **termite clearance** report. It is not unusual in older areas that have retained value for the purchaser to obtain the property for the purpose of a teardown and rebuild. In this case the buyer would not require a termite clearance report. However, when a buyer plans to reside in the premises and is obtaining a new loan as part of the purchase, the lender will usually require a termite clearance report even if the principals do not request one. The escrow officer is to make sure all conditions are met before the loan is funded and before any funds are disbursed at the closing.

If a pest control and certification is part of the transaction, the escrow officer will receive a copy of the termite clearance report. The loan documents often require the escrow officer to have a copy prior to the ordering of the funding of the loan. The report will include a structural pest control report. In some areas, the pest control firm also can give a report on the roof, electrical system, foundation, or a soil report. Most often, however, these separate types of inspections are handled by specifically licensed professionals, for example, a roofing contractor, or a licensed electrician.

The termite report (see Figure 10.4) indicates two areas, one for corrective work that usually must be corrected prior to the close of escrow, as the buyer's lender will require the work to be completed. The second area of the termite report is the preventive work that if performed will prevent future problems but that is not currently required to obtain a clearance report. Local practices differ, but usually the seller pays for Section 1 and the buyer pays for the optional Section 2 items disclosed on the report.

The initial pest control inspection is normally conducted much earlier in the escrow time period. The initial report is a statement as to the present condition and provides a written report as to the areas that need correction, such as replacement or repair. The coastal areas and much of Northern California have

FIGURE 10.4

Sample "Termite" Report

STRUCTURAL PEST CONTROL REPORT

(1) Within ___calendar days, after acceptance of the offer, Seller shall furnish Buyer at the expense of the Seller, a current written report of inspection by _____ Termite and Pest Control, a registered Structural Pest Control Company, of the main building, detached garage(s) or carport(s), if any, and the following other structures on the Property:

(2) If requested by Buyer or Seller, the report shall separately identify each recommendation for corrective work as follows: "Section 1": Infestation or infection which is evident. "Section 2": Conditions that are present which are deemed likely to lead to infestation or infection.

(3) If no infestation or infection by wood destroying pests or organisms is found, the report shall include a written Certification as provided in Business and Professions Code 8519(a) that on the inspection date "no evidence of active infestation or infection was found."

(4) Work recommended to correct conditions described in "Section 1" shall be at the expense of the Seller.

(5) Work recommended to correct conditions described in "Section 2," if not requested by Buyer.

(6) If inspection of inaccessible areas is recommended in the report, Buyer has the option to accept and approve the report, or within ___ calendar days after receipt of the report to request in writing further inspection be made within ___calendar days. If further inspection recommends "Section 1" and/or "Section 2" corrective work, such work shall be at the expense of the respective party designated in subparagraph (4) and/or (5). If no infestation or infection is found, the cost of inspection, entry, and closing of the inaccessible areas shall be at the expense of Buyer.

(7) Inspections, corrective work, and certification under this paragraph shall not include roof covering(s).

(8) Work shall be performed with good workmanship and materials of comparable quality and shall include repair of leaking shower stalls and pans, and replacement of tiles and other materials removed for repair. It is understood that exact restoration of appearance or cosmetic items following all such work is not included.

(9) Work to be performed at Seller's expense may be performed by Seller or through others, provided that (a) all required permits and final inspections are obtained, and (b) upon completion of repairs a written Certification is issued by a registered Structural Pest Control Company showing that the inspected property "is now free of evidence of active infestation or infection."

(10) Funds for work agreed to be performed after close of escrow shall be held in escrow and disbursed upon receipt of a written Certification as provided in Business and Professions Code 8519(b) that the inspected property "is now free of evidence of active infestation or infection."

a fairly moist climate with mildew and dry rot that affects wood in a negative manner. Much of the inland valleys in California are predominantly desert-like with very low humidity and attract pests that prefer the more arid regions. Throughout California, the subterranean termite is a major pest that usually must be eradicated from the premises prior to the close of escrow.

The initial report often shows fascia boards in need of replacement in order to obtain a clear report from the termite company. Some homeowners do the work themselves or hire a handyman or carpenter to make these types of repairs. When the repairs are separate from the termite company, the escrow officer may have to pay more than one vendor bill. If the escrow officer sees that the termite bill is low indicating that it appears that the reports were not made by the termite company but may have been performed by another entity, it would be wise for the escrow officer to ask. This is a situation where a mechanic's lien is highly possible to have been overlooked. It is important to determine that anyone who has performed work on the premises has been paid and signed a release so that no lien would be valid after the close of escrow. The escrow officer should make inquiry as to who performed any work on the premises during the escrow period, the method of payment for such work, and to make provisions for final payment to any vendor that would need to be made by escrow after the closing.

■ AGREEMENTS AND REPORTS THAT CAUSE ESCROW PROBLEMS

Escrow officers are to remain neutral during the transaction, but often other parties place them in a position that steers them away from neutrality. When the buyers have not selected how they will hold title, the escrow officer is often asked to make a recommendation or explain the consequences of the various methods for holding title. The mere act of asking the escrow officer is placing him or her in a situation that could have far-reaching tax and legal consequences. Therefore, the escrow holder is prohibited from giving legal advice and must steer the parties to seek the correct authority that will give the individual(s) the proper information. The buyer in a transaction is often given a title company printed explanation of the various options on how to hold title.

Another problem for the escrow holder can be the real estate agents who represent one side of the transaction, but who consequently get involved with the other principal. One agent may be handling all of the transaction, so that there is sometimes no help from the other side. Or an aggressive agent may be overstepping his or her level of expertise and the level of his or her employment. The phrase seen in the next text box should be placed into each escrow instruction so that it is clear—to the escrow holder, the principals, and others—who is representing each principal. This is the verification confirmation of the written authority of the employment contracts that each agent has with each principal.

> **AGENCY CONFIRMATION:** The following agency relationships are hereby confirmed for this transaction:
>
> Listing Agent: **Bay Area Broker, Inc.** is the agent of the Seller.
>
> Selling Agent: **Broker Realty, Inc.** is the agent of the Buyer.

■ REPAIRS

Many times repairs are necessary before the escrow can close. In the original purchase agreement, it is not uncommon for the buyer to have required the seller to make specific repairs to the property. In a residential transaction, the buyer may request the seller to replace a broken garage door spring and to repair the garage door. In an agricultural land transaction, the buyer may require the seller to fill in a small ravine-type settling crevice or to clear brush off the land. In the sale of an apartment building, the buyer may require the seller to replace all broken windows and broken light globes outside each of the units.

During the course of the escrow, an appraisal is usually performed. The work requirements on the appraisal report may be none or just a few. Some appraisal reports contain a long list of repairs that must be made to the premises. An apartment building appraisal might require replacing the magnasite deck, securing the hand railings, or replacing the fire extinguisher boxes. These items will go to the lender who will normally automatically require whatever the appraiser listed as in need of repair.

When a new **insurance policy** is written, the insurance agent typically walks the property to determine if the company will insure the property. In the case of an apartment building or office building, the insurance agent may require the carport or parking area to have repairs to avert trip and fall claims by insisting that the asphalt be corrected where oil leaks have caused holes in the surface. In the case of a swimming pool, a city inspector and the insurance agent may require a special height or type of fence to be placed around the pool to comply with a specific city code.

The lender may place additional requirements on the property to comply with FHA or DVA government type loan programs. Items that were not noted as problems on the appraisal report may become requirements from the lender prior to the funding of the loan. For example, a perfectly good roof on a 100-year-old home where no leaks are visible and the appraiser did not note any roof problem and the seller did not disclose a roof problem of any kind, may still require a roof certification from a licensed roofing contractor. This is common for a well-made, older home built with a slate roof or similar long-life products. Natural rock and stone materials that were used many years ago may last for many years to come, but many have to be confirmed by an expert in that field. The inspection bill would normally be placed into the escrow to pay after the close of escrow.

■ WORK COMPLETED AFTER CLOSE OF ESCROW

Sometimes repairs cannot be made before the escrow closes. An example is in the case where tenants are in possession and may be in the process of a court legal eviction action. The current tenants may not cooperate with access to the premises. Repairs made prior to the close of escrow could be ruined by those in possession. To avert this problem, the escrow holder may have an instruction that involves the work being completed after the close of escrow.

This is a case where the escrow instructions would call for an escrow amendment to be drawn up between the parties. The instruction would be for the escrow to hold funds due to the seller after the close of escrow until the occurrence of some specific event. The event may be a sign-off and release by the buyer to release the funds to the seller, such as when the seller evicts a hostile tenant and the buyer actually obtains physical possession of the premises. The event may be a clearance report from an outside vendor, such as a pest control or retrofit firm. The lender must be made aware of the amendment and the item held after the close of escrow. As in the case of a tenant-occupied property where the seller is continuing an eviction against the tenant after the close of escrow, the fact that the buyer is not taking possession at the close of escrow is a material fact of the transaction and must be disclosed. In cases where the eviction has been filed with an eviction attorney and is being processed it is often not a problem with the lender in allowing the loan to close. The problem occurs if the escrow does not notify the lender of the event.

Also, work may be completed after the close of escrow for the buyer, with the buyer's funds, and not involve the seller in any manner. When a purchaser is completing a 1031 tax-deferred exchange and the property being purchased has a slightly lower sales price than the property sold for the exchange, the buyer may equalize the prices by performing IRS-approved necessary work. The buyer may place funds into escrow that are above the amount of the contract price with the seller but are part of the total purchase price. The additional funds are used for capital improvements, such as installing insulation in the attic space and a new roof, installing central heating or air conditioning, or replacing the appliances. In this case the buyer wants the funds held by the escrow until the buyer signs that the work is completed and the escrow is to release the payment to the vendor. The installation of these capital improvements enhances the value of the property and if part of the sales contract, should influence the appraised value of the property.

■ ORDERING INSURANCE BY FAX

In former years, most of the escrow portion of the real estate transaction was handled in person or by messenger. The escrow officer would prepare a document; the title company representative would pick up and deliver the document, often both ways, via hand carrying. Today's technology changes the way business is conducted. While some title company representatives still help by hand carrying some items, if called upon, paid messenger services are more often utilized. An independent, licensed, bonded, insured messenger service handles most of the pick up and delivery for real estate documents.

Many parts of the escrow transaction are transmitted electronically. The escrow instructions are keyed into a computer with printer output. The copies may be delivered to the parties for signature, as escrow requires original signatures on a set of escrow instructions. After that, however, most all items are handled via fax. The escrow will fax the prospective new lender a certified copy of escrow instructions. The escrow officer will order all other items, using the lane guide for location, via fax. The beneficiary demand will be ordered from the existing lender of record via fax. The insurance policies will be ordered via fax, covering flood, earthquake, contents, and homeowners policies. In a later section of this chapter, the electronic signature that is often used for some types of escrow documents is discussed. For the most part, the fax is the most used document transmitter for escrow. The faxed copy usually shows at the top of the page the date, time, and fax transmission number from where it was generated.

■ IRREVOCABLE DEMAND

During the normal course of the sale of one property, it is typical for the seller to purchase another property using the net proceeds from the sale of the first property for the closing on the second property. In the normal course of events, with inexperienced parties handling such a transaction, unnecessary delays will occur. The first escrow would proceed to closing, then a check would be issued to the seller for the proceeds. The seller would take those proceeds to his or her bank and deposit these funds, then try to convert the funds to a cashier's check to take to the second escrow. However, the bank will usually place a hold on any large deposit, especially escrow checks, which are often drawn on out-of-state bank accounts. Once the funds are available at the bank and a cashier's check is issued, the party would take these funds to the second escrow and make a deposit into that escrow account. The second escrow is under the good funds law and would have to hold the funds from this buyer until the funds are available for disbursement under the good funds law, as described on page 293. The delay could amount to a week or more depending upon weekends and holidays.

The delay is unnecessary if the parties managing the transaction are aware of the process and regulations that must be followed. Instead of following the procedure described above, the seller of the first escrow could have the escrow officer of the second escrow prepare an **irrevocable demand order** on the first escrow. The demand states that all funds due to the seller are to be transferred in total to the second escrow. This usually happens with a wire transfer, if different banks are used. A **wire transfer** can move the funds on the same day as the closing so that no delay occurs.

The key knowledge for the principal to remember is to use the same title company on the first escrow when opening the second escrow. If the seller knows that he or she will purchase another property, check to find the names of several title insurance companies in the area where the purchase is likely to occur. Then when the first property goes into escrow, the seller/principal can instruct all parties to the first escrow to use one of the several title companies that the seller names that is also in business in the new area.

In the case where the same title insurance company is named, the title insurance company can verify with its own records that it already has the funds from the first closed escrow. This is even better than a wire transfer between two different companies. Then the title company can automatically transfer the seller's net proceeds funds from the first escrow directly into the second escrow upon the close of the first escrow. Then, any leftover funds not used to close the second escrow are disbursed from the second escrow. The seller receives no funds from the close of the first escrow, only a closing statement that shows the costs and expenses and the amount of dollars transferred to the second escrow. The second escrow would show the amount received from the first escrow along with any initial deposit or other funds the buyer deposited into the second escrow. From all the funds deposited into the second escrow, the costs and expenses would be shown, including the amount of the check given to the buyer for unused funds from the first escrow.

The use of an irrevocable demand usually assures the second escrow that there will be enough funds to close the second escrow in case of prorations going over a weekend or holiday where additional days are calculated and additional funds are needed from the buyer to pay normal prorations. The seller would receive a 1099-S IRS tax form to show the funds received from escrow.

■ ELECTRONIC DOCUMENT/SIGNATURE

As technology has changed in modern times, so too has the way business is transacted. In the past, a document had to be the original copy with original signatures in order to be recorded. Today, however, electronic media changes documents from paper to digital format. A discussion of **electronic signature** for recordation of documents is found in Chapter 12. But when processing a file, the escrow officer will send and receive many types of digital information. Common documents that escrow will receive via fax are often the statement of information, the beneficiary demand statement, and escrow amendments. The escrow officer could receive e-mail instructions and a scanned copy of an escrow document by e-mail. The escrow officer should always check with the title company and recorder's office as to the acceptance of any electronic document, including the electronic signature. The Internet has much information available regarding the acceptance of electronic signatures, especially in banking and business practices.

WEB LINK
@

See the following Web sites for an example: *www.alphatrust.com/solutions/banking* or *www.crogroup.com/electron.htm.*

Applicable Law

A law entitled Electronic Signatures in Global and National Commerce Act (E-SIGN) (Pub. L. 106-229) became effective October 1, 2000. An *electronic signature* is an electronic sound, symbol, or process, attached to or logically associated with a contract or other record and executed or adopted by a person with the intent to sign the record. Electronic signature describes a category of electronic processes that can be substituted for a handwritten signature. E-SIGN governs transactions relating to the conduct of business, consumer, or commercial affairs between two or more persons. It legitimatizes electronic contracts, signatures, and record keeping in many situations. E-SIGN makes it easier for system institutions to use e-commerce and potentially realize cost savings.

With the parties' agreement, you can now engage in e-commerce in many situations. E-SIGN does not, however, allow electronic communications for a notice of default, acceleration, repossession, foreclosure, eviction, or the right to cure when an individual's primary residence secures the loan. E-SIGN also does not apply to all writing or signature requirements under the Uniform Commercial Code. E-SIGN preempts only those statutes and regulations that relate to business, consumer, or commercial transactions. E-SIGN sets up different standards for e-commerce with businesses and with consumers. Although both businesses and consumers must agree to e-commerce, E-SIGN provides certain protections and compulsory procedures for consumer transactions. Under E-SIGN, *consumer* means an individual who obtains, through a transaction, products or services used primarily for personal, family, or household purposes. Under E-SIGN, some system loans qualify as consumer transactions, while others are business transactions.

E-SIGN also allows parties to a transaction to decide document integrity and signature authentication technologies. It requires electronically stored documents to accurately reflect the information in the original, whether in paper or electronic form, and be accessible to all people entitled to review the original in a form capable of accurate reproduction. It also sets up special technological and business process standards for electronic promissory notes secured by real estate.

Electronic Communications

A message can be transmitted electronically and displayed on equipment as visual text. An example is a message displayed on a personal computer monitor screen. This does not include audio-response and voice-response telephone systems.

Proposed §609.950(c) states, in part, that system institutions must ensure that their communications with parties other than consumers demonstrate good business practices in the delivery of credit and closely related services and in obtaining goods and services.

Compliance with the Electronic Signatures in Global and National Commerce Act (Public Law 106-229) (E-SIGN). §609.910.

(a) *General.* E-SIGN makes it easier to conduct e-commerce. *Electronic business (e-business) or electronic commerce (e-commerce)* means buying, selling, producing, or working in an electronic medium. With some exceptions, E-SIGN permits the use and establishes the legal validity of electronic contracts, electronic signatures, and records maintained in electronic rather than paper form. It governs transactions relating to the conduct of business, consumer, or commercial affairs between two or more persons. E-commerce is optional; all parties to a transaction must agree before it can be used.

(b) *Consumer transactions.* E-SIGN contains extensive consumer disclosure provisions that apply whenever another consumer protection law, such as the Equal Credit Opportunity Act, requires the disclosure of information to a consumer in writing. Consumer means an individual who obtains, through a transaction, products or services, including credit, used primarily for personal, family, or household purposes. You must follow E-SIGN's specific procedures to make the required consumer disclosures electronically. E-SIGN's special disclosure rules for consumer transactions do not apply to business transactions. Under E-SIGN, some system loans qualify as consumer transactions, while others are business transactions. You will need to distinguish between the two types of transactions to comply with E-SIGN.

(c) *Specific exceptions.* E-SIGN does not permit electronic notification for notices of default, acceleration, repossession, foreclosure, eviction, or the right to cure, under a credit agreement secured by, or a rental agreement for, a person's primary residence. These notices require paper notification. The law also requires paper notification to cancel or terminate life insurance.

(Continued on next page)

(d) *Promissory notes.* E-SIGN establishes special technological and business process standards for electronic promissory notes secured by real estate. To treat an electronic version of such a promissory note as the equivalent of a paper promissory note, you must conform to E-SIGN's detailed requirements for transferable records. A transferable record is an electronic record that:

(1) would be a note under Article 3 of the Uniform Commercial Code if the electronic record were in writing;

(2) the issuer of the electronic record has expressly agreed is a transferable record; and

(3) relates to a loan secured by real property.

(e) *Effect on State and Federal law.* E-SIGN preempts most State and Federal statutes or regulations, including the Farm Credit Act of 1971, as amended, and its implementing regulations, that require contracts or other business, consumer, or commercial records to be written, signed, or in nonelectronic form. Under E-SIGN, an electronic record or signature generally satisfies any provision of the Act, or its implementing regulations, that requires such records and signatures to be written, signed, or in paper form. Therefore, unless an exception applies or a necessary condition under E-SIGN has not been met, an electronic record or signature satisfies any applicable provision of the Act or its implementing regulations.

(f) *Document integrity and signature authentication.* Each system institution must verify the legitimacy of an e-commerce communication, transaction, or access request. Document integrity ensures that the same document is provided to all parties. Signature authentication proves the identities of all parties. The parties to the transaction may determine how to ensure document integrity and signature authentication.

(g) *Records retention.* Each system institution may maintain all records electronically even if originally they were paper records. The stored electronic record must accurately reflect the information in the original record. The electronic record must be accessible and capable of being reproduced by all persons entitled by law or regulations to review the original record.

■ WIRING FUNDS: GOOD FUNDS LAW AND SPECIAL RECORDING

Prior to January 1, 1990, the title insurance companies and independent escrow companies suffered losses because lenders and buyers could withdraw funds that had been deposited for the purpose of closing the escrow just prior to the

FIGURE 10.5

Escrow Funds— Received and Disbursed

FUNDING:

- Electronic Wire Transfer (same day disbursement)
- Cashier's Check (one business day prior to distribution of funds)
- Personal Check, local (three business days from escrow bank deposit date)
- Personal Check, nonlocal (five business days from escrow bank deposit date)

DISBURSEMENT PROCESS:

- Funds received by Title Company Payoff Section of Accounting Department with instructions from the lender
- Cleared funds before Title Officer sets up recording; no disbursements prior to recording
- After recording, the Payoff Section disburses funds as follows:
    - Title charges
    - Recording fees
    - Demands
    - Taxes
    - Reconveyance
    - Balance goes to escrow account for escrow disbursements

recording. In the meantime, when the recording was completed, the title and escrow companies found that they were in a predicament because they had already written disbursement checks against the funds that were withdrawn, such as the cost of the recording fee. It was common practice for lenders to claim that they had made a mistake and placed a stop payment on their check. Buyers could do the same thing on the checks they had brought to escrow to close the transaction at the time they signed loan documents. The title and escrow companies had great liability and very little control to prevent the "stop payment" problem.

As of January 1, 1990, the **good funds law** became effective to stop the previous practices and to protect the industry from losses. Section 12413.1 of the California Insurance Code, as shown in the next text box, gives more control to the title insurance companies when acting in an escrow or subescrow capacity. The law imposed mandatory holding periods upon escrow deposits, depending upon the type of funds received by the escrow holder. The law requires that *all* funds must be deposited and collected by the title insurance company's escrow and/or subescrow account prior to disbursement of any funds, see Figure 10.5. It establishes a holding period, depending upon the method of funding to the title company, which must expire before *any* funds may be disbursed.

Along with the good funds law is the issue of special recording. A **special recording** is any document recorded at the county recorder's office by a title company at any time other than at 8:00 A.M. The county recorder's offices in California have instituted more stringent regulations about when a recording may be handled and how the document must appear. Many government offices, including the county recorder's office, are not open for normal business on any Friday, or are open only every other Friday. This means that if an escrow is to close on a Friday, the funds to pay off any existing lien holder must be paid over the weekend. Escrow would have to compute the interest over the weekend if an escrow is recorded on a Friday because the grant deed to transfer ownership would take place on the Friday, but the funds could not get to the lender under the good funds laws.

California Insurance Code 12413.1

No title insurance company, controlled escrow company, or underwritten title company shall disburse funds from any escrow account until the day established by the following:

(a) Except for funds deposited by cash or by electronic payment, deposits accorded next day availability pursuant to Part 229 of Title 12 of the Code of Federal Regulations may not be disbursed until the business day following the business day of deposit.

(b) Except for drafts, deposits not accorded next day availability pursuant to Part 229 of Title 12 of the Code of Federal Regulations shall not be disbursed until the day on which these funds must be made available to depositors under the federal regulation specified in this subdivision.

(c) Funds deposited by cash or by electronic payment may be disbursed following deposit on the same business day as the business day of deposit.

(d) Notwithstanding the provisions of subdivision (b), deposits other than drafts may be disbursed on the business day following the business day of deposit if the financial institution to which the funds have been deposited informs the title insurance company, controlled escrow company, or underwritten title company in writing that final settlement has occurred on the deposited item. For the purposes of this subdivision, an electronically transmitted document that specifies that final settlement has occurred constitutes written notice as to an individual item.

(e) Where a draft, other than a share draft, has been received and submitted for collection, no title insurance company, controlled escrow company, or underwritten title company shall disburse funds from an

(Continued on next page)

escrow account with respect to the draft until the proceeds of the draft have become available for withdrawal from the financial institution to which the draft has been submitted for collection. For purposes of this subdivision, "available for withdrawal" means when the draft has been submitted for collection and payment received. Notwithstanding this subdivision, disbursement of funds represented by share drafts shall be governed by subdivisions (b) and (d), if applicable.

(f) For purposes of this section, "escrow account" means any depository account with a financial institution to which funds are deposited with respect to any transaction wherein one person, for the purpose of effecting the sale, transfer, encumbering, or leasing of real or personal property to another person, delivers any written instrument, money, evidence of title to real or personal property, or other thing of value to a third person to be held by that third person until the happening of a specified event or the performance of a prescribed condition, when it is then to be delivered by that third person to a grantee, grantor, promisee, promisor, obligee, obligor, bailee, bailor, or any agency or employee of the latter.

(g) Except as provided in subdivision (h), for purposes of this section, any word or term used herein or relevant to interpretation of this section, including, but not limited to, "available for withdrawal," "check," "electronic payment," and "business day," which is defined in Part 229 of Title 12 of the Code of Federal Regulations on January 1, 1990, shall have the meaning there given as the regulations existed on January 1, 1990.

(h) For purposes of this section, "financial institution" means any financial institution specified in Section 12413.5.

(i) No title insurance company, controlled escrow company or underwritten title company shall be liable for a violation of this section if the violation was not intentional or resulted from bona fide error notwithstanding the maintenance of procedures reasonably adapted to avoid that error. Examples of bona fide errors include, but are not limited to, clerical, calculation, computer malfunction and programming, and printing errors.

(j) Nothing in this section shall be deemed to prohibit the recordation of documents prior to the time funds are available for disbursement with respect to a transaction provided the parties to the transaction consent in writing prior thereto.

(k) Nothing in this section is intended to amend, alter, or supersede other sections of this code, or other laws of this state or the United States, regarding an escrow holder's duties and obligations.

■ POSSESSION AGREEMENTS

In some transactions, the buyer already has possession because the buyer is the existing tenant of the premises. The contract may have been written up some time ago as a lease with option to purchase. Or the binding agreement may be new and the tenant and landlord have decided to change to buyer and seller. In other transactions, the buyer may take occupancy prior to the close of escrow either with or without rent. Because of lien priority, where the buyer already has possession at the close of escrow, and concerns about mechanics' liens, having a written **possession agreement** defines the rights and obligations of the parties. Should the transaction not close escrow for any reason, the owner would not want the buyer to be able to place a lien on the premises.

In some cases, the seller may retain possession after the close of escrow. This may be a problem if not disclosed to the lender as part of the escrow instructions. Many types of loan programs require that the buyer personally reside on the premises as a condition of the loan. In these cases, the escrow instructions should indicate the same type of wording as the legal contract between the parties indicates, which is similar to the following:

OCCUPANCY: Buyer does intend to occupy Property as Buyer's primary residence.

When the seller rents back from the buyer, escrow is often involved in the collection of the rent during the escrow that is taken from the seller's account and given to the buyer as a credit. The seller's existing house payment is usually a lower dollar amount than the buyer's new house payment. The rent for the seller is normally at least the amount of the buyer's new payment for which the buyer would become liable after the close of escrow. The parties to the transaction should keep in mind the fact that should the seller not move at the end of the rental period, a standard eviction would have to take place according to the landlord/tenant regulations. This may take four to eight weeks for a normal eviction, provided that a rental agreement was executed separate from the sales contract, in which the terms and conditions of the rental were written and clearly delineated. If the rental is combined with the sales contract information, then should the seller not move out at the end of the period and fail to pay rent, the buyer's recourse would be to begin a lawsuit for breach of contract. An eviction action usually takes less than two months. A breach of contract suit could take many months, even several years. A separate written contract for the sales agreements and a separate written contract for the rental agreement should be handled outside of escrow. Escrow would only refer to the terms and conditions contained in the document that are handled outside of escrow and of no concern to the escrow officer.

The amount charged per day or per month would be in writing as part of the escrow instructions. The amount of any security or any other deposits would be in writing as part of the escrow instructions. Escrow would charge the appropriate party the per-day rate up to the date of close of escrow. After written instruction that possession has been obtained by the correct party, then the security deposit check for any refund can be created by escrow and the funds sent to the appropriate party.

In most real estate transactions, possession is normally the date of close of escrow. The deed records at 8:00 A.M. on the date of close of escrow. After 8:00 A.M. the escrow officer, after confirmation of recording from the title insurance company, will start issuing checks to all the appropriate vendors. This allows the seller to physically receive the funds after 8:00 A.M. and use the funds to pay for the cost of moving, including a professional moving company or a rental truck. To allow the seller time to get personal property off of the premises, possession is often given to the buyer at 5:00 P.M. on the day of close of escrow. The buyer is paying for the new loan for that entire day for proration purposes. In this case, no per diem rent is charged for the date of close of escrow. The words used in the purchase contract are seen in the next text box, and if the parties desire otherwise, the wording would need to reflect their desires.

> **POSSESSION AND KEYS:** Possession and occupancy to be delivered to Buyer on date of recordation at 5:00 P.M. When possession is available to Buyer, Seller shall provide keys, and/or means to operate all property locks, mailbox, security systems or alarms, and association facilities, as applicable.

THINK ABOUT IT

Disclosure: Real Estate Agent versus Escrow Officer

Local headlines earlier show that virtually everyone in the area knew that a mother and her four children had been murdered ten years earlier in a home now for sale. The seller, the real estate agents, the local escrow officer, and the neighbors knew the gory details. The out-of-area buyer did not know anything about the episode until after the close of escrow when the neighbor told the buyer that the seller had asked the neighbors not to mention anything about the incident to anyone. Can the buyer sue for nondisclosure of a material fact under *Easton v. Strassburger*, 152 Cal. App. 3d 90, 199 Cal. Rptr. 383 (1984)?

Answer: The buyer may sue and claim that the price offered would have been lower if the buyer had been told the truth about the property. However, the court will require the buyer to show the actual loss in market value to the property. If a value is established, the recovery would be against the real estate agent and not against the escrow officer. The real estate licensee has to disclose a death on the premises only up to three years after the fact. The escrow officer is not a real estate licensee and has no duty to disclose any known fact to the buyer (*Reed v King*, 193 Cal. Rptr. 383).

■ CHAPTER SUMMARY

The escrow officer processes the escrow file toward the closing. For the file that is ready to close escrow, various documents, forms, and disclosures must be made to consummate the transaction. Some disclosures relate to the physical premises, as is shown from a professional inspection, termite report, or appraisal report. Other items must comply with governmental regulations, such as smoke detectors, permits, and flood or earthquake disclosures. The disclosures must be made to not only the principals but may involve third-party entities, such as a new lender for the buyer. The escrow officer must disclose in advance requirements regarding the handling of the funds, including acceptable deposit funds and how hand disbursements will be handled. Some disclosures are between the principals outside of escrow, such as the transfer disclosure statement (TDS), while others are handled through the escrow, such as a possession agreement between the parties. The discovery of various items found after escrow is opened may require a written amendment to the escrow prior to the close of escrow.

■ CHAPTER 10 QUIZ

1. The escrow officer most often handles the items found on a physical inspection
   a. after the escrow officer has personally inspected the premises.
   b. by informing the lender of the items found on the physical inspection report.
   c. after the close of escrow by paying the vendor who performed the inspection.
   d. by listing the items found in a detailed report given to the seller.

2. The work required for repairs or replacement discovered during the escrow may
   a. be completed outside of escrow and paid for outside of escrow.
   b. be completed outside of escrow and paid by escrow after the close of escrow.
   c. not be completed during the escrow period, and may be performed and paid for after the close of escrow.
   d. be all of the above.

3. An irrevocable demand is used
   a. as a physical inspection report.
   b. to disclose items about the property.
   c. to transfer funds from one escrow to another.
   d. to place insurance on the property.

4. The good funds law pertains to the escrow
   a. good faith initial deposit of the buyer.
   b. receipt and release of funds received and distributed by escrow.
   c. net proceeds that the seller will receive after the close of escrow.
   d. interest received on the deposit of the buyer during the escrow period.

5. The buyer's walk-through is
   a. performed just prior to the close of escrow to ensure the property is basically in the same condition as when originally purchased.
   b. performed at the opening of the escrow so the buyer may physically determine the condition of the property after the seller has accepted the offer to purchase.
   c. conducted only after a licensed, insured, bonded physical inspection report has been performed on the premises.
   d. instituted as part of the escrow instruction to protect the escrow officer from the results found during the escrow officer's physical inspection of the premises.

6. The escrow officer needs to obtain which type of insurance endorsement for the lender during the escrow period?
   a. Hazard and fire
   b. Flood and earthquake
   c. Contents and homeowners
   d. All of the above

7. Possession agreements are used when
   a. the premises are occupied by the tenant.
   b. the seller will rent back the premises after the close of escrow even though the loan requirement is for owner-occupied premises.
   c. the buyer rents the property prior to the close of escrow.
   d. the premises are tenant-occupied and the tenant will remain in possession after the close of escrow.

8. When the escrow officer is presented with a lien on the buyer for nonpayment of child support, the best action to take would be to
   a. draw an escrow amendment to disclose the fact to all parties to the transaction.
   b. notify the buyer so the buyer can take action to rectify the situation.
   c. notify the seller immediately.
   d. notify the real estate agents so they can handle the situation, thus relieving the escrow of any liability in connection with the matter.

9. Which statement is *NOT* correct?
   a. A fixture is usually personal property.
   b. Real property can become personal property.
   c. Personal property can become real property.
   d. A fixture is always real property.

10. Which are common disclosures made to a buyer during the escrow period?
    a. Flood
    b. Seismic
    c. Environmental
    d. All of the above

PREPARING TO CLOSE: ESCROW MATH

■ KEY TERMS

arrears	impound account	overage
closing costs	loan origination fee	prorations
documentary transfer	Mello-Roos	reconveyance deed
tax	messenger service	settlement statement
hazard insurance	mortgage insurance	
HUD-1 form	premium (MIP)	

■ CHAPTER OVERVIEW

The escrow officer is responsible for much of the calculating of charges and fees between the parties. The legal contractual obligations created by the clauses in the escrow instructions and related documents, including loan documents and deed, are equally as important. The agents, principals, and third parties, such as a beneficiary, rely on the expertise of the escrow officer's mathematical skills. Chapter 11 is concerned primarily with the mathematics contained in a typical escrow.

Either principal may pay any charge, unless the loan or some regulation prohibits a particular party from such. In most transactions, the fees are typically paid by the party who benefits from the item. Local custom and practice are the main determinants of who pays which fees. Overall, in Northern California the buyer pays more fees, and in Southern California the seller pays more of the fees. Again, because fees are freely negotiable between the parties, transactions vary and closing statements differ.

■ LEARNING OBJECTIVES

At the conclusion of Chapter 11, you will be able to

- understand prorations;

- give a definition for each escrow debit and credit for the buyer and the seller;

- outline the steps to calculate the amount to charge for an escrow item on a per day basis;

- differentiate between buyer and seller expenses and between a debit and credit item; and

- explain the federal regulation HUD-1 settlement statement and RESPA.

■ IS EVERYTHING IN?

The escrow officer is the individual responsible for checking to see that all documents and funds are in place before ordering the title company to record the grant, trust, and reconveyance deeds. The escrow officer must make sure that all deeds are properly prepared and executed. Most California county recorder offices require specific sizes of deeds and other documents. Documents recorded are copied and photographed for the title insurance industry. The title plant needs uniform measurements. All documents are preferred to match current fax machine size paper—8½" × 11" page size.

If any item is not in the escrow file, then the escrow holder is not in a position to close escrow. One principal may have all items in place with escrow, typically the seller. The other party, often the buyer, may have overlooked a document and not be in a position to close. Both parties will normally have everything in place that is under their power and control because the buyer and the seller want the escrow to close. However, because much of the file is dependent upon third parties who are not the principals, the escrow holder is often not in a position to close escrow.

Toward the end of the escrow period, the escrow is often awaiting, for example, the insurance policy endorsement from the buyer or the beneficiary demand statement from the seller. The appraisal report may not yet be clear of work requirements; the final termite certification may not have yet been submitted to escrow; and the loan documents may not be ready for the buyer to sign. The most common holdup at the close of escrow is the new lender; the buyer's new loan is delaying the close of escrow. Until the new loan has actually been funded, the money is not available to pay off the seller's existing creditors. The last event in the escrow is commonly the funding of the loan, followed immediately by the recordation of the deed for the escrow to actually close.

The escrow holder is not finished with the escrow when the deeds are recorded but when all disbursements have been made and the escrow trust account has been cleared out, and final documents, including the settlement statement, have been delivered to the principals. To be in position to close the escrow, it is the responsibility of the escrow officer to prepare for the closing by making sure all required items have been received.

■ CHECKLIST TO CLOSE

Because the escrow officer checks to make sure he or she has all the beneficiary demands, judgment lien documents, deeds, funds, and reports, the escrow company or the title insurance company handles much of the work performed by an attorney in other states. In many states, an attorney prepares the warranty deed to transfer ownership of the property and brings this document to the closing meeting. In California, the escrow officer prepares the grant deed that transfers ownership.

In California, the escrow officer does not usually prepare the trust deed, which is prepared by the lender, in the case of a new first trust deed loan. However, if the seller is extending credit to the buyer and the buyer is executing a second trust deed, the escrow officer often prepares both the trust deed and the trust note according to the terms and conditions dictated in the escrow instructions that were negotiated between the parties. Likewise, the **reconveyance deed** is prepared by the trustee and delivered to the escrow holder to go to the title company. This deed is already signed and notarized and ready for recordation.

How then does the escrow holder keep track of all the necessary items required to be in the position to close escrow? The escrow file consists of some form of coversheet that lists all the commonly used preprinted items, along with blank spaces to add particular items unique to the specific escrow. When an escrow officer has the file ready to close, an internal audit is usually conducted. A senior escrow officer or some other internal personnel will typically review the checklist to ensure compliance with the necessary items required. In Northern California where the title company may be performing the escrow, a review by title personnel could be possible.

A typical file checklist is shown in Figure 11.1. The part of the file that is most often reviewed is the **HUD-1 form** or closing **settlement statement** that shows the math calculations. Should an escrow actually close and not enough funds were collected due to incorrect math calculations, the escrow officer must work to try to rectify the error. The collection for the shortage would begin with a call to the buyer along with a letter requesting the amount of the shortage. If the buyer does not respond, the escrow company may be forced to take legal action for which the expense of the legal system may exceed the amount to be recovered. In the case of an **overage** of funds for either the buyer or the seller after the close of escrow, the escrow officer would merely issue a check to balance the escrow account back to a zero balance.

Thus, as the escrow nears the end, it is the responsibility of the escrow officer to review the entire file to determine the current status of the escrow and to determine what is yet to be received or performed.

■ WHO PAYS WHAT?

All costs and fees are freely negotiable between the parties. The buyer, seller, title company, escrow officer, lender, or another may pay any amount, including the closing costs and the down payment. The buyer may receive funds to close the escrow as a gift from another individual not involved in the escrow. Sometimes a coborrower may pay the cash required for escrow while the other coborrower qualifies for the loan. The exception to this is when the loan program or lender has specific loan requirements.

If not prescribed by any other requirement, the allocation of who pays for what is set by local custom and practice within an area. In Northern California typically the buyer pays for the title insurance costs, and in Southern California the seller pays for the CLTA title insurance policy. The inland valleys of Central California have been made up predominantly of migratory California residents moving out of the big cities. If these buyers already owned property in California, they probably brought with them the escrow practices they were used to when they bought and sold their previous property. Much of the area between Bakersfield and Sacramento is a mix of Northern and Southern Californians. As they bring their past with them, the midsection of the state typically is a mix of both practices to form a new custom. In the Chico area, for instance, the escrow is performed by the title company, as is Northern California practice. However, the escrow company uses many Southern California practices.

FIGURE 11.1

Escrow Checklist

Item	Ordered	Received	Buyer	Seller	Lender	Comments
Initial deposit						
Increased deposit						
Funds to close						
Signed escrow instructions						
Preliminary title						
Check legal description						
Verify vesting						
Pest control clearance						
Prorations						
Calculate closing costs						
Disbursement authorization						
Buyer's insurance						
Termite clearance						
Loan commitment						
Loan documents						
Beneficiary demand						
Lender requirements						
Insurance requirements						
Commission authorization						
Personal property						
Grant deed						
Trust deed						
Trust note						
Reconveyance deed						
Notary expiration date						
Contingency						
PCOR						
HUD-1 (HUD-1A)						
HOA documents						
IRS forms						
Disclosures						

Because the allocation of expenses is negotiable, the closing statement presented in this chapter will show both a Southern California and a Northern California settlement statement. The discussion of how the amount is calculated would remain the same in all areas of the state. The mathematical computation shown here is designed to familiarize the individual with the correct method for determining the expense amounts. Each item typically found on the closing statement is shown individually.

■ COMPUTER-GENERATED ESTIMATED CLOSING STATEMENTS

Multiple-Listing Service (MLS) Cost Sheet

In some escrow situations, the real estate agent may not have given the principals a written net sheet or estimated closing costs statement. Most multiple-listing service (MLS) computer printouts available to agents have predetermined costs and expenses already programmed on them, as is shown in Figure 11.2 for the seller and in Figure 11.3 for the buyer. The agent just puts the sales price and amount of commission into the computer and a printed form is ready and available to give to the principal. This form is not an itemized escrow closing statement, only an estimate. Note that the seller has authorized paying a real estate brokerage commission of 5.5 percent of the sales price. The MLS form will determine the split between the broker handling the seller and the broker who handles the buyer's part of the transaction. In this case, the listing broker is retaining 3 percent of the sales price, and 2.5 percent goes to the selling broker, who handles the purchaser. Also, note that the buyer has authorized ½ of 1 percent only to his or her own selling broker. The listing agent receives nothing from the buyer and 3 percent from the seller as commission. The selling agent received 2.5 percent paid from the seller's proceeds and ½ percent paid by the buyer under a California buyer-broker agreement.

Real Estate Software Program Cost Sheets

Many agents use special real estate software, such as Top Producer or Agent 2000, to generate cost sheets. The same buyer cost sheet and seller net sheet data are used. The printout comes with a photo of the agent, company logo, and other preprogrammed materials for a nicer presentation of the information. The calculations for these programs are in different formats and may generate different amounts for the principals. A visit to these online Web sites would show, if you access their programs, that differences are not only in the format but are in the actual math calculations. It is no wonder that consumers are confused by closing costs when the real estate professionals present the data in so many different ways. In the case of a broker-owned escrow, the escrow officer should be familiar with the different formats and calculations presented to the principals.

Federal Housing and Urban Development (HUD-1) Estimated Cost Sheet

The estimated closing costs can get even more confusing for the buyer. Federal law requires the lender to give the buyer an estimate of the closing costs, within three days of receipt of a loan application, on a HUD-1 form for a buyer-seller transaction or on a HUD-1A for a refinance transaction. The Real Estate Settlement Procedures Act (RESPA) originated in 1974 and has various amendments, which made the mandate effective as of 1976. The act also requires the

FIGURE 11.2

MLS Seller Net Sheet

Sales Price $300,000, commission 5.5%

Estimated Seller's Proceeds

January 1, 2005   Prepared by: Dr. D. Grogan
Prepared For: Kirk Klient and Kate Klient   Real Estate Services, Inc.
               6789 Main Blvd #17
               Anytown, CA 90000

Property Selling Price		**$300,000.00**
Encumbrances:		
First loan (7%)	$100,000.00	
Second Loan		
Other (Property Tax Proration 14 days)		$246.62
Homeowners Association Dues		$70.00
Estimated Closing Costs		
Title Insurance	$1,500.00	
Escrow Fees	$ 785.00	
Sub Escrow Fees	$ 125.00	
Fee for Service (5.5% of Sales Price)	$16,500.00	
Reconveyance	$500.00	
Statement and/or Demand	$50.00	
Notary, Recording & Drawing	$100.00	
County Transfer Tax ($1.10 per $1,000)	$ 330.00	
City Transfer Tax ($0 per $1,000)	—0—	
Termite Inspection	$45.00	
Miscellaneous	$250.00	
Home Warranty	$300.00	
HOA Documents	$250.00	
HOA Transfer	$200.00	
Loan Interest Proration	$160.48	
Total Encumbrances		**$99,683.38**
Total Estimated Closing Costs		**$21,095.48**
Net Cash to Seller		**$179,221.14**

I understand that the above is an estimate only and not the actual costs that would be incurred if an actual sale consummated. The estimated amounts above are not guaranteed in any way.

_____
Seller   Date

_____
Broker/Sales Associate   Date

Information deemed to be reliable although not guaranteed.

FIGURE 11.3

MLS Buyer Cost Sheet

Sales Price $300,000, buyer-broker commission 0.50%, Condo dues $150/month

Buyer's Closing Costs	

January 1, 2005

Prepared For: Brian Byer and Barbara Byer   Prepared By: GREATER SOUTH BAY
6789 Main Blvd.   Sunbelt Real Estate Services
Anytown, CA 90000

Property Selling Price		**$300,000.00**
Down payment		$45,000.00
Loan Information:		
First Trust Deed (6.5%—30 yr.)		$240,000.00
Second Trust Deed (8%—5 yr.)		$15,000.00
Estimated Closing Costs		
Title Insurance (ALTA)	$920.00	
(See Chapter 4 for ALTA rates)		
Escrow Fees ($200 + $1.95/$1K)	$785.00	
Fee for Service (Buyer/Broker Commission)	$1,500.00	
Hazard Insurance	$1,050.00	
Loan Fees ($0 + 1.00 points)	$2,550.00	
Interest Prorations (14 days—First)	$606.62	
Interest Proration (Second)	$46.62	
Property Tax Proration (14 days @ $3.33/day)	$246.62	
HOA	$70.00	
Impound cost		
Tax Impound (12 months)	$2,550.00	
Mortgage Insurance Impound (5 months)	$500.00	
Estimated Closing and Impound Costs	+ $10,824.86	
Estimated Total Needed to Purchase	**$310,824.86**	
Less: Deposit Paid	– $5,000.00	
Estimated Cash Needed to Close Escrow:	**$305,824.86**	
Monthly Costs:		
First Trust Deed (Principal & Interest)	$1,696.00	
Impound—Taxes	$312.50	
Impound—Insurance	$87.50	
Monthly MIP Payment	+ $100.00	
Total Payment to Holder First		$2,196.00
Second—Interest Only		$100.00
Monthly Association Dues		+ $150.00
Total Monthly Payment:		**$2,446.00**

I understand that the above is an estimate only and not the actual costs that would be incurred if an actual sale consummated. The estimated amounts above are not guaranteed in any way.

_____   _____
Buyer   Date

_____   _____
Broker/Sales Associate   Date

Information deemed to be reliable although not guaranteed.

lender to provide the borrower with an annual percentage rate (APR) prior to being committed to the loan.

For real estate transactions, the different cost sheets provided to the buyer are often a problem. The original RESPA law covered only federally related loans on one-unit to four-unit properties, and excluded some transactions; however, virtually all transactions today use the standard, software-computer generated RESPA form as standard practice. The estimated costs in the computer program that most lenders use are based on national averages, not on actual local estimated costs. This is also true for the prequalification phase of the transaction. For example, a national average expense for utilities in most other states where snow and a lot of cold weather are common, lowers the amount of loan for which the buyer may qualify based upon the higher heating costs for fuel in those states. For Hawaii, Florida, and the southwestern states, including much of California, those "averaged" figures are totally misrepresentations of the actual amount. The mountain areas of Northern California would more closely match the national average figures used for winter fuel costs.

The same is true for not only the prequalification items but also for the estimated closing costs. In fact, some areas of California have higher closing costs because of the various local items charged in the transaction that are not an expense in other states, such as the city transfer tax or a Mello-Roos fee.

RESPA was enacted with the intent that the APR would allow the buyer to compare one lender's loan offering against another lender's loan. In order for a buyer to truly compare more than one loan, the buyer would have to place a loan application with each lender. In the real estate industry, the more times a credit report is run on an individual, the lower the FICO credit score and the worse loan terms that may be offered to the buyer. In other words, comparison shopping could cause harm to the borrower's credit rating.

One confusing result of the federal law is that at the time of submitting the loan application, the HUD-1 form is based upon the loan that the borrower is applying for and not the resulting loan that the borrower may actually obtain at the close of escrow. The borrower may originally apply for a 90 percent loan, where the loan is 90 percent of the appraised value of the property. The subsequent appraisal may be less than the agreed-upon sales price between the parties. The lender makes the loan based upon the appraised value based upon the appraiser's frequent contact with real estate prices at a level of expertise that the lender is relying on before placing any funds into escrow. This is referred to as the loan-to-value ratio or LTV.

Because the cash down payment and loan fees would be vastly different from the loan applied for compared to the actual loan the transaction is approved for, the HUD statement could not possibly be accurate information for disclosure purposes. Yet, the form must be prepared prior to even knowing what kind of loan the buyer will ultimately be approved to obtain. This makes the form and initial disclosure almost irrelevant to any facts in the transaction. The estimated closing cost form is not the same as the final closing statement that reflects the actual costs at the close of escrow. The federal government is investigating reforms concerning HUD/RESPA disclosures. When new laws are implemented, changes will be made to current procedures.

Currently, the HUD-1 form is mailed directly to the borrower. The real estate licensee does not have a chance to compare the estimated closing costs given to the borrower by the agent with the ones that are received directly from the proposed lender. Neither of these two compare with the actual closing statement that escrow will ultimately prepare with the final figures. Another HUD-1 form is required with the final closing statement that shows the actual closing costs that were charged at the close of escrow. The fact that there is the preliminary HUD-1 with the estimated closing costs and the final actual closing statement is often confusing to the general public. The real estate professional needs to know how the calculations are correctly determined and the differences between the various documents that the consumer will receive, but also needs to be able to explain the differences at a basic, understandable level to the consumer. A detailed explanation of each line on the HUD-1 form is given in Chapter 12 because it is prepared after the close of escrow. The estimated HUD-1 statement described in this chapter is prepared well in advance of the close of escrow, usually at the time of the loan application at the beginning of the escrow processing period.

Buyer Funds and Agent

One way for the real estate professional to deal with the estimated **closing costs** that would show who would pay for which items and how much the fee would be is to have escrow prepare an estimated closing costs statement for the principals. Because escrow is so busy and the fee received for the amount of work escrow does is not great, a special fee for this statement may be charged. Whether for a small additional fee or not, it would be wise for the real estate professional to have the escrow prepare an estimated closing statement for the seller after the beneficiary demand has been received and have the seller sign and receive a copy of the document. Likewise, after the lender has given a more firm commitment on the loan that may be given for that particular property and for that particular buyer, it would be advisable to then provide an estimated closing costs statement for the buyer to sign and to acknowledge a receipt of a copy of the estimate. This reconfirms the need for the final funds needed by the buyer to close the escrow and opens the discussion with the real estate profession on making sure the buyer understands that a personal check will not be acceptable the day before the close of escrow. The good funds law indicates that a personal check from the buyer would probably hold up the close of escrow. By utilizing the expertise of the escrow department that handles many escrows, a more accurate estimate of the actual costs is likely.

■ WILL THE SELLER'S PROCEEDS BE SUFFICIENT TO PAY EXISTING LIENS?

One problem that may arise is inaccurate information on the existing loan of record. Chapter 6 discussed the seller's liens and Chapter 8 discussed the purchase of foreclosure property, giving additional depth on the subject of the seller's loan payoff. However, it cannot be emphasized enough that the real estate professional must check the numbers carefully.

When sellers are behind on payment or only recently purchased the property that they are now selling, it is common that there may not be adequate funds to close the escrow. Sellers who indicate that they owe three back payments may, in fact, owe six months. Even if the seller correctly represents the amount of back payments due, unless the agent has experience in seller foreclosures, it is unlikely that enough of the garbage fees, for example, associated with a foreclosure have been figured into the ultimate payoff amount. The trustee costs in a foreclosure, in addition to the lender late fees, penalties, and accrued interest that is unpaid, all add large extra sums to the seller's payoff. When sellers indicate they are behind three months on a loan payment of only $1,000 a month, expect to calculate at least $10,000 extra into the costs to pay off the loan, in addition to the current unpaid principal amount of the loan. Especially in these types of situations, a foreclosure or property that has been recently "flipped," an estimated closing statement by the escrow officer would be recommended.

■ PRORATIONS

The escrow officer is responsible for the accurate calculation for each item to be divided between the parties, called **prorations.** This means that each party is to pay his or her own proportion of the expense, cost, or fee that is charged for each item in the real estate transaction. The basic real estate principles course usually teaches one of two methods to help remember the monthly payment. The first is the "Pity Me" for PITI-MI, meaning the payment consists of the Principal, Interest, Taxes, and Insurance, plus the Mortgage Insurance. The other method a real estate principles instructor may teach is the A-PITI acronym to remember the monthly payment. This is sometimes taught to help the learner remember the components of a payment and is pronounced as shown in Figure 11.4.

FIGURE 11.4

Monthly House Payment

"It is 'A PITI' (A Pity) to have to make the payment." This means:

A = Association dues

P = Principal of the current unpaid balance

I = Interest on the loan

T = Taxes on the property

I = Insurance on the property

The principal loan balance is not prorated in escrow. The seller's unpaid loan amount after having made the last payment remains the same. The buyer is obtaining a new loan for a certain amount and that amount is referred to as the principal owed by the buyer. But all other components of the monthly payment involve prorations. In addition to these recurring monthly charges, many nonrecurring closing costs are charged to the buyer and to the seller as part of the escrow fees and charges, such as rents and title fees. The escrow will calculate these charges that are shown on the closing statement, which are explained in more detail below for each item.

Before going into the detail of each item, it is important to first understand what period of time a house payment covers. The public does not normally concern itself with the details of the ongoing monthly payment, and the issue only surfaces when an escrow is involved. The information contained in Figure 11.5 shows whether the component of the monthly payment is made in advance or in arrears for a normal monthly payment and the proration where escrow opens on January 17 and closes on April 17. All payments are due on the first day of each month.

When the seller made the last monthly payment to the lender on April 1, the interest, property taxes, and insurance portion of the payment would be from March 1 to April 1. With close of escrow (COE) on April 17, no May 1 payment will be made by the buyer. The lender will want the interest due from April 1 to April 17, and escrow will be given the daily rate to charge the seller on the beneficiary demand statement. Escrow will charge the seller the daily interest rate and the daily rate on the existing, recorded property taxes.

The amount of insurance is collected monthly, so when the annual premium becomes due, the lender has adequate funds to pay for coverage for the subsequent year. Because the insurance policy is already currently in effect, the amount collected monthly in advance would be part of the refund from the lender, shown as a credit to the seller. The insurance company would be notified to cancel coverage and would issue any refund due directly to the seller after the close of escrow.

FIGURE 11.5

Monthly Loan Payment Breakdowns

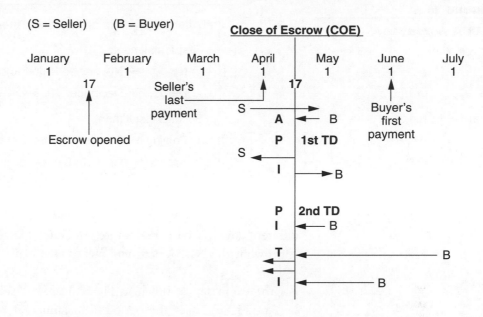

The lender cannot have the first monthly payment due less than 30 days from close of escrow, April 17. Thus, the first payment could not be due prior to May 17. Because all payments are to be due on the first day of the month, the next first would be June 1. The June 1 payment will pay the loan interest from May 1 to June 1. Escrow will need to collect the daily rate from April 17 to May 1.

■ PRORATION OF PROPERTY TAXES

Property taxes in California are calculated on the government's fiscal year. The state government's calendar does not begin January 1 or end December 31. Instead, the tax year calendar begins on July 1 and ends June 30 of each year. Real property tax payments are split into two installments in California, with one period from July 1 through December 31 and another period from January 1 through June 30. The purchase contract and escrow instructions usually contain the wording found in the next text box:

> THE FOLLOWING PRORATIONS AND/OR ADJUSTMENTS ARE TO BE MADE AS OF: CLOSE OF ESCROW
>
> Real Property Taxes based on latest available tax bills.

With any loan payment, real estate or otherwise, a payment due late is set for one particular day, and a grace period varies so that the delinquent date is a

FIGURE 11.6

NDFA Acronym

When it comes to paying taxes, there is:

First Installment:

No   =   **No**vember 1: due and payable

Darn   =   **D**ecember 10: 5 P.M.—delinquent

Second Installment:

Fooling   =   **F**ebruary 1: due and payable

Around   =   **A**pril 10: 5 P.M.—delinquent

different day. In a basic real estate principles course, most real estate professionals learn what the NDFA acronym means (see Figure 11.6).

For the example, as shown in Figure 11.5, the seller would have paid the taxes by April 10 to cover the period from January 1 to June 30 of the current year. The seller would have paid for the period that the seller owned the property but also would have paid for the period from April 17 to June 30 after the buyer owned the property. Escrow will collect the funds from the buyer to reimburse the seller.

The seller's property taxes are $1,200 per year divided by 12 months, equaling $100 per month. The seller paid from April 17 to May 1 for the buyer, plus paid the full month of May and June. The $100 per month divided by 30 days is $3.33 per day (or $1,200 per year divided by 360 days, equaling $3.33 per day). The buyer owes the seller for April 17, 18, 19, 20, 21, 22, 23, 24, 25, 26, 27, 28, 29, and 30, or 14 days. Escrow will multiply $3.33 times 14 days and debit, or charge, the buyer $46.62 and give these funds to the seller as a credit for the month of April, plus $100 for the month of May and $100 for the month of June, for a total debt of $246.62 from the buyer to the seller.

The next payment for the buyer for property taxes would be paid by December 10 for the period from July 1 through December 31 for the current year. The buyer will often have a loan where the lender will set up an **impound account,** or collect in advance for a buyer's bill. The buyer's taxes are calculated according to Proposition 13 (Prop 13) in California. This means that the base taxes for the general tax levy are equal to 1 percent of the sales price, plus local assessments. If the local assessments are one-quarter of 1 percent, then the total property tax for the buyer would be 1.25 percent times the sales price of $300,000, or $3,750 per year, with $1,875 due for each of the two property tax payments.

Escrow cannot charge for any bill that is not already due and payable as a lien against the property. The preliminary title report will show that the existing property tax lien is the seller's existing $1,200 a year, or $100 per month. That is the only amount that can be used to calculate the prorations at the close of escrow. As calculated above, the buyer will reimburse the seller $246.62 for the property taxes already paid in advance by the seller.

However, the buyer will be charged the new property tax amount based on Prop 13 from the date of close of escrow, April 17. The buyer's $3,750 per year in property tax is calculated by dividing the taxes by 360 days per year for a rate of $10.42 per day. The buyer will owe April 17 to May 1, plus the full month of June to pay the tax assessor until the June 30 period that ends for that half-year tax period. The annual $3,750 property tax for that half-year installment is $1,875 for the buyer. The $1,875 divided by 6 months equals $312.50 per month. The buyer owes for April 17, 18, 19, 20, 21, 22, 23, 24, 25, 26, 27, 28, 29, and 30. The escrow will collect from the buyer as a debit to the buyer's closing costs of $10.42 per day times 14 days for April for an amount of $145.88, plus the month of May for an amount of $312.50, plus the month of June for an amount of $312.50. The buyer would owe for the tax collected a total amount calculated by adding the three together for a total of $788.88. Escrow does not collect or pay this amount to the tax collector. The escrow does not collect this amount and pay it to the lender for the impound account to pay the tax bill when it becomes due. Instead, the buyer will normally receive a separate supplemental tax bill directly from the tax collector a few months after escrow closes as an additional bill paid outside of escrow. Remember the buyer already paid the seller the sum of $246.62 at the close of escrow and later will have to pay the $788.88, less the $246.62 already paid, or $542.26 due as the supplemental tax bill a few months after close of escrow.

If the lender has an impound account, the annual tax of $312.50 per month would be collected with each monthly payment, beginning when the first payment is due on June 1. But the lender will receive a copy of the supplemental tax bill and have to pay that amount out of the impound account. The lender cannot disburse what has not been collected from the borrower. Thus, the borrower would have the $788.88 calculated into the monthly payment so the lender would collect an amount equal to the amount needed to pay out the regular tax bill, any special assessments, and the supplementary tax bill. The next property tax bill will be $1,875 due by December 10 for the second half-year installment. If the lender collects for an impound account monthly, the amount paid would be $312.50 per month.

The clause in the escrow instructions authorizing the escrow officer to handle the real property taxes is usually something similar to that found in the following text box:

SUPPLEMENTAL TAX INFORMATION: The tax assessor has the right to reassess the subject property after close of escrow and issue a supplemental tax bill to the Buyer, who shall be solely responsible for same. In the event the Seller receives a supplemental tax bill for prior tax year(s) before close of escrow, charge the Seller's account. Supplemental tax bills for any tax period prior to close of escrow is the sole responsibility of the Seller. If any such supplemental tax bill has been issued for this current tax year, it is the Seller's responsibility to forward said bill to the new Buyer, and the Buyer's responsibility for payment of same. In such event, said supplemental bill will be added to the current tax bill and prorated accordingly at close of escrow. TAX BILLS ISSUED AFTER THE CLOSE OF ESCROW SHALL BE HANDLED DIRECTLY BY AND/OR BETWEEN BUYER AND SELLER.

■ PRORATION OF LOAN INTEREST

Real estate loans do not allow the borrower to pay interest in advance. If a borrower obtained a real estate loan today and won the lottery tomorrow, the amount that would be due is the unpaid principal plus the interest for one day. Some loans, specifically FHA loans, allow the borrower to be charged a full 30 days' interest as one term or condition of the loan. In the absence of a prepayment penalty, a real estate loan may be paid off at any time with a charge of interest only for the actual days that the money was used, unlike many consumer, credit card, and auto loans that add the interest on the entire contract in advance. If a consumer bought a $10,000 car with $5,000 interest, the contract would be written up for $15,000. If the borrower won the lottery and paid the loan off 45 days after obtaining the car or furniture, the amount paid would be $15,000. A real estate loan is handled differently. For a borrower who obtained a loan for $100,000 with interest over 30 years of $150,000, the entire amount paid over 30 years is $250,000. However, if the borrower paid off the loan in 45 days, the borrower would owe only the current unpaid balance of $100,000 plus 45 days interest on that loan.

When the seller in the example shown in Figures 11.2 and 11.5 made the last house payment due on the first day of April, the seller was paying interest in **arrears,** or for the previous period of time. The interest was paid for the period from March 1 to April 1. The seller would ordinarily pay the April interest on the May 1 payment. Because the seller will never make a May payment because he or she would no longer own the property at that time, the escrow must collect the interest on the loan for the bank.

From the beneficiary demand, the escrow officer determines that the seller's existing unpaid loan balance is $100,000 with interest at 7 percent per annum.

The $100,000 times 7 percent interest equals $7,000 per year divided by 360 days per year equals $19.44 per day. The interest was paid by the seller only through March 30. The seller owes interest on the loan for April 1, 2, 3, 4, 5, 6, 7, 8, 9, 10, 11, 12, 13, 14, 15, 16, and 17. Even though the escrow closed on April 17, the lender most likely did not receive the principal and interest payoff on the 16th, therefore the borrower/seller is charged for the day of close of escrow. The title company will wire transfer the seller's existing lender on the 17th. The escrow will collect from the seller the $19.44 per day times the 17 days the seller used the funds for a total debit of $160.48 taken from the seller's proceeds.

The buyer's first payment cannot be due prior to 30 days after close of escrow. Escrow closes on April 17, so the first payment could not be until May 17. Because the loan payment is due on the first day of each month, the next 1st of a month after May 17 is June 1. The payment made by the buyer on June 1 covers the interest on the loan from May 1 to June 1. The escrow collects the interest for the period from April 17 to May 1.

The buyer's new loan is a first trust deed of 80 percent of the sales price of $300,000. The $240,000 loan carried an interest rate of 6.5 percent. Escrow calculates $240,000 times 6.5 percent to obtain the annual interest of $15,600 per year divided by 360 days a year for a rate of $43.33 per day. The borrower used the money on April 17, 18, 19, 20, 21, 22, 23, 24, 25, 26, 27, 28, 29, and 30. Escrow will charge the buyer $43.33 times 14 days for a total of $606.62 as a debit, or charge to the buyer.

If the seller carried back a 5 percent second trust deed due in five years at 8 percent interest per annum, the escrow would collect for that also. In the example in Figure 11.3 for the $300,000 sales price, hypothetically adding a 5 percent second trust deed would mean a loan amount of $15,000. If the agreement was for payment of interest only, no principal reduction would be made. The $15,000 times the 8 percent interest would mean annual interest of $1,200, or a monthly payment of $100 per month on an ongoing basis until the due date when the entire unpaid principal of $15,000 would be due. The first payment on the second trust deed would be made on May 1 and would not have to wait a full 30 days until June 1. The unpaid interest for the period from April 17 to May 1 would have to be collected in escrow and paid to the seller/beneficiary. The $100 per month divided by 30 days would result in a $3.33 daily interest payment. The 14 days from April 17 to May 1 times the $3.33 per day would result in an escrow calculation of $46.62. Interest collected through escrow for interest proration for the buyer is the only time that interest is paid in advance, rather than paid in arrears.

■ PRORATION OF HOMEOWNER ASSOCIATION DUES AND FEES

In the example shown in Figure 11.2, the escrow closed on April 17. The seller would have already paid the HOA dues on April 1. The seller paid from April 1 to May 1. This means that the seller paid from April 18 to April 30 for the period when the buyer owns the property. Therefore, the buyer must reimburse the seller. The escrow officer collects the sum due from the buyer and credits the funds to the seller. If the HOA dues are $150 per month, the escrow officer would divide by 30 days per month to obtain the daily rate of $5 per day. The seller already paid $150 from April 1 to May 1; the seller owned the property April 1 to April 16. On April 17 the buyer already owned the property so the buyer owes April 17, 18, 19, 20, 21, 22, 23, 24, 25, 26, 27, 28, 29, and 30, for a total of 14 days. The $5 per day times 14 days means that the buyer owes the seller $70. The seller would receive a credit of $70 and escrow would debit the buyer's closing costs $70. The buyer would owe $150 on May 1 to the home-owners' association.

■ INSURANCE POLICY

The insurance is not prorated through escrow. If the seller has an existing policy that runs to a future date, the insurance company will be notified by escrow, the sales agent, or the policy holder to cancel the policy. Any refund due to the seller is handled outside of escrow. The insurance company may mail a refund of unused premium payments directly to its insured. Because many sellers sell one property and purchase another, it is common for the new property being purchased to have the new insurance policy and the same insurance carrier. In this case, instead of a refund handled after the close of escrow, the insurance company will calculate the amount due on the new property purchase, calculate the refund from the old policy, and then bill escrow for the difference.

The new lender for the buyer's new loan will require insurance coverage naming the lender as coinsured so that any loss is payable to the lender and the borrower/insured. The escrow officer would be presented with a bill for a one-year premium for an insurance policy covering the premises. The borrower may have only basic **hazard insurance** for the typical fire coverage, or the principal may have additional insurance policies, such as flood insurance, earthquake insurance, and/or mortgage insurance. The annual premium would be a debit for the buyer.

If the buyer has an impound account with the lender, the lender will usually require at least a two-month insurance reserve collected in escrow. The escrow impound chart in Table 11.1 shows that if the buyer's first payment is June 1, the lender will collect five months for the impound account. If the hazard insurance is 0.35 percent times the sales price, then the annual premium for the

TABLE 11.1

Escrow Impound Chart

Docs Drawn	First Payment Due Date	Months to Impound	Required Payment
January 2–31	Mar 1	1	1st & 2nd 04/05
February	Apr 1	1	1st & 2nd 04/05
March	May 1	2	1st & 2nd 04/05
April	Jun 1	3	1st & 2nd 04/05
May	Jul 1	4	1st & 2nd 04/05
June	Aug 1	5	1st & 2nd 04/05
July	Sept 1	6	1st & 2nd 04/05
August	Oct 1	7	1st & 2nd 04/05
September	Nov 1	8	1st & 2nd 04/05
Oct 1–18	Dec 1	9	1st & 2nd 04/05*
Oct 19–31	Dec 1	3	1st Inst 04/05
November	Jan 1	3	1st Inst 04/05
December	Feb 1	4	1st Inst 04/05[†]
Jan 1	Mar 1	1	1st Inst 04/05
Jan 2–31	Mar 1	1	1st & 2nd 04/05

*Any loan funding on or after October 22 must have first half 04/05 taxes paid. Loan funding on October 22—impound 3 months.

[†]Any loan funding on or after January 2nd must have first and second installments of 04/05 taxes paid.

$300,000 sales price shown in Figure 11.3 would be $1,050. The monthly collection would be $1,050 divided by 12 for an amount of $87.50 per month added to the payment for hazard insurance. If the lender required five months collected by escrow, the lender would receive a reserve of $87.50 times five for a total of $437.50.

If the buyer does *not* place a 20 percent down payment, the lender will usually require mortgage insurance, which usually has two collections for escrow. The first is the one-time, up-front premium, referred to as UFMIP for up-front mortgage insurance premium. For the example in Figure 11.3 the premium would not be calculated for the $300,000 sales price, but only based on the loan amount. The escrow would calculate $240,000 times 2.25 percent, for example, for an amount of $5,400. Some loans allow this amount to be financed with the loan, while others require the amount to be paid at the close of escrow. If the UFMIP is financed, the loan amount would be increased, along with the monthly payment to cover the increased cost. In the example in Figure 11.3 the original loan amount of $240,000 would be increased to include the $5,400 UFMIP for a total loan amount of $245,400. Or the buyer could pay the $5,400 UFMIP in cash at the closing, and it would then appear as one of the items under the closing costs. The UFMIP is not shown on Figure 11.3.

The second **mortgage insurance premium (MIP)** is the ongoing monthly amount collected with the monthly payment by the lender and paid to the insurance carrier. The amount is calculated at the rate of 0.5 percent for any loan over 15 years. In the example shown in Figure 11.3 for the $300,000 sales price, the monthly premium would be calculated on the loan amount of $240,000 times 0.5 percent for an annual amount of $1,200 divided by 12 months in a year, for a monthly amount of $100 added to the payment. Five months would be collected for the impound account.

■ THE RENTAL STATEMENT

If the property has rental income, escrow is often involved in transferring funds from the seller to the buyer. If the property is a condominium, as shown in the Figure 11.2 example, that is rented for $1,800 per month, but the buyer planned to occupy the premises and obtained an owner-occupied loan requiring the buyer to take possession of the premises, escrow would not be involved in any manner. The seller would need to notify the tenant with at least a 60-day notice to vacate the premises. If the tenant failed to move, an unlawful detainer eviction proceedings would begin and take about 45 days. The January 17 opening of escrow could still close by April 17 under this scenario.

The seller would handle outside of escrow any security deposit refund unless the lender required otherwise. The new lender would require the former tenant to vacate the premises by the close of escrow. The tenant's security deposit that was placed with the seller some time ago at move-in would have priority over the new lender's trust deed loan because the deposit date was prior to the date of recording the new trust deed. The date and time of recordation prevails. The title insurance company's ALTA policy, as discussed in Chapters 4 and 5, would assure the lender that it is, in fact, in first priority position.

If the tenant in occupancy is to remain as a tenant for the new buyer of the property, then escrow would be involved in two areas. A copy of the rental agreement would pass from the seller to the buyer. The buyer would serve the tenant with a formal change in terms of tenancy form indicating that the next month's rent payment would be paid to the new buyer instead of in the name of the seller. Often, the same property management company may handle the rental forms, so that the tenant would see no difference in where he or she makes the monthly rent payment. The escrow officer would look at the rental document and furnish the seller with a rent statement to show the amount of security deposit that the seller is holding on behalf of the tenant. The seller is allowed to deduct from the tenant's existing security deposit any sums due—such as previous unpaid tenant-caused plumbing bills. The seller would prepare a security deposit disposition form to show the amount collected from the tenant and the amount of any charges the seller is deducting from the tenant's deposit. If the tenant had a deposit of $2,500, but the seller deducted $500, then the seller would provide escrow and the buyer and the tenant with a statement showing that $2,000 is being transferred to the buyer through escrow. Escrow would debit the seller and credit the buyer with the $2,000.

In addition, the seller would have collected the April rent of $1,800 on April 1. Because the buyer owned the property for 14 days of April, the escrow would divide the $1,800 by 30 days to determine the $60 per day rate. Escrow would debit from the seller the $60 per day times 14 days for an amount of $840 that the seller collected in advance that represents the April 14 to May 1 rent already collected by the seller. The $840 would be credited to the buyer to give the buyer the sum due for the April rent. The tenant rent of $1,800 would be due on May 1 and paid directly to the buyer to cover the rent period in advance from May 1 to June 1.

■ DOCUMENTARY TRANSFER TAX AND MELLO-ROOS

Documentary Transfer Tax

A **documentary transfer tax** may be assessed on all new money in a real estate transaction where the transfer of real property is involved. The rate is $0.55 per $500 of new money. If a buyer assumes an existing loan, that seller already paid the transfer tax when the seller purchased the property so no tax is due on that part of the transaction. The new cash that the subsequent purchaser places into escrow to assume the existing loan is known as "new money" and would be subject to the tax. A new loan for a buyer would be subject to the tax.

California allows not only the county to charge the transfer tax, but it also allows individual cities within a county to adopt an ordinance for a transfer tax. The chart shown in Table 11.2 shows the cities in California that charge and shows the rate they are currently charging for the transfer of real property and the wording used in the escrow instructions.

Mello-Roos

In California, after the Proposition 13 tax limits had been in place for many years, a new law was created as a special property tax assessment by the Mello-Roos Community Facilities Act of 1982. The law requires the real estate licensee to disclose the fact of a **Mello-Roos** tax as soon as practical in the transaction and contains penalties should the licensee not comply. The law states that the seller is mandated to disclose a Mello-Roos tax to a prospective purchaser. Failure to disclose the fact means the buyer can cancel the transaction and cause a lawsuit or loss of a DRE license. Escrow is not required to make any such disclosure. Because the buyer can cancel, the escrow officer should ascertain if the disclosure has been met before proceeding with further work on the transaction.

TABLE 11.2

Documentary Transfer Tax Rate Chart

The cities listed charge a city transfer tax in addition to their respective county transfer taxes, as indicated. Information was obtained from sources deemed reliable but is not guaranteed. Rates are subject to change without notice. Please contact the county recorder to verify the current rate in your area.

County Rate per $1,000	County Tax	Monument Fee	City	Transfer Tax
Alameda	$1.10	Yes—$10	Alameda Albany Berkeley Hayward Piedmont Oakland San Leandro	$ 5.40 $ 8.50 $15.00 $ 4.50 $13.00 $15.00 $ 6.00
Contra Costa	$1.10	Yes—$10	El Cerrito Richmond San Pablo	$ 7.00 $ 7.00 $ 7.00
Fresno	$1.10	None	None	
Los Angeles	$1.10	Yes—$10	Culver City Los Angeles Pomona Redondo Beach Santa Monica	$ 4.50 $ 4.50 $ 2.50 $ 2.20 $ 3.00
Marin	$1.10	None	San Rafael	$ 2.00
Orange	$1.10	None	None	
Placer	$1.10	None	None	
Riverside	$1.10	Yes—$10	Riverside	$ 2.20
Sacramento	$1.10	None	Sacramento 0.275% of sales price	
San Bernardino	$1.10	Yes—$10	None	
San Diego	$1.10	Yes—$10	None	
San Francisco	$1.10	None	San Francisco: $100,000–$250,000 $251,000–$1,000,000 $1,000,001+	 $ 5.00 $ 6.80 $ 7.50
San Joaquin	$1.10	None	Stockton	$ 3.00
San Mateo	$1.10	None	San Mateo	$ 5.00
Santa Clara	$1.10	Yes—$10	Mountain View Palo Alto San Jose	$ 3.30 $ 3.30 $ 3.30
Solano	$1.10	Yes—$10	Vallejo	$ 3.30
Sonoma	$1.10	Yes—$10	Cotati Cloverdale Petaluma Rohnert Park Santa Rosa Sebastopol	$ 1.90 $ 1.10 $ 2.00 $ 1.10 $ 2.00 $ 2.00
Stanislaus	$1.10	Yes—$10	None	
Ventura	$1.10	Yes—$10	None	
Yolo	$1.10	None	Davis West Sacramento Winters Woodland	$ 1.10 $ 1.10 $ 2.20 $ 1.10

■ LENDER'S FEES

Many loans do not have a prepayment penalty, but they often have other charges if the escrow officer is not aware of normal operations for specific types of loans. For example, an FHA loan has no prepayment penalty. However, if the existing FHA lender is not notified at least 30 days in advance of the loan payoff, and if the payoff funds are not received by the lender's cutoff on the first day of the month, the lender is allowed to and will charge one full additional month's interest on the unpaid loan balance. The lender's loan documents come with a cover sheet that gives written notice to the escrow holder for specific lender charges and fees that are to be paid by escrow. The documents have instructions on the prepayment penalty, if any, prepaid interest usually shown as a dollar amount for each individual day, and any up-front loan fees such as **loan origination fee,** points, or other items. This document must get to escrow as part of the calculations needed by the escrow officer.

■ SIGNING THE LOAN DOCUMENTS

The escrow officer will work closely with the new lender to determine when the lender will print the loan documents from the lender's computer program. In the case where the seller is carrying back a loan for the buyer, the escrow officer would already have prepared the trust deed and note and should be able to calculate the prorations.

The loan process was discussed in Chapters 7 and 8. Once printed, the loan documents may be signed at the office of the real estate agent, where a notary public is usually available. Or the loan documents may be signed at the lender's offices. Loan documents may be delivered to escrow for the buyer/borrower to sign. Most escrow offices have at least one notary public available for the execution of documents. It is becoming common business practice for loan documents to be delivered directly to a location set up by the principal, with a messenger who acts as a traveling notary. In Northern California, loan documents are most often delivered to the title company and escrow department for signing.

■ BALANCE NEEDED BY BUYER

After the escrow is opened and the documents are executed, the escrow officer calculates a preliminary closing statement to determine what will be needed for closing. The escrow officer will already have the charges for many of the escrow costs, such as the cost to draw documents for a second trust deed and note. The escrow will have the charges and fees from the new lender as per the loan document cover sheet. The seller's existing lender will have provided a written beneficiary demand statement showing any prepayment penalty for early payoff and the dollar amount to charge the seller for each day up to a specific date. The escrow officer will need to obtain the final title company charges and fees to determine the seller's net and the buyer's costs.

At this point, when everyone has submitted the fees and charges to be paid through escrow, the escrow officer would prepare an independent preclosing worksheet of all charges for each principal. After checking all calculations, the escrow officer usually has another person at the escrow company audit the file before final closing to ensure that nothing has been overlooked.

The buyer is then notified by escrow of the amount of funds that needs to be received by escrow. According to the good funds law, to expedite the closing, the funds may be delivered by wire transfer or by a cashier's check. All funds must have been cleared prior to escrow ordering the title to record the deed. The real estate professional will often obtain the amount of funds needed from the escrow officer and give the borrower specific instructions on how much is due and the form that is needed to complete this step in the closing process of the escrow.

■ MESSENGER SERVICE

The **messenger service** used for escrow and title is extremely important. These licensed, bonded couriers have possession of critical documents at various stages of the transaction. For example, the messenger will pick up the signed, notarized deed. If the deed were taken to the county recorder's office at this point, the transaction would be a closed escrow. Therefore, the safekeeping of the document handled by the messenger is important.

The messenger is normally the entity that delivers the check for the loan payoff to the existing lender of record if a wire transfer is not used. Many lenders are not set up for receipt of a wire transfer, or do not know how to instruct a wire transfer, such may be the case with a private individual where the holder of the second trust deed is the former owner of the property on an owner carryback loan. Messengers are subject to all the normal problems that come from traffic jams and accidents that are beyond the control of the driver. A delay of one hour could cause a recordation to be delayed four or five days, changing the proration figures on the escrow items due to a holiday weekend.

Escrow usually collects an extra few days of interest, especially if recordation is to be near a Friday or holiday weekend. If the messenger cannot make the cutoff time for the existing lender of the seller, escrow would have enough funds to pay for extra days. If the messenger did meet the cutoff date time, then the escrow or lender would return unused funds to the principal. This process may take a couple of weeks after close of escrow for the lender to process the refund directly to its former borrower.

In the case of the buyer, the escrow would need enough extra funds to pay for Friday, weekend, or holiday weekend days. The new lender will demand interest for each day the funds are used. If the new loan funds on a Thursday but the grant deed to transfer ownership does not record until the following Tuesday because of a Monday holiday, then escrow will need extra funds. The borrower will be charged from the Thursday date that the funds were used, not from the Tuesday recording date for transfer of ownership.

Another common service, as mentioned above, is the traveling notary public who picks up the loan documents and meets with the borrower(s), together or individually, at virtually any location. One party may be at his or her place of employment while the other principal may be at home or at his or her job. After the documents are signed and notarized, the messenger delivers the documents back to the lender or to escrow or to the title insurance company for recordation, depending upon the instructions given to the messenger.

■ PREPARING TO RECORD

The date and time of the proposed close of escrow is used by the escrow officer to determine the amount of cash the borrower needed to bring into escrow at the final meeting. As discussed earlier, the good funds law prevails so that the buyer's funds and the new lender's funds have time to clear the bank. The escrow officer will have calculated all fees, charges, and expenses for each party.

All California recordings are set by recordation for 8:00 A.M. Virtually all special recordings at times other than 8 A.M. have disappeared throughout the state at most county recorders' offices. This means that as of 8 A.M. on the day of recordation the buyer owns the property. Therefore, the buyer receives the rent for the day of closing. The buyer is charged interest on all loans and pays the association dues and insurance for the date of close of escrow. The seller is charged for items through the day before the close of escrow, except for the loan interest on the seller's existing loan. The seller's existing lender does not receive the payoff funds at 8 A.M. on the day of closing, but the funds are transferred later that day or on the next day. The lender does not instruct the trustee to record the Deed of Reconveyance until after receipt of the payoff funds and then only after the funds have cleared. This process can take up to two weeks after close of escrow to allow the beneficiary to instruct the trustee, get the signature on the Reconveyance Deed, and have the deed recorded at the County Recorder's Office. A copy of the Deed of Reconveyance will be mailed back to the borrower from the County Recorder's Office weeks after the close of the escrow.

THINK ABOUT IT

The seller has paid the annual homeowner association dues of $1,130 for the calendar year. Escrow closes on June 22. Does the buyer owe the seller, or does the seller owe the buyer? Which party has a debit or a credit? How much would be owed and by whom?

Answer: $1,130 ÷ 360 days per year = $3.14 per day. The seller paid in advance from January 1 to December 31, but only owned the property until June 22. The seller will want a refund for the funds paid in advance.

The buyer owes the seller for the remaining 9 days in June (June 22, 23, 24, 25, 26, 27, 28, 29, and 30) plus 30 days each for July, August, September, October, November, and December (30 days × 6 months = 180 days).

Add the 9 days for June plus the 180 days for the balance of the year = 189 days. $3.14 per day × 189 days = $593.46 that the escrow officer would collect from the buyer as a debit and give to the seller as a credit.

■ CHAPTER SUMMARY

This chapter discussed the details of escrow prorations for charges and fees between the principals. Each party normally has certain debits or credits involved with the closing statement, the HUD-1. The escrow officer is given the per diem fee to charge the party, or the escrow agent will calculate the rate per day to use for buyer or seller expenses. Common escrow mathematics involves prorations of loan interest, property taxes, and homeowner association fees. After the mathematics is completed, the escrow officer sets the file up to record by notifying the title insurance company that escrow is in a position to close. The escrow officer must be keenly aware of how the various escrow prorations and costs are calculated. The escrow officer performs many of the mathematical calculations using escrow specific software. Third parties provide the figures directly to the escrow officer in many cases, but the experienced escrow officer will question figures that look unusual or are subject to question. When figures submitted to escrow do not look correct, the escrow officer would follow up to ascertain the correct amount to charge the parties in the escrow.

The escrow officer may call the real estate agents and alert them to what appears to be an unusual dollar amount for an item. Experienced real estate professionals will check their files to determine if the party agreed to specific amounts or extra fees and costs. This chapter also discussed escrow mathematics for property taxes, loan interest, association dues, and insurance along with buyer and seller debits and credits for closing costs.

■ CHAPTER 11 QUIZ

1. The most common transfer of ownership method used in California is termed
   a. actual notice.
   b. constructive notice.
   c. closing meeting.
   d. settlement meeting.

2. On the settlement closing statement, the sales price is reflected as a
   a. credit to the buyer and debit to the seller.
   b. credit to the seller and debit to the buyer.
   c. credit to the buyer and credit to the seller.
   d. debit to the seller and debit to the buyer.

3. Which is true regarding unpaid property taxes of the seller?
   a. Escrow would debit the seller and pay the taxes.
   b. A mechanic's lien would be on the property for the unpaid taxes after closing.
   c. The buyer would assume the unpaid taxes as a tax lien.
   d. The lender would collect for the unpaid taxes in the impound account.

4. The HUD-1 settlement statement shows the
   a. buyer's closing costs and prorations for the buyer and the seller's closing costs and prorations for the seller.
   b. estimated appraisal and credit report fees.
   c. estimated seller costs for a new loan.
   d. charges of the lender only and excludes other fees.

5. The escrow holder would use a checklist for the purpose of
   a. relieving and eliminating liability for the escrow holder.
   b. safeguarding that all instructions have been met.
   c. determining what is left to do to close the escrow.
   d. accomplishing all of the above.

6. When escrow prorates the interest charge on the loan for the lender, the normal procedure is to
   a. debit the seller for interest from the close of escrow back to the prior month's loan payment.
   b. debit the buyer for interest from the close of escrow up to the first payment to be made on the new loan.
   c. use the figures for interest given on the beneficiary demand and the loan documents.
   d. do all of the above.

7. Which is correct for prorating the actual day of recordation?
   a. The seller is charged for property taxes and association dues.
   b. The insurance is usually prorated between the two principals, and the per day amount is split between the buyer and seller.
   c. The buyer is charged for the day for association dues, interest, taxes, and insurance.
   d. The buyer is charged for interest on the existing loan of record shown on the preliminary title report.

8. The preliminary audit by the escrow officer should verify
   a. legal description of the property.
   b. names of the parties and vesting.
   c. receipts and authorization of disbursements.
   d. all of the above.

9. The transfer of real property includes a documentary transfer tax that is at the rate of $0.55 per $500 of value plus
   a. the retail sales tax rate applied for the local area.
   b. an additional $20 for the county recorder's office for the supplementary tax fee.
   c. any local city transfer tax that may be applicable.
   d. a buyer registration and a seller registration fee, if a foreign investor.

10. The accurate calculation for each item to be divided between the parties is called a(n)
    a. impound account.
    b. proration.
    c. settlement statement.
    d. debit statement.

CHAPTER TWELVE

POSTCLOSING PROCEDURES

■ KEY TERMS

actual notice	jurat	Satisfaction of Judgment
attorney in fact	notary public	settlement charges
CAL-FIRPTA	paid outside of closing	settlement date
constructive notice	(POC)	termite report
Department of	power of attorney	title charges
Consumer Affairs	reconvey	transferor
electronic signature	sales/broker's	
HUD-1 form	commission	

■ CHAPTER OVERVIEW

Once the escrow has closed, the escrow officer still has much work to do. Chapter 12 discusses the various parties who have interests after the close of escrow for which the escrow or title company or the country recorder's office would provide documents. The buyer, seller, brokers, and lender receive a copy of the HUD-1 settlement closing statement showing charges and fees to the parties. Escrow issues the 1099 tax information and complies with FIRPTA and

CAL-FIRPTA, pays anyone obtaining proceeds from escrow, and forwards insurance policies to various parties.

■ LEARNING OBJECTIVES

At the conclusion of Chapter 12, you will be able to

- understand the procedures escrow handles after the close of escrow;

- give a definition for electronic signature;

- outline general sections required on the HUD-1 form;

- differentiate between when FIRPTA or CAL-FIRPTA withholding is required and when the exemptions exclude the withholding; and

- explain real estate fraud.

■ CLOSE OF ESCROW

The purpose of escrow is to hold documents and money in trust until the close of escrow as a disinterested third party. When the escrow holder is in position to close escrow, the next step is to actually do it. What, then, is the actual close of escrow? As has been discussed, escrow closers in different parts of the country and different areas of California do not handle the actual close of escrow in the same way.

Basic real estate principles and contract law indicate that there are two types of notice, *actual* or *constructive*. **Actual notice** is when an individual has personal knowledge of an event. The majority of escrow closers in the United States use actual notice as of the date of close of escrow. To legally transfer title, one of the required elements is that the deed be delivered during the lifetime of the grantor who is giving away the right of ownership. Another element is that the buyer is to have delivery of the deed and receipt of the document.

In those parts of the United States where actual notice and delivery are used, a closing meeting is scheduled, called the "settlement meeting." The buyer and seller attend the meeting, and the physical, paper deed is actually handed by the seller to the buyer in the presence of witnesses. If either party is not available, a representative appears in that party's place to give or receive the actual deed.

In California the custom is to predominantly use the second method of transfer of ownership. **Constructive notice** means that any recorded document at the county recorder's office gives constructive notice to the world that the act happened. Anyone could look at the public records and see the document.

Constructive notice is what the lender uses to evidence security for any loan. The lender does not meet with the buyer and count out the money and hand it to the buyer. The buyer takes the money and physically hands it to escrow or to the seller. Likewise, in most transactions in California, the seller does not personally meet with the buyer and hand him or her the physical deed. Instead, the trust deed shows on the face of the document the original amount of the debt and is recorded in the county recorder's office to give constructive notice to all the world that the property owner signed and agreed to the loan. Likewise, the buyer and the seller instruct the title company to record the grant deed that transfers ownership of the property between the principals, and the recorded grant deed tells the entire world that the transfer occurred. Many parties in a California real estate transaction may have handled escrow only with a mortgage, warranty deed, and attorney, because they have only had non-California property transfers. These individuals are expecting a California escrow to be handled the same way most of the other states do business, and the escrow officer and other transaction professionals need to be aware of the differences to be better able to answer questions.

The actual close of escrow happens in the following manner throughout the other states, with only the last few items common practice in California:

- Seller meets with buyer and delivers the deed.

- Seller meets with buyer to deliver the deed with an attorney present (frequently the real estate agents, title company representative, and lender are also present).

- Buyer and seller meet at the real estate office to deliver the deed and keys.

- Buyer and seller meet at an attorney's office to deliver the deed and keys.

- Buyer and seller meet at the title insurance company office to deliver the deed that the title insurance company will record.

- If the buyer gets a new loan, the buyer and seller may meet at the offices of the new lender.

- The seller executes a notarized deed well in advance of the actual closing and delivers it to escrow to hold until all escrow instructions have been complied with; escrow gives all deeds (grant deed, trust deed, etc.) to the title company; the escrow officer instructs the title company to record the deed at the county recorder's office. No meeting takes place between the parties. The recorded document gives the public constructive notice that the transfer happened.

FIGURE 12.1

Power of Attorney

- The documents must be notarized.

- If the power of attorney is executed outside the United States, the American consulate in that county must notarize the document.

- Title companies will not normally allow use of a power of attorney over six months old.

- The form allowed in California is not the same wording on the power of attorney document as used for a general power of attorney or used in other states or used for general, non-real estate matters.

- To be valid, the form allowed in California must contain the words: "to mortgage, transfer in trust, or to otherwise encumber or hypothecate."

- The party signing is called the **attorney in fact.**

- Individuals using the power of attorney to sign for another must execute all documents in their own personal handwriting.

- The individual signing the power of attorney for another must have prior approval by the lender and must sign the document with an exact order: writing the name of the person they are signing for, followed by a comma, then writing their own name, followed by a comma, then include the following words for each signing: "His (or her) attorney in fact."

■ THE RECORDING PROCESS

In the preparation to close the escrow, the escrow officer will review documents, such as the preliminary title report, beneficiary demand statement, and loan documents, in addition to the items to be recorded. Common documents that are recorded include the grant deed, the trust deed, and the deed of reconveyance. However, escrow is involved with many other documents that may need recordation, such as an *assignment of trustee* or a *power of attorney*.

In the case of use of a **power of attorney** in a real estate transaction, escrow must notify all third parties when such a document will be used. Most frequently, a lender making a new loan under a trust deed will not allow use of a power of attorney for execution of the original loan documents, and especially the trust note. While a power of attorney is allowed, a general power of attorney will *not* be allowed. In most cases, the lender will require the use of a *special power of attorney*. Some of the information concerning use of a power of attorney in a real estate transaction is outlined in Figure 12.1. The escrow officer should receive written instructions for third parties on the acceptance of a particular document by sending a fax of the signed document to the third party in advance for review and approval.

Often the escrow contains a requirement, either by the lender of the new loan or an instruction from a principal, that instructs escrow to pay off a lien through escrow. In this case, the escrow will instruct title to record items such as a **Satisfaction of Judgment,** as shown in Figure 12.2, or a Release of Mechanic's Lien, as shown in Figure 12.3.

After verification of all the purchaser's funds necessary to close the escrow, the escrow officer notifies the title company that the documents the escrow officer has previously delivered to the title company are now to be recorded at the county recorder's office. This is the point that is often referred to as the "perfect escrow" because all conditions have been met. This does not mean that up until this point anything during the open escrow period was perfect. The perfect escrow comes from the meaning of "to perfect" the transaction, meaning consummation and completion. All documents have been reviewed for recordation and insurability, the documentary transfer tax funds are attached for payment, and the recording fees are attached for payment. At this point the documents are recorded at the county recorder and the transaction is closed. Now the escrow officer has much work to perform to complete the escrow file.

Many escrows involve two or more persons acting as principals to transfer ownership out of their names or to act as a borrower. With busy lifestyles of individuals, it is not always possible for all of the parties to meet at one time to execute the same document. In fact, it is very common for parties to sign at a different date and at a different time. The principals may sign separately at the escrow company, which has a **notary public** to execute the required seal or stamp on documents. In these cases, when there is a separate signing, the notary **jurat** must also be a separate for each, such as the sample shown in Figure 12.4.

■ ELECTRONIC RECORDING

In most cases a document evidencing transfer of ownership is recorded at the public recorder's office to give the world constructive notice that the transfer has taken place. To be recorded, the document must be signed by the maker, and it is usually dated. The document has a public notary seal or stamp affixed that indicates the acknowledgment by the notary as to the identity of the **transferor** who is authenticating the signature.

An **electronic signature,** discussed in more detail in Chapter 10, is one form of electronic document. Instead of the document containing an original signature, the document is an electronic copy of the document that contains the electronic signature. Recently, the California State Legislature had a proposed AB1732, referred to as the Torlakson Bill. The purpose of the bill was to allow any

FIGURE 12.2

Satisfaction of Judgment

RECORDING REQUESTED BY
Pacific Ocean Title Company

AND WHEN RECORDED MAIL THIS DEED AND
UNLESS OTHER WISE SHOWN BELOW MAIL TAX STATEMENTS TO
Name
Address
City & State
Zip
Title Order No.   Escrow No.

Book
Page
File No.

Recorded on
_____at_____
Official Records
County of _____, California
Conny B. McCormack
Registrar-Recorder/County Clerk

Fees:
$ _____
B.

SPACE ABOVE THIS LINE FOR RECORDER'S USE

SATISFACTION OF JUDGMENT

IN THE _____ COURT OF _____

_____
PLAINTIFF

No.: _____

_____
DEFENDANT

The Judgment herein having been paid, full satisfaction is hereby acknowledged of said

Judgment entered _____in Book _____Page _____, of Judgments, in

favor of _____ and against

_____

and the Clerk is hereby authorized and directed to enter full satisfaction of record of said action.

DATED:_____, 20_____.

_____

_____
Attorney (s) for Judgment Creditor

STATE OF CALIFORNIA
COUNTY OF_____
On this the _____day of _____ , 20___
before me, the undersigned officer, personally
appeared _____, known to me
to be the same person whose name is subscribed
to the within instrument, and duly acknowledged
to me that _____ executed the same.

_____
Signature of Notary

_____
Name (Typed or Printed) of Notary

FOR NOTARY SEAL

OR STAMP

_____
Deputy Clerk of the Above-Entitled Court

FIGURE 12.3

Release of Mechanic's Lien

RECORDING REQUESTED BY
Pacific Ocean Title Company

AND WHEN RECORDED MAIL THIS DEED AND
UNLESS OTHER WISE SHOWN BELOW MAIL TAX STATEMENTS TO
Name
Address
City & State
Zip
Title Order No.　　　　Escrow No.

Book
Page
File No.

Recorded on
_____at_____
Official Records
County of _____, California
Conny B. McCormack
Registrar-Recorder/County Clerk

Fees:
$ _____
B.

SPACE ABOVE THIS LINE FOR RECORDER'S USE

RELEASE OF MECHANIC'S LIEN

That Notice of Mechanics Lien executed by _____

_____, naming as obligors (including the owners or reputed owners)

_____

Recorded_____, 20_____, as Instrument No. _____ in Book _____, Page _____,

Official Records of the County of _____, State of California, upon that Real

Property in said County and State described as:

(legal description here)

Is hereby released, the claim having been fully paid and discharged.
APN or AIN:　xxx-xxx-xx

Dated:_____

_____

_____

_____

_____

STATE OF CALIFORNIA
COUNTY OF_____
On this the _____day of _____ , 20___
The undersigned, a Notary Public in and for said
County and State, personally appeared _____
_____, known to me
to be the person ___whose name _____subscribed
to the within instrument and acknowledged that
_____executed the same.

_____
　　　Signature of Notary
_____
　　Name (Typed or Printed) of Notary

FOR NOTARY SEAL OR STAMP

FIGURE 12.4

Notary Jurat for Two Signatures

STATE OF CALIFORNIA
COUNTY OF_____

_____ being first duly sworn,
deposes and says: That _____ the
_____ claimant named in the foregoing
claim of lien, that _____ he has read the same and
knows the contents thereof, and that the statements
therein contain are turn and that it contains, among
other things, a correct statement of _____ demand,
after credits and offsets.

Dated: this ____day of _____, 20___ at _____
(City & State)

_____
(Signature of Affiant)

Subscribed and sworn to before me

_____
_____

Notary Public in and for said State

STATE OF CALIFORNIA
COUNTY OF_____

_____
being first duly sworn, deposes and says: That _____
_____ the claimant
herein, is a _____ that affiant is _____
and for that reason ____ makes his affidavit on behalf
of said _____ that he was read the same
and knows the contents thereof, and that the statements
therein contained are true and that it contains among
other things, a correct statement of the demand of
claimant, after deducting all just credits and offsets.

Dated: this ____ day of _____, 20___ at _____
(City & State)

_____
(Signature of Affiant)

Subscribed and sworn to before me

_____
_____

Notary Public in and for said State

**FOR NOTARY SEAL
OR STAMP**

**FOR NOTARY SEAL
OR STAMP**

California county recorder's office to set up a system to accept electronic documents for recording. Various versions of the bill were proposed, with one specifically allowing a real estate licensee to do electronic recording.

In the case of this bill, the California Association of REALTORS® Governmental Affairs Department asked for a legal opinion from the state's legislative counsel. The opinion received stated that the bill was unnecessary. Under existing law, the counsel concluded, any county recorder's office could already accept electronic documents for recording. After obtaining the opinion, the author of the bill withdrew the bill. Therefore, existing law does allow for electronic recording of documents.

■ NOTIFICATION BY THE TITLE COMPANY

Once the escrow company has set up the recording, the title insurance company and the escrow company confirm everything one last time. The title company confirms receipt of all the documents. The title company also receives the loan funds and collects the change of ownership form. The documents that are to be recorded are then transmitted to the county recorder's office.

Upon confirmation that all documents have been actually recorded, the subescrow department pays off the existing demands and taxes, and then collects the title fees from the proceeds. The recordation is now completed, the escrow is closed. Now is when the escrow officer has a great deal of postclosing work left to do; namely, write all the checks to all the vendors, including the brokers.

■ FINAL CLOSING STATEMENT—THE HUD-1 FORM (RESPA)

The **HUD-1 form** consists of items numbered from 100 to 1400 that is a prescribed format with various sections of the two-page form as shown in Figure 12.5. A detailed explanation of each line is given below and each section and page is explained.

Sections marked with the letters A through I are the transaction names of the parties to the transaction, such as the name of the buyer, seller, lender, escrow, and title company, plus the type of loan and date of close of escrow, or **settlement date.**

The first page consists of two sections. Section J is a summary of the borrower's transaction for all funds with lines numbered in the 100s to 300s; Section K is a summary of the seller's transaction for all funds with lines numbered in the 400s to 600s. The items on the first page show the down payment, loan amount, and total of the closing costs and fees taken from the bottom of page two, on line 1400.

The second page is an itemized statement of all costs and fees for both the seller and the buyer for the lines numbered 700 to 1400. The page has one column for the borrower and one for the seller where any item could be paid by only one party or the other party or split and paid by both.

■ EXPLANATION OF HUD-1 SETTLEMENT STATEMENT   The first page of the HUD-1 Settlement Statement summarizes all the costs and adjustments for the borrower and seller. Section J is the summary of the borrower's transaction and Section K is the summary of the seller's side of the transaction. It is not required that one side receive a copy of the information on the other side.

FIGURE 12.5

HUD-1 Settlement Statement

A. **Settlement Statement**	**U.S. Department of Housing and Urban Development**	OMB Approval No. 2502-0265

B. Type of Loan

1. ☐ FHA 2. ☐ FmHA 3. ☐ Conv. Unins.	6. File Number:	7. Loan Number:	8. Mortgage Insurance Case Number:
4. ☐ VA 5. ☐ Conv. Ins.			

C. Note: This form is furnished to give you a statement of actual settlement costs. Amounts paid to and by the settlement agent are shown. Items marked "(p.o.c.)" were paid outside the closing; they are shown here for informational purposes and are not included in the totals.

D. Name & Address of Borrower:	E. Name & Address of Seller:	F. Name & Address of Lender:

G. Property Location:	H. Settlement Agent:
	Place of Settlement:	I. Settlement Date:

J. Summary of Borrower's Transaction		**K. Summary of Seller's Transaction**	
100. Gross Amount Due From Borrower		**400. Gross Amount Due To Seller**	
101. Contract sales price		401. Contract sales price	
102. Personal property		402. Personal property	
103. Settlement charges to borrower (line 1400)		403.	
104.		404.	
105.		405.	
Adjustments for items paid by seller in advance		Adjustments for items paid by seller in advance	
106. City/town taxes to		406. City/town taxes to	
107. County taxes to		407. County taxes to	
108. Assessments to		408. Assessments to	
109.		409.	
110.		410.	
111.		411.	
112.		412.	
120. Gross Amount Due From Borrower		**420. Gross Amount Due To Seller**	
200. Amounts Paid By Or In Behalf Of Borrower		**500. Reductions In Amount Due To Seller**	
201. Deposit or earnest money		501. Excess deposit (see instructions)	
202. Principal amount of new loan(s)		502. Settlement charges to seller (line 1400)	
203. Existing loan(s) taken subject to		503. Existing loan(s) taken subject to	
204.		504. Payoff of first mortgage loan	
205.		505. Payoff of second mortgage loan	
206.		506.	
207.		507.	
208.		508.	
209.		509.	
Adjustments for items unpaid by seller		Adjustments for items unpaid by seller	
210. City/town taxes to		510. City/town taxes to	
211. County taxes to		511. County taxes to	
212. Assessments to		512. Assessments to	
213.		513.	
214.		514.	
215.		515.	
216.		516.	
217.		517.	
218.		518.	
219.		519.	
220. Total Paid By/For Borrower		**520. Total Reduction Amount Due Seller**	
300. Cash At Settlement From/To Borrower		**600. Cash At Settlement To/From Seller**	
301. Gross Amount due from borrower (line 120)		601. Gross amount due to seller (line 420)	
302. Less amounts paid by/for borrower (line 220)	( )	602. Less reductions in amt. due seller (line 520)	( )
303. Cash ☐ From ☐ To Borrower		**603. Cash** ☐ To ☐ From Seller	

Section 5 of the Real Estate Settlement Procedures Act (RESPA) requires the following: • HUD must develop a Special Information Booklet to help persons borrowing money to finance the purchase of residential real estate to better understand the nature and costs of real estate settlement services; • Each lender must provide the booklet to all applicants from whom it receives or for whom it prepares a written application to borrow money to finance the purchase of residential real estate; • Lenders must prepare and distribute with the Booklet a Good Faith Estimate of the settlement costs that the borrower is likely to incur in connection with the settlement. These disclosures are manadatory.

Section 4(a) of RESPA mandates that HUD develop and prescribe this standard form to be used at the time of loan settlement to provide full disclosure of all charges imposed upon the borrower and seller. These are third party disclosures that are designed to provide the borrower with pertinent information during the settlement process in order to be a better shopper.

The Public Reporting Burden for this collection of information is estimated to average one hour per response, including the time for reviewing instructions, searching existing data sources, gathering and maintaining the data needed, and completing and reviewing the collection of information.

This agency may not collect this information, and you are not required to complete this form, unless it displays a currently valid OMB control number.

The information requested does not lend itself to confidentiality.

Previous editions are obsolete	Page 1 of 2	form **HUD-1** (3/86) ref Handbook 4305.2

FIGURE 12.5

HUD-1 Settlement Statement (Continued)

L. Settlement Charges

				Paid From Borrowers Funds at Settlement	Paid From Seller's Funds at Settlement
700.	**Total Sales/Broker's Commission based on price $**	@	% =		
	Division of Commission (line 700) as follows:				
701.	$	to			
702.	$	to			
703.	Commission paid at Settlement				
704.					
800.	**Items Payable In Connection With Loan**				
801.	Loan Origination Fee	%			
802.	Loan Discount	%			
803.	Appraisal Fee	to			
804.	Credit Report	to			
805.	Lender's Inspection Fee				
806.	Mortgage Insurance Application Fee to				
807.	Assumption Fee				
808.					
809.					
810.					
811.					
900.	**Items Required By Lender To Be Paid In Advance**				
901.	Interest from	to	@$	/day	
902.	Mortgage Insurance Premium for		months to		
903.	Hazard Insurance Premium for		years to		
904.			years to		
905.					
1000.	**Reserves Deposited With Lender**				
1001.	Hazard insurance	months@$	per month		
1002.	Mortgage insurance	months@$	per month		
1003.	City property taxes	months@$	per month		
1004.	County property taxes	months@$	per month		
1005.	Annual assessments	months@$	per month		
1006.		months@$	per month		
1007.		months@$	per month		
1008.		months@$	per month		
1100.	**Title Charges**				
1101.	Settlement or closing fee	to			
1102.	Abstract or title search	to			
1103.	Title examination	to			
1104.	Title insurance binder	to			
1105.	Document preparation	to			
1106.	Notary fees	to			
1107.	Attorney's fees	to			
	(includes above items numbers:		)		
1108.	Title insurance	to			
	(includes above items numbers:		)		
1109.	Lender's coverage	$			
1110.	Owner's coverage	$			
1111.					
1112.					
1113.					
1200.	**Government Recording and Transfer Charges**				
1201.	Recording fees: Deed $	; Mortgage $	; Releases $		
1202.	City/county tax/stamps: Deed $	; Mortgage $			
1203.	State tax/stamps: Deed $	; Mortgage $			
1204.					
1205.					
1300.	**Additional Settlement Charges**				
1301.	Survey	to			
1302.	Pest inspection to				
1303.					
1304.					
1305.					
1400.	**Total Settlement Charges (enter on lines 103, Section J and 502, Section K)**				

Section 100 summarizes the borrower's costs, such as the contract cost of the house, any personal property being purchased, and the total settlement charges owed by the borrower from Section L.

Beginning at line 106, adjustments are made for items (such as taxes, assessments, or association dues) that the seller has previously paid. If the buyer will benefit from these items after settlement, the buyer will usually repay the seller for that portion of the cost.

Here is an example of the calculation:

J. Summary of Borrower's Transaction		
100. Gross Amount Due From Borrower		
101. Contract sales price		100,000.00
102. Personal property		
103. Settlement charges to borrower (line 1400)		4,000.00
104.		
105.		
Adjustments for items paid by seller in advance		
106. City/town taxes	to	25.00
107. County taxes	to 7/31	40.00
108. Assessments	6/30 to 7/31 (owners assn)	
109.		
110.		
111.		
112.		
120. Gross Amount Due From Borrower		104,065.00

Assume in this example, the cost of the house is $100,000 and the borrower's total settlement charges brought from Line 1400 of Section L are $4,000. Assume that the settlement date is July 1. Here the borrower has agreed to pay the seller for the $40 homeowners' association dues that have been paid for the month of July and for the Mello-Roos charge of $25. This is added for a gross amount due from the borrower of $104,065.

Section 200 lists the amount paid by the borrower or on behalf of the borrower. This will include the deposit of earnest money put as an initial deposit toward closing costs and the down payment with the agreement of sale. The loan(s) is shown and any loan being assumed.

Beginning at Line 210, adjustments are made for items that the seller owes (such as taxes, assessments) but for which the borrower will pay after settlement. The seller will usually pay the buyer or escrow will credit this portion at settlement.

200. Amounts Paid By Or In Behalf Of Borrower		
201. Deposit or earnest money		2,000.00
202. Principal amount of new loan(s)		80,000.00
203. Existing loan(s) taken subject to		
204.		
205.		
206.		
207.		
208.		
209.		
Adjustments for items unpaid by seller		
210. City/town taxes	to	
211. County taxes	1/1 to 6/30 $1,200/year	600.00
212. Assessments	1/1 to 6/30 $200/year	100.00
213.		
214.		
215.		
216.		
217.		
218.		
219.		
220. Total Paid By/For Borrower		**82,700.00**

In this example, assume the borrower paid an earnest deposit of $2,000 and is getting a loan for $80,000. A tax of $1,200 and an assessment of $200 are due at the end of the year. The seller will pay the borrower for six months or one-half of this amount. Line 220 shows the total $82,700 to be paid by or for the borrower.

Section 300 reflects the difference between the gross amount due from the borrower and the total amount paid by/for the borrower. Generally, line 303 will show the amount of cash the borrower must bring to settlement.

300. Cash At Settlement From/To Borrower		
301. Gross Amount due from borrower (line 120)		104,065.00
302. Less amounts paid by/for borrower (line 220)		(82,700.00)
303. Cash [X] From [ ] To Borrower		21,365.00

In this example, the borrower must bring $21,365 to settlement.

A. Specific Settlement Costs

This part of the statement discusses the settlement services which the buyer will be required to get and pay for and which are itemized in Section L of the HUD-1 Settlement Statement.

700. Sales/Broker's Commission: This is the total dollar amount of the real estate broker's sales commission, which may be paid by either principal. This commission is typically a percentage of the selling price of the home, but may be a flat fee.

L. Settlement Charges

700.	Total Sales/Broker's Commission based on price $	@	% =	Paid From Borrowers Funds at Settlement	Paid From Seller's Funds at Settlement
	Division of Commission (line 700) as follows:				
701.	$	to			
702.	$	to			
703.	Commission paid at Settlement				
704.					

800. Items Payable in Connection with Loan: These are the fees that lenders charge to process, approve, and make the mortgage loan.

801. Loan Origination Fee: This fee is usually known as a "loan origination fee" but sometimes is called a "point" or "points." It covers the lender's administrative costs in processing the loan. Often expressed as a percentage of the loan, the fee will vary among lenders. Generally, the buyer pays the fee, unless otherwise negotiated.

802. Loan Discount: Also often called "points" or "discount points," a loan discount is a one-time charge imposed by the lender or broker to lower the rate at which the lender or broker would otherwise offer the loan to you. Each "point" is equal to 1 percent of the loan amount. For example, if a lender charges two points on a $80,000 loan this amounts to a charge of $1,600 ($80,000 × 1% = $800 × 2).

803. Appraisal Fee: This charge pays for an appraisal report made by an appraiser.

804. Credit Report Fee: This fee covers the cost of a credit report, showing the borrower's credit history. The lender uses the information in a credit report to help decide whether or not to approve a loan and how much money to lend to the borrower and under what terms and conditions.

805. Lender's Inspection Fee: This charge covers inspections, often of newly constructed housing, made by employees of the lender or by an outside inspector. (Pest or other inspections made by companies other than the lender are discussed in line 1302.)

806. Mortgage Insurance Application Fee: This fee covers the processing of an application for mortgage insurance.

807. Assumption Fee: This is a fee that is charged when a buyer "assumes" or takes over the duty to pay the seller's existing loan.

808. Mortgage Broker Fee: Fees paid to mortgage brokers would be listed here. A computerized loan origination (CLO) fee would also be listed here.

800. Items Payable In Connection With Loan			
801. Loan Origination Fee	%		
802. Loan Discount	%		
803. Appraisal Fee	to		
804. Credit Report	to		
805. Lender's Inspection Fee			
806. Mortgage Insurance Application Fee to			
807. Assumption Fee			
808.			
809.			
810.			
811.			

900. Items Required by Lender to Be Paid in Advance: The buyer may be required to prepay certain items at the time of settlement, such as accrued interest, mortgage insurance premiums, and hazard insurance premiums.

901. Interest: Lenders usually require borrowers to pay the interest that accrues from the date of settlement to the date that the first monthly payment would pay for interest on the loan.

902. Mortgage Insurance Premium: The lender may require the borrower to pay the first year's mortgage insurance premium or a lump sum premium that covers the life of the loan, in advance, at the settlement.

903. Hazard Insurance Premium: Hazard insurance protects the borrower and the lender against loss due to fire, windstorm, and natural hazards. Lenders often require the borrower to bring to the settlement a paid-up first year's policy or to pay for the first year's premium at settlement.

904. Flood Insurance: If the lender requires flood insurance, it is usually listed here.

900. Items Required By Lender To Be Paid In Advance				
901. Interest from	to	@$	/day	
902. Mortgage Insurance Premium for		months to		
903. Hazard Insurance Premium for		years to		
904.		years to		
905.				

1000–1008. Escrow Account Deposits: These lines identify the payment of taxes and/or insurance and other items that must be paid at settlement to set up an escrow account. The lender is not allowed to collect more than a certain amount. The individual item deposits may overstate the amount that can be collected. The aggregate adjustment makes the correction in the amount on line 1008. It will be zero or a negative amount.

1000. Reserves Deposited With Lender				
1001. Hazard insurance	months@$	per month		
1002. Mortgage insurance	months@$	per month		
1003. City property taxes	months@$	per month		
1004. County property taxes	months@$	per month		
1005. Annual assessments	months@$	per month		
1006.	months@$	per month		
1007.	months@$	per month		
1008.	months@$	per month		

1100. Title Charges: Title charges may cover a variety of services performed by title companies and others. Each particular settlement may not include all of the items listed.

1101. Settlement or Closing Fee: This fee is paid to the settlement agent or escrow holder. Responsibility for payment of this fee is negotiated between the seller and the buyer.

1102–1104. Abstract of Title Search, Title Examination, Title Insurance Binder: The charges on these lines cover the costs of the title search and examination.

1105. Document Preparation: This is a separate fee that some lenders or title companies charge to cover their costs for preparation of the final legal papers, such as a deed of trust, note, or deed.

1106. Notary Fee: This fee is charged for the cost of having a person who is licensed as a notary public swear to the fact that the persons named in the documents did, in fact, sign them.

1107. Attorney's Fees: The principals may be required to pay for legal services provided to the lender, such as an examination of the title binder. Occasionally, the seller will agree in the agreement of sale to pay all or part of this fee. The cost for attorney may also appear here. If an attorney's involvement is required by the lender, the fee will appear on this part of the form, or on lines 1111, 1112, or 1113.

1108. Title Insurance: The total cost of owner's and lender's title insurance is shown here.

1109. Lender's Title Insurance: The cost of the lender's policy is shown here.

1110. Owner's (Buyer's) Title Insurance: The cost of the owner's policy is shown here.

1100. Title Charges			
1101. Settlement or closing fee	to		
1102. Abstract or title search	to		
1103. Title examination	to		
1104. Title insurance binder	to		
1105. Document preparation	to		
1106. Notary fees	to		
1107. Attorney's fees	to		
(includes above items numbers:		)	
1108. Title insurance	to		
(includes above items numbers:		)	
1109. Lender's coverage	$		
1110. Owner's coverage	$		
1111.			
1112.			
1113.			

1200. Government Recording and Transfer Charges: These fees may be paid by either principal, depending upon the agreement of sale. The buyer usually pays the fees for legally recording the new deeds (line 1201). Transfer taxes, which in some localities are collected whenever property changes hands or a loan is made, are set by state and/or local governments. City, county, and/or state tax stamps may have to be purchased as well (lines 1202 and 1203).

1200. Government Recording and Transfer Charges			
1201. Recording fees: Deed $	; Mortgage $	; Releases $	
1202. City/county tax/stamps: Deed $	; Mortgage $		
1203. State tax/stamps: Deed $	; Mortgage $		
1204.			
1205.			

1300. Additional Settlement Charges

1301. Survey: The lender may require that a surveyor conduct a property survey. This is a protection to the buyer as well. Usually the buyer pays the surveyor's fee, but sometimes this may be paid by the seller.

1302. Pest and Other Inspections: One fee is to cover the cost for an inspection for termites or other pest infestation of your home including the cost to correct existing damage. Another fee is for preventive work.

1303–1305. Lead-Based Paint Inspections: This fee is to cover inspections or evaluations for lead-based paint hazard risk assessments and may be on any blank line in the 1300 series.

1300. Additional Settlement Charges		
1301. Survey to		
1302. Pest inspection to		
1303.		
1304.		
1305.		

1400. Total Settlement Charges: The sum of all fees in the borrower's column entitled "Paid from Borrower's Funds at Settlement" is placed here. This figure is then transferred to line 103 of Section J, "Settlement charges to borrower" in the Summary of Borrower's Transaction on page 1 of the HUD-1 Settlement Statement and added to the purchase price. The sum of all of the settlement fees paid by the seller is transferred to line 502 of Section K, Summary of Seller's Transaction on page 1 of the HUD-1 Settlement Statement.

1400. Total Settlement Charges (enter on lines 103, Section J and 502, Section K)		

Paid Outside of Closing ("POC"): Some fees may be listed on the HUD-1 to the left of the borrower's column and marked "POC," that is, **paid outside of closing (POC).** Fees such as those for credit reports and appraisals are often paid by the principal and not by escrow. Other fees such as those paid by the lender to a mortgage broker or other settlement service providers may be paid after closing/settlement. These fees are usually included in the interest rate or other settlement charge. They are not an additional cost to the borrower. These types of fees will not be added into the total on Line 1400.

■ FOREIGN INVESTORS: FIRPTA AND CAL-FIRPTA

The Internal Revenue Service requires that escrow furnish each transaction with a 1099-S for each seller who receives proceeds from the close of an escrow. The escrow officer would prepare the form and furnish a copy in the seller's closing statement along with a copy sent to IRS. The information that must be provided includes not only the name of the seller but also must show the individual's tax ID number and states the amount of consideration received in the transaction.

At the federal level, the law states that no more than 20 days after a transfer has been made, 10 percent of the total consideration must be withheld at closing and remitted to IRS. After November 3, 2003, a foreign person must provide a tax identification number (TIN) for disposition of real property.

CAL-FIRPTA is the California Foreign Investment Real Property Tax Act that became effective in 1991 that followed the federal FIRPTA of 1980 (26 U.S.C., Sec. 897). The purpose of the law was to regulate the withholding of taxes for nonresident foreigners who might make a profit from U.S. business activity in real property but who might not pay any taxes on the profit made. The law wanted to make sure that all investors and owners of real property pay the withholding tax on the profit. The California version includes those who make a profit from the sale of real property in California and take the funds either out of the country or even to another state without paying any California tax. As of 2004, California requires 3½ percent of the total consideration to be withheld from seller proceeds.

Escrow is required by law to automatically withhold funds for taxes and to send the amount indicated in the law to the tax authority on behalf of the taxpayer. If the amount withheld exceeds the amount actually due, the taxpayer may file for a tax refund. Rarely is the amount less than what would be required to be withheld according to the legal formula. If that case did happen, however, the taxpayer would still owe the difference. The law allows the escrow holder to be exempt from any liability in regards to the tax amount due, provided that escrow complied with the withholding law.

Under FIRPTA, the real estate broker is liable for full disclosure to the seller that proceeds will be withheld. As a required disclosure, failure of the broker to make this mandatory disclosure would subject the broker to being held accountable for the amounts due for the taxes, along with any penalties that would be due on the amount. FIRPTA obligates the escrow, title, brokers, and any attorney in the transaction to inform all parties of the risks and consequences of this requirement. The typical escrow instructions would include wording similar to that shown in Figure 12.6.

■ ESCROW HOLDER RELATIONSHIP

When an escrow is opened, the escrow holder is a dual agent who acts for both the buyer and the seller. After the conditions of the escrow have been met, the role of the escrow holder changes to being an agent for each of the individual parties to the transaction with respect to the particular aspect of the escrow, such as agent for the seller regarding funds, and agent for the buyer regarding the deed, and agent for the lender regarding the loan documents.

FIGURE 12.6

CAL-FIRPTA Notice and Disclosure

Property Address: _____   Escrow No.: _____

In accordance with law (AB2065)(Chapter 02-488) Revised Revenue and Taxation Code Section 18552, a Buyer may be required to withhold an amount equal to 3⅓% of the sales price, in the case of a disposition of California real property interest by either:

1. A Seller who is an individual or when the disbursement instructions authorize the proceeds to be sent to a financial intermediary of the Seller, OR,

2. A Seller is a Corporation, which has no permanent place of business in California.

For failure to withhold, the Buyer may become subject to a penalty in the amount equal to the greater of Ten Percent (10%) of the amount required to be withheld or Five-Hundred Dollars ($500.00).

However, notwithstanding any other provision included in the California statutes referenced above, no Buyer will be required to withhold any amount or be subject to penalty for failure to withhold if:

1. The Total Consideration of California subject property is $100,000.00 or less, OR

2. The Seller executes a written certificate, under the penalty of perjury, certifying that the Seller is a Corporation with a permanent place of business in California, OR

3. The Seller, who is an individual, executes a written certificate, under the penalty of perjury, to any of the following:

   a. The property is the Seller's principal residence.

   b. The Seller is selling the property at a loss for California Income Tax purposes.

   c. The Seller is selling the property as part of an Internal Revenue Code Section 1031 exchange.

   d. The Seller is selling the property because of an involuntary conversion and will replace the property within the provisions of Internal Revenue Code Section 1033.

The new law does not contain language allowing for request for either a waiver of withholding or reduced withholding as previously allowed under CAL-FIRPTA.

The undersigned parties acknowledge that the escrow holder is required to provide to Buyer(s) written notification of California withholding requirements. This notification instructs the Buyer(s) to withhold 3⅓% of the total consideration of the California real property herein, when CAL-FIRPTA is applicable.

If either the Buyer or the Seller require any additional information, they are advised to contact the California Franchise Tax Board at (916) 845-4900.

THE SELLER IS SUBJECT TO PENALTY FOR KNOWINGLY FILING A FRAUDULENT CERTIFICATE FOR THE PURPOSE OF AVOIDING THE WITHHOLDING REQUIREMENT.

_____   _____
         Buyer's signature   Seller's signature

The status of the escrow holder is a limited agency or specific agency and not a general agency. Escrow assumes no liability for any failure to do or not to do any item in the escrow instructions, especially regarding third party actions. The escrow holder cannot make any other party do or not do some act that would aid and comply with the escrow. Escrow cannot acknowledge the existence of the escrow to any party other than those involved in the specific transaction.

The escrow holder has the duty and responsibility of acting as a fiduciary to the principals and to third parties that affect the escrow. Naturally, the escrow holder's primary duty is to comply with the terms and conditions of the escrow instructions.

Should the escrow not close, the term "fallout" is used to describe that the transaction fell out of escrow. In the case of this cancellation, the parties may agree to sign a document instructing the escrow officer on what to do with the funds and documents. The parties that mutually agree to cancel the escrow do not, however, terminate the rights of the parties to the transaction in the underlying agreement, usually the purchase agreement contract. When the escrow officer is faced with conflicting instructions, the interpleader is used, as discussed in Chapter 3. The escrow holder has no liability for a fall out so long as the written instructions were followed. Liability for the escrow officer is only when escrow either did not follow the escrow instructions, which is deemed breach of contract, or the escrow officer was negligent in the performance of the escrow instructions for the duties that were to be performed as a fiduciary.

After the close of escrow, when all items have been complied with, the escrow holder is still responsible for certain duties. The major commitment of the escrow holder is the duty to continue to act as a fiduciary. Because the statute of limitations on negligent performance of fiduciary duties is two years, the escrow officer must not discuss with anyone other than the principals or authorized third parties named in the transaction any part of the escrow information for a minimum of two years after the close of escrow.

■ BUYER RECEIVES

After the close of escrow, the escrow officer will prepare the closing documents to be given to the buyer. During the course of the escrow, the buyer would have already received a copy of the **termite report** that indicated the current condition of the improvements. At that time, the work had not been completed. The final termite clearance indicating the work is completed is found in the closing packet that the buyer will receive from escrow after the close of escrow.

Along with the HUD-1 closing/settlement statement showing all the credits and debits that were charged to the buyer in the escrow, the buyer will usually always receive a check payable from the escrow trust account. Prior to the close of escrow, the buyer would have been notified of the funds that the escrow officer needed in order to close escrow. The amount requested is usually more than the actual amount needed. In anticipation of probable delays, escrow asks for more funds than are actually needed in anticipation of possible change in date of recordation. Any unused funds for actual costs must be refunded to the party from whom they were received. A check from escrow after the recordation brings the account back to zero so that after escrow draws all funds from the buyer's account nothing is left.

The buyer's copy of the insurance policy binder is normally given from escrow to the buyer showing evidence of various types of coverage, depending upon the escrow. Some policies were optional, such as earthquake insurance, while other endorsements may have been required by the lender prior to closing of escrow, such as evidence of flood insurance. The buyer pays for but does not normally receive a binder for the mortgage insurance policy. The buyer would, however, receive a binder for the policy of title insurance that may also be included in the closing documents.

Several weeks after the close of escrow, the buyer will receive additional items in the mail. The buyer may receive a buyer's copy of the hazard insurance policy. The grant deed comes from the county recorder's office by mail after the close of escrow. The transfer document might be a recorded all-inclusive trust deed (AITD) or some other document. Other documents, such as the fraud disclosure information statement, may accompany the recorded deed.

■ SELLER RECEIVES

The seller would receive a copy of the final termite completion report after the work had been completed. The seller would also receive a copy of the HUD-1 document. The settlement statement for each principal does not show the charges that the other principal paid. It is important to remember that for both the buyer and the seller, if any referral fee was paid, it must be disclosed, in writing, on the HUD-1 if the escrow involved a federally related loan. Because failure to disclose could be construed as an illegal kickback, any licensee involved would be subject to investigation and license revocation for violation of a federal law.

The seller is usually most interested in the net proceeds check from the conclusion of the sale or exchange of the property. The seller often needs to receive the proceeds check, get the check converted to cash, then use that cash for the costs of moving. In nonresidential, and especially with income-producing property, this is less likely to be the case. Because the proceeds check is usually for a large amount, the seller may have to wait until the bank honors the proceeds check, under the bank's other good funds laws, before the seller has access to these funds. Knowing that this is normal banking procedure, it is often a good idea to have the seller's proceeds handled by wire transfer directly into the seller's bank account if there is an immediate need for use of the funds. This would give greater service on the transaction to the seller and could avert possession problems after the close of escrow.

The seller will also, like the buyer, receive a document directly from the county recorder's office for the recorded reconveyance deed, which is evidence of the payoff of any loan. The fraud information sheet would accompany the recorded deed.

The escrow is also obligated to file the 1099-S information with the Internal Revenue Service. This form for the amount of the proceeds actually paid to the seller could not be completed prior to the close of escrow. The form may be computer generated months after the close of escrow, according to the time line set out by the IRS for delivery of tax information to taxpayers. In any case, the form is not usually given immediately after close of escrow, but is mailed to the seller at a later date.

■ LENDER RECEIVES

The lender also receives documents after the close of escrow. The escrow would provide the lender with a copy of the hazard insurance policy binder naming the lender, along with any other insurance policy binders applicable, such as required flood insurance, voluntary earthquake insurance, or similar documents. In most cases, the buyer pays the premium for a mortgage insurance policy, if such is part of the transaction, but the lender receives the actual insurance policy because it covers the lender in case of default on the loan so the lender gets the binder.

Any lender coverage title insurance policy would also go to the lender after close of escrow. This is usually the ALTA title insurance policy, but additional insured or special construction or other types of binder coverage might be applicable to a particular transaction. The title insurance company would get the appropriate document to the lender, frequently from escrow.

The lender will receive a copy of the HUD-1 document and will review the closing settlement statement after the close of escrow to determine that all items were as represented. If, at the last minute, an amendment went into escrow where the seller credited the buyer with funds, or a deposit was made into escrow from a third party for the closing costs or down payment, then the lender would most likely send the file to the fraud audit department to determine if any impropriety was evident. The lender must perform this act if the mortgage insurance policy is to be valid. A thorough review of all funds passing through all hands is performed, including any illegal kickbacks from any parties.

From the county recorder's office, the lender will also receive in the mail the actual recorded deed showing evidence of the debt. The lender would already have the original copies of the loan documents with the original signatures on the trust note or mortgage. But the recorded trust deed comes directly from the county recorder's office several weeks after the close of escrow. Because so many loans are sold after the close of escrow to investors on the secondary money market, it is common for other documents to be recorded after the close of escrow in conjunction with the escrow transaction, such as a loan servicing agreement.

The most common document that is used to transfer ownership of the debt is the Assignment of the Deed of Trust as is shown in Figure 12.7. This document is recorded at the county recorder's office in the county in which the real property is located, not where the seller of the trust deed or where the buyer of the trust deed does business. When the loan was funded one or more days prior to the close of escrow, the debtor, in California called the trustor, signed the trust note and trust deed to be recorded that indicated the name of the entity from which the money was borrowed, called the beneficiary. When the trust note is sold to another entity, this assignment of trust deed form is used to show the world, as constructive notice, evidence of the transfer of the entity to which the loan is to be repaid, the new beneficiary. The form shows the legal description of the real property, along with the name of the trustor, the trustee, and the beneficiary. Because loans are transferred frequently during the life of the loan, more than one assignment of the loan is not unusual. The borrower is not affected, other than possibly changing where the monthly payment is mailed. And as discussed earlier, if the same entity retains the loan servicing, the buyer may mail the payment to the same place the payment was mailed to prior to the assignment.

Institutional lenders commonly use the Assignment of the Deed of Trust to transfer ownership of the debt, as discussed above. However, private individuals who make loans on real property commonly use another recorded document called the Substitution of Trustee form as shown in Figure 12.8. The title company furnished a free copy of the trust deed to the escrow officer who drew up the original trust deed. Now, at payoff, a new trustee is being substituted for the one named in the preprinted deed. This may save the parties funds at the close of this escrow, as an institutional trustee usually charges a higher fee than a private individual might charge. Anyone who is not involved in the transaction can serve as the new trustee and go to escrow to sign off that the beneficiary has notified the trustee that the debt is no longer applicable to the borrower, trustor, or the property. By recording the Substitution of Trustee form, the new trustee would be the individual who would be responsible for signing the deed of reconveyance to show evidence of release from the debt that is now paid off.

FIGURE 12.7

Assignment of Deed of Trust

RECORDING REQUESTED B Y
Pacific Ocean Title Company

**AND WHEN RECORDED
MAIL THIS DEED AND**
UNLESS OTHER WISE SHOWN BELOW MAIL TAX
STATEMENTS TO
Name
Address
City & State
Zip
Title Order No.   Escrow No.

Book
Page
File No.

Recorded on
_____at_____
Official Records
County of _____, California
Conny B. McCormack
Registrar-recorder/County Clerk

Fees:
$ _____
B.

SPACE ABOVE THIS LINE FOR RECORDER'S USE

ASSIGNMENT OF DEED OF TRUST

FOR VALUE RECEIVED, the undersigned hereby grants, assigns and transfer to _____

_____ all beneficial interest under that certain Deed of Trust dated

_____ executed by _____, Trustor

to _____. Trustee, and recorded as

Instrument No. _____ on _____ in book _____ page _____, of Official

Records in the County Recorder's office of _____County, California, described

land therein as:

        (legal description)

TOGETHER with the note or notes therein described or referred to, the money due and to become
Due thereon with interest and all rights accrued or to accrue under said Deed of Trust.

APN or AIN: xxxx-xxx-xxx

Dated:_____

STATE OF CALIFORNIA
COUNTY OF_____
On this the _____day of _____ , 20___
The undersigned, a Notary Public in and for said
County and State, personally appeared _____
_____, known to me
to be the person ___whose name ____subscribed
to the within instrument and acknowledged that
_____executed the same.

_____
        Signature of Notary
_____
        Name (Typed or Printed)

**FOR NOTARY SEAL OR
STAMP**

FIGURE 12.8

Substitution of Trustee

RECORDING REQUESTED BY
Pacific Ocean Title Company
**AND WHEN RECORDED MAIL
THIS DEED AND**
UNLESS OTHER WISE SHOWN BELOW MAIL TAX
STATEMENTS TO
Name _____
Address _____
City & State _____
Zip _____

Book
Page
File No.

Recorded on
_____at_____
Official Records
County of Los Angeles, California
Conny B. McCormack
Registrar-Recorder/County Clerk

Fees:
$ _____
B.

SPACE ABOVE THIS LINE FOR RECORDER'S USE

SUBSTITUTION OF TRUSTEE

NOTICE IS HEREBY GIVEN that, Pursuant to the provisions of the California Civil Code
_____
hereafter referred to as "Claimant" (whether singular or plural), claims a lien upon the real property and buildings, improvements or structures thereon, described in Paragraph Five (5) below, and states the following:

(1) That demand of Claimant after deducting all just credits and offsets is _____
together with interest thereon at the rate of _____% per annum from _____, 20_____.

(2) That the name of the owner(s) or reputed owner(s) of said property, is (are)
_____
(name, or state "unknown")

(3) That Claimant did from _____, until _____
perform labor and/or supply materials as follows: _____
(general statement of a kind of work done or materials furnished, or both)
_____
for the construction, alteration or repair of said buildings, improvements or structures, which labor, or materials, or both of them, were in fact used in the construction, alteration, or repair of said buildings, improvements, or structures, the location of which is set forth in Paragraph Five (5) below.

(4) Claimant furnished work and materials under contract with or at the request of:
_____
_____

(5) That the property upon which said lien is sought to be charged is situated in the City of
_____, County of _____, State of California, commonly known as
_____and more particularly described as:
(Street address)
_____
_____

DATED: This _____ day of _____, 20_____   Firm Name: _____

(Verification for Individual Claim)   (Verification for other than Individual Claim)

■ BROKER RECEIVES

After the close of escrow the real estate broker, if used in the transaction, receives a closing packet of information. In the documents received, a copy of the HUD-1 for the buyer or the seller, depending upon which was represented by that broker, is given to the broker with another copy for the salesperson employed under the broker. Licensees should always keep evidence of this form in the closed escrow file. In addition, the broker will also receive a copy of any last-minute signed amendments or other documents. A copy of the final termite completion report will also go to the real estate broker.

The broker will receive the commission check after the close of escrow. Escrow would also issue a 1099 form at a later date to evidence payment of funds to the broker and report the earnings to IRS.

■ PAYING BILLS

In addition to paying the brokerage commission to the licensed agent after the close of escrow, other vendors are awaiting payment from the escrow. Escrow is not authorized to make any payment to anyone prior to the actual recording at the close of escrow. Once the escrow has closed, the escrow officer is obligated to make payment to the various vendors as soon as is applicable. Because escrow usually awaits release of the closing proceeds funds from the title insurance company, some delay may occur for the escrow company to obtain the funds from which to issue checks.

Typical vendor checks that escrow would issue after the close of escrow include payment to the termite company, insurance premium payment, home warranty company policy payment, repair bill payment, if any, and similar items. The escrow officer may have been instructed to issue a check from the seller's proceeds for the amount of tenant security deposits directly to the buyer's property management firm.

■ RECONVEYANCE

Once the documents are recorded, it is normal for escrow to be in possession of documents that need to be delivered between various parties. The individual will receive the original from the county recorder's office at a later date. The word **reconvey** means to convey back to where the item came from. This idea is used after the close of escrow in conveying documents back to the appropriate parties to the transaction.

The formal reconveyance deed was discussed earlier in the chapter on lenders and was reviewed as one of the documents the seller would receive from the county recorder's office after the close of escrow.

■ TITLE POLICIES

The ALTA title insurance policy is received by the lender and the buyer after the close of escrow to show evidence of coverage. The various endorsements were discussed in Chapter 5 in detail. The lender wants assurance from the title company that the lender's legal interest in the property is secure and that no other lien would have priority above the rights of the new loan. The buyer may have purchased extended ALTA coverage. This is especially true for new construction where the first purchaser wants to ensure that no mechanic's lien interests are remaining on the premises.

The CLTA title insurance policy is issued after the close of escrow to assure the buyer that no other evidence of any interest is held in the property except what was previously disclosed to and agreed upon by the buyer prior to the close of escrow. The buyer may have voluntarily agreed to a new loan. Also, the buyer agreed to the property tax lien that remains on the property.

■ FRAUD AND AUDIT FILE

The **Department of Consumer Affairs** serves as the central reporting agency for real estate fraud. The department has many free services, including counseling on real estate matters, information on recorded documents, referrals to other governmental agencies to assist where appropriate, or handling investigative matters beyond the scope of the department's purview. The department also handles investigation of and mediation for complaints. Working closely with the DRE legal department when licensees are involved and with the district attorney for matters with the public, the Department of Consumer Affairs legal department has relationships with all prosecuting agencies on matters involving real estate fraud.

When a document has been recorded in Los Angeles County, as just one example, the county recorder's office will include a document from the Department of Consumer Affairs that states the information that is the same as or very similar to the wording shown in Figure 12.9. In addition, the Los Angeles County Registrar-Recorder/County Clerk sends a letter to each party shown in the data contained on the recorded document stating that the letter is about recorded document notification. The letter specifically indicates that the enclosed deed or trust deed was recorded at the county recorder's office. In an effort to protect homeowners from fraud, the parties are instructed that they may review the

FIGURE 12.9

**Consumer Affairs
Real Estate Fraud**

To protect yourself and your property, call the Department of Consumer Affairs if any of the following apply:

1. You have no knowledge of the document you received.

2. You don't understand the document you received.

3. You have had a problem with the transaction the document relates to.

4. The information contained on the document is incorrect.

5. The information contained on the document was changed after you signed it.

6. You did not sign the document.

7. You believe the person signing the document was incompetent at the time of signing.

8. You believe the person was deceased at the time of signing of the document.

9. You believe there was fraud in the transaction.

10. You believe there was misrepresentation in the transaction.

11. You have experienced problems involving a home improvement contract.

12. You did not sell, borrow, or make a gift of your property to another.

document to ensure its accuracy and to make sure that the document is authentic. The letter further goes on to explain in clearly understandable terms that the enclosed document is a signed deed that means that someone else may own all or some part of the property. If the document is a deed of trust, the consumer is notified in the letter that someone has pledged the property as security for a loan and that nonpayment of the loan gives the lender the right to foreclose on the property. It further states the obvious, that if the lender institutes a foreclosure, the property will be sold and that the consumer will be forced to move out of the property. The informational letter indicates that the consumer should take no action if they are already aware of the document and have no problem with the transaction. Otherwise a telephone number is given that directs the consumer to contact the Department of Consumer Affairs office for assistance and information on the free services provided to the public. The same information available may be seen at this Web site: *http://consumer-affairs.co.la.ca.us*.

WEB LINK

THINK ABOUT IT

Closing Cost Error

As a licensed real estate agent in California you like the sales part of each transaction but are not particularly fond of the mathematics involved. To help build your confidence and reduce office liability, your office manager required you to print a copy of your buyer's cost sheet and have the copy signed by the buyer placed into the file. You used the MLS form at first, but later used the real estate specific Top Producer software program. The buyer signed each and you reviewed the numbers carefully against the lender's estimated closing costs form mailed directly to your buyer.

At the close of escrow you review the HUD-1 RESPA form that shows the exact figures used at the closing. In reviewing the figures you find a mistake that would result in a $50 credit to the buyer. What would you do?

Answer: You would first go to your office manager or broker to determine if your $50 credit is correct, as a double check on your math computation. Then you would contact the escrow holder to correct the mistake for your buyer. The mistake may have come from the title company calculations, or the new lender may have miscalculated a charge or fee. You would also go over the figures with your buyer and explain the steps you are taking to correct the situation.

■ CHAPTER SUMMARY

The closing procedures involve a series of steps that lead to the transfer of ownership. The closing is the final step in the transfer of ownership to real property. However, when the deed that transfers ownership is recorded, the escrow officer has many tasks left to complete. The escrow will prepare a package of documents for the buyer, another for the lender, and another for the seller.

After recordation of the closing documents, the escrow officer prepares the disbursement checks and prepares orders for others to handle outside of escrow, such as the reconveyance deed for the loan paid off, or the grant deed placing ownership into a family trust. Prior to release of any funds, an internal audit at the escrow company is performed to reduce error and ensure quality control of the funds of the principals, the lender, and the title company. Checks are typically written to vendors, such as the termite company, and to pay the brokerage commission and the seller's net proceeds. Often a small amount is written to the buyer for an excess collected that was not used in the escrow to pay actual expenses.

■ CHAPTER 12 QUIZ

1. The buyer would receive all the following after the close of escrow *EXCEPT* the
   a. HUD-1 settlement statement.
   b. insurance binder.
   c. reconveyance deed.
   d. termite clearance report.

2. The sales price on the HUD-1 settlement statement would be shown as
   a. neither a debit nor a credit to the buyer.
   b. debit to the seller.
   c. credit to the buyer.
   d. none of the above.

3. The electronic signature problem was reviewed at the state legislature level for
   a. a legal opinion.
   b. validity of the new statute.
   c. verification of authenticity.
   d. an approval by the legislative body.

4. The termite clearance is furnished to the
   a. buyer.
   b. seller.
   c. lender.
   d. All of the above

5. The FIRPTA and CAL-FIRPTA laws and regulations apply to the
   a. buyer's cash down payment paid through escrow, excluding final closing costs.
   b. seller's proceeds.
   c. broker's commission rate charged to the seller.
   d. lender's loan fees, loan origination fee, points, and other charges paid by the seller.

6. The real estate fraud and/or audit file is used to
   a. safeguard the public against loss of property from fraudulent recorded deeds.
   b. ensure that the lender has full disclosure of the buyer's cash through escrow.
   c. warn the general public of possible loss of ownership of the property.
   d. do all of the above.

7. Which would the seller receive after the close of escrow?
   a. Substitution of trustee
   b. Assignment of trust deed
   c. Reconveyance deed
   d. Notary jurat

8. The seller would be exempt from paying IRS taxes at the close of escrow under the FIRPTA laws if the
   a. transaction is over $100,000.
   b. transaction is under $100,000.
   c. person selling U.S. property is not a U.S. citizen, has no U.S. bank accounts, and pays taxes in another country.
   d. seller is a business entity in another state and plans to pay its California income taxes for business operations within the state of California within the next three years.

9. When escrow collects and pays taxes from the seller's proceeds under FIRPTA, the amount of the tax is
   a. 3⅓% of the sales price.
   b. 10%.
   c. $500.
   d. $100,000.

10. Who would receive a copy of the HUD-1 settlement statement after the close of escrow?
    a. Buyer   c. Lender
    b. Seller   d. All the above

SPECIAL ESCROWS

13

HOMESTEAD, PROBATE, FOREIGN INVESTORS, AND FOR SALE BY OWNER

■ KEY TERMS

Abandonment of
  Homestead
administrator
beneficiary
CAL-FIRPTA
California Homestead
  Act
creditor

declaration of
  homestead
devisees
estate
FIRPTA
for sale by owner
  (FSBO) transaction

homestead
petition
probate
trust
will

■ CHAPTER OVERVIEW

The escrow officer and an escrow company may establish a specialized niche market with expertise in unique escrow business opportunities. This would require familiarity with forms, procedures, and business practices of that specialized field to work with the real estate professionals who depend on escrow having knowledge to assist the team of persons involved in closing the escrow.

The **California Homestead Act** is involved in escrow when a foreclosure action arises and the homeowner has legal rights to protect his or her equity in the property before lien priority creditors may receive funds. Probate action requires escrow to obtain a court release to pass assets and funds to subsequent entities who have a **beneficiary** interest to receive funds after approval. Foreign investors make up an increasing number of real estate investors, and escrow is often involved in establishing whether or not the parties receiving funds at the close of escrow have cleared tax liability. Also, the escrow officer who works with for sale by owner (FSBO) transactions needs special knowledge for the handling of the transaction so as to not give legal, tax, or real estate advice.

■ LEARNING OBJECTIVES

At the conclusion of Chapter 13, you will be able to

- explain the requirements for a valid homestead;

- differentiate between the various steps involved in a probate;

- distinguish between the process and the procedures required by the probate court;

- explain the differences for an escrow involving a foreign investor; and

- outline the key points when working with a for sale by owner (FSBO) transaction.

■ HOMESTEAD

The word **homestead** may be used in three different ways when applied to real estate practices. Escrow professionals must be aware of all three meanings, although most transactions would involve only two of the types of homesteads.

The first type is defined by federal law, The Homestead Act, put into action over 140 years ago to help develop the raw lands of the newly formed midwestern portions of the United States. Occasionally, the escrow and title search of property in those areas may involve an original patent from the government for ownership. This means that the property has been in the same hands for generations and has not changed legal, recorded ownership since becoming part of this country. This first homestead involved acquiring title to property.

The second type of homestead is the protection of equity granted to homeowners to avoid a forced sale of their homes. Escrow would be involved in this type of homestead when title shows a valid, recorded document is a lien on the property. This would be important on a judgment lien sale and on a refinance loan.

FIGURE 13.1

Homestead Requirements

- Homestead must be recorded at county recorder's office.
- Claimants declare themselves as heads of household.
- Claimants must reside on the premises at the time of filing.
- Homestead must describe the premises.
- The property may be a single-family unit, multiple-family unit, condominium, stock cooperative, community apartment project, mobile home, or boat.

The third type of homestead involves a reduction of property taxes. Escrow would calculate the prorations based upon whether or not a homestead has been filed by the owner and placed on the property to reduce the property taxes.

The Homestead Act of 1862 was the basis for widespread development of land becoming improved by individuals over much of the center of the United States. People were drawn from all over the world as well as the settled East Coast to "go West young man" because the U.S. government allowed individual members of its society to own the land, even if they were not citizens of the United States. This basic concept is still true today.

The original concept to qualify for a legal homestead required that the person had to be over age 21. The individual had to file a **declaration of homestead** with the county recorder or land office in which the real property was located. The maximum amount of land that could be obtained under this form of acquiring title to real property was 160 acres. The person had to pay a small fee and agreed to actually reside on the premises for a minimum of five years. After completion of all requirements, the individual received a U.S. government patent, not a deed, that conveyed ownership from the government to the individual. Large grants of land were awarded to individuals, companies (railroads), towns, and other entities. This law encouraged property ownership with the government giving property to the people.

The California Homestead Act is not related to the Homestead Act of 1862. Instead it is designed to help people keep property they already own. Today a homestead is designed to protect the equity a homeowner has in his or her personal residence so that the individual is not forced by a **creditor** to sell the property to pay a debt. One kind of homestead is called the *dwelling house exemption*. The other kind of homestead is referred to as the *formal declared homestead* (see Figure 13.1).

A sample form of the Declaration of Homestead is found in Figure 13.2. The form is filed at the country recorder's office where the property is located, not where the owner of the property may currently be living, if different from the property location. Once recorded the document remains in place and in full

FIGURE 13.2

Declaration of Homestead

RECORDING REQUESTED BY
First City Title Company

AND WHEN RECORDED MAIL THIS DEED AND UNLESS OTHER WISE SHOWN BELOW MAIL TAX STATEMENTS TO
Name
Address
City & State
Zip
Title Order No.   Escrow No.

Book
Page
File No.

Recorded on
_____at_____
Official Records
County of _____, California
Conny B. McCormack
Registrar-recorder/County Clerk

Fees:
$ _____
B.

SPACE ABOVE THIS LINE FOR RECORDER'S USE

DECLARATION OF HOMESTEAD
(JOINT DECLARATION OF HUSBAND AND WIFE)
_____ and _____
(Name of Husband)   (Name of Wife)

do severally certify and declare as follows:
(1) They are husband and wife.

(2) _____ is the head of a family, consisting of himself and wife and _____
(Name of Husband)

(3) They are now residing on the land and premises located in the City of _____, County of

_____, State of California, and more particularly described as follows:

(4) They claim the land and premises hereinabove described together with the dwelling house thereon, and its appurtenances, as a Homestead.
(5) No former declaration of homestead has been made by them, or by either of them, except as follows:

_____

(6) The character of said property so so9ught to be homesteaded, and the improvements thereon may generally be described as follows: _____

IN WITNESS WHEREOF, they have hereunto set their hands this _____day of _____, 20_____.

_____   _____
(Husband)   (Wife)

STATE OF CALIFORNIA
COUNTY OF_____
On this the _____day of _____ , 20___
The undersigned, a Notary Public in and for said
County and State, personally appeared _____
_____, known to me
to be the person ___whose name ____subscribed
to the within instrument and acknowledged that
they executed the same.

_____
Notary Public in and for said State

STATE OF CALIFORNIA
COUNTY OF _____
_____ and _____
husband and wife,, each, being first duly sworn, deposes
and says. That he/she is one of the declarants of the
foregoing declaration of homestead; that he/she has
read the foregoing declaration and knows the contents
thereof, and that the matters therein stated are true of
His/her knowledge _____
(Husband)
_____
(Wife)
Subscribed and Sworn to before me on:_____
_____
Notary Public in and for said State

FOR NOTARY SEAL OR STAMP

FOR NOTARY SEAL OR SPAMP

effect until the owner either sells the property, files another Declaration of Homestead, or files an Abandonment of Homestead form with the county recorder's office.

A form called the **Abandonment of Homestead,** as shown in Figure 13.3, is used to terminate a recorded homestead that has been filed on a property. It is not necessary to file abandonment if the property owner sells the property. Escrow would not be involved with the abandonment of homestead when the escrow is for the sale of the property, but escrow may often be involved when a refinance escrow is used. If the homeowner has a homestead recorded on the property and is asking the lender for a new loan, the lender may require that the homestead be removed from title prior to the recordation of the new lien.

Escrow should be aware of the laws regarding the California homestead in order to work with and be in a better position to discuss the homestead with the lender. The rules in California are that a homestead does *not* protect against a foreclosure sale for a **trust** deed sale. The trust deed holder has priority over the homestead. A homestead never defeats a trust deed or a mechanic's lien foreclosure. A homestead is not terminated when a spouse dies. The surviving spouse can remain in title and retain the homestead to protect the equity in the property. The amount of the exemption may be reduced, due to divorce or the death of one of the owners-occupants, but the homestead is still valid for the property.

Almost all states have some type of homestead law to protect the homeowner against debts and judgments resulting from a forced sale of the property. Some states have what is known as a "probate homestead," which allows a surviving spouse to keep the home for life. California does not recognize a probate homestead, but clients of an escrow who come from states where this is common practice may be confused on how a homestead is applied in California law.

■ PROBATE OBJECTIVES AND PROCESS

With a rapidly aging population in California, it is likely that numerous escrow opportunities will arise in the area of the specialized field of probate, which requires knowledge in this technical area where the court system often dictates the handling of this type of transaction. The following three basic groups open escrow for the majority of probate escrows:

1. Professional conservator

2. Probate attorney

3. Real estate licensee with attorney

FIGURE 13.3

Abandonment of Homestead

RECORDING REQUESTED BY
First City Title Company

AND WHEN RECORDED MAIL THIS DEED AND
UNLESS OTHER WISE SHOWN BELOW MAIL TAX
STATEMENTS TO
Name
Address
City & State
Zip
Title Order No.   Escrow No.

Book
Page
File No.

Recorded on
_____at_____
Official Records
County of _____, California
Conny B. McCormack
Registrar-Recorder/County Clerk

Fees:
$ _____
B.

SPACE ABOVE THIS LINE FOR RECORDER'S USE

ABANDONMENT OF HOMESTEAD

KNOW ALL MEN BY THESE PRESENTS; That _____, to wit,_____

_____
(names or name)

do certify as follows:

(1) _____
(we are or I am)

(2) _____ hereby abandon the homestead on the land and premises hereinafter
(we or I)

described. The declaration of the homestead herein abandoned was recorded on _____
in Book_____, Page_____ of Official Records, in the office of the County Recorder of
_____ County, California.

(3) The land and premises hereinabove referred to are located in the City of _____
_____, County of _____, State of California, and are more particularly
described as follows:

(legal description)

Together will all tenements and appurtenances thereunto belonging.
IN WITNESS WHEREOF, _____have hereunto set _____hand _____ this_____
Day of _____, 20____
APN or AIN: xxx-xxx-xx
Dated:_____   _____
                                         _____
STATE OF CALIFORNIA   _____
COUNTY OF_____
On this the _____day of _____ , 20___

The undersigned, a Notary Public in and for said
County and State, personally appeared _____
_____, known to me
to be the person ___whose name ____subscribed
to the within instrument and acknowledged that
_____executed the same.

FOR NOTARY SEAL OR STAMP

_____
Signature of Notary

_____
Name (Typed or Printed)

TABLE 13.1

How to Settle an Estate

Search for decedent's information	Files, records, safe deposit box, safe, will, burial instructions, assets, bills, insurance policies, death benefits
Obtain legal documents	Will, certified copy of Death Certificate
Establish	Executor, heirs, beneficiaries
Obtain asset valuation as of date of death	(1) Real property appraisal; (2) personal property appraisal; (3) total gross estate value under or over $600,000 per person
Determine how title is held	Spousal Property Petition if outright transfer by will or intestate succession
File federal estate tax return	Form 706, within 9 months of death
Transfer property	Joint tenant, community property, trust beneficiaries
Court approval	Disbursement of all items

In California every court-ordered transfer, such as a probate sale, requires an escrow. **Probate** occurs when a person dies and the estate of the deceased must be disbursed. The bills of the deceased must be paid, government taxes made current, and ownership to real and personal property must be transferred. Probate includes the following items:

- Proving to the court that the will is valid

- Identifying and making an inventory of the property

- Having all property appraised

- Paying all debts, bills, obligations, and taxes

- Obtaining court approval to distribute items as directed in the will

The process and manner in which a person needs to establish how to settle an estate is shown in Table 13.1.

Not all property of the deceased must go through probate, as when title of the deceased is held in a living trust. This first step in handling the affairs of the deceased is to establish if the estate does or does not have to go through probate. An **estate** that can establish filing under the "small estates" proceeding can have title cleared by filing an affidavit to avoid probate where the beneficiary of the estate can establish either (1) personal property valued at not more than $25,000, and/or (2) real property valued at not more than $100,000. Property exempt from probate in California includes the following:

- Property held as a joint tenant

- Property held in a living trust

- Property left to a surviving spouse

- Property passed where the total estate is under $600,000 per person

A **will** becomes a matter of public record and must be submitted to a court for approval for handling the matters of the deceased.

In the same manner that an escrow for a living person is established, so also should the escrow for a deceased person have documents prior to opening of escrow. (See Figure 13.4 for an example of a probate advisory.) The following list of documents would be created outside of escrow to establish a contractual relationship between the parties or their representatives:

- Agency Relations Disclosure

- Agent's Inspection Disclosure (California Civil Code §2079 and §1102)

- Probate Listing Agreement (Exclusive authorization and right to sell probate)

- Probate purchase agreement and receipt for deposit

- Probate advisory

- Buyer's inspection advisory

- Seller's advisory

■ PROBATE PROCEDURES

The probate process must be handled according to a specific legal process. All probate proceedings are subject to the jurisdiction of the court. Probate court action is required when events occur making it necessary to

- collect debts owed to the deceased person;

- clear title to real or personal property that is held in the name of the deceased;

- pass clear title to assets to heirs;

- settle a dispute between people who each claim entitlement to the deceased person's assets; and

- resolve all disputes as to whether the deceased person's will is valid.

Title received by the successors will be approved by the superior court of California that establishes the vesting for heirs and others. The closing of escrow is subject

FIGURE 13.4

Probate Advisory

CALIFORNIA
ASSOCIATION
OF REALTORS®

PROBATE ADVISORY
For Probate, Conservatorship and Guardianship Properties

The sale of the Property described as (address) _____,
pursuant to the attached Probate Purchase Agreement (C.A.R. form PPA-11), is made under authority of the California
Probate Code. The Seller is not the title owner, but instead is a representative of a probate estate, a guardianship or a
conservatorship. The sale may require a court order. Many obligations imposed upon sellers, particularly sellers of real
property containing one-to-four dwelling units, may not be applicable to the sale of this property. However, even though the
seller is exempt from many obligations, the seller must still comply with many others. Further, any real estate licensee
representing Buyer or Seller in the transaction may have duties independent of the principals. This Advisory is intended to
inform Buyer and Seller of their rights and obligations independent of those established by the attached agreement.

EXEMPTIONS:

1. **TDS, NHD, Mello-Roos:** Seller is <u>exempt</u> from providing Buyer with the Real Estate Transfer Disclosure
   Statement (TDS), Natural Hazard Disclosure Statement (NHD), and a Mello-Roos district lien disclosure, pursuant to
   California Civil Code either for "transfers pursuant to court order" or for "transfers by a fiduciary in the course of the
   administration of a decedent's estate, guardianship, conservatorship, or trust."

2. **Earthquake Guides:** Seller is <u>exempt</u> from providing either a Homeowner's or Commercial Property Owner's Guide
   to Earthquake Safety.

3. **Smoke Detectors:** The sale is <u>exempt</u> from the State requirements that, for <u>single family residences</u>, operable smoke
   detectors be in place and that a written statement of compliance be provided to Buyer.

REQUIREMENTS:

1. **Disclosures:** Seller is <u>not exempt</u> from common law and statutory duties concerning fraud and deceit, even though
   the specific TDS form is not required to be completed. Seller remains obligated to disclose known material facts
   affecting the value and desirability of the property.

2. **Hazard Zones:** Seller is <u>not exempt</u> from applicable statutory obligations to disclose earthquake fault zones, seismic
   hazard zones, state fire responsibility areas, very high fire hazard severity zones, special flood hazard areas and flood
   hazard zones pursuant to the Public Resources Code, Government Code and United States Code, even though,
   pursuant to the Civil Code, the specific NHD form is not required to be completed.

3. **Water Heaters:** The sale is <u>not exempt</u> from the State requirement that water heaters be properly anchored, braced
   or strapped.

4. **Lead-based Paint:** The Seller is <u>not exempt</u> from the federal obligation to (i) disclose known lead-based paint and
   lead-based paint hazards, (ii) provide Buyer copies of reports or studies covering lead-based paint and hazards on the
   property, (iii) provide Buyer with the pamphlet "Protect Your Family From Lead In Your Home," and (iv) give Buyer a
   10-day opportunity to inspect for lead-based paint and hazards, if the Property contains residential dwelling units and
   was constructed prior to 1978.

5. **Data Base Disclosure:** The sale is <u>not exempt</u> from the requirement that residential sales contracts contain a notice
   regarding the availability of information about registered sex offenders.

Buyer and Seller acknowledge receipt of copy of this page, which constitutes Page 1 of _____ Pages.
Buyer's Initials (_____) (_____)   Seller's Initials (_____) (_____)

R E B S / I N C
Published and Distributed by:
REAL ESTATE BUSINESS SERVICES, INC.
a subsidiary of the CALIFORNIA ASSOCIATION OF REALTORS®
525 South Virgil Avenue, Los Angeles, California 90020
PRINT DATE

REVISED 10/99

OFFICE USE ONLY
Reviewed by Broker
or Designee _____
Date _____

EQUAL HOUSING
OPPORTUNITY

PROBATE ADVISORY (PAK-11 PAGE 1 OF 2)

Source: Reprinted with permission, CALIFORNIA ASSOCIATION OF REALTORS®. Endorsement not implied.

FIGURE 13.4

Probate Advisory (Continued)

Property Address: _____ Date: _____

6. **Tax Withholding:** The sale is <u>not exempt</u> from the obligation of the buyer to withhold a portion of the purchase price under federal law if the transferor is a "foreign person" or under state law if the transferor had a last known street address outside of California. **Federal:** For federal purposes, a non-resident alien includes a fiduciary. An administrator or executor of an estate is treated as a non-resident even if all beneficiaries are citizens or residents of the United States. **State:** If the decedent was a California resident at the time of death, the estate is treated as a California resident regardless of the residency of the executor or administrator.

7. **Brokers:**
   A. Inspection: The sale is <u>not exempt</u> from the Broker's obligation to conduct a reasonably competent and diligent visual inspection of the accessible areas of the property and disclose to Buyer material facts revealed by such an inspection in the sale of residential property containing one-to-four dwelling units. Brokers may do so on C.A.R. form AID-11.

   B. Agency: The sale is <u>not exempt</u> from the obligation to provide agency relationship disclosure and confirmation forms in the sale of residential property containing one-to-four dwelling units.

<u>**OTHER CONSIDERATIONS:**</u>

1. **Local Law:** Local law may impose obligations on the transfer of real property (such as the installation of low flow toilets or shower heads, or installation of smoke detectors). Local law should be consulted to determine if sales made under the authority of the California Probate Code are exempt from such requirements.

2. **Death:** If the Property is being sold under authority of the Probate Code because of the death of an owner of the Property and if Buyer has concerns about the manner, location or details of the death, then Buyer should direct any specific questions to the executor or administrator of the estate.

3. **Stock Cooperatives:** If the Property is part of a stock cooperative (Co-op), Buyer may be required to seek approval of the Board or Owner's Association of the Co-op prior to transfer of title. If this is not a contingency of the sale, failure of Buyer to gain approval of the Co-op board will not provide grounds for cancellation or rescission of the sale.

4. **Court Confirmation/Independent Authority:**

   The representative of a decedent's estate may receive authority to sell the Property under the Independent Administration of Estates Act (IAEA). In order to do so, the representative must first petition the Probate Court. The Petition may be made at the time the representative is approved or any other time. Notice of the Petition is given to heirs, devisees, executors and other interested persons, any of whom may object.

   If IAEA authority is granted it may be full or limited. If only limited authority has been granted, the sale must be confirmed by the court. If full authority has been granted, the representative must first give a notice of the proposed sale to the devisees and heirs of the decedent and other interested parties. If no objection is received, the sale may proceed. If any noticed person objects, the sale may require court confirmation. Note: A representative with full authority has the option of proceeding to court for confirmation even if not required to do so under the Probate Code.

Date _____   Date _____

Buyer _____   Seller _____

Buyer _____   Seller _____

REVISED 10/99
Page 2 of _____ Pages.

OFFICE USE ONLY
Reviewed by Broker
or Designee _____
Date _____

EQUAL HOUSING
OPPORTUNITY

PROBATE ADVISORY (PAK-11 PAGE 2 OF 2)

to receipt of a court order confirming the sale. The purpose for probate is to settle the estate of a deceased in order to

- establish the validity of a will or no testamentary deposition of property;

- establish the proper identity of heirs, **devisees,** and beneficiaries;

- protect the right of creditors;

- provide for the payment of all applicable taxes;

- preserve the assets during the legal process; and

- distribute property legally to the appropriate parties.

Because the deceased cannot handle his or her own affairs, another individual must take care of the estate for the deceased. If the deceased named the person to handle the estate, the individual is referred to as the *executor.* If the deceased did not select someone to represent him or her by naming the person in the will, then the court appoints an individual, called the **administrator.** The administrator is also the person the court would name if the estate had no will. Someone has to file the final income tax form to clear the estate. The checklist for settling a simple estate is shown in Table 13.2.

The title company will require the following documents to close the probate escrow:

- Notice of proposed action

- Order authorizing independent administration of the estate

- Letters testamentary

- Copy of the will

- Letter from attorney stating that the value of the estate does not exceed $600,000 and therefore exempts it from federal or state estate tax

The escrow instructions must show that the close of escrow is subject to the receipt of a certified copy of the court order confirming the sale. The certified copy must be forwarded to the title insurance company and is recorded at the county recorder's office where the property is physically located, not where the deceased died, at the close of escrow.

The real estate professional may represent the decedent's estate for the real property or may represent the buyer. The forms listed below are commonly used in a probate transaction. (See Figures 13.5 to 13.7 for examples of some of these forms.) The real estate professional and escrow officer specializing in handling the probate escrow should become familiar with the following:

TABLE 13.2

Checklist for Settling a Simple Estate

☑	Item	Comment
1.	Locate will	Make copies
2.	Order certified copy of death certificate	Minimum five copies
3.	Determine estate representative	Name or court appointed
4.	Determine heirs and beneficiaries	Names, ages, addresses
5.	Determine decedent's legal residence	State probate varies
6.	Obtain insurance, Social Security, and death benefits	Collecting benefits and approvals
7.	Arrange tax forms	Federal and state income tax returns, estate and/or inheritance tax return
8.	Assemble and list all estate assets	Bank accounts, cash, savings accounts, uncashed checks, money market funds, promissory notes, stocks, bonds, retirement accounts, copyrights, patents, real property, antiques, insurance, collectibles, vehicles, household goods
9.	Determine title interests	Community or separate property, joint tenancy, etc.
10.	Establish asset valuation	Co-owner share for real and personal property
11.	List debts and obligations unpaid at death	Illness expenses, funeral expense, income taxes, property taxes, liens and encumbrances, debts, court costs and filing fees, appraisal fee, attorney fee
12.	Determine priority of debts	Lien priority rules
13.	Pay debts after estate funds available	Lien priority rules
14.	Prepare and file tax returns	U.S. estate tax return and income tax returns
15.	Determine method of transferring assets	Joint tenancy beneficiary, transfer for under $600,000, surviving spouse, trust beneficiaries, probate approval where required

- **Petition** for Probate (Probate Code §§8802, 10450)

- Notice of Petition to Administer Estate (Probate Code §8100)

- Notice of Hearing (Probate Code §§1211, 1215, 1216, 1230)

- Order for Probate (Probate Code §§8006, 8400)

- Duties and Liabilities of Personal Representative (Probate Code §8404)

- Letters (Probate Code §§1001, 8403, 8405, 8544, 8545, and Code of Civil Procedures §2015.6)

- Creditor's Claim (Probate Code §§9000 et seq., 9153)

- Notice of Administration to Creditors (Probate Code §§9050, 9052)

- Allowance or Rejection of Creditor's Claim (Probate Code §9000 et seq., 9250–9256, 9353)

- Inventory and Appraisal (Probate Code §§1620–1616, 8800–8980)

- Inventory and Appraisal Attachment (Probate Code §§301, 2610–2613, 8800–8920, 10309)

- Notice of Proposed Action: Objection—Consent (Probate Code §10580)

- Waiver of Notice of Proposed Action (Probate Code §§10583, 10584)

- Citation (Probate) and Proof of Service (Probate Code §§1240, 1241, 1242)

- Spousal Property Petition (Probate Code §13650)

- Notice of Hearing (Probate Code §§1211, 1215, 1216, 1230)

- Spousal Property Order (Probate Code §13656)

- Report of Sale and Petition for Order Confirming Sale of Real Property (Probate Code §§2540, 10308)

- Order Confirming Sale of Real Property (Probate Code §§2543, 10313)

- Affidavit RE Real Property of Small Value (Probate Code §13200)

- Petition to Determine Succession to Real Property (Probate Code §13151)

- Order Determining Succession to Real Property (Probate Code §13154)

- Affidavit of Surviving Spouse Succeeding to Title to Community Property (Probate Code §13540)

- County Assessor's Office, Preliminary Change of Ownership Report (PCOR) (California Revenue and Taxation Code 480.3)

- Executor's Deed

- Order of Final Distribution

■ WORKING WITH FOREIGN INVESTORS

As was explained under homestead, U.S. citizenship is not a requirement for ownership of real property in the United States. Some foreigners have made a fortune by investing in real estate in America. Eventually they sell the property, and the funds are taken back to their homeland. Others have invested in U.S. real property and have continued to live in America as foreigners. Escrow is often involved in several levels of paperwork when dealing with a foreign investor.

FIGURE 13.5

Petition for Probate

DE-111

ATTORNEY OR PARTY WITHOUT ATTORNEY *(Name, state bar number, and address):*	TELEPHONE AND FAX NOS.:	*FOR COURT USE ONLY*

ATTORNEY FOR *(Name)*:

SUPERIOR COURT OF CALIFORNIA, COUNTY OF

STREET ADDRESS:

MAILING ADDRESS:

CITY AND ZIP CODE:

BRANCH NAME:

ESTATE OF *(Name)*:

DECEDENT

PETITION FOR	☐ **Probate of Will and for Letters Testamentary** ☐ **Probate of Will and for Letters of Administration with Will Annexed** ☐ **Letters of Administration** ☐ **Letters of Special Administration** ☐ **Authorization to Administer Under the Independent Administration of Estates Act** ☐ **with limited authority**	CASE NUMBER: HEARING DATE: DEPT: TIME:

1. Publication will be in *(specify name of newspaper):*
   a. ☐ Publication requested.   b. ☐ Publication to be arranged.
2. **Petitioner** *(name of each):*   **requests**
   a. ☐ decedent's will and codicils, if any, be admitted to probate.
   b. ☐ *(name)* :
      be appointed (1) ☐ executor   (3) ☐ administrator
                           (2) ☐ administrator with will annexed   (4) ☐ special administrator
      and Letters issue upon qualification.
   c. ☐ that ☐ full ☐ limited   authority be granted to administer under the Independent Administration of Estates Act.
   d. (1) ☐ bond not be required for the reasons stated in item 3d.
      (2) ☐ $ bond be fixed. It will be furnished by an admitted surety insurer or as otherwise provided by law. *(Specify reasons in Attachment 2 if the amount is different from the maximum required by Probate Code section 8482.)*
      (3) ☐ $ in deposits in a blocked account be allowed. Receipts will be filed. *(Specify institution and location):*

3. a. Decedent died on *(date):*   at *(place):*
      (1) ☐ a resident of the county named above.
      (2) ☐ a nonresident of California and left an estate in the county named above located at *(specify location permitting publication in the newspaper named in item 1):*
   b. Street address, city, and county of decedent's residence at time of death *(specify):*

   c. Character and estimated value of the property of the estate:
      (1) Personal property: $
      (2) Annual gross income from
          (a) real property: $
          (b) personal property: $
                        Total: $
      (3) Real property: $ *(If full authority under the Independent Administration of Estates Act is requested, state the fair market value of the real property less encumbrances.)*
   d. (1) ☐ Will waives bond. ☐ Special administrator is the named executor and the will waives bond.
      (2) ☐ All beneficiaries are adults and have waived bond, and the will does not require a bond. *(Affix waiver as Attachment 3d(2).)*
      (3) ☐ All heirs at law are adults and have waived bond. *(Affix waiver as Attachment 3d(3).)*
      (4) ☐ Sole personal representative is a corporate fiduciary or an exempt government agency.
   e. (1) ☐ Decedent died intestate.
      (2) ☐ Copy of decedent's will dated: ☐ codicils dated: are affixed as Attachment 3e(2).
          ☐ The will and all codicils are self-proving (Prob. Code, § 8220).
                        (Continued on reverse)

Form Approved by the
 Judicial Council of California
 DE-111 [Rev. January 1, 1998]
 Mandatory Form [1/1/2000]   **PETITION FOR PROBATE**   **WEST GROUP** Official Publisher   Probate Code, §§ 8002, 10450

FIGURE 13.5

Petition for Probate (Continued)

ESTATE OF *(Name)*:

DECEDENT

CASE NUMBER:

3. f. **Appointment of personal representative** *(check all applicable boxes)*:

(1) Appointment of executor or administrator with will annexed:

> *Include in Attachment 3e(2) a typed copy of a handwritten will and a translation of a foreign language will.*

(a) ☐ Proposed executor is named as executor in the will and consents to act.

(b) ☐ No executor is named in the will.

(c) ☐ Proposed personal representative is a nominee of a person entitled to Letters. *(Affix nomination as Attachment 3f(1)(c).)*

(d) ☐ Other named executors will not act because of ☐ death ☐ declination ☐ other reasons *(specify in Attachment 3f(1)(d)).*

(2) Appointment of administrator:

(a) ☐ Petitioner is a person entitled to Letters. *(If necessary, explain priority in Attachment 3f(2)(a).)*

(b) ☐ Petitioner is a nominee of a person entitled to Letters. *(Affix nomination as Attachment 3f(2)(b).)*

(c) ☐ Petitioner is related to the decedent as *(specify):*

(3) ☐ Appointment of special administrator requested. *(Specify grounds and requested powers in Attachment 3f(3).)*

g. Proposed personal representative is a ☐ resident of California ☐ nonresident of California *(affix statement of permanent address as Attachment 3g)* ☐ resident of the United States ☐ nonresident of the United States.

4. ☐ Decedent's will does not preclude administration of this estate under the Independent Administration of Estates Act.

5. a. The decedent is survived by *(check at least one box in each of items (1)-(3))*

(1) ☐ spouse ☐ no spouse as follows: ☐ divorced or never married ☐ spouse deceased

(2) ☐ child as follows: ☐ natural or adopted ☐ natural adopted by a third party ☐ no child

(3) ☐ issue of a predeceased child ☐ no issue of a predeceased child

b. Decedent ☐ is ☐ is not survived by a stepchild or foster child or children who would have been adopted by decedent but for a legal barrier. *(See Prob. Code, § 6454.)*

6. *(Complete if decedent was survived by (1) a spouse but no issue (only a or b apply), or (2) no spouse or issue. Check the **first** box that applies):*

a. ☐ Decedent is survived by a parent or parents who are listed in item 8.

b. ☐ Decedent is survived by issue of deceased parents, all of whom are listed in item 8.

c. ☐ Decedent is survived by a grandparent or grandparents who are listed in item 8.

d. ☐ Decedent is survived by issue of grandparents, all of whom are listed in item 8.

e. ☐ Decedent is survived by issue of a predeceased spouse, all of whom are listed in item 8.

f. ☐ Decedent is survived by next of kin, all of whom are listed in item 8.

g. ☐ Decedent is survived by parents of a predeceased spouse or issue of those parents, if both are predeceased, all of whom are listed in item 8.

h. ☐ Decedent is survived by no known next of kin.

7. *(Complete only if no spouse or issue survived decedent)* Decedent ☐ had no predeceased spouse ☐ had a predeceased spouse who (1) ☐ died not more than 15 years before decedent owning an interest in **real property** that passed to decedent, (2) ☐ died not more than five years before decedent owning **personal property** valued at $10,000 or more that passed to decedent, (3) ☐ neither (1) nor (2) apply. *(If you checked (1) or (2), check only the **first** box that applies):*

a. ☐ Decedent is survived by issue of a predeceased spouse, all of whom are listed in item 8.

b. ☐ Decedent is survived by a parent or parents of the predeceased spouse who are listed in item 8.

c. ☐ Decedent is survived by issue of a parent of the predeceased spouse, all of whom are listed in item 8.

d. ☐ Decedent is survived by next of kin of the decedent, all of whom are listed in item 8.

e. ☐ Decedent is survived by next of kin of the predeceased spouse, all of whom are listed in item 8.

8. **Listed in Attachment 8** are the names, relationships, ages, and addresses, so far as known to or reasonably ascertainable by petitioner, of (1) all persons named in decedent's will and codicils, whether living or deceased, (2) all persons named or checked in items 2, 5, 6, and 7, and (3) all beneficiaries of a devisee trust in which the trustee and personal representative are the same person.

9. Number of pages attached: _____

Date:

▶ _____

(SIGNATURE OF ATTORNEY *)

* (Signature of all petitioners also required (Prob. Code, § 1020).)

I declare under penalty of perjury under the laws of the State of California that the foregoing is true and correct.

Date:

▶ _____

. . . .

(TYPE OR PRINT NAME)

(SIGNATURE OF PETITIONER)

▶ _____

. . . .

(TYPE OR PRINT NAME)

(SIGNATURE OF PETITIONER)

DE-111 [Rev. January 1, 1998]   **PETITION FOR PROBATE**   WEST GROUP   Page two
                                                                                       Official Publisher

FIGURE 13.6

Duties and Liabilities of Personal Representative

DE-147

ATTORNEY OR PARTY WITHOUT ATTORNEY (*Name, state bar number, and address*):

FOR COURT USE ONLY

TELEPHONE NO.:   FAX NO. (*Optional*):

E–MAIL ADDRESS (*Optional*):

ATTORNEY FOR (*Name*):

SUPERIOR COURT OF CALIFORNIA, COUNTY OF

STREET ADDRESS:

MAILING ADDRESS:

CITY AND ZIP CODE:

BRANCH NAME:

ESTATE OF (*Name*):

DECEDENT

DUTIES AND LIABILITIES OF PERSONAL REPRESENTATIVE
and Acknowledgment of Receipt

CASE NUMBER:

DUTIES AND LIABILITIES OF PERSONAL REPRESENTATIVE

When the court appoints you as personal representative of an estate, you become an officer of the court and assume certain duties and obligations. An attorney is best qualified to advise you about these matters. You should understand the following:

1. MANAGING THE ESTATE'S ASSETS

a. Prudent investments
You must manage the estate assets with the care of a prudent person dealing with someone else's property. This means that you must be cautious and may not make any speculative investments.

b. Keep estate assets separate
You must keep the money and property in this estate separate from anyone else's, including your own. When you open a bank account for the estate, the account name must indicate that it is an estate account and not your personal account. Never deposit estate funds in your personal account or otherwise mix them with your or anyone else's property. Securities in the estate must also be held in a name that shows they are estate property and not your personal property.

c. Interest-bearing accounts and other investments
Except for checking accounts intended for ordinary administration expenses, estate accounts must earn interest. You may deposit estate funds in insured accounts in financial institutions, but you should consult with an attorney before making other kinds of investments.

d. Other restrictions
There are many other restrictions on your authority to deal with estate property. You should not spend any of the estate's money unless you have received permission from the court or have been advised to do so by an attorney. You may reimburse yourself for official court costs paid by you to the county clerk and for the premium on your bond. Without prior order of the court, you may not pay fees to yourself or to your attorney, if you have one. If you do not obtain the court's permission when it is required, you may be removed as personal representative or you may be required to reimburse the estate from your own personal funds, or both. You should consult with an attorney concerning the legal requirements affecting sales, leases, mortgages, and investments of estate property.

2. INVENTORY OF ESTATE PROPERTY

a. Locate the estate's property
You must attempt to locate and take possession of all the decedent's property to be administered in the estate.

b. Determine the value of the property
You must arrange to have a court-appointed referee determine the value of the property unless the appointment is waived by the court. You, rather than the referee, must determine the value of certain "cash items." An attorney can advise you about how to do this.

c. File an inventory and appraisal
Within four months after Letters are first issued to you as personal representative, you must file with the court an inventory and appraisal of all the assets in the estate.

Page 1 of 2

Form Adopted for Mandatory Use
Judicial Council of California
DE-147 [Rev. January 1, 2002]

DUTIES AND LIABILITIES OF PERSONAL REPRESENTATIVE
(Probate)

Probate Code, § 8404

FIGURE 13.6

Duties and Liabilities of Personal Representative (Continued)

ESTATE OF *(Name):*	CASE NUMBER:
DECEDENT	

d. File a change of ownership
At the time you file the inventory and appraisal, you must also file a change of ownership statement with the county recorder or assessor in each county where the decedent owned real property at the time of death, as provided in section 480 of the California Revenue and Taxation Code.

3. NOTICE TO CREDITORS

You must mail a notice of administration to each known creditor of the decedent within four months after your appointment as personal representative. If the decedent received Medi-Cal assistance, you must notify the State Director of Health Services within 90 days after appointment.

4. INSURANCE

You should determine that there is appropriate and adequate insurance covering the assets and risks of the estate. Maintain the insurance in force during the entire period of the administration.

5. RECORD KEEPING

a. Keep accounts
You must keep complete and accurate records of each financial transaction affecting the estate. You will have to prepare an account of all money and property you have received, what you have spent, and the date of each transaction. You must describe in detail what you have left after the payment of expenses.

b. Court review
Your account will be reviewed by the court. Save your receipts because the court may ask to review them. If you do not file your accounts as required, the court will order you to do so. You may be removed as personal representative if you fail to comply.

6. CONSULTING AN ATTORNEY

If you have an attorney, you should cooperate with the attorney at all times. You and your attorney are responsible for completing the estate administration as promptly as possible. **When in doubt, contact your attorney.**

NOTICE: 1. This statement of duties and liabilities is a summary and is not a complete statement of the law. Your conduct as a personal representative is governed by the law itself and not by this summary.
2. If you fail to perform your duties or to meet the deadlines, the court may reduce your compensation, remove you from office, and impose other sanctions.

ACKNOWLEDGMENT OF RECEIPT

1. I have petitioned the court to be appointed as a personal representative.

2. My address and telephone number are *(specify):*

3. I acknowledge that I have received a copy of this statement of the duties and liabilities of the office of personal representative.

Date:

▶

_____   _____
(TYPE OR PRINT NAME)   (SIGNATURE OF PETITIONER)

Date:

▶

_____   _____
(TYPE OR PRINT NAME)   (SIGNATURE OF PETITIONER)

CONFIDENTIAL INFORMATION: If required to do so by local court rule, you must provide your date of birth and driver's license number on supplemental Form DE-147S. (Prob. Code, § 8404(b).)

DE-147 [Rev. January 1, 2002]   **DUTIES AND LIABILITIES OF PERSONAL REPRESENTATIVE**   Page 2 of 2
                                                          (Probate)

FIGURE 13.7

Report of Sale and Petition for Order Confirming Sale of Real Property

DE-260, GC-060

ATTORNEY OR PARTY WITHOUT ATTORNEY *(Name, state bar number, and address):*	TELEPHONE AND FAX NOS.:	FOR COURT USE ONLY

ATTORNEY FOR *(Name)*:

SUPERIOR COURT OF CALIFORNIA, COUNTY OF

STREET ADDRESS:

MAILING ADDRESS:

CITY AND ZIP CODE:

BRANCH NAME:

ESTATE OF *(Name)*:

☐ DECEDENT ☐ CONSERVATEE ☐ MINOR

REPORT OF SALE AND PETITION FOR ORDER CONFIRMING SALE OF REAL PROPERTY
☐ And Sale of Other Property Sold as a Unit

CASE NUMBER:

HEARING DATE:

DEPT.:   TIME:

1. **Petitioner** *(name of each)*:
   is the ☐ executor   ☐ special administrator   ☐ purchaser *(30 days have passed*
        ☐ administrator with will annexed   ☐ conservator   *since the sale—attach declaration)*
        ☐ administrator   ☐ guardian
   of the estate and **requests a court order** for
   a. confirmation of sale of the estate's interest in the real property described in Attachment 2e.
   b. ☐ confirmation of sale of the estate's interest in other property sold as a unit as described in Attachment 2c.
   c. ☐ approval of commission of *(specify)*:   % in the amount of: $ *(see local court rules)*.
   d. additional bond ☐ is fixed at: $ ☐ is not required.
2. **Description of property sold**
   a. Interest sold
       ☐ 100%   ☐ Undivided *(specify)*:   %
   b. ☐ Improved
       ☐ Unimproved
   c. ☐ Real property sold as a unit with other property *(describe in Attachment 2c)*.
   d. Street address and location *(specify)*:

   e. Legal description is affixed as Attachment 2e *(attach)*.
3. **Appraisal**
   a. Date of death of decedent or appointment of conservator or guardian *(specify)*:
   b. Appraised value at above date: $
   c. Reappraised value within one year prior to the hearing: $ ☐ Amount includes value of other property sold
       as a unit.   *(If more than one year has elapsed from date 3a to the date of the hearing, reappraisal is necessary.)*
   d. Appraisal or reappraisal
       ☐ has been filed.   ☐ will be filed.
4. **Manner and terms of sale**
   a. Name of purchaser and manner of vesting title *(specify)*:

   b. ☐ Purchaser is ☐ the personal representative ☐ the attorney for the personal representative.
   c. Sale was ☐ private ☐ public   on *(date)*:
   d. Amount bid: $ Deposit: $
   e. Payment
       ☐ Cash   ☐ Credit *(see Attachment 4e)*
   f. ☐ Other terms of sale *(see Attachment 4f)*
   g. ☐ Mode of sale specified in will ☐ petitioner requests relief from complying for the reasons stated in Attachment 4g.
   h. ☐ Terms comply with Probate Code section 2542 *(guardianships and conservatorships only)*

(Continued on reverse)

Form Approved by the
Judicial Council of California
DE-260, GC-060 [Rev. January 1, 1998]
Mandatory Form [1/1/2000]

REPORT OF SALE AND PETITION FOR ORDER CONFIRMING SALE OF REAL PROPERTY
(Probate)

WEST GROUP
Official Publisher

Probate Code, §§ 2540, 10308

FIGURE 13.7

Report of Sale and Petition for Order Confirming Sale of Real Property (Continued)

ESTATE OF *(Name)*:

CASE NUMBER:

5. **Commission**
   a. ☐ Sale without broker
   b. ☐ A written ☐ exclusive ☐ nonexclusive   contract for commission was entered into with *(name)*:

   c. ☐ Purchaser was procured by *(name)*:
      a licensed real estate broker who is not buying for his or her account.
   d. ☐ Commission is to be divided as follows:

6. **Bond**
   a. Amount before sale: $ ☐ none
   b. Additional amount needed: $ ☐ none
   c. ☐ Proceeds are to be deposited in a blocked account. Receipts will be filed. *(Specify institution and location)*:

7. **Notice of sale**
   a. ☐ Published ☐ posted as permitted by Probate Code section 10301 ($5,000 or less)
   b. ☐ Will authorizes sale of the property
   c. ☐ Will directs sale of the property

8. **Notice of hearing**
   a. Specific devisee
      (1) ☐ None
      (2) ☐ Consent to be filed
      (3) ☐ Written notice will be given
   b. Special notice
      (1) ☐ None requested
      (2) ☐ Has been or will be waived
      (3) ☐ Required written notice will be given

   c. Personal representative
      (1) ☐ Petitioner (none required)
      (2) ☐ Consent to be filed
      (3) ☐ Written notice will be given

9. **Reason for sale** *(need not complete if 7b or 7c checked)*
   a. ☐ Necessary to pay
      (1) ☐ debts
      (2) ☐ devises
      (3) ☐ family allowance
      (4) ☐ expenses of administration
      (5) ☐ taxes
   b. ☐ The sale is to the advantage of the estate and in the best interest of the interested persons.

10. **Formula for overbids**
    a. Original bid: $ _____
    b. 10% of first $10,000 of original bid: $ _____
    c. 5% of (original bid minus $10,000): $ _____
    d. Minimum overbid (a + b + c): $ _____

11. **Overbid.**   Required amount of first overbid *(see item 10)*: $

12. **Petitioner's efforts** to obtain the highest and best price reasonably attainable for the property were as follows *(specify activities taken to expose the property to the market, e.g., multiple listings, advertising, open houses, etc.)*:

13. Number of pages attached: _____
Date:

* (Signature of all petitioners also required (Prob. Code, § 1020).)

▶ _____
                                    (SIGNATURE OF ATTORNEY *)

I declare under penalty of perjury under the laws of the State of California that the foregoing is true and correct.
Date:

▶ _____
· ·
        (TYPE OR PRINT NAME)   (SIGNATURE OF PETITIONER)

▶ _____
· ·
        (TYPE OR PRINT NAME)   (SIGNATURE OF PETITIONER)

DE-260, GC-060 [Rev. January 1, 1998]   **REPORT OF SALE AND PETITION FOR ORDER**   WEST GROUP   Page two
                                          CONFIRMING SALE OF REAL PROPERTY   Official Publisher
                                                    (Probate)

The foreigner may be a nonresident alien or a nonresident alien fiduciary. The ownership entity may include a foreign partnership or foreign corporation not created under the laws of the United States or its territories. These individuals and business firms have rights and obligations that must be treated in specific ways. The major consideration for the escrow is the transfer of funds into or out of the United States.

Some of the reasons for foreign investments in the United States are the value of the dollar against foreign currencies and the exchange rate. Other foreign investors are attracted to real estate in the United States because of the strong political stability of the United States in the global economy. Because the cost of borrowing in some foreigners' countries is often less than in the United States, borrowed capital from their home country may be invested in U.S. property. It is often claimed that the greatest reason for investing in California real estate is as a hedge against inflation.

One concern for the escrow officer is the tax liability in the transaction. In some countries such as Japan, where the minimum tax rate may be as high as 62 percent, a U.S. corporate tax rate of only 34 percent may look favorable. Coupled with faster depreciation schedules on our real estate assets compared to some foreign countries, investors see an opportunity for stability, growth, and lower taxes. In the past, foreign investors made money in U.S. real estate, sold the asset, then took home the profits. The Tax Reform Act of 1986 changed all that.

As of January 1, 1987, U.S. investors had an incentive to sell their properties, which increased the supply of U.S. real estate available. Different investors preferred a wide range of properties. Predominantly, investors from Great Britain, Canada, Germany, the Netherlands, Japan, Mexico, and Pacific Rim countries bought agricultural land in the United States. California's fertile Imperial and San Joaquin Valleys attracted these investors. Industrial property buyers predominantly invested funds from Canada, Great Britain, Japan, the Netherlands, and Germany. Commercial property, such as shopping centers, banks, retail properties, office buildings, hotels, resorts, parking lots, and golf courses, were most attractive to investors from Japan, Canada, Great Britain, the Middle East, and Pacific Rim countries. Foreigners invest in the United States for the following reasons:

■ The value of the dollar against foreign currencies

■ Political stability to protect the asset and the future exchange rate

■ Global economy and regulation on foreign investment funds

■ Leverage—cost of borrowing funds

■ Diversification of investments

- Higher yield on U.S. properties

- Stability of the U.S. real estate market

- As a hedge against inflation

- Lack of quality real estate available in the home country

- Tax benefits for income tax, corporation tax, and capital gains tax

- Shorter depreciation schedule

- California modified tax law basing tax on gain made in California

- Tax Reform Act of 1986

On a national basis, those states that border Canada, such as the Northern New England states and the state of Washington, have more Canadian citizen investors than the other states. Likewise, Florida has more Cuban citizen investors than elsewhere. Similarly, California has more investment from Mexican citizens than most states.

For example, when escrow handles a party who has experience in the transfer of property in Mexico, an explanation may be needed to clarify the California escrow practices. In Mexico, transactions are handled this way: When purchasing property in Mexico the rules for a citizen of Mexico are different than for a non-Mexican citizen, unlike U.S. property ownership laws. The current Mexican owner is asked to sell directly. If both parties agree to the price and terms, a paper is written and signed by the parties before a notary public. When the buyer pays the seller the full price in cash, both parties go back to the notary public, who has a new deed notarized to indicate the change of ownership. No attorney, no escrow, and no real estate agents are involved in a transaction in Mexico. Because interest rates are so high in most foreign countries, the parties either pay cash for the purchase or do not buy property.

In Northern California from 1995–2000, most agricultural investment was predominately in Butte and Tehema counties. Both counties account for 24 percent of the total foreign land holdings in the state. In Southern California for the same period, agriculture investments grew in Fresno, San Luis Obispo, and Santa Barbara counties (Camarillo and Oxnard). At the same time, for nonagriculture investments, Japan is at the top, especially in Los Angeles County, but also in Anaheim and San Diego. In Northern California, San Francisco and Oakland were top on the list. Overall, Southern California leads the state in foreign real estate investors. California has a higher percentage of foreign investment in U.S. real estate than in foreign investment in the U.S. overall. This means that more California escrows will be involved with foreign investors than escrows handled elsewhere. California has 20 percent of the total U.S. foreign real estate investment. In 1988, the flow of foreign investment in U.S. nonagriculture real estate went from $4.5 billion to $9 billion. At the same time, the flow of nonagriculture real estate investment in California was between $1 and $1.5 billion. This is why federal and state legislators began to regulate the flow of funds out of the United States and out of the California economy.

The main concern was that unchecked foreign investments could jeopardize U.S. political and economic independence: the higher price a foreign investor might pay could force U.S. first-time homebuyers out of the market; control of local rental markets for residential or commercial real estate could force higher rents to U.S. firms and individuals; and, if the foreign investors pull the funds out to take the money home, the cash taken out of the United States could cause interest rates to increase and weaken the U.S. dollar. Therefore, the following laws were passed that apply to U.S. real estate that the escrow handler would have to include in the process before close of escrow:

■ *Foreign Investment Study Act of 1974.* This Act authorized the Secretary of Commerce and Secretary of the Treasury to conduct a two-year study of foreign investments in the United States. The study concluded that foreign investment actually improved the efficiency of U.S. markets. But the study recommended that data gathering be instituted to continue on a regular basis.

■ *International Investment Survey Act of 1976.* This Act authorized the president to collect and analyze periodic and comprehensive data on foreign investment in the United States. Not designed to restrict foreign investment, beginning with a 1976 benchmark, it allowed a comprehensive survey every five years. The Act was amended in 1981 to allow the benchmark survey after 1980 to be conducted in 1987.

■ *Agricultural Foreign Investment Disclosure Act of 1978.* This Act required all foreign investors who acquire or dispose of agricultural land in the United States to report the transaction to the Secretary of Agriculture within 90 days. The amount of acreage, price, citizenship, intended property use, location, and other information is reported. A transfer of less than ten acres is exempt, as is property where gross receipts from the sale of agricultural products grown on the property are under $1,000.

■ *Foreign Investment in Real Property Tax Act of 1980 (FIRPTA).* **FIRPTA** requires the payment of capital gains taxes by foreigners who sell U.S. real estate. All foreigners who acquired property after July 18, 1980, must file an annual report with IRS listing their holdings and the appraised value of the asset.

■ *Foreign Investment Tax Reform Act of 1984.* This Act changed the reporting requirements to include only foreigners who are not engaged in U.S. trade or business. To ensure that foreigners pay the U.S. capital gains tax realized from the sale of U.S. real estate, the Act requires that the foreigner must withhold part of the closing funds for the tax payment. Escrow is required to withhold and pay directly to IRS the amount of withholding as stated by the Act. The amount is usually 10 percent of the selling price of the property, or the foreign seller's maximum tax liability. Subsequently, California enacted a similar law, known as **CAL-FIRPTA,** that requires the mandatory payment of taxes to the state for the sale of property held by foreign investors.

Foreign investors need to have the following items before investing in California real property, and the escrow agent must request all items to comply with several laws:

- **Power of Attorney.** When a foreign investor sells California real estate, it is common for the proceeds to be used to purchase other property in California. A real estate exchange is a common occurrence, and, in this case, the funds are not leaving California. This fact would have to be proved to the tax collectors to affect the exchange. Otherwise, if the tax is paid to the government, the remaining funds may not be enough to close the escrow. If the foreign investor is not going to be present at the time of purchasing California property, he or she must get an attorney in the home country to obtain a lawful power of attorney. This power of attorney allows the foreign investor's agent to act on his or her behalf.

- **Corporation.** If the foreign investor is a corporation, the corporate bylaws and articles of incorporation must be provided to make sure the corporation is legitimate and current in its U.S. corporate taxes, including payroll and other taxes. The assets cannot be released until the government tax release is obtained.

- **Partnership.** If the foreign investor is a partnership, it must indicate what type of partnership: limited or general. The investor then has to provide documentation for proof of the type of partnership and that the partnership taxes are paid.

- **Secretary of State.** Both the corporation and partnership must file with the Secretary of State to transfer real property. The escrow agent must obtain a release from the state indicating that the entity is either tax exempt or that no tax is currently due.

- **Social Security Number.** The foreign investor must have a valid Social Security number and be current in the payment of U.S. taxes. The number allows the foreign investor to open a bank account in the state in which that person is planning to invest. If a foreign investor wants to buy property in California, he or she must have an open bank account in California.

- **California Bank Account.** The foreign investor has to have a wire transfer or other acceptable form of deposit to get the required money into a California bank account from his or her home country. Escrow cannot close based upon a check from a bank in a foreign country.

- **Down Payment.** Foreign investors are usually required to place 30 percent to 50 percent cash as a down payment for the purchase of U.S. real property. Lenders are less likely to place a loan for over 50 percent of the appraised value to foreign investors.

- **Property Size.** If a foreign investor is purchasing a one-unit to four-unit residential property, financing is available up to the typical maximum Fannie Mae loan limits with either fixed or adjustable rate loans. If the property has five or more units, the criteria for these jumbo loans often change whether the buyer is a domestic or foreign investor. Cash flow, rate of return of and on the investment, occupancy rates, age and condition of the property, and similar criteria are carefully reviewed.

- **Points.** Escrow can expect points to range from 3 percent to 5 percent when the purchaser is a foreign investor. The higher the risk, the more likely that higher points will be charged.

- **Disclosures.** All normal disclosures for a standard California real property transaction are required, including agency, buyer's affidavit, transfer disclosure statement, lead-based paint, seismic, and flood hazards.

■ WORKING WITH THE FOR SALE BY OWNER (FSBO) TRANSACTIONS

Because the escrow is an arrangement for completing a real estate transaction, the escrow officer would naturally try to reach that goal on all escrows, including that of the **for sale by owner (FSBO) transaction.** The principals there establish the terms of sale on a contract outside of escrow. For experienced real estate professionals who know investments and real estate practices and procedures, the FSBO escrow is often easy to do. However, most principals to the escrow do not understand the basics of a real estate transaction and may ask the escrow officer to give information that is beyond the scope of their expertise, such as tax, legal, or real estate advice.

The escrow officer who does not have a real estate license may not give real estate advice. Giving real estate advice when not licensed could subject the escrow officers and the firms by which they are employed with large penalties and fines from the California Department of Real Estate. Escrow officers cannot give tax advice unless they are so qualified and would have to pay any penalties and fines the principal would be subject to for giving advice on exchanges, net proceeds, or any tax issues. The escrow officer who practices law would have additional problems should the bar association begin a lawsuit action against the escrow company and the individual escrow officer for giving legal advice if not so qualified.

Keeping in mind that the escrow officer is, in fact, the expert on closing an escrow, the parties to a real estate sales transaction employ the escrow holder to assist them to open the escrow and to close the escrow. The valid escrow should have an independent legal contract executed between the principals outside of escrow. The escrow instructions should be established subsequent to the purchase contract agreement. The following list is helpful for the principal who is trying to close a FSBO escrow:

- Have an executed purchase contract between the principals with all signatures.

- Principals determine which escrow company to use to open escrow.

- Buyer's funds are deposited into escrow account.

- Furnish escrow with the following title information:
    - Seller: vesting, liens;
    - Buyer: vesting.

- Establish which principal pays which fees billed to escrow to pay.

- List all contingencies and determine what constitutes removal of the contingency or compliance with the item.

- List all third party requirements, such as lender's credit report, lender's appraisal, third party home inspection, termite clearance report, etc.

- Follow up on buyer's financing with the lender.

- Determine title insurance coverage.

- Just prior to close of escrow, complete a final physical inspection.

- Establish by mutual agreement what the instructions are should the escrow not close, such as escrow cancellation fee, title fee, searches, funds spent during the escrow, etc.

THINK ABOUT IT   What are the advantages and disadvantages in working with a for sale by owner (FSBO) transaction?

■ CHAPTER SUMMARY

The homestead laws protect the equity of the homeowner and are often involved in a real estate escrow where secondary financing is being placed on the property. Because the homestead would have lien priority over the new money lien, escrow frequently is asked to prepare an abandonment of homestead if a homestead is already recorded on the property.

The probate laws are exacting on the forms and procedures established by the legal system. The escrow officer must comply with all court actions to close the escrow and must establish a final release to close the escrow after releases from tax liabilities.

Working with foreign investors and for sale by owner transactions requires skill for the escrow officer in dealing with nonconforming individuals. These individuals must comply with local customary business practices to close the escrow according to California escrow practices.

■ CHAPTER 13 QUIZ

1. Which is *NOT* true?
   a. Probate is a court approved action.
   b. All property must go through probate.
   c. Some property is exempt from probate.
   d. Probate laws vary among states.

2. The California Homestead Law
   a. is an amendment to the earlier Homestead Act of 1862.
   b. involves acquiring title to real property.
   c. protects the equity in the personal residence of the property owner.
   d. transfers ownership to real property if improvements are made on the property with minimum occupancy period and if a fee is paid.

3. Foreign investors who make profits from the sale of real property in the United States
   a. cannot take any of the funds out of the country.
   b. must pay taxes on the profit before the net proceeds can leave the country.
   c. can avoid any tax due by having a U.S. citizen as a partner.
   d. must have court approval and IRS release to obtain the funds.

4. Which of the following tax laws affect foreign investors in real property ownership?
   a. The Tax Reform Act of 1986
   b. The Foreign Investment in Real Property Act of 1980
   c. The Agricultural Foreign Investment Disclosure Act of 1978
   d. All of the above

5. When the seller of real property by a foreign investor is a corporation or partnership, the escrow officer must obtain a release from the
   a. secretary of state.
   b. Health and Safety Code Enforcement.
   c. building inspector.
   d. federal probate court.

6. Which is *NOT* a true statement?
   a. The administrator of an estate is selected by the court.
   b. The executor of an estate is selected by the deceased.
   c. The probate action must be approved by a municipal judge.
   d. Probate may be waived for exempt property transactions.

7. The abandonment of homestead is
   a. used to terminate a recorded homestead previously filed on real property.
   b. automatically terminated when a spouse dies.
   c. automatically transferred to subsequent property purchased.
   d. extended to cover interests of junior lien holders.

8. An escrow is required for
   a. a declaration of homestead.
   b. an abandonment of homestead.
   c. every court ordered transfer.
   d. transfers between a buyer and a seller.

9. When the public has access to the detailed information on beneficiaries of an estate for individuals such as George Washington, Benjamin Franklin, and the lead guitarist for the Grateful Dead, Jerry Garcia, this means that
   a. the estate had a living trust naming the beneficiary heirs.
   b. a will established the administrator who passed the estate assets to heirs.
   c. community property and joint tenancy interests were published in a local newspaper of general circulation in the county were the decedent died.
   d. the estate underwent probate.

10. Which is NOT true regarding foreign investors?
    a. The International Investment Survey Act of 1976 was designed to restrict foreign investment in the United States.
    b. The foreign investor must have a valid Social Security number and be current on the payment of taxes.
    c. Foreign investors are predominantly bringing in funds to invest in the United States from Africa, India, and China.
    d. An escrow with a foreign investor must be handled by a specialized escrow at the foreign consulate for the country from which the investor brought the funds to the United States for real property acquisition.

14

SPECIALTY RESIDENTIAL PROPERTY

■ KEY TERMS

condominium (condo)
conventional suburban
   development (CSD)
cooperative
covenants, conditions,
   and restrictions
   (CC&Rs)

estoppel agreement
homeowners'
   association (HOA)
housing and community
   development (HCD)
maintenance fee
net listing

profit and loss (P&L)
   statement
promissory note
rental agreement
security agreement
teardown
time-share

■ CHAPTER OVERVIEW

Chapter 14 discusses the escrow documents needed to transfer ownership and close the escrow for residential property but not the standard single-family home that has previously been discussed. The most frequent escrows for non-owner-occupied escrows is for transfer of ownership of an apartment building. The escrow for this income-producing property is extensive in accounting and contract documents, many of which are noted by the escrow but with which the escrow is not concerned. The buyer and seller usually agree to the transfer of certain information or documents, and the new lender of the buyer also will request the information.

The condominium and cooperative unit ownership are discussed next, followed by the homeowners' association. For the condo, the unit owner has a grant deed showing ownership, whereas for the co-op, the unit owns shares of stock in a corporation.

Construction often involves not only the purchase of the existing property but also the tearing down of the existing improvements. This initial escrow usually has an escrow for the construction loan.

Mobile homes may be individually set on already owned land, or they may be placed on a pad in a mobile home park. The transfer of ownership of a time-share has special items of concern to ensure that the buyer is getting full insured title.

■ LEARNING OBJECTIVES

At the conclusion of Chapter 14, you will be able to

- understand the differences between an escrow for residential property and a specialized residential escrow;

- give a definition for time-share ownership;

- outline a mobile home escrow;

- differentiate between a condominium and a cooperative; and

- determine the distinguishing characteristics for new home construction.

■ APARTMENTS

The escrow company that handles income property has numerous specialized documents that the buyer or the lender require. Many of the documents are handled outside of escrow. Agreements are often referred to in an escrow clause stating that the item is to occur and that escrow is not to be concerned with the item.

The apartment escrow will require the four following items:

1. **Rental Agreement** for each unit

2. Rent roll for the current month so that escrow may prorate rents

3. Security deposit statement so escrow can transfer deposits

4. **Estoppel Agreement** signed by each tenant stating the amount of rents, the amount of deposit paid to the seller, and the length of the term of the tenancy.

In addition to the above, it is common for the lender of the buyer to request the following items:

- **Profit and loss (P&L) statement** on the property for the past three years showing income, expenses, and profit or loss

- Recent capital improvements, such as heating system or roof

The new buyer will want to also have the following, which may also be asked for by the buyer's lender:

- Personal property inventory with bill of sale to transfer ownership

- Smoke detector and fire extinguisher information

- List of vendors, such as plumber, gardener, trash service, cable service

- Tenant concessions, such as assigned parking, free rent, or appliances

- Copy of existing fire hazard insurance policy showing coverage to give to the new insurer, showing proof of previous coverage

To close the escrow, the issue of any nonpaying tenant must also be resolved. This may be handled by agreement between the parties where the escrow is not to close until the unit is vacant. Because the buyer may want the loan to close as soon as possible to obtain a low interest rate, escrow may receive instructions to hold sums due to the seller until after the close of escrow, and to not release said funds until the buyer signs off that the unit is vacant. In some cases, so long as the seller has paid the eviction attorney and the matter is already in a court unlawful detainer action, then the escrow will close and the buyer may just wait until the unit is vacant. Escrow may be asked to hold funds from the seller's proceeds after the close of escrow. The seller may agree to pay the buyer a specific amount per day for every day that rent would be paid by a tenant. The ending date on the payment is the date the seller has the unit vacant. Many different arrangements are made through escrow to ensure that a problem tenant is taken care of prior to being passed along to the buyer.

The following is a standard clause that is often used when an income property is placed into escrow. The purpose is for the buyer to approve contractual relationships prior to actual ownership. The consequences of the seller's actions could financially affect the buyer after the close of escrow.

CHANGES DURING ESCROW: Prior to the close of escrow, Seller agrees not to (1) rent or lease any vacant unit, or other part of the premises, (2) alter, modify, or extend any existing lease agreements, or (3) enter into, modify, or extend any service contract(s), without first having obtained Buyer's written approval.

■ CONDOMINIUMS

The typical sale of an individual **condominium (condo)** unit within a condominium project will result in the following list of steps, procedures, and items:

- Real estate purchase contract and receipt for deposit completed by the real estate licensees and principals to establish a binding, legal contract

- Escrow take sheet that includes association information

- Statement of information for all principals

- Sales escrow instructions

- Preliminary change of ownership report (PCOR)

- HUD-RESPA settlement statement

- Pest control report and clearance

- Request for demand for seller's existing liens

- Federal truth-in-lending disclosure statement showing annual percentage rate (APR)

- Home warranty policy

- Hazard insurance policy

- ALTA/CLTA title insurance policy

- Buyer's closing statement (estimated and final)

- Seller's closing statement (estimated and final)

- Transfer disclosure statement (TDS)

- Bylaws of the homeowners' association

- Articles of incorporation of the homeowners' association

- Homeowners' association rules and regulations

- Covenants, conditions, and restrictions (CC&Rs) of the homeowners' association

- Instruction to pay commission, if applicable

- Loan approval

■ COOPERATIVE

A **cooperative,** referred to as a co-op, is very similar to the condominium homeowner association, but with some specific differences. With a condo, each individual unit is individually owned, and the buyer obtains a recorded deed to show ownership. With a cooperative, the owner does not receive a deed, but instead receives shares of stock in a corporation. The corporation owns the common area and the individual units. The shareholder is entitled to use, rent, or sell a specific unit.

The use of cooperative ownership for real property varies among the states, but New York has over one-half of all cooperatives in the United States. California, however, has a significant number of projects where the ownership utilizes a cooperative. In many instances the property was previously converted from a highrise apartment building, such as the luxury units near the Santa Monica Promenade. In Torrance, California, 320 units located on Merrill Drive utilize the cooperative ownership. Another 203 units are located in Inglewood, Gardena, and Palos Verdes, California. The San Francisco Bay area and other highly populated, more expensive regions of California are more likely to have co-ops than areas around the Salton Sea, Fresno, Chico, and Lake Shasta.

A co-op has monthly fees that consist of a blanket loan payment, plus any maintenance and utility costs. The most difficult part of the co-op escrow is obtaining financing, as most lenders will not make a loan on a co-op. Many transactions involve sellers having to carry back part of their equity in the form of an extension of credit to the buyer as a loan that uses the unit as collateral. The steps for an escrow on a co-op include the following:

- Purchase contract between the principals.

- Title search is ordered.

- Request for demand is ordered.

- Property inspection is requested.

- Appraisal is performed.

- Title insurance issues a leasehold policy.

- Escrow prorates the property taxes and homeowners' association monthly dues that include the loan payment, insurance, and possibly some utilities.

Unique to the co-op is the fact that only one real property tax bill with only one assessor's parcel number (APN) for the entire property. Each unit shares in the total bill based upon the size of the individual unit. The escrow period usually runs about 45 to 60 days to close escrow. After the close of escrow the buyer would receive a stock certificate rather than a grant deed. The buyer would also receive a leasehold interest for an individual unit and possibly a designated parking and/or storage area. At the close of escrow the buyer would receive the following:

- Stock certificate
- Current history of the property
- Loan statement reflecting the amount owed on each unit
- Reserve study
- Financial statement used for the corporation
- Articles of incorporation
- Covenants, conditions, and restrictions (CC&Rs)
- General rules of occupancy
- Occupancy agreement
- Homeowner's statement for disclosures
- Termite report and clearance
- Home warranty policy, if applicable
- Management company fees for transfer and move in
- Recording fees
- Demand statement
- Memorandum of lease, recorded at the county recorder's office
- Form UCCI, which secures the stock certificate

■ HOMEOWNERS' ASSOCIATIONS

A **homeowners' association (HOA)** is a nonprofit corporation formed and organized to serve and represent individual unit owners who own a shared common area. The proportionate share of ownership is based upon the number of units owned of the whole. Many small associations have been formed where a particular city would not allow small lot splits, as are popular in beach communities in California. Instead of a lot split, two homes are built on one lot, and a homeowners' association is formed as part of the property ownership. Other complexes have hundreds of units that comprise numbers of full-time staff to serve the owners, often with resort-like amenities. When many types of diverse units are built resulting in the establishment of entire new towns, this is called **conventional suburban development (CSD),** a term that is relatively new. Some

CSDs are built on hundreds of acres in outlying areas while others are practically in the heart of downtown using redevelopment funding.

Each unit ownership in an association has mandatory membership in the home-owners' association. The escrow officer may contact the association governing body to obtain the necessary disclosure and transfer documents. The members elect the corporation board of directors to run the association governed by the officers, usually consisting of the president, vice president, secretary, and treasurer. Some large complexes have additional officers or have committees appointed for such items as social activities. Some homebuyers do not want the responsibility of automatically becoming a member of a volunteer-run corporation. Those in charge of the association may or may not have any experience in operating a large business. An HOA that consists of only 70 units with monthly dues of $300 per month may be a corporation that has annual revenues of $210,000 but has no leadership training criteria for leadership positions. In these cases, the board of directors often hires outside, professional assistance.

Most HOAs hire an outside property management firm to handle the day-to-day operations of maintenance, dues assessment and collections, notices, and operations. The property management fee is part of the annual budget and part of the amount paid in the monthly dues assessment. The management company has a professional staff of maintenance personnel, the ability to hire an independent audit of association books, good unit records, legal staff to deal with nonpaying unit owners, and, frequently, benefits such as communications in the form of a newsletter. Escrow would obtain the required disclosure and transfer documents from the association management company.

An HOA is not to be confused with a neighborhood association (NA), which consists of voluntary membership in the organization with the purpose of dealing with specific neighborhood concerns. A neighborhood association may take on a social cause, such as homeless groups in the area or issues of crime. The NA may tackle a political issue such as school rezoning districts or installation of speed bumps and traffic flow. Other NAs meet to fight for or against a rezoning of the neighborhood or a surrounding community that would affect values and lifestyle of the neighborhood, such as changing property zoned for low density into high density.

The HOA is responsible for common area maintenance, exterior building care or repair, common area driveway and parking areas, utilities such as trash and water, and blanket insurance. The areas under the direct control of the unit owner are the interior of the unit only, and all other areas are under the control of the HOA, including pipes running inside common walls. The maintenance of the structure, exterior, and common grounds are the responsibility of the HOA, including elevators, underground parking areas, planter boxes, pools, and the recreation meeting room.

Some HOAs are large, master-planned communities with various types of mixed uses. One association might consist of several hundred single-family homes, several clusters of multistory townhouse condominiums, and yet another grouping of one-story condominium duplexes. The growing demand for these types of communities is due to the homogeneity of architectural style for all the various types of home ownership, the diverse audience from the general public that would be attracted to the lifestyle, the more reasonable price of an individual unit when the amenities are included, and the amenities themselves. California tends to build these types of units with boat slips or around golf courses, and these communities attract many people who could not otherwise afford the lifestyle of the beach or golf areas. Most of these recreational-oriented HOAs have pools, tennis courts, and interior recreational facilities such as pool table, table tennis, and gym.

An escrow that has any type of homeowners' association connected with ownership of the property must have certain additional documents to be in compliance with the transfer of the individual unit. The original construction project created the recorded documents that the subsequent property owner must comply with. The title insurance company will access the homeowner information that will be required by the lender. Because the HOA is a corporation, the governing body is the articles of incorporation filed with the state of California and previously recorded. Along with this document are the bylaws of the corporation that lay out much of the daily operations. In addition, most HOAs have a set of rules and regulations that apply to each unit owner. Within one or more of these governing documents are conditions and restrictions over the unit owners, referred to as the **covenants, conditions, and restrictions (CC&Rs).**

Escrow instructions designate that the seller will furnish to the buyer and the buyer's lender specific documents through the escrow. When the HOA complex has a disproportionate number of rental units within the complex and with few owners of the units living on the premises, it may be difficult to obtain financing for the sale of the unit. The lender may see that over 50 percent of the units are rented and feel that the unit is an apartment complex and not a residential ownership unit. Escrow should be aware of the various reasons that an escrow involving the HOA would not close.

Another problem with HOA complexes is obtaining a lender that approves the complex. If the units were inspected at the time of construction for FHA or VA approval, then subsequent financing for these types of loans is fairly routine. However, most complexes were not inspected during construction and obtaining subsequent approval by the government-approved lender is often difficult or impossible because all or part of the construction may not meet the minimum building standards associated with government financing.

When a complex is new, it is common for the builder to obtain a loan commitment from one particular lender. After the units are 100 percent sold, one lender holds 100 percent of the loans, putting that lender at higher risk should the management fail to maintain the quality of ownership or should individual homeowners fail to maintain pride of ownership. When the first units are sold as a resale, it is common for the seller to think the existing lender will make a new loan to a qualified buyer. This is, however, most often not the case. Because of the percentage of loans already held in the complex, the seller's lender may not make the new loan. And when the buyer applies to other lenders for the first few resales, the new lender may question the track record for the complex. The new lender wants to make sure the units are not all rental and that the risk of default is low.

However, established units with regular turnover of unit ownership usually have no problem with obtaining several lenders who would finance a buyer on a unit. The new lender will always want to review the governing documents prior to making the loan commitment.

The Congress for New Urbanism, a 1993 San Francisco-based nonprofit organization, works with architects, developers, planners, and others to create coherent regional planning, walkable neighborhoods, and civic spaces. Escrows for units in these types of communities would involve transfer documents representing the community. See the following Web site: *http://www.cnu.org/pdf/code_catalog_8-1-01.pdf* or *http://www.cnu.org*.

WEB LINK

■ CONSTRUCTION

Most states are planning for growth and restricting rapid development without limitations on infrastructure. The ability to provide adequate schools, libraries, police and fire protection, and basic utilities is a concern in all states and is affecting construction in California. The escrow instructions for new construction commonly reflect the mandated disclosures associated with development, such as the Mello-Roos law for the financing of infrastructure.

In California, a recently signed law requires local governments and developers to secure an adequate long-term water supply before a new residential subdivision can be approved. Developments of 500 or more units are affected. Under the new law, the local government must verify in writing that the water supply is or will be available and, in the case of groundwater, that the landowner has the right to extract the water. Redevelopment and low-income projects are exempt.

When purchasing property for new construction, the developer must

- determine zoning needs;
- check with the city planning department;
- find the ideal location;
- purchase the property for immediate building; or
- purchase the property for future building.

The time line for initial building and for the completion of the project will determine the financing and the escrow. A construction escrow involves obtaining the property from the landowner for the purpose of building new construction for the future. The completed project may involve many escrows where the newly constructed units are sold to the public individuals. This is discussed in Chapter 15 as part of section on subdivisions. Other projects are developed as new construction, but held by the builder, as is the case of the large apartment complexes, discussed earlier in this chapter.

An individual may purchase a vacant lot in a built-up area with plans to construct a new home on it after tearing down an existing home. This is commonly referred to as a **teardown.** In this case, the following events would occur:

- Locate the property to analyze for possible development.
- Determine the present and any proposed zoning change for the future.
- Meet with architect to determine the cost of demolition and cost to build the new structure.
- Enter into purchase agreement contract with existing property owner.
- Open escrow with the existing property owner:
  - Outright purchase with new financing for the purchase may be utilized with subsequent construction loan made after transfer of ownership.
  - Purchase may be contingent upon approval to build.
- Hire architect to create the blueprints and obtain city planning department approval to build the proposed structure.
- Pay city building department permit fee for the actual permit, the plan check, energy fees, seismic evaluation, and any civic fees for parks, schools, or such.

- Obtain construction loan with lender who specializes in home construction loans:
    - Submit plans for approval with proof of permit fees.
    - Await appraisal approval for construction from proposed plans.
    - Expect 75 percent loan-to-value (LTV) ratio for construction loan.
    - Escrow acts as a "stake holder" to retain the lender's funds until meeting specific loan criteria, such as construction completion phase or resale of a unit, as in the case of a blanket loan or some other escrow instruction.
    - Loan interest is calculated only on the funds used, not total loan approval amount. No interest is paid until funds are actually disbursed.
    - Escrow of construction loan:

        Draw basis: percentage of funds released as a percentage of the construction is completed with formal approval signoff.

        10 percent upon completion of foundation.

        20 percent upon completion of framing.

        20 percent upon completion of plumbing, heating, and electrical.

        20 percent upon completion of exterior roof and walls.

        20 percent upon completion of interior finishes.

        10 percent upon end of mechanic's lien release period.

    - Equity line: Funds are placed into account for the property owner to release independent of bank approval of the construction phase.
    - Escrow on long-term loan. The construction loan is converted into long-term loan at the end of the construction phase.

Once a purchase has been made between the existing property owner and the person who wishes to develop the property, it is common to experience several areas of concern in the escrow process. The first escrow was the purchase from the existing property owner.

A subordination clause is often used in escrow instructions when the purchase is vacant land for future construction. This clause is used to change the priority of a financial arrangement. The lender that provided the funding for the construction loan wants to ensure that this loan has first loan priority. The trust deed on vacant land would subordinate to the new loan for the construction.

The second escrow is the holding escrow. Once the property has been purchased from the existing seller, the new property owner will determine the highest and best use for the property. The owner would need to obtain plans and secure a construction loan. The lender will usually fund the loan into a "holding escrow."

where the money is released on a draw based on the portion of the building finished by the contractor. The escrow holder acts as a stake holder who has written instructions to hold the funds until directed to release funding upon the lender's approval.

After construction, when the construction is completed, escrow will be involved in paying off the construction loan and creating a new, long-term, permanent financing loan on the completed individual home. This involves a third escrow.

Escrow involving construction may have several other areas of concern for the person involved in this type of real estate and escrow. The first area is the problems associated with putting together a compatible team. The person who wants to develop property should have an architect and contractor who work well together and who are in good communications with the property owner and with escrow.

The second area that can cause problems in closing an escrow when the closing is contingent upon obtaining final approval is neighbor complaints. In most communities, a neighbor has the right to file a formal complaint against proposed construction. In these cases, a hearing is held by the government agency to determine the validity of the complaint. Some construction is approved for completion, and some is not. The hearing's outcome would determine the final outcome of the escrow.

■ MOBILE HOMES

Mobile homes are grouped into several categories, each with differing escrows. Not every escrow holder will handle an escrow involving a mobile home. Some escrow officers specialize in only one type of mobile home escrow. The types of mobile home escrow transactions involving the transfer of ownership to a mobile home include the following:

- ■ The mobile home park, consisting of the common area, the pads on which the units are situated, and such items as a laundry area, pool or recreation area, and utilities.

- ■ New Dealer. Here the sale of the mobile homes is classified as "mobile" and is handled similarly to the transfer of ownership of an automobile.

- ■ Mobile home in a park with a new loan obtained through an institutional lender.

- ■ Mobile home sold with seller carryback financing.

■ Mobile home placed on a permanent foundation with land. This sale of a mobile home unit is treated as real property, as if it were no longer mobile.

A mobile home park is the transfer of improved land with amenities that enhance the value of the property and that are subject to real property taxation. The paved driveway and parking areas, interior streets often lushly landscaped or even adjoining a golf course or lake or ocean, street lights, the slab in place on which a unit may be placed, and the utility outlets for each pad are part of the ownership transfer that the escrow is handling. With an aging population, the demand for newer and more modern mobile home parks has been accommodated by developers who choose to target the senior buyer. Most developers have mentored a relationship with an experienced escrow holder to handle the paperwork required for transfer of ownership of the entire park, whether occupied or built for speculation. In this case, the escrow officer would be seeking release for clear title to the property that showed no mechanics' liens, utility easement claims, or other development problems that would keep the escrow from closing.

For the sale of individual mobile home units, the California Health and Safety Code, Chapter 5, Section 18035 cites what is required by law for a mobile home dealer sale. Whether the unit seller is working under the California Department of Real Estate (DRE) or the Department of Motor Vehicles (DMV) is of little concern to the escrow holder, whose main concerns are the transfer documents and the funds. If the unit is under DMV, the paperwork and fees for a transfer would be different than if the unit was governed by the rules and regulations of the DRE. The mobile home escrow officer will need to complete a checklist, similar to the ones shown in Table 14.1 for personal property and Table 14.2 for real property.

Escrow will obtain a copy of the registration of the individual mobile home, usually from the dealer or agent. The buyer has a signed purchase order and a conditional sales contract to evidence the purchase. The escrow officer would deposit any cash from the buyer into an established escrow account as the escrow agent for the transaction. The escrow officer completes the notice of escrow opening from the California Department of **Housing and Community Development (HCD).** This form is referred to as the HCD 481.8, and it is shown in Figure 14.1. The escrow instructions will include a clause that is the same as or similar to the one shown below to comply with the January 1990 law requiring delivery through escrow to the buyer of the park rental agreement:

> Escrow holder shall order a copy of the park rental agreement to be held in this escrow file, but shall have no liability and/or responsibility as to the contents contained therein.

TABLE 14.1

Mobile Home Transfer (Personal Property)

1. Escrow instructions	Signed by buyer and signed by seller.
2. Certificate of Registration for the mobile home	Check the last issue date for expiration to obtain the last one issued.
3. Certificate of Title	If unencumbered, owner has this. If not clear, order payoff statement with #4.
4. Conditional Lien Release	Beneficiary completes and returns with #3.
5. Search	Informal search for status of unit as of the date of the search. Formal search gives updates for 120 days of any activity on the unit.
6. Notice of Escrow Opening	HCD report 481.8 required for a dealer transaction. Places a 120-day moratorium on the unit. Written extension for 2nd period allowed only if by written request.
7. Mobile Home Park Rental Agreement	If unit is to be located in a park.
8. Smoke Detector form	Executed by buyer or seller.
9. Power of Attorney from Buyer	Used to execute forms for buyer.
10. Power of Attorney from Seller	Used to execute forms for seller.
11. DMV Certificate of Title/HCD 480.5	Application for Registration.
12. Notice of Sale	Signed by seller. The close of escrow date.
13. Designation of Co-owner term	
14. Tax Clearance Certificate	If unit is on real property tax roll.
15. Certification of Retail Value and Purchase Price (HCD 476.4)	Unit is on the In-Lieu Tax Roll. Value obtained from Kelly Blue Book or HCD.
16. Certificate of Registration and Conditional Lien Release	If 2nd lien holder on the mobile home unit is to be paid off, obtain payoff demand and forms.
17. Insurance policy	Buyer to furnish.
18. Lender's instructions	Check carefully and obtain buyer approval.
19. Security Agreement, and Promissory Note and Bill of Sale	Draw documents listing personal property (skirting, deck, awning, step, shed, etc.).
20. Money	To close escrow.
21. Statement of Facts	If unit placed on private property.

TABLE 14.2

Mobile Home Transfer (Real Property)

1. Certificate of Title and Registration	Must have the last date issued.
2. Payoff lien(s)	Obtain demand statement.
3. Decal plates	Seller obtained the DMV-issued plates.
4. Certified copy of recorded HCD 433A	Recorded at county assessor's.
5. Taxes	Obtain release for fees paid.
6. Grant deed	Recorded at county recorder's office.
7. Termite report	Lender requirement for unit and grounds.
8. Statement of Facts	If unit is on private property, HCD gets copy.

FIGURE 14.1

Mobile Homes HCD 481.8

STATE OF CALIFORNIA
BUSINESS, TRANSPORTATION AND HOUSING AGENCY
DEPARTMENT OF HOUSING AND COMMUNITY DEVELOPMENT
DIVISION OF CODES AND STANDARDS
REGISTRATION AND TITLING PROGRAM

NOTICE OF ESCROW OPENING

SECTION 1 - INSTRUCTIONS

To report the opening of escrow to the Department, send this completed form, Notice of Escrow Opening, HCD 481.8a, with the recording fee of $35.00 to the department. Retain the Notice of Escrow Closing, form HCD 481.8b and the Notice of Escrow Cancellation, form HCD 481.8c with your escrow file. Refer to these forms for further instructions.

If a multiple section manufactured home, mobilehome, or multi-unit manufactured housing is currently registered under more than one decal or license plate, list each decal number or license plate number with its corresponding serial number and HUD Label or HCD Insignia Number. If a multiple section manufactured home, mobilehome, or multi-unit manufactured housing is currently registered under only one decal, list the decal number on the first line. List the serial number for each section and the corresponding HUD Label or HCD Insignia Number.

SECTION 2 - DESCRIPTION OF UNIT

Manufacturer Trade Name (Make): _____   Date of Manufacture: _____

Section	Decal or License Number(s)	Serial Number(s)	HUD Label or HCD Insignia Number(s)
1			
2			
3			
4			

SECTION 3 - ESCROW INFORMATION

Escrow File Number:	Date Escrow Opened:

Company Name: _____ Telephone No.:_____

Address: _____
         Street Address or P.O. Box   *City*   *State*   *Zip*

SECTION 4 - BUYER/DEALER INFORMATION

Buyer(s) Name(s): _____

Dealer Name: _____ Dealer License Number: _____

Dealer Address: _____

SECTION 5 - ESCROW AGENT CERTIFICATION

I certify under penalty of perjury under the laws of the State of California that the foregoing is true and correct.

Executed on _____ at _____, _____
         Date   *City*   *State*

Signature of Escrow Agent _____

Printed Name of Escrow Agent _____
HCD 481.8a (7/97)

As in any other type of home ownership transfer, the escrow holder will write all lien holders for a demand for a loan status report and a Statement of Conditional Lien Release (HCD 481.7), as shown in Figure 14.2, or a Statement of Anticipated Formal Assumption (HCD 481.6), as shown in Figure 14.3. The lien holder(s) then has five days from date of receipt to complete the forms and forward the form and the title to the escrow agent. The escrow holder will have a 120-day moratorium period for the mobile home record.

During the moratorium period, the escrow holder receives notice of any change in the record. The escrow officer cannot process transfer of ownership or registration card requests during the moratorium period. Only the registration renewal fee could be processed during the moratorium time, and even then the new registration card would be held until the end of the moratorium period.

A written demand would go from escrow to the county tax collector for any mobile home unit situated on real property, where a lease-space agreement is not present, to determine ownership of the land and status of payment of the real property taxes. A Mobile Home Tax Clearance Certificate, as shown in Figure 14.4, would go from the tax collector to the escrow holder if no taxes are due, or a Conditional Tax Clearance Certificate, as shown in Figure 14.5, if the taxes have not been paid. Form HCD 495.0 is the request for voluntary transfer of a mobile home to local property taxation that might be used in the transaction.

In the case where the mobile home is sold so that it becomes treated as real property and no longer as a vehicle of personal property, certain forms must be filed through escrow. The HCD Form 433 is used when a mobile home is being placed on a permanent foundation, whether a new mobile home or a used mobile home. Dealers frequently sell new mobile home units where the individual unit owners place them on land they own. The county agency will generate the HCD 433 Form when the permits are issued for the unit and after the unit has been properly inspected. It is the county's responsibility to actually record the form with the HCD. Escrow will obtain a copy of the recorded form from the county, then send a certified copy to HCD at the close of escrow. The purpose of this is to remove the mobile home unit from the HCD records because the unit is now considered real property and is subject to real property taxation regulations.

When the financing is handled with a **security agreement** and a **promissory note,** these documents are not recorded at the close of escrow as a grant deed would be recorded at the county recorder's office. The two documents would be delivered to the beneficiary (institutional lender or seller) by registered mail. The HCD does not receive a copy of these two financing documents. By listing the beneficiary on the certificate of title as the legal owner, the beneficiary's interest is secured. This is similar to any DMV lien holder interest and similar to the way

FIGURE 14.2

Statement of Conditional Lien Release (HCD 481.7)

STATE OF CALIFORNIA
BUSINESS, TRANSPORTATION AND HOUSING AGENCY
DEPARTMENT OF HOUSING AND COMMUNITY DEVELOPMENT
DIVISION OF CODES AND STANDARDS
REGISTRATION AND TITLING PROGRAM

CONDITIONAL LIEN RELEASE

SECTION I.   ESCROW COMPANY INFORMATION

Company Name: _____

Address: _____
       Street Address or P.O. Box   *City*   *State*   *Zip*

Escrow Agent's Name: _____   Escrow File Number: _____

SECTION II.   LIENHOLDER INFORMATION

Lienholder Status (check one): ☐ Legal Owner   ☐ First Junior Lienholder   ☐ Second Junior Lienholder

Lienholder Name: _____

Address: _____
       Street Address or P.O. Box   *City*   *State*   *Zip*

SECTION III.   REGISTERED OWNER(S) INFORMATION

Name(s): _____   Loan Number: _____

SECTION IV.   DESCRIPTION OF UNIT

Manufacturer Trade Name: _____   Manufacture Year: _____

Manufacturer Serial Number(s): _____

Decal (License) Number(s): _____

SECTION V.   LIENHOLDER CERTIFICATION

I certify under penalty of perjury under the laws of the State of California that the foregoing is true and correct and that in order to release or transfer our lien, I/we the aforementioned lienholder, require a total payment in the amount of $_____. This payoff figure will expire on _____ and is subject to the conditions outlined on the attached lien status report. Upon receipt of payment and compliance with condition(s) outlined on the attached lien status report, the undersigned does hereby agree to release all rights, title or interest in the unit described above.

Executed on _____ at _____
          Date   *City*   *State*

Name of Lienholder: _____

Signature of Authorized Agent: _____

SECTION VI.   ESCROW AGENT CERTIFICATION

I hereby certify under penalty of perjury under the laws of the State of California that the foregoing is true and correct and that the above-named lienholder has been paid in full according to the terms and conditions set forth in the lien status report.

Executed on _____ at _____
          Date   *City*   *State*

Signature of Escrow Agent: _____

HCD 481.7 (7/97)

FIGURE 14.3

Statement of Anticipated Formal Assumption (HCD 481.6)

STATE OF CALIFORNIA
BUSINESS, TRANSPORTATION AND HOUSING AGENCY
DEPARTMENT OF HOUSING AND COMMUNITY DEVELOPMENT
DIVISION OF CODES AND STANDARDS
REGISTRATION AND TITLING PROGRAM

STATEMENT OF ANTICIPATED FORMAL ASSUMPTION

SECTION I.   ESCROW COMPANY INFORMATION

Company Name: _____

Address: _____
        Street Address or P.O. Box   *City*   *State*   *Zip*

Escrow Agent's Name: _____   Escrow File Number: _____

SECTION II.   LIENHOLDER INFORMATION

Lienholder Status (check one):   ☐ Legal Owner   ☐ First Junior Lienholder   ☐ Second Junior Lienholder

Name: _____

Address: _____
        Street Address or P.O. Box   *City*   *State*   *Zip*

SECTION III.   BORROWER(S)/REGISTERED OWNER(S) INFORMATION

Name(s): _____   Loan Number: _____

Address: _____

SECTION IV.   DESCRIPTION OF UNIT

Manufacturer Trade Name: _____   Year: _____

Manufacturer Serial Number(s): _____

Decal (License) Number(s): _____

SECTION V.   BUYER INFORMATION

Name(s): _____

Address: _____

SECTION VI.   LIENHOLDER CERTIFICATION

I certify under penalty of perjury under the laws of the State of California that the foregoing is true and correct and that based on information and belief, on or before the close of escrow, the buyer, shown above, will assume the full indebtedness of our lien for the described unit, currently in the name of the above-mentioned borrower(s)/registered owner(s). Upon the execution of the formal assumption of the lien by the buyer, we the aforementioned lienholder, grant our approval for the buyer or his or her designee to be recorded as the new registered owner(s).

I/We certify under penalty of perjury under the laws of the State of California that the foregoing is true and correct.

Executed on _____ at _____
            Date   *City*   *State*

Lienholder Name: _____

Signature of Authorized Agent: _____

HCD 481.6 (7/97)

FIGURE 14.4

Mobile Home Tax Clearance Certificate

MOBILE HOME TAX CLEARANCE CERTIFICATE

COUNTY OF _____

Serial Number	
Location of Mobile Home	Assessor s Parcel No.

Previous Owner	Applicant
Name:	Name:
Address:	Address:

I hereby certify that the following has been paid:

❑ Delinquent License Fees
❑ Property Taxes applicable to the mobile home
identified above through the fiscal year 19____–19____
❑ A security deposit for payment of the Property Taxes
for the fiscal year 19____–19____

This certificate is VOID on and after _____

County Tax Collector

DATED _____, 19_____   By _____

FIGURE 14.5

Conditional Mobile Home Tax Clearance Certificate

CONDITIONAL TAX CLEARANCE CERTIFICATE

Mobile home

Date Requested: _____

_____

Escrow Company Name & Address   Escrow #   Name & Phone Number of Escrow Officer

_____

Name & Address of Current Registered Owner (Seller)   Location of Home Now

_____

Name of Buyer (Applicant) & Address to which future tax statements should be mailed   Parcel Number of Home

AFTER ESCROW

_____

Make   Year

Parcel Number of Home

_____

Manufacture's Serial Numbers   Legal License No.

_____

CERTIFICATION OF TAX COLLECTOR

To pay taxes in accordance with various provisions of law and to satisfy provisions of section 18092.7 of the Health and Safety Code, the total amount of $ _____ must be paid on or before _____.
If not so paid, the amount of $_____ must be paid on or before _____.

THIS CERTIFICATE IS VOID ON AND AFTER _____
(date)

Executed on _____ at _____
(date)   (City, State)

County tax collector for _____County, State of California.

Issued on _____   _____
(date)   Buyer or Escrow Officer

CERTIFICATION OF ESCROW OFFICER

I hereby certify under penalty for perjury that the tax liability stated above has been paid in full on or before the date required and all terms of this statement of conditional tax clearance have been complied with. A copy of this certification has been returned to the tax collector with the payment.

Executed on _____ at _____
(date)   (City, State)

Escrow closed on _____   _____
(date)   Buyer or Escrow Officer

in which a mortgage is handled. The registration card will be forwarded to the buyer who becomes the owner, similar to the automobile registration form held by the owner of a car.

With a mobile home that is on a permanent foundation, the close of escrow may be established as the date of the county recordation for real property taxation purposes. However, for a mobile home that is not on a permanent foundation or not on the land owned by the unit buyer, there is no date of recordation of any documents to establish the close of escrow date. The escrow officer establishes the date of close of escrow after the buyer's funds are deposited with escrow and after the buyer and the seller have signed all required documents and agreed to the approval for the closing.

When escrow closes, the escrow officer completes the closing statement showing the costs and expenses of the buyer and another statement for the seller. Upon completion of the transfer application and close of escrow, the moratorium will be removed from the unit. A letter will be put into the file for the particular mobile home unit to show the transfer of ownership along with the file status report showing the new owner information, with a copy mailed to the escrow company.

After the escrow officer balances the file and forwards the required documents to HCD, the funds are disbursed. Escrow prepares the closing statement and the closing letter. The escrow officer will mark his or her calendar to call HCD to make sure all documents were received or to see if any additional items were required. See Figure 14.4 and Figure 14.5 for examples of the different forms.

■ TIME-SHARES

A **time-share** escrow involves 25 to 30 documents depending upon the state in which the transaction takes place. Each state differs in the type of documents required. The grant deed is common in California, but the bargain and sale deed is common in Nevada as is the warranty deed. Financing is often with a promissory note and deed of trust in California. Some states use a property report and a public offering statement. Compared to other types, the time-share escrow has many restrictions stated in the documents. The escrow time may be as short as ten days to two weeks. The steps in closing a time-share escrow are shown below:

- Document for the sales transaction information contact.

- Request preliminary title information.

- Request loan, taxes, and association status and documents.

- Prepare necessary recording document for the appropriate state.

- Collect the sale proceeds/closing costs from the buyer.

- Pay off existing loan or loan transfer document.

- Set up new loan, especially owner-seller financing documents.

- Prorate income and expenses, taxes, and association fees, if applicable.

- Obtain policy of title insurance.

- Request recording of the deed(s).

- Notify time-share management company of the transfer.

- Disburse net sale proceeds to seller and others (broker, association, etc.).

When an original time-share is presented to the public, group meetings are held. Incentives giving something for free may be part of the transaction and are usually handled outside of escrow and directly with the offeror. Once the time-share is already owned, the resale of the time-share has several distinct characteristics not common in other types of escrows.

An owner of a time-share could receive a fee simple deed that would be recorded in the county in which the property is located. This would afford the time-share owner the same rights as those held with other deeded real estate. The owner could sell, rent, bequeath, or give away the property.

Another type of time-share ownership is referred to as the right-to-use. Here the owner has a lease, license, or club membership that allows the purchaser to use the property for a specified period of years. This type of ownership is used outside the United States in countries where a foreigner cannot hold deeded ownership. Some countries do not allow their own citizens to hold title to real property, and only the sovereign can own real estate.

A **net listing** is designed to provide the seller with a fixed dollar amount at the close of escrow, regardless of the sales price. Because this often appeals to the time-share owner, it is a common arrangement for the time-share escrow. In California, the commission to the broker has to be disclosed to the principals prior to the close of escrow. When the escrow closing is about to occur, the escrow officer is then able to draw up the final closing costs, including the commission.

Most state licensing agencies discourage use of the net listing, including California. But for time-share escrows it is often the only way a broker can obtain a listing. Because a net listing can lock the seller into a low price, the broker might have an increased incentive to close the sale. The seller is giving up the ability to freely negotiate a price with the buyer. If the market price increases, the listing broker is the only party to the transaction who benefits. Conversely, if there is not a wide enough profit margin, the broker will not have an incentive to sell that time-share compared to another listing that would give the broker a larger commission. The best time for a seller of a time-share unit to enter into a net listing commission arrangement is when the broker already has a ready, willing, and able buyer so that escrow opens and closes quickly.

The owner of a time-share is responsible for the maintenance fee that is usually billed through a management company. Each time-share owner receives a copy of the annual proposed budget and the annual fee is usually billed once a year, in December. The **maintenance fee** pays for the unit furniture, common area and unit equipment, property taxes, insurance, utilities, housekeeping, pool area, and grounds. Some time-shares include use of an automobile, boat, golf course, or other items. The amount of annual dues is not normally prorated in escrow. If the seller has already paid the dues for the year, the buyer usually does not reimburse any unused portion. The total purchase price usually reflects the amount that includes the annual maintenance fee. It is important for escrow to be sure that all transfer documents are completed for proper membership in the resort that the time-share ownership is affiliated with by proper notice to the association and correctly completing transfer documents.

A policy of title insurance is an insured statement of the condition of title relative to the ownership of the real property. A title insurance policy for a time-share ownership guarantees that the buyer owns what the deed says is owned. The intent of the policy is to protect the holder of the policy against title defects, liens, and encumbrances as of the date the policy is issued.

The appeal for a time-share is the ability to trade, or exchange, the time-share ownership unit for other dates at the same or at another location. Time-share resale companies specialize in handling this market niche.

THINK ABOUT IT

The buyer of a mobile home park wants to upgrade the park to increase the income above what the seller is receiving. The seller has a very casual management style in the handling of the park. The mobile home nearest the entrance is a dilapidated, very old trailer with who knows how many cats running around the unit. The owner of that trailer claims to own no animals.

The buyer puts an amendment into the escrow that the run-down unit must be removed prior to close of escrow. The seller claims that the resident pays all rent and fees on time, complies with the park rules, and that the seller cannot terminate the lease for the unit due to the Mobile Home Residency Law.

Can the buyer or the seller give the tenant a Notice of Termination?

Answer: No. However, if someone buys the unit, the owner can require that the unit be moved from the park because it is significantly run-down and the purpose is to upgrade the park.

■ CHAPTER SUMMARY

This chapter discussed the various escrow documents needed to transfer ownership for residential apartments, condos, co-ops, mobile homes, and time-shares. For an apartment building, the principals usually agree to transfer tenant-related documents and tenant funds. The new lender will require detailed information about the tenants, the property, and the buyer.

The chapter also discussed construction escrow that involves both the purchase of the existing property and the teardown of the existing improvements. The construction loan escrow involves not only the existing property owner and the person who performs the construction but also the construction financing entities and subsequent purchaser of the property with the new improvements.

Many property ownership rights in California include some form of association, including some single-family homes. The condominium and cooperative unit ownership and the mobile home and time-share ownership may involve an association. The transfers of these types of property ownership were discussed in this chapter.

Mobile homes can be individually set on already owned land, or they may be placed on a pad in a rented mobile home park space. Mobile homes are divided into several types of escrows. Escrow officers typically specialize in only particular types of mobile home escrows.

■ CHAPTER 14 QUIZ

1. The escrow process for construction for a new home would include all of the following *EXCEPT*
   a. escrow to purchase the property on which to perform the construction.
   b. holding escrow to disburse the construction financing.
   c. neighborhood escrow to hold funds pending area approval for construction design.
   d. after construction escrow for long-term financing loan escrow.

2. Which is a true statement?
   a. A co-op is the same as a condominium.
   b. A condominium is the same as a town house.
   c. A town house is the same as a single-family residence.
   d. None of the above is correct.

3. The normal length of time for a time-share escrow is most nearly
   a. 10 days to 2 weeks.
   b. 30 days.
   c. 60 days.
   d. 90 days.

4. A net listing commission agreement paid by escrow is often associated with a(n)
   a. apartment building.
   b. condominium unit.
   c. mobile home or time-share.
   d. single-family residence.

5. The HOA is responsible for
   a. interior of individual unit.
   b. exterior of individual unit.
   c. common area.
   d. both b and c above.

6. Which is *NOT* correct?
   a. A co-op is ownership of a share of stock in a corporation that entitles the shareholder to a specific unit.
   b. An apartment is ownership of the common area, with tenants owning the space of the interior of each unit by virtue of the lease agreement.
   c. A condominium is ownership that includes the unit along with joint ownership of common area improvements and common area land.
   d. A time-share entitles the owner to use or occupancy of a unit or lot in a multiownership structure with annual fees entitling the owner to a specific period of time.

7. A manufactured home is one that
   a. is built entirely in a factory and then transported to the site and installed.
   b. is built on the site from pieces delivered to the site for assembly.
   c. most commonly is a tilt-up, preconstructed, cement home, constructed and assembled off-site.
   d. includes units assembled at the site and those made elsewhere and assembled at a factory.

8. When an escrow officer handles an escrow involving a mobile home, the entity most frequently involved in the documents is
   a. HUD.
   b. VA.
   c. HCD.
   d. HOA.

9. Which documents are used in a condominium escrow?
   a. Articles of Incorporation
   b. Bylaws
   c. Covenants, conditions, and restrictions
   d. All of the above

10. The condominium escrow would have a
   a. HUD insurance warranty.
   b. RESPA settlement statement.
   c. declaration of statement of specific week of ownership.
   d. rent income statement and proration allocation.

15

NONRESIDENTIAL SPECIALTIES

■ KEY TERMS

accommodator
Alcoholic Beverage
   Control (ABC)
bill of sale
bulk sales transfer
commercial property
   escrow
constructive receipt
covenant not to
   compete
emblements

Employment
   Development
   Department (EDD)
exchanger
Farmer's Home
   Administration
   (FmHA)
financing statement
goodwill
industrial property
inventory
IRC 1031 tax exchange

off-sale general license
personal property
priority drawing
real property
relinquished property
replacement property
stock in trade
subdivision process
transferor
transferee
undeveloped land

■ CHAPTER OVERVIEW

The residential real estate market generates a great deal of escrow work, with the majority of transactions being single-family homes, followed by income properties such as apartment buildings. However, the escrow officer who obtains experience in a specialized field of nonresidential escrow practices is almost guaranteed life-time employment so long as demand remains for the specialty property. Most escrow holders do not handle many of the types of transactions discussed in this chapter. If an escrow holder does handle one type of the kinds of transactions in this chapter, this would not mean that they would agree to handle a different kind of transaction. Vast differences arise between new home sales and development when compared to office buildings, commercial and industrial property, agricultural property and undeveloped land, and bulk sale business opportunities with or without a liquor license.

Each transaction type covered in this chapter has unique phrases and clauses that the escrow officer would need to understand, and those phrases and clauses are often not available in standard escrow computer programs. A few selected examples of the various transactions mentioned in this chapter are given with specific details that highlight the differences between escrow types.

Subdivision escrows are described with sample clauses. A commercial property escrow is included to give general business opportunity escrow data, which may often be part of a bulk sales transfer. Not all transfers of property require an escrow. The transfer of a liquor license always requires an escrow.

Some escrows handle transactions with an exchange and an accommodator, whether residential, commercial, or industrial property.

■ LEARNING OBJECTIVES

At the conclusion of Chapter 15, you will be able to

- understand the difference between the previously discussed residential sale escrow and the sale escrow instructions used to transfer property ownership from a developer/builder to a homebuyer;

- give a definition for what type of transaction requires an escrow;

- list the types of documents used for a subdivider/builder home sale to a buyer;

- differentiate between real and personal property; and

- explain the requirements for an escrow involving a commercial, retail property.

■ SUBDIVISIONS

The **subdivision process** involves the conversion of land into a completed project. The subdivision team usually consists of city planners, a contractor, architect, engineer, and lender, in addition to the escrow holder and the principals. Commonly, the project will require approval from the California Department of Real Estate under the Subdivision Map Act or the Subdivided Lands Act often with a final public report filing with the Real Estate Commissioner's office.

A purchaser of specialized property does not assume title insurance coverage. Upon a sale, the owner of the property changes and the financing often changes to a new lender. Lenders often require as part of the loan approval process that they be specifically named as coinsured on the insurance policies. Lenders are concerned about liability, especially in construction where so many subcontractors are used to create the end product. Typically a construction project will require a 39-month policy where escrow prorates the premium on the basis of the last 36 months.

> The parties to this escrow have satisfied themselves outside of escrow that the transaction covered by this escrow is not in violation of the Subdivision Map Act or any law regulating land division, zoning ordinances or building restrictions which may affect the land or improvement that are the subject of this escrow. You, as escrow holder, are relieved of all responsibility and liability in connection with such laws, ordinances, restrictions or regulations and are not to be concerned with any of their enforcement.

Earlier, Chapters 4 and 5 discussed title insurance for residential sales or refinance coverage. Figure 15.1 explains typical words used in title insurance policy coverage for new construction when a contractor handles development of new tract homes offered for sale to the public. The civil code indemnity agreement, loss of priority, and effect on trust deed lenders are defined, along with the legal terms off-site work and on-site work. Sample construction loan title insurance policy coverage packages follow the new construction definition of terms. Four basic types of construction loan title insurance packages are most requested by construction lenders: the LP-9 shown in Figure 15.2, the LP-10 shown in Figure 15.3, and the LP-3 and LP-4 shown in Figure 15.4.

There are many and varied reasons for a lender's preference of one package over another, such as access assurance, existing improvements or not, etc., so that it's basically up to the discretion of the lenders as to which type of construction loan insurance package they require.

FIGURE 15.1

Explanation of New Construction Indemnities

NEW CONSTRUCTION INDEMNITIES

AN INDEMNITY AGREEMENT

An Indemnity Agreement, as defined in California Civil Code Section 2772, is as follows:

> "A contract by which one engages to save another from legal consequence of the conduct of one of the parties or of some other person."

In a construction loan situation, an Indemnity Agreement, simply stated, is an agreement whereby the owner, general contractor, or both, indemnify the title company against loss from mechanics' liens having priority over the construction of improvements prior to the recordation of the security instrument.

WHAT IS A LOSS OF PRIORITY?

A loss of priority is any work of improvement commenced on a construction site prior to the recordation of the lender's construction Deed of Trust.

WHAT EFFECT DOES THE INDEMNITY HAVE ON THE LENDER'S DEED OF TRUST?

The Indemnity Agreement is a separate agreement between the borrower, general contractor, or both, and the title company. This agreement does not involve the lender or trustee of the Deed of Trust. Approval of the Indemnity Agreement by the title company enables the title company to issue mechanic's lien risk insurance to the construction lender.

Issuance of mechanic's lien risk insurance is considered by title companies to be a very high-risk area, particularly where there is a loss of priority. Because of the added risk, title companies make a thorough investigation of the construction project before making any decisions on the issuance of mechanic's lien risk insurance. To help the title insurance company make this decision, the following items are needed for evaluation of their risk exposure:

Indemnity Agreement/Loss of Priority

1. Indemnity Agreement properly executed.
2. Current financial statements from all indemnitors.
3. Cost breakdown of the construction project.
4. Information as to how the loan is structured and disbursements safeguarded.
5. Current preliminary title report.

FIGURE 15.1

Explanation of New Construction Indemnities (Continued)

LEGAL DEFINITION OF LOSS OF PRIORITY

OFF-SITE WORK

In general, off-site work includes architectural project layout, demolition, grading, streets, curbs and gutters, street lighting systems, etc. If that work is financed by a loan secured by a deed of trust recorded prior to commencement of the work, which loan was given for the sole or primary purpose of financing such improvements, liens have priority over the deed of trust unless the loan proceeds are controlled in the manner set forth in C.C.3137. However, if the improvements are financed out of an overall construction loan or out of the developer's own funds the question of priority depends upon the date of commencement of the work.

ON-SITE WORK

On-site work refers to the actual structure. There is some overlap in that grading can be either on-site or off-site work, in the case of the building up of the pad on which the structure will be set. The important point to remember is that as to on-site work the deed of trust will have priority over the mechanic's lien if no work was started or materials delivered to the job site prior to the recordation of the construction loan.

If the land has been in any way disturbed, it must be assumed that there is a loss of priority. For instance, the installation of a utility pole bringing in electrical and telephone lines to the job site for later hook-up to the job office is the start of work. Holes may have been dug or drilled to obtain core samples for the architect or the engineer. An engineer may have staked the property or put in corner monuments in preparation for the work. That is generally sufficient. There may have been preliminary grading. That could be enough. A load of lumber may have been placed upon the site. That is sufficient. In short, the property must be completely untouched in order to have priority. There may be some slight variation, such as in the case of demolition of existing buildings and cleaning of the site which may not necessarily mean the start of work of improvements, but each of these exceptions must be individually ruled upon.

To provide the best protection to the lender on the property of the insured Deed of Trust, title companies prefer that no work be commenced on the project until after the construction Deed of Trust has been recorded. If an owner feels that he must commence work prior to recordation of the Deed of Trust, it is essential that he first consult with the title company in order to obtain an approval for the issuance of mechanic's lien risk insurance.

When the project has been completed and the Notice of Completion has been recorded, many owners and contractors request that retention funds held by the lender be released prior to the expiration of the statutory lien period. Before the lender will disburse these funds it will usually require the title company to issue an ALTA rewrite policy or issue some form of mechanic's lien endorsement. Before the title company can issue this type of insurance, there must be an approved Indemnity Agreement and the insurer must be satisfied that all bills for labor and material have been paid or that there are sufficient funds in the loan account to pay any remaining construction invoices.

FIGURE 15.2

The LP-9 Package and Commentary Explanation

THE LP-9 PACKAGE

TIME/EVENT	POLICIES, INSPECTIONS, ETC
(1) Trust Deed Records	(Priority Inspection) (CLTA Loan Policy)
Construction in Progress **(2)**	(Quite often the title company is asked) (to issue a Foundation endorsement,) (in which case the title company) (would need to make a "Foundation) (Inspection." This is not, however,) (part of the construction loan) (insurance package.)
Completion of Project (Notice of Completion) **(3)**	(ALTA Inspection) (ALTA Loan Policy with) (100 and 116 Endorsements)

Note: Provided construction is not in progress (Loss of Priority), otherwise it would require indemnities, etc.

Commentary for LP-9 Package

1. Immediately prior to the recording of the "construction" deed of trust, a "priority inspection" is made to ascertain that construction has not begun (not even by one minute) prior to said trust deed recording.

   At that time, provided construction is not in progress, the initial policy of the LP-9 package is issued—a CLTA Loan Policy (insuring the validity, etc., of said trust deed), together with an endorsement concerning priority of the insured trust deed over later recorded mechanics' liens ("priority insurance"). If, by "priority inspection," it is determined that construction has started prior to recordation of the "construction" trust deed ("loss of priority"), the title insurance company would immediately notify the construction lender by phone that construction has started and priority of its pending construction loan has been lost and that the title insurance company, therefore, would be unable to issue said policy until the situation has been resolved, e.g., by indemnity agreement, cessation of labor, etc.

2. Quite often, between the time the trust deed records and the time the project is completed, we are asked to issue an assurance (by endorsement) concerning the location, etc., of the foundation of the improvement.

3. When the project is completed, the title insurance company generally receives a notice of completion for recording and a request for the final policy of the LP-9 package. The title company is then to "date the file down" and make an "ALTA inspection." Once this is accomplished, the title insurance company will convert (thus the term "ALTA conversion") the initial policy (CLTA Loan Policy) into an ALTA Loan Policy (insuring the subject trust deed) as of a later date endorsement.

FIGURE 15.3

The LP-10 Package and Commentary Explanation

THE LP-10 PACKAGE

	TIME/EVENT	POLICIES, INSPECTIONS, ETC
(1)	Prior to Recording	Prestart Inspection
(2)	Trust Deed Records	(Priority Inspection) (ALTA Loan Policy) (with no endorsements)
(3)	Construction in Progress	(The title company may be asked to issue) (a foundation endorsement. The title) (insurance company would need to) (make a "Foundation Inspection.") (This is not, however, part of the) (construction loan insurance package.)
(4)	Completion of Project (Notice of Completion)	(ALTA Inspection) (ALTA Loan Policy with) (100 and 116 Endorsements)

Note: Provided construction is not in progress (Loss of Priority), otherwise it would require
   indemnities.

Commentary for LP-10 Package

1. Because the initial policy in the LP-10 construction loan insurance package is an ALTA Loan Policy, and since the ALTA Loan Policy is an extended coverage policy (containing affirmative assurances relating to access, certain off-record matters, etc.), prior to the recordation of the "construction" deed of trust, and usually prior to the writing of the preliminary title report, the title insurance company makes a "prestart inspection" to determine if any condition exists "on ground" which would prohibit the title insurance company from issuing the requested policy.

2. Then, on the morning of recording of the "construction" deed of trust the title company makes another inspection, only this time it's a "priority inspection" to ascertain that construction has not begun (not even by one minute) prior to said deed of trust recording.

3. At that time provided construction is not in progress, the title company issues the initial policy of the LP-10 package—an ALTA Loan Policy (insuring the validity, etc., of said deed of trust), but with no endorsement. The ALTA Loan Policy format contains an assurance concerning priority of the insured trust deed over later recorded mechanics' liens ("priority insurance"). If, by "priority inspection," the title company determines that construction has started prior to recordation of the "construction" trust deed ("loss of priority"), the title company will immediately notify the construction lender by phone that construction had started, priority of their pending construction loan had been lost, and that the title company therefore would be unable to issue said policy until the situation had been resolved, e.g., by indemnity agreement, etc.

FIGURE 15.3

The LP-10 Package and Commentary Explanation (Continued)

4. Between the time the trust deed records and the time the project is completed, the title company is asked to issue an assurance (by endorsement) concerning the location, etc., of the foundation of the improvement (102 series endorsement).

When the project is completed, the title company generally receives a Notice of Completion for recording and a request for the final policy of the LP-10 package. The title company will "date the file down" and make an "ALTA inspection." Once this is accomplished, the title company will reissue (thus the term "ALTA rewrite") the initial policy (ALTA Loan Policy) as of a later date, together with a 100 and 116 endorsement.

The basic difference, but not the only differences, between the LP-9 and the LP-10 packages lies in the type of policy initially issued (when the "construction" trust deed records) because the final policy in either case is essentially the same endorsement.

The basic difference between the LP-3 and the LP-4 packages lies also in the type of policy issued when the "construction" trust deed records. In addition, neither the LP-3 nor the LP-4 requires any further policy to be issued while, as mentioned above, the LP-9 and the LP-10 packages both require that a final policy be issued.

Several construction notices may appear on the title search or may be presented to the escrow for recordation during a transaction. The Notice of Nonresponsibility form as shown in Figure 15.5 is not used for most sale escrows, but it is often used when an owner buys a larger parcel of land, then obtains lot splits, and hires a contractor to build a spec (speculation) home for resale. When the property owner finds the subsequent buyer and enters escrow with that buyer, the property owner might request that the Notice of Nonresponsibility be used when that buyer uses the property owner's contractor to make additional improvements. For example, on a residential property, the owner has the home finished, and the parties agree on a sales price. Then, the buyer wants the seller's contractor to complete the front and back yard landscaping, including sprinklers, planters, and a cement lawn curb. In this case the form might be used to protect any potential lien that would be placed on the property if for any reason the contractor did not get paid.

The most common use of the Notice of Nonresponsibility is for nonresidential property. In most commercial properties, the occupant is not the property owner. The owner leases the premises to some owner of a business. When the business owner needs to make changes, alterations, or repairs to the premises, the business

FIGURE 15.4

The LP-3 and LP-4 Packages and Commentary Explanation

THE LP-3 PACKAGE

TIME/EVENT	POLICIES, INSPECTIONS, ETC
Prior to Recording	Prestart Inspection
Trust Deed Records	(Priority Inspection) (ALTA Loan Policy*) (with no endorsements)

THE LP-4 PACKAGE

TIME/EVENT	POLICIES, INSPECTIONS, ETC
Trust Deed Records	(Priority Inspection) (CLTA Loan Policy) (with 101 endorsements*)

* Provided construction is not in progress (Loss of Priority)—otherwise we would require indemnities, etc.

Commentary for LP-3 and LP-4 Packages

Many times (especially on very expensive projects) a lender is willing to loan money for construction purposes (for a relatively short period of time), but the lender does not want its money "tied up" for a lengthy period of time.

Another lender, e.g., an insurance company, may be willing to loan money for a longer period of time but may not want to become involved in the construction portion of the project. In these instances the initial lender would loan the money to finance the construction phase, and then, when the project is completed, the owner borrows money from another lender (for a long term) to pay off the construction lender. The construction lender's trust deed would be reconveyed, and the new ("take out') money would be secured by a new deed of trust.

In this type of situation, the lender would often only require an LP-3 or an LP-4 construction loan insurance package.

The LP-3 package is identical to the initial steps and issuance of the LP-10 package but this is as far as it goes. There is no ALTA rewrite in this package.

The LP-4 package is identical to the initial steps and issuance of the LP-9 package, but this is as far as it goes. There is no ALTA conversion in this package.

FIGURE 15.5

Notice of Nonresponsibility

RECORDING REQUESTED BY
First City Title Company

**AND WHEN RECORDED MAIL
THIS DEED AND**
UNLESS OTHERWISE SHOWN BELOW MAIL TAX
STATEMENTS TO
Name
Address
City & State
Zip
Title Order No.   Title No.

Book
Page
File No.

Recorded on
_____at _____
Official Records
County of _____, California
Conny B. McCormack
Registrar-Recorder/County Clerk

Fee
_____
$5

SPACE ABOVE THIS LINE FOR RECORDER'S USE

NOTICE OF NONRESPONSIBILITY

TO ALL WHOM IT MAY CONCERN: NOTICE IS HEREBY GIVEN:

(1) That _____, to wit, _____(am-are) the
          (I-we)   (Insert name or names)
_____ of certain
                    (Insert herein the nature of title or interest)
property located in the City of _____, County of _____, State of California,
and more particularly described as; Lot_____ in Block _____Tract No._____ as, per map recorded
in Book _____, Page _____ of _____. Records of County, State of California.

(2) That _____have obtained knowledge that _____(I-we)
                        (Insert brief description of improvements, repair or alteration)
_____
  on said property (in the course of construction –are being made).

(3) That ten (10) days have not elapsed since _____ obtained this knowledge.

(4) That _____ (I-we) will not be responsible for the _____
(erection, alteration or repaid) _____ of said
_____ (building-improvement) or for the material or labor used
or to be used thereon, or which has been performed, furnished or used in any manner or way
upon said land, or upon the _____ (building-improvement) thereon, or addition thereto,
or for the services of any architect.

(5) That _____ _____ the
                    (Insert name or names)   (is-are)
purchaser ___ of said property under a contract of purchase.

(6) That the street address of said property is_____, City of
_____, California, and that _____ _____
                                    (Insert name or names)   (is-are)
the lessee___ of said property.

Dated:_____   _____

                                        _____

State Of California
County of _____

_____being first duly sworn, deposes and says: That the above and within notice is
a true and correct copy of a notice posted in a conspicuous place on Lot _____ of Tract No. _____, in the City of
_____, County of _____, State of California on the ____ day of _____, 20 ____ by
_____and that the facts stated therein are true of _____ own knowledge, and that
_____ is making this affidavit for and on behalf of the person___ for whose protection said notice was given

                                        _____

Subscribed and sworn to before me this _____day of _____, 20____.

FOR NOTARY SEAL OR STAMP

_____
Notary Public in and for said County and State

owner hires a contractor or workers to make the improvements. These workers, if unpaid, could file a lien on the property if unpaid. The owner of the premises wants to protect himself or herself against such an action. A commercial lease usually always indicates that the tenant may not make any tenant improvements, even at tenant expense, without the written permission of the owner. The owner may require permits from the city, additional insurance coverage, and a bond for completion of the work. The purpose of the notice, however, is to notify the property owner of work that will be performed so that the owner can post the Notice of Nonresponsibility on the premises to notify all persons that the property owner is not going to pay for any work should the person who hired the workman not pay for the work. This is strictly a protection against mechanics' liens.

Another document that may be seen in an escrow involving construction or a contractor is the Notice of Cessation form as shown in Figure 15.6. A property owner may have had new construction performed on the premises with an independent contractor. A property owner may have had some type of remodel or alteration performed on the property as part of the sale. In nonresidential properties, it is often part of the negotiations to include such property alterations in a sale, or as part of a long-term lease, a lease-to-own situation, or in a build-to-suit transaction. The subsequent owner or tenant may have the seller or landlord pay for work to alter the property. The new business owner may ask the seller or landlord to pay for the improvements and allow payments over a period of time. Many sellers or landlords agree because the interest rate for such a loan is usually good and because the premises are being updated and improved so that in case of future default on this loan, the asset collateral is improved.

The Notice of Cessation form is used when work is stopped and the contractor is no longer approved for any future work or expenses on the premises. The tenant or new owner might post this notice, and the seller or landlord might also have this form recorded to give the world constructive notice that work has stopped. The date for work stoppage prevents mechanic's lien issues, and the title insurance company is always concerned about the date work began on the premises, more than the date work finished. Special insurance clauses and a physical inspection may be part of the transaction.

■ OFFICE BUILDINGS

Like apartment buildings, office buildings generate income. The commercial tenant, unlike the residential tenant, usually has greater responsibility and liability for the premises. The escrow for an office building will reflect the differences.

FIGURE 15.6

Notice of Cessation

RECORDING REQUESTED BY

AND WHEN RECORDED
MAIL THIS DEED AND
UNLESS OTHER WISE SHOWN BELOW MAIL TAX
STATEMENTS TO
Name
Address
City & State
APN/AIN #

Book
Page
File No.

Recorded on
_____at _____
Official Records
County of _____, California
Conny B. McCormack
Registrar-recorder/County Clerk

Fees:
$ ____
B.

SPACE ABOVE THIS LINE FOR RECORDER'S USE

NOTICE OF CESSATION - INDIVIDUAL

BE IT KNOW THAT:

Ivan Gonzales, Trustee for the Gonzales Family Trust dated July 1, 1988, owner/agent upon being duly sworn, states upon oath the following in reference to this Notice of Cessation:

1.   The date on or about when the cessation of labor commenced was the 29th day of August, 2003 as per a fax received from Alex Con Smith (310) 555-1212 @ 8:10 am.

2.   Such cessation has continued until the recording to this Notice of Cessation.

3.   The name and address of the owner is Ivan C. Gonzales, the address is 123 Elm Street, Coastal Inlet, CA 99999.

4.   The nature of the interest or estate of the owner is Trustee for 100% ownership for the Gonzales Family Trust dated July 1, 1988.

5.   A description of the site sufficient for identification, containing the address of the site, if any, is: 123 Elm Street, Coastal Inlet, CA 99999.

6.   A legal description of the property is: Parcel # 4444-014-014, according to Tract #336, Block 6 Lot 25.

7.   The name of the original contractor for the work of improvement as a whole is as follows:
Taylor Smith and Alex Con Smith, California Contractors license #40960, 1715 W. 220th St., Coastal Inlet, CA. 99999 (310) 555-1213 Class B-General Building Contractor Cert: HIC
Alex Con Smith, Contractor representative of A. H, Building P O Box 4782, Coastal Inlet, CA 99999 (310)555-1212 American Contractors Indemnity Company Contractors Bond # 16111 $50,000.00.
This the 29th day of August, 2003.

_____
Ivan C. Gonzales, Trustee

STATE OF CALIFORNIA
COUNTY OF LOS ANGELES
I, Ivan C. Gonzales, Trustee, of the Grogan Family Trust dated July 20, 1989, declare under
penalty of perjury under the laws of the State of California, that I have read the above Bonded
Stop Notice, and I know it is true of my own knowledge, except as to those things stated upon information and belief, and as to those I believe it to be true.
Executed on this the 29th day of August 2002, at Coastal Inlet, California.

_____
Ivan C. Gonzales, Trustee

Sworn to and subscribed before me, this 29th day of August, 2003

_____
Notary Public

My Commission Expires:_____

The office building escrow will require the seller to furnish the borrower the same type of information that a buyer of an apartment building would require, such as the following:

- Copies of the rental agreements/leases, showing the following:
  - Name of occupants, address, contact information
  - Business name, corporate headquarters, locations of the firm
  - Tax identification or Social Security number
  - Length of term of the lease
  - Type of business and environmental issues concerning the business operation
  - Insurance policies for each tenant, coinsurance naming landlord/property owner(s)
  - Amount of current rent and amount paid above rent for other itemized items, such as common area, utilities, maintenance, etc.
  - Rent increase schedule, escalation clause, method/index used for rent raise
  - Payment history of all existing tenants
  - Record of any violations, citations, legal action regarding any tenant
- Profit and loss statements
- Any written change in terms of tenancy
- Itemized list of all tenant deposits
- Description of concessions given to each tenant
- Written limitation on liability for hazardous materials, attractive nuisance, or similar
- Sign restrictions
- Noncompetitive covenant clause between businesses
- Tenant association documents
- Past and current maintenance records, employees, independent crews
- Vendor contracts, such as vending machines, gardener, glass cleaner, holiday decorating
- Parking history, assignments, present condition information

The common areas of an office building are usually under the supervision of a building owner for maintenance of any elevator or escalator system, lobby and premises security patrol, and restrooms for the public and for employees of the tenants. Any equipment, furniture, and fixtures being transferred will be written into the escrow instructions as well as the purchase agreement. The escrow officer will need to prepare documents to transfer ownership of personal property.

An escrow for a large office building could involve the transfer of the following kinds of **personal property** that are part of the assets of the property: patrol vehicles for security staff; radio communications system between lobby desk and security officers; couches and furniture, including lamps and tables in employee lounge areas as well as the lobby area; and some office furnishings such as desks, tables, and even large plant arrangements.

■ COMMERCIAL PROPERTIES

The **commercial property escrow** is primarily interested in retail business. Many lenders require various special policies depending upon the type of property that is acting as security for the loan. For example, a mandatory special insurance premium for plate glass coverage is prorated and collected by the escrow officer through escrow.

The escrow instructions for a commercial retail property would include many of the same phrases, clauses, and forms that have previously been discussed for the standard residential transaction. The following list is typical for the commercial transaction, and only new or different items are explained in detail:

- Sale escrow instructions naming the parties, consideration, legal description, terms of the transaction.

- Instructions to Escrow:
  - Buyer and property to qualify for new loan.
  - Appraisal contingency.
  - Closing costs are to be paid as allocated in the instructions.
  - Preliminary title report.
  - Fire insurance.
  - Preliminary change of ownership report (PCOR).
  - Notary fees.
  - Zone disclosure.
  - Facsimile transmittals.
  - Miscellaneous charges.
  - Good funds disclosure.
  - Supplemental tax information.

- IRS 1099-S reporting disclosure.
- Liquidated damages.

■ Additional escrow instructions and provisions:

- Escrow holder has no obligation to verify any signatures of any of the parties involved.
- Assignment of insurance policy.
- Escrow is not responsible in any way for any personal property tax.
- Escrow may deposit any authorized funds in connection with closing.
- The parties are to satisfy themselves, outside of escrow, of any violations from any sources and with any enforcements.
- The purchase agreement is effective only between the parties signing the purchase agreement and not of any concern to the escrow holder.
- Escrow is not responsible for any physical inspection of real or personal property.
- All parties authorize escrow to record and deliver instruments.
- Escrow is authorized to insert dates on documents and instruments.
- Escrow is to conduct no lien or title search of personal property.
- Escrow is not concerned with the usury law for any loan or encumbrance.
- The parties to the escrow agree to deliver all documents and funds to close the escrow according to the terms of the escrow.
- Escrow is to provide title to subject property.
- Escrow is not concerned with any terms of any new loan or loan documents.
- The parties are to furnish escrow with the information necessary to comply with the Federal Tax Reform Act and the California Revenue and Taxation Code, and the Internal Revenue Service and the California State Franchise Tax Board.
- The parties agree that escrow is responsible as an escrow holder only and is not a party to the transaction and has no legal relationship with any party.
- Escrow is instructed to comply with the Change of Ownership form.
- All parties acknowledge that escrow has the absolute right to withhold and stop all proceedings when any controversy or conflict arises until escrow receives written notice of the settlement of the issue.
- All notices, demands, and instructions must be in writing to escrow.
- If escrow is not closed within 90 days, the parties authorize escrow to withhold $50 per month from funds on deposit until all funds are

disbursed, and then escrow is instructed to automatically cancel the escrow.

- Escrow holder shall terminate six months from the set date for close of escrow to interplead according to a valid court of competent jurisdiction.

- Escrow holder is to notify the parties of any dishonored check or precarious matters made to escrow.

- All parties agree to release escrow from all liability of any kind or nature and to indemnify escrow from any loss, damages, claims, judgments, or costs of any kind or nature resulting from or related to the release or discharge of hazardous or toxic wastes on the subject property whether in the past, the present, or that may occur in the future.

- Escrow is instructed to destroy all documents after five years from close of escrow or date of cancellations or date of last activity.

- Agency confirmation.

- Condition of the property.

- Fixtures.

- Walk-through inspection.

- Possession and keys.

- Transfer Disclosure Statement (TDS).

- Smoke detectors.

- CAL-FIRPTA (Chapter 12)

   From seller's proceeds, withhold 3⅓ percent of the gross sales price, under California Revenue and Taxation Code, Section 18662 and 18668.

   Escrow and buyer are to contact the Franchise Tax Board "withholding at source unit."

- End of Memorandum Items:

  - Prorations are to be as of close of escrow.

  - Seller authorizes escrow to pay the documentary transfer tax required for any deed.

  - Seller authorizes escrow to pay brokerage and loan commissions on separate instructions.

- CAL-FIRPTA Notice and Disclosure (Chapter 12).

Another common event in the sale of commercial property is an escrow that deals with some type of franchise operation. The franchise may be a retail chain of restaurants, insurance or real estate office, or even the corporate offices for industrial-type property, as discussed in the next section. In these cases, the escrow often instructs the escrow officer to obtain a release from the franchisor so that the buyer of the business does not carry over any debt or obligation from the seller.

■ INDUSTRIAL PROPERTIES

The escrow for an **industrial property** may involve only raw land, may involve the long-term lease of land with the tenant constructing the building improvement, or may involve both the building improvement and the land. The leasing and development of industrial-zoned property requires knowledge of land sales, **inventory**, and environmental issues.

Because the principals involved in an escrow involving industrial property are often interested in the various tax aspects of the transaction, the timing of the escrow process is critical to the transaction. To effect an **IRC 1031 tax exchange,** the escrow officer must be very cognizant if the intent of the principals is to close the escrow for tax purposes. If the closing of the escrow is tax driven and the principal loses the tax benefit for any reason, it is highly likely that the escrow will not close. Even though the escrow officer is not liable for any of the tax ramifications for the principals, the escrow officer is responsible for trying to meet the obligations as instructed in the escrow instructions, which often include meeting specific deadlines to benefit the principal for tax purposes.

The various commercial or industrial franchises often become a part of the escrow that must be handled prior to the close of escrow. As an example, for a gas station franchise, the law requires that all the subground tanks meet new environmental guidelines to prevent future tank leakage. Enforcement of the gasoline tank requirements has caused some gas stations to be sold because the existing owner did not have the revenue to meet the new guidelines. The cost to dig up the old tanks, remove the contaminated soil, replace surrounding soil with uncontaminated dirt, and install the newly approved, very expensive sealed tanks is often more than some gas station businesses can afford. This caused many industrial escrows to be opened for the change of ownership of these gas stations. Because some of these properties were not sold for future gas station usage, only the seller was involved in environmental releases for the escrow. Some properties were upgraded and continued as gas stations. The new pumps used in them are predominantly digital and tied to inventory control, and the new pump systems monitor contamination under the ground and gas fume escape at the pump. Due to the legal enforcement surrounding gas stations, different types of environmental safety systems became available for any gas station that remained in operation for that purpose.

Besides environmental safety considerations, the escrow holder must be familiar with three different franchise options. The first franchise option signifies that the major oil company owns and controls the real estate on which the station is located and the individual only leases the facility from the dealer. The dealer pays monthly rent to the oil company to operate the facility. Rents vary from site to site. Each dealer is an independent business operator and must abide by the franchise company's formal written contract, termed the "Franchise Agreement and Lease Terms." Should the buyer of the property be a major oil company, then the seller would have to agree to allow the buyer to inspect the premises for planning for the new franchise ownership. The buyer would request specific terms in the escrow instructions that would comply with the franchise operation.

The second franchise option is when the individual "owns." The individual leases or buys the land and the station from a third party and has only a Motor Fuel Agreement with the oil company. The escrow instructions would remain the same for the transfer of the land, and the transfer of ownership for the building would be handled the same as any other commercial property transfer for improvements. In this type of escrow it is not uncommon for the buyer to state that the entire transaction is contingent upon approval by the franchisor and therefore the escrow officer would become involved in checking to see if the buyer has obtained the approval required to close the escrow.

The third franchise option could also involve construction. The escrow may involve the purchase of the land, with either no improvements on the land or where improvements will be removed by demolition. The escrow will include the land purchase and the new construction on the site. The oil company normally assists the buyer with determining whether the site is viable for motor fuel operations and helps the buyer to obtain the required permits and approvals. The escrow usually will refer to the escrow being contingent upon obtaining city approval for construction on the site. The oil company, in these cases, already has a department that has model station layouts with ingress and egress paths, engineering designs, and financing of the construction with competitive options.

Another option is to add a convenience store operation in conjunction with the gas station operation. The new construction or purchase of an existing convenience store operation would have many items involved in the escrow including bulk sales, inventory, and fixtures. In general, for all three options, many of the following are requirements for the gas station operation that are often spelled out within the escrow instructions:

- City planning department inspection and approval for the business operation:
  - Trash and disposal approval
  - Lighting and reflectors, neighborhood glare

- Sign ordinance compliance
- Six-foot wall between subject property and adjacent residential property
- Planted area and landscaping approval (minimum 5 percent of surface site)
- Public telephone visible from the street with 24-hour access
- Conditional use permit, if necessary; no paint, body/fender repair, tire work on the premises as part of the approval process
- Air and water facility available to the public at no cost

■ Fire department and fire prevention division approval for the underground tanks:
- Distance from property line and foundation
- Depth of excavation (minimum two feet)
- Surrounding material in which tanks are set and material covering, including surface
- Corrosion protection stipulations
- Piping
- Annual testing of tanks

■ Payment of all federal, state, city, or other local tank fees

■ Registration with the State Board of Equalization—Fuel Taxes Division in Sacramento

■ AGRICULTURAL PROPERTY

The real estate licensee who handles farms, vineyards, groves, and such has to be able to handle both the farmer owning 20 to 160 acres but also capable of successful negotiations with the international or domestic agribusiness corporations that handle today's agricultural brokerage. Two key elements increase the successful agricultural broker operations: (1) a college degree in some area of agriculture and (2) actual working experience in the field in which the broker specializes. The field of agricultural property brokerage involves having a working knowledge of soil conditions, water rights, crop yield, machinery, and government subsidy programs as well as tax laws.

Few escrow officers statewide specialize in agricultural escrows. Often the agricultural broker will begin by working with one particular escrow officer so that an ongoing relationship builds for both. The broker often trains the escrow officer in not only the style of escrow operation that the broker prefers but in the many disclosures that relate specifically to agricultural lands, such as fertilizer, landslide, and flooding.

Often the escrow officer who handles agricultural property works with many government agencies. Many farmlands are on government-owned, leased land. The federal government lands are handled through the Forest Service, the Park Service, the Department of Agriculture, the Army Corps of Engineers, and the Bureau of Land Management. The state level has similar agencies that often require their approval prior to the close of escrow, such as the Coastal Commission. The land in California around airports, navigable waterways, the California desert, and areas around Yosemite, and Lake Tahoe all involve farms, grazing land, crops, timber, and other resources.

The agricultural broker may work with urban planners and governments to slow the growth of urban development to retain as much dairy, farmlands, deserts, and forests as possible. The escrow officer would need a working knowledge not only of the agricultural business but also of landlord-tenant rights and responsibilities for the long-term lease for agricultural use. The escrow will most likely call for a survey showing physical boundaries for hazard, flood, crop, and title insurance purposes. In addition, if government financing is used, such as through a program administered by the **Farmer's Home Administration (FmHA)** or similar agency, detailed paperwork is always involved.

The **emblements,** which are the growing crops, are considered personal property and require special wording in the escrow to preserve the rights of the owner of the annual, harvestable crop. The trees on which fruit crops grow are **real property** because they have roots connected to the ground. The escrow may involve the owner of the real property, the trees; the owner of the leasehold interest in the emblements, the annual crops; and a developer who plans to build on the land. In some instances, the value of the crop exceeds the value of the raw land.

■ UNDEVELOPED LAND

The value of raw land may be the current use of the land, the future use of the land, or the value of off-site amenities that go with the land. The current crop or dairy yield may be sufficient to support a buyer seeking the property for the current use. This type of value is discussed under agricultural property.

Some land may be rezoned or is in the process of being redeveloped so that the future value of the undeveloped land may substantially increase. Individuals who work with undeveloped lands often work with city planning, and this requires an understanding of variances, spot zoning, conditional-use, a buffer zone, watershed plains. All parties to the transaction require knowledge of the terms used as the standard language for an escrow involving undeveloped land. Often these escrows are based on speculation and not on current value. A buyer may pay more than the property is worth in anticipation of future increased value.

Individuals handle the majority of purchases of undeveloped property, such as desert land, where the owner carries the loan. Because conventional loan financing is virtually nonexistent for this type, the entire transaction is often an all-cash transaction, if the seller does not finance the subject property. The purchaser often buys the property with the intent of subdividing the property into smaller lots. Because the local government agencies may not agree with the splits and local buyers may not be interested in purchasing smaller lots, demand may be low.

Undeveloped land in California is predominantly either flat lands or hillside lands. The flat lands are those with a slope of 5 percent or less and are considered the most desirable for both agriculture and for building improvement. Because both progrowth and antidevelopment groups seek the land, proposed changes to existing use often can create conflict. The cost to build is less for flat lands. Hillside property has complex issues such as foundation supports, anchoring into loose soil, drainage, and frequently unusable portions of the land, such as bluffs or cliffs. A property view may offset the extra cost to build the more complex building requirements that accompany hillside development property.

The typical issues that will become part of the escrow disclosures are often part of the paperwork inside or outside the escrow. The following is a list of typical disclosures involved with vacant investment property escrows:

- Geological survey to identify special requirements for soil percolation performed by certified engineer for earthquake, flood, and stability

- Flood zone as conducted by the federal emergency management agency (FEMA) that maps areas where flood insurance will be required

- Seismic zones and earthquake fault lines and special studies zone disclosure

The sale transfer of vacant land is similar to the single-family resident transaction, and it rarely involves a lender, so no pest control or hazard insurance is required. In escrow, taxes and special assessments are prorated as they are in any residential transaction. In 1997 the Torlakson-Kopp Bill became effective requiring expanded mandatory disclosures. As a result, the statutory Natural Hazard Disclosure Statement, effective June 1, 1998, is required. A common, but not legislated, disclosure is the Property Disclosure Report (PDR) generated by the title insurance company that is used in many land escrows.

The June 1 Act of 1938 reserves the government's right to mineral and oil rights upon private lands. The provision is described in the Act of Congress as reserved in the patent of June 1, 1938. The Act protects the right of an individual to cross property not otherwise accessible to get to "landlocked" property. Most access to undeveloped land is on unimproved roads for which the adjoining property owners are responsible. Easements are an important part of the escrow as are title insur-

	Real Estate	Bulk Sales
Parties	Seller/Buyer	Transferor/**Transferee**
Property	Real property	Personal business property
Instrument	Deed	Bill of Sale
Taxes	Real property taxes Documentary transfer tax City conveyance taxes	Personal property tax Sales tax Unemployment insurance tax
Title	Preliminary title report	Certificate of information
Search	Title insurance	UCC search
Lien	Trust deed Trust note	Security agreement Financing statement
Default	No Notice of Sale	Public Notice of Sale
Change	Recorded title	Bill of Sale—Not recorded
Lien Payoff	Recorded evidence in county where property is located	File Evidence of Lien in Sacramento or File termination or release
Document	Reconveyance Deed	UCC-2

ance facets that the principals desire as a result of having an escrow involving undeveloped land.

Escrow should be aware that an investor who wants to divide a parcel of land into lots for resale must comply with the California Subdivision Law regarding density, zoning, minimum lot sizes, and other items. An official plat map must be filed with the tax assessor's office. It is not unusual for a local water municipality to have a special Mello-Roos assessment for improvements. Other considerations that may be part of the escrow instructions might include vegetation and wildlife preservation, building requirements, zoning, and even an economic impact report for government officials.

FIGURE 15.7

Allocation of Bulk Sales Price

Inventory*	$ _____
Fixtures and Equipment	$ _____
Leasehold Improvements	$ _____
Goodwill[†]	$ _____
Covenant Not to Compete[‡]	$ _____
Liquor License	$ _____
Total Consideration	$ _____

* Inventory in stock

† Location, length of time in business

‡ Not to exceed 10 percent of the purchase price

■ BULK SALE

A **bulk sales transfer** is the sale of a business and the real property being transferred in bulk. Bulk sales transfer is defined and regulated by Division 6 of the California Uniform Commercial Code (UCC). The purpose of the law is to notify creditors who would be affected by certain bulk transfers. The transfer of a business does not require that an escrow holder handle the transaction, unless a liquor license is involved. Then, an escrow is required, as discussed in the next section. Because the purpose of the law is to protect creditors and the buyer of the business from commercial fraud, the experienced escrow officer would have escrow instructions that dictate avenues that would allow for the business transfer so as to not defraud creditors or the buyer of the business. The difference between a real estate transaction and a bulk sales transfer is shown in Table 15.1, and the allocation of bulk sales price is shown in Figure 15.7.

The escrow of the sale of a business commonly involves the buyer obtaining a loan for the personal property and the business operation. The loan is placed on the real and the personal property that is used to secure the loan through a Security Agreement and **Financing Statement**. This part of the transaction is regulated under Division 9 of the UCC.

Section 6102 of the California UCC defines a bulk sale as any transfer in bulk, and not in the ordinary course of the business, a substantial part of the materials, supplies, merchandise, or other inventory of an enterprise, including those who manufacture what they sell, or that of a baker, café, or restaurant owner, garage owner, or dry cleaner. Businesses that are exempt from the Section 6106 regulation are primarily service-oriented businesses, such as a beauty shop, laundromat, business school, or real estate office.

It is normal for escrow instructions to include a **covenant not to compete** agreement between the principals. The escrow officer often executes this document as part of the escrow. In some escrows, the written document is handled outside of escrow for which escrow is of no further concern regarding this matter. The covenant must restrict both the time limit period and the distance. Typical wording might include:

> The seller, John Jacques Jones, of JJ's Enterprises does covenant and promise not to compete in a same or similar business after the close of escrow of the above named business for a period of three years from the date of close of escrow within a three mile radius from the business location at 123 Grand Blvd., Any City, California.

When an escrow holder performs a bulk sales transfer, the consideration paid is not for any real property but is for the purchase of the personal property. No title insurance policy is required. Other types of government agency and property searches are usually requested by the parties. The escrow officer's checklist would include the following:

- County search: Doing Business As (DBA) search, pending litigation, real property records, and lien search

- State search: Uniform Commercial Code (UCC) 3 to determine seller debts secured by business equipment, accounts payable, or inventory

- Releases:
  - State Board of Equalization Sales and Use Tax certificate of payment
  - State of California Employment Development Dept. (EDD)—Benefit payments section and Unemployment Insurance
  - Notice to creditors of bulk sale (Sections 6104 and 6105 UCC)

■ LIQUOR LICENSE

An escrow is required when a liquor license is transferred. For any transfer of ownership involving the **Alcoholic Beverage Control (ABC),** the law is very specific about requiring an escrow. The escrow officer who specializes in this type of transaction must know that there are two types of liquor licenses. The first is the issuance of a new license, and the second is the transfer of ownership of an existing license.

The California Department of Alcoholic Beverage Control Section codes are as shown in the text box below.

ABC Code Sections

23001 Purpose of the Act

23049 Legislative Intent

24044 Remodel versus new construction

24070 Person to person; premises to premises; intercounty

Rule 64 Premises under construction

Rule 68 Transfer of general license

(Continued on next page)

| 24073 | Recording Notice of Intention |
| 24076 | Limited partnership application |

The California ABC issues a new license only where it can be shown that the population has increased enough to allow another license in that particular county and area. California allows new applications to be submitted only during a short period of time, which was between September 8 and 19 in 2003. For the 2002 application period that would issue a new liquor license for 2003, a total of 578 applications were filed with the ABC. The following year, September 2003 for the 2004 licenses, 792 applications were taken for new licenses. Should the escrow officer open an escrow that is contingent upon the purchaser of property obtaining a new liquor license, a high likelihood is that the escrow may not close because the number of licenses given is often less than the number who try to obtain an ABC-approved new license. The obtaining of a license is referred to as the **priority drawing.**

A priority drawing is held in the California counties where the demand exceeds the supply. In year 2002 only 7 counties held a priority drawing, while in year 2003 only 17 did so. In year 2004 the following counties held priority drawings to determine whether or not a new liquor license could be obtained: Butte, El Dorado, Fresno, Kings, Los Angeles, Madera, Nevada, Orange, Placer, Riverside, Sacramento, San Diego, San Luis Obispo, Santa Barbara, Sutter, Tulare, and Yolo. The following information gives the population required in California to support a general liquor license:

One on-sale general liquor license for every 2,000 people

One off-sale general liquor license for every 2,500 people

The ABC Act, Section 23985, requires a 30-day posting period for a liquor license. Each applicant must complete an ABC investigation that takes about 45 to 50 days, and then the law will not allow issuance of the license for a minimum of 30 days. Each license is on a 12-month renewal basis. Escrow should plan the calendar to incorporate the legal time line requirements. Each ABC licensee must possess a seller's permit from the sales tax division of the State Board of Equalization. It is a misdemeanor to sell without this permit. The collection and payment of liquor tax and sales tax is held to be critically important to the state revenue. At the federal level, the individual must obtain a basic permit and completed contract with the United States Treasury Department under the Bureau of Alcohol, Tobacco, and Firearms. Normally a local, city business license is required to conduct operations. Escrow would need to determine if the license is for an existing location or a license that was at a different location that is being moved to another location for the liquor license.

If the purchase of a retail business includes a liquor license, according to Sections 24071.1 through 24075 of the ABC Act, an escrow must be established with some person, corporation, or association that is not a party to the transfer. The full amount of the purchase price must be placed into escrow. Escrow agreements must provide for payment only after the transfer of the license is approved by the ABC, according to Section 24074.3. The law requires that within 30 days of application, the applicant furnish the ABC a statement of the purchase price that has been deposited with the escrow holder. The applicant must also submit a copy to the **transferor** and a copy to the escrow holder.

WEB LINK
@

At the time of filing the application for either the off-sale or on-sale general license, or the off-sale beer and wine license, or the on-sale beer and wine license, or the on-sale beer license, or the on-sale general license for seasonal business, the applicant must present a copy of the Notice of Intention to Transfer (form ABC-227 as seen in Figure 15.8). See Figure 15.9 for the California Department of Alcoholic Beverage Control (ABC) Web site at *http://www.abc.ca.gov* for information about liquor license applications in California. The purpose of a Notice of Intended Transfer is to allow outstanding creditors to take steps to protect their interests. This permits creditors to take legal steps to protect their own interest within the legal jurisdiction covering the debt obligation. The licensee and applicant must enter into an agreement directing the escrow holder to pay the claims of bona fide creditors, after any tax due is first paid.

Some of the items that must go on the form include the licensee's name(s), address of the premises, licensee's address, applicant's name, business location address, kind of license intended to be used, the entire cost of the transaction, and the total consideration paid for the business and for the license. An original on-sale and **off-sale general license** cannot transfer for two years from the site of origin. It also cannot be sold for more than $12,000 for two years following the date of issuance. Licenses transferred intercounty cannot transfer for two years and cannot sell for more than $10,000.

All escrow agents who handle the transfer of a liquor license must be licensed and incorporated for the purpose of conducting business as an escrow holder. Any escrow must remain open until the ABC approves the qualifications of the applicant and of the premises. The escrow holder must not release any funds in the escrow in exchange for a promissory note or in exchange for any other consideration of less value to the creditors than the funds exchanged. The only exception is when a guarantor is used; then an escrow is not required.

The ABC may refuse to transfer a license when the applicant or licensee owes money to the Board of Equalization for sales and use taxes. The escrow officer would obtain a written release from the agency prior to the close of escrow. The same is true for the Franchise Tax Board for income taxes, all applicable property

FIGURE 15.8

Notice of Intention to Transfer (Form ABC-227)

RECORDING REQUESTED BY

WHEN RECORDED MAIL TO:
NAME

MAILING ADDRESS   (Street number and name)

CITY   STATE   ZIP CODE

DO NOT WRITE IN THE SPACE ABOVE.   *Government Code*
Section 27361.6 reserves space above for exclusive use of County Recorder.

NOTICE OF INTENDED TRANSFER OF RETAIL ALCOHOLIC BEVERAGE LICENSE UNDER SECTIONS 24073 AND 24074 CALIFORNIA BUSINESS AND PROFESSIONS CODE
Read instructions before completing.

1. LICENSEE(S) NAME(S) *(Seller)*

2. PREMISES ADDRESS TO WHICH LICENSE(S) HAS/HAVE BEEN ISSUED

3. LICENSEE'S MAILING ADDRESS   *(If different)*

4. APPLICANT(S) NAME   *(Transferee or Buyer)*

5. PROPOSED BUSINESS ADDRESS *(If different than Item 2)*

6. MAILING ADDRESS OF APPLICANT

7. KIND OF LICENSE INTENDED TO BE TRANSFERRED

8. ESCROW HOLDER/GUARANTOR NAME

9. ESCROW HOLDER/GUARANTOR ADDRESS

10. TOTAL CONSIDERATION TO BE PAID FOR THE BUSINESS AND LICENSE; INCLUDING INVENTORY, WHETHER ACTUAL COST, ESTIMATED COST, OR A NOT-TO-EXCEED AMOUNT

CASH	$
CHECKS	
PROMISSORY NOTES	
TANGIBLE AND/OR INTANGIBLE PROPERTY	
TOTAL AMOUNT	$

The parties agree that the consideration for the transfer of the business and the license(s) is to be paid only after the Department of Alcoholic Beverage Control has approved the proposed transfer. The parties also agree and herein direct the above-named escrow holder to make payment or distribution within a reasonable time after the completion of the transfer of the license as provided in Section 24074 of the California Business and Professions Code.

LICENSEE'S SIGNATURE *(Transferor or Seller)*	DATE SIGNED
APPLICANT'S SIGNATURE *(Transferee or Buyer)*	DATE SIGNED

*One copy of this notice, **CERTIFIED** by the County Recorder, together with an additional copy must accompany the application for the transfer of the license.*

ABC-227 (8/99)   State of California, Department of Alcoholic Beverage Control

FIGURE 15.9

**Liquor License
Web Site**

Source: California Department of Alcoholic Beverage Control

taxes, and for the **Employment Development Department (EDD)** for employment taxes. Escrow is authorized to pay any taxing agency the money owed to that agency prior to the close of escrow and to obtain the release for such payment, according to Section 24049 of the Business & Professions Code (B&P).

If there is any purchase price or consideration in connection with the transfer of a business operated under a retail license, an escrow must be established with some person, corporation, or association not a party to the transfer before the filing of such transfer with the Department (B&P 24074) when a liquor license is transferred.

■ PERSONAL PROPERTY PLUS REAL PROPERTY

Often in the transfer of ownership of a business, both real and personal property are involved. The escrow officer would draw the deed to transfer the ownership to the real property and would also have to execute a bill of sale for ownership of the personal property. The **bill of sale** is given to the buyer after the close of escrow, just as the deed is mailed from the country recorder's office after closing and recordation.

In Chapter 11, real property taxes and assessments were explained. Personal property also is subject to taxes. All personal property taxes that appear on the secured tax roll are payable along with the first installment of the real property taxes, on or before December 10. All personal property taxes that appear on the unsecured tax roll are due on the tax lien date. Some local differences occur in California. For example, Section 1700 of the Revenue and Tax Code allows a local county to have its Board of Supervisors make a resolution to provide for the payment of personal property taxes to be treated in the same manner as the real property taxes. In other words, such a resolution would allow a one-half payment for the personal property tax to be made along with each of the two tax installments for real property taxes.

■ INTERNAL REVENUE CODE 1031 EXCHANGES AND ACCOMMODATORS

A 1031 tax-deferred exchange is important to an investor because it allows for the preservation of assets by allowing the property owner to exchange one investment property for a different investment property and be legally able to defer all the tax on the profit from the sale of the first property and postpone paying tax on that gain by bringing the gain into the second property. Naturally, upon the sale of the second property, the tax would be due on both the gain from the first and the gain from the second property. However, many investors keep rolling over the equity in a property perpetually during the life of the original owner. The investor continues to build wealth. Upon the demise of the original owner, any tax liability through inheritance will be limited to the gains from the date of the inheritor's acquisition, not during the years of ownership.

The basic steps are these: The taxpayer finds a buyer for the first property and sells it through a qualified intermediary, who is often an "accommodator." The taxpayer finds a replacement property and has the intermediary purchase that property. The intermediary then exchanges the two properties, selling the first property to a separate individual, and handling the exchange for the new property purchased. The typical exchange is a four-party exchange, involving three principals and one independent intermediary. The actual exchange includes the taxpayer, the buyer of the relinquished property, the seller of the replacement property, and the intermediary.

The intermediary acts as a clearing house for each property involved with the exchange. The intermediary acquires the **relinquished property** from the taxpayer, as per the exchange agreement, and then conveys that property to an outside buyer. To complete the exchange, the intermediary acquires the **replacement property** from an independent seller, then conveys that property to the taxpayer.

The intermediary receives the net proceeds from the buyer of the relinquished property, and the taxpayer receives a credit. The intermediary then uses the net proceeds to purchase the replacement property from the seller. To meet IRS 1031 requirements, escrow must see that the taxpayer does not receive either actual or even **constructive receipt** of the exchange proceeds.

The IRS rule for an exchange is that the exchange period begins on the day the relinquished property is transferred and ends on the earlier of 180 days (not six months—count the actual days) thereafter, or alternatively, the due date (including extensions) of the tax return for the taxable year in which the transfer of the relinquished property occurs.

In many exchange transactions, the escrow agent performs the relatively straightforward function of holding documents and funds to effect an exchange. The escrow agent works with the representatives of the exchangers to complete these tasks. However, sometimes the escrow officer must complete the entire exchange transaction without the help of a tax professional and without the aid of a tax attorney. The principals and the real estate agents rely heavily on the experienced escrow officer to structure the exchange to meet the tax requirements. The wording for a typical exchange escrow would be the same as or similar to the wording in the next text box:

> **Exchange Escrow Clause**
> The buyer agrees to cooperate with the exchanger in completing an exchange qualifying for nonrecognition of gain under Internal Revenue Code Section 1031 and the applicable provisions of the California Revenue and Taxation code. The **exchanger** reserves the right to convert this transaction to an exchange at any time before the closing date. The exchanger and the buyer agree, however, that consummation of the transaction contemplated by this agreement is not predicated or conditioned on completion of such an exchange. If the exchanger elects to complete an exchange, the buyer shall execute all escrow instructions, documents, agreements, or instruments reasonably requested by the exchanger to complete the exchange. The buyer shall incur no additional liabilities, expenses, or costs as a result of or connected with the exchange.

An **accommodator** is a company established to assist a taxpayer in qualifying for a tax-deferred exchange under the Internal Revenue Code Section 1031. The function of the accommodator is to act as the qualified intermediary in a real property exchange transaction. The actual 1031 code reads:

No gain or loss shall be recognized if property held for productive use in a trade or business or for investment (not including **stock in trade** or other property held primarily for sale) is exchanged for property of a like-kind to be held either for productive use in trade or business or investment . . .

THINK ABOUT IT

The owner of 80 acres in the unincorporated county area near Golf Cart City bought the lot as an investment for $50,000 with a barely livable, very old wooden house. After ten years of living on the property, it is now inside the city limits and the owner is approached by a developer with an offer for $1 million cash plus the "model" condominium unit free-and-clear to live in after all units are sold, including the unit upgrades, furnishings, and attached fixtures. The seller accepts the offer.

Escrow opens, and the preliminary title report is received by the buyer. The city council has zoned the area that includes the undeveloped land for one single-family detached home per acre. The developer calls escrow to cancel because the offer was contingent upon securing financing for the development of the condominium project.

Another developer opens escrow with the same seller on the same property with the same escrow company for $300,000.

What are the rights of the seller to sue the city for the loss of value?

Answer: A zoning ordinance is a legitimate exercise of a government's right to police power. The restriction on population density of an area is to reasonably protect the public health, welfare, and safety for sanitation, police, and fire protection and prevention, adequate schools, libraries, etc., and other infrastructure needs. The ordinance is nondiscriminatory since it applies to *all* property owners in the area. If the value is lowered too much, the property owner might sue the city for confiscation, but in this case even though the decrease in value is substantial, the seller is realizing a profit.

■ CHAPTER SUMMARY

The nonresidential escrow includes most of the procedures used for a residential escrow, such as the statement of information, the title search, and recordation of documents. This chapter discussed the title and document forms used for subdivisions that are handled and used for different circumstances. The office building, commercial, and industrial property escrow usually includes more detail on disclosures of hazardous materials and often includes governmental approvals for property use as part of the escrow. The agricultural and undeveloped land escrow often involves water rights and changing the use of the property. The escrow for a business opportunity involves the stock and trade of the business, and it often includes construction or improvement alterations. The bulk sales transfer of a business that involves any type of liquor license is required to have an escrow. When handling a business escrow, the escrow officer needs a clear understanding of the difference between personal property, which would involve the use of a bill of sale to transfer ownership, and real property, which uses a deed. The exchange can be a complicated transaction, or it may be a relatively simple escrow, depending upon the number of properties involved. In any case, the tax aspects of an IRC 1031 exchange are part of the clauses for such an escrow. The escrow officer may seek legal counsel for many types of escrows discussed in this chapter.

■ CHAPTER 15 QUIZ

1. To transfer ownership, the sale of personal property included in the sale of real property for a business would include a
   a. trust deed.
   b. grant deed.
   c. bill of sale.
   d. billing statement.

2. When transferring the interests in a business opportunity escrow, the escrow officer is instructed to obtain a release from the
   a. California Franchise Tax Board.
   b. Documentary Tax Board.
   c. City Transfer Tax Board.
   d. Environmental Impact Report Board.

3. Undeveloped land sales transactions often involve a clause in the escrow of the seller to give to the buyer a(n)
   a. transfer disclosure statement (TDS).
   b. property disclosure report (PDR).
   c. all-inclusive trust deed (AITD).
   d. alcoholic beverage board report.

4. Which transaction is required to have an escrow?
   a. Subdivision
   b. Office building
   c. Agricultural property
   d. Liquor license

5. The tax rules for an exchange can be found under section
   a. IRS 1021.
   b. IRS 1031.
   c. IRS 1041.
   d. IRS 1051.

6. When handling any type of escrow involving construction and development, the escrow officer should be aware that the title insurance company will usually require
   a. a warranty deed for the seller to guarantee the project.
   b. a guarantee deed for the buyer to gain special protection.
   c. special endorsements.
   d. mechanics' liens.

7. The escrow for an office building might include an escrow clause regarding
   a. pools.
   b. parking.
   c. subtenant audit.
   d. state license transfer.

8. The noncompetitive covenant *NOT* to compete in a same or similar business is most often a clause that would be part of which type of escrow?
   a. Subdivision
   b. Commercial property
   c. Undeveloped land
   d. Exchange

9. The sale of undeveloped land might frequently involve the
   a. California Franchise Tax Board.
   b. City Business License Transfer.
   c. Coastal Commission.
   d. sales tax and employee tax releases.

10. Which would probably *NOT* be involved in an escrow involving a bulk sales transfer?
    a. ABC
    b. DBA
    c. TDS
    d. UCC

ONLINE RESOURCES AND WEB LINKS

WEB LINK
@

The following documents can be found at the Dearborn Real Estate Education Web site at *www.dearbornRE.com* (click on the Instructor Resources link, then scroll down to the link entitled California Real Estate Escrow).

    Escrow Instructions for Northern California
    Escrow Instructions for Southern California
    Sample Loan Escrow Instructions
    Sample Preliminary Title Report

To access the California Escrow Law, which is part of the California Financial Code, go to the California Law Web site at *www.leginfo.ca.gov/calaw.html*. The Escrow Law is contained in Division 6 of the Financial Code.

WEB LINK
@

To access the regulations for the Escrow Law, go to the California Code of Regulations Web site at *http://ccr.oal.ca.gov/* and click on the California Code of Regulations link. The Escrow Law regulations are contained in Title 10: Investment, Chapter 3: Commissioner of Corporations, Subchapter 9: Escrow Agents.

WEB LINK
@

For information on the licensing and regulation of escrow agents in California, go to the California Department of Corporations Web site at *www.corp.ca.gov/index*.

The following list contains only the Internet resources that have been mentioned in this book, and others that may be of interest to readers. You are encouraged to explore other resources, including the numerous online property listing services and lenders.

Online definition of escrow
    http://real-estate-law.freeadvice.com/commercial_real_estate/escrow.htm

Federal Deposit Insurance Corporation (FDIC) regulations
    http://www.fdic.gov/regulations/laws/rules/

State Bar of California
http://www.calbar.ca.gov/state/calbar_home.jsp

California Escrow Association
http://www.ceaescrow.org

American Escrow Association
www.a-e-a.org

Information about the Lane Guide
www.laneguide.com

Federal Housing Administration maximum loan amounts
https://entp.hud.gov/idapp/html/hicast1.cfm

California Department of Veterans Affairs
http://www.cdva.ca.gov

Listing of properties available through the Federal Housing Administration
http://www.hud.gov/homes/index.cfm

Escrow Max
www.escrowmax.com

Structural Pest Control Board
http://pestboard.ca.gov/forms.htm

Information regarding the acceptance of electronic signatures
www.alphatrust.com/solutions/banking
www.crogroup.com/electron.htm

Department of Consumer Affairs
http://consumer-affairs.co.la.ca.us

The Congress for New Urbanism
http://www.cnu.org

California Department of Alcoholic Beverage Control
http://www.abc.ca.gov

GLOSSARY

abandonment The voluntary giving up of rights of ownership or another interest (such as an easement) in real property. This can occur by failing to use the property with an intention to abandon (give up the interest). (Chapter 13)

Abandonment of Homestead Used to terminate a recorded homestead that has been filed on a property. (Chapter 13)

abstract attorney An attorney who specializes in real property transactions. In many eastern U.S. states, abstract attorneys often handle the escrow and title functions in the transfer of real property. (Chapter 1)

abstract of judgment A summary of the essential provisions of a court judgment. (Chapter 4)

abstract of title A summary of the public records relating to the title to a particular piece of land. A compilation of abstracts of deeds, trust deeds, and other pertinent data that affect the title to a real property of title. It is a form of title evidence made for the purpose of title examination. (Chapter 4)

abstract (of documents) A statement in abbreviated form; a statement of the important parts of a deed, trust deed, or other legal instrument for the title examiner to interpret. It is a substitute for the photoprint copy of the document. (Chapter 4)

acceleration clause A clause in a deed of trust or mortgage that allows the lender to demand "accelerated" (early) payment of the outstanding loan balance for various reasons. The most common reasons for accelerating a loan are: (1) the borrower's failure to make loan payments and (2) the borrower's transfer of title (sale of the property) to another individual without informing the lender. (Chapter 6)

access A means by which property is approached or a method of entrance into or upon a property. It is also a general or specific right of ingress and egress to a particular property. (Chapter 5)

accommodator (intermediary) A party to an IRC 1031 exchange transaction. Pursuant to an exchange agreement, an accommodator acquires relinquished property, holds money from the sale of the relinquished property, acquires replacement property, and then transfers the replacement property to the exchanger. The basic steps are that the taxpayer finds a buyer for the first property and sells it to the buyer through a qualified intermediary. (Chapter 15)

accrued To increase or accumulate; interest on loans is said to accrue daily. (Chapter 6)

acknowledged Same as acknowledgment. A written declaration by a person executing an instrument, given before an officer authorized to give an oath (usually a notary public), stating that the execution is of his or her own volition. (Chapter 9)

acknowledgment A signed statement by the named person that he or she has signed that document of his or her own free will. This acknowledgment must be performed before a duly authorized officer (such as a notary public). (Chapter 4)

actual notice When an individual has personal knowledge of an event. (Chapters 11, 12)

adjustable-rate mortgage (ARM) A mortgage in which the interest rate changes periodically, according to corresponding fluctuations in an index. All ARMs are tied to indexes. (Chapter 7)

administrator A person appointed by the probate court to carry out the administration of a decedent's estate when the decedent has left no will. If a woman is appointed, she is called an administratrix. The individual court appoints if the deceased did not select someone to represent him or her by naming the person in the will. The administrator is also the person the court would name if the estate had no will. (Chapter 13)

adverse possession A process of acquiring title to real property by possession for a certain (statutory) period of time, in addition to fulfilling other conditions. (Chapter 9)

affiant A person who makes an affidavit. (Chapter 6)

affidavit A written statement or declaration, sworn to before an officer who has authority to administer an oath. (Chapter 6)

agent A person who acts for another by proper authorization. (Chapter 3)

agreement of sale A written contract entered into between the seller (vendor) and buyer (vendee) for sale of real property (land) on an installment or deferred payment plan. It is also known as an agreement to convey, a long form security agreement, or a real estate installment contract. (Chapter 3)

Alcoholic Beverage Control (ABC) The state department that implements the laws regulating liquor licenses and controls the issuance and transfer of said licenses. (Chapter 15)

AKA Also known as. (Chapter 4)

alienation clause A clause in a note or trust deed permitting the payee to declare the entire unpaid balance immediately due and payable upon subsequent transfer of the property. Also referred to as a "due-on-sale" clause. (Chapter 8)

all-inclusive rate Rate that includes charges for title insurance, searching or abstract fees, and examination fees. (Chapter 8)

all-inclusive trust deed (AITD) A junior deed of trust securing a promissory note, the face amount of which is the sum of the liability secured by prior trust deeds plus the cash or equity advanced by the AITD lender. (Chapter 8)

ALTA (American Land Title Association) Organization composed of title insurance firms that set standards for the industry, including title insurance policy forms used on a national basis. It is a national association and most large title insurers are members. Policy forms sponsored by the organization are used in most states. (Chapter 5)

ALTA owner's policy An owner's extended-coverage policy that provides buyers and owners the same protection the American Land Title Association (ALTA) policy gives to lenders. (Chapter 5)

ALTA title policy A type of title insurance policy issued by title insurance companies that expands the risks normally insured against under the standard type of policy. It includes unrecorded mechanics' liens, unrecorded physical easements, facts a physical survey would show, water and mineral rights, and rights of parties in possession. (Chapter 5)

American Escrow Association (AEA) Assists members in networking various individual state interests into a national coalition. The AEA is expected to be called upon to help establish closing practices for real estate transactions worldwide since the fall of the Berlin wall opened up private ownership of property. (Chapter 2)

amortization The loan payment consists of a portion that will be applied to pay the accruing interest on a loan, with the remainder being applied to the principal. Over time, the interest portion decreases as the loan balance decreases, and the amount applied to principal increases so that the loan is paid off (amortized) in the specified time. (Chapter 5)

amortization schedule A table that shows how much of each payment will be applied toward principal and how much toward interest over the life of the loan. It also shows the gradual decrease of the loan balance until it reaches zero. (Chapter 5)

annual percentage rate (APR) This differs from the note rate on your loan. It is a value created according to a government formula intended to reflect the true annual cost of borrowing, expressed as a percentage. For example, 6 percent add-on interest would be much more than 6 percent simple interest, even though both would say 6 percent. Federal Truth-in-Lending statutes require APR to be disclosed. (Chapter 7)

appraisal A written opinion of the value of a property. It is primarily based on an analysis of comparable sales of similar homes nearby. (Chapter 8)

appraised value An opinion of a property's fair market value, based on an appraiser's knowledge, experience, and analysis of the property. Because an appraisal is based primarily on comparable sales, and the most recent sale is the one on the property in question, the appraisal usually comes out at the purchase price. (Chapter 10)

appraiser An individual qualified by education, training, and experience to estimate the value of real property and personal property. Although some appraisers work directly for mortgage lenders, most work independently. (Chapter 2)

appurtenance Something that belongs or is attached to something else. Something that belongs to another thing, such as a barn, dwelling, garage, or orchard; it is incidental to the land to which it is attached. (Chapter 13)

ARB Map An office "subdivision" or map made by a title company for its own convenience in locating property in an area in which all the descriptions are by metes and bounds. On this "subdivision" the "lots" are given "arbitrary" numbers. The deeds and other instruments affecting these lots are posted to what is called an "arbitrary account." The word "arbitrary" is often shortened to "arb." If the system is so devised as to permit assigning new numbers to new tracts as they are "cut out" it is a "progressive arb." (Chapter 5)

arrears The state of being behind; used when describing payment of past-due interest and loan payments. (Chapter 11)

assessed value The value placed on land and improvements as a basis for taxation. In California this is usually accomplished by the tax assessor's office. (Chapter 6)

assessment The placing of a value on property for the purpose of taxation. (Chapter 6)

assessor A public official who establishes the value of a property for taxation purposes. (Chapter 9)

assessor's identification number (AIN) *See* assessor's parcel number (APN). (Chapter 3)

assessor's parcel number (APN) A number used to specify the portion of a large tract or lot. (Chapter 3)

asset Items of value owned by an individual. Assets that can be quickly converted into cash are considered "liquid assets." These include bank accounts, stocks, bonds, mutual funds, and so on. Other assets include real estate, personal property, and debts owed to an individual by others. (Chapter 9)

assignee One to whom a transfer of interest is made. For example, the assignee of a deed of trust or contract. (Chapter 7)

assignment The transfer, in writing, of a person's interest in an asset to another person or entity, such as an assignment of stock, a deed of trust, and a note or a lease. When ownership of your mortgage is transferred from one company or individual to another, it is called an assignment. (Chapter 5)

assignor One who makes an assignment. For example, the assignor of a deed of trust or contract. (Chapter 5)

assumption An agreement to undertake a debt or obligation originally contracted by another. (Chapter 6)

attorney-in-fact The party signing. One who is authorized by another to perform certain acts for another under a power of attorney; written authorization of this power should always be recorded in the county where the power is to be used. An agent authorized to act for another under a "power-of-attorney." (Chapters 9, 12)

balloon payment The final lump sum payment that is due at the termination of a balloon mortgage. (Chapter 9)

barrister An early European lawyer. (Chapter 1)

base The examiner's notes, report, and title policy, or a copy thereof, used as a starting point in making an examination for reissue of the policy at a later date. (Chapter 5)

beneficiary The beneficiary is the lender or the one to whom an obligation is owed. Used in a trust deed. The recipient of benefits, often from a deed of trust; usually the lender of a sum of money. (Chapters 6, 13)

beneficiary demand Written instructions by a beneficiary under a deed of trust stating and demanding the amount necessary for issuance of reconveyance, whether a full or partial amount. (Chapter 6)

beneficiary statement A report from the lender, usually in writing, setting forth the terms and conditions of a loan already of record, such as amounts still owed, interest rate, monthly payments, etc. (Chapter 6)

bilateral escrow instructions A single set of escrow instructions signed by both the buyer and seller (as practiced in Southern California); often signed at the opening of escrow, not at the end. (Chapter 3)

bill of sale A written document that transfers title to personal property. For example, when selling an automobile to acquire funds that will be used as a source of a down payment or for closing costs, the lender will usually require the bill of sale (in addition to other items) to help document this source of funds. The document with which ownership of personal property is transferred. (Chapter 15)

binder An early agreement to purchase a home from a seller. It is usually ensured with earnest money. (Chapter 5)

blanket policy Policy covering an entire tract of land or subdivision from which policies are issued on separate parcels. Also called "base." (Chapter 5)

Board of Land Commissioners A board appointed by U.S. Congress in 1851 to settle California land disputes. The board held the power to rule upon and make settlements for all claims to private land ownership in California. (Chapter 1)

borrower One who obtains a loan and owes money to a lender. (Chapter 5)

branch A subordinate or division office, as opposed to an affiliate, agent, subsidiary, or underwritten firm associated with the headquarters. (Chapter 6)

breach An action that breaks a law, rule, or agreement. (Chapter 10)

breach of contract Failure to perform a contract, in whole or part, without legal excuse. (Chapter 10) *See also* breach.

broker Broker has several meanings in different situations. Generally, a broker is anyone who acts as an agent, bringing two parties together for any

type of transaction, and earns a fee for doing so. Most REALTORS® are "agents" who work under a "broker." In the mortgage industry, broker usually refers to a company or individual who does not lend the money for the loans, but brokers loans to larger lenders or investors. (Chapter 12)

bulk sales transfer The sale of a business and the real property being transferred in bulk. (Chapter 15)

bulk transfer The transfer of stock in trade. (Chapter 1)

business opportunity The assets for an existing business enterprise, including its goodwill. As used in real estate law, the term includes "the sale or lease of the business and goodwill of an existing business enterprise or opportunity." (Chapter 2)

buyer One who purchases or acquires property. (Chapter 2)

buyer affidavit A sworn statement written down for the buyer and made under oath. (Chapter 7) *See also* affidavit.

CAL-FIRPTA This is the California Foreign Investment Real Property Tax Act that became effective in 1991 that followed the federal FIRPTA. The purpose of the law was to regulate the withholding of taxes for nonresident foreigners who might make a profit from U.S. business activity in real property but who might not pay any taxes on the profit made. (Chapter 12)

California Department of Housing and Community Development (HCD) The escrow officer completes the Notice of Escrow Opening required by HCD. (Chapter 14)

California Department of Veterans Affairs (Cal-Vet) Provides real estate loans available to armed forces veterans from California, at low interest rates. (Chapter 7)

California Escrow Association (CEA) Served as advisors when community college real estate escrow education providers began a program to award separate certificates in escrow in addition to the Real Estate Certificate. (Chapter 2)

California Homestead Act Involved in escrow when a foreclosure action arises and the homeowners have legal rights to protect their equity in the property before lien priority creditors may receive funds. (Chapter 13)

canceling escrow Terminating escrow by mutual written instructions. (Chapter 2)

capacity The legal ability of people or organizations to enter into a valid contract. A person entering into a contract will have full, limited, or no capacity to contract. (Chapter 3)

CC&Rs *See* covenants, conditions, and restrictions.

certificate of title In areas where attorneys examine abstracts or chains of title, a written opinion, executed by the examining attorney, stating that title is vested as stated in the abstract. (Chapter 4)

certified escrow instructions Where the escrow holder can electronically send escrow instructions that are certified to the buyer's lender and send the data to the title insurance company for preparation of the preliminary title report. (Chapter 7)

chain of title A continuous succession of land ownership, like connected links of chain. Each link represents a single owner. (Chapters 1, 4)

CLAP Often referred to as a memory aid for items needed by the escrow officer. It stands for the following: Cash, Loans, Agreements, and Possession. (Chapter 3)

clear title A title that is free of liens or legal questions as to ownership of the property. (Chapter 1)

close of escrow (COE) The date the documents are recorded and title passes from seller to buyer. On this date, the buyer becomes the legal owner, and title insurance becomes effective. (Chapter 2)

closer Some states refer to the persons who perform the close of escrow as the *settlement agent*, because they handle the settlement costs and the closing document, often referred to as the settlement statement. Other states call the individual the *closer*. (Chapter 2)

closing The final procedure in the real estate sales process, where the sale and pertinent loan are completed by the execution of documents for recording. In some areas, this procedure is known as the "closing of escrow." (Chapter 2)

closing costs The numerous expenses incurred in completing the transfer of ownership of real estate.

These costs are in addition to the price of the property. Closing costs can be separated into what are called "nonrecurring closing costs" and "prepaid items." Nonrecurring closing costs are any items that are paid just once as a result of buying the property or obtaining a loan. "Prepaids" are items that recur over time, such as property taxes and homeowners' insurance. A lender makes an attempt to estimate the amount of nonrecurring closing costs and prepaid items on the good faith estimate, which it must issue to the borrower within three days of receiving a home loan application. (Chapter 11)

closing statement A final accounting of the closed escrow showing the actual figures used to compute the completed escrow; may be filled out on a RESPA or HUD form; legally required to be given to the buyer and seller at the end of every real estate transaction. (Chapter 6)

CLTA (California Land Title Association) The second most common title insurance policy, which is usually purchased at the time of transfer of title. (Chapter 5)

collateral Marketable real or personal property pledged by a borrower as security for a loan. (Chapter 4)

collateral assignment The assignment of a security instrument, such as a trust deed, to secure performance of an obligation by the assignor. The assignee holds title for security purposes only. (Chapter 5)

commercial property escrow Included to give general business opportunity escrow data that may often be part of a bulk sales transfer. (Chapter 15)

commission A real estate agent's earnings for handling a property transaction; usually computed as a percentage of the selling price and negotiable between the seller and the agent. (Chapter 7)

commissioner Commissioners are usually political appointments by the state governor. Thus, the term of each commissioner is generally the same length as the term of the governor. Examples are the Insurance Commissioner or the Real Estate Commissioner. Each commissioner oversees that government agency and enforces pertinent legislation. (Chapter 2)

commitment A binding contract with a title company to issue a specific title policy, showing only those exceptions contained in the commitment and any intervening matters after the date of the commitment and prior to the effective date of the policy. The commitment contains all information included in the preliminary title report, plus a list of the title company's requirements to insure the transaction. It also includes the standard exceptions from coverage that will appear in the policy. (Chapter 7)

community property In some states, especially the Southwest including California, property acquired by a married couple during their marriage is considered to be owned jointly, except under special circumstances. Each spouse has an interest in the property whether each appears in title or not. This is an outgrowth of the Spanish and Mexican heritage of the area. (Chapter 1)

competent Having the legal power to deal with something. (Chapter 3)

complete escrow When all necessary instruments and funds are deposited into escrow and it is possible to carry out the escrow instructions, it is referred to as a complete or "perfect" escrow. (Chapter 1)

condemnation The taking of private property by the government for public use—as for a street or a storm drain. The owner is justly compensated. This right or power of government to take property for a necessary public use is called "eminent domain." (Chapter 5)

condominium A multifamily or other structure in which units are individually owned and in which owners of individual units also own an undivided interest in common areas. Apartment or other type of property in which the owner has fee title to the part actually occupied, with a proportionate interest in areas used by all occupants, such as walkways and parking areas. (Chapter 14)

conservator Generally, an individual or trust institution appointed by a court to care for property. Specifically, an individual or trust institution appointed by a court to care for and manage the property of an incompetent adult, in the same way as a guardian cares for and manages the property of a minor. (Chapter 13)

consideration The inducement for entering into a contract; it consists of either a benefit to the promisor or a loss or detriment to the promisee. (Chapter 3)

constructive notice Notice given by the public records. Generally, the law presumes that one has the same knowledge of instruments recorded as if one were actually acquainted with them. Means that any recorded document at the county recorder's office gives constructive notice to the world that the act happened. (Chapters 4, 11, 12)

constructive receipt A term referring to the control of proceeds by an exchanger even though funds may not directly be in their possession. (Chapter 15)

contingency Dependent upon conditions or events specified but not yet accomplished. Property may be sold contingent upon the seller or buyer meeting a predetermined condition. (Chapter 7)

contiguous land Being in actual contact; adjoining or touching. (Chapter 5)

contract An agreement between two or more parties to do or not to do a certain thing. (Chapter 3)

contract of sale An agreement to purchase property wherein legal title is retained by the seller until the buyer has paid the purchase price in accordance with the terms of the contract. (Chapter 8)

covenant not to compete An agreement not to compete within a specified area in which the business being sold is located. Requires a dollar amount to be allocated to its creation. (Chapter 15)

conventional A loan secured by a mortgage or deed of trust that is not insured or guaranteed by a governmental agency. (Chapter 7)

conventional suburban development (CSD) A newer term used when many types of diverse units are built, or where virtually entire new towns are established. (Chapter 14)

convey To transfer title in property from one person to another. (Chapter 9)

conveyance An instrument in writing, such as a deed or trust deed, used to transfer (convey) title to property from one person to another. (Chapter 4)

cooperative Multiple-family housing with each occupant being entitled to perpetual use of his or her own unit and receiving a share certificate giving him or her a proportionate interest in the entire property. Referred to as a co-op, it is very similar to the condominium homeowner association, with specific differences that warrant study. (Chapter 14)

corporation An entity authorized by law and established by a group of people, the stockholders, that is endowed with certain rights, privileges, and duties similar to an individual. (Chapter 9)

corporation grant deed A grant deed used by a corporation. A corporation is a legal entity created under state law, consisting of an association of one or more individuals but regarded under the law as having an existence and personality separate from such individuals. (Chapter 9)

county assessor One who sets value of property for taxation purposes. (Chapter 13)

covenant (1) A formal agreement or contract between two parties in which one party gives the other certain promises and assurances, such as the covenant of warranty in a warranty deed. (2) Agreements or promises contained in deeds and other instruments for performance or non-performance of certain acts, or use or nonuse of property in a certain manner. (Chapter 14)

covenants, conditions, and restrictions Commonly called "CC&Rs" the term usually refers to a written recorded declaration that sets forth certain covenants, conditions, restrictions, rules, or regulations established by a subdivider or other landowner to create uniformity of buildings and use within tracts of land or groups of lots. The restrictions also can be established by deed. CC&Rs are sometimes referred to as "private zoning." (Chapter 14)

coverage Matters insured under the policy. (Chapter 4)

credit (1) The deduction of a payment made by a debtor from an amount due. (2) The right-hand side of an account on which such amounts are entered. A bookkeeping entry on the right side of an account, recording the reduction or elimination of an asset or an expense or the creation of or addition to a liability or item of equity or revenue. (Chapter 11)

creditor A person or entity to which money is owed by another. (Chapter 13)

credit report fee A fee to obtain a person's credit report. (Chapter 11)

cut-out The term applied when a parcel or a portion of the property is taken or "cut-out" from a larger parcel on an arbitrary map. (Chapter 5)

date of acceptance The date the seller accepts the offer or the buyer accepts the counteroffer. (Chapter 10)

date of closing Date title is transferred to buyer. (Chapter 5)

date down A reexamination of the title records to cover the time period from the original completion of the title examination down to the present (usually the time of recording of the documents of the title order). (Chapter 5)

debit (1) An item of debt as recorded in an account. (2) The left-hand side of an account or accounting ledger where bookkeeping entries are made. A bookkeeping entry on the left side of an account, recording the creation of or addition to an asset or an expense or the reduction or elimination of a liability or item of equity or revenue. (Chapter 11)

debtor One who owes a debt. (Chapter 6)

decedent A deceased person. (Chapter 13)

Declaration of Homestead The recorded document that protects a homeowner from foreclosure by certain judgment creditors. (Chapter 13)

Decree of Distribution A probate court decree that determines how the estate of a decedent shall be distributed. (Chapter 9)

deed Written document by which an estate or interest in real property is transferred from one person to another. The person who transfers the interest is called the "grantor." The one who acquires the interest is called the "grantee." Examples of deeds are grant deeds, administrators' deeds, executors' deeds, quitclaim deeds, etc. The deed to use depends on the language of the deed, the legal capacity of the grantor, and other circumstances. (Chapter 4)

deed of trust   A written document by which the title to land is conveyed as security for the repayment of a loan or other obligation. It is a form of mortgage. The landowner or debtor is called the "trustor." The party to whom the legal title is conveyed (and who may be called on to conduct a sale thereof if the loan is not paid) is the "trustee." The lender is the "beneficiary." When the loan is paid off, the trustee is asked by the beneficiary to issue a reconveyance or "recon." This deed of reconveyance corresponds to the release that the holder of a mortgage executes when the mortgage is paid off, called the satisfaction of mortgage. (Chapter 12) *See also* trust deed.

default   Failure to perform a duty or pay an obligation. (Chapter 14)

defective title   (1) Title to a negotiable instrument obtained by fraud. (2) Title to real property that lacks some of the elements necessary to transfer good title. (Chapter 1)

deficiency judgment   A personal judgment in a judicial foreclosure action for the remaining amount due after the sale of the security. (Chapter 8)

demand for payoff   A letter or statement furnished by the beneficiary that shows the current unpaid loan balance and the total amount due and payable to retire the lien, such as a mortgage or a trust deed. The total amount due may include past due late fee, prepayment penalties, interest, or other items in addition to the principal amount; used when the loan is to be paid off in full through escrow. (Chapter 6)

Department of Consumer Affairs   Serves as the central reporting agency for real estate fraud. The department has many free services, including counseling on real estate matters, information on recorded documents, and referrals to other governmental agencies to assist where appropriate

or to handle investigative matters beyond the scope of the department's purview. (Chapter 12)

Department of Veterans Affairs (DVA)   Loan is handled through a loan broker, just as the FHA loan. The Veterans Administration does not take government funds and make real estate loans. The lender makes the loan, and only in case of default does the DVA become involved. (Chapter 7)

demise   A transfer to another of an estate for years, for life, or at will. (Chapter 15)

Department of Corporations   Lays out specifically the what, who, where, when, and how of being an escrow agent. These regulations identify those activities that are considered escrow functions and those excluded from following these rules. (Chapter 2)

deposit   (1) Money given by the buyer with an offer to purchase. Shows good faith. Also called "earnest money." (2) A natural accumulation of resources (oil, gold, etc.) that may be commercially recovered and marketed. (Chapter 2)

deposit receipt   A written contract used when accepting "earnest money" to bind an offer for property by a prospective purchaser. (Chapter 3)

description   The exact location of a piece of real property stated in terms of lot, block, tract, part lot, metes and bounds, recorded instruments, or U.S. Government survey (sectionalized). This is also referred to as "legal description of property." (Chapter 2)

devise   A gift or disposal of real property by last will and testament. A disposition of real property by will. (Chapter 13)

devisee   One who receives real property by will. (Chapter 4)

devisor   One who disposes of real property by will. (Chapter 4)

disbursement   The release of monies held in an escrow account; usually on the day when escrow closes. (Chapter 2)

disclosure   In real estate, revealing all the known facts that may affect the decision of a buyer or tenant. A broker must disclose known defects in the property for sale or lease. A builder must give to a potential buyer the facts of his or her new development. (Are there adequate school facilities, an airport nearby?) A broker cannot be an agent for both buyer and seller unless both know (disclosure) and agree. (Chapter 3)

discount points The amount of money the borrower or seller must pay the lender to get a mortgage at a stated interest rate. This amount is equal to the difference between the principal balance on the note and the lesser amount that a purchaser of the note would pay the original lender for it under market conditions. A point equals 1 percent of the loan. (Chapter 12)

document An original or official paper relied upon as a basis, proof, or support of anything. (Chapter 12)

documentary transfer tax A tax a state enabling act allows a county to adopt that applies to all transfers of real property located in the county. Notice of payment, commonly known as "documentary stamps," is entered on the face of the deed or on a separate paper filed with the deed. A tax on transfers of title to real property. (Chapter 11)

double escrow A real estate transaction procedure in which the closing of one escrow is dependent upon the closing of another one; also called a "concurrent escrow," commonly used in exchanges and in instances where the buyer depends on funds he or she expects to get from the sale of another property. (Chapter 2)

due-on-sale clause A clause that calls for an obligation to become due upon the sale of a property previously put up as collateral for a promissory note; frequently broadened to become a due-on-transfer clause; also called an acceleration clause. (Chapter 6)

due-on-sale disclosure If there is a due-on-sale clause in any existing loan, the lender may demand full payment of the entire loan as a result of the sale of the property. All parties agree that they are not relying on any representation by the other party or the broker about the enforceability of such a clause in existing notes or deeds of trust to be executed as a result of this sale. All parties have been advised by the broker to seek legal advice. (Chapter 6)

earnest money Down payment made by a purchaser of real estate as evidence of good faith; a deposit or partial payment. (Chapter 3)

easement An easement allows another person the right to use your land for a specific purpose. The most usual easements are those granted to public utility or telephone companies to run lines on or under your private property and to neighboring houses to use a common driveway to give access to their homes. (Chapters 4, 5)

egress A means for departing from one's own property without trespassing on another person's property, as applied to an easement. (Chapter 5)

electronic funds transfer Sometimes referred to as "electronic settlement." A fast, efficient, and secure method of transferring money between the parties to a transaction and throughout a chain. (Chapter 1)

electronic signature A digitized, bitmapped representation of an actual handwritten signature that can be captured and stored in a computer by (1) digitally scanning a paper document containing the signature; (2) signing with a stylus and digital writing pad connected to a computer; (3) copying a computer file containing the bitmapped signature. It can be authorized by an individual to be the legally binding equivalent of the individual's handwritten signature. (Chapters 1, 10, 12)

emblements The growing crops; considered personal property and require special wording in the escrow to preserve the rights of the owner of the annual, harvestable crop. Annual crops produced for sale. (Chapter 15)

eminent domain It is another word for condemnation, the right of the government to take private property for a public purpose. An example of this would be to make way for a road. The Constitution requires the government to pay fair compensation if it takes property. (Chapter 5) *See also* condemnation.

Employment Development Department (EDD) The state department that collects employee taxes from businesses that pay employees' wages. (Chapter 15)

encroachment The presence of an improvement such as a building, a wall, a fence, or other fixture that overlaps onto the property of an adjoining owner. When a building, a wall, a fence, or other fixture encroaches upon (overlaps) the land of an adjoining owner, there is said to be an "encroachment," provided this adjoining owner has not consented to such location on his or her land. (Chapter 4)

encumbrance A lien affecting the land and improvements, such as a mortgage or trust deed. (Chapter 4)

endorsement Addition to or modification of a title insurance policy that expands or changes coverage of the policy, fulfilling specific requirements of the insured. (Chapter 5)

engineer A person with an engineering background who acts as a conveyancer for handling the transfer of title for property. The engineer conducts title searches to determine the rights of ownership and oversees surveyors who establish property line boundaries and parcel measurements. (Chapter 1)

Equal Credit Opportunity Act A federal law requiring lenders to ensure that credit is available with fairness, impartiality, and without discrimination. (Chapter 10)

equitable title Title of the purchaser under a contract of sale or the right to acquire the legal title. (Chapter 9)

equity (1) A legal doctrine based on fairness, rather than strict interpretation of the letter of the law. (2) The market value of real property, less the amount of existing liens. (3) Any ownership investment (stocks, real estate, etc.) as opposed to investing as a lender (bonds, mortgages, etc.). (Chapter 13)

escroue The French word that is the origin of the word "escrow." The French referred to a scroll or a roll of writing as escroue. (Chapter 1)

escrow An independent third party, who acts as the agent for buyer and seller, or for borrower and lender. This third party carries out instructions of both parties and disburses documents and funds. Escrow closes and the transfer of property or document is completed upon fulfillment of certain conditions specified in the written instructions. The necessary deeds and other instruments are recorded at the close of escrow. (Chapters 1, 3, 4)

escrow agent The neutral third party holding funds or something of value in trust for another or others. Someone qualified to perform all the steps necessary to prepare and carry out escrow instructions, which might involve such tasks as obtaining title insurance; securing payoff demands; prorating taxes, interest, rents, etc.; and disbursing the funds held in escrow. Also known as an "escrow officer." (Chapter 2)

escrow holder Handles all types of escrows. Most are qualified to perform services for particular transactions. (Chapter 3)

escrow instructions Instructions from a buyer, seller, or lender to the escrow company as to what conditions must be met before escrow can close. (Chapter 11)

escrow law This law describes the legal requirements for those who act as an escrow agent. (Chapter 2)

escrow number The file number assigned to an escrow by the escrow officer for identification purposes. (Chapter 6)

escrow officer The individual who works for or is employed by the escrow agent, a firm or company. (Chapter 3) *See also* escrow agent.

estate (1) The interest or nature of the interest that one has in property, such as a life estate, the estate of a deceased, real estate, etc. (2) A large house with substantial grounds surrounding it, giving the connotation of belonging to a wealthy person. The degree, quantity, nature, and extent of a person's interest in property. (Chapters 3, 4, 13)

estoppel agreement Signed by each tenant stating the amount of rents, the amount of deposit paid to the seller, and the length of the term of the tenancy. A doctrine that bars one from asserting rights inconsistent with a previous position or representation. (Chapter 14)

examination The process of determining the vesting of title, and encumbrances and liens thereon. (Chapter 4)

examiner A person who examines the title to real property determining the vesting of title and the liens and encumbrances that affect the property. (Chapter 4)

exception An interest in real property excluded from the conveyance remaining in the grantor, or an interest that had been excluded in a prior conveyance. (Chapter 5)

exchange A reciprocal transfer of real property that has certain tax advantages over a sale. Definite procedures must be followed in order to qualify the transfer as an exchange. (Chapter 15)

exchanger Reserves the right to convert this transaction to an exchange at any time before the closing date. (Chapter 15)

exclusion Also known as "exception." The deduction or subtraction from inclusion. (Chapter 4)

execute To complete, to make, to perform, to do, to follow out; to execute a deed, to make a deed, including especially signing, sealing, and delivery; to execute a contract is to perform the contract, to follow through to the end; to complete. (Chapter 6)

execution An order directing a sheriff, constable, marshal, or court-appointed commissioner to enforce a money judgment against the property of a debtor. This officer, if necessary, may sell the property to satisfy the judgment. (Chapter 9)

executor A person appointed in a will and affirmed by the probate court to cause a distribution of the decedent's estate in accordance with the will. (The one who makes the will is called a testator.) If a woman is appointed, she is referred to as the executrix. (Chapter 13)

executrix A female person or legal entity who is designated in a will as the representative of a decedent's estate. (Chapter 13)

exemption An immunity from some burden or obligation. (Chapter 2)

facsimile An exact and precise copy. (Chapter 15)

FDIC Abbreviation for Federal Deposit Insurance Corporation. (Chapter 2)

Federal Housing Administration (FHA) A Federal agency created by the National Housing Act of 1934 for the purpose of expanding and strengthening home ownership by making private mortgage financing possible on a long-term, low-down payment basis. The vehicle is a mortgage insurance program, with premiums paid by the homeowner, to protect lenders against loss on these higher-risk loans. Since 1965, FHA has been part of the Department of Housing and Urban Development (HUD). (Chapter 5)

fee An estate of inheritance. (Chapter 3)

fee simple An estate under which the owner is entitled to unrestricted powers to dispose of the property and which can be left by will or inherited. Commonly, a synonym for ownership. The highest form of ownership anyone can have in land—freely transferable and inheritable. Also known as "absolute fee," "fee estate," or just "fee." You acquire a fee estate when you purchase a piece of land. Originally, a "fee" was an estate in land held by a feudal lord. (Chapter 4)

FHA insurance An undertaking by FHA to insure the lender against loss arising from a default by the borrower. (Chapter 7)

fiduciary One who holds something of value in trust for another. (Chapter 2)

Financial Institutions Reform, Recovery, and Enforcement Act (FIRREA) This act restructured the savings and loan association regulatory system; enacted in response to the savings and loan crisis of the 1980s. (Chapter 15)

financing statement A personal property security instrument that replaced a chattel mortgage upon adoption of the Uniform Commercial Code. The document that is filed with the Secretary of State as a public record of security interest in personal property (like recording a deed of trust). (Chapter 15)

fire insurance Insurance against loss or damage by fire to specific property. (Chapter 15)

FIRPTA If the seller is a "foreign person" under the Foreign Investment of Real Property Tax Act (FIRPTA), every buyer must, unless an exemption applies, deduct and withhold 10 percent of the gross sales price from seller's proceeds and send it to the Internal Revenue Service (IRS). (Chapter 15)

fixture A thing that was originally personal property but has become attached to and is considered as part of the real property. (Chapter 15)

foreclosure The sale of property used as security for a debt after default in payment. (Chapter 2)

forfeiture A loss of some right, title, estate, or interest in consequence of a default under an obligation. (Chapter 5)

forfeiture of title A common penalty for the violation of conditions or restrictions imposed by the seller upon the buyer in a deed or other proper document. For example, a deed may be granted upon the condition that if liquor is sold on the land, the title to the land will be forfeited (that is, lost) by the buyer (or some later owner) and will revert to the seller. (Chapter 5)

for sale by owner (FSBO) transaction The parties themselves established through contract outside of escrow that no licensed agent is involved. (Chapter 13) *See also* FSBO.

franchise A right or privilege conferred by law or contract. (Chapter 15)

FSBO "For Sale By Owner" pronounced FISBO, the principals often believe that the original agreement is all that is needed. (Chapter 3)

full disclosure In real estate, revealing all the known facts that may affect the decision of a buyer or tenant. A broker must disclose known defects in the property for sale or lease. (Chapter 12)

general index An index (kept in the plant) of all matters affecting persons or corporations and their rights to do business and all matters of a general nature that cannot be entered on the lot books because no specific property is mentioned. (Chapter 4)

good funds law State law requiring assurance by escrow companies of receipt of loan funds, deposit, or electronic wiring, prior to closing a transaction, thus eliminating a practice in which lenders obtained several days of float on the loan proceeds. (Chapter 10)

goodwill The value of the clientele known to patronize the business being transferred. The price paid by a buyer of a business over and above the value of the assets. (Chapter 15)

grant A transfer of real estate, between individuals, by deed. A transfer of real estate from a sovereign is accomplished by patent or royal decree. (Chapter 1)

grant deed One of the many types of deeds used to transfer real property. Contains warranties against prior conveyances or encumbrances. When title insurance is purchased, warranties in a deed are of little practical significance. (Chapter 2)

grantee The person to whom a grant is made. (Chapter 9)

grantor The person who makes a grant. (Chapter 1)

grantor-grantee index The record of the passing of title to all the properties in a county as kept by the county recorder's office. Property is checked by tracing the names of the sellers and buyers (chain of title). Title companies usually have more efficient methods of keeping records according to property description. (Chapter 5)

hazard insurance Real estate insurance protecting against fire, some natural causes, vandalism, etc., depending upon the policy. Buyer often adds liability insurance and extended coverage for personal property. Fire insurance policy that often includes liability insurance and extended-coverage insurance. (Chapter 11)

heirs The persons designated by law to succeed to the estate of a decedent who leaves no will. (Chapter 9)

homeowner policy A combined property and liability insurance policy designed for residential use. A variety of packaged policies are designed for owners of single-family dwellings, for tenants, and for condominium owners. (Chapter 5)

homeowners' association (HOA) A nonprofit association created to own or lease common areas and make improvements in a condominium or planned unit development; serves as the administrative and legislative arm of the unit owners. A nonprofit corporation formed and organized to serve and represent individual unit owners who own a shared common area. (Chapter 14)

homestead A statutory protection from execution or the establishment of title by occupation of real property in accordance with the laws of various states or the federal government. (Chapter 13)

home warranty Same as home warranty insurance. Private insurance insuring a buyer against defects (usually in plumbing, heating, and electrical) in the home he or she has purchased. The period of insurance varies and both new and used homes may be insured. (Chapter 10)

Housing and Community Development (HCD) This is where the escrow officer completes the Notice of Escrow Opening. (Chapter 14)

HUD-1 form HUD stands for Department of Housing and Urban Development. (Chapter 11) *See also* Real Estate Settlement Procedures Act (RESPA).

HUD-1 settlement statement A document that provides an itemized listing of the funds that were paid at closing. Items that appear on the statement include real estate commissions, loan fees, points, and initial escrow (impound) amounts. Each type of expense goes on a specific numbered line on the sheet. The totals at the bottom of the HUD-1 statement define the seller's net proceeds and the buyer's net payment at closing. It is called a HUD-1 because the form is printed by the Department of Housing and Urban Development (HUD). The HUD-1 statement is also known as the "closing statement" or "settlement sheet." (Chapter 11)

hypothecate To give a thing as security without giving up possession. (Chapter 8)

impound account Funds collected by a lender from a borrower to guarantee payment of such items as taxes and hazard insurance premiums when due. A trust type of account established by lenders for the accumulation of borrowers' funds to meet periodic payments of taxes, FHA mortgage insurance premiums, and/or future insurance policy premiums required to protect their security. Impounds are usually collected with the note payment. (Chapter 11)

impounds A trust type of account established by lenders for the accumulation of borrower's funds to meet periodic payments of taxes, mortgage insurance premiums, and/or future insurance policy premiums required to protect their security. (Chapter 3)

incompetent Incapable of managing one's affairs. (Chapter 9)

indemnity Insurance against possible loss or damage. A title insurance policy is a contract of indemnity. (Chapter 15)

indemnity agreement An agreement to compensate another party for a potential loss; a "hold-harmless" agreement. (Chapter 15)

I/C (individual/corporation) An index kept in the plant of all matters affecting persons or companies that cannot be entered in the property accounts because no specific property is mentioned. (Chapter 4)

independent escrow Does the basic escrow mechanics of a transaction, it is consistent to the procedure and reliability for doing only one job that is used in the transfer of property by the full-time escrow company. (Chapter 2)

industrial property May involve only raw land, may involve the long-term lease of land with the tenant constructing the building improvement, or may involve both the improvement building and the land. (Chapter 15)

ingress A right to enter someone else's property without being considered a trespasser. (Chapter 5)

insurance commissioner Commissioner is very much involved in regulating operations for title insurance company escrow operations. Although only a department of the title insurance business entity, the title company escrow department in Northern California handles the bulk of escrows. (Chapter 2)

injunction An order of a court prohibiting some act, or compelling an act to be done. (Chapter 5)

inspection A visit to and review of particular premises. A purchaser should always inspect the property before closing. (Chapter 10)

institutional lender A financial intermediary or depository, such as a savings association, commercial bank, or life insurance company that pools money of its depositors and then invests funds in various ways, including trust deeds and mortgage loans. (Chapter 5)

instrument A writing, such as a deed, made and executed as the expression of some act, contract, or proceeding; the term "document," rather than "instrument," is used. (Chapters 1, 4)

insurance policy A plan for cooperatively sharing risks with a group so that the consequences of severe loss will not fall too heavily on any individual. (Chapter 10)

interim loan A short-term loan under circumstances anticipating a subsequent long-term loan. (Chapter 5)

interspousal grant deed A document used when the transfer is between individuals in a marriage. (Chapter 9)

intestate (1) Deceased without leaving a legally valid will. (2) Property not disposed of by will or bequest. (Chapter 13)

inventory Stock in trade; merchandise held for sale or used in manufacture of items for sale in the day-to-day function of a business. (Chapter 15)

involuntary lien A lien created by operation of law. (Chapter 5)

IRC 1031 tax exchange A real estate transaction with tax consequences that the principles want the escrow holder to state in the instructions that it is the intent to affect an exchange under the federal tax code, where escrow will insert a hold harmless clause alleviating escrow from any subsequent consequences. (Chapter 15)

irrevocable Not to be revoked or withdrawn. (Chapter 10)

joint escrow instructions The document used in California that licensed agents obtain from the California Association of REALTORS® Winforms® designed to include the purchase agreement and escrow instructions for the transaction. (Chapter 3)

joint protection policy A title insurance policy insuring the interest of both owner and lender. (Chapter 5)

joint tenancy An estate owned by two or more persons in equal shares created by a single transfer. Upon the death of a joint tenant, the surviving joint tenants take the entire property and nothing passes to the heirs of the deceased. (Chapter 4)

judgment The final determination of a court of competent jurisdiction of a matter presented to it; money judgment providing for the payment of claims presented to the court, awarded as damages, etc. (Chapter 6)

judgment lien A lien against the property of a judgment debtor; an involuntary lien. (Chapter 6)

judicial foreclosure A type of foreclosure that requires court proceedings; mortgage foreclosures require court proceedings while deed-of-trust foreclosures generally do not; state laws dictate. (Chapter 9)

junior lien A subordinate lien. (Chapter 8)

jurat A certificate evidencing the fact that an affidavit was properly made before an authorized officer. The certificate of an officer before whom a writing was sworn to, such as a notary public; also, that part of an affidavit stating where, when, and before whom the affidavit was sworn. (Chapter 12)

jurisdiction The right of a court to make a decision concerning the subject matter in a given case; the power to hear and determine a matter. (Chapter 15)

land contract (land sale contract) An installment contract for the sale of land. The seller (vendor) holds legal title, and the buyer (vendee) has equitable title until the sales price is paid in full. (Chapter 8)

land grant A gift of public land by the federal government to a state or local government, corporation, or individual. (Chapter 1)

lane guide A reference book that provides the contact information for various lien holders, including name, mailing address, telephone number, fax number, and e-mail address. (Chapter 6)

lawful object The legal system will not enforce an illegal contract. If a contract violates a law, it may be held to not have lawful object, therefore, be illegal and unenforceable in a court of law. (Chapter 3)

legal description A description of land recognized by law, based on government surveys, spelling out the exact boundaries of the entire piece of land. It should so thoroughly identify a parcel of land that it cannot be confused with any other. The exact location of a piece of property stated in terms of lot, block, and tract, part lot, metes and bounds, or U.S. government survey (sectionalized). This is also referred to as a legal description of property. (Chapter 4)

lender Any person or entity advancing funds that are to be repaid; a general term including all mortgagees and beneficiaries under deeds of trust. (Chapter 8)

lessee The tenant under a lease. (Chapter 15)

lessor The landlord under a lease. (Chapter 5)

levy A seizure of property by judicial process. (Chapter 10)

licensee Licensee means any person holding a valid unrevoked license as an escrow agent. (Chapter 11)

lien An encumbrance against property for money, either voluntary or involuntary. All liens are encumbrances, but all encumbrances are not liens. A charge upon property for the payment or discharge of a debt or duty. (Chapter 4)

lien information sheet A document provided to escrow by the seller giving lien holder information so that escrow can contact each for current status. (Chapter 6)

life estate An estate measured by the life of a natural person. (Chapter 9)

limited partnership A partnership composed of one or more general partners and one or more limited partners, whose contribution and liability are limited. (Chapter 15)

liquidated damages clause A clause in a contract by which the parties by agreement fix the damages in advance for a breach of the contract. (Chapter 10)

liquor license A state approved permit from the ABC Board to sell alcoholic beverages. (Chapter 15)

lis pendens A notice recorded in the official records of a county to indicate that a lawsuit is pending affecting the lands described in the notice. (Chapter 5)

listing An employment contract between a broker and his or her client. (Chapter 3)

loan application The loan application is a source of information on which the lender bases a decision to make the loan; defines the terms of the loan contract; gives the name of the borrower, place of employment, salary, bank accounts, and credit

references; and describes the real estate to be mortgaged. It also stipulates the amount of loan being applied for and repayment terms. (Chapter 7)

loan approval When a loan is approved. (Chapter 7)

loan commitment A lender's agreement to lend a specified amount of money; must be exercised within a certain time limit. (Chapter 7)

loan conditions Regulations imposed on a loan such as term, rates, etc. (Chapter 7)

loan docs Documents used to process a loan. (Chapter 7)

loan documents *See* loan docs.

loan fees Costs charged by a lender for giving out a loan; may include points, tax service fees, appraisal fee, etc. (Chapter 11)

loan officer A person or firm that acts as an intermediary between borrower and lender; one who, for compensation or gain, negotiates, sells, or arranges loans and sometimes continues to service the loans; also called loan broker. (Chapter 7)

loan origination fee Any up-front loan fees. (Chapter 11)

loan processor The person who processes loans. This individual orders the credit report and appraisal and asks for a copy of the certified escrow instructions. The escrow officer works mostly with the loan processor. (Chapter 7)

loan servicing disclosure A disclosure of the loan servicer's duties performed such as collecting payments that include interest, principal, insurance, and taxes on a note from the borrower in accordance with the terms of the note. (Chapter 8)

Lot Book Report A short title company report providing the property owner's name, the vesting, the property's legal description, and a plat map. A title company's set of books reflecting every document describing real property that has been recorded in the county in which the property is located; in some counties these books constitute the heart of the title plant. (Chapter 4)

maintenance fee Pays for the unit furniture, common area and unit equipment, property taxes, insurance, utilities, housekeeping, pool area, and grounds. Some time-shares include an automobile, boat, greens fees, or other items. (Chapter 14)

market value The price that real property would reasonably be expected to bring were it to be offered for sale with a reasonable sales effort over a reasonable period of time. (Chapter 6)

maturity date The end of a loan repayment period; a specific date in the future when full payment for a loan becomes due. (Chapter 4)

material fact A fact is material if it is one that the agent should realize would be likely to affect the judgment of the principal in giving his or her consent to the agent to enter into the particular transaction on the specified terms. (Chapter 10)

mechanic's lien A lien created by statute for the purpose of securing priority of payment for the price or value of work performed and materials furnished in construction or repair of improvements to land, and which attaches to the land as well as the improvements. (Chapters 5, 6)

Mello-Roos The law requires the real estate licensee to disclose the fact of a Mello-Roos tax as soon as practical in the transaction and contains penalties should the licensee not comply. The law states that the seller is mandated to disclose a Mello-Roos tax to a prospective purchaser. (Chapter 10)

messenger service Uses with escrow and title are extremely important. These licensed, bonded couriers have possession of critical documents at various stages of the transaction. (Chapter 11)

metes and bounds A term used in describing the boundary lines of land setting forth all the boundary lines together with their terminal points and angles (measurements and boundaries). Usually refers to a type of legal description in which all of the exterior liens of the parcel of land are described in succession to form a closed area. (Chapter 4)

mineral extraction Protection against damage to existing improvements resulting from exercise or use of a surface right for extraction or development of reserved mineral rights is available. (Chapter 5)

mineral rights Ownership of minerals found on a property. (Chapters 5, 9)

minor A person under 18 years of age. (Chapter 2)

moratorium Temporary suspension. (Chapter 14)

mortgage (1) To hypothecate as security, real property for the payment of a debt. The borrower (mortgagor) retains possession and use of the property. (2) The instrument by which real estate is hypothecated as security for the repayment of a loan. (Chapter 6)

mortgagee The party lending the money and receiving the mortgage; the lender under a mortgage. (Chapter 6)

mortgage insurance Insurance against loss to the mortgagee in the event of default and a failure of the mortgaged property to satisfy the balance owing plus costs of foreclosure. (Do not confuse with mortgage life insurance.) (Chapter 11)

mortgage insurance premium (MIP) The ongoing monthly amount collected with the monthly payment by the lender and paid to the insurance carrier. (Chapters 7, 11)

mortgage life insurance Insurance from which the benefits are intended by the policy owner to pay off the balance due on a mortgage upon the death of the insured or to meet the payments on a mortgage as they fall due in case of the death or disability of the insured. (Chapter 7)

mortgagor The party who borrows the money and gives the mortgage; the debtor under a mortgage. (Chapter 6)

multiple listing An organized real estate listing service under which brokers pool their listings. (Chapter 11)

multiple-listing service An association of real estate agents providing for a pooling of listings and the sharing of commissions on a specified basis. (Chapter 11)

mutual agreement The consent of all parties to the provisions of a contract. The voluntary cancellation of a contract by all parties is called mutual rescission. (Chapter 3)

negotiable Capable of being negotiated, assigned, or transferred in the ordinary course of business. (Chapter 11)

net listing Designed to provide the seller with a fixed dollar amount at the close of escrow, regardless of the sales price. (Chapter 14)

neutral Belonging to neither side nor advocating for the interest of one party. Escrow officers act as a neutral third party. (Chapter 1)

nominee A person designated to take the place of another. (Chapter 5)

notary public An official appointed by the secretary of state to administer oaths, to authenticate contracts, to certify acknowledgments, etc. A California notary public may act as such in any part of the state. A person who acknowledges oaths, such as the signing of a grant deed or deed of trust; must be duly appointed by the proper authorities. (Chapter 12)

note A unilateral agreement containing an express and absolute promise of the signer to pay to a named person, or order, or bearer, a definite sum of money at a specified date or on demand. Usually provides for interest and, concerning real property, is secured by a mortgage or trust deed. (Chapter 5)

notice of cessation A notice that work has ceased; a notice recorded within the time period that is specified by statute, limiting the time for filing mechanics' liens on an incomplete project. (Chapter 15)

notice of completion A notice that should be recorded to indicate completion of a work of improvement to real property. A valid notice of completion limits the time for filing valid mechanics' liens. (Chapter 15)

notice of default Recorded notice that a default has occurred under a deed of trust and/or note. (Chapter 4)

obligee One to whom an obligation (promise) is owed. (Chapter 12)

obligor One who legally binds (obligates) oneself, such as the maker of a promissory note. (Chapter 12)

off-record A defect in title to real property that is not apparent from an examination of public records. A recorded document may not effectively transfer title to property if it was forged, was never delivered to the grantee, or was signed by an incompetent party. (Chapter 5)

off-sale beer and wine License permits sale of only beer and wine, not consumable on premises. (Chapter 15)

off-sale general license License permits sale of any type of alcohol, not consumable on premises. (Chapter 15)

offer to purchase The proposal made to an owner of property by a potential buyer to purchase the property under stated terms. (Chapter 3)

official records A master set of books kept by the county recorder in which copies of all recorded documents in that county are stored; may be microfilmed. (Chapter 4)

on-sale beer and wine License permits sale of only beer and wine, consumable on premises. (Chapter 15)

on-sale general License permits sale of any type of alcohol, consumable on premises. (Chapter 15)

option A right to require an act to be done in the future. (Chapter 3)

optionee One who, for consideration, receives an option. (Chapter 3)

optionor One who, for consideration, gives an option. (Chapter 3)

order entry clerk Opens the title order in the title plant system; performs computer runs to capture records, verifies the legal description, and searches individual and corporate general indexes (GI). (Chapter 5)

ordinance A legislative enactment of a city or county. (Chapter 15)

owner carryback A term used to indicate that the seller is willing to take back a purchase-money mortgage. (Chapter 6)

ownership The right to use and enjoy property, or an (exclusive) interest in property. (Chapter 3)

overage Of funds for either the buyer or the seller after the close of escrow, the escrow officer would merely issue a check to balance the escrow account back to a zero balance. (Chapter 11)

paid outside of closing (POC) Some fees may be listed on the HUD-1 to the left of the borrower's column and marked "POC." Fees such as those for credit reports and appraisals are usually paid by the borrower before closing/settlement. They are additional costs to you. (Chapter 12)

policy of title insurance A type of insurance where coverage is paid in advance for past interests and ownership rights in real property to protect the future interest for a property owner. (Chapter 2)

parcel Any area of land contained within a single description. Generally, this refers to a piece of land, usually a specific part of a larger portion of land. (Chapter 4)

partial reconveyance The release of part of someone's interest in real property secured by a mortgage or deed of trust. (Chapter 5)

patent A conveyance of title to land by the federal or state government "with the exclusive right to use." (Chapter 4)

payee One who receives payments. (Chapter 5)

perfect escrow When all necessary instruments and funds are deposited into escrow and it is possible to carry out the escrow instructions, it is referred to as a complete or perfect escrow. (Chapter 1)

personal property Any property that is not land or improvements permanently affixed to land (real property). Examples: stocks, bonds, furniture, automobiles, clothing, promissory notes, etc. Items of tangible personal property are often referred to as chattel. Whatever is not real property; curtains, furniture, appliances, and other items not attached permanently to the property. (Chapters 3, 10, 15)

petition A formal written document requesting a right or benefit from a person or group in authority. (Chapter 13)

PIQ A title term referring to property in question. (Chapter 4)

PITI A payment that combines principal, interest, taxes, and insurance. (Chapter 11)

plant Consists of lot books or property accounts, maps, general index (or individual corporation files), and other records necessary for the issuance of title policies. (Chapter 4)

plat map A map of land subdivision or housing development. (Chapters 4, 5)

PMI (Private Mortgage Insurance) Insurance against a loss by a lender in the event the borrower (mortgagor) defaults. The insurance is similar to insurance by a governmental agency such as FHA, except that a private insurance company issues it. The premium is paid by the borrower and is included in the mortgage payment. (Chapter 7)

points A charge made by a lender. One point equals 1 percent of the loan. (Chapter 3)

police power The power to enact laws and regulations necessary for the common welfare. (Chapter 15)

policy of title insurance Once the chain of title is established the title company will produce a preliminary title report to indicate what was initially found and offer a title insurance policy. (Chapter 4) *See also* title insurance policy.

possession The day the buyer actually moves onto the property; may be different from the close-of-escrow or recording date. (Chapter 3)

possession agreement An agreement that gives the detail of the act of either actually or constructively possessing or occupying property. (Chapter 10)

power of attorney A document by which one person (called the "principal") authorizes another person (called the "attorney-in-fact") to act for him/her in a specific manner in designated transactions. (Chapter 12)

preliminary change of ownership report (PCOR) This form must be completed *prior* to the transfer of the subject property (California Revenue and Taxation Code 480.3). The form has four parts. (Chapter 9)

preliminary title report or prelim A written report issued by a title company, preliminary to issuing title insurance. It shows the recorded condition of title of the property in question. A report showing the current status of a property and the condition under which a title company is willing to insure title as of a specified date. (Chapter 4) *See also* commitment.

prepayment penalty An agreement to pay a penalty for the payment of a note before it actually becomes due. (Chapter 6)

prequalified A pending loan in which a loan officer opines that, based on a preliminary interview and credit report, the borrower will be able to meet the loan requirements—assuming the borrower is telling the truth about his or her financial situation and income status. (Chapter 7)

presumption That which may be assumed without proof. (Chapter 4)

principal One who employs an agent to act on his or her behalf; or the chief or foremost party in a particular transaction; or the amount of a loan exclusive of interest; or the assets constituting a trust estate. (Chapter 3)

priority drawing Should the escrow officer open an escrow that is contingent upon the purchaser of the property obtaining a new liquor license, there is a high likelihood that the escrow may not close because the number of licenses given is usually far less than those who try to obtain an ABC-approved new license. (Chapter 15)

priority inspection A title term referring to the type of inspection made in connection with insuring a new construction loan. In making the inspection of the property, the title company must be assured that the work of improvement had not yet begun when the lender's deed of trust was recorded. (Chapter 15)

priority of lien The order in which liens are given legal precedence or preference. (Chapter 6)

prior lien A lien that is senior to others. (Chapter 1)

private mortgage insurance (PMI) A special form of insurance designed to permit lenders to increase their loan-to-market-value ratio, often up to 97 percent of the market value of the property. Many lenders are restricted to 80 percent loans by government regulations, special loss reserve requirements, or internal management policies related to mortgage portfolio mix. (Chapter 7)

probate The process of legally establishing the validity of a will before a judicial authority. (Chapter 13)

profit and loss (P&L) Statement on the property for the past three years showing income, expenses, and profit or loss. (Chapter 14)

promisee An individual to whom a promise is made. (Chapter 10)

promise for a promise In the purchase agreement, the promise for a promise is the offer and acceptance between the principals. The buyer promises to perform by deliveries all the money necessary to close escrow. (Chapter 3)

promisor An individual who makes a promise. (Chapter 10)

promissory note Following a loan commitment from the lender, the borrower signs a note, promising to repay the loan under stipulated terms; the promissory note establishes personal liability for its payment; the evidence of the debt. (Chapter 14)

property Anything of which there may be ownership. (Chapter 3)

prorate To divide, distribute, or assess proportionately. (Chapter 7)

proration The allocation of property taxes, interest, insurance premiums, rental income, etc., between buyer and seller proportionate to time of use. Adjustments of interest, taxes, and insurance, etc., on a pro rata basis as of the closing or agreed-upon date. Fire insurance is normally paid three years in advance. If a property is sold during this time, the seller wants a refund on that portion of the advance payment that has not been used at the time the title of the property is transferred. Usually done in escrow by the escrow holder at the time of closing the transaction. (Chapter 11)

public records The transcriptions in a recorder's office of instruments that have been recorded, including the indexes pertaining to them. (Chapter 12)

public street access Having access to enter a public street. (Chapter 5)

qualified intermediary A party to an IRC S1031 exchange transaction that satisfies the "safe harbor" requirements of Reg. S1.1031 (k)-1g(4); a qualified intermediary is not the agent of the exchanger; money actually or constructively received by a qualified intermediary will not be attributed to the exchanger. (Chapter 15)

quiet title To free the title to a piece of land from the claims of other persons by means of a court action called a "quiet title" action. The court decree obtained is a "quiet title" decree. (Chapter 5)

quitclaim deed A deed operating as a release; intended to pass any title, interest, or claim that the grantor may have in the property, but not containing any warranty of a valid interest or title in the grantor. (Chapter 8)

real estate owned (REO) Properties acquired by lenders through foreclosures or deeds in lieu of foreclosures. (Chapter 8)

Real Estate Settlement Procedures Act (RESPA) A federal law requiring the disclosure to borrowers of settlement (closing) procedures and costs by means of a pamphlet and forms prescribed by the United States Department of Housing and Urban Development. (Chapter 11)

real property (immovable) Land, from the center of the earth and extending above the surface indefinitely, including all inherent natural attributes and any human-made improvements of a permanent nature placed thereon. For example, minerals, trees, buildings, appurtenant rights. Land and, generally, whatever is erected, growing, or affixed to the land. A term used to describe land and what is permanently attached to the land. (Chapters 3, 4, 10, 15)

recital clause In very old deeds this clause was used to show whom the property was received from and how the current grantor acquired title. (Chapter 9)

reconveyance deed (1) An instrument used to transfer title from a trustee to the equitable owner of real estate, when title is held as collateral security for a debt. Most commonly used upon payment in full of a trust deed. Also called a deed of reconveyance or release. (2) The recorded deed indicating that a real property lien under a trust deed has been paid in full; releases the trustor (borrower) from any further liability for that debt. (Chapters 6, 11)

recordation Filing for record in the office of the county recorder. (Chapter 5)

recording Filing documents affecting real property as a matter of public record, giving notice to future purchasers, creditors, or other interested parties. Recording is controlled by statute and usually requires the witnessing and notarizing of an instrument to be recorded. (Chapter 4)

redeem To buy back, repurchase, recover. (Chapter 8)

redemption Buying back one's property after a judicial sale. (Chapter 8)

refinance (refi) To renew, reorganize, or revise an existing loan by obtaining a new loan. This usually pays off the existing loan. (Chapter 8)

refinance transaction The process of paying off one loan with the proceeds from a new loan using the same property as security. (Chapter 8)

Regulation B A Federal Reserve System regulation covering the Equal Credit Opportunity Act. (Chapter 8)

Regulation X A Real Estate Settlement Act estimate. The HUD good faith estimate of closing costs is a federal law that requires the lender to disclose the estimated amount of fees, commission, costs, and expenses that the borrower will have to pay. It also gives the estimated monthly payment, including impounds. (Chapter 8)

Regulation Z *See* Truth-in-Lending Act (TIL).

reinstatement period The curing of all defaults by a borrower, i.e., the restoration of a loan to current status through payment of arrearages. (Chapter 8)

relinquished property The property "sold" by the exchanger. This is also sometimes referred to as the "exchange" property or the "downleg" property. (Chapter 15)

remaining balance The amount of principal that has not yet been repaid. (Chapter 8)

rental agreement An agreement to rent. (Chapter 14)

replacement property The property acquired by the exchanger; sometimes referred to as the "acquisition" property or the "upleg" property. (Chapter 15)

repossession When a borrower defaults on a loan, the lender has the legal right to take possession of the item on which the loan was based. (Chapter 8)

requests for notice of default A recorded request for notification of a recorded notice of default on a deed of trust. (Chapter 8)

rescission The act of canceling or annulling the effect of a document. (Chapter 8)

reservation Right reserved by the grantor in conveying property, or a right that had previously been reserved. (Chapter 9)

RESPA *See* Real Estate Settlement Procedures Act.

restrictions Often called "restrictive covenants." Provisions in a deed or other instrument whereby an owner of land prohibits or restricts certain use, occupation, or improvement of the land. (Chapter 14)

rider A supplement to; an addition to; an endorsement to a document. (Chapter 7)

right of first refusal A provision in an agreement that requires the owner of a property to give another party the first opportunity to purchase or lease the property before he or she offers it for sale or lease to others. (Chapter 5)

right of rescission A borrower's right to cancel a credit contract within three business days from the day he or she entered into the loan contract. (Chapter 8)

right of survivorship In joint tenancy, the right of survivors to acquire the interest of a deceased joint tenant. (Chapter 2)

right of way A right of way is a form of an easement granted by property owners that gives the right to travel over their land and to have the reasonable use and enjoyment of their property by others as long as it is not inconsistent with the owners' use and enjoyment of the land. These principles had their origin in traditional common law, which governed, for example, the free flow of water or allowed neighboring landowners to travel over another's property (an informal "road system"). Although ownership rights of property are lessened by an easement, society at large benefits due to the additional freedom of movement. (Chapter 4)

sales/broker's commission This is the total dollar amount of the real estate broker's sales commission, which is usually paid by the seller. This commission is typically a percentage of the selling price of the home. (Chapter 12)

satisfaction of judgment Performance of the terms of an obligation. The release from the court that a judgment lien has been paid in full. (Chapters 6, 12)

satisfaction of mortgage The recorded document indicating that a mortgage lien on real property has been paid in full. (Chapter 6)

schedule rate A schedule of prices for title insurance policies. (Chapter 4)

seal An impression upon a document that lends authenticity to its execution, i.e., a corporate seal or notary seal. (Chapter 9)

search In title industry parlance, a careful exploration and examination of the public records in an effort to find all recorded instruments relating to a particular chain of title. (Chapter 9)

searcher A person who, after checking title plant and other records, assembles all the facts and documents concerning the title to the PIQ for submission to a title examiner. (Chapter 4)

secondary financing A loan secured by a second mortgage or trust deed on real property. These can be third, fourth, fifth, sixth mortgages or trust deeds, on and on, ad infinitum. (Chapter 6)

second mortgage A mortgage that has a lien position subordinate to the first mortgage. (Chapter 11)

secured loan A loan that is backed by collateral. (Chapter 8)

security agreement Document now used in place of a chattel mortgage as evidence of a lien on personal property. A financing statement may be recorded to give constructive notice of the security agreement. Property pledged to ensure payment of a debt; collateral. (Chapter 14)

security deposit A deposit made to ensure performance of an obligation. (Chapter 10)

seller affidavit A sworn statement written down and made under oath before a notary public or other official authorized by law to administer an oath. "Pledged one's faith." The form indicates that the sales price of the property is subject to withholding tax unless the transaction complies with some exemption. (Chapter 6) *See also* affidavit.

seller carryback An agreement in which the owner of a property provides financing, often in combination with an assumable mortgage. (Chapter 14)

servicer An organization that collects principal and interest payments from borrowers and manages borrowers' escrow accounts. The servicer often services mortgages that have been purchased by an investor in the secondary mortgage market. (Chapter 8)

servicing The collection of mortgage payments from borrowers and related responsibilities of a loan servicer. (Chapter 8)

setback A portion of property that must be set aside and not built on to keep building improvements a certain distance from lot boundaries. (Chapter 5)

settlement charges Charges and costs to conclude a real estate transaction. (Chapter 12)

settlement date The date used to conclude a real estate transaction. The closing date. (Chapter 12)

settlement statement *See* HUD-1 settlement statement.

short pay (short sale) A short sale is the sale of real property where the fair market sale price is less than the existing unpaid loan balance. (Chapter 8)

short sale A sale of secured real property that produces less money than is owed the lender; also called a short pay, in that the lender releases its mortgage or trust deed so that the property can be sold free and clear to the new purchaser. (Chapter 8)

short-term rate A reduced rate for title insurance applicable in cases where the owner of a property has been insured previously or where any lender has been insured somewhat recently on the property. (Chapter 5)

special assessments *See* assessments.

special power of attorney A written instrument whereby a principal confers limited authority upon an agent to perform certain prescribed acts on behalf of the principal. Also called "specific power of attorney." (Chapter 12)

stakeholder A person entrusted to hold the stakes for two or more persons with conflicting interests. Escrow clerks act as the neutral stakeholders for real property transactions. (Chapter 1)

starter A copy of the last policy or report issued by a title insurer describing the title to land upon which a new search is to be made. In some states, this is called a "back title letter" or "back title certificate." (Chapter 4)

statement of information A brief written statement of facts relied upon by title insurers to assist in the identification of persons executing the statement. (Chapter 5)

statute of limitations A law specifying time limits for initiating enforceable legal action. (Chapter 12)

stock in trade Merchandise held for sale or used in the manufacture of items for sale in the day-to-day function of a business. Also referred to as "inventory." (Chapter 15)

street improvement bonds Interest-bearing bonds issued, usually by a city or county, to secure the payment of assessments levied against land to pay for street improvements. The property owner may pay off the particular assessment against the property or may allow the assessment to "go to bond" and pay installments of principal and interest over a period of years, usually at the city or county treasurer's office. The holder of a bond receives payments from these offices. (Chapter 4)

subdivision A housing development that is created by dividing a tract of land into individual lots for sale or lease. A tract of land divided, by means of a map, into lots, generally for residential purposes. Involves the conversion of land into a completed project. (Chapters 4, 15)

subdivision process The division of a parcel of land into house lots. (Chapter 15)

subject to Usually referred to as the condition of title that exists at the time of acquisition by the buyer, such as subject to a deed of trust of record. (Chapter 6)

subordinate Taking second place; to be of lesser priority, such as a newly created deed of trust being subordinate to an existing one. (Chapter 4)

subordination agreement A written agreement that changes the priority of documents, making, for example, one deed of trust subordinate to another. (Chapter 4)

substitution of trustee Here a new trustee is substituted for the original trustee. (Chapters 4, 9)

surety A party that binds itself with another, called the principal, for the performance of an obligation. (Chapter 1)

surface rights Rights to enter upon and use the surface of a parcel of land, usually in connection with an oil and gas lease or other mineral lease.

They may be "implied" by the language of the lease (no explicit reservation or exception of the surface rights) or "explicitly" set forth. (Chapter 5)

survey A drawing or map showing the precise legal boundaries of a property, the location of improvements, easements, rights of way, encroachments, and other physical features. An ALTA survey additionally shows the exact location of all improvements, encroachments, easements, and other matters affecting the title to the property in question. A title insurance company may require a survey whenever the company is requested to issue an ALTA extended coverage policy. (Chapter 5)

surveyor A person who measures the boundaries of a parcel of land, its area, and sometimes its topography. (Chapter 1)

survey plat map The process by which boundaries are measured and land areas determined; the on-site measurement of lot lines, dimensions, and position of houses on lots, including the determination of any existing encroachments, easements, and party walls. (Chapter 5)

take-off Photocopies of or abstracts of all instruments or other matters filed each day in the recorder's office and in the clerk's office that affect the title to real property. (Chapter 4)

take sheet The escrow holder will often transfer the information contained on the purchase agreement. Its purpose is to assist the escrow holder with the information needed to prepare the escrow instructions by outlining the data required in an orderly fashion. (Chapter 3)

tax collector One who collects the taxes on the property. (Chapter 5)

tax identification number (TIN) A number placed on the documents to be recorded, such as a Social Security number. (Chapter 3)

tax lien A debt of either real property taxes, state or federal income taxes, or other types of government taxes, such as inheritance or estate taxes, that are an encumbrance for the property owner. (Chapter 6)

tax sale Property on which current county taxes have not been paid is "sold to the state." No actual sale takes place; the title is transferred to the state and the owner may redeem it by paying taxes, penalties, and costs. If it has not been redeemed within five years, the property (referred to as "tax sold property") is actually deeded to the state. (Similar "sales" to cities take place for unpaid city taxes.) (Chapter 4)

taxes (real property) An assessment on real property that can become a lien against that property if not paid at the appropriate time. (Chapter 5)

teardown An individual may purchase a single lot in a built-up area that already has an existing home or some other type of improvement on the lot and wish to "tear down" the existing improvements to construct a new home on that parcel of land. (Chapter 14)

tenancy in common A type of ownership that does not pass ownership to the others in the event of death when there are two or more individuals on the title to a piece of property, as opposed to joint tenancy. (Chapter 4)

termite clearance Clearance of termite inspection; approval of the termite inspection. (Chapter 10)

termite report A statement made by a licensed structural pest control company indicating corrective work to remedy a structure's current infestation and preventive work to inhibit future or threatened infestation. (Chapter 12)

testate Having made a legally valid will before death. (Chapter 13)

testator One who has made a legally valid will before death. (Chapter 13)

three-day right of rescission The period in which the borrower may rescind. The borrower must sign to acknowledge receipt of the rescission notice and disclosures, but need not sign anything saying that he/she has not rescinded, after the lapse of the rescission period. (Chapter 8)

time-share Escrow involves 25 to 30 documents depending upon the state in which the transaction takes place. Each state differs in the type of documents required. (Chapter 14)

title A legal document evidencing a person's right to or ownership of a property. (Chapters 3, 4)

title charges May cover a variety of services performed by title companies and others. Your particular settlement may not include all of the items below or may include others not listed. (Chapter 12)

title defect Any circumstance that adversely affects the right of whole ownership to real property by the owner of record. (Chapter 4)

title insurance Insurance to protect a real property owner or lender up to a specified amount against certain types of loss; e.g., defective or unmarketable title. (Chapter 11) *See also* vesting.

title insurance company A company that specializes in examining and insuring titles to real estate. (Chapter 4)

title insurance policy There are generally two types in use. The first is a loan policy that insures the validity, enforceability, and priority of a mortgage or deed of trust (and assignment); the second is an owner's policy that insures ownership of a particular interest or estate in real property. It is a contract to indemnify against loss through certain defects in the title. (Chapter 4)

title officer Does independent validation of documents and records found; will verify the information. (Chapter 4)

title ownership The legal evidence of ownership in a property. (Chapter 1)

title plant A storage facility of a title insurance company in which it has accumulated complete title records of properties in its area. Record rooms, containing copies of all recorded instruments. (Chapter 4) *See also* plant.

title report *See* preliminary report, title report, or prelim.

title search A review of all recorded documents affecting a specific parcel of land to determine the present condition of title. An experienced title officer, or attorney, reviews and analyzes all material relating to the search, then determines the sufficiency and status of title for insurance of a title insurance policy. (Chapters 4, 5)

title searcher A person who reviews all recorded documents affecting a specific piece of property to determine the present condition of title. (Chapter 5)

title technician Assembles the title plant records; compiles file data in a specific order; and forwards the file to the title examiner. (Chapter 5)

title unit Will date-down the file to indicate items recorded or disclosed since the last title examination; writes the policy of title insurance; generates schedules, endorsements, supplements, transmittals; and makes corrections on the legal description or vesting. (Chapter 5)

Torrens system A governmental title registration system that uses certificates of title issues by a public official, called the "registrar of title," as evidence of title. No longer used in California. (Chapter 4)

tract index An index of records of title according to the description of the property conveyed, mortgaged, or otherwise encumbered or disposed of. (Chapter 5)

trade fixture Articles of personal property annexed to real property but that are necessary to the carrying on of a trade and are removable by the owner. (Chapter 10)

transfer disclosure statement A disclosure of the title of property being conveyed from one person to another. (Chapter 10)

transfer of ownership Any means by which the ownership of a property changes hands. Lenders consider all of the following situations to be a transfer of ownership: the purchase of a property "subject to" the mortgage, the assumption of the mortgage debt by the property purchaser, and any exchange of possession of the property under a land sales contract or any other land trust device. (Chapter 10)

transfer tax State or local tax payable when title passes from one owner to another. (Chapter 11)

transferee The buyer of a business. (Chapter 15)

transferor The seller of a business. (Chapters 6, 12, 15)

Treaty of Guadalupe Hidalgo The treaty was signed on February 2, 1848, by Nicholas P. Trist for the United States and by a special commission representing the collapsed government of Mexico at the end of the Mexican War. Under the treaty, Mexico ceded to the United States Upper California and New Mexico (including Arizona) and recognized U.S. claims over Texas, with the Rio Grande as its southern boundary. The United States in turn paid Mexico $15 million, assumed the claims of American citizens against Mexico, recognized prior land grants in the Southwest, and offered citizenship to any Mexicans residing in the area. (Chapter 1)

trust A fiduciary relationship in which a trustee holds title to property for the benefit of others. A legal title to property held by one party for the benefit of another. (Chapter 13)

trust deed An instrument used in California to secure debt for a real estate loan where bare legal title is transferred from the borrower/trustor to the trustee in case of default or payoff with instructions given to the trustee by the lender/beneficiary. Lenders and sales agents refer to the trust deed; escrow and title refer to the deed of trust. (Chapters 6, 7) *See also* deed of trust.

trustee (in a deed of trust) A fiduciary that holds or controls property for the benefit of another. The entity holding bare legal title who performs two duties; when the debt is paid in full the trustee takes instruction from the beneficiary to issue the reconveyance deed to retire the debt; or, when the loan is in default by the trustor, the beneficiary instructs the trustee to begin foreclosure with the authority for the trustee to transfer title to the subsequent purchaser. (Chapter 6) *See also* deed of trust.

trust note The loan documents include the trust note that contains the terms and conditions of the loan. (Chapter 9)

trustor (in a deed of trust) The borrower under a deed of trust. The debtor under a trust deed. (Chapter 6) *See also* deed of trust.

Truth-in-Lending Act (TIL) Federal statutes and regulations (Regulation Z) that are designed primarily to ensure that prospective borrowers and purchasers on credit receive credit cost information before entering into a transaction. (Chapter 8)

undeveloped land In California this is predominantly either flat lands or hillside land. (Chapter 15)

unilateral escrow instructions Two sets of escrow instructions (used in Northern California); buyers sign one set, and sellers sign the other one. Usually signed at the closing of escrow rather than at the opening. (Chapter 3)

unlawful detainer A legal action to recover possession of real property. (Chapter 11)

usury The charge of a greater rate of interest for the loan of money than is permitted by law. (Chapter 8)

valid Sufficient in law; effective. (Chapter 9)

variable interest rate An interest rate that fluctuates with the current cost of money; subject to adjustment if the prevailing rate moves up or down. (Chapter 5)

vendee One who is purchasing property under a land sale contract. (Chapter 5) *See also* agreement of sale.

vendor One who is selling property under a land sale contract. (Chapter 5) *See also* agreement of sale.

vendor's lien An implied lien given by law to a vendor for the remaining unpaid and unsecured part of a purchase price. (Chapter 5)

verification An affidavit attached to a pleading or other document that states that the matters set forth are true. (Chapter 6)

vest To give title to or to pass ownership to property. (Chapter 4)

vested Having the right to use a portion of a fund such as an individual retirement fund. For example, individuals who are 100 percent vested can withdraw all of the funds that are set aside for them in a retirement fund. However, taxes may be due on any funds that are actually withdrawn. (Chapter 6)

vestee Current recorded owner. (Chapter 5)

vesting (1) To give immediate, fixed right in property, with either present or future enjoyment of possession; also denotes the manner in which title is held. (2) The manner in which the owner of real property holds title. For example, John Jones, a single man. (Chapters 3, 4, 7)

veterans administration (VA) An agency of the federal government that guarantees residential mortgages made to eligible veterans of the military services. The guarantee protects the lender against loss and thus encourages lenders to make mortgages to veterans. Now called the "Department of Veterans Affairs." (Chapter 7)

voluntary lien Any lien placed on property with consent of, or as a result of, the voluntary act of the owner. (Chapter 4)

walk-through A final inspection of a property just before closing. This assures the buyer that the property has been vacated, that no damage has occurred, and that the seller has not taken or substituted any property contrary to the terms of the sales agreement. (Chapter 10)

warranty An assurance or undertaking that certain defects do not exist. (Chapter 9)

warranty deed A deed used in many states to convey fee title to real property. (Chapter 10)

wild deed A deed in which none of the parties named have any apparent interest in the property described. A disposition of property effective upon the maker's death; often referred to as "last will and testament." (Chapter 4)

will A legal declaration of how a person wishes his or her possessions to be disposed of after death. (Chapter 13)

wraparound A loan that is really a combination of loans, the existing loan(s) and a new second loan. (Chapter 8)

Zone Disclosure Statement fee The only disclosure that escrow is usually involved with. It is billed to and paid through escrow. (Chapter 3)

zoning Local government regulations relating to the use of the property. (Chapter 5)

ANSWER KEY

Chapter 1
Background

1. a	(page 11)	6. d	(page 10)
2. d	(page 11)	7. c	(page 3)
3. c	(page 8)	8. b	(page 13)
4. b	(page 3)	9. b	(page 8)
5. a	(page 9)	10. a	(page 14)

Chapter 2
Escrow: The Profession and the People

1. b	(page 22)	6. b	(page 25)
2. a	(page 39)	7. d	(page 23)
3. c	(page 41)	8. a	(page 21)
4. d	(page 22)	9. c	(page 32)
5. c	(page 30)	10. c	(page 37)

Chapter 3
Opening the Escrow

1. a	(page 58)	6. a	(page 62)
2. b	(page 58)	7. d	(page 62)
3. a	(page 58)	8. d	(page 62)
4. d	(pages 63, 72)	9. c	(page 66)
5. b	(page 61)	10. c	(page 67)

Chapter 4
Title Insurance: Consumers and Real Estate Professionals

1. c	(page 76)	6. b	(page 80)
2. b	(page 80)	7. d	(page 78)
3. a	(page 88)	8. d	(page 86)
4. c	(page 80)	9. a	(page 79)
5. d	(page 76)	10. a	(page 78)

Chapter 5
Title Insurance: Technical Documents

1. c	(page 107)	6. c	(page 117)
2. b	(pages 135–136)	7. d	(page 139)
3. a	(page 110)	8. d	(page 138)
4. d	(pages 110–111)	9. b	(page 138)
5. b	(page 133, see "cut-out" in glossary)	10. b	(page 139)

Chapter 6
Seller's Escrow and Liens

1. a	(page 145)	6. a	(page 142)
2. d	(page 146)	7. b	(page 144)
3. b	(page 142)	8. c	(page 150)
4. c	(page 159)	9. d	(page 154)
5. d	(page 151)	10. a	(page 144)

Chapter 7
Loan Escrow and Buyer Escrow

1. b	(page 196)	6. d	(pages 175–176)
2. c	(page 174)	7. a	(page 188)
3. c	(page 174)	8. b	(page 192)
4. a	(page 194)	9. a	(page 189)
5. d	(page 183)	10. d	(page 191)

Chapter 8
Loan Escrows

1. d	(page 230)	6. b	(page 213)
2. d	(pages 204–206)	7. a	(pages 225, 228)
3. c	(pages 208, 223)	8. a	(page 202)
4. c	(page 203)	9. d	(page 203)
5. b	(page 204)	10. d	(pages 223, 226)

Chapter 9
Preparing Documents

1. a	(page 241)		6. b	(page 261)
2. b	(page 235)		7. c	(page 255)
3. c	(page 238)		8. d	(page 249)
4. d	(page 241)		9. c	(page 247)
5. d	(page 261)		10. b	(page 252)

Chapter 10
Processing and Disclosures

1. c	(page 269)		6. d	(page 288)
2. d	(page 269)		7. c	(page 296)
3. c	(page 288)		8. b	(page 277)
4. b	(page 293)		9. a	(page 271)
5. a	(page 278)		10. d	(page 275)

Chapter 11
Preparing to Close: Escrow Math

1. b	(page 325)		6. d	(pages 313–314)
2. b	(pages 307–308)		7. c	(page 313)
3. a	(page 314)		8. d	(page 303)
4. a	(page 310)		9. c	(page 321)
5. d	(page 303)		10. b	(page 311)

Chapter 12
Postclosing Procedures

1. b	(page 350)		6. d	(page 356)
2. b	(page 337)		7. c	(page 351)
3. a	(page 333)		8. b	(page 348)
4. d	(pages 349–351)		9. a	(page 348)
5. b	(pages 346–347)		10. d	(page 349)

Chapter 13
Homestead, Probate, Foreign Investors, and For Sale by Owner

1. b	(page 369)		6. c	(page 379)
2. c	(page 365)		7. a	(page 367)
3. b	(page 384)		8. c	(page 369)
4. d	(page 384)		9. d	(page 370)
5. a	(page 385)		10. b	(page 385)

Chapter 14
Specialty Residential Property

1. c	(pages 400–402)		6. b	(page 393)
2. d	(page 395)		7. a	(page 392)
3. a	(page 411)		8. c	(page 403)
4. c	(page 412)		9. d	(page 394)
5. d	(page 397)		10. b	(page 394)

Chapter 15
Nonresidential Specialties

1. c	(page 444)		6. c	(page 419)
2. a	(page 431)		7. b	(page 429)
3. b	(page 437)		8. b	(page 439)
4. d	(page 418)		9. c	(page 437)
5. b	(page 445)		10. c	(page 440)

INDEX